BRIAN DON...
in
THE CONQUEST OF PAIN
MONDAY EVENING   DECEMBER 11, 1944

"Great Stars . . . . Great Radio Plays"

ROSALIND RUSSELL
in
"HYMN FROM THE NIGHT"
MON. EVE.   SEPT. 18th

"Great Stars . . . . Great Radio Plays"
IN CAVALCADE'S 1944 FALL SERIES

THE HISTORY OF THE CAVALCADE OF AMERICA

WRITTEN BY MARTIN GRAMS, JR.

PRESENTED BY

Copyright © 1998
Martin Grams, JR.

All rights reserved.
No part of this book may be reproduced in any form,
except for the inclusion of brief quotations in a review,
without permission in writing from the author of publisher.

ISBN: 0-7392-0138-7

Library of Congress Catalog Card Number: 99-94220

Printed in the USA by

MORRIS PUBLISHING

3212 East Highway 30 • Kearney, NE 68847 • 1-800-650-7888

Dedicated to -

My family, who manages to put up with all of my little inconsistencies such as taking up all the space on the kitchen table and hogging the computer for hours on end.

And to all of the *Cavalcade of America* fans out there, who not only called me on the phone every week asking when this book would be done, but encouraging me to complete this project.

TABLE OF CONTENTS

Introduction *iii*

The History of the *Cavalcade of America* 1

The Broadcast Log (Radio Episodes)

The Broadcast Log (Television Episodes)

The Books

Broadcast Times

Awards

Index

Homer Fickett (director): "I remember the time we did 'Abe Lincoln in Illinois,' and used modern recording for the scene when the train starts. Three people wrote in to protest that trains of 1860 didn't make an air brake noise. Then I recall when we did a special play for Washington's birthday. A Colonial butcher named John Honneyman posed as a Tory spy for Washington and told him when to cross the Delaware. It was Christmas time, you remember, and the soldiers sang Tannenbaum. After the broadcast, several people wrote in and said those soldiers were certainly smart because 'Tannenbaum' wasn't written until two months after Washington crossed the Delaware."

INTRODUCTION

Someone once wrote that history never repeated itself. It is the historians who often repeat themselves. And so did the *Cavalcade of America*. For over twenty years, this DuPont-sponsored program presented dramas of American history, using the top talent of Hollywood and Broadway in the leading roles. That is what this book is about.

When I first began this project, my original intention was to document as much of the series as possible, because no one had ever done so. A few friends even told me that *Cavalcade* was (and still is) "very unpopular." They are probably correct. There is not much interest in an anthology series dealing with American history, especially when there are other shows more popular. I will admit that if I had a choice between a *Suspense* episode where the villian will get their head cut off by an axe or a drama about Washington crossing the Delaware, I would choose the former of the two.

After I began this project, however, I found there was a lot more to *Cavalcade* than just American history. And it is those same convictions I hope you will discover for yourself when you are done reading this book. I do have to pause a moment to thank a handful of people, who without their help, this book would never be.

The numerous staff at DuPont who helped me with my project, granted me permission to use the DuPont name throughout this book, and opened numerous files regarding *Cavalcade* that have rarely been seen. They allowed me to zerox copies of scripts, contracts, flyers, and other memorabilia related to *Cavalcade*. Barbara S. Pandos, U.S. Programs Manager; Jon Williams and his staff at the Hagley Library and Museum; Marie Beletti of the DuPont External Affairs; Derek Teague for his vast knowledge in New York and Hollywood actors; Rosemary Rice; Raymond Edward Johnson; Jay Hickerson who often helps contribute logs and information over the years; Colleen Lyons who helped supply a little research that added those tid-bits people like; Terry Salomonson who sent me some information regarding *Cavalcade*; Dave Siegel for the articles he sent from old issues of *Radio Guide* and other old magazines; Berry Hill in New York for access to his *Cavalcade* books; Bill Yunick for logs and recordings he sent me; Les Waffen of the National Archives in Washington, D.C. for filling in a few blanks in my manuscript, and last but not least, Harvey, who did the index at the end of this book. A handful of people asked me to supply an index at the end of this book, and it was Harvey who proofed my manuscript and made the index possible. A big hand to everyone involved.

I hope this book answers any questions you may have about this great Hollywood program. It was truly one of the great radio / television programs of the first half of the twentieth century. Although forgotten in the minds of most people, it still remains a piece of broadcasting history, and a preservation of American dreams. This is the history of the *Cavalcade of America*.

THE BIRTH OF A NATION

Sixty years ago when DuPont chemists were toiling over their bunsen burners and squinting into their retorts to bring into the world such strange, new materials as nylon and Lucite, the public thought of DuPont as a gunpowder manufacturing gargantuan, making goods of destruction. Some smart advertising agency executives sold the twenty-six men on DuPont's executive committee, the idea of advertising by radio, the constructive things DuPont was making for society. "Better things for better living through chemistry" was the motif behind the advertising plan and was soon heard as DuPont's slogan on the weekly program.

Cavalcade of America reached a milestone. In 1935 it presented its first script, "No Turning Back," a two-part documentary concerned with the tenacious spirit of the Pilgrims and of their descendants. Carlyle Stevens, the original narrator, struck the note the program was to play on consistently. "As you watch the American Cavalcade pass in review," he said, "you find much that is not pomp and circumstance. A certain doggedness and perseverance, a willingness to stick it out at all costs, is the most distinguished attribute of the American."

Dixon Ryan Fox: "At eight o'clock on Wednesday evening, October 9, 1935, those of us who were gathered around our radios listened for the first time to a half-hour program called *The Cavalcade of America*, sponsored by E.I. Du Pont De Nemours and Company. Some of us who had been concerned in the preparation of the program listened with a keen - in fact a nervous - interest. We hoped that the people of the United States, the millions upon millions of them who were drawing up their chairs to choose entertainment out of the air, would agree with us that one of the best uses they could make of a half-hour, once a week, would be to listen to a series of spoken dramas which revealed the spirit of America, as it had issued from American hearts and minds during the past three hundred years. The original engagement was made for eight weeks. We wondered and waited."

There was no relation to the 1929 NBC series entitled *Cavalcade*, which was broadcast over NBC during the late twenties and early thirties. That program was one of the earliest musical variety shows noted for it's rhyming scripts, and produced by Edwin L. Dunham. But the DuPont program, featured dramas of American history, and premiered as an eight-week experimental presentation. If it would succeed, the *Cavalcade of America* would become a permanent fixture in the American home.

Dixon Ryan Fox: "The DuPont Company, which itself is almost as old as the Republic, felt that this was the kind of program with which it could appropriately associate its name. Those of us who had been called into counsel, men primarily interested in education and in the history of our country, believed that it was what people ought to want."

Radio was still an infant in 1935. Few people in radio thought it would succeed. Likely to be tagged as "long-haired" and an "educational program," those in the know felt that a show devoted to historical drama would find a very small listening audience. After all - ninety-five percent of the programs heard over the air was music, news reports, and more music. But *Cavalcade* proved that Americans were interested in their country and it's great names. The producers of the show were far-sighted enough to see that if the program was to have any real value, it could not be a dry, dusty, rehash of what teachers taught in grade schools.

Dick Ryan Fox: "The program was originally conceived and steadily developed in patriotic faith, informed by understanding and responsible research, to remind us of the purposes and motives on which our fathers and mothers based and built this nation. In it we heard the inspiring voices of the past, when men and women of public spirit and lofty resolution faced and conquered difficulties which might have wrecked out national undertaking before we could inherit it. We listened to the authentic life of America, vastly more stirring and persuasive because it was true."

The central thought of the originators of the program was to show how American character had been illustrated in our history. Each broadcast was to deal with a different trait or tendency. In the early days the theme was didactically stated in titles like that of the opening script. With time, however, although the underlying intention was unchanged, the presentation became less dogmatic. From being essentially a thesis play in which the moral was underscored, the typical "Cavalcade" script became a play-drama, comedy, fantasy, melodrama, still with a serious purpose, but with a new sense of entertainment values.

Walter Hampden, Fay Bainter and Franchot Tone were a few of the Hollywood stars to make appearances during the opening weeks of *Cavalcade*. By the end of the sixth week, letters had poured into the mail office of NBC, and the DuPont Company received almost as many as NBC. The listeners were tickled pink with the dramas. Far more interesting than music on other radio stations.

One listener wrote: "This program was typical in that it stressed basic values in American life and made them the goal of human endeavor. You are rendering the country a most significant service which is thoroughly appreciated by many of us."
- J.W. Heckert, Oxford, Ohio

The program was a success, accomplishing the task it was first sent out to do. *Cavalcade* was designed to re-awaken in the public mind a consciousness of those ideals and inheritance that were most basically American. With this objective, the show was submitted to a permanent time slot, and longer broadcast run. While most radio directors and actors had to contend with the fear of their program being "pulled" from the air for any number of reasons, especially losing the sponsor, the *Cavalcade of America* did not have to contend with such worries. *Cavalcade* was a "DuPont program" as most performers referred to. DuPont had no intention to dropping sponsorship, and it was this very reason why the program never had a brief broadcast run on the air.

The early broadcasts (the first hundred or so episodes), primarily dealt with American traditions and human traits. "The Will to Explore" and "Perseverance" were a few of the topics. The opening narrator would speak briefly about those traits, and then introduce two, short, fifteen-minute dramas of American history exemplifying those traits. This policy changed as the years went by. *Cavalcade* script writers and the officials felt that the program was better understood when presented in one, thirty-minute drama.

In the summer of 1936, the script writers of *Cavalcade* decided to present musical numbers. One episode presented the life of Victor Herbert, and how he came to write some of his most famous compositions. Another episode featured music from Hollywood films. And during July and August of 1936, the producers decided to present a six-part presentation entitled "The Development of Band Music in America." These episodes were very well received by newspaper critics and listeners alike.

Kenneth Webb, author of many early *Cavalcade* scripts and a successful Broadway playwright, served as *Cavalcade*'s first director.

Kenneth Webb: "Thousands of letters which have been received from interested listeners, including parents, teachers and students, have been most gratifying to those in charge of the program. The painstaking research done by the authors together with conscientious editing by such well known historical authorities as Dr. Dixon Ryan Fox, President of Union College, and Dr. Arthur M. Schlesinger of the Department of History at Harvard University have been repaid by the fact that dozens of schools throughout the country have asked for weekly announcements of forthcoming broadcasts. Many have even made the *Cavalcade of America* 'required listening' for classes in history, social science, chemistry, dramatics, geography and commerce."

DuPont hired an agency to run the program, Batten, Barton, Durstine & Osborn, Inc. From their New York offices, BBD&O hired the writers, actors, musicians, and directors for the entire broadcast run, until 1953 when *Cavalcade* would leave the air.

Kenneth Webb: "Since our first broadcast in 1935, *Cavalcade of America* has had five historians. The first was the late Dr. Dixon Ryan Fox, President of Union College, a trustee of the NY State Historian Society and a member of many other outstanding historical organizations. He was also the author and editor of many history books. James Truslow Adams became the second historian for *Cavalcade* in 1938. He was the editor-in-chief of the Dictionary of American Biography and a contributor to the Encyclopedia Britannia. Mr. Adams also wrote several popular books on historical subjects. Arthur Schlesinger, who followed Mr. Adams, was the Associate Professor of American History at Harvard University.

The stories and scripts were conceived by authors from historical records, novels, and on occasion movies, and selected by a Planning Board that worked in close harmony with the sponsor. After the story had been okayed by the Planning Board it was scheduled for broadcast some six or eight weeks ahead. Then the research department got busy digging out all the facts concerning the person and his/her period. The material had to be authenticated by the sponsor, Planning Board, and Research Department before the final acceptance. (These meetings, by the way, consisted of hours of long discussion and hundreds of ideas that were tossed across the table.)

Dick Ryan Fox: "It would immediately be apparent that this had involved an immense amount of inquiry in unconventional historical material. Professor Arthur M. Schlesinger, of Harvard University, and I have had the responsibility not only to suggest episodes, but also to see that the scripts turned in by the many writers were faithful to the facts. This did not mean that all the dialogue was an exact transcript from the record. Often times an historical character's beliefs and mental attitudes had to be indicated more succinctly than he had stated them in any one place. Now and then characters had to be invented to voice what we know was the sentiment of some group or element in American society. But, with the minimum of error that care could establish, we tried to insure that it was the real voice of America, or some part of America, that was heard in each speech. The authors themselves had shown a scholarly resourcefulness in discovering material and a fine conscientiousness in using it, as well as dramatic skill in fashioning the program. There was no question that they, and particularly the producers with their corps of actors and musicians, had made a broad and deep contribution to America's understanding of its heritage."

Throughout its career *Cavalcade* had paid tribute to the pioneers who laid the foundations of America, to the leaders of science, the arts, politics who are building its superstructure, and to everyday people who were its heart and pulse.

Dick Ryan Fox: "One of its fascinations had been in its freshness. It would have been much easier to rehearse the familiar matter of the textbooks, to say again what everybody knows about the great heroes of American history. That had been done before. Those in charge had followed another plan. The dazzling geniuses, the supermen, appear now and then, though in aspects and episodes by no means so well known. For the most part, however, the designers of *Cavalcade* had dipped into the common mass for their instances of heroism, virtue, ingenuity and public service. They had drawn their stories from the great folk of America, the same folk on which we must, and happily can, with full faith now rely. They had tried to analyze the American character and find instances which vividly illustrated American traits and ideals."

Ideas for scripts came from many sources. It was up to a story committee at the agency that handled the show to decide which ideas were suitable. The committee consisted of Homer Fickett, producer (later director); Kenneth Webb (director) George Kondolf, story editor; Julia Boyd, librarian of Princeton University, who was a historical consultant; and Arthur Pryor, agency radio department head. Until his death in July of early forties, John Anderson, drama critic of *The Journal-American*, also was a member.

The committee throws the ideas around and recommends the ideas they selected to the sponsor (du Pont). Once the sponsor approves, the committee chooses a writer who gets

Cavalcade of America

presents

FRANK MORGAN

in

"Names On The Land"

**MONDAY EVENING
DECEMBER 24, 1945**

NATIONAL BROADCASTING COMPANY

Coast to Coast Network

8.00-8.30 .... E.T.   9.30-10.00 .... M.T.
7.00-7.30 .... C.T.   8.30- 9.00 .... P.T.

Coast to Coast Network

Originating from Hollywood

Cavalcade of America

presents

GEORGE SANDERS

in

"The Magnificent Meddler"

**MONDAY EVENING
DECEMBER 17, 1945**

NATIONAL BROADCASTING COMPANY

Coast to Coast Network

8.00-8.30 ... E.T.   9.30-10.00 .... M.T.
7.00-7.30 .... C.T.   8.30- 9.00 ... P.T.

Consult Your Local Radio Timetable

Originating from Hollywood

to work on an out-line for a script. Often, before the writer can go ahead with the development of the idea, he must track it down like a news reporter to see if there's really a script in it.

During the 1936 - 37 season, *Cavalcade* dramatized biographies of Thomas Edison, Admiral Peary, Stephen Girard, and James Fenimore Cooper. A documentary on dynamite, the origin of eye-seeing dogs, and the story behind dyes were a few of the historical presentations.

During the summer of 1937, from July to September, the program changed it's title to *The Cavalcade of Music*. This was a twelve-part presentation of the best musicians in America, their lives and music. Irving Berlin, George Gershwin, Jerome Kern, Victor Herbert, and Cole Porter were a few.

On June 29, 1938, the *Cavalcade of America* broadcasted it's one-hundred and forty-first episode. This was scheduled to be the final broadcast of the series. As a closer, DuPont agreed to dramatize an episode about Eluthere I. du Pont, the founder of the DuPont Company. At the end of the broadcast, the announcer thanked the listening public for tuning in to the program, and the gratifying letters that were received over the months. The announcer asked any listeners who wanted to continue hearing these top-quality dramas, to write and ask.

The responses were plentiful, and six months later, on December 5, 1938, *Cavalcade* returned to the air. There was now a couple of changes. Gabriel Heatter was made an announcer. The dramas themselves now dealt with biographies on American figures, dismissing the previous presentations of American vows such as the 4-H movement and Child Welfare. These biographies were "pure American" as described on one such episode. Paul Bunyan, Will Rogers, Knute Rockne, Stephen Foster, Mark Twain and Patrick Henry. Six months later, in May of 1939, *Cavalcade*, once again, left the air. The final broadcast was a repeat performance of the Eluthere I. du Pont drama, the same that closed the previous season.

TIME FOR A CHANGE

BBD&O officials noticed something in particular with this last season. Biographies of American heroes were well received, more than previous broadcasts. DuPont decided to go for more of a change. Why not incorporate Hollywood stars in the lead roles, and hire a permanent historical consultant crew? This was the change that revolutionized *Cavalcade*. The new season would begin in January of 1940 and start with a bang.

> **Dick Ryan Fox:** "Now, after more than two years of growing interest, it was hard to realize that there could have been any doubt. Prizes and ceremonial commendation, deliberate endorsement of important educators, all welcome as they have been, have meant less to those in charge, I think, than the thousands of grateful letters from the plain people of every state. They know that it is their story, that their own forebears and forerunners were the participants in this *Cavalcade* here rehearsed."

Marquis James, twice winner of the Pulitzer Prize in the Field of Historical Biography, was one of the three historical advisors. James was widely known as a meticulous scholar and was a fearless researcher who never pulled his punches when he was certain of his facts - and he always was. Carl Carmer, a specialist in the folklore of this continent, was the second researcher. Carmer was the prominent author of "Listen for a Lonesome Drum" in 1935, and was enthusiastically received by thousands of readers who found his fresh treatment of history as exciting as fiction. Only a few months back, in the fall of 1939, his book "The Hudson" became one of the nation's best-sellers. The third and final of the three researchers was Professor Frank Monaghan of Yale University. Although James and Carmer supplied the story material, it was Dr. Monaghan who passed on his historical aspects. Monaghan himself, would write numerous scripts for the *Cavalcade of America*.

Dr. Frank Monaghan: "I believe that the *Cavalcade of America* program was of high interest to all teachers in the field of American studies - civics, government, literature and history. In those days of world chaos it was increasingly important that every student become better acquainted with the colorful and sturdy traditions of America's past. That was the basic concept of the *Cavalcade of America*: to present a dramatic and significant pattern of the characters, forces and ideas that had contributed most to the building of the American nation."

Homer Fickett: "We did have some peculiar quirks, mostly dealing with historical data. That was one reason we had Dr. Monaghan as an advisor. Sometimes, in spite of every precaution to make *Cavalcade* a perfect performance, we stubbed our toes."

Press release dated January 1940:

"Around the drama each week, one hears the professional voice of Dr. Frank Monaghan, who is announced as professor of history at Yale. He sets the stage in a manner somewhat reminiscent of Cecil B. DeMille but not so nearly effectively. He also rings down the curtain with a teaser question. For example, 'What woman in American history made a midnight ride of just as much importance as Paul Revere?' Her life, of course, is the subject of next week's drama."

The historians were retained to check the authenticity of each script, so a huge reference library was employed. By the time a script reached the air, it is was authentic as time and thought could make it. None but original scripts are used on the program and some of these were bought from unknown writers. In the search for good originals, a badly written script with a basically fine idea was not discarded. *Cavalcade*'s rewrite man worked on it until the script was up to the standard of the show. Unlike most dramatic programs, *Cavalcade*'s stories had to be worked backwards. An idea or a personage was presented as a possibility for dramatization, and the search for the elements of a good story in the background was conducted.

Carl Carmer: "Two volumes of *Cavalcade* scripts had been published by the Milton Bradley Company of Springfield, Mass. Those two books contain many of the scripts heard on the air during *Cavalcade's* first two years."

Newspapers with a circulation of 17,500,000 carried advertisements of *Cavalcade*, mainly in cities where broadcasting stations in the hook-up were located. 715,000 pieces of mail had been sent to customers, stockholders, business leaders, educators, and anyone else who might have an interest in the program. This guaranteed that on the evening of January 2, papers would be put down in hundreds of thousands of homes, and busy fingers would seek to bring the program in. In this way was a radio audience built.

Broadcast from New York, the *Cavalcade of America* presented Hollywood stars in the lead roles. Burgess Meredith, Walter Huston, Ethel Barrymore, and Thomas Mitchell were a few. And within weeks after the new 1940 season premiered, the listening audience rose in quantity.

Homer Fickett: "One of my worst problems is created by cast members falling asleep between the Western show at 5:30 and the repeat broadcasts at 8:30."

In the theatre, just before *Cavalcade* went on the air January 2nd, someone with a worrying nature asked one of the agency men if he were sure the timing was accurate. "We won't be cut off the air in the middle of the commercial!" the worrier gasped, horrified by the thought. "Timing doesn't bother us in the least," was the calm reply. "After twelve years of putting shows on the air, timing becomes second nature. the show is speeded up or slowed down almost automatically. There's nothing to it."

Kenneth Webb: "Dr. Frank Monaghan, a former professor of history at Yale, was the fourth of *Cavalcade*'s historians. He was also historical director of the NY World's Fair and The Freedom Train. Dr. Francis Ronalds became the historian for *Cavalcade* during the war in 1944. A former professor of history at Indiana University, Dr. Ronalds was curator of historic sites for the U.S. Park Service in the Department of Interior. Much attention was given to the details in the scripts by Dr. Ronalds for in addition to being heard on the air, the scripts were often reprinted in educational, scientific and historical publications."

Kenneth Webb was the first director of *Cavalcade*, and he also wrote numerous scripts for the series. Following Webb was Homer Fickett, a soft-spoken, hard-working producer on *Cavalcade*, who was the original producer of *March of Time*, and Kate Smith's first commercial radio program. Fickett was a plump, dynamic little man who looked enough like Winston Churchill to be his American twin. When *Cavalcade* returned to the radio for the 1938-39 season, Kenneth Webb had bowed out of directing. Homer Fickett moved up to directing, where he remained until September of 1943, when Paul Stewart took over. Stewart was a radio actor, best remembered for being a member of Orson Welles' Mercury Theater Company. Stewart directed *Cavalcade* for two years, until the summer of 1945, when Jack Zoller took over the directing duties.

JACK ZOLLER, MAN OF ACTION

Jack Zoller was born in Cincinnati, September 9, 1908. Married to the former Letitia Payne of Washington, D.C., in 1948, who once worked as his assistant. He was the father of two boys, Christopher and Michael. A balding thin man, gray at the temples and neatly mustached, Zoller's manner was reticent and guarded, but pleasantly relieved by a quiet geniality. He was a man of inward smiles and soft speech, and likable. His associates at NBC called him Jack.

Jack Zoller: "If you must know, I started out to be a doctor. I had the bedside manner, a little black valise, and even studied barbering to learn surgery the easy way. All I needed was the degree. I even got as far as the University of Cincinnati, Ohio, with that idea in mind. But then one day I met Patia Power, the mother of Tyrone Power. Patia was directing a little theatre group in Cincinnati. She suggested that I come around and consider a part. I did. When the bug bit me I forgot all about wanting to be a doctor. My first role was playing the young minister in 'Servant in the House.' Young Tyrone, age ten, played the page boy. After this ran its curse I followed with the lead in Phillip Barry's 'You and I'."

One thing led to another, and it wasn't long before Jack abandoned the test tubes and burners for the more alluring smell of grease paint. He joined a Shakespearean repertoires company with Robert Mantell, but found that it wasn't worth the trouble.

Jack Zoller: "One season in tights and wigs was enough. After that, in 1927, I joined a regular stock company in Cincinnati. Our opening bill was 'The Devil in the Cheese' and now Patia Power was working with us as a character actress. After our tour, and back in Cincinnati, I found out about a strange new thing called 'Radio,' and learned that WLW was looking for actors and was actually paying them to learn the business. Before you could give a two weeks notice I was working at WLW along with other people new to the business . . . Jane Froman, Lum and Abner, Little Jack Little, Ed Byron, Red Skelton and loads of others. After two or three years there, I set out for the big city. In New York I had good luck and managed to get on most of the bigger network programs."

In 1932, he returned to WLW as actor/director. In 1933 he went to Hollywood as assistant director with an independent picture company. He did one picture which was of the B minus class. The company failed, so he went back to WLW again. During the following few years Zoller appeared in the cast of the Broadway show "All Editions," starring Regis Toomey, and worked in a variety of assignments as actor-director, both in radio and pictures, including MGM's *Crossroads* (1942) with William Powell and Hedy Lamarr. The part he played in the Broadway show "All Editions," prophetically enough, was that of a radio director.

When the war came, he enlisted in the Army and directed radio programs on the West Coast as a Staff Sergeant. After his discharge, he joined NBC. In February of 1945, he became director of *Cavalcade of America*, where he remained until the end of the

broadcast run. He was also a member of the Lambs Club in New York, a theatrical club. Zoller stood in the insulated control room, looking like frozen alertness. He was calm, smiling and only his fingers wagged furiously in some kind of radio code. His gray eyes meanwhile swiftly apprehended the split-second clocks, the engineers along side him, the actors grouped on the stage, and the musicians off near one wing - all kneading with him one more show for millions of radio listeners. The clocks particularly seemed to press their weight in that intense atmosphere. Radio directors often develop ulcers, but that scourge of the profession has never claimed Zoller, possibly because of his disciplined thinking and deportment. He is the antithesis of the nail-biting, rush-around radio director.

"As for my not having ulcers," he quietly quipped during a lull in the control room, "let's just say that is one of the miracles of our modern radio age. There's no glamour here. Just work, but highly interesting to me. I keep regular hum-drum office hours, nine to five generally, the same as any other advertising executive. And there's always plenty to do. We have to plan our shows two to three weeks in advance." Zoller's directing duties does not mean standing in a control booth and waving fingers. Zoller's task as director also meant selection of cast, both star and AFRA, having a good judgment of music, rehearsal and production of the show on the air, and the final responsibility for quality control and broadcast. His directorship includes the selection of scripts with story editor John Driscoll, casting the right voices, running the actors through their rehearsals and going into huddles with the musicians, technicians and account executives.

"While every Tuesday is an opening night for us," he went on, "there is no popping of champagne corks or cheerio parties. After the performance, I commute to my little home in Mt. Vernon, and relax with some newspapers or a good book. Next morning I'm back at work again." Zoller, the man behind the scenes, does have his one big moment before every show.

Jack Zoller: "That's during the half-hour warm-up session before the studio audience," he said. "We always have one Hollywood guest star on the Cavalcade program, and I come out to introduce the illustrious one to all assembled. If it's a beautiful lady like Rosalind Russell she might plant a great big kiss on my cheek and then the applause really gets thunderous. And oh boy! - my wife kids me about that sort of thing. One wonders how I can take all that glamour!"

RELUCTANT PRAISE FOR THE WRITER

Cavalcade has long been a writer's studio. Its story committee believed that a dramatic radio program rises or falls largely because of the quality of its writing. Realizing that a good script can't be whipped up in the time it takes to make an omelet (radio's daily delusion), *Cavalcade* allows more time for the writing of a script than is customary. This is, of course, good for the script. It is also good for the writer. Says George Kondolf: "I am happy to say that the present fees paid by the agency for writers have enabled us to attract better authors and have allowed them to give more time to *Cavalcade* and the scripts."

Stephen Vincent Benet, Robert Sherwood, Maxwell Anderson and Carl Sandburg had written original scripts for *Cavalcade*. Among "names" who, like Sherwood and Anderson, Paul Peters and Arthur Arent, came to *Cavalcade* from the theatre were Victor Wolfson, Isabel Leighton and Frank Gabrielson.

Mr. Kondolf, who has always felt that writing for the stage is about the most difficult technique in the world, believes that you can teach a playwright the special tricks of radio writing in little time. And this despite the cherished myth that radio writers, unique in the species of penmen, are a race apart, beamed directly from heaven, stop-watch in hand.

When once the story committee had selected a vehicle for a certain Monday night's airing, the ample budget (trade papers list it in the neighborhood of $7,500 weekly by 1950) allowed practically free rein in choice of players.

Another reason for *Cavalcade*'s excellence was a vivacious young lady named Mary Cummings. During the mid-to-late forties through the mid fifties, she was the story editor. It was she who did the original digging, sifting, accepting and rejecting. By 1952, after seven hundred some scripts already broadcasted, there was some problem of finding original material for each show. This Miss Cummings did by pursuing magazines, newspapers, ballads, legends, and history books in addition to investigating the merit of ideas submitted by the many people who were interested in the show.

The demand for scripts to be used by the Board of Education was greater than that requested from any other show. Many schools have used *Cavalcade* scripts or records to supplement their history courses. At one time, the Rockefeller Foundation made a series of records for this purpose.

Since each story presented was one based on a true event and presented as it happened, there was the problem of finding true events that lend themselves to interesting dramatic presentation. Then again, the story editor may use only for the central character or happening, one which contributed to the growth of America and democracy. Thus the job of story editor required an exacting attention to detail, an infinite amount of patience, and an ability to recognize interesting story material. Mary Cummings attained her present position in a rather unorthodox manner. She was not an ambitious young writer or even a writer at all and she had had no formal education in the radio field.

Cummings was talking to a friend of hers over coffee a while back and asked for advice as to what type of work she should go into. She had tried several jobs but had not found any about which she could really become enthusiastic. The friend happened to be connected with an advertising agency and suggested that she try writing for radio. This struck Miss Cummings as being amusing, since she had had no experience. But finally she was persuaded to do so.

Her first script was sold. Encouraged by this, she wrote some more scripts and they also were sold. She then began to specialize in mystery writing and finally in straight dramatic writing. Her ability in this field won her acclaim and shortly afterwards, she became story editor of *Cavalcade of America*. A native of New York and a graduate of Ithaca College, laughed when she recalled the attitude she had when she began in the radio field but it was very serious when she expresses her gratitude to the friend who first suggested that she attempt to write.

STAR OF STAGE AND SCREEN

Long before Orson Welles became a "genius" he was satisfied with featured parts in *Cavalcade* programs. Way back when Richard Widmark gave little evidence of being a "menace," or when Agnes Moorehead's "suspense" was confined to obtaining supporting radio roles, these present-day stars were just frequent *Cavalcade* players. Other "unknowns" at the time were Skippy Homeier, John McIntire, and Ona Munson.

The idea behind casting seems to be that of deciding exactly who, from all the ranks of fine performers, will be able to enact the part to perfection. New York being the "radio home" of the show, *Cavalcade* drew on theatrical talent for its stellar parts, or summon Hollywood scintillates willing to travel back to Manhattan. The program premiered in New York, later broadcasts originating from Hollywood on sporadic occasional airings, and returning to New York after. Eventually, the program was heard from Hollywood for long periods of time. "Of course, more stars are available in Hollywood," Fickett stated, "and that's the reason we come out here to put on broadcasts."

Finally, a star must be fitted to the script. For *The Lux Radio Theatre*, the movie of choice was arranged from the studios, then the stars who appeared in the original film, whenever possible, were invited on the program. For *Suspense*, on occasion, the stars were chosen first, and the stories written later. For *Cavalcade*, the story was written first, then the star chosen. If, as often happens, there are relatives of the subject still alive, a copy of the script is sent to them for their approval. (On occasion, the original relatives played a role in the drama, and/or spoke after the presentation to the listening audience.) It was a policy of the program not to deal with personages who were still alive, though stories built around contemporary ideas and happenings did bring in the names of many living people.

On June 27, 1950, Susan Douglas, a rising young actress, portrayed Gloria Chomiak, Wilmington High School student who won the national "I Speak for Democracy" contest. Other real-life Wilmingtonians portrayed on the program were Winnie Lawrence, friend of Miss Chomiak, George Chomiak, her Uncle, Mabel Wright, dramatics teacher at the Wilmington High School, Clarence Fulmer, principal of the School, Mary Elizabeth Power, staff member of the Journal Every-Evening; and Harvey Smith, announcer on radio station WDEL.

The bright talent of Broadway, though it was inspiring to the listener, could be a headache to a radio producer, according to Jack Zoller. Don't get him wrong, Broadway luminaries were well folks, but they're so darn busy. "The eastern broadcast goes on the air at eight o'clock and curtain time for most Broadway stars is eight-thirty," explained Zoller. "We have to keep elevators waiting and taxi-cabs waiting so they can make it. Then on the repeat broadcast it's the same thing. We repeat to the west at 11:30 p.m., eastern time - just about the time the curtain is coming down on a Broadway hit. That means more elevators and taxicabs. And it's a little distracting to the actor, too. You know New York - so much can happen between Broadway and Rockefeller Center!" Take Orson Welles as an example. When Welles learned to his amazement that Cecil B. DeMille hired an ambulance to get from one part of New York to another, in time to do his hosting duties on *The Lux Radio Theatre*, and that this procedure was not illegal, Welles took up the same performance.

The Hollywood guests were pictured as pleasant, congenial people, but they sometimes got nervous before a microphone. Here they work with accomplished, glib radio performers, and if they fluff a line or sound dullish it would be a bad situation. There were no retakes on a radio show. But the star's fee was good, usually about $3,500, a figure that should bolster any performer's morale. Do the Hollywood stars ever get temperamental? Rarely, but there have been complaints when they feel that the scripts were unsuitable for their personalities. When Humphrey Bogart commented his dislike for his lines in a script, they were rewritten to suit his personality.

Nearly 1,000 man-hours each week and eleven-and-a-half hours of rehearsal time are spent in the preparation of this half-hour show. All the activity centers around the director, whose direction is both vigorous and rigorous, while the *Cavalcade* players included such skilled actors as Frank Readick, Edwin Jerome, Will Greer, and Karl Swenson. The star, however, practically always comes from Broadway or Hollywood. Walter Hampden was the first star; Bob Hope, Robert Montgomery, Clark Gable, Jackie Cooper, and Loretta Young were later stars.

The company generally met on a Tuesday for a first reading rehearsal, during which parts were assigned and the mood of the script was set. The mike rehearsals followed on Thursday and on Monday. Now scene by scene was worked out in detail so that the script would connote a series of pictures and the effect would be of people at a specific moment in a specific place in a specific world. New ideas were constantly added to the script so that by the time the dress rehearsal took place on Monday afternoon, it was quite different from what it was at first.

But the script was not rewritten for the last time until the dress rehearsal was over and what's known as a "hash session" takes place. The director gives the cast these eleventh-hour changes when they return at 6:15 for the final run-through before broadcast.

The *Cavalcade* play like all radio dramas was limited as a dramatic form. It could not develop character, for instance. It must observe certain taboos, for another. And because its policy is to celebrate the achievement of American life, it cut itself off from the possibilities of satire.

What *Cavalcade* could not do, however, was less significant than what it could do. Not a small part of its success came from its realization that the dramatic impulse was essentially the same, whatever the medium of expression - that a sense of plot, character, language, social forces was more fundamental than a knowledge of the meaning of a music bridge or a cross fade were important, of course, but they were the trees in the forest, not the forest itself, no matter what your trade loyalty. *Cavalcade* scripts had been matched and sometimes surpassed by scripts on other dramatic programs. Sometimes *Cavalcade* scripts failed. However, sustained achievement sustained over a period of twenty plus years, *Cavalcade* was in the first rank.

Juano Hernandez played Booker T. Washington in "The Burning Bush."

The Cavalcade broadcast of "Citizen Mama" starred Irene Dunne.

AND NOW A WORD FROM OUR SPONSOR . . .

Who bank-rolls *Cavalcade*'s elaborate production is a natural question from any listener.

Years ago, when DuPont chemists were toiling over their bunsen burners and squinting into their retorts to bring into the world such strange, new materials as nylon and Lucite, the public though of DuPont as a gunpowder manufacturing gargantuan, making goods of destruction. Some smart advertising agency executives sold the twenty-six men on DuPont's executive committee the idea of advertising by radio the constructive things DuPont was making for society - "Better things for better living through chemistry" was the motif behind the advertising plan and was then heard as DuPont's slogan on the weekly show. Did the idea of radio work out satisfactorily for DuPont? Well, the program ran for more than twenty years and had a Crossley rating between 12 and 13.

In the radio business this is what was known as an "institutional" program. In other words, it doesn't try to sell the product of its sponsor as much as it tries to build up good will and familiarize the public with the sponsor's name. Many radio programs were failures because, although they were good shows, they didn't send the sponsor's sales up. *Cavalcade* didn't have to worry about that - all it needed to do to be a success was give an inspiring and entertaining half-hour once-a-week, and to that end it hired radio's most capable actors. America's best-known authors, and every now and then an unusual guest star.

Ideas for the stories presented on *Cavalcade* usually come from the story editor, John Driscoll or Mary Cummings (depending on the years), who researched the stories and wrote a proposed outline. The outline was then discussed by *Cavalcade*'s production staff, which consisted of the director, producer, story editor and other members of the radio department of the agency, BBD&O, Inc., which produced the show.

If this group approved the idea for the story, the story editor and the radio account executive for *Cavalcade* at the agency, took it to be approved by the Radio Division of the DuPont Company. The story was then assigned to a free-lance radio script writer. A date was set for the receipt of the first draft. This draft was then discussed and criticized in the same way as the outline. A first draft was also sent to *Cavalcade*'s historian, Dr. Francis J. Ronalds, who checked the story for authenticity. The necessary changes were made by the author, and the script was then scheduled for broadcast.

At this time various other people, including the casting directors, publicity writer and composer of music, went into action. The producer of *Cavalcade* worked closely with director Jack Zoller to cast the leading roles. When the stage or screen star had been contacted, Jack Zoller and the assistant director, began casting the supporting roles for the play. This usually took place from three to six weeks prior to the airing of the show.

In the meantime, publicity on the show was under way. Each week, items on the stars and the story were sent to columnists. A radio brief, outlining the story idea and naming the star, went to all NBC stations carrying *Cavalcade*. A general release, often times with added items of interest which took place at a previous broadcast, were mailed to newspapers throughout the country. Various organizations and clubs, colleges, school systems, groups of nurses or scientists, who might be interested in a particular script, were informed of the broadcast with letters.

"Spot" announcements to be read by an announcer on the various stations were sent out. At rehearsal, the star records special promotional announcements which were sent to NBC stations. These were sent out on the network's closed circuit. Ardon Cornwell, who wrote the original music for each *Cavalcade* drama, composed and orchestrated music suitable to the theme of the show, and went over it with conductor Donald Voorhees.

The show then went into rehearsal. On the Tuesday before the scheduled broadcast, the director, assistant director, engineer, sound man, composer, conductor of the orchestra, the publicity writer and the star and cast assemble in the studio. They all sit around a table for a "reading rehearsal" first. Following the "reading rehearsal," pictures of the star and the cast are taken to be sent to radio and screen magazines for publication. At this time, too, records for the special promotional announcements are cut. During the rehearsal of play before the microphone the director, Jack Zoller works to obtain the proper interpretation of their parts from the cast and the proper balance of voices and sound. As soon as the mike rehearsal is completed, a record is cut of the show.

The record was played at the agency for the production staff, who may make suggestions for improving certain parts of the program. The show was then almost ready for the air. When the star and the cast assemble for rehearsal on Tuesday afternoon, they were given the revisions in the script. At this time the orchestra was on hand, and the show went into dress rehearsal. Following the dress rehearsal, attended by members of the production staff and representatives of the Du Pont Company, another short meeting was held to obtain any last minute suggestions.

Air-time for *Cavalcade*: just prior to the "stand-by" signal, Ted Pearson (later Cy Harrice), the narrator, or Bill Hamilton the announcer, went in front of the curtain to tell the theatre audience something of the background of *Cavalcade* and to introduce the cast. Following the first broadcast, which was aired to all eastern and midwestern states, the *Cavalcade* group is free for two and one-half hours, during which time they usually have dinner. When special guests have attended the broadcast, they come backstage to meet the star and cast, and often have their pictures taken with them. These pictures are used for publicity for magazines, newspapers and other periodicals.

The production staff, star, cast, and orchestra all return to the theatre a half-hour early for the repeat broadcast at 11:30 p.m. EST which was heard in all the mountain and western time zone states. Midnight on Tuesdays means that another *Cavalcade* program has been broadcast to about eight million listeners, and Wednesday means that all the wheels start moving again on next week's show.

Dr. James R. Angell, President Emeritus of Yale, says:

"There is an old saw to the effect that history never repeats itself, and from this assertion the inference is often drawn that the past can teach us nothing of value for the future. Taken literally the *assertion* is true, but the *inference* is quite wrong.

"We are living in a period when world-shattering events are following one another with unprecedented rapidity, and the importance of a knowledge of history and of the prodigious forces which are at work in it was never greater.

"The new Cavalcade program offered by the Du Pont Company over the facilities of the National Broadcasting Company promises to set a brilliant new pattern for sponsored radio productions. Drawing upon distinguished writers and scholarly historians, supported by skilled and experienced producers, it presents on the air the most significant personalities and the most dramatic events in the centuries-old history of the western world, culminating in the creation and development of the United States.

"To students in schools and colleges and to all thoughtful persons who would grasp the meaning of our troubled times, the program offers complete authenticity for illuminating material of absorbing interest.

"I predict for it an outstanding success which I feel sure will not be overlooked by other sponsors. Indeed, I anticipate that it will open a new chapter in the evolution of commercial radio by showing how fine entertainment may be combined with the enlargement of knowledge and the enrichment of understanding."

TO GIVE YOU AN EXAMPLE OF THE STAFF INVOLVED IN *CAVALCADE OF AMERICA* . . .

This is a list of BBD&O creative people who worked all or part of their time on *The Cavalcade of America* in 1948 and their duties. This does not include the guest stars, supporting cast, or the numerous performers in the orchestra!

1. Arthur Pryor, Jr. (12 1/2%) - BBD&O Vice President in charge of radio. His job was the genera supervision of BBD&O *Cavalcade* personnel, scripts and production.

2. Maurice Collette (20%) - Account Representative. Collette was general supervision and planning.

3. Harold Blackburn (100%) - Radio Account Representative. Blackburn's responsibility for scheduling of scripts, selection of regular cast and stars, obtaining of suitable rehearsing and broadcasting facilities, in and out of town, personnel of theater, financial arrangements, number and location of stations, station relations, scheduling of meetings, BBD&O's operation on commercials, and publicity.

4. William Millard (100%) Junior Radio Account Representative, Assistant to Harold Blackburn. Millard was transferred to another account in June of 1948, and replaced by John Brady for the fall season. By early 1949 Millard was back on *Cavalcade*, and Brady moved on to other prospects.

5. John Brady (50%) Junior Radio Account Representative, Assistant to Harold Blackburn. See above entry in William Millard for his contribution to the series.

6. John Driscoll (100%) Story Editor. Research for suitable subjects for scripts, submission of subjects in suitable form to BBD&O Story Committee and then to Du Pont, assignment of okayed subjects to writers, follow-up of writers to get scripts finished to meet the schedule, revision of scripts as necessary.

7. George Kondolf (47 1/2%) Producer and Script Editor in charge of supervision of selection of subjects for scripts, of writers, of cast, both AFRA and star. Judgment of rehearsal and production of show on the air. His *Cavalcade* duties relinquished in September.

8. Gwen Owen (10%) Reader. Gwen read and researched potential material for *Cavalcade* scripts.

9. Dr. Francis Ronalds (100%) Historian advisor on historical accuracy of scripts.

10. George Albee (100%) Writer of commercials.

11. Jack Zoller (100%) Who could forget the director? His job, selection of cast, both star and AFRA, judgment of music, rehearsal and production of show on the air, final responsibility for quality of broadcast.

12. Gladys Franklin (85%) Assistant Director. Actual employment of cast, responsibility for cast during rehearsals and broadcast. Timing and physical revision of scripts and commercials.

13. Edwin Marshall (25%) Negotiations and closings with stars.

14 and 15. Kenneth Webb (5%) and David White (2%) Supplies Hollywood negotiations for talent.

16. Wayne Tiss (4%) Vice-President in charge of Hollywood office General advisory, scripts and production. Negotiations with Hollywood writers and stars.

17. Kay Winn (27 1/2%) Negotiations for rights and executions of contracts with publishers, writers and stars.

18. William Maloney (4 1/2%) Head of BBD&O Publicity. General supervision of *Cavalcade* publicity.

19. James McGarry (20%) Head of BBD&O Publicity. Supervision and planning of *Cavalcade* publicity.

20. Doris Porter (82 1/2%) Writes and sends publicity to list of columnists, radio editors. NBC general publicity - contacts and cooperates with special groups interested in individual *Cavalcade* broadcasts. Gets stories and pictures of special nature at theater and distributes them to DuPont plant publications and other potential users.

21 and 22. T.P. Coyle and A.J. Scannel (Each 1%) Publicity. Writer and consultant.

23. James Fitzpatrick (15%) Publicity. Mechanical production of publicity material. Preparation of clipping books and evaluation reports.

24. Frank Silvernail (12 1/2%) Head of BBD&O Radio Time Buying. Supervision of preparation of list of stations, rates, discounts, time.

25. John Bestecki (3%) Radio Time Buying. Preparing of lists of stations, rates, discounts, time.

26. Eleanor Olsen (25%) Distribution of *Cavalcade* tickets and obtaining tickets to other air shows as requested. Teletype operator.

27. T.D. Anderson (9%) Research. Comparison and evaluation of ratings, times, networks and programs.

28. Will Force (8%) Copywriter. Copy for *Cavalcade* programs, literature and advertisements.

29. August Schnitzler (6%) Artist. Layouts for *Cavalcade* programs, literature and advertisements.

30. Herbert West (1%) Head of Television Department. Preparation of data for consideration of television for DuPont.

31. Thomas Wright (2%) Television. Preparation of data for consideration of television for DuPont.

32. Chester Kulesza (5%) Television. Preparation of data for consideration of television for DuPont.

33. R.C. Pond (1%) Decoration and signs for theater.

34. Nestor Thayer (11%) Billing. Computation of fees to AFRA actors and musicians, preparation of authorizations for payments for publishers, authors, musicians and actors.

35 to 41. (100%) Radio Plan Board includes Fred B. Manchee, Chairman
        Charles H. Brower   Arthur Pryor, Jr.
        Wickcliffe Crider   Carroll P. Newton
        Robert Foreman   Herbert West

42. Bill Hamilton (100%) Commercial spokesman.

It was difficult for even members of DuPont to imagine how much time, effort and how many people were engaged in bringing the popular network program to the air.

Walter S. Carpenter, Jr. (President of DuPont): "We were surprised to learn that approximately seventy-five people from the NBC network, from our advertising agency, Batten, Barton, Durstine and Osborn, Inc., of New York, and from the DuPont Company, contribute in one way or another to preparing for a *Cavalcade* broadcast. Many of them are working full time on *Cavalcade*, some are consultants, and others are talent who need appear only for rehearsals and the actual broadcast."

HERE'S THE STORY BEHIND "THE NEXT VOICE YOU HEAR"

MGM's big movie of 1950 was *The Next Voice You Hear* by George Albee, who wrote the commercials for DuPont's *Cavalcade of America* radio program. When asked, George said he didn't know whether writers were born or made, but that he started at a very early age in life. He wrote his first story when he was twelve. Its title was "Kala, or The Mysterious Mountain" and he hammered it out on an old *Chicago* type-writer which belonged to his doctor father. And hammered is the right word; for the ribbon on the machine was 10 years old and George had to hold the carriage and whack each letter eight times.

Albee, although he was born in Wisconsin, where his grandfather was president of the state normal school, was brought up in southern California. He attended Manual Arts High School at Berkeley, California, graduating in 1927. After college he played his way through Japan and down the China coast to the Philippines with a jazz band.

George Albee: "Returning home, I made a series of one-reel motion pictures at colleges and universities, saved my money and went to Europe. There I spent a year and a half in England, France, and North Africa - total cost, above and beyond steamship fare, five hundred dollars. I do not advise anyone else to try this since it involved, among other things, crossing the Mediterranean in the hold of a freighter with a hundred diseased and dying Arabs."

Back in Los Angeles, Albee went to work for Universal Studios. He wrote the dialogue for an early talking picture called *Hell's Heroes*. After one look at the print, he hastily moved to New York state where he lived ever since, in an old Dutch farmhouse in the Catskills. But perhaps the picture was not quite as bad as he thought, for it had since been given several awards and in an interview printed in *Collier's* magazine, its director, William Wyler, spoke of it as one of the best "westerns" he had ever made.

The story behind Albee's picture for MGM illustrated the old adage that "big oaks from little acorns grow." One day George was having lunch in the dining room of the Hotel DuPont with Dr. Allston Morris, resident physician of Delaware Hospital. He was trying to induce Dr. Morris to come to work for the DuPont Medical Division - which young Morris later did. During lunch the two men were chatting about the state of the world and George said he wished God would come on the radio and give people such a bad scare that they would behave themselves. Morris laughed and between the two of them, over coffee, he and Albee dreamed up a lot of miracles that might do the job.

George Albee: "A few evenings later I spent the evening in New York with a friend, Dale Eunson, author of the play 'Guest in the House' and fiction editor of *Cosmopolitan* magazine. He asked me why I did not write for magazines and I replied that because they refused to print stories with any originality in them."

As an example, Albee mentioned the story idea he had had in Wilmington. "Write it," said Eunson, "and we'll buy it."

"I'll bet you ten bucks you won't," said Albee.

"I'll bet you ten bucks we will," said Eunson.

So Albee went home and in four days wrote the story - while in bed with a cold. He admits he laughed so hard at his own humor that he nearly fell out of bed. *Cosmopolitan* bought the tale five minutes after it left the editor's desk. Within a month the State Department had published it in eleven foreign languages and shortly after this, MGM's new production chief, Dore Schary, bought it for his studio.

George Albee: "I believed the picture would never be made because of technical difficulties. Late in 1949, however, Dore Schary was in New York for the preview of *Battleground*. He got to bed late after the premiere and had a restless night. At dawn, Schary jumped out of bed shouting, 'I know how to make it! I know how to make it!' (laughs)"

- NEW FEATURES
- NEW STARS
- VIVID DRAMA
- FINE MUSIC

It's bigger, faster moving, and even better than ever—this 4th consecutive year of the *Cavalcade of America*. Outstanding among the new features of this current broadcast series are JAMES TRUSLOW ADAMS, noted author and historian who will act as historical consultant in the selection and preparation of story material; THOMAS CHALMERS, narrator, whose varied career on the stage, screen and in opera recently attained a new high in public recognition through his rôle as narrator in the documentary film, "The River"; and GABRIEL HEATTER, noted for his epic news commenting, who will relate stories from the interesting world of chemistry. DON VOORHEES and his 30-piece symphonic orchestra will provide the musical setting.

Into millions of American homes—Du Pont again brings vivid, colorful, absorbing, and little-known stories of real Americans. Heroes, humorists, kings of sport, statesmen, scientists, explorers —all come to life for radio listeners, to make people thrill with pride for the American Cavalcade.

CAVALCADE of AMERICA

**CBS NETWORK
EVERY MONDAY**

**EASTERN TIME ZONE
8 p. m.**

WADC	Akron	WABC	New York
WOKO	Albany	WDBO	Orlando
WCAO	Baltimore	WCAU	Philadelphia
WLBZ	Bangor	WJAS	Pittsburgh
WEEI	Boston	WPRO	Providence
WGR	Buffalo	WRVA	Richmond
WCHS	Charleston, W.Va.	WHEC	Rochester
WBT	Charlotte	WTOC	Savannah
WKRC	Cincinnati	WMAS	Springfield
WGAR	Cleveland	WFBL	Syracuse
WJR	Detroit	WDAE	Tampa
WDRC	Hartford	WJSV	Washington
WMBR	Jacksonville	WORC	Worcester
WQAM	Miami	WJNO	W. Palm Beach

**CENTRAL TIME ZONE
7 p. m.**

WGST	Atlanta	WHAS	Louisville
WAPI	Birmingham	WREC	Memphis
WDOD	Chattanooga	WCCO	Minneapolis
WBBM	Chicago	WLAC	Nashville
KRLD	Dallas	WWL	New Orleans
KRNT	Des Moines	KOMA	Oklahoma City
KTRH	Houston	KFAB	Omaha-Lincoln
WFBM	Indianapolis	KTSA	San Antonio
KMBC	Kansas City	KMOX	St. Louis
	KTUL	Tulsa	

MOUNTAIN TIME ZONE
(Rebroadcast)
10 p. m.

KLZ	Denver	KSL	Salt Lake City

PACIFIC TIME ZONE
(Rebroadcast)
9 p. m.

KARM	Fresno	KSFO	San Francisco
KNX	Los Angeles	KIRO	Seattle
KOIN	Portland	KFPY	Spokane
	KVI	Tacoma	

At nine o'clock in the morning, in the New York office of the studio, he telephoned to the West Coast and ordered the people there to get to work on a tentative picture script. William Welman, the studio's ace director, asked to have the picture assigned to him. Its star was a young actor named James Whitmore, who played the part of the tough sergeant in *Battleground* and who was being built for stardom by M-G-M.

It was Albee who wrote the radio commercials for the DuPont *Cavalcade of America* episodes. Every week he turned out a new two-page draft, which would later be edited, briefed, and carefully placed in the latest script to be broadcast.

"SOUNDS LIKE A COVERED WAGON"

Sound effects for *Cavalcade* are a story all of their own. Present day mechanics in that field can master almost any sound of a current nature they have to cope with, but when it comes to reproducing an 1885 grindstone, or a Dutch bowling match on the New Amsterdam Green, then research of a very exacting and accurate nature was required for this was a show in which radio paints its settings with sound - it had to be good. Jack Paine was Studio Engineer for *Cavalcade*.

> **Jack Paine:** "The job of studio engineer is comparable to that of a motion picture cameraman. The studio engineer can fade, cross-dissolve, or blend sounds the same way a cameraman can fade, cross-dissolve or blend picture images. The engineer can intensify dramatic effect similar results with special angle shots and trick lens."

Such a comparison serves to suggest the responsibilities and importance of the engineer in a dramatic program such as *Cavalcade*. Sound effects, dialogue, and music must be blended or accentuated to exactly the right degree in order to achieve the intended dramatic effect. One slip, and the mood of an entire scene might be shattered. Jack doesn't seem to mind being an unsung hero at all. In fact, he's quite happy about his assignment with *Cavalcade*. And, somehow or other, besides being a busy engineer and an equally busy father, he has found time to visit all forty-eight of the forty-eight states. He joined the studio engineer job for *Cavalcade* in the fall of 1947.

One of the most fascinating jobs in radio - according to Al Scott, was to be a sound effects man. Al ought to know, for he's been a sound effects man at NBC for twelve years, and spent more than four years as a sound technician on the Du Pont *Cavalcade*.

Al had to be something of an actor, as well as sound man, for he was called upon each week during the warm-up to *Cavalcade* to give a demonstration of sound effects for the studio audience. This was more important in some shows than others, for the audience laughing at the antics of a sound man has broken up many a tense, dramatic broadcast. So, studio audiences are warned by Scott about unusual effects, especially such a thing as free-for-all fight. For these rough and tumble effects, Al smashes wooden boxes, among other things, to make it sound as though someone were having a chair broken over his head.

Many sound effects are surprising to an audience. In creating the sound of a horse galloping, Al uses a couple of leather cups on a hard surface of in a box of sand, pacing the rhythm to the speed called for in the script. He crinkles a piece of Cellophane very close to the mike to make the sound of an egg frying or logs burning in the fireplace. Wind, rain and thunder are on records, but he loves to tell *Cavalcade* audience that to make snow, all you do is tear up white paper and throw it into the air.

Al Scott: "Often the most obvious way of devising a sound effect is to use the real thing. When it is impossible to use the real thing I depend on special recordings or on ingenious inventions of my own."

In addition to *Cavalcade*, Al had created sound effects on many other top NBC shows. A few of them were *The March of Time*, *Mr. District Attorney*, *The Aldrich Family* and *Big Story*. On television he supplied the sound effects for *Howdy Doody*.

RELUCTANT PRAISE FOR THE WRITER (PART TWO)

A glance at the authors of the past broadcasts reveals an enviable list of names. Drawing writing talent from the varied literary field, *Cavalcade* has had as authors of its scripts many famous playwrights, short-story writers, novelists, poets and radio writers.

Kenneth Webb, successful playwright, wrote and directed *Cavalcade* during its first four years, beginning in 1935. Among the Broadway stage hits on which Webb collaborated were "Gay Divorce," "One of the Family," and "Zombie." Maxwell Anderson, author of "Winterset" and "Knickerbocker Holiday"; Philo Higley, who wrote "Remember the Day"; Arthur Miller, Pulitzer Prize winner and author of "All My Sons" (who admits that he only wrote scripts for *Cavalcade* because he needed the money); and Alexander Woollcott, famous drama critic and author, were others in the same field who contributed scripts.

Both Woollcott and Carl Sandburg narrated *Cavalcade* shows in addition to writing scripts. Sandburg also collaborated with Stephen Vincent Benet on *Cavalcade*'s "Listen to the People." Benet's famous Christmas play about the Nativity, "A Child is Born" was broadcast on *Cavalcade*. Another famous play, which was repeated several times, was Marc Connelly's adaptation of his book "The Green Pastures."

Looking still further down the list of *Cavalcade* authors are the names of the poet, Norman Rosten; short-story writer Mignon Eberhart; Albert Payson Terhune, so famous for his animal stories, and Henry Fisk Carlton, author of the beloved "Snow Village" sketches.

Many of the authors who wrote some of the early *Cavalcade* scripts have remained in radio. Writer-director Norman Corwin had several scripts broadcast, as did Jerry McGill, later author-director-producer of *Big Town*, and Robert Tallman, who co-pilots radio's popular *The Adventures of Sam Spade*. Tallman also penned scripts for *The Whistler* and *Suspense*. Morton Wishengrad, writer of the radio expose of Communism titled "Communism, U.S. Brand," also wrote for *The Eternal Light*. Erik Barnouw was president of the Radio Writers Guild. Barnouw taught radio writing at Columbia University and was the author of two books on the art of radio writing.

Other *Cavalcade* writers include short-story writer Mignon Eberhart; Albert Payson Terhune, famous for his animal stories, Louis Bromfield, novelist.

Irve Tunick has been writing network shows for years. His first show was *The World is Yours*, done by the Smithsonian Institute in cooperation with NBC around the middle thirties. Tunick wrote free lance for such programs as *Transatlantic Calls* (CBS), *Words at War* (NBC), *Listen America* (ABC) and *School of the Air* (CBS). While writing for *Cavalcade*, he was also busy writing for the Sunday afternoon program *The Eternal Light* on NBC, and the historical *You Are There* for CBS. He also wrote numerous CBS documentaries.

Tunick has written special institutional shows for American Legion Auxiliary, National Conference of Christians and Jews, and Disabled American Veterans. He has won a first place award in one division in 1948 for *The Friend of Peter Stuyvesant* on CBS, written for National Conference of Christians and Jews. In August of 1949, General Wainwright presented him a special citation for shows done during the past three years for Disabled American Veterans.

Ann Barly, the author of the best selling book "Patrick Calls Me Mother," wrote a number of *Cavalcade* radio plays, as did novelist Louis Bromfield. Robert E. Sherwood, who penned "Abe Lincoln in Illinois" was still another *Cavalcade* writer. Arch Oboler, who later became a Hollywood producer and one of the first to bring mystery stories to radio was an early contributor. John Driscoll alternated with Ken Webb in writing most of the scripts for the first four years, and wrote for *Cavalcade* almost from the very beginning, except for interruptions for war service.

In addition to his work on *Cavalcade*, Driscoll has edited scripts on other musical and dramatic programs including "The March of Time." Shortly before the war he was loaned by DuPont to the War Department to write with Norman Corwin and edit a thirteen-week four-networks series, titled *This is War!*, which Corwin directed. Extra-curricular activities have included some writing for and of the theatre for the late John Anderson of the New York Journal. One of Driscoll's original scripts was used as the basis for the film, *Knute Rockne - All American* (1940), which starred Ronald Reagan and Pat O'Brien. His other motion picture work, during another leave of absence, was helping to prepare the shooting script for the picture *The Hucksters* (1947) for which he received a screen credit of "Technical Director."

During the war, Driscoll served as a Lieutenant in the Navy, first in the Office of the Secretary of the Navy and later as assistant Navigator on the U.S.S. Iowa where he also delivered daily newscasts. By the end of the war he was on the staff of Admiral Nimitz. He also completed a staff course at the Naval War College.

THIS IS THE ANNOUNCER SPEAKING

Ted Pearson, narrator for *The Cavalcade of America*, got his start in radio in 1926 as a singer for a Chicago radio station. He went from singing to announcing to "general handy-man" about the studio and finally became a producer of several musical programs.

Ted went back to announcing, and was heard on the *Armour Hour, The Chicago Symphony* broadcast, and the famous *Empire Builders* for Great Northern Rail Road.

Ted came to New York in 1934 as one of the first free-lance announcers in radio and got a job with Fred Waring's "Pennsylvanians." In 1937 Ted went to Hollywood under contract to MGM, and made two pictures while there. One was *Navy, Blue and Gold* (1937) with Robert Young and James Stewart, the other was *Test Pilot* (1938) starring Myrna Loy, Clark Gable, Spencer Tracy and Lionel Barrymore. While in Hollywood, Ted also announcer for the *Good News* show and in 1941 he returned to New York and his first love . . . radio. In early 1950, Pearson left *Cavalcade*. . . perhaps because of an off-the-clock incident.

A memo addressed to Ted Pearson, dated January 13, 1950 suggested the reason for his leave of absence. The following are excerpts from a memo from producer Harold L. Blackburn, dictated following the Wilmington origination (Christmas broadcast) to those concerned with the DuPont account in the office of Batten, Barton, Durstine & Osborn, Inc.

"I am deeply concerned over the reports of the actions of Ted Pearson following the rehearsal in Wilmington on Monday."

"I suppose we could pass this over by feeling that as far as the broadcast was concerned everything was in order and OK. However, it goes beyond that. What any of the personnel of the program do away from the theatre of broadcasts in New York short of publicly scandalizing themselves does not concern us. However, when we are out of town we are in the spotlight. All of us collectively and individually represent our client, our agency and the advertising business and personal department assumes much greater importance under these conditions."

"I propose that we continue him on probation and recommend that we write him a formal letter telling him that his personal conduct on out of town shows from the minute he leaves New York until he returns is as vital as his conduct at air performance, and if at any time he acts in a manner unbefitting the occasion we would expect his resignation without notice."

Blackburn's recommendation had been accepted in part. The letter also informed Pearson that if he had desire to, he could "continue on the show except for out of town performances. The boys who were exposed to the Wilmington situation just feel they can not run the risk of a 'repeat performance' on out of town shows."

Bill Hamilton, the tall, dark and handsome announcer had boyhood ambitions to becoming a doctor. He even attended pre-medical college at Ohio State University. But somewhere along the line he discovered that a radio career was the thing for him. An audition proved how right he was, and so in 1935 he started to work as an announcer for WCOL in Columbus, Ohio.

Bill held a variety of announcing jobs for Ohio for the next few years. During the war, he became an officer in the U.S. Navy. After leaving the service, he joined The DuPont Company as radio manager. Six months later, he began announcing for *Cavalcade of America*.

In the fall of 1948, Bill decided he would like to spend all his time as an announcer, so he came to New York to free-lance. His first job - you've guessed it - was announcing *Cavalcade*. Bill's colleague on the show, Ted Pearson, narrated the plays, while Bill, familiar with DuPont products, delivered all the commercial messages. His was also the first voice heard on the program each week, when he informs the radio audience that they are to *The Cavalcade of America*.

Hamilton was also announcer on *Celebrity Time* on CBS-TV. He never failed a subject but still spent eight years as an undergraduate. You see, Bill started out at Ohio State in 1931. He had to work a quarter semester to be able to afford school for the next quarter. This kept up until Bill finally graduated in 1939. Incidentally, Hamilton's reunion since 1939 was at the Ohio State-Michigan game on November 25, 1950.

WHAT SWEET MUSIC DO I HEAR?

Donald Voorhees was a veteran of radio. Voorhees was conducting on the air even before the formation of the National Broadcasting Company in 1926. Voorhees started his musical career early. His first music lessons were on the violin, when he was five. Two years later he started to study the piano and then the organ. His early studies were in Allentown, PA., where he was born, and in Harrisburg, PA. Voorhees later studied with the late Dr. J. Fred Wolle, founder of the Bach Bethlehem Choir.

At eleven, Voorhees was playing the organ and leading the choir in his family's church. At twelve, he played the piano in the Lyric Theater in Allentown, PA. When he was fifteen, while still in high school, he became conductor of the theater's orchestra. At that time the Lyric Theater housed many tryouts of Broadway musicals, and Voorhees met many producers and artists.

Just two days after his graduation from high school, when he still pondered whether to go into choral work or the theater, he received an unexpected telephone call asking him if he would come to New York to direct the orchestra for a Broadway show. He accepted at once, and several days later the seventeen-year-old musician conducted the opening performance of "Broadway Brevities of 1920" starring Eddie Cantor. This was the beginning of a series of engagements to conduct many of the hit shows of the 1920's. George White's "Scandals," "The Right Girl," "Rain or Shine," and five editions of Earl Carroll's "Vanities" were among a few he conducted.

In 1924 Voorhees started conducting concerts on station WEAF, later WNBC, New York, from the stage of the Earl Carroll Theater. In 1928 he turned his full attention to radio and had directed music on many of radio's leading musical and variety shows since.

Voorhees, married, had at least one daughter and son. He had been a dog fancier and at one time had 150 Scotch terriers in his kennels. During *Cavalcade*, however, he had only one house pet.

Many honors have been given to Voorhees, including two honorary doctorates in music. In the annual poll of radio and music critics conducted by *Musical America Magazine* he has been singled out year after year for honors.

For years one of the Voorhees trademarks was his pencil, used instead of a baton. In 1948, however, he returned to the baton, so that the large orchestra and chorus would be sure to see his beat. (Rumor has it that he almost poked an eye out of one of the musicians during a performance.) But pencil or baton, Voorhees has been a leading figure in music on the air throughout the development of radio.

As the dramatic material of *Cavalcade* programs gradually became more complex, more varied transitional music was needed. In keeping with the exacting historical accuracy imposed on the *Cavalcade* scripts, the music too was derived by painstaking research from authentic melodies popular at the period being dramatized. In the episode "Daniel Boone" the incidents were separated by music which he must undoubtedly have heard during his lifetime. A Civil War scene was given flavor by a tune which people were whistling in 1861. George Washington must not be allowed to dance a minuet by Paderewski! To find the right music for specific historical dates involved endless research in musical libraries, and once found, the melody had to be arranged to suit the requirements of program timing and of being played by a modern symphonic orchestra. This authenticity idea was carried so far that supersensitive musicians working with *Cavalcade* objected to using a charming snatch of sea-music from Debussy, written in the nineteenth century, to portray the sea which Amerigo Vespucci crossed in the fifteenth century!

Ardon Cornwell, who composed much of the original music for *Cavalcade*, found that a sense of drama was just as important as musical ability in his job. To anyone not a musical composer, Ardon's job on *Cavalcade* seems an amazing one. He must read and re-read the script to capture the thought and impressions which the author wished to convey to the listener - even when he was handed a second revision and asked to discard the first!

Ardon then composes a theme with variations, or several different themes, to set the different moods of the play. In nearly every show a sound effect of galloping horses, a fight, an explosion, a glass breaking, or a woman crying must be picked up and carried with music (and not become a silent sound effect because of a bang of a drum or the sound of violins). Then, without too obvious a change, with music, set the mood for the next scene. Any changes in the script mean changes in the music.

Ardon came to New York and made his beginning in radio in 1930, following a stint teaching piano at Weltman Conservatory in Malden, Mass. He has done the arrangements and featured orchestrations on such shows as *The Maxwell House Show Boat*, *The Texaco Fire Chief* program with Ed Wynn, *The March of Time*, *Exploring the Unknown*, as well as arrangements for the "Ipana Troubadours," Albert Spaulding and Lawrence Tibbett.

DU PONT
Cavalcade
of America

presents

EDWARD G. ROBINSON

in

"The Doctor With Hope in His Hands"

**MONDAY EVENING
MARCH 11, 1946**

NATIONAL BROADCASTING COMPANY
Coast to Coast Network

8.00-8.30 .... E.T.   9.30-10.00 .... M.T.
7.00-7.30 .... C.T.   8.30- 9.00 .... P.T.
Consult Your Local Radio Timetable

DU PONT
Cavalcade
of America

presents

CLAIRE TREVOR

in

"Builders Of The Bridge"

**MONDAY EVENING
NOVEMBER 5, 1945**

NATIONAL BROADCASTING COMPANY
Coast to Coast Network

8.00-8.30 .... E.T.   9.30-10.00 .... M.T.
7.00-7.30 .... C.T.   8.30- 9.00 .... P.T.
Consult Your Local Radio Timetable

Originating from Hollywood

On Broadway, Ardon composed the music for the two shows, "Virginia" and "Between the Devil." He has also completed a number of long works for symphony orchestra which include the following: "Peter Pan" (with narration and coloratura soprano parts), a "Currier and Ives Suite" for orchestra, a "Violin Concerto," and a group of four "Songs for Orchestra." His "Panorama of Victor Herbert" and his symphonic arrangement of "Dixie" have been performed by the Kansas City Symphony Orchestra.

One of his most important works, as he described, was an untitled opera based on a Biblical subject, not for publication. (Anyone know if he ever completed this work?)

Another musical genius who lent a hand was Donald Bryan. Bryan first displayed an interest in a trumpet at the age of seven. He had very little idea where it would lead to, other than a series of fascinating sounds. Due course of time, however, revealed that Don was destined to play the same instrument under such varying batons as those of Ben Bernie and Arturo Toscanini, as well as conducting the orchestra for *Cavalcade*.

Don began his musical career studying under Erwin Franko Goldman, who now conducted the summer concerts in Central Park in New York. He continued to play the trumpet while attending Lehighton, (PA) High School, Manlius Military Academy, Muhlenberg College and Columbia University. He was also a soloist with the Allentown, PA band for several years. (Yes, it is a coincidence that Voorhees was from Allentown, Pennsylvania as well.)

After a brief sojourn teaching rural school in PA, Don organized a dance band which later became the nucleus of the original Ben Bernie Band. He remained with Bernie as assistant conductor until 1930 when he joined the Fred Waring orchestra in Hollywood. During the next ten years Don spent several seasons with Toscanini and the NBC Symphony Orchestra, the season of 1941-42 conducting *Cavalcade* and later led other orchestras on well-known musical and dramatic radio programs. In 1942 he became musical director for station WMCA in NY.

Arthur Pryor, Jr., son and grandson of famous band leaders, was born in a theatre in St. Joe, Missouri - a showman by both heritage and training. He was, for some years, associate conductor and business manager for his father's band. In 1927 he heard the call of radio, then a curiosity hardly aspiring to the status of either art or industry. As producer of radio shows with the advertising agency trained by the Du Pont Company, he has been closely connected with the evolving successes of *Cavalcade*.

Translating the mood of *Cavalcade* scripts into musical ideas is the task of Kirk Alexander, brilliant young composer whose performance as musical director of Princeton's famous Triangle Club, and whose arrangements of orchestral scores for the Berkshire Playhouse productions at Stockbridge, brought him to the attention of *Cavalcade*. After the historical drama has progressed from story conference to outline form and thence to a definite dramatic structure with its form fairly well determined, Alexander studies it to see how its varying moods can be established and its themes developed in musical terms. Conferring with the producer of the show, he evaluates suggestions as to their musical feasibility. Often it is found that a few bars of music will convey an impression more forcibly than an entire scene. Transitions are made an integrated part of the drama, rather than a mere lowering of the curtain between scenes; as for instance a bell tone grows out of an orchestral interlude and continues as a sound effect for the beginning of the next indicent.

DID YOU HEAR WHAT I HEARD?

George McAneny,
> **(President of The American Scenic and Historic Preservation Society):**
> "Checking *Cavalcade* scripts to see that Caesar's clock does not strike was a far more difficult and laborious task than the general public probably thought. Certainly the harassed "historical consultant had often sympathized with Pontius Pilate's 'What is truth?' but unlike Pilate, he had to stay for an answer."

Listeners who wrote in to point out historical errors in a broadcast of *Cavalcade* did so for various reasons. Some were descendants of depicted characters whose family pride of family tradition had been outraged by mis-information - or delight in showing what they considered to be their superior erudition. Some who wrote in were honestly interested in seeing that the true facts were adhered to. Fortunately for the consultant, usually the writers received their knowledge from an Encyclopedia or some secondary work on the subject.

George McAneny: "It was this latter type that, though the most positive in showing up an 'error' were often wrong. They were those who wrote 'We have caught you out in an awful howler. You spoke of the United States of America in 1777, when you should have said the United Colonies.' In replying, we were tempted to ask if they have ever read the Declaration of Independence."

Most listeners did not really understand what was meant by a source. If an individual writer gained a wide reputation as an authority on any given subject, he was in the producers' minds as a source. It was necessary to know where, what and how to look up "facts." This was not as simple as it sounded. It was also often necessary to know who was the best authority on a given period or person.

All historians were, of course, subject to error. Some amazing ones occurred. For example there was a well known life of Thomas Jefferson that had the Declaration of Independence debated in Carpenter's Hall instead of the State House. Consequently, if there were no available sources to consult on a given question, not one but every secondary work should be studied, and in the event of discrepancies, the standing of the author, date of publication, and even the publisher of the work taken into account in deciding whose story should be followed.

Most mistakes were caught in the script written weeks before the broadcast date. However, scripts were re-written many times and each re-write had to be checked. It was often necessary to make changes the day of the broadcast. Once they were only able to catch what would have been an extremely bad error two hours before broadcast time, thanks to the kindness of the Keeper of the Manuscripts at the New York Public Library, who allowed the consultant to continue on after closing time.

Jack Zoller: "Once we changed the number of stars in David Porter's flag fifteen minutes before *Cavalcade* went on the air. This confusion arose over the fact that the official flag of our country from 1795 to 1818 had fifteen stars and fifteen stripes, despite the fact that new States had been added to the Union."

It was much easier and certainly more pleasant to tell about all the "accidents" one has prevented being broadcast than it was to confess the errors one had made. The historian can not be responsible for a sound effects man assassinating President McKinley with three shots when only two were really fired, but alas, he was a long way from being infallible even about subjects he fondly believed he "really knew about." For instance, he happened to live surrounded by Eighteenth Century muskets, but he allowed Eli Whitney to use a firing pin in assembling a 1798 musket. He likes to think that he read pan for pin, but that was a very lame excuse indeed.

Some letters of protest have their amusing side. For instance, there was a member of the Daughters of the Confederacy, who assured us that the daughter of Jefferson Davis would never have demeaned herself to have even contemplated marriage with a Yankee, or the person who *knew* L'Enfant did not design the Nation's Capitol because a plaque in Pennsylvania stated that Andrew Ellicott was its designer. However, to answer this objection, only to learn a month later that a new life of L'Enfant, "Planner of the City Beautiful," had just been issued which would have made all that work unnecessary.

The fact that usually no real purpose is served by hurting individual or group sensibilities had to be kept constantly in mind. We must also take into account that for dramatic effect, scenes that could have happened are sometimes introduced. The problem here is whether such a scene logically could have happened or whether the protagonists in the scene are in character.

George McAneny: "Perhaps the most frustrating part of the job is researching possible stories that are finally discarded. It often takes more digging to lay the ghost of an old legend than it does to check the facts of a true story. Which is a reminder that the historian should say a good word for the badgered, but patient script writer, who must inwardly rage at some of his pedantic strictures which at times put him in agreement with the feelings of Samuel Butler, who once said, 'I do not mind lying, but I hate inaccuracy'."

Assassin: Mr. President?

McKinley: How do you do? Oh, I'm sorry. I didn't notice your right hand is bandaged. May I offer you this one?

Assassin: No, Mr. President. Let me offer you *this* one!

(Sound - three bullets)

(Crowd reaction) - (key music)

"Three bullets" said the *Cavalcade* script. And three bullets the NBC sound effects man gave the listening public in "The Statler Story." Out in La Farge, Wisconsin one listener solemnly counted each bang and reached for pen and paper.

"The papers of the time and our history books say the assassin, Czolgosz, fired only at President McKinley twice" . . . he wrote to DuPont. And he was right!

Such inaccuracies had been rare in *Cavalcade*'s two decades on the air. A series of distinguished consultants had seen to that. The late Dr. Dixon Ryan Fox, President of Union College, was first. By the sixteenth season, Dr. Francis Ronalds of Princeton, New Jersey, curator of historic sites for the U.S. Park Service as the historical consultant.

But in spite of this expert surveillance, a boner does occasionally find its way into a *Cavalcade* script, and from there over the airwaves to the home of an amateur historian with a sharp ear for mistakes.

In a broadcast about the Declaration of Independence, an actor quoted, "certain *in*alienable rights." A listener who knew his famous documents correctly insisted that the word should have been "*un*alienable." A few weeks later when the Declaration was again quoted, great care was taken to make sure the right word was used. This time another listener protested: "Shouldn't the word have been *in*alienable?" Du Pont's Radio Section, which handled such letters, was prepared to answer that.

Some inaccuracies which listeners thought they spotted were not inaccuracies at all. During a story dealing with the Civil War period, NBC's sound effects man brought a chugging train into a station with a great squealing of brakes. "Don't you know that trains of that time had mechanical brakes?" asked a listener. "What I heard was air brakes." The sound engineer questioned about this, maintained that the sound he had created was definitely mechanical.

In a script dealing with a World War I nurse, the heroine was referred to as "Lieutenant." A lady in Florida drew attention to the fact that nurses had no rank until World War II. Actually, she was right. But it was an intentional error. Nurses' titles of that period were so cumbersome that the scriptwriter used the more familiar term, "lieutenant." Such alterations of fact are considered dramatic license and are used to make the story easier to understand.

Scripts of the *Cavalcade* shows were used in many schools to supplement history courses. They must be as correct as historical research could make them. And, with few exceptions, they were. It was the exceptions, however, that make interesting reading and cause headaches. "People have come to expect authenticity from *Cavalcade*," producer Jack Zoller said. "We can't get by with the slightest slip - and after all, we're only human."

Kenneth Webb: "It is of special interest that the program has been designed for and has received the approbation of all ages and widely separate groups."

Homer Fickett: "Beginning with the first broadcast on October 9, 1935, *Cavalcade*'s stories were told in two episodes, one historical and the other of the present day. Originally *Cavalcade* dramatized traits and characteristics of the American people as best exemplified in the lives of famous Americans. After the first year, this was altered slightly to include little-known facts in American history or heroic or unusual acts by little-known Americans, as well as famous ones."

It is interesting to note that an early *Cavalcade* story on George Washington was unique in that it ignored the Revolutionary War, and outlined the hero's remarkably prophetic experiments in agriculture. And when Edison was ethered there wasn't a whisper about his famous light bulb. The story of the founding of the *New York Tribune* and the love life of Nathaniel Hawthorne were a few odd scripts listeners did not expect to hear on *Cavalcade*.

Originally *Cavalcade* drew its themes from historic fact; later from both past and present, placing greater emphasis on the past; during it's last few seasons it was largely concerned with the present, although an occasional script still dealt with an event of the past that had sharp contemporary significance. 95 % of its heroes have been real rather than fictional.

Jack Zoller: "Changes have also been made in the type of casting for the show. Guest stars were used for the first four broadcasts in 1935. Thereafter, until January 1940, *Cavalcade* broadcasts were presented by a stock company. Since 1940, famous stars of stage, screen and radio have been heard in the leading roles."

Kenneth Webb: "Only once did *Cavalcade* divert for any length of time from the format of presenting stories in the form of plays. This was in the summer and early fall of 1937 when our show became *The Cavalcade of Music*, and the music of well-known living American composers was presented. Devoting one program to each composer, the music of George Gershwin, Richard Rogers, Victor Herbert, Irving Berlin, Jerome Kern, Cole Porter and others were featured."

And the cost of each radio production? Variety Magazine reported in February of 1944 that the budget for The *Cavalcade of America* moved from $5,000 to $7,000 per show (exactly one year before) to $11,500. By 1950, *Cavalcade* productions were costing much more. Stars were being paid between $500 to $5,000, depending on the box office. And by 1950, there was only one live performance, for the East Coast. The program was then recorded for playback to the West Coast. And by 1950, *Cavalcade* was performed on the stage at the Belasco Theater in New York. The seating capacity was 938.

WHAT YOU NEVER HEARD

Here are a few actual submissions from faithful viewers and listeners:

". . . there is another story from down in Georgia - now only seven years old. Is a seven-year story too hot to handle sufficiently ripe to present on television or radio? This one is "Columbians in Georgia." It has never been published as it was and I would have to get a practical guarantee from you that you would publish it on *Cavalcade of*

America before I would consent to write this true story into a play. I suggest that you get a real human story about "The Art Colony" at Stone Mountain and how it was built, from Steffen Thomas, artist sculptor Stone Mountain, Ga. . ."

- *Mrs. May Frank Duffey,*
Atlanta, Georgia

". . . Splendid "Duel at the Corral" tonight at 7:30. Suggest you announce these are true episodes. I also suggest the life of Wild Bill Hickock as a source of really good scenarios. . ."

- *W.B. Bitterbusch,*
Brooklyn 17, New York

" . . . I have a television script on the Civil War, relating to the almost forgotten episode of General Fitz-John Porter, USV, who was cashiered from the Union Army in disgrace and who thirty years later was restored to rank and honor, for having disobeyed an order of his superior officer on the field of battle, on August 26, 1862 at Warrenton Junction, Virginia. Supporting the reinstatement of General Porter to his rank in the Union Army, General Grant wrote in his report to President Chester A. Arthur: '. . . Porter was right in all that he did and said in the camp under Pope, and that had Porter been in command of the Union Army on that field of operations, there would have been no Antietam, no Chancellorsville, no Gettysburg, no Appamatox, and that the fighting would have ended then and there. August 29, 1862.' Would your department be interested in looking at this unusual and detailed script of the Civil War? The script runs to about 5,000 words."

- *Mr. Archie Kilpatrick,*
Penacook, New Hampshire

Author's Note: This letter created a disposition and was rejected because of the implied criticism of Army brass.

"I have the history of Blennerhassett Island, written out for each character, and wondered if your director would like to see it. If so, please notify me and give me his address to send it to him."

- *Mrs. Ray Tavenner,*
Parkersburg, West Virginia

"Please find enclosed some information which I have compiled about my own ancestor, Jonas Catell, III, who served during the entire Revolutionary War and lived and died in Gloucester County, New Jersey. This information is on file in the offices of the Gloucester County Historical Society, Gloucester County Court House, Woodbury, NJ. His descendants have fought in all the Wars to the present time and have been prominent in the affairs of the United States. Among the prominent men was the United States Senator from New Jersey, Arthur Cattell, who served in President Andrew Johnson's cabinet after the assassination of President Lincoln . . . I trust the above information will be of interest to you."

- *Mrs. John J. Madeline,*
Woodlynne 6, New Jersey

"I have listened to your broadcasts of better things for better living. Have you discovered anything that will deaden the sound of streetcars coming in my bedroom windows? I am a few doors off a streetcar line and in summer it is most annoying."

- Bertah Weick
Detroit, Michigan

There were numerous scripts written and submitted. Some were tossed aside and dramatized months after they were completed. Others were never dramatized at all. For the broadcast of March 9, 1942, Madeleine Carroll was originally scheduled to star in a radio adaptation of the great contemporary American novel, "The Age of Innocence," by Edith Wharton. The story poked satire at New York's "society" of the late nineteenth century. It was a circumscribed, stuffy existence typified in the character of young Newland Archer. Into his dull orderly life flashed Ellen Olenska, who could not enter the charmed circle because she represented another stratum of society which his family's "code" had denied him.

Another script written was "Man of the Forest," the story of Gifford Pinchot, one of America's most avid soil conservationists. Gregory Peck was scheduled to star in that script.

Fay Bainter was originally scheduled to star in "Cross Creek," the story of one woman's adventures in a unique and charming community. When Marjorie Kinnan Rawlings left New York for Cross Creek, Florida, to vary her successful writing career with orange growing, she expected to learn a lot. But she hardly expected to meet as fascinating a group of people as she did. The inhabitants of Cross Creek had a reputation for being aloof and slightly belligerent towards newcomers. Aunt Martha Mickens was the only one who welcomed her formally. The others, she met when circumstances forced an introduction - Widow Slater, when the latter's cow broke down the author's fence; Mr. Martin, when Mrs. Rawlings shot his prize pig; and Moe, when she needed him most. There were others, too, whom she found a little strange until she became used to their way of thinking, wherein every man's worth and dignity were respected more than his money, and everybody helped everybody else according to the need. She found Cross Creek a wonderful place.

Alcott's popular novel "Little Women" was also adapted for *Cavalcade*, but that script, just like the others, were never broadcast.

ENTER THE TELEVISION AGE

Judging by the BBD&O list of those who worked on the *Cavalcade* program, DuPont had intentions as early as 1948 to make the transition to television. DuPont was a growing industry that changed with the times. And television was a "ground-breaker." Besides, it would not look good if DuPont were to reject such a growing medium. After all, was it not DuPont that began sponsoring it's own program when radio was still an infant?

S.S. VanKeuren, Vice-President of Hal Roach Studios, Inc., sent Wayne Tiss at BBD&O a four-episode proposal, dated September 1, 1950.

"Enclosed herewith please find a detailed cost breakdown on each of the four stories submitted to us for the *Cavalcade of America* program . . . It is our opinion that "Anna Zenger" and "No Greater Love" could be photographed in two days, but that "Clear and Present Danger" and "The Interchangeable Mr. Whitney" would require three photographic days due to the number of members of the cast and the number of sets . . . We have used a figure of seventy-five dollars per day for principal players, as per our conversation . . . You will note that there is quite a difference in the budget for each one of the four pictures, occasioned for the most part by the varying number of people in the cast, wardrobe and set requirements, together with the extra day needed for photography. However, the average per picture, for the four pictures, comes to a figure less than $15,000.00."

The figures were submitted, however Hal Roach Studios never produced any films for *Cavalcade*.

One production memo dated 1951 strongly suggested Raymond Massey and Walter Reed as host for a television series:

"Our specific recommendation for a star is Raymond Massey. However, as you will see on the chart, there are many names other than Massey that we discussed . . . some of them have greater prestige, some are more famous, and some are more expensive. Of course, we have not contacted Massey as we did not want to go forward in connection with this unless it was acceptable to you. If Massey was acceptable to DuPont, but not available, we would make other recommendations of the same style and type for your approval. Let me give a word about Mr. Massey which will explain why we think be would be ideal to act as the permanent host and to perform in perhaps eight of the shows.

"Mr. Massey is a distinguished actor, both stage and screen; his brother is (or was) the Prime Minister of Canada which gives him some personal background prestige; he is identified in many people's minds with Abraham Lincoln because he has portrayed the part so many times; he has personal presence and dignity, and he is old enough and experienced enough to play the lead in any of the shows that are to be dramatized.

"Next I should like to give you our thinking on subject material. We should like to begin by suggesting that the pictures be divided into three general classifications, although we are not suggesting the classifications appear on the air in sequence as we believe they should be interchanged. The classifications are: Historical (8 in number), Contemporary (14 in number) and The Future (4 in number). Pictures dealing with the future would be based on technical knowledge that is now available. For instance if we were dealing with the atomic era our guest star might be David Lillienthal, or a man of comparable prestige. At the opening of the show Mr. Massey would chat with Mr. Lillienthal and set the stage for the dramatization that was to follow . . . at the end of the show we would perhaps close with Mr. Lillienthal and Mr. Massey.

"Our second and alternative recommendation involves a much less expensive actor and of considerably less prestige than Mr. Massey. Ruth Burch, our casting director, with a full understanding of what we were driving at, suggested a man like

Walter Reed, who could be used in the same manner as Westinghouse uses Miss Furness. Mr. Reed is an excellent actor . . . he's attractive and has a good background. He is still early in his career and without recognition or fame. It is obvious that if he were to become host for the DuPont shows he would not have anywhere near the immediate drawing power that a man in the class of Mr. Massey would. However, if DuPont were thinking on a more long range basis, and decided to pursue a course where they would use a man like Mr. Reed and build him with the show, they would probably be able to make a long term contract with options extending well into future so they would be protected price-wise when the time came that Mr. Reed would have built into an important star. By then Mr. Reed would be identified as a spokesman for DuPont, and we believe strongly that television can build stars even more rapidly than motion pictures. A new good example of this is William Lundigan for Chrysler Corporation.

"The question of cost was discussed pro and con as we are well aware of the economics involved. Our suggestion is that we contact with DuPont to produce 26 shows for $33,000 each. The cost of the star would be in addition . . ."

The television episodes of *Cavalcade* were video taped, instead of a "live" performance, for numerous reasons. The most important reason was because the episodes could be broadcast on numerous stations across the country at different days and times - a convenience for the various stations that were unable to carry a "national" broadcast. The video edition of *Cavalcade of America* was following its radio format in dramatizing episodes from American history. The program on film was much more rewarding in the seeing than in just the hearing. The initial program told the story of how Benjamin Franklin outwitted the British commanders, General William Howe, by prolonging truce talks until General George Washington had a chance to extricate his entrapped troops on Manhattan Island.

Numerous story suggestions were thrown around, lists of *Cavalcade* radio broadcasts were made, some lists went as far as to detail plot descriptions, others just titles and dates. When *Cavalcade* first premiered over the television airwaves, only adaptation of the radio broadcasts were dramatized. A few that appeared on the lists that did not make it to the transition of television were . . .

"Edwin Booth" 9/29/37 (102) and "Edwin Booth" 3/31/41 (220), "The Seeing Eye" 12/2/36 (59) and 11/17/37 (109), "Children, This is Your Father" 10/15/45 (449), "The Law West of the Pecos" 6/11/45 (439), "The Purple Heart Comes to Free Meadows" 2/21/44 (371), "David Crockett" 5/19/41 (227), "Wild Bill Hickok" 11/6/40 (199), "The Story of Penicillin" 4/24/44 (380), "Young Tom Jefferson" 5/25/42 (280), "The Redemption of Lottie Moon" 6/13/50 (660), "Joe Palmer's Beard" 9/13/49 (621), "The Devil's Staircase" 4/7/52 (738), "Metal of the Moon" 1/23/51 (684), "Woman Alone" 6/16/47 (528), "The Stirring Blood" 3/10/47 (514), "Abigail Opens the White House" 2/24/47 (512), "Angels on Horseback" 3/23/42 (271), "A Race for Lennie" 1/29/45 (410), "The Doctor With Hope in his Hands" 3/11/46 (470), "The Unheroic Hero" 2/21/49 (600), "When Cupid Was a Pup" 4/1/46 (473), "Gettysburg" 9/13/48 (577)*

* Civil War stories apparently were not very favorable for *Cavalcade* television, however, when this episode was proposed, it should be noted that the idea of "filmed on location" was suggested.

There were plenty of original story suggestions proposed for television, that were never broadcast on radio's *Cavalcade*. Below is a list of just a fraction of titles and plots, subjects which had been researched but abandoned following story conferences.

"The Lady of Halstead Street" . . . the Jane Addams story. She gave up home and love to do work for others.

"Burbank of the Wheat Fields" . . . Mark Alfred Carlton developed a rust-proof wheat which has been the savior of the world's wheat crop.

"Laboratory Heroes" . . . doctors, human guinea pigs, who experiment on themselves to perfect scientific and medical knowledge and discoveries. Rejected for fear that a program dramatizing men and women who "attempt suicide" was too horrifying to the American public.

"Her Honor, the Mayor" . . . the story of Dorothy McCullough Lee, present mayor of Portland, Oregon, who solved her city's vice and crime problems.

"Operation Bootstrap" . . . "Scio, Ohio, factory employees help rebuild a factory after it burned down.

"Young Man with a Bat" . . . baseball story of Mickey Mantle and his father. Permission had to be received by Mantle to write such a script, which was never given.

"This is an Emergency Call" . . . magnificent heroism of Mrs. Mildred Lothrop, telephone operator, during sudden flood which threatened her community and her four children's lives.

"Buffalo Bill" . . . young Cody's first attempt to play himself on the stage was a hilarious failure, but it succeeded in spite of him and marked the beginning of "westerns" - the ever-popular western show. The rights to dramatize the life of Buffalo Bill was not acquired.

"Ed Mowery, Newspaperman" . . . Pulitzer Prize winner of 1953, Mowery, in answer to plea from convict, uncovered evidence which proved him innocent and won his release from penitentiary.

"Ten Gallon Hat" . . . "how John B. Stetson invented the hat that became the West's best friend.

"Dr. Morton" . . . demonstrated the first use of ether in surgical operation. Rejected because the decision holders felt it to be too complicated when dealing with operations on television.

"Dr. Wiley and Pure Food and Drugs" . . . government chemist who caused laws to be enacted protecting this country's health.

"Harriet Beecher Stowe" . . . author and abolitionist.

"Jonathan Letterman" . . American army surgeon, introduced first ambulance service in the Civil War.

"Samuel Gridley Howe" . . . opened first school for the blind. Taught deaf-blind child, Laura Bridgman, to communicate with others and made her what Helen Keller became to a later generation.

"Mt. Rushmore" . . . how the gigantic sculpture came to be made. There was a proposal to keep costs down for this broadcast by featuring stock footage of the giant heads of Washington, Jefferson, Lincoln, and Roosevelt, however permission had to be granted to feature such footage of the famed sculpture.

"George Elery Hale and the Big Eye" . . . how Hale's dream of a 100-inch telescope came true at Palomar Observatory.

"Judge Harold Medina" . . . the history-making ordeal during the trial of eleven communists.

"Samuel J. Colt" . . . inventor of the revolver - conceived and first utilized a standard machine production. He was the first large-scale employer to assume responsibility for the well-being of his employees.

"Levi Strauss" . . . I'll admit that this would have been an interesting one. The inventor of Levis during the California gold rush days.

"Currier and Ives" . . . printmakers, Americana. They rose to fame, only to succumb to the march of progress in the form of a new illustration process, the Ben Day, invented by boy who worked for them.

"Charles Goodyear" . . . the discoverer of the vulcanizing process for rubber.

"The XYZ Affair" . . . no, this was not the origin of the "examine your zipper" quip. This was the dramatic affair in which Talleyrand tried to extract bribes from Americans, to which our minister Charles Pinckney replied, "Millions for defense, but not one cent for tribute."

"Coleman Sellers" . . . the inventor of photographic motion pictures (later purchased and improved by Edison.)

The following were proposals that made it to the first draft of a script, but never made it off of the proposal table.

"The Post Office Story" . . . approved on April 1, 1955, this script concerned a woman named Miss Mary Wallace of Springfield, Ohio, in June of 1942 who found in her mail one day, a returned letter. She didn't recognize the name of the addressee, a Senora Inez Lopez De Molinaldi of Buenos Aires, Argentina. Although the letter contained information about the three dolls she had recently purchased and added to her collection, there was also a section about the illness of a relative. Regardless of the fact that the letter was addressed to "Miss Mary Wallace, 1808 East High Street, Springfield, Ohio." She turned the letter over to post office officials and the FBI. What the FBI agents discovered was too shocking. It was a letter from an enemy agent, a saboteur, within the country, an Axis operative in Argentina, with information about ships of our Pacific Fleet.

Note: The lady with a doll shop mentioned the types of dolls in her letters as codes for types of navy ships - thus a big china doll would mean a battleship near the Chinese cost, etc. interesting isn't it?

"The Flying Enterprise" . . . this was the story of Captain Carlsen, who for thirteen days in 1952, clung to his doomed ship, "The Flying Enterprise." He taught the world a lesson in courage and devotion to duty. This American merchant ship cracked all the way across the deck and down the sides. Captain Carlsen ordered the passengers and crew to leave the ship, and inspected the boat himself. He saw that she would be afloat for sometime, and as his duty as a captain, stayed with the ship. After thirteen days and two storms later, hungry and wet, Carlsen had to abandon his ship. The wheelhouse doors exploded from the pressure of air and water. Back in New York, Carlsen reported to Hans Isbrandtsen, the owner of "The Flying Enterprise." "I'm sorry I didn't bring the ship back." Then after a slight pause, "When can I go out again?"

Note: "The Flying Enterprise," at the present time, was very well known. It was rejected, however, because it had previously been done on television for another program, possibly Reader's Digest.

"Art For America's Sake" . . . Norman Rockwell, artist of "The Four Freedoms," the boy scout calendars, and numerous covers for *The Saturday Evening Post* was America's best-loved painter, yet most of his life he had been in conflict with the "art artists" who felt he was just an illustrator catering to the public. Then at 3 am on July 16, 1942, he had an idea. Rockwell went into his studio and composed four paintings depicting the Four Freedoms, as his contribution to the War. When they were finished and published in the *Post*, the O.W.I. printed 4,000,000 copies and distributed them around the country. Four Freedoms War Bond Shows were put on and $132,992,539 worth of bonds were sold. Even the "art artists" had to admit Rockwell's work was good, and Rockwell had proved to himself that art for America's sake is true art.

Note: It's not clear exactly why this script was never filmed, something concerning a lack of drama and "possible conflict."

"Doctor Commando" . . . this was the story, done of *Cavalcade* as a radio program on February 26, 1952, about General Sams, Chief of the Public Health and Welfare Section of the United Nations Command in the Far East. Although broadcast over the radio, it was rejected because of "No story elements," and the possibility of a very high budget - in short, cost was a factor.

"One Man's Dream" . . . Jim White is the only man, living or dead, who was responsible for the founding of an entire National Park. He was the discoverer, explorer and the driving force in bringing about the Carlsbad National Park, site of the Carlsbad Caverns. Jim was a young cow hand of nineteen in 1901 when he discovered and began exploring the caverns. Then he tried to interest other people, but nobody believed him. For years he buttonholed celebrities and tried to get them to do something about his find. Finally, in 1923, Jim's efforts were realized when the cave was proclaimed, "The Carlsbad Cave National Monument."

Note: Jim White died a few years before this script was written. His family was agreeable to the idea of a television show and had informed the writer who suggested this project to DuPont - including the fact that they would make material and extensive stock footage available to meet production costs. Still, the script was rejected because it was "Not too exciting."

"The Consulate Story" . . . this was the story of a day in the life of John Sutherland, chief clerk in a U.S. Consulate in a small Asiatic country bordering Red China. But it's a very special day - the last day of a long but commonplace career. For now in his sixties, Sutherland has reached the end of the rope. There will be no speeches, no gold watches, no ceremonies. He is merely a minor figure in a minor post - a man who feels his life has been pretty much of a waste. Rejected because of a "lack of excitement, cloak and dagger. We want no episodes containing 'Is life worth living'?"

When *Cavalcade* was first seen on television, the show was seen on alternate Wednesdays, not every week. *Cavalcade of America*, it was announced in a press release in October of 1952, would later present Peter Zenger's fight for freedom of the press, the early romantic days of Lincoln, the love story of Andrew Johnson and the adventures of Lydia Darragh, the Philadelphia widow who spied on the British during the Revolution. The reason for alternate Wednesdays was simple. DuPont did not want to back all of their money into such a project without a "trial run." If the television series failed, they still had the radio program. But the television series prospered, and for *Cavalcade*'s second season on television, the program was broadcast weekly, instead of by-weekly. And the radio program promptly left the airwaves.

The DuPont concern for the television series also merited a garland all its own. In *Cavalcade*, there were no disconcerting middle commercial to break the mood of the historical drama. Critics called this move as "good salesmanship" and "appreciated."

At one point, the television series under went a change. Dr. Ralph J. Bunche, United Nations Under Security General, gave permission for the new *Du Pont Cavalcade Theatre* to dramatize a portion of his youth for the series. The story was scripted by Joel Murcott, and dealt with Dr. Bunche's boyhood with his grandmother, Mrs. Lucy Johnson, after he was orphaned at the age of 12. According to Warren Lewis, the producer, the series was going to differ from its predecessor, *The Cavalcade of America*, in that it would deal with stories of contemporary American life instead of historical figures. Already completed was "The Story of Nancy Merki," who was stricken with poliomyelitis at the age of eight but overcame the handicap and nine years later became a United States Olympic swimming champion.

The episode dealing with Alcoholics Anonymous, "One Day at a Time," featured a curiosity none of the television episodes had. The producer of that episode expressed the author of the script not be revealed in the credits.

Teachers, minister, mothers and public officials had sanctioned the program, as have all leading radio editors. In 1937 it was designated "The Radio show most acceptable and worthwhile for the general family." Even College and University radio stations still broadcast repeats of this program as education and entertainment fare on summer evenings and Sunday afternoons.

George McAneny: "It is far easier to fool the ear, than the eye. 'I thought he said the wrong date, but I must have been mistaken,' as against, 'Look at that American Officer of the Virginia Line in 1781 carrying a Civil War saber.' On radio, that brave martyr to Yellow Fever, Nurse Clara Maas could be buried to simple sound effects. On television we had to find out just how many men were in the firing squad. Whether the corporal in charge also fired, whether Krags or Springfields were used by regulars in 1898, how much smoke they made, and so on. As a matter of fact, this seemingly simple showing of a line of rifle barrels took a whole lot of digging at the Library of the War College in Washington."

Cavalcade Guests } *Some come to perform some to admire*

The grandson and granddaughter of Charles Harvey, who constructed the Soo Canal, meet Marsha Hunt and Bill Holden, who played the leading roles in "Builder of the Soo."

Stage and screen star Ralph Bellamy relaxes while Director Jack Zoller and lovely actress Louise Allbritton go through a last-minute rehearsal.

This young lady visitor from one of the Du Pont plants watches Lee Bowman of the movies rehearse a tense moment.

Two famous guests, Donna Reed and Dane Clark, inspect one of the sound-effect de-

YOU KNOW THE MAKING OF A RADIO EPISODE,
NOW HERE'S THE MAKING OF A TELEVISION EPISODE

During Christmas week 1955, everyone at BBD&O involved in the selection of scripts for the *DuPont Cavalcade Theater* was looking for a story that would be appropriate for presentation on June 5th, the eve of the twelfth anniversary of D-Day. Meanwhile at *Collier's* that same week, Associate Editor Cornelius Ryan was looking for a good drama-packed article idea for publication in the summer. Fate, or whatever it is that occasionally rubs two creative heads together for sensational results, led Ryan into the Overseas Press Club where a mutual friend introduced him to join John Driscoll, script supervisor for BBD&O. The pair spent the evening discussing various war experiences - Driscoll as assistant navigator on the U.S.S. Iowa, Ryan as a correspondent covering the European invasion. Their talk finally got around to the Battle of St. Lo, considered by many as the bloodiest battle of the invasion, and Ryan recounted the story of Major Tom Howie an the part he played in that battle.

There was Ryan's story idea - and Driscoll's script for DuPont. "The Major of St. Lo" had reached two great audiences - in the pages of June 8 of *Collier's* and on the June 5 *Cavalcade* over ABC-TV. It may reach still a third great audience for several Hollywood film companies gained interest in it as a possible property for a feature length movie.

The drama recounted the advance on St. Lo by Major Howie's third Battalion of the 29th Division. Howie, whose combat record qualified him for a staff job, declined in favor of fighting along with his men. When the story idea came to Ryan that night, Driscoll suggested that if *Collier's* went for it, he would like to submit a synopsis to DuPont and the *Cavalcade* producer for approval. *Collier's* accepted Ryan's story outline at once and scheduled it for the June 8 issue. So John Driscoll then took it to DuPont, and the client thought it had excellent television possibilities. The synopsis then went to producer Warren Lewis, of Four Star Productions, for approval and budget breakdown.

Lewis, at this time, was very high on a story of the Korean War which he was trying to work into his schedule for the very near future. But upon reading "The Major of St. Lo," he immediately prepared a budget for it and dropped the Korean drama. Next, the approval of the War Department was received through Major Thomas Clagget, chief of Radio-TV branch of P.I.O. Footage from an Army film about Howie's division, the 29th, was made available. Dick Bluell, Four Star script editor, flew in from the coast to New York for a conference with Driscoll and Ryan, and the latter, who had authored the *Collier's* article, was assigned to write the treatment for the script. The *Cavalcade* production was now under way.

At this point, BBD&O account executives and public relations people met with advertising and personnel from *Collier's* to coordinate promotion on "The Major of St. Lo." Here is the program they set up and followed through:

1. A special layout within the *Collier's* Story consisting of production stills especially staged by Four Star, showing different phases of the capture of St. Lo. These were taken

two weeks before the actual shooting of the film by photographer Robert Landry, who while a war correspondent, actually took pictures of the fighting around St. Lo that were used in *Life* magazine. The box next to the pictures contained a 150-word promotion for *Cavalcade*.

2. A slide was made of the *Collier's* article and used over ABC-TV Network May 29, for the last fifteen second of *Cavalcade* with live audio, to plug the magazine and the program the next week. Also, a copy of this slide was sent to all *Cavalcade* stations with copy for promotional announcements plugging the article and tele-play.

3. A special mailing was sent by Elliot F. Alexander, DuPont *Cavalcade* public relations man at BBD&O to all promotion managers of stations carrying *Cavalcade* containing a special press release plugging the *Collier's* story, a proof of the story, and a letter explaining how they could capitalize locally on all the national promotion being done. This letter outlined the strategy as follows:

* Press screening and luncheon at the Overseas Press Club in New York for local syndicated columnists such as Hal Boyle, Bob Considine, etc. Also represented will be the 29th Division, and possibly other units active in the St. Lo campaign.
* We will contact the national headquarters of all veterans groups such as the American Legion, Veterans of Foreign Wars, AMVETS, etc., and pass on to them all available information. A follow-up on your part is all that is necessary to get maximum coverage.
* New York papers are being sent biographical material about the production, casting, and people behind the scenes. Enclosed you will find two pages of such facts that should prove interesting to your local press.
* *Collier's* will have on all stands, banners and streamers publicizing both the article and *Cavalcade*. Contact the local *Collier's* distributor and combine your promotional efforts.
* Tie-in on any local D-Day celebration by preparing an exhibit or placing posters in strategic places to help publicize the show.
* The Public Information Officer of the Army (Radio and Television Department) will forward material on the program to base papers and Army publications all over the country. Follow this up by a call to all military bases in your area.
* Set-up an interview over the station with a member of the Armed Forces, stationed locally, who was actually at St. Lo. Plug *Cavalcade* on the news shows the weekend before D-Day and also whenever possible on your daytime programs.
* On the May 29 *Cavalcade* an announcement will be made over the network promoting "The Major of St. Lo" with audio and a slide of the actual cover and double page spread of the June 8 edition of *Collier's*.
* TV Guide, in the edition of June 2, will run a half-page picture taken during the production of the "Major."
* ABC-TV is sending out to all stations carrying this tele-play, an ad mat suitable for use in your local newspapers.
* Included in all *Collier's* advertising for circulation, will be plugs for *DuPont Cavalcade Theater* including one minute and twenty-second spots, on both radio and television.
* Special film trailers, both twenty-second and one minute in length are being specially produced, and you should receive them some time next week.

"The Major of St. Lo" was shot well over *Cavalcade* budget, with Hollywood facilities and Army equipment called into service. Battle scenes called for 92 extras, seven Patton tanks along with many trucks, jeeps and artillery pieces. 24,000 rounds of blank ammo were used and 10,000 rounds of mortar fire. Forty-eight major earth detonations were prepared and exploded. Sixteen Hollywood sets were used, and these included Atlanta's old Peach Tree Lane from *Gone With the Wind* and a bombed-out village scene originally prepared for "GI Joe" which was re-adapted for "The Major" at a cost of $4,000.

But extraordinary as the production itself, was the promotion campaign. This entire hard-hitting drive was accomplished within normal publicity budget limits through everyone's contribution of extra time and effort. DuPont, BBD&O and *Collier's* all worked together for maximum audiences. And they all shared the harvest.

Harold Blackburn, DuPont account executive, Jock Elliott, DuPont account supervisor, Cornelius Ryan, author and associate editor of *Collier's*, and John Driscoll, script editor of BBD&O worked on this project. Jim Brown and Elliott F. Alexander at BBD&O worked out the promotion plans as seen above.

Take another example, "Smyrna Incident," one of the DuPont *Cavalcade*'s more popular episodes. From the inception of the idea to the final print, some 160 people contributed their special talents to make it a show that is historically accurate, dramatic and interesting to the television public. The story concerned the rescue in 1853 of Martin Koszta, a Hungarian who fought against tyranny in Austria, came to America, took out his first papers, and return to Smyrna, Turkey on business, only to be trapped by informers and imprisoned on an Austrian ship. His dramatic release, which threatened an international incident, was promoted by Commander Ingraham, captain of a U.S. man-of-war, who risked a show of force against heavy odds.

The writer and director, Robert Stevenson, who has written six and directed ten *Cavalcade* shows to this point, read everything he could find on the Koszta incident. Historians checked the script for accuracy. The producer got in touch with the Navy and brought in a consultant on naval affairs. The art director, Ernest Fegte, had to know about mosques and minarets, sailing ships and bazaars. The costume and property men located everything from authentic turbans and naval uniforms to guns and sulfur matches.

What looked like a ten-ring circus of carpenters, electricians and set decorators the day before the shooting began turned into disciplined order by 7 a.m. the next day. For every man was an expert in his field - the main actors and production staff had an average of 25 years' experience in motion pictures. Casting had been done with great care. Rehearsals, under Stevenson's direction, were meticulous in their emphasis on every detail. Then when all was ready, the filming was in the hands of the cameramen through whose eyes every scene must be shot. Director of photography, Hal Stine, prepared to shoot the entire episode within three days. Set Decorator Lou Diage checks scenery as two "Turks" wait for the director's call to set. Bob Stevenson made suggestions to the actors before doing a close-up shot as they discussed Koszta's capture. On the set at 6:45 every morning, Web Phillips must work on make-up with the cast and see that the appearances remains good under the hot arc lights. No reflections from sweaty brows are permitted. And finally, the production depended on the experience and scissors of the feature editor in the cutting room.

After all the scenes are shot and film is processed, Sherman Todd edited the show for the best continuity and flow for the television viewer. Throughout the production, a feeling of enthusiasm, permeating the barn-like stage, said "Nothing is more satisfying than creating a good show."

Commercials were filmed with the unbilled assistance of Don Carlos, technician; Elmer Dyer, director of photography; Joseph Denove, director. Joseph Denove headed his own movie company in Europe and made many films there. Dyer has long list of film credits, including such famous aerial epics as *Hell's Angels* (1930) and *Dawn Patrol* (1930). Carlos was a pioneer in lighting effects and 3-D photography. All three made their headquarters in Hollywood, and helped make several *Cavalcade* features.

The actual sequence of events in making a trailer for use on Du Pont's *Cavalcade* television show went like this:

1. The idea was developed by researchers, then was "polished" in a series of conferences in the DuPont Advertising Department.
2. Script writers went to work, making the draft of the story, which was reviewed by many experts before the final form was adapted.
3. A moving picture producer was engaged to do the actual filming. The cost and location was an important factor in the decision of who would do the actual filming, from the three or four studios hired on an almost rotating basis. The director would make detailed plans based on the final manuscript.
4. The producer sends out a scout to select locations that will serve as the best backgrounds for various action to be shown.
5. Actors and make-up men are engaged, locally if possible. Many technical details are also arranged far in advance.
6. Camera crews arrive at the plant and begin shooting sequences that may best tell the story outlined by advertising writers.
7. The film footage is sent to Hollywood for editing and "dubbing in" of sound-track narration, then added to the feature film.
8. The complete *Cavalcade* show is distributed to all of the network outlets and spot stations, where nearly thirteen million viewers tune in.

The commercials for television were titled, and filmed by various production studios from Pathescope Productions, Screen Televideo, Caravel Films, and Jack Denove. Subjects, much like those on radio varied from broadcast to broadcast. Cellophane, Freon, Fibers, Dyes, Bleaches, Rayon, Alathon, Maylar Film, Petchem, Titanium, Research, Safety, Agriculture, Wax, Medicine, and even Research at the Haskell Lab.

The staff at Denove attempted, whenever possible, to create authentic settings and workers. If for some reason they were unable to do so, they improvised. One excellent example is a letter from George P. Neilson, Jr. from Jack Denove Productions, Inc, dated December 22, 1953:

"One thing more - we plan to film Carl Johnson in a studio setting which resembles the area in the DuPont plant where he works. Would it be possible for your plant photographer to take a couple of these pictures and send them by 'Air Mail' to Jack Denove Productions, Inc., Samuel Goldwyn Studios, 1041 N. Formosa Avenue, Hollywood 46, California. If there is any questions, please do not hesitate to call me."

MEMO FROM A 1957 PRODUCER'S FILE

"Last evening, I telephoned Bill Cruikshank, President of Four Star, in an attempt to learn first hand whether or not his company planned to instigate a lawsuit against DuPont as well as Don Sharpe, if we awarded the new Lewis and Sharpe organization a contract for sixteen *Cavalcade* films for the 1956-57 season."
- Robb M. De Graff, dated July 24, 1956.

Throughout the early fifties, the original intention of DuPont was to take *Cavalcade of America* from radio to television. By utilizing simple steps, they were able to try a simple, non-costly broadcast run, consisting of historical tele-plays based off of original *Cavalcade* scripts. The success of the program proved well, and *Cavalcade* left the radio waves, staying on television on a more routine and permanent schedule. Eventually the television episodes lead to original tele-plays of historical events. The format, however, changed when it was decided that dramas of modern stories brought higher ratings than contemporary American history.

For the season of 1956 to 1957, DuPont intended to produce a series of sixteen films. Unlike previous seasons, threats and lawsuits cropped up, and DuPont became the middle man.

On September 12, 1956, an article appeared in the *Hollywood Reporter* reading:

FOUR STAR SUES TO STOP SHARPE-LEWIS FILMING CAVALCADE

"Four Star Films, owned by Dick Powell, Charles Boyer, David Niven, Don Sharpe, Warren Lewis and William Cruikshank filed suit in Santa Monica Superior Court yesterday against Sharpe, former president of the company and Warren Lewis, former producer, asking $500,000 damages and an injunction to stop the new Sharpe-Lewis Company from filming any of the DuPont *Cavalcade* programs.

Four Star contends hat Sharpe while employed by it as the salaried sales agent and executive producer for *Cavalcade* and as a member of the board of directors violated his obligation and that he and Lewis secretly conspired and agreed to seize for themselves a corporate business opportunity belonging to Four Star. Action was taken because of recent announcement that Sharpe-Lewis had been retained to make sixteen new *Cavalcade* films."

By December of 1956, all became clear. Before covering the specific relationships with Sharpe and Lewis, it is important to re-emphasize the general practice under which DuPont had operated in selecting an organization to produce television films. The overall objective had been to obtain the best quality entertainment at the best price. Consequently, Du Pont never felt wedded to any one producing organization. In the five seasons, since 1952, Du Pont had employed eight different producers (see television log).

The final cost of the *Cavalcade* episode "No Greater Love" was $20,700. The final cost of "The Palmetto Conspiracy" was $37,950. A difference in price between these episodes varied because of settings, cast, costumes, and so forth. "No Greater Love" was produced by Chertok, and "The Palmetto Conspiracy" was produced by Denove.

DuPont viewed a contract for producing television films as a business agreement with a supplier to deliver a specific amount of material, just as other contracts the Company made were viewed. The purpose of an option in a television film production contract was for the price protection. It allowed DuPont to buy additional films from a supplier at an established price. Each year, through DuPont's advertising agency, BBD&O had sought and evaluated proposals from a number of the best prospects. These usually included proposals from companies with whom they had been or were currently doing business. The decision for awarding contracts for future production had been based on the appraisal of past performance and potential of an organization, and, its ability to accomplish the over-all program objective.

DuPont's first contract with Don Sharpe on television films was on the West Coast in September, 1954. He met with Messrs, Dewey and De Graff, and Himan Brown of BBD&O. From his history, Sharpe impressed the agency with a number of irons in the television fire; a producer, and actor's agent, as well as an associate in a number of programs and production companies.

In July of 1954, BBD&O had screened a pilot film for DuPont of a proposed television series about contemporary Americans in which Frank Leahy was to be the host-narrator. DuPont made an offer to buy the film ("The Otto Graham Story") outright to place in DuPont's *Cavalcade of America* series. The deal was completed as a result of this September meeting. A contract was made with Don W. Sharpe, and DuPont subsequently telecast the film on November 9, 1954.

Later, the DuPont company learned of plans for subsequent projects. In early 1955, they saw a second film, "The Nancy Merki Story." DuPont made the same offer for this, but it was rejected.

Up to May of 1955, DuPont understood BBD&O had had a number of contracts with Sharpe, first on DuPont's proposal to buy the Merki film, and later, as they approached the time to discuss and evaluate producers for the 1955-56 season, on the subject of a whole series.

During April and May 1955, DuPont began to evaluate producers for the next season. Among the proposals for the forthcoming season they received, was one from Sharpe. It

The brightest stars of the screen perform weekly on the DuPont program

Henry Fonda and Robert Young enjoy themselves at a Cavalcade rehearsal. Fonda was starred the week after Young and stopped in to see how rehearsals went.

Dane Clark, newest movie heart-throb, takes last-minute directions from shirt-sleeved, hard-working Cavalcade director Jack Zoller.

Ida Lupino at the mike, Gayne Whitman, Cavalcade's announcer, center, and Walter Huston in Cavalcade's Hollywood NBC studios.

Here's Doug Fairbanks, Jr. (left), rehearsing his role in the recent timely Cavalcade drama about vaccination, "The Doctor and the President."

Another beauteous headliner on Cavalcade is lovely Janet Blair, shown with John Hodiak, recent groom of Academy Award winner Anne Baxter and a star in his own right.

was submitted on Four Star letterhead, and based on an idea for a series called "The American Story," ("Otto Graham" had been the pilot film). He proposed to use Warren Lewis as producer, and Four Star production facilities. It was also stated the contracting company would be Four Star.

After evaluating all proposals, the contract was awarded to Four Star, and Warren Lewis was specifically named as producer in the contract for twenty-six films. In December of 1955 or January 1956, DuPont learned that Sharpe had resigned as President of Four Star. Sometime in February of 1956, DuPont learned of the Official Films - Four Star merger. DuPont's first opportunity to talk personally with Sharpe about how these developments might affects work on their current *Cavalcade* series, was on February 17, 1956, when he and Lewis were in Wilmington for a story meeting.

DuPont was informed that Lewis would personally follow through as producer of the remaining films in the series. In addition, Sharpe told DuPont of a number of properties he was developing on his own, including "Adam and Eve," "Chicago 2-1-2," "Wire Service," etc. More of the same type conversation went on when Sharpe was in Wilmington on March 6. He told Messrs, Dewey and De Graff of the big plans and the high prospects he had for his properties. He discussed the possibility of setting up his own company to produce any series he sold. He definitely was cool and non-committal about any interest in doing DuPont's *Cavalcade* series in the future.

On March 13 and 14, DuPont began gathering information that would enable them to prepare a proposed budget for the first half of 1957. Warren Lewis was asked about future plans for such projects and his implied that he was somewhat "in the middle," and that things were not too pleasant at Four Star. At that time, DuPont felt wedded to no one producing organization. They did appreciate Lewis' efforts on the series. They had also decided on a new type of program. They wanted to "open up" their stories to include fiction, and to add "name" actors. So, as usual, DuPont planned to obtain proposals from a number of potential producers, through the agency.

Their original plan was to spend a week in Hollywood in late May, discussing ideas and/or proposals with various producers for the new series. On May 3, DuPont executives met Sharpe in New York. He was elated about obtaining partial sponsorship of "Wire Service" and talked specifically of plans to set up a company to produce it. They asked him if he was interested in producing a new series for DuPont. He said yes. This was the first time that DuPont executives knew he was interested in going after their business. Later, the agency asked him for a written proposal.

On May 7, Walter Tibbals of Four Star called a DuPont executive to say he had talked with John Hoagland of BBD&O about DuPont's new series and stated Four Star was interested in making a proposal. The agency then formally requested a proposal from Four Star as they had done in the case of five or six other producers. Merrs, Dewey and De Graff (with Messrs, Elliott, Tiss, Stefan and Rowe of BBD&O) spent from June 18 to 22 in Hollywood discussing ideas and proposals for the new series with eight producers. Included were Sharpe and Lewis and Four Star.

The June 18th discussion with Sharpe and Lewis reviewed their written proposal to BBD&O of May 25th, along with supplementary data presented that day. A major portion of the discussion dealt with two areas. One, verifying a basic price for films because of union increases. Two, resolving re-use of films at no fee. At the conclusion of this meeting, no commitment was made by DuPont. On June 19th, DuPont reviewed the Four Star proposal with Bill Cruikshank, President, and Walter Tibbals, Vice President. This was the first time they had ever met Cruikshank and they were very favorably impressed. No commitment was made.

After their meeting, they agreed among themselves - that even at this early stage of evaluation - any decision between Four Star and Sharpe and Lewis would be a difficult one. In their opinion, they had a lot to offer.

By the end of that week, before their leaving the West Coast, they had made no commitment with a producer. Sharpe and Lewis, Four Star and Volcano all made especially interesting and attractive proposals. Upon their return to Wilmington, and after a report of evaluation of the trip was prepared, they were inclined to favor Sharpe and Lewis. This they told other producers, including Four Star, along with the fact that no commitment had yet been made for the production of our 1956-57 series of sixteen films.

In early July, DuPont was put on notice by Four Star, in a telegram to BBD&O, that they might be included in possible litigation against Sharpe and Lewis. Since DuPont executives could not seem to get clarification on just what it was all about, R.M. De Graff called Bill Cruikshank, President of Four Star, on July 23, 1956, for clarification. He stated this was a "family quarrel," and no suit was really contemplated. He said they certainly didn't plan to include DuPont or BBD&O in any litigation.

After discussion and counsel from DuPont's legal department, the latter wrote an opinion that if they decided to give Sharpe and Lewis the contract based on merit, this was a good business risk for DuPont. They also felt as did BBD&O, that they should at least try to obtain a personal indemnification from Don Sharpe - in case there was a suit.

R.M. De Graff went to New York on July 12 to specifically ask Sharpe for a personal indemnification. He agreed. Following this period and up to the end of July, Sharpe "backed and filled" on his request several times. Eventually, he agreed to a "watered down" version which DuPont's legal department said was worth while, but at least showed good faith and intent.

The "official" commitment to Sharpe and Lewis for production of the new series and therefore made on or about July 31, when BBD&O management (Duffy and Manche) agreed with DuPont that this was a good business risk on their part.

By this point, DuPont decided to cancel the *Cavalcade* program. Two years before *Cavalcade* went off television, the program was entitled *The DuPont Cavalcade Theater*. During the final year, the series was entitled *The DuPont Theater*. During the final year, dramas of modern-day people, instead of American historical figures, were being dramatized. A lawsuit was brewing at which DuPont had no involvement, and had no intention to get drawn in. Someone at BBD&O looked at all of these factors and suggested a more pleasing program for DuPont to sponsor, filmed in color. DuPont optioned and the *Cavalcade of America*, after twenty-two years on the air, was canceled.

Producer Jack Zoller attempted to put into words what *Cavalcade of America* hoped to convey to the listeners. "It's a show full of hope for everyone," he said. "Its philosophy is one of positiveness. We want to show that America today is a country of opportunity no less than it was in the days of Edison and Ford."

Homer Fickett: "While our DuPont *Cavalcade* radio program has changed its format from time to time since its first broadcast in 1935, we have never deviated from the original purpose of the show - to present a series of entertaining and educational broadcasts to tell the story of America, its people and its history."

Jack Zoller: "In addition to the stories of thrilling new achievements that were constantly coming to light, skilled historians and researchers will continue to find significant, if little known, incidents in our past that help tell the *Cavalcade of America*. We told the stories of men and women of every creed and color. Every state in the union and every nationality has been represented. Every profession has been covered. Still those who worked on *Cavalcade* felt that the surface had hardly been scratched."

NOTES ON THE CAVALCADE RADIO LOG

As with previous publications, the information listed within these pages came from a variety of sources. All of which were compiled, compared, and often collaborated by newspapers, magazine articles, photo collections, and even the recordings themselves. When I began this project, I received over a dozen different broadcast logs from many so-called "authorities." I found that not one broadcast log featured the same information the others had, and with varying degrees of difference. My broadcast log below is a combination of sources that can not be disproved. i.e. the actual recordings and most importantly, all 781 scripts bound and preserved at the Hagley Library in Wilmington, Delaware. I am most grateful to the staff at Hagley, who allowed me permission to zerox, write, and often question the accuracy of the information contained herein.

1. The titles listed for each broadcast are the "official" script titles, as they were typed on the front of each and every script cover. I took precision care to ensure the proper spelling of these titles, so "Child Welfare in the United States" is the correct title, not "Child Welfare in the U.S." I know that is being picky since the same meaning surface from both titles, but I wanted this to be as accurate as possible.

Often times the announcer(s) would bill a different title during the broadcast than what was listed on the front page of the script. On great occasion that was an accident, but on a few instances, as you will find when flipping through these pages, a few scripts had two official titles instead of one. (One script was untitled as no drama was presented. A speech was given instead. Watch out for that one!) The first hundred or so scripts featured two fifteen-minute dramas, each individually titled, including a third and official script title that dealt with the entire broadcast. The titles of those short dramas are listed as "Part One," "Part Two," etc.

2. The writers of the scripts were often confusing. Last names were given for many of the early broadcasts. I researched as best I could to find the first names of some writers, but there are about a dozen or so whose first names elude me. They are listed _?_ followed by their last names. My apologies for those blanks that will be found throughout the log, but such information appears to be elusive.

3. Many of the scripts to the early broadcasts actually listed the first date the script was written, and all of the dates the script was revised by historians. Keep in mind that all of the scripts were rewritten and changes made hours before each broadcast. Du Pont dropped the practice of listing those dates after the first couple years. During the final year, Du Pont began putting an asterick (*) beside all of the fictional characters on the scripts. You will find those also listed.

4. Cast lists were pieced together through photos of the rehearsals and the scripts themselves. You will find that many episodes (especially the early broadcasts) have no cast list, as no cast list is known, and was not documented. Again, I tried my best to fill in such blanks. All possible attempts to ensure correct spelling have been made.

5. Under many of the episode entries I have listed trivia and recollections from the directors, writers, and actors regarding those episodes. I hope they prove entertaining as well as informative.

6. All of the episodes broadcast originated from New York City except for the episodes marked **(HLYD)**, which were broadcast from Hollywood, California.

EPISODE #1 **"NO TURNING BACK"** Broadcast on October 9, 1935
    Starring: Walter Hampden
    Part One: "The Return of the Mayflower"
    Part Two: "The Grasshopper Plague"
    Written by Ruth Woodman, _?_ Larem, and Kenneth Webb.
    Dwight Weist is the announcer and Frank Singiser is the commercial announcer.
    Produced by Arthur Pryor and directed by Kenneth Webb.
    Music composed and conducted by Harold Levy.
    Story: The *Mayflower* left England in August of 1620 with another ship, the *Speedwell*. After turning back twice because of leaks on the *Speedwell*, the passengers and crew of the *Mayflower* had to make a monumentous decision. Should they turn around or continue the journey alone? If they choose to continue, there would be no turning back.

EPISODE #2 **"THE WILL TO CONQUER DISTANCE"** Broadcast on October 16, 1935
    Part One: "Theo. Judah and Pass Thru Sierras"
    Written for *Cavalcade* by Ruth Woodman.
    Part Two: "First Airmail Across Sierras"
    Written for *Cavalcade* by Kenneth Webb and Homer Fickett.
    Dwight Weist is the announcer and Frank Singiser is the commercial announcer.
    Produced by Arthur Pryor and directed by Kenneth Webb.
    Music composed and conducted by Harold Levy.
    Story: The exploration of Theodore Judah and the discoveries he made as he journeyed through the Sierra Mountains. His mission was accomplished, paving the way for communication across the nation.

EPISODE #3 **"THE SPIRIT OF COMPETITION"** Broadcast on October 23, 1935
    Starring Franchot Tone in the leading parts of this evening's broadcast.
    Part One: "The Oklahoma Run"
    Part Two: "Mississippi Steamboat Race"
    Written for *Cavalcade* by Ruth Woodman.
    Dwight Weist is the announcer and Frank Singiser is the commercial announcer.
    Produced by Arthur Pryor and directed by Kenneth Webb.
    Music composed and conducted by Harold Levy.
    Melodies that were popular in the gay nineties were featured as an opener.
    Story: The first story regards the young engineer who found the path for the transcontinental railway over the Sierras. The second involves the air mail pilot who blazed a sky trail high above those mountains. The spirit of competition brought better travel conditions, faster transportation of merchandise, progress and advancement, just as the Oklahoma land race hoped to conquer a wilderness.

    Trivia: Several distinguished visitors were with Franchot Tone in the studio during the actual "on-air" performance. One of them was actress Joan Crawford, whose marriage to Franchot Tone was announced two days before. Tone's father and mother, Dr. and Mrs. Frank J. Tone were also in the studio. It was especially fitting that Dr. Tone should be present at this program dedicated to the achievements of chemistry, because only a few days ago, he received the Acheson Medal and Prize awarded by the Electro-Chemical Society for his outstanding accomplishments in electrothermics.

EPISODE #4   "**THE WILL TO REBUILD**"   Broadcast on October 30, 1935
Stars Frank Craven as Josiah Quimby in the first story and as Henry Fowler in the second
Part One: "The Sacramento Fire"
Written for *Cavalcade* by Ruth Woodman.
Part Two: "The Dust Storm"
Written for *Cavalcade* by Homer Fickett and Kenneth Webb.
Dwight Weist is the announcer and Frank Singiser is the commercial announcer.
Produced by Arthur Pryor and directed by Kenneth Webb.
Music composed and conducted by Harold Levy.
The *Cavalcade* orchestra took us back to California in the early years of the Gold Rush with the 1849 Overture as an opener.
Story: Here is a re-creation of two outstanding examples of the will to rebuild - events characteristic of thousands of similar happenings in American history. The Gold Rush encouraged numerous people to migrate to California, buying plots of land and staking claims to property. A disaster soon crept that caused the competing men and women to join forces, utilizing an identical will to achieve, to build and rebuild, a reflection of traditional American spirit.

EPISODE #5   "**FAITH IN EDUCATION**"   Broadcast on November 6, 1935
Part One: "The Bound Boy in Colonial Massachusetts"
Written for *Cavalcade* by Henry Fisk Carlton.
Part Two: "The Story of Horace Mann"
Written for *Cavalcade* by Henry Fisk Carlton, Dixon Ryan Fox and Kenneth Webb.
Dwight Weist is the announcer and Frank Singiser is the commercial announcer.
Produced by Arthur Pryor and directed by Kenneth Webb.
Music composed and conducted by Harold Levy.
The opening song was the "Triumphal March of Grieg."
Story: Each one of us, has at some time or another, said in his heart, "I wish that I might do something for the world, something that will make it just a little better place to live in for the generations to come." This episode shows how the loving ambition and the abiding courage in the life of a poor woman changed an evil situation into a highway of opportunity for millions who came after her.

EPISODE #6   "**WOMAN'S EMANCIPATION**"   Broadcast on November 13, 1935
Starring Fay Bainter in both dramas, dealing with women's emancipation.
Part One: "The Story of Elizabeth Cady Stanton"
Part Two: "The Story of Winning the Vote"
Written for *Cavalcade* by Kenneth Webb.
Dwight Weist is the announcer and Frank Singiser is the commercial announcer.
Produced by Arthur Pryor and directed by Kenneth Webb.
Music composed and conducted by Harold Levy.
Opening musical score featured melodies from the operetta "Apple Blossoms."
Story: When the signers of the Declaration of Independence founded our American Republic with the statement that "All men are created equal," they did not seem to include women. In spite of examples set by such representative leaders of their sex as Abigail Adams, John Adams' loyal wife whose letters and pamphlets did much to light the torch of freedom, who coined the phrase "inherent rights," used so often in the colonists' demands for justice. Here are two true stories of women who influenced the American public with their stand for women's rights.

EPISODE #7 **"WILLINGNESS TO SHARE"** Broadcast on November 20, 1935
Part One: "The Boston Port Bill"
Written for *Cavalcade* by Ruth Woodman, from an outline by Kenneth Webb.
Part Two: "American Red Cross Incidents"
Written for *Cavalcade* by Ruth Woodman.
Dwight Weist is the announcer and Frank Singiser is the commercial announcer.
Produced by Arthur Pryor and directed by Kenneth Webb.
Music composed and conducted by Harold Levy.
The opening song introducing tonight's drama was the 1900 melody "Down South."
Story: No one can deny that one of our most notable American trails was our willingness to help others, whether their need is caused by man or by nature. From the days of the early settlers to our present times, the American people have always been quick to organize in times of emergency. This willingness to help others is the subject of the two stories heard on this broadcast.

Dwight Weist: "It is with pleasure that Du Pont quotes from a letter written by Mr. Roger Fenn, Headmaster of the Fenn School of Boston, and Chairman of the Radio Committee of the Massachusetts Civic League. Mr. Fenn writes 'Your program, the *Cavalcade of America*, represents a milestone in the development of family radio entertainment. On behalf of the Radio Committee of the Massachusetts Civic League, I congratulate you.' End of quotation. This comment, typical of many which have been received since this series of broadcasts started, again makes us feel that these true stories of traditional American spirit and character are appreciated by radio listeners."

EPISODE #8 **"COMMUNITY SELF RELIANCE"** Broadcast on November 27, 1935
Revised on November 23, 1935.
Part One: "The Mayflower Compact"
Part Two: "The Vermont Flood"
Written for *Cavalcade* by Ruth Woodman.
Dwight Weist is the announcer and Frank Singiser is the commercial announcer.
Produced by Arthur Pryor and directed by Kenneth Webb.
Music composed and conducted by Harold Levy.
Features excerpts from the overture to Wagner's opera "The Flying Dutchman."
Story: At Thanksgiving time, when our nation and our people reflect on the many things for which we should be thankful, we cannot fail to include thanks for the American spirit of self-reliance, which is so well illustrated in these dramas involved. The early days of our country, beginning with the good ship Mayflower, sailed for sixty-five days in 1620 to begin a new life - a community that solved their own problems without asking for outside aid.

EPISODE #9 **"HEROISM IN MEDICAL SCIENCE"** Broadcast on December 4, 1935
Part One: "Long and Discovery of Anesthesia"
Part Two: "Georgia and the Panama Canal"
Written for *Cavalcade* by Kenneth Webb.
Dwight Weist is the announcer and Frank Singiser is the commercial announcer.
Produced by Arthur Pryor and directed by Kenneth Webb.
Music composed and conducted by Harold Levy.
The opening songs were a group of Stephen Foster songs.
Story: Many years ago when Thomas Jefferson was President and everything beyond the Allegheny Mountains was a wilderness, the Du Pont company began to play part in the establishment of chemical science in the United States. Here *Cavalcade* presents a feeling of reassurance in the knowledge that the same ideals of American character live today - in the cities, on the farms . . . marching forward.

EPISODE #10 **"THE WILL TO EXPLORE"** Broadcast on December 11, 1935
Part One: "Lewis and Clark Expedition"
Part Two: "Greeley Polar Expedition"
Written for *Cavalcade* by Kenneth Webb.
Dwight Weist is the announcer and Frank Singiser is the commercial announcer.
Produced by Arthur Pryor and directed by Kenneth Webb.
Music composed and conducted by Harold Levy.
Opening song was Charles Wakefield Cadman's "From the Land of the Sky Bluewater."
Story: America has fostered men of exploration, the will to explore and expand, the will to cross into unknown territory. Dangerous as it may seem, this paved the way for more people to span across the globe and settle their homes. Lewis and Clark explored the vast wilderness of the West, in an attempt to find a passage to the West. Greeley, on the the other hand, led an expedition into the frigid cold weather to make a world record.

Trivia: This episode was originally written with two script titles, because the writer, Kenneth Webb, could not make up his mind which title he wanted to use. Before the actual broadcast, however, the title "Courageous Curiosity" was discarded.

EPISODE #11 **"DEFIANCE OF NATURE"** Broadcast on December 18, 1935
Part One: "Erie Canal"
Part Two: "Holland Tunnel"
Written for *Cavalcade* by Ruth Woodman.
Dwight Weist is the announcer and Frank Singiser is the commercial announcer.
Produced by Arthur Pryor and directed by Kenneth Webb.
Music composed and conducted by Harold Levy.
Story: When it comes down to Man versus nature, man usually has to contend to the sanctuary of his home until the elements of Mother Nature rears her angry head. But there have been occasions when man was not content, and waged war with the waters. Case in point: The construction of the first important waterway built in the United States, the Erie Canal, and the design of the Holland Tunnel, which provided a direct link from Canal Street in Manhattan to New Jersey.

EPISODE #12 **"THE HUMANITARIAN URGE"** Broadcast on December 25, 1935
Revised on December 24, 1935.
Part One: "The Mary Ellen Case"
Part Two: "The Juvenile Court Story"
Written for *Cavalcade* by Ann Barley.
Dwight Weist is the announcer and Frank Singiser is the commercial announcer.
Produced by Arthur Pryor and directed by Kenneth Webb.
Music composed and conducted by Harold Levy.
The opening songs were some melodies from "Hansel and Gretel."
Story: The Humanitarian Urge - that has often been the motive power spurring on heroes in the *Cavalcade of America*. Generous lives spent in the care of the weak, the young, the oppressed, have been common in the annals of the nation. No more devoted champions of humanity can be found than those Americans who have loved and toiled for children. An example is the fact that the lot of the child has been strange and illogical. Valued by their families in all ages, children have had slight recognition by the state until recently. A Roman father might kill his child, if he pleased. A Medieval father might let him go to a fatal Dance of Death through a plague stricken city.
This episode brings true stories of the traits of character that have built our nation - and it is safe to say that nothing more important to the welfare and progress of America than our growing appreciation of America's children - as illustrated in these two dramas.

EPISODE #13 **"THE DECLARATION OF INDEPENDENCE"** Broadcast January 1, 1936
Written for *Cavalcade* by Kenneth Webb.
Dwight Weist is the announcer and Frank Singiser is the commercial announcer.
Produced by Arthur Pryor and directed by Kenneth Webb.
Music composed and conducted by Harold Levy.
The opening song was Victor Herbert's "American Fantasy"
Story: Freedom. Our dearest heritage was won only after a long and determined struggle. And the document which sets forth our reasons for founding an independent nation did not spring into being spontaneously, as many think. The true events of how this all started, the debates and concerns of the writing of the Declaration of Independence. It's impact and influence is historical.

EPISODE #14 **"WOMEN IN PUBLIC SERVICE"** Broadcast on January 8, 1936
Part One: "Jane Addams at Hull House"
Part Two: "Kentucky Volunteer Nurse Story"
Written for *Cavalcade* by Ann Barley.
Dwight Weist is the announcer and Frank Singiser is the commercial announcer.
Produced by Arthur Pryor and directed by Kenneth Webb.
Music composed and conducted by Harold Levy.
The following songs were featured as an opener before the dramas. The 1892 song "After the Ball," the 1899 song "On the Banks of the Wabash" and the 1896 song "Sweet Rosie O'Grady."
Story: The part women play in public volunteer service has been an age-old tale. Some have become legends in their won right, others have become the silent unsung heroes. Jane Addams was one of the first to recognize such conditions and against oppression and prejudice, fought to maintain her position and authority. Since then, volunteer work has established a regular meaning across the country. The Red Cross and the Salvation are always willing to accept help whenever disaster calls.

EPISODE #15 **"BUILDING AND ARCHITECTURE"** Broadcast on January 15, 1936
Revised on January 13, 1936.
Part One: "The Building of Independence Hall"
Part Two: "The Building of Empire State"
Written for *Cavalcade* by Edward Longstreth.
Dwight Weist is the announcer and Frank Singiser is the commercial announcer.
Produced by Arthur Pryor and directed by Kenneth Webb.
Music composed and conducted by Harold Levy.
Story: Architecture designs not only curve the way for buildings of acclaim and accomplishment, but they leave their mark in the streets we walk through every day of the year. Who doesn't know what the Empire State Building looks like, or where the building is located? Who doesn't know what important event occurs in Independence Hall? These are the stories of their construction and design. Landmarks of America that will stand long after our generation and the future generations.

EPISODE #16 **"SPEED OF WORDS"** Broadcast on January 22, 1936
Part One: "Clipper Ship / Pony Express"
Part Two: "Trans-Continental Telegraph / Trans-Atlantic Cable / The Telephone / Via Wireless / Radio-Phone"
Written for *Cavalcade* by Edward Longstreth.
Dwight Weist is the announcer and Frank Singiser is the commercial announcer.
Produced by Arthur Pryor and directed by Kenneth Webb.
Music composed and conducted by Harold Levy.
The opening song was "On the Trail" from Ferde Grofe's 1933 "Grand Canyon Suite."

Story: Communication is probably the most important saw in our civilization. The need for a "fast and safe" way to connect the East and West Coast was more than important. Without it, builders would work blind, talent scouts could not hire the expertise, and loved ones would be lost. The Pony Express was the first of such methods, but lasted only eighteen months before it's termination, caused by the Trans-Continental Telegraph. Wire was much better than young men and horses, it established a speed of words.

EPISODE #17   "ENTERPRISE"   Broadcast on January 29, 1936
Part One: "Tudor and Ice Business"
Part Two: "Air Route Across Pacific"
Written for *Cavalcade* by Ann Barley.
Dwight Weist is the announcer and Frank Singiser is the commercial announcer.
Produced by Arthur Pryor and directed by Kenneth Webb.
Music composed and conducted by Harold Levy.
The opening song was Percy Grainer's 1728 "Country Gardens."
Story: From expansion comes enterprise. The visionaries who saw money in the founding of our country. Just who do you think sold land to the flock of migratory during the Gold Rush? Who visited small towns and sold tonic elixirs from peddler carts? Some were crooked, of course, but it was the visionaries who were honest and ambitious who were laughed at. But among all the scorn, they found a way.

EPISODE #18   "LOYALTY TO FAMILY"   Broadcast on February 5, 1936
Part One: "Elizabeth Harper and Trip to Ohio Territory"
Part Two: "Modern Story"
Written for *Cavalcade* by Ann Barley.
Produced by Arthur Pryor and directed by Kenneth Webb.
Dwight Weist is the announcer and Frank Singiser is the commercial announcer.
Music composed and conducted by Harold Levy.
The scene was set from a few opening songs from Frederick Knight Logan's American Indian melody "Pale Moon."
Story: Loyalty to the family, the basic unit of our country's social structure, has been a great force for good in America. Countless men and women of distinction have said that their first lessons in human usefulness were learned from a devoted family group. Since it is largely in the hands of women that the care of our families has been placed, it is to the history of American womanhood that we look tonight for the highest examples of unselfish devotion.

EPISODE #19   "ABRAHAM LINCOLN - A TRUE AMERICAN"   Broadcast on Feb. 12, 1936
Written for *Cavalcade* by Jerry McGill, Dr. Dixon Ryan Fox, and Kenneth Webb.
Dwight Weist is the announcer and Frank Singiser is the commercial announcer.
Produced by Arthur Pryor and directed by Kenneth Webb.
Music composed and conducted by Harold Levy.
Story: The great Emancipator had a life unlike any other American. Born in the backwoods, raised by a loving family, educated by a wise friend, Abe Lincoln never let anyone down. He saved a young man's life during a trial. He failed at running a general store. He ran for President and lived through a blood bath that eventually took his life. On the evening of his birthday, *Cavalcade* presents a few events in the life of Lincoln.

EPISODE #20   "THE BRIDGE BUILDERS"   Broadcast on February 19, 1936
Revised on February 14, 1936.
Part One: "The Story of John A. Roebling"
Part Two: "Modern Bridges"
Written for *Cavalcade* by Jerry McGill.
Dwight Weist is the announcer and Frank Singiser is the commercial announcer.

Produced by Arthur Pryor and directed by Kenneth Webb.
Music composed and conducted by Harold Levy.
Story: The question of how to cross a mass of water was answered three ways. Go around it, sail across it, or build a bridge. Your introduction of Mr. John Roebling, a man with a vision, and a passion for bridges. His techniques and designs are still utilized with even the most modern bridges built today.

Dwight Weist: "Many of our listeners have been kind enough to write us telling why their families like this program - how their children use information from these stories in their school work. It is most encouraging to receive mail like this. Thus, the *Cavalcade of America*, portrayed from week to week on this Du Pont radio program - is something that Du Pont has seen, known, been a part of."

EPISODE #21   **"HEROES OF THE SEA"**   Broadcast on February 26, 1936
  Part One: "The Clipper Ship *Flying Cloud* reaches San Francisco in 89 days"
  Part Two: "The rescue of the British Freighter *Antinoe* by the *President Roosevelt* - Captain Fried commanding"
  Written for *Cavalcade* by Merrill Dennison.
  Dwight Weist is the announcer and Frank Singiser is the commercial announcer.
  Produced by Arthur Pryor and directed by Kenneth Webb.
  Music composed and conducted by Harold Levy.
  The opening song was the 1838 melody "Life on an Ocean Wave."
  Story: Some of the greatest feats accomplished by man was in the ocean. Donald McKay, a Canadian, did most of his work in East Boston. He built the famed *Flying Cloud* that attempted to set a record across the ocean. Other men, such as Captain Fried, commanded a ship to accomplish an act of bravery that has been unequaled in the history of the seven seas.

EPISODE #22   **"SONGS THAT INSPIRED THE NATION"**   Broadcast on March 4, 1936
  Revised on March 3, 1936.
  Part One: "Stephen Foster' Old Folks at Home" (composed in 1851)
  Part Two: "Dan'l Decatur Emmett's Dixie"
  Part Three: "John Philip Sousa's Stars and Stripes Forever"
  Part Four: "Irving Berlin's Alexander's Ragtime Band"
  Part Five: "Carrie Jacobs-Bond's End of a Perfect Day"
  Written for *Cavalcade* by Kenneth Webb.
  Dwight Weist is the announcer and Frank Singiser is the commercial announcer.
  Produced by Arthur Pryor and directed by Kenneth Webb.
  Music composed and conducted by Harold Levy.
  Music of Francis Hopkinson was featured as an opener.
  Story: Americans have been moved by patriotic songs. Their composers were inspired to write what they felt needed written. And those songs, in turn, inspired others to do likewise. From Irving Berlin to John Philip Sousa, these are the true events leading to the compositions of such musical interludes.

EPISODE #23   **"PERSEVERANCE"**   Broadcast on March 11, 1936
  Part One: "Elias Howe and the Sewing Machine"
  Part Two: "The Wright Brothers"
  Written for *Cavalcade* by Merrill Dennison.
  Dwight Weist is the announcer and Frank Singiser is the commercial announcer.
  Produced by Arthur Pryor and directed by Kenneth Webb.
  Music composed and conducted by Harold Levy.

(cont'd)

Story: The first drama is based on the events leading to Elias Howe, New Englander, who invented the sewing machine. The second drama involves Wilbur and Orville Wright, both men in their twenties, who launched the first successful flight at Kitty Hawk, with witnesses attending. Persistence has it's price, and ambition gives its own reward. The perseverance of these men allows our society to do today, what they dreamed yesterday.

EPISODE #24   "THEY ALSO SERVE"   Broadcast on March 18, 1936
    Part One: "Story of Gloucester Fisherman"
    Part Two: "Story of Fireman and Policeman"
    Written for *Cavalcade* by Edward Longstreth
    Dwight Weist is the announcer and Frank Singiser is the commercial announcer.
    Produced by Arthur Pryor and directed by Kenneth Webb.
    Music composed and conducted by Harold Levy.
    Songs featured were Charles W. Cadman's 1806 "At Dawning" and the 1913 song "I Hear a Thrush at Eve."
    Story: Along the line of march, watching and waiting patiently, are the women whose courage and devotion make possible the advancement of our race. Wherever men go out to wrestle a livelihood from the jealous elements, women wait at home for their safe return. The wild areas that beat against our shores team with fish from which we realize vast sums of money every year. Such examples of the past and present are presented.

EPISODE #25   "CONSERVATION"   Broadcast on March 25, 1936
    Part One: "The Story of Johnny Appleseed"
    Written for *Cavalcade* by Ruth Woodman.
    Part Two: "A Modern Story of A Fire in Woods"
    Written for *Cavalcade* by Jerry McGill.
    Dwight Weist is the announcer and Frank Singiser is the commercial announcer.
    Produced by Arthur Pryor and directed by Kenneth Webb.
    Music composed and conducted by Harold Levy.
    Story: We are often impressed that leaders are builders rather than conquerors. They have subdued the wilderness and made it blossom with the fruits of civilization. They have planted and protected. They have conserved America's resources. High among our unsung heroes stands John Chapman, known to his own generation by his nickname, Johnny Appleseed. With a modern story of how we preserve nature's beauties.

EPISODE #26   "WINNING FAME FOR AMERICAN LITERATURE"   Aired on April 1, 1936
    Second revision was on March 31, 1936.
    Part One: "The Story of Mark Twain"
    Part Two: "The Story of Louisa May Alcott"
    Written for *Cavalcade* by Ann Barley.
    Dwight Weist is the announcer and Frank Singiser is the commercial announcer.
    Produced by Arthur Pryor and directed by Kenneth Webb.
    Music composed and conducted by Harold Levy.
    The following songs rung up the curtain: Ferde Grofe's 1926 "Mississippi Suite," "Father of Waters," and the 1917 song "Huckleberry Finn."
    Story: Samuel Clemens, also known to millions as Mark Twain, lived a good portion of his life along the Mississippi River, where he based many of his fictional stories. Louisa May Alcott, author of the well-known book "Little Women," based her own life's experiences in her novel. Both fought for recognition, and became the two most famous authors in America.

On the next page: Two advertisements of various *Cavalcade* broadcasts.

DU PONT Cavalcade of America

presents

IDA LUPINO

in

"Star in the West"

**MONDAY EVENING
FEBRUARY 25, 1946**

NATIONAL BROADCASTING COMPANY
Coast to Coast Network

8.00-8.30 .... E.T.   9.30-10.00 .... M.T.
7.00-7.30 .... C.T.   8.30- 9.00 .... P.T.
Consult Your Local Radio Timetable

Originating from Hollywood

DU PONT Cavalcade of America

presents

DICK POWELL
and
JANET BLAIR

in

"Children Of Ol' Man River"

**MONDAY EVENING
FEBRUARY 4, 1946**

NATIONAL BROADCASTING COMPANY
Coast to Coast Network

8.00-8.30 .... E.T.   9.30-10.00 .... M.T.
7.00-7.30 .... C.T.   8.30- 9.00 .... P.T.
Consult Your Local Radio Timetable

Originating from Hollywood

EPISODE #27 **"OPPORTUNITY"**   Broadcast on April 8, 1936
  Part One: "The Story of Benjamin Franklin"
  Part Two: "The Story of Cyrus H.K. Curtis"
  Written for *Cavalcade* by Ann Barley.
  Dwight Weist is the announcer and Frank Singiser is the commercial announcer.
  Produced by Arthur Pryor and directed by Kenneth Webb.
  Music composed and conducted by Harold Levy.
  The opening song was Oley Speaks' 1914 melody "Sylvia."
  Story: Opportunity knocks on everyone's door. If you take a stab at what comes your way, prosperity slides into your pocket. We all know Benjamin Franklin took every chance he could to make money. But how about Cyrus Curtis? Curtis founded the Curtis Publishing Company in 1890. He started his first publication, *Young America* as a twelve-year-old newsboy. By the early 1920's, Curtis purchased *The New York Post*, *The Philadelphia Inquirer*, and *The Philadelphia Press*.

EPISODE #28 **"RAILROAD BUILDERS"**   Broadcast on April 15, 1936
  Part One: "The Hoosac Tunnel Story"
  Part Two: "The Union and Central Pacific R.R. Story"
  Written for *Cavalcade* by Merrill Dennison.
  Dwight Weist is the announcer and Frank Singiser is the commercial announcer.
  Produced by Arthur Pryor and directed by Kenneth Webb.
  Music composed and conducted by Harold Levy.
  A special arrangement of well-known railroad songs were featured as an opener.
  Story: As in a previous broadcast, we realize again the tremendous part played by the railroads in the building of America. But backing the railroads were men, dreamers, planners and do-ers. The men who helped open up the country, made it accessible to millions, bridged its rivers, tunneled its mountains and conquered its deserts. Men whom nothing could daunt in the performance of their prodigious tasks.

EPISODE #29 **"SAFETY FIRST"**   Broadcast on April 22, 1936
  Revised on April 21, 1936.
  Part One: "The Founding of Life Insurance Companies"
  Part Two: "The Fire Prevention Story"
  Part Three: "The Modern 'Safety First' and Fire Fighting Story"
  Written for *Cavalcade* by Edward Longstreth.
  Dwight Weist is the announcer and Frank Singiser is the commercial announcer.
  Produced by Arthur Pryor and directed by Kenneth Webb.
  Music composed and conducted by Harold Levy.
  An overture based on themes used during previous broadcasts of *Cavalcade of America*.
  Story: The instinct for self-preservation in an intelligent people finds expression in the slogan, "Safety First." Or, as Poor Richard puts it, "An ounce of prevention is worth a pound of cure." Benjamin Franklin, the creator of Poor Richard, was one of the most prudent men America ever produced. In his Pennsylvania "Gazette" for December 1733, he published an article on fires and how to extinguish them. He deplored the fact that the city had no fire company. This is the story that prompted Franklin to create the first fire company and profit by offering fire insurance.

EPISODE #30 **"SELF RELIANCE"** Broadcast on April 29, 1936
   Part One: "Eliza Lucas and Indigo Planting"
   Part Two: "Modern School Teacher and Blizzard"
   Written for *Cavalcade* by Ann Barley.
   Dwight Weist is the announcer and Frank Singiser is the commercial announcer.
   Produced by Arthur Pryor and directed by Kenneth Webb.
   Music composed and conducted by Harold Levy.
   The opening melodies featured were the 1917 song "Nobody Knows the Trouble I've Seen" and the 1918 song "Sometimes I Feel Like a Motherless Child."
   Story: Compared with the attitude of foreign civilizations, the self-reliance of American women is one of the most remarkable features of American life. America's advancement has been aided greatly by the willingness of her women to accept responsibility. Eliza Lucas, beautiful and spirited daughter of the South, settled in the colony of Carolina in 1738. Her story and the story of another woman torn from the latest pages of a newspaper are the dramas of the evening.

EPISODE #31 **"THE ARTISTIC IMPULSE"** Broadcast on May 6, 1936
   Revised on May 5, 1936.
   Part One: "Story of Rise in American Art with Examples of Benjamin West, Gilbert Stuart and Peale"
   Part Two: "The Story of Whistler"
   Written for *Cavalcade* by Edward Longstreth.
   Dwight Weist is the announcer and Frank Singiser is the commercial announcer.
   Produced by Arthur Pryor and directed by Kenneth Webb.
   Music composed and conducted by Harold Levy.
   Opening songs were Dvorak's "Songs My Mother Taught Me" and Brahams' "Lullaby."
   Story: Benjamin West was an American painter who became famous for his large pictures of historical subjects. Many critics today agree with the painter Gilbert Stuart, who scorned West's "ten-acre pictures." His studio in London became a "school" for many American artists, including Ralph Peale, Samuel F. B. Morse, Charles Willson Peale, and Rembrandt Peale.

EPISODE #32 **"TILLERS OF THE SOIL"** Broadcast on May 13, 1936
   Written for *Cavalcade* by Edward Longstreth.
   Dwight Weist is the announcer and Frank Singiser is the commercial announcer.
   Produced by Arthur Pryor and directed by Kenneth Webb.
   Music composed and conducted by Harold Levy.
   Story: America leads all other countries in the world in agriculture. And in the fertile soil our democracy has its roots. On the farm the family is a self-reliant unit, a little township all in itself. From early colonial times, the first settlers on our Eastern seaboard had to wrest food and shelter from the great wilderness surrounding them. But sturdy of muscle and determined in spirit, they pressed inland until the spring of 1790, the first year of our country's constitutional existence.

EPISODE #33 **"HARDINESS"** Broadcast on May 20, 1936
   Revised on May 19, 1936.
   Part One: "Steve Hanks and the Lumber Story"
   Part Two: "Colonel Lucas and the Oil Story"
   Written for *Cavalcade* by Ann Barley.
   Dwight Weist is the announcer and Frank Singiser is the commercial announcer.
   Produced by Arthur Pryor and directed by Kenneth Webb.
   Music composed and conducted by Harold Levy.
   The opening song played a suggestion of the locale of the first story, an overture of "By the Waters of the Minnetonka."   **(cont'd)**

Story: In the development of her great national resources, America has been fortunate in finding strong and hardy workers. Men who have tamed the forests and the great rivers of this continent; men who have toiled at extracting rich minerals - have laid the bulwarks of American advancement. Two stories of notable achievement in the development of our natural resources is Stephen Beck Hanks and Colonel Lucas.

EPISODE #34   **"RESOURCEFULNESS"**   Broadcast on May 27, 1936
Revised on May 26, 1936.
Part One: "John Ames takes printing press across Isthmus to California"
Part Two: "The Story of Coast Guard"
Written for *Cavalcade* by Ann Barley.
Dwight Weist is the announcer and Frank Singiser is the commercial announcer.
Produced by Arthur Pryor and directed by Kenneth Webb.
Music composed and conducted by Harold Levy.
The opening song was Victor Herbert's 1901 "Pan Americana."
Story: A presentation of two stories, both displaying American resourcefulness. The first opens in 1849, the year of the great California gold rush. Hurrying to reach California, thousands of Americans rushed to Panama, and crossing the Isthmus, embarked on west coast vessels . . . for San Francisco. From two Americans in a canoe manned by natives with paddles, to the United States Coast Guard, the goal is still the same. To accomplish their tasks with determination, and letting no obstacle - large or small - stand in their way.

EPISODE #35   **"SONGS OF HOME"**   Broadcast on June 3, 1936
Revised on June 2, 1936.
Written for *Cavalcade* by Kenneth Webb.
Dwight Weist is the announcer and Frank Singiser is the commercial announcer.
Produced by Arthur Pryor and directed by Kenneth Webb.
Music composed and conducted by Harold Levy.
Songs featured throughout the program: the 1823 melody "Home Sweet Home," the 1853 song "My Old Kentucky Home," the 1878 composition "Carry Me Back to Old Virginny," and the 1873 song "Home on the Range."
Story: At one time or another, we have whistled one of those songs. Whether we were in the car traveling home from work, or walking through the front door after a long business trip. How these songs came to be written and why they mean so much to the American home is just part of the story.

Trivia: There was no program on June 10, due to a Republican Convention.

EPISODE #36   **"HEROES OF TEXAS"**   Broadcast on June 17, 1936
Written for *Cavalcade* by Jerry McGill.
Dwight Weist is the announcer and Frank Singiser is the commercial announcer.
Produced by Arthur Pryor and directed by Kenneth Webb.
Music composed and conducted by Harold Levy.
Story: In 1820, Moses Austin, a Missouri banker, asked Spanish officials in San Antonio to let him establish a colony of Americans in Texas. The Spanish government granted his request, but Austin died before he could organize the colony. His son, Stephen F. Austin, carried out the plan and brought 300 families to Texas.

On the next page: William Sanderson, a very talented artist, sketched these drawings of various broadcasts from *Cavalcade*'s early years.

TRANSCONTINENTAL
JOURNEYS

HEROES OF TEXAS

EPISODE #37 "STEAMBOAT BUILDERS" Broadcast on June 24, 1936
Script first written on May 18, 1936, and revised on May 25, June 15 and 24, 1936.
Part One: "John Fitch invents the steamboat"
Part Two: "Robert Fulton makes it practical"
Part Three: "Eliphalet Nott and the anthracite engine"
Written for *Cavalcade* by Edward Longstreth.
Dwight Weist is the announcer and Frank Singiser is the commercial announcer.
Produced by Arthur Pryor and directed by Kenneth Webb.
Music composed and conducted by Harold Levy.
The opening songs were Victor Herbert's "Yesterthoughts" and "Punchinello."
Story: The Steamboat is a term used for steam-driven vessels that sail on rivers. In 1787, John Fitch demonstrated the first workable steamboat in the U.S. The first financially successful steamboat was Robert Fulton's *Clermont*. Eliphalet Nott came to the rescue by advancing the steam boat engine with anthracite (coal).

EPISODE #38 "AMERICAN JOURNALISM" Broadcast on July 1, 1936
Script first written on May 25, 1936, and revised on June 5 and 25, 1936.
Part One: "The Story of Horace Greeley"
Part Two: "The Story of Henry Mortimer Stanley"
Written for *Cavalcade* by Ann Barley.
Dwight Weist is the announcer and Frank Singiser is the commercial announcer.
Produced by Arthur Pryor and directed by Kenneth Webb.
Music composed and conducted by Harold Levy.
Story: Horace Greeley founded and edited the *New York Tribune*, a prominent American newspaper that played an important part in molding public opinion. His advice to the unemployed in New York was "Go West, Young Man." A coined phrase that has become a legend. And that is what American journalism is. A legend that has shaped our country, and reported the leading events of the centuries.

EPISODE #39 "VICTOR HERBERT, MASTER OF MELODY" Broadcast on July 8, 1936
Script first written on June 12, 1936 and revised on July 2 and 7, 1936.
Written for *Cavalcade* by Kenneth Webb.
Dwight Weist is the announcer and Frank Singiser is the commercial announcer.
Produced by Arthur Pryor and directed by Kenneth Webb.
Music composed and conducted by Harold Levy.
Songs featured in this broadcast are: Herbert's 1846 composition "Low Backed Car," "Prince Ananias" is played on the piano, "Slumber on my Little Gypsy Sweetheart," the 1903 song "March of the Toys" from "Babes in Toyland," "Only Girl," and the 1917 song "Eileen."
Story: Victor Herbert was an American composer and conductor, often called "the prince of operetta." He was the first American composer to write an original score for a movie. This is the story of how he started his musical career, and gained world-wide fame through his music and operettas.

THE CAVALCADE OF AMERICA

Better Things for Better Living . . . through Chemistry

EPISODE #40 "THE DEVELOPMENT OF BAND MUSIC IN AMERICA" (PART ONE)
Subtitled: "THE SMALL BANDS: SOUSA, GILMORE AND PRYOR"
Broadcast on July 15, 1936
Script first written on July 7, 1936, and revised on July 13 and 14, 1936.
Written for *Cavalcade* by Kenneth Webb.
Frank Singiser is the announcer.
Produced by Arthur Pryor and directed by Kenneth Webb.
Music composed and conducted by Arthur Pryor.
Songs featured in this broadcast: "Semper Fidelis," the anvil chorus from "Il Travatore," a song from Victor Herbert's 1906 "The Red Mill," the 1905 song "The Whistler and his Dog," Johann Strauss' "The Beautiful Blue Danube," and Richard Wagner's "Ride of the Valktries."

Trivia: This was the first of a special summer series "The Cavalcade of America in Music." These programs described the origin and development of orchestral and band music in America. They contained dramatic episodes, and examples of popular concert music. To inaugurate the first of the summer programs, Du Pont featured "America's foremost band master" Arthur Pryor and his band.

EPISODE #41 "THE DEVELOPMENT OF BAND MUSIC IN AMERICA" (PART TWO)
Subtitled: "FROM THE GAY NINETIES ON"   Broadcast on July 22, 1936
Script first written on July 13, 1936, and revised on July 17, 1936.
Written for *Cavalcade* by Kenneth Webb.
Frank Singiser is the announcer.
Produced by Arthur Pryor and directed by Kenneth Webb.
Music composed and conducted by Arthur Pryor.
Songs featured in the order of their appearance were: "Military Man" from Shirley Temple's film *Poor Little Rich Girl*, "Slavonic Rhapsody," selections from Rudolf Friml's "The Vagabond King," and Bucalossi's 1782 "The Hunting Scene."
Story: During the period affectionately termed "The Gay Nineties," the two-step was America's most popular dance, and John Philip Sousa's marches, especially the "Washington Post" were in demand. In 1889, Sousa, then the leader of the United States Marine Band was asked to write the march in commemoration of the occasion and to play it for the first time during an award ceremony in a public school in Washington. Band music was extremely popular in the gay nineties - not just Sousa's - but other conductors.

EPISODE #42 "THE DEVELOPMENT OF BAND MUSIC IN AMERICA" (PART 3)
Subtitled: "AMERICAN BANDS TRAVEL"   Broadcast on July 29, 1936
Script first written on July 17, 1936, and revised on July 24 and 28, 1936.
Written for *Cavalcade* by Kenneth Webb.
Frank Singiser is the announcer.
Produced by Arthur Pryor and directed by Kenneth Webb.
Music composed and conducted by Arthur Pryor.
Songs performed in the order of their appearance: John Philip Sousa's "El Capitan," Reginald DeKoven's "Robin Hood," college songs such as Yale's "Down the Field," Harvard's "Harvardiana," Amherst's "Lord Geoffrey Amherst," Princeton's "Cannon Song," and U.S. Navy's 1806 song "Anchors Aweigh." Also featured were Orth's "In a Clock Store," and a selection from Richard Wagner's "Siegfried."
Story: From the days when the caveman beat on hollow logs, through the centuries to our modern concert bands, rhythm has been man's most natural method of musical expression. Marching feet and beating hearts are part of our rhythmic evolution. These are the stories of the band masters and the operettas they wrote, which made popular from coast to coast.

EPISODE #43 **"THE DEVELOPMENT OF BAND MUSIC IN AMERICA"** **(PART FOUR)**
Subtitled: **"BANDS TODAY"** Broadcast on August 5, 1936
Script first written on July 10, 1936, and revised on August 3, 1936.
Written for *Cavalcade* by Kenneth Webb.
Frank Singiser is the announcer.
Produced by Arthur Pryor and directed by Kenneth Webb.
Music composed and conducted by Arthur Pryor.
Songs performed in the order of their appearance: Victor Herbert's "The Rose of Algeria," Sousa's "Stars and Stripes Forever," and Sibelius' "Finlandia."
Story: This week at the eighth annual Music Camp at Interlochen, Michigan, the American Bandmasters Association held their annual meeting. Founded in 1930 by Edwin Franko Goldman, this Association has done much to develop standard instrumentation in bands rather than the former catch-as-catch-can method so that today, college and high school bands can procure the same careful musical arrangement that is used by the concert bands. Many interesting episodes have taken place during the tours of the great concert bands. These are a few of them.

EPISODE #44 **"THE DEVELOPMENT OF BAND MUSIC IN AMERICA"** **(PART FIVE)**
Subtitled: **"THE CONCERT BAND COMES INTO ITS OWN"**
Broadcast on August 12, 1936
Script first written on August 3, 1936, and revised on August 7 and 10, 1936.
Written for *Cavalcade* by Kenneth Webb.
Frank Singiser is the announcer.
Produced by Arthur Pryor and directed by Kenneth Webb.
Music composed and conducted by Arthur Pryor.
Songs featured in the order of their appearance: "On Jersey Shore," Victor Herbert's "Badinage," a selection from Kreisler's operetta "Apple Blossoms," an overture from "Rienzi," and a sextet from "Lucia."
Story: On the death of Patrick Sarsfield Gilmore, America's first well known band master, a new conductor was sought to take his place with the 22nd Regiment Band of New York, which had become known as Gilmore's Band. His name was Victor Herbert, a well known and great cellist.

EPISODE #45 **"THE DEVELOPMENT OF BAND MUSIC IN AMERICA"** **(PART SIX)**
Subtitled: **"INTRODUCING THE INSTRUMENTS"** Broadcast August 19, 1936
Script first written on August 3, 1936, and revised on August 13 and 18, 1936.
Written for *Cavalcade* by Kenneth Webb.
Frank Singiser is the announcer.
Produced by Arthur Pryor and directed by Kenneth Webb.
Music composed and conducted by Arthur Pryor.
Songs featured in the order of their appearance: Pryor's "The Heart of America," Bizet's "L'Arlisienne Suite," Victor Herbert's "Fortune Teller," Pryor's "The Lion Chase," a Sousa march, and the Grand Scene of "Andre Chenier."
Story: During this summer series, a presentation of dramatizations of such great bandmasters as Patrick Sarsfield Gilmore and John Philip Sousa. This broadcast concerns the instruments that make up a concert band. This episode shows you how instrumentation is planned and arranged.

EPISODE #46 **"THE EVOLUTION OF DANCE MUSIC IN AMERICA"** Broadcast 8 / 26/ 36
Script first written on August 19, 1936, and revised by August 25, 1936.
Written for *Cavalcade* by Harold Sanford.
Frank Singiser is the announcer.
Produced by Arthur Pryor and directed by Kenneth Webb.
Music composed and conducted by Donald Voorhees.

Songs featured in the order of their appearance: the 1834 song "Turkey in the Straw," a segue to "The Washington Post," a segue to "In Old New York" from "Red Mill," "The Dixieland Jazz Band," "Alexander's Ragtime Band," Paul Whiteman's "Whispering," "Three O'Clock in the Morning," "The Charleston," "Nobody's Sweetheart," Hoagy Carmichael's popular 1937 song "Stardust," "Carioca" from the Fred Astaire and Ginger Rogers film *Flying Down to Rio*, and the 1936 melody "Stompin' at the Savoy."
Story: From the days of the marching bands, popular music made out feet stomp at the beat of harmony. Patriotic or otherwise. Soon Dixieland and Marti Gras music became a popular trend, followed by the release of musical discs. Radio brought music to the American home, and when sound invaded the film industry, it was the actors who began making music of their own. This is the story of how music became popularized as the years passed by.

Note: This episode, and the handful preceding it, were all written only days before each broadcast, and not weeks like the majority of the other scripts featured on this program!

EPISODE #47 "AMERICAN MUSICAL COMEDY AND OPERETTA"
Broadcast on September 2, 1936
Script first written on August 31, 1936, and revised on September 1, 1936.
Written for *Cavalcade* by Harold Sanford.
Frank Singiser is the announcer.
Produced by Arthur Pryor and directed by Kenneth Webb.
Music composed and conducted by Donald Voorhees.
Songs featured in the order of their appearance: the 1898 song "Gypsy Love Song," Rudolf Kriml's "Allah's Holiday" from his operetta "Katinka," Jerome Kern's 1917 "Till the Clouds Roll By," "A Pretty Girl is Like a Melody," the title song from the 1919 musical "Irene," "The Love Nest" from the show "Mary," Jerome Kern's "Look for the Silver Lining," "George Gershwin's 1924 song "Somebody Loves Me," the 1925 "Garrick Gaieties" songs "Mountain Greenery," the 1929 melody "Without a Song," "Great Day," a segue to the 1931 song "Crystal Candelabra" and "The Night was Made for Love" both from the musical love story "The Cat and the Fiddle," Cole Porter's 1932 song "Night and Day," the 1932 song "Wintergreen for President," "Small Hotel," the Rogers and Hart song "There's a Small Hotel," and excerpts from Jerome Kern's "Show Boat."
Story: In this episode, we take a musical trip tracing the tuneful development of American operetta and musical comedy from the turn of the century to the present day.

EPISODE #48 "MODERN AMERICAN ORCHESTRAL MUSIC" Broadcast Sept. 9, 1936
Script first written on September 3, 1936, and revised on September 8, 1936.
Written for *Cavalcade* by Harold Sanford.
Frank Singiser is the announcer.
Produced by Arthur Pryor and directed by Kenneth Webb.
Music composed and conducted by Donald Voorhees.
Songs featured in the order of their appearance: the 1915 song "Underneath the Stars," the 1920 song "Dardanella," Victor Herbert's 1922 song "Parade of the Wooden Soldiers," Gershwin's 1924 song "Rhapsody in Blue," and Victor Herbert's "Kiss in the Dark."
Story: The true events leading up to the compositions of the songs listed above. How Victor Herbert's music made it to the stage, and the friendship of Paul Whiteman and Victor Herbert. These songs are not songs of the past, but of songs old and new, originally composed for special occasions, and now part of our bloodline. Modern American orchestral music from the masters of the art form.

EPISODE #49 "THE ORCHESTRA OF TODAY AND HOW IT GREW"
Broadcast on September 16, 1936
Script first written on September 14, 1936, and revised on September 15, 1936.
Written for *Cavalcade* by Harold Sanford.
Frank Singiser is the announcer.
Produced by Arthur Pryor and directed by Kenneth Webb.
Music composed and conducted by Donald Voorhees.
Songs featured in the order of their appearance: Irving Berlin's 1936 hit "Let's Face the Music and Dance," "Chinatown, My Chinatown," "Swanee," the All Star Trio's "Canadian Capers," "My Baby's Arms," Zez Confrey's song "Kitten on the Keys" is performed on the piano, George Gershwin's 1930 "I Got Rhythm" and "Embraceable You," "Margie" is performed on the banjo and orchestra, "Cocktails for Two," "When the Day is Done," "Roses of Picardy," a segue to "A Cup of Coffee, Sandwich and You," Rimsky-Korsakoff's "Capriccio Espagnole," the 1920 song "Japanese Sandman," and Arthur Schwartz's 1931 song "Dancing in the Dark."
Story: A broadcast featuring numerous references of how the modern pop music orchestra has evolved in the last fifteen years, and how radio has contributed to these changes. The music, although performed on stage and available on sheet music, was more popular when first heard on the early days of radio.

EPISODE #50 "MUSIC OF THE MOVIES"   Broadcast on September 23, 1936
Script first written on September 21, 1936, and revised on September 22, 1936.
Written for *Cavalcade* by Harold Sanford.
Frank Singiser is the announcer.
Produced by Arthur Pryor and directed by Kenneth Webb.
Music composed and conducted by Donald Voorhees.
Songs featured in the order of their appearance: "The Way You Look Tonight" from the Fred Astaire and Ginger Rogers film *Swingtime*, "Poor Pauline" from *The Perils of Pauline*, the 1915 "Birth of a Nation" theme from the film of the same name, "Covered Wagon" and "Oh Susanna," from the 1923 motion picture *Covered Wagon Days*, "Charmaine" from the 1925 film *The Big Parade*, De Sylva, Brown and Henderson's "Sonny Boy" from the 1928 film *The Singing Fool*, "Singing in the Rain" from the 1929 film *Hollywood Revue*, "A Little Kiss Each Morning" from Rudy Vallee's first musical movie *The Vagabond Lover*, "The Rogue Song" from 1930, *Isn't It Romantic* from the 1932 Maurice Chevalier film *Love Me Tonight*, the 1933 song "Forty-Second Street" from the film of the same name, "Shuffle Off to Buffalo," Walt Disney's "Who's Afraid of the Big Bad Wolf?" from the 1933 animated cartoon of the same name, "The Continental" from the 1934 film *The Gay Divorce*, the theme from "Carmen," "One Night of Love," Jerome Kern's "Lovely to Look At" from the 1935 film *Roberta*, Bo Jangles of Harlem Theme" from Jerome Kern's *Swing Time*, and Irving Berlin's 1935 hit "Cheek to Cheek" from the film *Top Hat*.

EPISODE #51 "SHOWMANSHIP"   Broadcast on Sept. 30, 1936
Script first written on June 12, 1936, and revised on July 27, September 11 and 23, 1936.
Written for *Cavalcade* by Katherine Seymour.
Frank Singiser is the announcer.
Produced by Arthur Pryor and directed by Kenneth Webb.
Music composed and conducted by Donald Voorhees.
Story: Not only was P.T. Barnum the most famous showman of his time, he is also known for opening his own circus in 1871, later called "The Greatest Show on Earth." But what most people don't know is that Barnum was also active in politics. He was elected to the Connecticut legislature in 1865 and 1866, and served one term as mayor of Bridgeport, Conn., in 1875 and 1876. This is the life of the famous temperance lecturer and exhibitor.

EPISODE #52 "A HELPING HAND"   Broadcast on October 7, 1936
Script first written May 4, 1936, revised June 5, July 20, September 11 and 24, and October 2 and 6, 1936.
Part One: "The Story of Elizabeth Lee Schyler"
Part Two: "The Story of the Traveler's Aid Society"
Written for *Cavalcade* by Ann Barley.
Frank Singiser is the announcer.
Produced by Arthur Pryor and directed by Kenneth Webb.
Music composed and conducted by Donald Voorhees.
Story: The dramas concern a hospital of many years ago - a place of startling contrast to the fine institutions of today - completely equipped with every modern aid and staffed by skilled doctors, interns and nurses. Research chemistry has helped in this progress by providing such products as bases for medicines that help cure illness and allay pain, and safety x-ray film, an important aid to diagnostic work . . . a helping hand in the cure of disease and illness.

EPISODE #53 "SENTINELS OF THE DEEP"   Broadcast on October 14, 1936
Script first written on July 24, 1936, and revised on September 25, 1936.
Written for *Cavalcade* by Jerry McGill.
Frank Singiser is the announcer and Fred Uttal is the commercial announcer.
Produced by Arthur Pryor and directed by Kenneth Webb.
Music composed and conducted by Donald Voorhees.
Donald Voorhees and his orchestra plays the fifth movement of the "Schehezarde" suite by Rimsky-Korsakoff's to ring up the opening curtain.
Story: The keepers of the lighthouses and lightships have made the coasts of America the safest in the world. Thousands of ships set their courses by the beacons of our lighthouses or the radio beams of our lightships, but over two hundred years ago, before the first lighthouse was built to guide the sailing ships of the eighteenth century into the harbor of Boston, it was a far different story.

EPISODE #54   "JOHN WINTHROP, PIONEER OF CHEMICAL SCIENCE"
Broadcast on October 21, 1936
Script first written on July 24, 1936, and revised on Sept. 25, and October 19, 1936.
Written for *Cavalcade* by Laurence Hammond.
Frank Singiser is the announcer and Fred Uttal is the commercial announcer.
Produced by Arthur Pryor and directed by Kenneth Webb.
Music composed and conducted by Donald Voorhees.
Story: John Winthrop was the son of an American colonial leader, and was himself the colonial Governor of Connecticut. In 1662 Winthrop got a charter from King Charles II of England that gave Connecticut the right to govern itself and elect its own rulers. Winthrop also practiced medicine; wrote on scientific subjects; and was a merchant and farmer. His work in chemical science has resulted in establishing chemistry of today.

Trivia: No broadcast on October 28, due to political speech under auspices of Democratic National Committee.

EPISODE #55   "EDWARD MacDOWELL, PIONEER IN AMERICAN MUSIC"
Broadcast on November 4, 1936
Script first written on July 24, 1936, revised on September 25, and October 29, 1936.
Written for *Cavalcade* by _?_ Glover.
Frank Singiser is the announcer and Craig Stevens is the commercial announcer.
Produced by Arthur Pryor and directed by Kenneth Webb.
Music composed and conducted by Donald Voorhees.

Songs featured: MacDowell's "Concerto in A Minor," "Scotch Poem," "Sea Pieces," and a piano plays a few bars of "To A Water Lily" from his 1896 "Woodland Sketches."
Story: As an American composer and pianist, Edward Alexander MacDowell has reflected the rich harmonies of the European romantic composers, notably Edward Grieg of Norway. During his lifetime, many people considered him the greatest composer in the history of American music.

EPISODE #56 **"TRANSCONTINENTAL JOURNEYS"** Broadcast on November 11, 1936
Script written Jan. 21, 1936, revised June 5 and 16, Sept. 25, and Nov. 5 and 10, 1936
Written for *Cavalcade* by Jerry McGill.
Frank Singiser is the announcer and Craig Stevens is the commercial announcer.
Produced by Arthur Pryor and directed by Kenneth Webb.
Music composed and conducted by Donald Voorhees.
The opening melody was the 1934 song "Wagon Wheels."
Story: The progress of transportation, like all other phases of American endeavor, has been swift and sure. The modern luxury liner, the streamlined train and the swift transports of the skyways are a far cry from the days of the Yankee Clipper Ships, the stage coach or the Covered Wagon trains. Yet the heyday of these sailing ships and horse drawn vehicles lies within the memory of living men and women

EPISODE #57 **"THE STORY OF RUBBER"** Broadcast on November 18, 1936
Written for *Cavalcade* by Laurence Hammond.
Frank Singiser is the announcer and Craig Stevens is the commercial announcer.
Produced by Arthur Pryor and directed by Kenneth Webb.
Music composed and conducted by Donald Voorhees.
Story: In 1832, Charles Goodyear began experimenting with a crude form of rubber, called India Rubber, to find a way to make the substance useful for manufacturing. Indian rubber becomes brittle when cold and sticky when hot. One day in 1839, Goodyear made an accident that gave him the solution of his puzzle - how to vulcanize rubber, making it strong and resistant to heat and cold.

EPISODE #58 **"SONGS OF SENTIMENT"** Broadcast on November 25, 1936
Script first written October 21, 1936, revised on October 26, November 19 and 23, 1936.
Written for *Cavalcade* by Jerry McGill.
Frank Singiser is the announcer and Craig Stevens is the commercial announcer.
Produced by Arthur Pryor and directed by Kenneth Webb.
Music composed and conducted by Donald Voorhees.
The opening melody was the 1833 "Long, Long Ago."
Story: Stories of the events leading up to the writing of the 1843 song "Old Oaken Bucket," the 1873 song "Silver Threads Among the Gold," the 1893 song "Sweet Marie" and the 1892 song "After the Ball."

EPISODE #59 **"THE SEEING EYE"** Broadcast on December 2, 1936
Script first written on November 18, 1936, and revised on November 23 and 30, 1936.
Written for *Cavalcade* by Ruth Adams Knight.
Frank Singiser is the announcer and Craig Stevens is the commercial announcer.
Produced by Arthur Pryor and directed by Kenneth Webb.
Music composed and conducted by Donald Voorhees.
The opening song was "A Fine Romance" from Jerome Kern's film *Swingtime*.
Story: The first school for blind people was established in Paris in 1784. The first such school in the United States, the New England Institution for the Education of the Blind (now the Perkins School for the Blind) opened in Boston in 1832. On one historical day, a stranger came along with the idea of using German Shepherd dogs to assist leading the blind. But how to train the dogs was a problem . . .

EPISODE #60 **"THE STORY OF CHRISTMAS SEALS"** Broadcast on December 9, 1936
Script first written on November 11, 1936, revised on November 24, 1936.
Written for *Cavalcade* by Ann Barley.
Frank Singiser is the announcer and Craig Stevens is the commercial announcer.
Produced by Arthur Pryor and directed by Kenneth Webb.
Music composed and conducted by Donald Voorhees.
The opening song was Cole Porter's 1936 song "I've Got You Under My Skin."
Story: This is the story of how Miss Emily Bissell created a means of raising money to combat tuberculosis by making small sticky-backed stickers. Since Christmas Cards were always being passed around during the holidays, why not offer stickers that would seal the envelopes closed? The stickers Emily had printed up became "Christmas Seals."

Ann Barley: "The name of the sick boy in that drama was fictitious. More than one such incident really happened. It was used as a framework to give Miss Bissell, promoter of the seals, an immediate human interest. I outlined the idea to Miss Cole, and the publicity department for the National Tuberculosis Association, and she was quite pleased with it. In fact, she suggested the last scene in the script with the boy grown up. I suggested to Du Pont that December ninth was the anniversary of the Christmas Seal start. I suggested in part that it be played up more in narration, if that date were used."

EPISODE #61 **"THE MAN WHO HAD TWO CAREERS"** Broadcast on December 16, 1936
Script first written November 4, 1936, revised Nov. 23, and December 14 and 15, 1936.
Written for *Cavalcade* by Fairfax Downey and John T.W. Martin.
Frank Singiser is the announcer and Craig Stevens is the commercial announcer.
Produced by Arthur Pryor and directed by Kenneth Webb.
Music composed and conducted by Donald Voorhees.
Opening song was "The Song is You" from Jerome Kern's operetta "Music in the Air."
Story: A biography of the famous American inventor and painter. He received the patent for the first successful electric telegraph in the United States. He also invented the Morse code, used for many years to send telegraphic messages. In addition, Morse helped found the National Academy of Design and served as its first president.

EPISODE #62 **"A TRIBUTE TO ERNESTINE SCHUMANN-HEINK"** Aired Dec. 23, 1936
Script first written on November 27, 1936, and revised November 19, 1936.
Starring: Jeanette Nolan as Ernestine Schumann-Heink
Also featuring Helen Oelheim in the singing role of Ernestine.
Written for *Cavalcade* by Katherine Seymour.
Frank Singiser is the announcer and Craig Stevens is the commercial announcer.
Produced by Arthur Pryor and directed by Kenneth Webb.
Music composed and conducted by Donald Voorhees.
Songs featured in the order of their appearance: the drinking song "The Brindisi" from "Lucrezia Borgia," a selection from "Carmen," a lullaby from a Brahams solo, and the orchestra plays "Silent Night."

Trivia: Madame Ernestine Schumann-Heink died November 17, 1936. A month later the painstaking producers of radio's *Cavalcade of America* were on the air with a dramatization of the life-story of the grand old lady of opera. So impressive was the broadcast that as the last strains of music died away, Schumann-Heink's son, Ferdinand, who had listened attentively to the program, turned to friends and said quietly, "I felt as though my mother were there." To Jeanette Nolan, twenty-five-year-old radio actress, and Helen Oelheim, dark-haired young Metropolitan contralto, fell the task of playing the role which "Mother Schumann" had lived. They were hugely successful.

EPISODE #63   "YANKEE INDEPENDENCE"   Broadcast on December 30, 1936
Written for *Cavalcade* by Henry Fisk Carlton, based on his 1932 story "The Charter Oak."
Frank Singiser is the announcer and Craig Stevens is the commercial announcer.
Produced by Arthur Pryor and directed by Kenneth Webb.
Music composed and conducted by Donald Voorhees.
The opening song was the 1916 song "Poor Butterfly."
Story: The story of Connecticut's determined effort to keep its identity and protect its charter was one that has become a New England tradition. The facts of the story of the Charter Oak are clouded in legend but many believe that the main events were substantial. New England was colonized by people who put self-government above all ideals. though officially under the rule of the British crown, extensive rights and privileges were given to the colonists by their charters.

Trivia: This script was first written *and* revised on December 29, 1936, the day before the actual broadcast!

EPISODE #64   "WINNING PRESTIGE FOR THE AMERICAN STAGE"
also "THE STORY OF THOMAS JEFFERSON"   Broadcast on January 6, 1937
Script first written on December 8, 1936, and revised on December 30, 1936.
Written for *Cavalcade* by Katherine Seymour.
Frank Singiser is the announcer and Craig Stevens is the commercial announcer.
Produced by Arthur Pryor and directed by Kenneth Webb.
Music composed and conducted by Donald Voorhees.
Story: These are episodes from the life of the first American actor who actually took comedy seriously, with scenes from his famous success - "Rip Van Winkle."

Trivia: This broadcast featured two official script titles, both of which are listed above.

EPISODE #65   "JOHN HYATT, FATHER OF PLASTICS"   Broadcast on January 13, 1937
Script first written on December 7, 1936, revised on Dec. 30, 1936 and January 6, 1937.
Written for *Cavalcade* by _?_ Hall.
Frank Singiser is the announcer and Craig Stevens is the commercial announcer.
Produced by Arthur Pryor and directed by Kenneth Webb.
Music composed and conducted by Donald Voorhees.
Story: In the late 1860's, John W. Hyatt, a printer from Albany, NY, developed a material to replace the scarce ivory used to make billiard balls. In 1870, John and his brother received a patent for the material, which they later named "Celluloid." This was the first synthetic plastic material to receive wide commercial use.

EPISODE #66   "SONGS OF THE SEA"   Broadcast on January 20, 1937
Written for *Cavalcade* by Jerry McGill.
Frank Singiser is the announcer and Craig Stevens is the commercial announcer.
Produced by Arthur Pryor and directed by Kenneth Webb.
Music composed and conducted by Donald Voorhees.
Songs featured in the order of their appearance: the 1838 song "Life on an Ocean Wave," "Haul the Bowline," the 1880 "Blow the Man Down," the 1840 song "Rocked in Cradle of the Deep," "The Stormy Winds Do Blow," "Homeward Bound," and the 1806 song "Anchors Aweigh."
Story: This musical drama tells the story and experiences a young man is witness to when he goes out to sea. His voyage on the waves is accompanied with music and homely tunes that are synonymous with life on the ocean.

EPISODE #67 **"PIONEER WOMAN PHYSICIAN"** Broadcast on January 27, 1937
Script first written on December 29, 1936, and revised on January 25, 1937.
Written for *Cavalcade* by Ann Barley.
Frank Singiser is the announcer and Craig Stevens is the commercial announcer.
Produced by Arthur Pryor and directed by Kenneth Webb.
Music composed and conducted by Donald Voorhees.
Story: Your introduction to Elizabeth Blackwell, the first woman in the United States to receive a medical degree. She helped break down prejudice against women in medicine. In 1857, Elizabeth and her sister Emily, also a doctor, opened their own hospital in New York City. The sisters later expanded the hospital to include a medical school for women.

EPISODE #68 **"MINUTE MEN OF THE AIR"** Broadcast on February 3, 1937
Script first written on January 15, 1937, and revised on January 28, 1937.
Written for *Cavalcade* by Innis Osborn.
Frank Singiser is the announcer and Craig Stevens is the commercial announcer.
Produced by Arthur Pryor and directed by Kenneth Webb.
Music composed and conducted by Donald Voorhees.
The opening song was Irving Berlin's 1932 "Soft Lights and Sweet Music."
Story: Interwoven with the story of the amateur radio operators of America - "hams," as they call themselves - is the history of the American Radio Relay League, which was founded by Hiram Percy Maxim, famous engineer and inventor. Mr. Maxim became interested in amateur radio in 1870, through the activities of his son. Father and son together developed one of the most dominant amateur stations in their part of the country. Their value has proven many times over when the two dramas presented here include a flood episode and the heroism of a blind boy.

EPISODE #69 **"THE MAN WHO COULDN'T GROW OLD"** Broadcast February 10, 1937
Script first written on January 9, 1937, and revised on February 3, 1937.
Written for *Cavalcade* by Ann Barley and Fairfax Downey.
Frank Singiser is the announcer and Craig Stevens is the commercial announcer.
Produced by Arthur Pryor and directed by Kenneth Webb.
Music composed and conducted by Donald Voorhees.
Story: Episodes in the life of Peter Cooper, the great educator and inventor.

EPISODE #70 **"THE OUNCE OF PREVENTION"** Broadcast on February 17, 1937
Script first written on December 29, 1936, revised Jan. 26, 1937, Feb. 5 and 12, 1937.
Written for *Cavalcade* by Edward Longstreth.
Frank Singiser is the announcer and Craig Stevens is the commercial announcer.
Produced by Arthur Pryor and directed by Kenneth Webb.
Music composed and conducted by Donald Voorhees.
Opening song was "You Are Love" from Jerome Kern's "Showboat."
Story: Smallpox was the first disease conquered by human beings. Vaccination wiped it out. Smallpox had been one of the world's most feared diseases, as it has killed hundreds of millions of people and scarred and blinded millions more. This is the story of Edward Jenner, an English physician, who in 1796 developed the first vaccine - one that prevented smallpox.

On the next page: William Sanderson, a very talented artist, sketched these drawings of various broadcasts from *Cavalcade*'s early years.

SAMUEL F. B. MORSE

THE MAN WITH TWO CAREERS

THE SEEING EYE

EPISODE #71 "WINNING RECOGNITION FOR AMERICAN SINGERS"
Broadcast on February 24, 1937
Script first written on January 19, 1937, and revised on February 4 and 23, 1937.
Written for *Cavalcade* by Katherine Seymour.
Frank Singiser is the announcer and Craig Stevens is the commercial announcer.
Produced by Arthur Pryor and directed by Kenneth Webb.
Music composed and conducted by Donald Voorhees.
Songs featured in this episode: "Bohemian Girl," "La Traviata," "Lohengrin," and the 1823 song "Home, Sweet, Home."
Story: Lillian Nordica, the famous American prima donna, attempts to found an American School of Music. This is the true story behind her amazing adventure.

EPISODE #72 "NATIONAL PARKS PIONEERS" Broadcast on March 2, 1937
Script first written on February 2, 1937, and revised on February 10 and 24, 1937.
Written for *Cavalcade* by Innis Osborn and Fairfax Downey.
Frank Singiser is the announcer and Craig Stevens is the commercial announcer.
Produced by Arthur Pryor and directed by Kenneth Webb.
Music composed and conducted by Donald Voorhees.
Story: The discovery of Yellowstone Park and episodes in the life of its discoverer, the famous scout, Jim Bridgar. With an epilogue on the idea of Stephen Tyng Mather who helped make the National Parks public playgrounds.

EPISODE #73 "STEPHEN GIRARD" Broadcast on March 10, 1937
Script first written on February 2, 1937, and revised on February 18, and March 8, 1937.
Written for *Cavalcade* by Edward Longstreth.
Frank Singiser is the announcer and Craig Stevens is the commercial announcer.
Produced by Arthur Pryor and directed by Kenneth Webb.
Music composed and conducted by Donald Voorhees.
The opening song was "The Night Was Made for Love" from Jerome Kern's "The Cat and the Fiddle."
Story: Stephen Girard was termed by his contemporaries as "The Perfect Citizen." This is his biography, the life of the great philanthropist, merchant and banker. The extraordinary life of this man tells numerous true tales of courage and amusement.

EPISODE #74 "JAMES FENIMORE COOPER: FIRST AMERICAN NOVELIST"
Broadcast on March 17, 1937
Script first written on February 8, 1937 and revised on March 9, 1937.
Written for *Cavalcade* by Katherine Seymour.
Frank Singiser is the announcer and Craig Stevens is the commercial announcer.
Produced by Arthur Pryor and directed by Kenneth Webb.
Music composed and conducted by Donald Voorhees.
Story: Best known for his "Leather-Stocking Tales," Cooper wrote five novels about Natty Bumppo, spent his life as a frontiersman, and became the first author to seriously portray American frontier scenes and characters. His conservative ideas about society are reflected in many of his writings. His works show his concern for the freedom of individuals and the rights of property owners. Case in point: his most popular novel of all, "The Last of the Mohicans," which he wrote in 1826.

EPISODE #75 **"THE HOUSE OF GLASS"** Broadcast on March 24, 1937
Script first written on December 29, 1936, revised Feb. 5, March 12 and 19, 1937.
Written for *Cavalcade* by Edward Longstreth.
Frank Singiser is the announcer and Craig Stevens is the commercial announcer.
Produced by Arthur Pryor and directed by Kenneth Webb.
Music composed and conducted by Donald Voorhees.
The opening song was "Only a Rose" from Rudolph Friml's "The Vagabond King."
Story: People who live in glass houses should not throw rocks. Unless your name is Henry William Stiegel. Stiegel was an important early American manufacturer of fine glass. His factories were the first in the American Colonies to make glassware as good as that being imported from Europe. At the height of his success, Stiegel lived in a large house, wore elaborate clothes, and was called a baron. But his extravagant living and his risky investment in new factories brought financial ruin.

EPISODE #76 **"THE McGUFFY READERS"** Broadcast on March 31, 1937
Script first written on March 8, 1937.
Written for *Cavalcade* by Ruth Adams Knight.
Frank Singiser is the announcer and Craig Stevens is the commercial announcer.
Produced by Arthur Pryor and directed by Kenneth Webb.
Music composed and conducted by Donald Voorhees.
Story: This is the biography of William Holmes McGuffey, whose contributions to the education of the youth of America came through his famous readers.

EPISODE #77 **"ADMIRAL PEARY DISCOVERS THE POLE"** Broadcast on April 7, 1937
Script first written March 27, 1937, and revised on April 3 and 6, 1937.
Written for *Cavalcade* by Jerry McGill.
Frank Singiser is the announcer and Craig Stevens is the commercial announcer.
Produced by Arthur Pryor and directed by Kenneth Webb.
Music composed and conducted by Donald Voorhees.
Story: How American explorers Robert E. Peary led the first expedition usually credited with reaching this pole. The expedition included Matthew Henson, who was Peary's assistant, and four Eskimos. They made the trip by dog team in 1909. American explorers Richard E. Byrd and Floyd Bennett are credited with reaching the pole by airplane in 1926, but it was Peary's determination that put him in the history books.

EPISODE #78 **"SONGS OF THE GAY NINETIES"** Broadcast on April 14, 1937
Starring: Lillian Russell
Written for *Cavalcade* by Jerry McGill.
Frank Singiser is the announcer and Craig Stevens is the commercial announcer.
Produced by Arthur Pryor and directed by Kenneth Webb.
Music composed and conducted by Donald Voorhees.
Songs featured in this broadcast are "Ra-Ra-Boom-De-Ay," the 1896 song "A Hot Time in the Old Town Tonight," the 1894 song "I Don't Want to Play in Your Yard," Lillian Russell sings the 1892 song "Daisy Bell" and the 1902 song "Come Down My Evening Star," and "Brown October Ale" from Reginald DeKoven's "Robin Hood."
Story: *Cavalcade* invites the listening audience to spend an evening in the theatre and musical halls of New York in the Mauve Decade. New Yorkers meet country folk. And listeners hear the hustle of the doorman, the ticket man, and singers in an evening of music and laughter.

EPISODE #79   "THE GOLDEN TOUCH"   Broadcast on April 21, 1937
Script first written on March 8, 1937, and revised on April 6 and 20, 1937.
Written for *Cavalcade* by Edward Longstreth.
Frank Singiser is the announcer and Craig Stevens is the commercial announcer.
Produced by Arthur Pryor and directed by Kenneth Webb.
Music composed and conducted by Donald Voorhees.
Story: John A. Sutter had a vision. He saw a town founded with saw mills and general stores. Families with children and schools for the children to attend, and his saw mills to give jobs to the fathers of those families. But after Sutter began the foundation of his dream, one of his men discovered small yellow dust in the nearby river. It was gold. And everyone - and I mean everyone - abandoned Sutter's dream for a more prosperous vision. "Sutterville" never became a reality, but his vision did come true - in one way. A future town would be established, and California soon became known as "The Golden State."

Trivia: This script was originally scheduled for broadcast on May 12, 1937 on the East Coast, but when the primary script for this date became "unavailable," this script was pulled off the shelves and presented a few weeks sooner than originally scheduled.

EPISODE #80   "GEORGE WASHINGTON, SCIENTIFIC FARMER"   Aired April 28, 1937
Script first written on April 3, 1937 and revised on April 22, 1937.
Written for *Cavalcade* by Katherine Seymour.
Frank Singiser is the announcer and Craig Stevens is the commercial announcer.
Produced by Arthur Pryor and directed by Kenneth Webb.
Music composed and conducted by Donald Voorhees.
Story: Never mind the cherry tree. Growing up at Ferry Farm, young George Washington helped manage a plantation worked by twenty black slaves. He was observant and hard-working. He learned how to plant and produce tobacco, fruit, grains, and vegetables. The future hero of the American Revolution becomes the forerunner of scientific farming.

EPISODE #81   "SONGS OF THE SOUTH"   Broadcast on May 5, 1937
Script first written on April 22, 1937, and revised on May 3 and 4, 1937.
Written for *Cavalcade* by John T.W. Martin and _?_ Smith.
Frank Singiser is the announcer and Craig Stevens is the commercial announcer.
Produced by Arthur Pryor and directed by Kenneth Webb.
Music composed and conducted by Donald Voorhees.
Songs featured were the 1860 song "Dixie," "Cotton Pickin' Time," the 1877 song "Roll Out, Heave Dat Cotton," the 1912 song "Memphis Blues," Anton Dvorak's "New World Symphony" is played on a piano, a soprano of the 1864 song "Beautiful Dreamer," "Poor Little Lamb," a quartet sings "Let the Heavenly Light Shine on He," the orchestra plays the 1850 song "Camptown Races," "Old Man River," and the 1878 song "Carry Me Back to Ole Virginny."
Story: Down south, where the cotton plantations reside, slaves picked the fields singing folk melodies that developed from African chants. Their music gave them spiritual help and guidance, and broke the monotony of work. Those songs have since marked their place in the Music of America - from "Show Boat" to the old minstrel stage shows.

EPISODE #82 **"THE STORY OF DYNAMITE"** Broadcast on May 12, 1937
    Script first written Jan. 9, 1937, revised Jan. 20, March 1, 17, April 7, and May 7, 1937.
    Written for *Cavalcade* by Innis Osborn and John T.W. Martin.
    Frank Singiser is the announcer and Craig Stevens is the commercial announcer.
    Produced by Arthur Pryor and directed by Kenneth Webb.
    Music composed and conducted by Donald Voorhees.
    The opening song is "Moonlight in Kalva" from Jerome Kern's operetta "Good Morning Dearie."
    Story: Alfred Bernhard Nobel was a Swedish chemist and industrialist, best remembered for inventing dynamite. He established Nobel Prizes, using profits from the manufacture of chemical explosives to provide funds for the prizes. Liquid nitroglycerin is a powerful explosive that is dangerous because of its tendency to explode when handled roughly. Nobel tried many ways of making the nitro safe to use. Thanks to his work, the Nobel Prizes, first awarded in 1901, remain the most honored prizes in the world.

EPISODE #83 **"THOMAS A. EDISON, THE MAN"** Broadcast on May 19, 1937
    Script first written on February 24, 1937, and revised on May 4, 1937.
    Written for *Cavalcade* by Edward Longstreth.
    Frank Singiser is the announcer and Craig Stevens is the commercial announcer.
    Produced by Arthur Pryor and directed by Kenneth Webb.
    Music composed and conducted by Donald Voorhees.
    Story: These are the little known incidents in the life of the famous inventor. Edison looked for many different solutions when attempting to solve problems. When he created new or improved devices, he made a variety of designs. Edison obtained 1,093 United States patents, the most the U.S. patent office has ever issued to one person.

EPISODE #84 **"SONGS OF THE AMERICAN INDIAN"** Broadcast on May 26, 1937
    Script first written on April 26, 1937, and revised on May 17 and 24, 1937.
    Written for *Cavalcade* by Lone Bear.
    Frank Singiser is the announcer and Craig Stevens is the commercial announcer.
    Produced by Arthur Pryor and directed by Kenneth Webb.
    Music composed and conducted by Donald Voorhees.
    Songs include an Indian Chant by Lone Bear, "The Sun Rise Call," "Indian Lullaby," "Sioux Serenade," "Blanket Song," and music of the "Pawnee Spirit Song" is heard in the distance.
    Story: In an age-old tribal call to council, we can hear Karuks Pahitu, or Lone Bear, grandson of White Eagle, last hereditary chief of the Pawnees, as he bids you welcome. A college graduate and winner of a Julliard School of Music Scholarship, Lone Bear is a splendid example of the present generation of American Indians. Thanks to careful research of the folk lore of his people, *Cavalcade* was able to present some of the authentic customs and legends of the Red Man.

EPISODE #85 **"THE STORY OF AMERICAN DYES"** Broadcast on June 2, 1937
    Script first written on April 17, 1937, and revised on May 4 and 25, 1937.
    Written for *Cavalcade* by Kenneth Webb.
    Frank Singiser is the announcer and Craig Stevens is the commercial announcer.
    Produced by Arthur Pryor and directed by Kenneth Webb.
    Music composed and conducted by Donald Voorhees.
    Story: The need for an American Dye Industry, its inception and successful growth as reflected in the lives of the members of a typical American family.

EPISODE #86 **"THE EIGHTH WONDER OF THE WORLD"** Broadcast on June 9, 1937
Written for *Cavalcade* by Innis Osborn and John T.W. Martin.
Frank Singiser is the announcer and Craig Stevens is the commercial announcer.
Produced by Arthur Pryor and directed by Kenneth Webb.
Music composed and conducted by Donald Voorhees.
The opening melody was the 1924 song "I'll See You in my Dreams."
Story: The Grand Coulee Dam is the largest concrete dam and the greatest single source of water power in the U.S. The United States Bureau of Reclamation designed and built the dam, which was completed in 1942. It took less than eight years to build. This is the story of the ideas and struggle to get it started and work in full swing.

Note: The dam was not completed until a few years after this broadcast aired. This was just the story of what was at that time, the construction of the largest concrete dam ever.

EPISODE #87 **"STARS OF DESTINY"** Broadcast on June 16, 1937
Script first written on April 14, 1937, and revised on May 7 and June 14, 1937.
Written for *Cavalcade* by Edward Longstreth.
Frank Singiser is the announcer and Craig Stevens is the commercial announcer.
Produced by Arthur Pryor and directed by Kenneth Webb.
Music composed and conducted by Donald Voorhees.
The opening song was "Night and Day" from Cole Porter's "The Gay Divorcee."
Story: The life of David Rittenhouse, scientist, inventor, astronomer and patriot.

EPISODE #88 **"THE PINE TREE SHILLING"** Broadcast on June 23, 1937
Script first written on May 11, 1937, and revised on June 2, 1937.
Written for *Cavalcade* by Osmond Molarsky.
Frank Singiser is the announcer and Craig Stevens is the commercial announcer.
Produced by Arthur Pryor and directed by Kenneth Webb.
Music composed and conducted by Donald Voorhees.
Story: A story of the early days of the American colonies when there was no regular monetary system. The coinage of the first money in the colonies is documented, as well as the life of Captain Hull, best remembered as the first mint-master in the U.S.

EPISODE #89 **"LUTHER BURBANK, THE PLANT WIZARD"** Broadcast on June 30, 1937
Script first written on May 14, 1937, and revised on June 10, 1937.
Written for *Cavalcade* by Osmond Molarsky.
Frank Singiser is the announcer and Craig Stevens is the commercial announcer.
Produced by Arthur Pryor and directed by Kenneth Webb.
Music composed and conducted by Donald Voorhees.
Story: Luther Burbank was an American plant breeder, nurseryman, and horticulturist. He introduced and developed many new fruits, vegetables, flowers, and grasses. His most famous creations include the Burbank potato and the Santa Rosa plum. Although Burbank had no direct impact on genetics or plant breeding, his accomplishments were examples of evolution in action, and earned him the nickname of "The Plant Wizard."

EPISODE #90 **"THE CAVALCADE OF MUSIC"** Broadcast on July 7, 1937
"THE MUSIC OF IRVING BERLIN"
Script first written on June 29, 1937, and revised on July 2 and 6, 1937.
Featuring Conrad Thibault as soprano.
Written for *Cavalcade* by _?_ Wright.
Frank Singiser is the announcer.
Produced and directed by Kenneth Webb.
Music composed and conducted by Donald Voorhees.

Songs heard in the order of their appearance: the 1912 song "Alexander's Ragtime Band," the 1919 Ziegfeld Follies song "A Pretty Girl is Like a Melody," Conrad Thibault sings the 1922 song "Lady of the Evening," "The Waltz Melody," Irving Berlin's 1932 song "Soft Lights and Sweet Music" from the musical "Face the Music," the 1933 song "Heat Wave," the 1936 song "Lets' Face the Music and Dance" and "On the Avenue Melody."
Story: Irving Berlin composed many of the most famous American popular songs. From about 1910 to the early 1930's, Berlin wrote songs for many Broadway musicals. In 1935, Berlin moved to Hollywood, California, where he wrote songs for a number of motion-picture musicals. This is the life of Irving Berlin and his composition.

Trivia: This was the first of another summer series of music, as *Cavalcade* had done the summer before. Conrad Thibault was hired to star in the first few broadcasts of this summer series, to lead the lyrical music.

EPISODE #91   "THE CAVALCADE OF MUSIC"   Broadcast on July 14, 1937
"GEORGE GERSHWIN"
Script first written on July 13, 1937, and revised on the same day this was broadcast.
Featuring Conrad Thibault as soprano.
Written for *Cavalcade* by _?_ Wright.
Frank Singiser is the announcer.
Produced and directed by Kenneth Webb.
Music composed and conducted by Donald Voorhees.
Songs heard in the order of their appearance: the 1923 song "Rhapsody in Blue," "Swanee," the 1924 composition "Somebody Loves Me," Conrad Thibault sings the 1929 composition "Soon," the 1924 song "Fascinating Rhythm," the 1926 song "Someone to Watch Over Me," Thibault sings the 1932 song "Who Cares," the 1930 song "I Got Rhythm," "Embraceable You," "Shall We Dance?" "I've Got Beginners Luck," Conrad Thibault sings "They Can't Take That Away From Me," "Shall We Dance," and a reprise of "Rhapsody in Blue."
Story: The life and music of George Gershwin, a young man whose tunes brought joy to America even as they lifted our so-called popular music to a new level. Gershwin was our interpreter of what is called the jazz idiom. Not a musician in the land will forget that day in 1923 when Gershwin completed a composition for Paul Whiteman to play before an audience of critical music lovers in Aeolian Hall, New York, an auditorium dedicated to classical music.

Trivia: A program of songs of Richard Rodgers was originally scheduled for this date. The music of George Gershwin had been planned for the week after. But the day before yesterday, Monday the twelfth of July, newspapers all over the nation headlined the unhappy fact that George Gershwin had passed away. So as a special tribute, the musical presentations were switched, a script rushed into production, in memory of Gershwin's legacy that he left behind.

EPISODE #92   "THE CAVALCADE OF MUSIC"   Broadcast on July 21, 1937
"RICHARD RODGERS"
Script first written June 29, 1937 and July 2, 1937, and revised on July 8 and 16, 1937.
Featuring Conrad Thibault as soprano.
Written for *Cavalcade* by _?_ Wright.
Frank Singiser is the announcer.
Produced and directed by Kenneth Webb.
Music composed and conducted by Donald Voorhees.
Songs featured in this broadcast: the 1935 song "My Romance," the 1929 melody "Without a Song," "Mountain Greenery," "Here in My Arms," Conrad Thibault sings

"My Heart Stood Still," "The Blue Room," Conrad Thibault sings "Blue Moon," the 1926 song "With a Song in My Heart," "There's a Small Hotel," Conrad Thibault and the Orchestra perform "I Wish I Were in Love Again," "Where or When," and the 1937 song "Johnny One Note."

Story: Composers who have made and were making America sing and dance - such men as George Gershwin, Vincent Youmans, Arthur Schwartz, Cole Porter and others including a young man name Richard Rogers, whose life and music were presented on this broadcast. In writing two successful variety shows for Columbia University in New York, Richard Rogers and his lyric-writing partner, Lorenz Hart, startled blasé critics of light music by showing Broadway something new...

EPISODE #93 "THE CAVALCADE OF MUSIC" Broadcast on July 28, 1937
"VINCENT YOUMANS"

Script first written on June 30, 1937, and revised on July 22 and 26, 1937.
Featuring Conrad Thibault as soprano.
Written for *Cavalcade* by _?_ Wright.
Frank Singiser is the announcer.
Produced and directed by Kenneth Webb.
Music composed and conducted by Donald Voorhees.
Songs featured in this broadcast: "I Want to Be Happy," the 1924 song "Tea for Two," Conrad Thibault sings the 1929 song "Without a Song," "Time on my Hands," "Great Day," Conrad Thibault sings "Through the Years," the 1925 song "Sometimes I'm Happy," "The Carioca," Conrad Thibault sings the 1926 song "More Than You Know," and "Hallelujah."
Story: This broadcast features the music of Vincent Youmans, who as any musician familiar with the lighter music will tell you, is one of our most skilled tunesmiths. While in a popular vein, Youmans' music seems to have a permanence not often found in its field. The musical numbers from his musical "No, No, Nanette" was at one time, playing in a half dozen cities.

Trivia: This broadcast completed Conrad Thibault's group of appearances on this summer series of *The Cavalcade of Music*.

Conrad Thibault: "It was a pleasure to work with Donald Voorhees and I've certainly found the program worthwhile from my standpoint. Not just musically either. I've known of Du Pont for a long time but I'm sure I have a better understanding of the great number of fields the company serves than I had before. So, I'll just say thank you Don [Voorhees] and thank you Du Pont. I hope I see you all again."

EPISODE #94 "THE CAVALCADE OF MUSIC" Broadcast on August 4, 1937
"RUDOLPH FRIML'S MUSIC"

Script first written on July 22, 1937, and revised on August 2, 1937.
Featuring Francia White as soprano.
Written for *Cavalcade* by _?_ Wright.
Frank Singiser is the announcer.
Produced and directed by Kenneth Webb.
Music composed and conducted by Donald Voorhees.
Songs performed in the order of their appearance: the 1917 song "You're In Love," Francia White sings "Giannina Mia" from the operetta "The Firefly," the 1915 song "Allah's Holiday" from Otto Harbach's musical play "Katinka," "Chansonette," Francia White sings "Indian Love Call" from "Rose Marie," "Only a Rose" from the operetta "The Vagabond King," "Closing Melody," "Song of the Vagabonds," and a few bars from Jerome Kern's songs were played at the end of the program as a teaser.

Story: "You could fill many, many hours with familiar and well-loved music by Rudolf Friml," said one musician. "His is a sure melodic touch. He writes so that everyone can understand - his most delicate or stirring tunes are always clear-cut and musically." Rudolph Friml has contributed much to our enjoyment of light music, and he did a great deal more in the coming years.

Trivia: Taking Conrad Thibault's place for the vocal songs is Francia White.

EPISODE #95   **"THE CAVALCADE OF MUSIC"**   Broadcast on August 11, 1937
"JEROME KERN'S MUSIC"
Script first written on July 22, 1937, and revised on August 10, 1937.
Featuring Francia White as soprano.
Written for *Cavalcade* by _?_ Wright.
Frank Singiser is the announcer.
Produced and directed by Kenneth Webb.
Music composed and conducted by Donald Voorhees.
Songs featured in the order of their appearance: "Old Man River," the 1917 song "Till the Clouds Roll By," Francia White sings the 1932 song "I Told Every Little Star," "Kalua" from the 1921 musical "Good Morning Dearie," "Why Was I Born" from the 1929 musical "Sweet Adeline," Francia White sings "Smoke Gets In Your Eyes," "Lovely to Look At" from the musical "Roberta," "You Are Love," Francia White sings the 1936 song "The Way You Look Tonight," and the 1937 song "Can I Forget You."
Story: Undoubtedly Jerome Kern has written millions of notes on sheets of music manuscript paper; and without any doubt at all, millions of complimentary words about him and his music have been written throughout the world. For Jerome Kern has one of the best success records of any composer over the last thirty years. One of his greatest works was the score for the musical dramatization of the best-selling novel "Show Boat."

EPISODE #96   **"THE CAVALCADE OF MUSIC"**   Broadcast on August 18, 1937
"SIGMUND ROMBERG'S MUSIC"
Script first written on July 22, 1937, and revised August 11, 16 and 17, 1937.
Featuring Francia White as soprano.
Written for *Cavalcade* by _?_ Wright.
Frank Singiser is the announcer.
Produced and directed by Kenneth Webb.
Music composed and conducted by Donald Voorhees.
Songs featured in the order of their appearance: the 1917 song "Will You Remember," Francia White sings "Lover Come Back to Me," "One Alone" from "The Desert Song," "Softly as in a Morning Sunrise," the 1935 song "When I Grow Too Old to Dream," the 1867 melody "Mary Had a Little Lamb," Francia White sings "One Kiss," and "Road to Paradise" from "Maytime."
Story: Almost twenty years ago, Sigmund Romberg's operetta "Maytime" opened and ran for 492 performances. His musicals have included "The New Moon," "The Desert Song," and "May Wine," all of which became classics running for years on the stage. Here are the best songs from those musicals, all written and composed by Romberg.

Trivia: During the rehearsal of this broadcast, early in the afternoon, Sigmund Romberg sent a telegram to singer Francia White: "I remember vividly your beautiful singing in the Pacific Coast revival of 'Desert Song' last season and am looking forward with great pleasure to hearing you tonight with Don Voorhees and his fine orchestra. Stop. Best wishes to Don Voorhees as well as to yourself. Stop."

EPISODE #97 "THE CAVALCADE OF MUSIC"   Broadcast on August 25, 1937
"ARTHUR SCHWARTZ'S MUSIC"
Script first written on July 22, 1937, revised on August 17 and 24, 1937.
Featuring Francia White as soprano, and guests Arthur Schwartz, Owen Davis and Laurence Stallings. Donald Voorhees actually speaks in this broadcast.
Written for *Cavalcade* by _?_ Wright.
Frank Singiser is the announcer.
Produced and directed by Kenneth Webb.
Music composed and conducted by Donald Voorhees.
Songs featured in this broadcast are: the 1929 song "I Guess I'll Have to Change my Plans," the 1931 song "Dancing in the Dark," the 1930 song "Something to Remember You By," Francia White sings "Love is a Dancing Thing," "An Old Flame Never Dies," "You and the Night and the Music," Francia White sings "My Heart is Dancing," "If You Were Someone Else," "Good-bye Jonah," and eight bars of a Victor Herbert number as a teaser for next week's program.
Story: When Arthur Schwartz graduated from New York University he studied law, was admitted to the bar and practiced for over three years. But he'd always had a strong urge to write music - especially the musical comedy type. So his close friends were not surprised when young Schwartz started writing tunes that quickly won him a place in Broadway's big time . . .

Trivia: The script for this broadcast was still being revised an hour before broadcast!

EPISODE #98   "THE CAVALCADE OF MUSIC"   Broadcast on September 1, 1937
"VICTOR HERBERT'S MUSIC"
Featuring Francia White as soprano.
Written for *Cavalcade* by _?_ Wright.
Frank Singiser is the announcer.
Produced and directed by Kenneth Webb.
Music composed and conducted by Donald Voorhees.
Songs featured are: "Sweethearts Waltz," the 1905 song "If I Were on the Stage," Francia White's 1905 song "Kiss Me Again," excerpts from "Natoma," the 1914 song "When You're Away," the 1929 song "Pagan Love Song," and Francia White sings the 1917 song "Thine Alone" and a song from "Naughty Marietta."
Story: One of Victor Herbert's favorite works was his opera "Natoma." The New York opera companies would not produce it, but Herbert finally managed to have it open in Philadelphia. With Mary Garden and John McCormack in the principal roles, the opera was a success, and one of Victor Herbert's greatest ambitions realized.

Trivia: This episode marks the farewell appearance of Francia White, who had appeared as lead singer in the last few broadcast.

EPISODE #99   "THE CAVALCADE OF MUSIC"   Broadcast on September 8, 1937
"NACIO HERB BROWN'S MUSIC"
Script first written on August 31, 1937, and revised on September 3 and 7, 1937.
Featuring Francia White as soprano.
Written for *Cavalcade* by _?_ Wright.
Frank Singiser is the announcer.
Produced and directed by Kenneth Webb.
Music composed and conducted by Donald Voorhees.
Songs featured: "Singing in the Rain" from the movie *Hollywood Revue of 1929*, "The Moon is Low" from the movie *Montana Moon*, "Pagan Love Song" from *The Pagan*, "Paradise" from *A Woman Commands*, "The Wedding of the Painted Doll" from *Broadway Melody of 1930*, "A New Moon Over My Shoulder" from the movie *Student*

Tour, "Temptation" from *Broadway Melody of 1930*, and two tunes as previews of next week's release of *Broadway Melody of 1938*, "Your Broadway and Mine" and "Feelin' Like a Million."
Story: You've seen the movies, you've heard the music, now know the story of how Nacio Herb Brown came to write the music he did, and how much his contribution to the art of writing music for the screen became a legacy. Songs from the films he composed are featured within this broadcast.

Trivia: This episode also features Dr. Frank G. Whitmore, Dean of the School of Chemistry and Physics at PA State College, interviewed by Dr. Harrison E. Howe.

EPISODE #100 **"THE CAVALCADE OF MUSIC"** Broadcast on September 15, 1937
"COLE PORTER"
Script first written on July 26, 1937, and revised on September 9, 1937.
Featuring Conrad Thibault as guest artist.
Written for *Cavalcade* by _?_ Wright.
Produced by Arthur Pryor and directed by Kenneth Webb.
Frank Singiser is the announcer.
Music composed and conducted by Donald Voorhees.
Songs featured are the 1919 composition "Old Fashioned Garden," the 1929 song "You Do Something to Me," the 1930 song "What is This Thing Called Love?" "You're on Top," "I Get a Kick Out of You," "Anything Goes," and "It's De Lovely." Thibault sings "Easy to Love," the 1936 song "I've Got You Under My Skin," and "Night and Day."
Story: Cole Porter was an American songwriter famous for his witty lyrics and imaginative melodies. Having studied music in Paris during the early twenties, his experiences there provided him with the material for his "Paris" in 1928, his first Broadway success. He showed an early talent for music and had a song published when he was only eleven years old.

EPISODE #101 **"THE CAVALCADE OF MUSIC"** Broadcast on September 22, 1937
"DON VOORHEES"
Script first written on September 18, 1937, and revised on September 21, 1937.
Featuring Conrad Thibault as guest artist.
Written for *Cavalcade* by _?_ Wright.
Produced by Arthur Pryor and directed by Kenneth Webb.
Frank Singiser is the announcer.
Music composed and conducted by Donald Voorhees.
Songs featured: Paul Whiteman's "Whispering," Arthur Schwartz's 1931 song "Dancing in the Dark," Rimsky-Korsakov's "Capriccio Espagnol," Schwartz's "Louisiana Hayride." Thibault sings "Vision Fugitive" and "Standin' in De Need O' Prayer," and the 1920 song "Japanese Sandman."
Story: Donald Voorhees, who conducts the orchestra for *Cavalcade*, was the final entry in the "Cavalcade of Music" series. Voorhees played pieces of music from other performers, and a short biography about Voorhees is told in musical form.

On the next page: William Sanderson, a very talented artist, sketched these **drawings of various broadcasts from *Cavalcade*'s early years.**

SARAH JOSEPHA HALE

OLIVER WENDELL HOLMES

EPISODE #102   **"EDWIN BOOTH: PIONEER AMERICAN ACTOR"**   September 29, 1937
Script first written July 13, 1937, and revised September 21, 1937.
Written for *Cavalcade* by John Driscoll.
Produced by Arthur Pryor and directed by Kenneth Webb.
Frank Singiser is the announcer, and Dwight Weist is the commercial announcer.
Music composed and conducted by Donald Voorhees.
Opening song was an overture of "Make Believe" from Jerome Kern's "Show Boat."
Story: Edwin Booth was called by many the greatest of American actors. Through his continued efforts and his intentional reputation, the stage in this country was elevated to its rightful prominence in the English speaking world. In all walks of life, Americans have been recognized for their perseverance and their ability to succeed against odds. As with Edwin Booth, the artist, so it is with the practical man and the scientist.

EPISODE #103   **"MARY LYON, PIONEER WOMAN EDUCATOR"**   Aired October 6, 1937
Written for *Cavalcade* by Katherine Seymour.
Produced by Arthur Pryor and directed by Kenneth Webb.
Frank Singiser is the announcer, and Dwight Weist is the commercial announcer.
Music composed and conducted by Donald Voorhees.
Story: 1937 marked the one hundredth anniversary of the founding of Mount Holyyoke Seminary - the first endowed, permanent institution for the education of women in the United States. These are the highlights in the career of Mary Lyon, whose heroic pioneering efforts paved the way for our American women's colleges of today.

Trivia: A dramatization of Cotton Mather and Zabdiel Boylston, two doctors who believed that they found an inoculate against small pox and wanted to test their serum, was originally scheduled for this date. Stubbornness and obstinacy could not prevail against the objections of New Englanders, and one by one, they overcame the objections of the people. Finally one of the selected men stood forth and offered himself as a test case. He was successfully treated, and the public won him over, on the strength of the experiment. This script was never broadcast.

EPISODE #104   **"WILLIAM PENN AND THE HOLY EXPERIMENT"**   October 13, 1937
Script first written on June 16, 1937, revised on September 27, 1937.
Written for *Cavalcade* by Edward Longstreth.
Produced by Arthur Pryor and directed by Kenneth Webb.
Frank Singiser is the announcer, and Dwight Weist is the commercial announcer.
Music composed and conducted by Donald Voorhees.
Opening song was "Here in Your Arms" from the motion picture *Dearest Enemy*.
Story: How William Penn came to America in the seventeenth century and founded Pennsylvania, the colony that contributed much towards the achievement of our independence. This Quaker pioneer greatly influenced the trend of our national thought and the structure of our constitutional government.

Trivia: There are two versions of this broadcast; the presentations vary from East Coast and the West Coast. Attending the opening ceremonies for the East Coast broadcast was Mr. Henry Butler Allen, Director of the Franklin Institute, Mr. Lamont du Pont, President of the Du Pont Company and Dr. C.M.A. Stine, Vice President of the Du Pont company. All three spoke from Philadelphia, heard after the dramatization. In order to make up the time for the speeches, Donald Voorhees and his orchestra did not play any opening song.

For the West Coast production, however, these men did not give any speeches, so Voorhees and his Orchestra played "Here in Your Arms," from the motion picture *Dearest Enemy*. This filled in the time frame that would have been used for the speeches heard on the East Coast production.

EPISODE #105 **"JOHN JACOB ASTOR"** Broadcast on October 20, 1937
and "PIONEER IN AMERICAN COMMERCE"
Script first written on July 23, 1937, and revised on October 5 and 19, 1937.
Written for *Cavalcade* by John Driscoll.
Produced by Arthur Pryor and directed by Kenneth Webb.
Frank Singiser is the announcer, and Dwight Weist is the commercial announcer.
Music composed and conducted by Donald Voorhees.
Opening song was a small overture of "By the Waters of Minnetonka."
Story: Typical of so many foreign-born pioneers, John Jacob Astor's loyalty to his adopted homeland helped its growth to greatness. John Jacob Astor, in the early days of the young republic, saw the vision of American Commerce taking an equal place with that of the other nations of the world.

Trivia: This broadcast featured two official script titles, both of which are listed above.

EPISODE #106 **"CLARA LOUISE KELLOGG"** Broadcast on October 27, 1937
and "FIRST AMERICAN PRIMA DONNA"
Script first written September 10, 1937, and revised October 8 and 26, 1937.
Starring Maria Silveira, who sang the parts of Clara Louise Kellogg.
Written for *Cavalcade* by Katherine Seymour.
Produced by Arthur Pryor and directed by Kenneth Webb.
Frank Singiser is the announcer, and Dwight Weist is the commercial announcer.
Music composed and conducted by Donald Voorhees.
Songs featured (in order of their appearance) were: Verdi's "Cara Nome," the closing soprano aria from the first act of "Rigolleto," "The Jewel Song," "Way Down Upon the Swanee River," the first act of "Faust" is played in the background, and the ballad "Come Buy Me Flowers."
Story: America's first prima donna, Clara Louise Kellogg, who was also the first American singer to defy tradition by obtaining all her musical training in her native land. She was the first American to achieve world-wide recognition in the field of opera - and through her pioneering efforts she blazed a trail for other talented American singers to follow.

Trivia: This broadcast features two official script titles, both of which are listed above.

EPISODE #107 **"ELMER AMBROSE SPERRY"** Broadcast on November 3, 1937
and "THE LAST OF THE OLD-TIME INVENTORS"
Script first written on July 19, 1937, and revised October 1, 18, and November 1, 1937.
Written for *Cavalcade* by _?_ Southworth, John T.W. Martin and John Driscoll.
Produced by Arthur Pryor and directed by Kenneth Webb.
Frank Singiser is the announcer, and Dwight Weist is the commercial announcer.
Music composed and conducted by Donald Voorhees.
Opening song was "Whispers in the Dark," from the movie *Artists and Models*.
Story: Not so many years ago, inventors did not have the benefit of trained assistants and technical knowledge. Elmer Ambrose Sperry was one of the last of the old-time inventors who thought something might work and tried it, carrying out his results to the best of his ability. The dramatization begins with Sperry's amazing race on a railroad tricycle ahead of a freight train, one of his first boyhood inventions. He continues with the first exciting tests of some of his outstanding creations including the gyro-pilot and gyroscopic compass now used on airplanes, and comes to a close with Sperry's achievement of the famous Lindbergh Air Beacon in Chicago.

Trivia: At the conclusion of this broadcast, the theatre audience was invited to remain for a special showing of the twenty-minute sound picture "The Wonder World of Chemistry." There was a five-minute intermission between the program and the picture.

More trivia: This broadcast featured two official script titles, both of which are listed above.

EPISODE #108   **"JOHN BARTRAM'S GARDEN"**   Broadcast on November 10, 1937
Script written July 23, 1937, revised October 19 and November 8, 1937.
Written for *Cavalcade* by Edward Longstreth.
Produced by Arthur Pryor and directed by Kenneth Webb.
Frank Singiser is the announcer, and Dwight Weist is the commercial announcer.
Music composed and conducted by Donald Voorhees.
The opening song was Cole Porter's 1919 melody "Old Fashioned Garden."
Story: The life of John Bartram, one of the greatest natural botanists that ever lived. Bartram began the collection, cultivation, and hybridization of plants at a time when experimentation in plant culture was practically unknown in America. He traveled throughout the American colonies and abroad collecting and improving his specimens. Gradulay his developments became a basis for many of the plant species common in America today. Bartram's garden was a favorite haunt of George Washington, Benjamin Franklin and Alexander Hamilton.

Trivia: At the conclusion of this broadcast, the theatre audience was invited to remain for a special showing of the twenty-minute sound picture "The Wonder World of Chemistry." There was a five-minute intermission between the program and the picture.

EPISODE #109   **"THE SEEING EYE"**   Broadcast on November 17, 1937
Script first written on November 18, 1936, and revised on November 23 and 30, 1936.
Written for *Cavalcade* by Ruth Adams Knight.
Produced by Arthur Pryor and directed by Kenneth Webb.
Frank Singiser is the announcer, and Dwight Weist is the commercial announcer.
Music composed and conducted by Donald Voorhees.
Story: The first school for blind people was established in Paris in 1784. The first such school in the United States, the New England Institution for the Education of the Blind (now the Perkins School for the Blind) opened in Boston in 1832. On one historical day, a stranger came along with the idea of using German Shepherd dogs to assist leading the blind. But how to train the dogs was a problem . . .

EPISODE #110   **"SARA JOSEPHA HALE"**   Broadcast on November 24, 1937
Script first written on October 27, 1937, and revised November 15 and 22, 1937.
Written for *Cavalcade* by Ruth Adams Knight.
Produced by Arthur Pryor and directed by Kenneth Webb.
Frank Singiser is the announcer, and Dwight Weist is the commercial announcer.
Music composed and conducted by Donald Voorhees.
Story: Sara Hale was no flamboyant feminist, and emphatically not a suffragist. She led subtle and thoroughly polite crusades for many social reforms. She fought - always in the best of literary taste for better wages and working conditions for women, civic attention to public health and sanitation, the establishment of public playgrounds, and the retention of property rights by married women. She eventually presided over the editorial course of Ladies' Magazine in Boston.

EPISODE #111 **"OTTHAR MERGENTHALER"** Broadcast on December 1, 1937
and "THE INVENTION OF THE LINOTYPE"
Script first written July 7, 1937, and revised on November 1 and 23, 1937.
Written for *Cavalcade* by _?_ Grantham and Kenneth Webb.
Produced by Arthur Pryor and directed by Kenneth Webb.
Frank Singiser is the announcer, and Dwight Weist is the commercial announcer.
Music composed and conducted by Donald Voorhees.
Story: Ottmar Mergenthaler invented the Linotype typesetting machine. His device with a keyboard that composed matrices (molds) for letters, and cast an entire line of type at once. He demonstrated his first successful trial in front of others, resulting in the patent of the Linotype in 1884. These are the events leading up to that event.

Trivia: This broadcast features two official script titles, both of which are listed above.

EPISODE #112 **"THE CONSTITUTION OF THE UNITED STATES"** December 8, 1937
Script first written December 20, 1935, revised November 15 and December 6, 1937.
Written for *Cavalcade* by Kenneth Webb.
Produced by Arthur Pryor and directed by Kenneth Webb.
Frank Singiser is the announcer, and Dwight Weist is the commercial announcer.
Music composed and conducted by Donald Voorhees.
Opening song was "Virginia," the march from the operetta of the same name.
Story: On December 7, 1787, Delaware led the way towards the founding of a new nation, the United States of America. Yesterday, twelve states joined with Delaware to celebrate the 150th anniversary of the first state to ratify the Constitution of the United States. In Dover, Delaware, representatives of the thirteen original states met to unveil a memorial plaque in honor of the Delaware signers of the Constitution. Here, *Cavalcade* presents the story of the Constitution's birth.

Trivia: Twenty-four members of the New York Alumnae Chapter of Phi Chi Theta Sorority were in attendance for the East Coast performance. A group from the Nutley Junior High School Travel Club attended the repeat performance for the West Coast.

EPISODE #113 **"THE GLORY OF THE VANQUISHED"** Broadcast on December 15, 1937
Script first written November 3, 1937, revised November 18, and December 13, 1937.
Written for *Cavalcade* by Ruth Adams Knight.
Produced by Arthur Pryor and directed by Kenneth Webb.
Frank Singiser is the announcer, and Dwight Weist is the commercial announcer.
Opening song: Cole Porter's melody "In the Still of the Night," from the film *Rosalie*.
Music composed and conducted by Donald Voorhees.
Story: The biography of Dr. Edward Livingston Trudeau, founder of the Adirondack cottage Sanitarium now Trudeau Sanitarium at Sarnac Lake, New York. Dr. Trudeau worked as a pioneer, and the result of his research has proved beneficial to thousands suffering from the disease. The same spirit that inspired men like Trudeau is found today in many laboratories throughout the country where research chemists are constantly working to add to our daily comforts and conveniences.

Trivia: This year marked the thirteenth Anniversary of the use of Christmas Seals to raise funds for the fight against tuberculosis. As a promtional tool to increase sales of Christmas Seals, thus allowing the listeners to help in the work which had been started by such men as Edward Livingston Trudeau, *Cavalcade* broadcasted a biography about Dr. Trudeau and his work.

EPISODE #114 **"THE MASTER NAVIGATOR"** Broadcast on December 22, 1937
Script first written August 31, 1937, revised on December 14 and 21, 1937.
Written for *Cavalcade* by Katherine Seymour.
Produced by Arthur Pryor and directed by Kenneth Webb.
Frank Singiser is the announcer, and Dwight Weist is the commercial announcer.
Music composed and conducted by Donald Voorhees.
Story: Known for his extensive revision of "The Practical Navigator," which he renamed "The New American Practical Navigator" in 1802, Nathaniel Bowditch, an American mathematician and astronomer, explained the principals of navigation and the most practical methods of applying them. This book is still called "the seaman's Bible."

EPISODE #115 **"ERNESTINE SCHUMANN-HEINK"** Broadcast on December 29, 1937
Starring: Jeanette Nolan as Ernestine Schumann-Heink and Helen Olheim, Prima Donna Contralto of the Metropolitan Opera Company, who sings the Ernestine role.
Written for *Cavalcade* by Katherine and Adele Seymour.
Produced by Arthur Pryor and directed by Kenneth Webb.
Frank Singiser is the announcer, and Dwight Weist is the commercial announcer.
Music composed and conducted by Donald Voorhees.
Songs featured were a selection and aria from "Carmen," a few bars of Brahms' "Lullaby" is hummed, and the Drinking Song, also known as "The Brindisi" from "Lucrezia Borgia." Voorhees and his Orchestra perform "Silent Night."

Trivia: Ordinarily there were few repetitions in the *Cavalcade* series, but requests for a second performance of the Schumann-Heink drama became so numerous that the producers decided to air the show again. Miss Oelheim agreed to sing, but Jeanette Nolan had disappeared, and there was no voice as satisfactory as hers. Early last spring Miss Nolan and her husband, John McIntire, likewise a member of the *Cavalcade* company, had departed for Montana to fulfill an ambition to write the great American play. They were living one hundred miles from the nearest town - Kalispell, Montana - in the Yaak River country, in the northwest corner of the state. Moreover, they were grimly determined to stay there until their play was finished.

An accident brought them back. McIntire became ill and had to go east as far as the Mayo Clinic at Rochestra, Minnesota for an operation. Then his doctors advised him not to return to Montana, suggested instead that he spend the winter in New York. So the reluctant playwrights returned, and to the vast relief of *Cavalcade*'s producers made themselves available for a repeat performance of the drama of Schumann-Heink.

EPISODE #116 **"JAMES BUCHANAN EADS, PIONEER AMERICAN ENGINEER"**
Broadcast January 5, 1938. Script first written June 14, 1937, revised June 15, 1937, December 27, 1937, and January 4, 1938.
Written for *Cavalcade* by Ann Barley.
Produced by Arthur Pryor and directed by Kenneth Webb.
Frank Singiser is the announcer, and Dwight Weist is the commercial announcer.
Music composed and conducted by Donald Voorhees.
The opening song set a special setting of the famous 1917 spiritual "Deep River."
Story: This is the life of a bridge engineer, James Buchanan Eads, who in his day won acclaim throughout the civilized world. James was one of the first American engineers to be consulted by Europeans. His writings on river currents and the control of waters were accepted everywhere as masterpieces of their kind. And his perseverance and daring have been a model for men who have since built roadways of steel and concrete over American waters. The thrilling account of how James built the St. Louis Bridge and the Mississippi jetties made him the first engineer to build a steel bridge across the Mississippi River.

EPISODE #117 **"BLAZING TRAILS FOR SCIENCE"** Broadcast on January 12, 1938
Script first written July 16, 1937, revised January 3, 1938 and January 10, 1938.
Written for *Cavalcade* by Edward Longstreth.
Produced by Arthur Pryor and directed by Kenneth Webb.
Frank Singiser is the announcer, and Dwight Weist is the commercial announcer.
Music composed and conducted by Donald Voorhees.
Story: This is a biography of Robert Hare, the little-known inventor of the oxygen-hydrogen blowpipe, and many other scientific improvements developing from it.

EPISODE #118 **"THE BIG BROTHERS"** Broadcast on January 19, 1938
Script first written Nov. 4, 1937, revised Dec. 10, 1937, and Jan. 10, 13, and 18, 1938.
Guest of the evening, Mr. Martin Lewis, associate editor of the magazine, *Radio Guide*.
Written for *Cavalcade* by Osmond Molarsky.
Produced by Arthur Pryor and directed by Kenneth Webb.
Frank Singiser is the announcer, and Dwight Weist is the commercial announcer.
Music composed and conducted by Donald Voorhees.
George Gershwin's "A Foggy Day" from the film *A Damsel in Distress* is played.
Story: A true story from modern life, about the Big Brothers, an organization that has brought a new life and untold happiness to so many little brothers - at times when their futures hung between a career of crime and wasted existence on the one hand, and a life of usefulness and service to their families and friends on the other. Case in point: typifying a case where the Big Brothers society helped steer a young man from a life of crime.

Martin Lewis: "*Cavalcade of America* was conceived originally as a series of dramatizations which could reflect the real spirit of America. Because *Cavalcade* has done that, and because, in addition, it has demonstrated that history is something more than the material of which textbooks are made, *Radio Guide* magazine takes pleasure in paying tribute to one of the truly distinguished radio programs of our times. Notable not only for its devotion to its purpose, but for the accuracy of its presentation of historical events, *Cavalcade of America* combines the warmth and vitality of living drama with the dignity and integrity of scholarship."

Trivia: Mr. Lewis awarded *Cavalcade* with Radio Guide Magazine Medal of Merit on the air shortly after his speech, which he presented before the drama.

EPISODE #119 **"THE PATHFINDER"** Broadcast on January 26, 1938
Script first written on August 31, 1937, revisions made on January 3, 11, and 25, 1938.
Written for *Cavalcade* by John Driscoll.
Produced by Arthur Pryor and directed by Kenneth Webb.
Frank Singiser is the announcer, and Dwight Weist is the commercial announcer.
Music composed and conducted by Donald Voorhees.
The opening overture was the ever popular melody "My Little Gray Home in the West."
Story: As a geologist, botanist and topographer, John C. Fremont combined his technical knowledge with his daring as a pioneer in the western wilderness. His zeal and conscientiousness may be compared with the earnest endeavors of the research chemist, who finds no effort too great in striving for the goal he had set himself in improving our daily living conditions.

EPISODE #120 **"FRANCIS SCOTT KEY"** Broadcast on February 2, 1938
Starring: Bill Adams and House Jameson
Written for *Cavalcade* by John Driscoll.
Produced by Arthur Pryor and directed by Kenneth Webb.
Frank Singiser is the announcer, and Dwight Weist is the commercial announcer.
Music composed and conducted by Donald Voorhees.
"The Star Spangled Banner" is played during this broadcast.
Story: The devotion of the people of this country to our flag in nowhere better symbolized than in the fervent stanzas of "The Star Spangled Banner." More than a century has lapsed since it was written, but it has always remained in the hearts of American citizens as the official national anthem, although it wasn't until March 3, 1931, that is was so designated by a special act of Congress. This is the story and events leading up to Francis Scott Key writing the famous song that remains a favorite.

EPISODE #121 **"OLIVER WENDELL HOLMES"** Broadcast on February 9, 1938
Script first written October 18, 1937, revised Dec. 10, 1937, Jan. 17, and Feb. 8, 1938.
Written for *Cavalcade* by John Driscoll.
Produced by Arthur Pryor and directed by Kenneth Webb.
Frank Singiser is the announcer, and Dwight Weist is the commercial announcer.
Music composed and conducted by Donald Voorhees.
Story: Incidents in the life of this versatile man who was known as a poet, doctor, and wit. The saving of the famous U.S.S. Constitution, known affectionately as "Old Ironsides" and Homes' contribution to the prevention of puerperal fever are the high spots.

EPISODE #122 **"THE LOUISIANA PURCHASE"** Broadcast on February 16, 1938
Script first written November 23, 1937, revised on January 26, and February 14, 1938.
Written for *Cavalcade* by Osmond Molarsky and Kenneth Webb.
Produced by Arthur Pryor and directed by Kenneth Webb.
Frank Singiser is the announcer, and Dwight Weist is the commercial announcer.
Music composed and conducted by Donald Voorhees.
The opening song was "Neath the Southern Moon" from Victor Herbert's "Naughty Marietta."
Story: The annexation of one of the largest areas of American territory, the story of the Louisiana Purchase. The development of our country's natural resources in this territory has been fostered in no small degree. Here *Cavalcade* presents the events leading up to the purchase of the vast territory from France, with particular emphasis on the part played in the negotiations by Pierre Samuel Du Pont.

EPISODE #123 **"NOAH WEBSTER: THE NATION'S SCHOOLMASTER"**
Broadcast on February 23, 1938.
Script first written on December 7, 1937, revised February 8 and 21, 1938.
Written for *Cavalcade* by Ruth Adams Knight.
Produced by Arthur Pryor and directed by Kenneth Webb.
Frank Singiser is the announcer, and Dwight Weist is the commercial announcer.
Music composed and conducted by Donald Voorhees.
The opening song was the 1914 melody "They Didn't Believe Me."
Story: Noah Webster lived to be a patriarch of eighty-five. The storm which centered about his textbooks and his dictionary died away and his American version of the Bible occupied his old age. He died May 28, 1843, but he lives on in the memory of America as both teacher and preacher - the Nation's Schoolmaster.

Trivia: One hundred and seventy-five representatives of the American Pulp and Paper Association was in attendance in the audience for this broadcast.

EPISODE #124 **"ANNE SULLIVAN MACY"** Broadcast on March 2, 1938
Helen Keller made a special appearance on this broadcast.
Written for *Cavalcade* by Ruth Adams Knight.
Produced by Arthur Pryor and directed by Kenneth Webb.
Frank Singiser is the announcer, and Dwight Weist is the commercial announcer.
Music composed and conducted by Donald Voorhees.
Opening song was "The Song is You" from Jerome Kern's operetta "Music in the Air."
Story: The life of Mrs. Macy, a partly blind teacher-companion of Helen Keller, who devoted her time and personal hours to the subject of education. Through her work with Miss Keller, Mrs. Macy actually revolutionized teaching of the blind and deaf. *Cavalcade* salutes the remarkable achievements of Macy as an educator.

Kenneth Webb: "One of the greatest tributes paid to these dramatizations was the remark of Miss Helen Keller on the occasion of the broadcast devoted to the life of her beloved teacher, Mrs. Anne Sullivan Macy: 'I thought it thrilling, tender and dignified.' She could hardly have chosen three more suitable adjectives to sum up the ideals in charge of the building and direction of the program."

EPISODE #125 **"THE LAST OF THE SCOUTS"** Broadcast on March 16, 1938
Script first written on December 23, 1937, revised February 21, March 8 and 9, 1938.
Written for *Cavalcade* by Ruth Adams Knight.
Produced by Arthur Pryor and directed by Kenneth Webb.
Frank Singiser is the announcer, and Dwight Weist is the commercial announcer.
Music composed and conducted by Donald Voorhees.
The opening song was the 1934 melody "Wagon Wheels."
Story: There is no period of American history more glamorous than that of the early days of the West. William F. Cody, Indian fighter, Pony Express rider, buffalo hunter, Army scout and the man who revealed the fabulous life of the plains not only to America but to the world, was known best as "Buffalo Bill."

Trivia: The original title of this script was "Buffalo Bill," changed before the final revision of the script was written.

> Listen to the story of "Buffalo Bill" to be aired Wednesday over CBS at:
> 8:00 p.m. EST — 7:00 p.m. CST
> Later for the West Coast at:
> 9:00 p.m. PST — 10:00 p.m. MST

EPISODE #126 **"CAPTAIN ROBERT GRAY AND THE COLUMBIA RIVER"**
Broadcast on March 16, 1938.
Script first written on February 2, 1938, revised Feb. 23, March 14 and 15, 1938.
Written for *Cavalcade* by _?_ Southworth.
Produced by Arthur Pryor and directed by Kenneth Webb.
Frank Singiser is the announcer, and Dwight Weist is the commercial announcer.
Music composed and conducted by Donald Voorhees.
The opening song was "Thine Alone" from Victor Herbert's Irish operetta "Eileen."
Story: Robert Gray was the first person to sail around the world under the United States flag. His voyage established an important trade route for U.S. merchants. In 1792, Gray set out and sailed into the mouth of the Columbia River, which he named after his ship. Gray's entrance into the river became a basis for U.S. claims to the Oregon Territory.

EPISODE #127 **"JOHN JAMES AUDUBON"** Broadcast on March 23, 1938
Script first written December 20, 1937, revised February 23, March 21 and 23, 1938.
Written for *Cavalcade* by Ann Barley.
Produced by Arthur Pryor and directed by Kenneth Webb.
Frank Singiser is the announcer, and Dwight Weist is the commercial announcer.
Music composed and conducted by Donald Voorhees.
Opening song was "One Song" from Walt Disney's movie *Snow White and the Seven Dwarfs*.
Story: John James Audubon was the first to study and paint the birds of North America. His lifelike paintings of birds in their natural surroundings brought him fame and fortune. But when he first wanted to publish his works, he could find no American publisher. He had to visit England and Scotland to struggle for recognition.

Trivia: In the theatre audience for this broadcast were twenty-five students from Finch Junior College in New York.

EPISODE #128 **"CHARLOTTE CUSHMAN"** Broadcast on March 30, 1938
Written for *Cavalcade* by John Driscoll.
Produced by Arthur Pryor and directed by Kenneth Webb.
Frank Singiser is the announcer, and Dwight Weist is the commercial announcer.
Music composed and conducted by Donald Voorhees.
As an opening overture, Voorhees and his orchestra played two old favorites, the 1780 song "Drink to Me Only With Thine Eyes" and the 1902 melody "Sally in Our Alley."
Story: A re-enactment of the career of America's first great actress who was one of the most versatile players in the history of the American Theatre. Beginning in opera, Charlotte Cushman one night lost her voice during a performance. Then she became an actress, and besides appearing in great feminine roles essayed such parts as "Romeo" in London and other great Shakespearean heroes. Her immortality in the theatre was recaptured in the presentation of a scene from her most famous performance - as "Meg Merrilies" in "Guy Mannering." The story of a life that developed with our theatre.

EPISODE #129 **"THE SEARCH FOR IRON"** Broadcast on April 6, 1938
Script first written December 17, 1937, revised Feb. 24, March 16, and April 5, 1938.
Written for *Cavalcade* by Ruth Adams Knight.
Produced by Arthur Pryor and directed by Kenneth Webb.
Frank Singiser is the announcer, and Dwight Weist is the commercial announcer.
Music composed and conducted by Donald Voorhees.
Opening song was "Heigh Ho" from Walt Disney's *Snow White and the Seven Dwarfs*.
Story: The story of a pioneering mother and her seven sons and grandsons, Hepzibeth Merritt and their struggles in Minnesota before her boys discovered the great deposits of iron in the world famous Mesabi Iron Range.

EPISODE #130 **"THOMAS JEFFERSON AND AMERICAN EDUCATION"**
Broadcast on April 13, 1938
Written for *Cavalcade* by Edward Longstreth and Kenneth Webb.
Produced by Arthur Pryor and directed by Kenneth Webb.
Frank Singiser is the announcer, and Dwight Weist is the commercial announcer.
Music composed and conducted by Donald Voorhees.
Opening song was the march "Virginia," from the musical comedy of the same name.
Story: A dramatization of the founding of the University of Virginia, an institution established by Thomas Jefferson according to his ideals for American education and the assistance rendered him in this plan by Pierre Samuel Du Pont de Nemours.

EPISODE #131 **"THE 4-H CLUB MOVEMENT"** Broadcast on April 20, 1938
Written for *Cavalcade* by John Driscoll.
Produced by Arthur Pryor and directed by Kenneth Webb.
Frank Singiser is the announcer, and Dwight Weist is the commercial announcer.
Music composed and conducted by Donald Voorhees.
Opening song was Jerome Kern's "What's Good About Goodnight" from the new film *The Joy of Living*.
Story: The 4-H is an educational program that helps young people develop new skills, explore possible career choices, and serve their communities. This is a prime example of how a small boy and the farm he resides on, influences this national farm youth organization in helping to make a happier and fuller life.

EPISODE #132 **"MARIA MITCHELl: FIRST AMERICAN WOMAN SCIENTIST"**
Broadcast on April 17, 1938.
Script first written February 28,1938, revised March 15 and April 18, 1938
Written for *Cavalcade* by Katherine Seymour.
Produced by Arthur Pryor and directed by Kenneth Webb.
Frank Singiser is the announcer, and Dwight Weist is the commercial announcer.
Music composed and conducted by Donald Voorhees.
The opening song was the recent 1937 release "Star Dust."
Story: Incidents in the life of America's first great woman scientist who has achieved a lasting place in the scientific development of our country through her work in astronomy and her professorship at the newly founded Vassar College.

EPISODE #133 **"SONGS OF THE MISSISSIPPI"** Broadcast on May 4, 1938
The singers for this broadcast included Everett Clark, Charles Harrison, Phil Dewey, and Alden Edkins.
Written for *Cavalcade* by John Driscoll.
Produced by Arthur Pryor and directed by Kenneth Webb.
Frank Singiser is the announcer, and Dwight Weist is the commercial announcer.
Music composed and conducted by Donald Voorhees.
Music featured (listed in order of appearance) was: "Waters of the Minnetonka," the 1877 song "Roll Out Heave That Cotton," the 1865 song "One More River to Cross," the 1912 song "Waitin' For the Robert E. Lee," the 1910 song "Steamboat Bill," "Down the Mississippi," Ferde Grofe's "Mardi Gras," and "Old Man River."
Story: A week after this broadcast, in Memphis, Tennessee, the annual Cotton Carnival was celebrated. As a salute to King Cotton, Du Pont presented an evening of songs featuring many of the melodies which have been inspired by the traditions of the great river Mississippi. The melodies and legends which have arisen from the traditions of the river include such greats as "Old Man River" and "Robert E. Lee."

EPISODE #134 **"THE COLONIZATION OF CALIFORNIA"** Broadcast on May 11, 1938
Written for *Cavalcade* by John Driscoll and Winifred Willis.
Produced by Arthur Pryor and directed by Kenneth Webb.
Music composed and conducted by Donald Voorhees.
Frank Singiser is the announcer, and Dwight Weist is the commercial announcer.
Music composed and conducted by Donald Voorhees.
The opening song was the 1915 classic "In a Monastery Garden."
Story: Junipero Serra was a Franciscan missionary who in 1769 founded the first mission in present-day California. He founded the California Missions and laid the foundation for the colonization of the state of California.

EPISODE #135 **"BENJAMIN FRANKLIN"** Broadcast on May 18, 1938
Script first written on April 27, 1938, and revised on May 16, 1938.
Written for *Cavalcade* by Mann Page.
Produced by Arthur Pryor and directed by Kenneth Webb.
Frank Singiser is the announcer, and Dwight Weist is the commercial announcer.
Music composed and conducted by Donald Voorhees.
Opening song was "I Live the Life I Love," from one of the Mask and Wig productions of the University of Pennsylvania.
Story: Stories from the life of America's "First Citizen" emphasizing Dr. Franklin's ceaseless passion for invention and portraying the genial side of this amazing American personality.

EPISODE #136 **"CHILD WELFARE IN THE UNITED STATES"** Aired on May 25, 1938
Written for *Cavalcade* by Ruth Adams Knight.
Produced by Arthur Pryor and directed by Kenneth Webb.
Frank Singiser is the announcer, and Dwight Weist is the commercial announcer.
Music composed and conducted by Donald Voorhees.
The opening song was Jerome Kern's "Just Let Me Look At You," from the film *The Joy of Living*.
Story: The growth of child care in the United States through organizations, that are striving to improve child care methods and reach a better understanding of juvenile needs. This episode also features dramatizations of events leading up to the founding of the Child Welfare organization stressing the good work it has done for orphaned or destitute American children.

EPISODE #137 **"SAMUEL SLATER"** Broadcast on June 1, 1938
Written for *Cavalcade* by _?_ Southworth.
Produced by Arthur Pryor and directed by Kenneth Webb.
Frank Singiser is the announcer, and Dwight Weist is the commercial announcer.
Music composed and conducted by Donald Voorhees.
The opening song was George Gershwin's last song, "Love Walked In" from "The Goldwyn Follies."
Story: Samuel Slater worked for six years as an apprentice and manager in an English textile mill. At the mill, he learned the workings of the spinning machine developed by the British inventor Richard Arkwright. Slater left England in disguise because the British government prohibited any person who had knowledge of the design and operation of spinning machines from leaving the country. In 1790, Slater agreed to build the Arkwright machine from memory for Almy & Brown, a Rhode Island textile firm that wanted to use the mechanical cotton spinning techniques. Now remembered as the founder of the textile industry in the United States, Slater performed what is probably one of the greatest feats of memory.

EPISODE #138 **"KING COAL: THE STORY OF ANTHRACITE"** Broadcast June 8, 1938
Written for *Cavalcade* by John Driscoll.
Produced by Arthur Pryor and directed by Kenneth Webb.
Frank Singiser is the announcer, and Dwight Weist is the commercial announcer.
Music composed and conducted by Donald Voorhees.
The opening song was "Let Me Whisper."
Story: A feature of highlights in the early history of our country's most valuable mineral "King Coal." Of bituminous or soft coal, our nation possesses vast deposits. Of anthracite or hard coal, we have the earth's greatest supply. It was the discovery and use of anthracite that constituted America's unique contribution to the history of coal.

EPISODE #139 **"DOCTOR JOHN GORRIE"** Broadcast on June 15, 1938
Written for *Cavalcade* by Ruth Adams Knight.
Produced by Arthur Pryor and directed by Kenneth Webb.
Frank Singiser is the announcer, and Dwight Weist is the commercial announcer.
Music composed and conducted by Donald Voorhees.
The opening song was the 1914 song "When You're Away" from Victor Herbert's operetta, "The Only Girl."
Story: The true story of John Gorrie, doctor, scientist and public benefactor who perfected the world's first ice-making machine. It's result benefits to mankind are numerable, especially as an aid in medical treatment.

EPISODE #140 **"THE SWEDES LAND IN DELAWARE"** Broadcast on June 22, 1938
Script first written on May 27, 1938, and revised on June 20, 1938.
Written for *Cavalcade* by John Driscoll.
Produced by Arthur Pryor and directed by Kenneth Webb.
Frank Singiser is the announcer, and Dwight Weist is the commercial announcer.
Music composed and conducted by Donald Voorhees.
The opening song was Victor Herbert's 1905 melody "Kiss Me Again."
Story: The dramatization of the coming of the Swedish colonists to America, their settlement near Wilmington, Delaware, their erection of Fort Christina and the work of their great Governor, Johan Printz - how the colony contributed to the rise of the State of Delaware and how the spirit of the Swedish people rose above pioneering hardships.

Trivia: Planned as a part of the Swedish Tercentenary Celebration a special feature of this broadcast was the fact that it was short-waved to the steamer "Kungsholm" at sea where the Crown Prince of Sweden and his party were enroute to America for the celebration.

EPISODE #141 **"ELUTHERE IRENEE DU PONT"** Broadcast on June 29, 1938
Script first written May 25, 1938, and revised June 17 and 28, 1938.
Written for *Cavalcade* by Mann Page.
Produced by Arthur Pryor and directed by Kenneth Webb.
Frank Singiser is the announcer, and Dwight Weist is the commercial announcer.
Music composed and conducted by Donald Voorhees.
The opening song was "I See Your Face Before Me" from Arthur Schwartz's musical comedy "Between the Devil."
Story: While hunting one day with his friend, Colonel Toussard, a young French émigré named E.I. du Pont missed a shot because his American-made powder failed to fire. Thus he became convinced of America's need for a gunpowder manufacturing plant of its own. Black powder was essential to the pioneers, who depended upon it to obtain food and to protect themselves. Du Pont had learned how to make powder from the celebrated chemist, Lavoisier, who at one time had charge of the French Government's plant at Essone. Encouraged by his friend, Thomas Jefferson, E.I. du Pont built a powder mill in 1802 on the banks of the historic Brandywine Creek near the city of Wilmington, Delaware.

Dwight Weist: "During the one hundred and forty broadcasts of the *Cavalcade of America*, we have received many letters asking why in our stories of pioneers we have not dramatized the life of Eluethere Irenee du Pont de Nemours, the pioneer who, one hundred and thirty-six years ago, founded the company which bears his name. So this evening, as the final broadcast in this season we presented his colorful and dramatic story at the request of many of our listeners."

EPISODE #142 **"KNUTE ROCKNE"** Broadcast on December 5, 1938
Script first written Nov. 9, 1938, revised Nov. 15, 18, 22, 23, and 29, Dec. 2, 1938.
Starring: Jimmy Donnelly as Bob
Kingsley Colton as Knute Rockne (as a boy)
Frank Readick as Knute Rockne (as a man)
Kenny Delmar as Charles "Gus" Dorais
Ted Jewett as the friend of Knute Rockne's
Clayton Collyer as the substitute
Ted Jewett as the President of the Student Council
Ted de Corsia as the Student
Roy Lemay as Dan
Ronald Liss as Bill
Dwight Weist as Jimmy Crowley
Elliott Reid as George Gipp
Ted de Corsia as "Horseman"
Don Lawder as the manager
Kenny Delmar as the Halfback
Ed Jerome as the reporter
Written for *Cavalcade* by John Driscoll.
Produced by Louis Mason and directed by Homer Fickett.
Thomas Chalmers as the announcer, and Gabriel Heatter as the news commentator.
Music composed and conducted by Donald Voorhees.
The opening song was "At Long Last Love" from Cole Porter's musical comedy "You Never Know." A chorus sung three songs during the broadcast: "Notre Dame Our Mother," "Hike Song" and "Victory March."
Story: The story of the great, beloved football coach at Notre Dame emphasizing the nation-wide results which followed from Rockne's work of building men and men's character.

EPISODE #143 **"PETER STUYVESANT"** Broadcast on December 12, 1938
Script first written on November 22, 1938, and revised on December 9 and 10, 1938.
Starring: Dwight Weist as the first man
Agnes Moorehead as the first woman
Agnes Moorehead as the mother
William Johnstone as Johann
William Johnstone as Kieft
Abby Lewis as the second woman
Ted de Corsia as man four
Dwight Weist as Hans
Frank Readick as man three
Ted Jewett as William
Abby Lewis as Tina
Frank Readick as Hendrick
Ted de Corsia as Jochem
Frank Readick as Jan
Written for *Cavalcade* by _?_ McMorrow.
Produced by Louis Mason and directed by Homer Fickett.
Ted Jewett is the announcer and Gabriel Heatter is the news commentator.
Music composed and conducted by Donald Voorhees.
The opening song was "This Can't Be Love" from the musical success, "The Boys From Syracuse."
Story: Peter Stuyvesant was an irascible old Dutchman who became the last Governor of Dutch New Amsterdam prior to its surrender to the English when it was given the name, New York. The colonists refused to support Stuyvesant, and he was forced to give in.

EPISODE #144 **"WILL ROGERS"** Broadcast on December 19, 1938
Script first written November 15, 1938, revised Nov. 23, December 14 and 16, 1938.
Starring: Frank Readick as Texas Jack
Agnes Moorehead as the first woman
Dwight Weist as the performer
Abby Lewis as the third girl
Ted Jewett as the doorman
Dwight Weist as man two
Bill Adams as the second girl
Abby Lewis as the first girl
Ted Jewett as man one
Written for *Cavalcade* by Mann Page.
Produced by Louis Mason and directed by Homer Fickett.
Ted Jewett is the announcer and Gabriel Heatter is the news commentator.
Music composed and conducted by Donald Voorhees.
The opening song was "Sing For Your Supper," from the latest Rodgers and Hart musical, "The Boys From Syracuse." Featured in the drama was the 1906 song "Cheyenne" and the 1882 "Skater's Waltz."

Story: A biography of America's favorite humorist, Will Rogers. This journey back down memory lane to reach out again for that friendly handshake - that quiet chuckle - and wit from that common cowboy with a flair for words.

EPISODE #145 **"PAUL BUNYAN"** Broadcast on December 26, 1938
Script first written by November 18, 1938, and revised December 14, 21 and 23, 1938.
Starring: Bill Pringle as Paul Bunyan   Jack Grimes as Father Bunyan
Sara Fussell as Mother Bunyan   Ted Jewett as Big Sam
William Johnstone as Johnny Inkslinger   Arthur Anderson as Shot Gunderson
Arthur Anderson as the first voice   Buddy Buehler as the second voice
Jack Grimes as the third voice   Ted de Corsia as Ole Olsen
Junior O'Day as Bill   Charita Bauer as Janet
Brad Barker supplied the animal sounds of Babe, the big blue ox.
Written for *Cavalcade* by Philo Higley and Robert Tallman.
Produced by Louis Mason and directed by Homer Fickett.
Thomas Chalmers is the announcer and Gabriel Heatter as the commercial announcer.
Music composed and conducted by Donald Voorhees.
The opening song was Victor Herbert's 1903 song "The Parade of the Wooden Soldiers."
Story: On this Christmas broadcast, *Cavalcade* tells a whimsical, imaginative story in the spirit of the season. It is the tale of a legendary character in American folk-lore - Paul Bunyan. This legend is founded on tales told in the logging camps and north woods of America. (The only American legend that is not based on Oriental or European sources.) The tale of a giant with a voice as deep as thunder and a heart as pure as gold. Lusty, powerful and humorous, the legend of Paul Bunyan has been told for generations and is a fanciful interlude in the American scene.

Gabriel Heatter: "One of our learned professors says 'Paul Bunyan is the one genuine folk figure which America has produced, of purely native and non-European origin.' As a matter of fact, so firmly is the legend of Paul Bunyan implanted in the city of Bemigji, Minnesota, conducts an annual Paul Bunyan carnival - which this winter occurs from January 19th through the 22nd. Visitors come in from distant points to attend this winter carnival, see the demonstrations of logging equipment used in Paul Bunyan's time, and join in the sports and fun."

EPISODE #146 **"JOHN HONEYMAN"** Broadcast on January 2, 1939
Script first written on December 1, 1938, and revised on December 28 and 30, 1938.
Starring: Bill Adams as George Washington
Frank Readick as John Honeyman   Karl Swenson as James
Ted de Corsia as Nathan   Abby Lewis as Betsy
Agnes Moorehead as Martha   Ted Jewett as Oliver
Kingsley Colton as the first boy   Ted Jewett as the clerk
Alfred Shirley as Rall   Jack Grimes as Tommy
Arthur Hughes as the second boy   Karl Swenson as the voice
Ted Jewett as the first Hessian   Dwight Weist as the third Hessian
Kenny Delmar as Charles   Karl Swenson as the town crier
Karl Swenson as the second Hessian   Dwight Weist as first soldier
Kenny Delmar as the second soldier   Ted de Corsia as the Corporal
Written for *Cavalcade* by Henry Fisk Carlton.
Produced by Louis Mason and directed by Homer Fickett.
Thomas Chalmers is the announcer and Gabriel Heatter is the commercial announcer.
Music composed and conducted by Donald Voorhees.
The opening song was "Sing Out the News."
Story: The story of a plain and simple New Jersey tradesman, John Honeyman, who made it possible for George Washington to plan and carry out successfully the famous

Christmas night surprise attack on the British forces at Trenton. In posing as a Tory butcher supplying food for the British forces, this unsung hero won the confidence of the enemy and obtained information which was vital to the success of the American cause. Honeyman started a chain of events that led to a decisive turning point in the struggle for American Independence.

Trivia: The closing comments by Gabriel Heatter varied from the East Coast performance and the West Coast performance in this episode. For the East Coast, Heatter reminded the radio listeners to stop and visit the Du Pont exhibit at the 1939 New York World's Fair. For the West Coast production, Heatter closed describing to the West Coast listeners about the exhibit.

EPISODE #147   "EDWARD BOK"   Broadcast on January 9, 1939
Script first written on November 23, 1938, revised Dec. 23, 1938, and January 6, 1939.
Starring: Frank Readick as the editor
Abby Lewis as Louise
Bill Pringle as the baker
Junior O'Day as William
Ted de Corsia as voice six
Dwight Weist as voice two
Ted Jewett as voice four
Kenny Delmar as the Boston reporter
Bill Pringle as the first man
Ed Jerome as the second editor
Frank Readick as Stanford White
Ted de Corsia as Theo. Roosevelt
Ted Jewett as Curtis
Frank Readick as the second man
Kingsley Colton as Edward Bok
Frank Readick as the secret service
Kenny Delmar as voice one
Frank Readick as voice five
Abby Lewis as voice three
Ted Jewett as the second reporter
Kenny Delmar as Rudyard Kipling
Abby Lewis as Dr. Coolidge
Ted Jewett as the toastmaster
Elliott Reid as Tom
Written for *Cavalcade* by Ann Barley.
Produced by Louis Mason and directed by Homer Fickett.
Thomas Chalmers as the announcer and Gabriel Heatter as the commercial announcer.
Music composed and conducted by Donald Voorhees.
Story: Edward Bok was a great humanitarian, whose cause for freedom established him in American History forever. His deeds go unnoticed, but Bok is well remembered for his lesser accomplishment - author and publisher of the "Ladies Home Journal."

EPISODE #148   "STEPHEN FOSTER"   Broadcast on January 16, 1939
Starring: Ted Jewett as Stephen Foster
Agnes Moorehead as the mother
Kenny Delmar as Richard
Ed Jerome as the editor
Elliott Reid as the reporter
Agnes Moorehead as Mrs. Pentland
Frank Readick as the interlocutor
Dwight Weist as the servant
Ted de Corsia as Cooper
Ted Jewett as Mike
Abby Lewis as Jane
Bill Pringle as Joe
Frank Readick as Roark
Ted de Corsia as the deckman
Written for *Cavalcade* by John Driscoll and Robert Tallman.
Produced by Louis Mason and directed by Homer Fickett.
Thomas Chalmers is the announcer and Basil Ruysdael is the commercial announcer.
Music composed and conducted by Donald Voorhees.
Songs featured (in the order of their appearance) were: A banjo accompaniment of the 1848 song "Oh Suzanna," "Way Down Upon the Swanee River," the 1851 song "Old Folks at Home," and "Dear Friends and Gentle Hearts."
Story: Although Stephen Collins Foster began his career as a bookkeeper, he soon was spending all his time and energy at song writing. This was his means of expression, and his whole life is told through his music. Before his death he composed the music and wrote the words of more than one hundred and twenty-five popular songs and melodies.

EPISODE #149 **"ALEXANDER GRAHAM BELL"** Broadcast on January 23, 1939
Script first written on January 6, 1939, and revised on January 18 and 20, 1939.
    Starring: Junior O'Day as Alexander   Ronald Liss as Willie
    Kinsley Colton as Henry   ___?___ Kimmel as the girl
    William Johnstone as Mr. Bell   Frank Readick as Watson
    Agnes Moorehead as Mabel   Ted Jewett as Henry
    Kenny Delmar as voice one   Frank Readick as voice two
    Ted de Corsia as voice three   Ed Jerome as voice four
    Kenny Delmar as Pres. Garfield   Dwight Weist as the committee
    Agnes Moorehead as Mrs. Maples   Bill Adams as Hubbard
    Frank Readick as man one   Ed Jerome as man two
    Ted de Corsia as man three   ___?___ Kimmel as woman one
    Irna Phillips as woman two   Elinore Donahue as woman three
    Agnes Moorehead as the female operator   Bill Adams as the male operator
Written for *Cavalcade* by John Driscoll, Homer Fickett, and Ruth Adams Knight.
Produced by Louis Mason and directed by Homer Fickett.
Thomas Chalmers is the announcer and Basil Ruysdael is the commercial announcer.
Music composed and conducted by Donald Voorhees.
The opening song was "From Now On" from Cole Porter's musical success, "Leave it to Me."
Story: From the primeval days when men called to each other from hilltops, from the time when they lighted signal flares to one another on the summits of mountains, the story of civilization springs from the exchange of ideas. Men's desire to communicate with other men has been an interpenetrating force through the centuries. The projection of the human voice through the trackless infinity of space was originally conceived in the mind of an American citizen - a man who is the subject of this drama - a man who stands among the greatest scientific geniuses of any age.

EPISODE #150 **"MARK TWAIN"** Broadcast on January 30, 1939
Script first written on December 22, 1938, and revised on January 9, 25, and 27, 1939.
    Starring: Junior O'Day as Samuel Clemens   Ted de Corsia as the man
    Agnes Moorehead as Mrs. Clemens   Bill Pringle as the captain
    Bill Adams as Sam   Elliott Reid as Henry
    Elliott Reid as Charles   Dwight Weist as Tom
    Joan Tetzel as Livy   Ed Jerome as the hotel clerk
    Ted Jewett as Curzon   Ed Jerome as the second man
    Ted Jewett as the reporter
Written for *Cavalcade* by Ann Barley.
Produced and directed by Homer Fickett.
Thomas Chalmers is the announcer and Basil Ruysdael is the commercial announcer.
Music composed and conducted by Donald Voorhees.
Story: The life of the American humorist, Samuel Clemens, or as he is better known, "Mark Twain." Early in life, Twain came in contact with the lusty amusing folk who lived along the Mississippi River. He never forgot them, and even in writing done many years later, the quaint humor of the river characters enlivened his stories. From "Huckleberry Finn" to "Innocents Abroad," Twain took the broad, rich and zestful humor of the New World and forged it into immortal literature.

On the next page: William Sanderson, a very talented artist, sketched these drawings of various broadcasts from *Cavalcade*'s early years.

JUNIPERO SERRA—THE COLONIZATION OF CALIFORNIA

FRANCIS SCOTT KEY, THE STORY OF THE STAR SPANGLED BANNER

EPISODE #151 "**NATHAN HALE**" Broadcast on February 6, 1939
Script first written on December 2, 1938, and revised on February 1 and 3, 1939.
Starring: Elliott Reid as Nathan Hale   Junior O'Day as Prentiss
Kingsley Colton as Perry   Gene O'Donnell as Alice
Ted de Corsia as Pond   Alfred Shirley as Drew
Agnes Moorehead as Mrs. Chichester   Frank Readick as Simon
Kenny Delmar as Bos'n   Ray Collins as Cunningham
Kenny Delmar as Montressor   Ted Jewett as the voice
Frank Readick as the Corporal
Written for *Cavalcade* by Henry Fisk Carlton and John Driscoll.
Produced and directed by Homer Fickett.
Thomas Chalmers is the announcer and Basil Ruysdael is the commercial announcer.
Music composed and conducted by Donald Voorhees.
Opening song was one of the loveliest melodies, "I Have Eyes."
Story: Nathan Hale and his immortal words, "I only regret that I have but one life to lose for my country," have become an American legend, but in American history he was no legendary figure. Hale was a man devoted to the mission entrusted him during the days of the American Revolution when he offered up his life to the service of our country. He was a schoolmaster who was called from his quiet path to assume the role of a spy for the American Army and to complete a mission which, while it failed, nevertheless has enshrined Nathan Hale as one of America's great patriots.

EPISODE #152 "**ALLAN PINKERTON**" Broadcast on February 13, 1939
Script first written on January 19, 1939, and revised February 8 and 10, 1939.
Starring: Kingsley Colton as Allan Pinkerton
Bill Pringle as the conductor   Ed Jerome as voice five
Bill Adams as William   Agnes Moorehead as the woman
Bill Pringle as voice four   Ted de Corsia as voice three
Ted Jewett as voice two   Frank Readick as voice one
Bill Pringle as Smith   Kenny Delmar as Craig
Ted Jewett as the man   Ed Jerome as Taylor
Frank Readick as Slocum   Agnes Moorehead as Martha
Ted de Corsia as Fernandina   Kenny Delmar as Davies
Bill Adams as the porter   William Johnstone as voice six
Donald C. Pease, winner of the fellowship plan, holds the Du Pont fellowship in Chemistry Department of Columbia University, talks with Ruysdael.
Written for *Cavalcade* by _?_ Bierstadt.
Produced by Larry Harding and directed by Homer Fickett.
Thomas Chalmers is the announcer, and Basil Ruysdael is the commercial announcer.
Music composed and conducted by Donald Voorhees.
Opening song: melody "Never Again" from the new Noel Coward revue "Set to Music."
Story: The maintenance of constitutional liberty in America has always implied the preservation of law and order among free men. In principle, the struggle for American freedom did not strictly end with Lord Cornwallis' surrender at Yorktown. Many have been the patriots who devoted their lives - and are doing so today - to enforcing the guarantee of justice to our citizens. Allan Pinkerton was one of these. He founded the Pinkerton Detective Agency and his organization played an important part in assisting President Lincoln during the days of the Civil War.

EPISODE #153 "**KIT CARSON**" Broadcast on February 20, 1939
Script first written on February 2, 1939, and revised on February 17, 1939.
Starring: Bill Adams as Kit Carson   Ted de Corsia as the porter
Ted de Corsia as Brewerton   Elliott Reid as Mason
Kenny Delmar as the trapper   Kenny Delmar as the first man

Ted Jewett as Reward   Ted Jewett as Jones
Frank Readick as Kit   Bill Pringle as the third man
Ted Jewett as the second man   William Johnstone as Bill
Tom Collins as Young   Agnes Moorehead as Josefa
Written for *Cavalcade* by Philo Higley and Emily Neff.
Produced by Larry Harding and directed by Homer Fickett.
Thomas Chalmers is the announcer and Basil Ruysdael is the commercial spokesman.
Music composed and conducted by Donald Voorhees.
Story: Kit Carson was a man whose whole life was devoted to opening trails between the East and the Western frontier of our country which led to the development of California and other great states west of the Mississippi. The explorations of this man helped commerce and civilization to grow as our country expanded westward. Like many other pioneers in the middle of the nineteenth century, Carson was born with a wanderlust and a yearning to explore the vast regions stretching to the shores of the Pacific. To this end he left home, and spent the rest of his life, often in association with some of the greatest explorers of the day, blazing new trails throughout our western territory.

Trivia: This week the San Francisco 1939 World's Fair opened in California and as a salute to that state, *Cavalcade* presented a drama based on a man who spent his life opening trails to the west.

EPISODE #154   **"GEORGE GERSHWIN"**   Broadcast on February 27, 1939
Script first written on February 1, 1939, revised February 21 and 24, 1939.
Starring: Kenny Delmar as George Gershwin   Ed Jerome as Greek
Kingsley Colton as George   Bill Pringle as Remick
Agnes Moorehead as the receptionist   Ed Jerome as Perkins
Agnes Moorehead as Mrs. Gershwin   Ted de Corsia as Father
Tom Collins as Heyward   Tom Collins as Dreyfus
Ted Jewett as Damrosch   Ted Jewett as the stage manager
Frank Readick as Paul Whiteman
Written for *Cavalcade* by John Driscoll and Robert Tallman.
Produced by Larry Harding and directed by Homer Fickett.
Thomas Chalmers is the announcer and Basil Ruysdael is the commercial spokesman.
Music composed and conducted by Donald Voorhees.
Songs featured within the broadcast: "Swanee," the 1924 song "Rhapsody in Blue," the 1932 song "Wintergreen for President," and segues from "Porgy and Bess."
Story: Born and brought up in Manhattan's lower East Side, Gershwin felt the pulsing heart-beat of humanity which he came to reflect so admirably in his music. He composed music and America sang it, whistled it, and loved it. To him American music was more than popular songs of the day. He fashioned it into symphonic masterpieces like the "Rhapsody in Blue," and into operatic triumphs like "Porgy and Bess." For his contributions to the musical literature of our nation the name of George Gershwin belongs to the ages.

EPISODE #155   **"THE TEXAS RANGERS"**   Broadcast on March 6, 1939
Script first written on February 15, 1939.
Starring: Agnes Moorehead as Lottie   Frank Readick as Tom Dawson
Ted de Corsia as the first ranger   Bill Pringle as Jim Allen
Bill Adams as Milton   Tom Collins as the barber
Kenny Delmar as McNelly   Gene O'Donnell as Mrs. Morrison
Ted Jewett as the scout   Ted Jewett as the second cowboy
Ted Jewett as the third ranger   Tom Collins as the second ranger
Kenny Delmar as first ranger
Written for *Cavalcade* by John Driscoll and Mann Page.

Produced by Larry Harding and directed by Homer Fickett.
Thomas Chalmers is the announcer and Basil Ruysdael is the commercial announcer.
Music composed and conducted by Donald Voorhees.
The opening song was the "Rangers' Song" from "Rio Rita."
Story: One of the most adventurous and romantic traditions of the Southwest is the organization of law and order in the Lone Star State - the Texas Rangers. This is the story of Tom Dawson, one man who symbolizes all Texas Rangers. The story is developed in the days when our Southwestern frontier was being threatened by lawlessness and terror. The Texas Rangers, like the Canadian Northwest Mounted Police, formed a vital chapter in the development of our Southwest along the lines of order, peace and prosperity.

EPISODE #156   "MARIE DRESSLER"   Broadcast on March 13, 1939
    Starring: Agnes Moorehead as Katisha   Alfred Shirley as Mikado
    Agnes Moorehead as Marie Dressler   Ted Jewett as Sennett
    Frank Readick as voice three   Bill Adams as Jim
    Ted de Corsia as the fifth voice   Ted Jewett as voice six
    Bill Adams as voice four   Sarah Fussell as Nella
    Joan Tetzel as Frances   Ed Jerome as the office manager
    Sarah Fussell as Mabel Normand   Tom Collins as Pratt
    Abby Lewis as the first voice   Abby Lewis as Alice
    Ed Jerome as Berry   Ed Jerome as Pooh-Bah
    Frank Readick as Koko
Written for *Cavalcade* by Ann Barley and John Driscoll.
Produced by Larry Harding and directed by Homer Fickett.
Thomas Chalmers is the announcer and Basil Ruysdael is the commercial announcer.
Music composed and conducted by Donald Voorhees.
The opening song was "This Is It" from Arthur Schwartz's musical "Stars In Your Eyes."
Story: Born without beauty or obvious talent but with a fierce determination to succeed in her adopted profession, Marie Dressler struggled long and desperately and finally succeeded. She became a star on Broadway in "Tilly's Punctured Romance." But after a time she was reduced to poverty and oblivion. A world that forgot Marie Dressler rose in universal acclaim when, well past middle age, she again, through a talent and genius that she had developed for characterization, made a sensational comeback in the motion picture "Anna Christie." The name of Marie Dressler rightly belongs to the great tradition of the American theatre.

EPISODE #157   "THE AMERICAN CLIPPER"   Broadcast on March 20, 1939
    Script first written on February 20, 1939, and revised on March 15 and 17, 1939.
    Starring: Agnes Moorehead as Mrs. Blake   Elliott Reid as the boy
    Frank Readick as Bos'n   Ted de Corsia as the man
    Tom Collins as the ship's mate   William Johnstone as Jo
    Bill Pringle as Mr. Blake
Written for *Cavalcade* by John Driscoll and Philo Higley.
Produced by Larry Harding and directed by Homer Fickett.
Thomas Chalmers is the announcer and Basil Ruysdael is the commercial announcer.
Music composed and conducted by Donald Voorhees.
The opening song was the 1934 musical hit "Deep Purple."
Story: The speed of airplanes and the speed of ocean liners; the speed of express trains and the speed of automobiles; the speed of the telegraph, the telephone, the radio - all the flashing, dynamic force in modern communication and transportation is part of the American heritage of foresight and enterprise. And one of the greatest manifestations of this heritage occurred about the middle of the last century when, captained by young

men, the American Clipper Ships, carried the American flag, American commerce and ideas to every port in the seven seas.

Basil Ruysdael: "The letters we have received from listeners since we began the *Cavalcade* in October 1935, have been a constant source of inspiration, have helped much to encourage us to go on with these series from year to year. In the early days of the *Cavalcade* we wondered if we could successfully carry on this rather unique idea - a program high in information content, and so entertaining as to command the attention of a fair share of the great radio audience. However, the sincerity the enthusiasm of the letters that came to us from people in all walks of life, quickly dispelled our fears. Some wrote to compliment - some to make suggestions. All of these letters have been constructive. We deeply appreciate them - and we have tried to make personal acknowledgment of every letter that has come to us."

EPISODE #158 **"THE LEAGUE OF THE LONG HOUSE"** Broadcast on March 27, 1939
Script first written on March 13, 1939, and revised on March 22 and 24, 1939.
Starring: Ted Jewett as Mani   Bill Pringle as Sachem
Ted de Corsia as Hendrick   Kenny Delmar as Jean
Ted de Corsia as Algonquin   Ed Jerome as Champigny
Ted de Corsia as the first Frenchman   Frank Readick as the second Frenchman
Frank Readick as Williams   Alfred Shirley as Johnson
Agnes Moorehead as the woman   Tom Collins as the voice
Tom Collins as Demonville   Ed Jerome as Logan
Kenny Delmar as the second man   Kenny Delmar as Champlain
Frank Readick as Grant   Ted Jewett as Dunmore
Tom Collins as Butler   Bill Adams as Glen
Written for *Cavalcade* by _?_ Bierstadt and John Driscoll.
Produced by Larry Harding and directed by Homer Fickett.
Thomas Chalmers is the announcer and Basil Ruysdael is the commercial announcer.
Music composed and conducted by Donald Voorhees, opening song is "Pale Moon."
Story: The story of the rise and fall of an Indian confederacy in North America which was democratic in principle antedating the patriotic movement in the colonies which led to our Declaration of Independence and the founding of American Democracy.

Trivia: On this evening's broadcast, Logan's speech was given by special permission of Samuel Goldwyn, owner of the film rights to Robert W. Chambers' novel, "Cardigan."

EPISODE #159 **"THE PIONEER MOTHER: ELIZA ANN BROOKS"** April 3, 1939
Script first written on March 11, 1939 and revised on March 31 and April 2, 1939.
Starring: Agnes Moorehead as Eliza Ann Brooks   Kenny Delmar as Snow
Ted de Corsia as Mr. Brooks   Joan Tetzel as Vienna
_?_ Keller as Mrs. Tanner   Junior O'Day as Elisha
Abby Lewis as Mrs. Dennison   Abby Lewis as Mrs. Christian
Kingsley Colton as Orion   Tom Collins as Will Grange
Karl Swenson as Eliza Ann Brooks (age 80)   Ted Jewett as man two
Ted Jewett as the second Indian   Ed Jerome as the Indian chief
Ted de Corsia as man one   Ted de Corsia as the Indian
Sarah Fussell as Elmont   Tammy Grimes as Justus
Written for *Cavalcade* by Ann Barley.
Produced by Larry Harding and directed by Homer Fickett.
Thomas Chalmers is the announcer and Basil Ruysdael is the commercial announcer.
Music composed and conducted by Donald Voorhees.
The opening song was the 1934 song "Wagon Wheels."

Story: The characteristic American traits of family devotion and determination to succeed against odds and portrays them in the true story of a pioneer mother - Eliza Ann Brooks. Eliza was an inspiring woman who lived in an inspiring era - the era when America was developing westward beyond the Mississippi. She had an ideal and a motto which formed the basis of her story - and which was the keynote of her life. "Where there is no vision, the people perish." The true story of this pioneer mother in a loner prairie schooner with her family of six children, who crossed the American frontier to California alone.

EPISODE #160 **"JOHN HOWARD PAYNE"** Broadcast on April 10, 1939
Script first written on March 30, 1939, and revised on April 7, 1939.
Starring: William Johnstone as Colman   Agnes Moorehead as Miss Tree
Abby Lewis as Mary   William Johnstone as Irving
Kenny Delmar as the Captain   Ted de Corsia as the trooper
Frank Readick as Gale   Ed Jerome as Price
Ted Jewett as John Payne, Sr.   Elliott Reid as John Payne
Bill Pringle as the seaman   Elliott Reid as Ahmed
Ed Jerome as Ross
Written for *Cavalcade* by John Driscoll and Philo Higley.
Produced by Larry Harding and directed by Homer Fickett.
Thomas Chalmers is the announcer and Basil Ruysdael is the commercial announcer.
Music composed and conducted by Donald Voorhees.
The opening song was the latest 1939 musical hit "Heaven Can Wait." During the drama, the 1823 song "Home, Sweet, Home" was performed.
Story: The life of the American composer following his career as a child prodigy on the New York stage. His triumphs and failures in London and Paris and his wandering exile abroad inspired him to the nostalgic sentiment he wove into his song of the American song, "Home, Sweet, Home."

EPISODE #161 **"PATRICK HENRY"** Broadcast on April 17, 1939
Script first written March 16, 1939, revised March 27, April 5, 6, 10, 14, and 15, 1939.
Starring: Ted Jewett as Davies   Agnes Moorehead as the mother
Kingsley Colton as Patrick Henry   Ed Jerome as Colonel
Kenny Delmar as voice six   Dwight Weist as judge Tyler
Ted Jewett as voice four   Tom Collins as voice five
Ted de Corsia as voice three   Dwight Weist as voice two
Bill Pringle as voice one   Tom Collins as Randolph
Abby Lewis as Sarah
Dr. James Truslow Adams, historical advisor, gives a small speech during broadcast.
Written for *Cavalcade* by John Driscoll, Garrett Porter, and Katherine Seymour.
Produced by Larry Harding and directed by Homer Fickett.
Thomas Chalmers is the announcer and Basil Ruysdael is the commercial announcer.
Music composed and conducted by Donald Voorhees.
The opening song was "Our Love" based on Tchaikovski's "Romeo and Juliet."
Story: Events in the life of the great American patriot climaxed by his utterance in the Virginia House of Burgesses of the clarion keynote of American freedom "Give me Liberty or give me death."

EPISODE #162 **"BASEBALL"** Broadcast on April 24, 1939
Script first written March 11, 1939, revised March 22, 28, and April 5, 11, and 21, 1939.
Starring: Elliott Reid as Doubleday   Kenny Delmar as the first southerner
Dwight Weist as the second southerner   Tom Collins as Yankee one
Ed Jerome as Yankee two   Tom Collins as McGraw
Frank Readick as Christy   Bill Adams as Hulbert

Ed Jerome as man one
Frank Readick as voice three
Ted de Corsia as voice five
Bill Pringle as voice one
Abby Lewis as Sarah
Kenny Delmar as voice seven
Dwight Weist as voice eight
Elliott Reid as voice nine
Ted de Corsia as man two
Kingsley Colton as George
Frank Readick as the sportswriter
Bill Pringle as De Wolf Hopper

Frank Readick as Prex
Ted Jewett as voice four
Dwight Weist as voice two
Tom Collins as voice six
Tom Collins as Randolph
Kenny Delmar as the Priest
Tom Collins as the ball player
Elliott Reid as Mike
Ted Jewett as Smith
Ted de Corsia as Babe Ruth
Ted Jewett as Walsh

Written for *Cavalcade* by John Driscoll and Peter Lyon.
Produced by Larry Harding and directed by Homer Fickett.
Thomas Chalmers is the announcer and Basil Ruysdael is the commercial announcer.
Music composed and conducted by Donald Voorhees.
The opening song was the 1908 song "Take Me Out to the Ball Game."
Story: In a glass-enclosed case of the British Museum is an ordinary object, small and round. Thirty centuries ago an Egyptian youth squeezed some papyrus and grass into a hard mass, wrapped two strips of leather around it and sewed the whole together to make the first ball. And down in the mud flats of the sluggish Nile River the Egyptian boy unwittingly laid the foundation for an American game which would bring enjoyment and the ideals of sportsmanship to generations of men, women and children - a game whose anniversary was celebrated this spring - the one hundredth birthday of our national game - baseball.

EPISODE #163   **"WASHINGTON AND THE CROWN"**   Broadcast on May 1, 1939
Script first written April 10, 1939, and revised on April 19 and 28, 1939.

Starring: Bill Adams as George Washington
Kenny Delmar as Wayne
Ted de Corsia as Hamilton
Ted Jewett as voice two
Ted Jewett as Humphreys
Dwight Weist as the officer
Kenny Delmar as Livingstone
Agnes Moorehead as Patsy

Ted de Corsia as second Sentry
Ted de Corsia as the Sergeant
Dwight Weist as voice one
Kenny Delmar as officer two
Frank Readick as the Sentry
Ed Jerome as the Lieutenant
Bill Pringle as Gates
Tom Collins as Nicola

Written for *Cavalcade* by John Driscoll and Garrett Porter.
Produced by Larry Harding and directed by Homer Fickett.
Thomas Chalmers is the announcer and Basil Ruysdael is the commercial announcer.
Music composed and conducted by Donald Voorhees.
The opening song was Victor Herbert's tribute to America called "American Fantasy."
Story: How George Washington refused to become King George of America by defeating a plot among his officers which would have altered the course of American democracy.

Trivia: In conjunction with the hundred and fiftieth anniversary of the inauguration of George Washington as our first President, and as a salute to the opening of the New York World's Fair, *Cavalcade* presented a little-known drama about George Washington. This same script was later dramatized again, as the premiere episode of another radio series entitled *Inheritance*, under the title "George Washington Refuses the Crown."

EPISODE #164 "JULIETTE LOW" Broadcast on May 8, 1939
Script first written on April 6, 1939, and revised on April 18, 21, and May 5, 1939.
Starring: Charita Bauer as Terry   Joan Tetzel as Joan
Joan Tetzel as Clarissa   Joan Tetzel as Carmen
Charita Bauer as the French girl   Frances Carden as Martha
Sandra Gould as the older woman   Patricia Peardon as Marty
Charita Bauer as Juliette Low   Patricia Peardon as Ellen
Frances Heflin as Meg   Frances Heflin as Page
Frances Heflin as Kathleen   Frances Carden as Frances
Frances Carden as the Swedish girl   Patricia Peardon as English girl
Abby Lewis as Daisy   Frank Readick as Dr. Russell
Alfred Shirley as Baden-Powell
Written for *Cavalcade* by Ann Barley and John Driscoll.
Produced by Ann Harding and directed by Homer Fickett.
Thomas Chalmers is the announcer and Basil Ruysdael is the commercial announcer.
Music composed and conducted by Donald Voorhees.
The opening song is the 1939 popular rhythmic melody: "And the Angels Sing"
Story: Over a tired world today thoughtful men and women who have tried and failed are looking to youth to save the future. In some lands, short-sighted leaders are regimenting youth - exploiting them with deliberate and selfish purpose - heedless that history inevitably repeats itself. It was in America that one of the most selfless and idealistic youth movements the world has ever known was founded. This is the story of Juliette Low who envisioned and organized the Girl Scouts of America.

EPISODE #165 "MR. JUSTICE HOLMES" Broadcast on May 15, 1939
Script first written on April 27, 1939, and revised on May 10 and 12, 1939.
Starring: Bill Adams as Oliver Wendell Holmes   Ted de Corsia as Thomas
Frank Readick as the clerk   Dwight Weist as the lieutenant
Charles Webster as Abraham Lincoln   Ed Jerome as Wright
Alfred Shirley as Maitland   Kenny Delmar as voice one
Kenny Delmar as Pollock   Ted Jewett as voice two
Ted Jewett as Theodore Roosevelt   Ray Collins as Emerson
Agnes Moorehead as Fanny   Dwight Weist as Oliver Holmes, Sr.
Written for *Cavalcade* by John Driscoll and Robert Tallman.
Produced by Larry Harding and directed by Homer Fickett.
Thomas Chalmers is the announcer and Basil Ruysdael is the commercial announcer.
Music composed and conducted by Donald Voorhees.
The opening song was one of the loveliest of Jerome Kern's 1933 melodies, "The Touch of Your Hand." Featured during the drama was the 1861 song "John Brown's Body."
Story: There were two great Americans who bore the name, Oliver Wendell Holmes. One was the famous New England poet - the physician called by men of his generation "The autocrat of the breakfast table." His son was perhaps even greater. And the story of the second Oliver Wendell Holmes is not so much the record of a man's life as the development of a man's mind. And it is this story of one of America's paramount legal philosophers and scholars that is told. The life and thought of America's great scholar and philosopher, Mr. Justice Holmes of the United States Supreme Court, showing how his Back Bay Boston and literary youth, his days in the Civil War and his brilliant career in the law developed his mind and character so that in the zenith of his maturity Oliver Wendell Holmes became the greatest single force in the liberal development of American jurisprudence.

EPISODE #166 "DOLLY MADISON"   Broadcast on May 22, 1939
Script first written on April 10, 1939, and revised on May 17 and 19, 1939.
Starring: Agnes Moorehead as Dolly Madison   Arlene Francis as Martha
Bill Adams as George Washington   Frank Readick as Carroll
Ray Collins as James Madison   Ed Jerome as Meade
Kenny Delmar as Depeyster   Ted de Corsia as the negro
Bill Adams as Tom   Abby Lewis as the Dutch woman
Written for *Cavalcade* by Ann Barley and John Driscoll.
Produced by Larry Harding and directed by Homer Fickett.
Thomas Chalmers is the announcer and Basil Ruysdael is the commercial announcer.
Music composed and conducted by Donald Voorhees.
The opening song was the current popular melody "A New Moon - An Old Serenade."
Story: Dolly Todd lost her husband as well as her only son in an epidemic of fever plague that swept Philadelphia in 1793. After a few years she married one of America's brilliant statesmen, James Madison, destined to become President of the United States. It was as his wife, Dolly Madison by her charm and incisive mind aided our nation during the critical days of the War of 1812. The famous story of how she saved Washington's portrait from the British who were about to burn the White House is dramatized. For many years afterwards she represented the spontaneity, the fashion and the authority of an era of youthful exuberant America.

Trivia: In order to those who were particularly interested in the wonders of chemistry, Du Pont included eight pages of pictures and stories about the Wonder World of Chemistry in the June issue of The Du Pont Magazine. During this week, the issues were on the press, and ready for mailing about June tenth. Any listener interested in the article was able to drop Du Pont a note or letter and the Du Pont company would acknowledge it by sending them a free copy of the June issue of The Du Pont Magazine. This was also Du Pont's way of checking out the *Cavalcade* response for the show was about to leave the air the week after.

EPISODE #167 "ELUTHERE IRENEE DU PONT"   Broadcast on May 29, 1939
Starring: Elliott Reid as E.I. Du Pont   Kenny Delmar as Victor
Abby Lewis as Sophie   Ted Jewett as Toussard
Kenny Delmar as the workman   Kenny Delmar as Victor
Ray Collins as Lafayette   Bill Adams as Thomas Jefferson
Ted de Corsia as the guardsman   Alfred Shirley as Lavoisier
Ed Jerome as Du Pont
Written for *Cavalcade* by Mann Page.
Produced by Larry Harding and directed by Homer Fickett.
Thomas Chalmers is the announcer and Basil Ruysdael is the commercial announcer.
Music composed and conducted by Donald Voorhees.
The opening song was the 1934 song "I'll Follow My Secret Heart."
Story: While hunting one day with his friend, Colonel Toussard, a young French émigré named E.I. du Pont missed a shot because his American-made powder failed to fire. Thus he became convinced of America's need for a gunpowder manufacturing plant of its own. Black powder was essential to the pioneers, who depended upon it to obtain food and to protect themselves. Du Pont had learned how to make powder from the celebrated chemist, Lavoisier, who at one time had charge of the French Government's plant at Essone. Encouraged by his friend, Thomas Jefferson, E.I. du Pont built a powder mill in 1802 on the banks of the historic Brandywine Creek near the city of Wilmington, Delaware.

A message from the Du Pont Company: Tonight's broadcast, 167th appearance on the *Cavalcade of America* on the air, brings our present series to a close. This past year, as in other years, many listeners have taken the trouble to write us telling of their interest in the *Cavalcade* broadcasts. To those people, all of whom have been sent personal replies, Du Pont again expresses appreciation for their thoughtfulness and inspiration. It has been a privilege to contribute to the enjoyment of radio listeners throughout the nation, and to bring to American homes these true stories of American fortitude and idealism. As the curtain rings down, we also make grateful acknowledgment to all the people who have helped make the *Cavalcade of America* a success - the actors, the authors, the musicians, and the radio technicians. Each of them, and each individual in our radio audience, is playing a part in the American cavalcade that will never end.

Trivia: Many letters had complimented the music of Don Voorhees and his orchestra, some music lovers had suggested that Du Pont give the orchestra more of an opportunity to play. Those listeners were happy to know that starting Sunday, June 11th, Don Voorhees began a series of complete musical program on the Ford hour.

Replaced in this time slot was *Tune-Up Time*, featuring Walter O'Keefe, Andre Kostelanetz and his Orchestra, and Kay Thompson and her Rhythm Singers.

EPISODE #168 **"AMERIGO VESPUCCI"** Broadcast on January 2, 1940
Script first written Dec. 8, 1939, revised Dec. 14, 18, 20, 27, 28, and 29, 1939.
Starring: Burgess Meredith as Amerigo Vespucci   Ed Jerome as the priest
Jackie Kelk as Piero, the boy   John McIntire as Paul
Kenneth Delmar as the messenger   Ted de Corsia as the man
Paul Stewart as the second man   Paul Stewart as the sailor
Elliott Reid as Giovanni   Bill Adams as Waldseemuller
Stephen Schnabel as Columbus   Ian McCallister as Cardinal
Karl Swenson as Lorenzo   Ed Jerome as the Friar
Kingsley Colton as Amerigo (as a boy)   Alfred Shirley as Ringmann
Written for *Cavalcade* by John Driscoll and _?_ Milward.
Produced by Homer Fickett and directed by Bill Sweet.
Ted Jewett was the narrator and commercial announcer.
Music composed and conducted by Donald Voorhees.
Story: Drama of a great Italian dreamer, friend of the di Medicis, intimate of Paul the Philosopher who first conceived the idea that there were lands beyond the Western Sea of Darkness, business associate of Christopher Columbus - the map scholar for whom this continent was named, Amerigo, Americus, America.

Trivia: When *Cavalcade* returned to the airwaves in January of 1940, the historical program was then being broadcast over NBC by specially selected hook-ups from ninety-four stations coast-to-coast. The presentations first intended to be dramatized was not, however, broadcast as originally planned. Although the January 2 broadcast featured Amerigo Vespucci and how the New World was named, the broadcasts afterwards went out of sinc.

For the broadcast of January 9, the story of Squanto, strange friend of the Pilgrims was originally broadcast. As you can see below, it did not. The story of Father Jogues, "The Man in the Black Robe," was originally scheduled for January 16. As for other schedule changes, check the trivia under the next months' entries.

**On the next page: newspaper advertisement for a *Cavalcade* broadcast (top).
A small card that appeared in numerous magazines and newspapers (bottom).**

CAVALCADE
OF AMERICA
back on the air!

It's bigger, faster moving, and even better than ever—this 4th consecutive year of the *Cavalcade of America*. Into millions of homes—Du Pont again brings vivid, colorful, and little-known stories of real Americans—to make people thrill with pride for the American cavalcade.

EVERY MONDAY NIGHT
COLUMBIA NETWORK

8 PM Eastern Time   10 PM Mt. Time
7 PM Central Time   9 PM Pacific Time

Going to Visit New York?
HOW YOU CAN SEE A CAVALCADE BROADCAST

A limited number of tickets are available for the actual performance of Cavalcade of America radio shows. These can be obtained by application to: Radio Section, Du Pont, Wilmington, Delaware. Since the demand is great, it is well to make your request some weeks in advance, and to allow a choice of alternative dates if possible. The program is broadcast in New York on Tuesday evenings at 9 p.m.

EPISODE #169 "SAM HOUSTON, THE RAVEN" Broadcast on January 9, 1940

Starring: Walter Huston as Sam Houston
Kenny Delmar as Allen
Elliott Reid as the son
Ed Jerome as the first Allen
Ian MacAllaster as Green
Elliott Reid as Caesar
Kenny Delmar as the Speaker
Ted Jewett as Johnson
Paul Stewart as the second Allen
Ted Jewett as Mr. T.
Jeanette Nolan as Eliza
Agnes Moorehead as Mother
Ed Jerome as Overton
Bill Adams as William
Alfred Shirley as the Chief
Ted de Corsia as Stanbery
Ted de Corsia as Haralson
Helen Lewis as Sarah
John McIntire as Jackson
Stefan Schnabel as the Pastor
Paul Stewart as Lewis

Based on the 1929 book "The Raven: A Biography of Sam Houston" by Marquis James, and adapted for *Cavalcade* by John Driscoll and _?_ Milward.
Produced by Homer Fickett and directed by Bill Sweet.
Thomas Chalmers is the announcer and Basil Ruysdael is the commercial announcer.
Music composed and conducted by Donald Voorhees.
Story: The somber, dramatic figure of Sam Houston - named "The Raven" by his adopted Cherokee Nation - stalks across the plains and fields of America. As Governor of Tennessee, intimate of President Andrew Jackson, Houston's tragic destiny led him first to renounce his citizenship in the United States and join the Cherokee Indians, then to political ruin in the nation's capitol at the hands of his enemies, and finally to the brink of his greatest adventure - the welding of the United States with the great empire of Texas.

Trivia: Tonight's program was taken from the Pulitzer Prize biography of Houston by Marquis James, a member of Cavalcade's historical board.

EPISODE #170 "MEHITABEL WING" Broadcast on January 16, 1940

Starring: Jeanette Nolan as Mehitabel Wing
Ted de Corsia as the forth man
Elliott Reid as the soldier
Dan MacLaughlin as the foreman
Dan MacLaughlin as the Aide
Bill Adams as the third man
Ted de Corsia as the first man
Stephen Schnabel as Philipse
Ian MacAllister as the prosecutor
John McIntire as William
John McIntire as William
Bill Pringle as the fifth man
Elliott Reid as the sixth man
Kenny Delmar as the Bailiff
Ed Jerome as the governor
Ed Jerome as the second man
Kenny Delmar as Livingston
Alfred Shirley as Horsmanden
Ted Jewett as the Sgt.-At-Arms

Based on the Carl Carmer story "Without Indecorum," and adapted for *Cavalcade* by John Driscoll and _?_ Milward.
Produced by Homer Fickett and directed by Bill Sweet.
Thomas Chalmers is the announcer and Basil Ruysdael is the commercial announcer.
Music composed and conducted by Donald Voorhees.
Story: Mehitabel Wing, a Quaker girl from the Hudson Valley, whose love for her farmer husband during an immature, but significant crisis before the Revolutionary War, has been a neglected anecdote in America's progress toward individual liberties. The colonies and the young nation had escaped most of the sharp class conflicts and violent resolutions that had shaken Europe, because America had but a few of the burdens that came from feudal institutions. The story dramatized is about one of these - the land-owning families whose feudal fiefs, tenanted by men who were virtually serfs, spread over much of the fertile Hudson River Valley.

Carl Carmer: "I consider this a most significant broadcast. My book entitled 'The Hudson' from which Mehitabel's story is taken, is a tribute to the millions of unknown, ordinary Americans whom history has neglected, and whose lives are the materials for that great history of the common people which has never been written."

Trivia: This episode, the biography of Mehitabel Wing, who embarked a ride earlier and more dramatic than Paul Revere's, was originally scheduled for January 23, but instead, was broadcast a week earlier.

EPISODE #171 **"TISQUANTUM, STRANGE FRIEND OF THE PILGRIMS"**
Broadcast on January 23, 1940
Starring: Sam Jaffe as Squanto
Based on research supplied by Dr. Frank Monaghan, and adapted for *Cavalcade* by John Driscoll and Garrett Porter.
Produced by Homer Fickett and directed by Bill Sweet.
Thomas Chalmers is the announcer and Basil Ruysdael is the commercial announcer.
Music composed and conducted by Donald Voorhees.
Story: The story of an Indian, captured and sold into Spanish slavery by English traders. Escaping from Spain, Tisquantum went to London, lived there, learned the language and finally shipped back to New England where he found his village in ruins, his people lost. He went to live with another tribe whose chief was Massasoit. He and Massasoit welcomed the Pilgrims, concluded a peace treaty and through Tisquantum's aid, the Pilgrims were able to endure their first years in the New World, for if it had not been for Tisquantum, who taught them to hunt, fish and plant corn, this early important colonial venture might well have failed.

Trivia: This broadcast was originally scheduled for January 9, under the title "Squanto." Instead, the drama about the famed Indian who befriended the Pilgrims, was pushed ahead a few weeks due to what the researchers felt "lacked historical accuracy." Later, the script was retitled "The Pilgrims' Strange Friend," and finally to the title listed above.

EPISODE #172 **"THOMAS JEFFERSON"** Broadcast on January 30, 1940
Starring: John Beal as Tom Jefferson   Agnes Moorehead as Martha
Bill Adams as Lee   Jeanette Nolan as Frau Graaf
Alfred Shirley as the man   Bill Pringle as Hancock
Kenny Delmar as the first member   Elliott Reid as the second member
Ted de Corsia as the third member   Ted Jewett as the voice
Alfred Shirley as the fourth member   Ted Jewett as the fifth member
Gretchen Davidson as the salesman   Elliott Reid as Smith
Ted de Corsia as Jones   Kenny Delmar as Sherman
Ed Jerome as Livingston   Ian MacAllister as Adams
John MacIntire as Franklin
Based on a story by Marquis James, and adapted for *Cavalcade* by John Driscoll and _?_ Milward.
Produced by Homer Fickett and directed by Bill Sweet.
Thomas Chalmers is the announcer and Basil Ruysdael is the commercial announcer.
Featuring as the Juano Hernandez chorus, including such songs as "Death is a Robber," the 1863 song "Weepin' " and "Our Time is Comin'."
Music composed and conducted by Donald Voorhees.
Story: "I am the most unimportant member of the Continental Congress," says Thomas Jefferson. "All I do is write memorandums for committees." Jefferson really believed what he said, yet from his pen came the Declaration of Independence, the world's classic statement of Democracy. The tall, red-headed young Virginian, a very human individual

who played the violin to help himself concentrate and who moved to the outskirts of 1776 Philadelphia because the city was too noisy for him to think, set forth in the Declaration's great preamble the basic rights of all men everywhere.

Trivia: The title of this broadcast was originally "Thomas Jefferson Goes Shopping," later changed to "The Declaration of Independence." When it was pointed out that *Cavalcade* had already presented an episode with that title, it was changed again, this time "Thomas Jefferson" by broadcast.

More trivia: This script went under twelve revisions! The fifth was dated December 8, 1939, sixth December 20, 1939, seventh January 2, 1940, followed by January 15, 23, 25, 27, and finally January 29, 1940!

EPISODE #173   **"JEAN LAFFITE"**   Broadcast on February 6, 1940
Starring: William Johnstone as Jean Laffite
Karl Swenson as the second merchant
Ted de Corsia as Gambio
Charita Bauer as Catherine
Frank Readick as General Coffee
John McIntire as General Andrew Jackson
Braham as Captain MacWilliams
Alfred Shirley as Captain Lockyer
Bill Adams as Grymes
Ted Jewett as the first merchant
Kingsley Colton as the boy
Ed Jerome as the priest
Jeanette Nolan as Marie Louise
Karl Swenson as Pierre Laffite
Ed Jerome as Gov. Claiborne
Alfred Shirley as MacWilliams
Bill Adams as Livingston

Based on an outline by Marquis James, and adapted for *Cavalcade* by John Driscoll, _?_ Jackson, Garrett Porter, and Kenneth Webb.
Produced by Homer Fickett and directed by Bill Sweet.
Thomas Chalmers is the announcer and Basil Ruysdael is the commercial announcer.
Music composed and conducted by Donald Voorhees.
Story: Jean Laffite was the last of the great American freebooters and pirates, a group traditionally present in all frontier society and one which disappeared in American history only with the vanishing of the frontier. Laffite's decisive part in the War of 1812 at a time when the nation was in sore straits. It is a romantic story, dealing with the greatest British force ever sent by the mother country against her errant colonies; a ragged army of frontiersmen led by an Indian fighter named Andrew Jackson, and - the fateful weight that turned the balance in America's favor - Jean Laffite's picturesque band of faithful followers from the Louisiana swamps, an army of smugglers and jailbirds that successfully defended the entrance to the Mississippi Valley. Through the drama swaggers the arrogant figure of Laffite, a daring, suave pirate with a price on his head, whose patriotism led him to the defense of his country on the side of law and order.

Trivia: This episode was based on an outline written exclusively by Marquis James. James wrote his outline based on the knowledge from three previously written books, "Andrew Jackson: The Captain," "Andrew Jackson: Portrait of a President" and "The Life of Andrew Jackson," (c.1937) authored by James.

EPISODE #174   **"ABRAHAM LINCOLN: THE WAR YEARS"**   Broadcast February 13, 1940
Script first written on February 4, 1940, revised on February 8 and 9, 1940.
Starring: Raymond Massey as Abraham Lincoln
Based on the 1939 four-volume biography of the same name by Carl Sandburg, and adapted for *Cavalcade* by Robert E. Sherwood.
Produced and directed by Homer Fickett.
Music composed and conducted by Donald Voorhees.
Story: "I claim not to have controlled events, but confess plainly that events have controlled me." So spoke Abe Lincoln. Born near present-day Hodgenville, Kentucky,

the man destined to become our sixteenth President overcame trials and tribulations to keep the country whole. As a young lawyer defending a small boy from a murder charge, as a husband to Mary Todd, who stood his ground when the country went to turmoil and bloodshed, and the writing of the Gettysburg Address. Abe Lincoln was truly one of the great men of are time. And these are the incidents in the young life of Abe Lincoln, before he became President and helped end slavery in the U.S.

Trivia: This week, over 92 NBC-Blue radio stations broadcasted *Cavalcade* in what was probably its most ambitious radio venture to date. The radio version of Carl Sandburg's four-volume biography, was an episode well-linked to Lincoln's cycle from Springfield in a stovepipe hat in 1861 and back to Springfield in a cortege in 1965. The Gettysburg Address was mostly drowned out by staged crowd noises and by the palaver of two men in particular - one eating an apple.

Trivia: For the 8 p.m. broadcast (CST), actor Massey gave the invited broadcast audience of 2,500 a special treat. He not only acted the part of Lincoln, but he also dressed the part - down to his stage nose and wart, a half-four operation. Dressed in black tie, Massey gave the best Lincoln the radio had heard but took no curtain call. Instead, he darted out the stage door, piled into a police car (car number 115 of the Chicago Police for those purists of heart out there), and was sped five blocks from the Grand Chicago Civic Opera House, to the curtain-rising of the stage production *Abe Lincoln in Illinois*.

More trivia: Donald Voorhees did not use his regular orchestra members for this broadcast. Four days after last week's on-air performance, Voorhees arrived in Chicago to rehearse with Chicago musicians for this *Cavalcade* broadcast. He took with him a Scottish Terrier, one of his pets, along for the trip. Voorhees later was the judge at the Scottish Terrier Class at the Wilmington Dog Show on October 12, 1940.

EPISODE #175   **"ANNE ROYALL"**   Broadcast on February 20, 1940
Starring: Ethel Barrymore as Anne Newport Royall
Based on exclusive material gathered by author Bessie Rowland James from her new biography, and adapted for *Cavalcade* by John Driscoll, Edward Longstreth and Kenneth Webb.
Produced and directed by Homer Fickett.
Thomas Chalmers is the announcer and Basil Ruysdael is the commercial announcer.
Music composed and conducted by Donald Voorhees.
Story: Anne Newport Royall, a fiery, crusading journalist active during the first half of the 19th century, might have become the most famous woman editor in America had she lived a century later. Her name, unknown today, was once a byword in many parts of the country. In these days of widely-syndicated women columnists it is difficult to fully comprehend the stature of Anne Royall, who treated national affairs as if they were her own household problems in a day when American women were confined to the drawing room, if not the kitchen.

Trivia: An adaptation of Carl Carmer's 1939 story "The Hudson" (pages 148 - 153) was originally scheduled for broadcast on this date under the title "The Cruise of the Experiment." For reasons unknown, the drama was never dramatized. To fill in the time slot for this date, "Anne Royal," which was originally scheduled for broadcast the week after (March 27, 1940), was pushed ahead a week.

More Trivia: The title of this script was originally "The People vs. Anne Newport Royall."

And More Trivia: This *Cavalcade* broadcast was prepared by Mrs. Marquis James, wife of the Pulitzer Prize novelist and an able biographer in her own right.

EPISODE #176   **"ENOCH CROSBY - THE SPY"**   Broadcast on February 27, 1940
    Starring: Henry Hull as Enoch Crosby
    Ian MacAllister as Gaolor
    Frank Readick as the orderly
    Kenny Delmar as Lafayette
    Bill Pringle as Lincoln
    Alfred Shirley as the voice
    Ian MacAllister as Robbert
    Jeanette Nolan as Katy
    Kenny Delmar as the Aide
    Ed Jerome as Washington
    John McIntire as Jay
    Ray Collins as Townsend
    Dwight Weist as Adjutant
    Ted Jewett as Rawlings
    Ted Jewett as Hamilton
    Dwight Weist as the officer
    Ray Collins as O'Hara
    Frank Readick as Skinner
    Alfred Shirley as Harcourt
    Bill Pringle as Young
    Ted Jewett as Duer
    Ray Collins as Cooper
Adapted for *Cavalcade* by John Driscoll and Garrett Porter from material suggested by Dr. Frank Monaghan, and suggestions of James F. Cooper's story "The Spy."
Produced and directed by Homer Fickett.
Thomas Chalmers is the announcer and Basil Ruysdael is the commercial announcer.
Music composed and conducted by Donald Voorhees.
Story: The Crosby story begins when the independence of the United States was scarce ten weeks old, with New York City held by the British, and General Washington's forces roaming the nearby territory. A pack peddler of silks, muslins and tobacco, Crosby passed freely through the loosely held lines of the opposing armies. Fabled by both British and patriots as a Tory spy, the wily Crosby supplied a steady stream of misinformation about Continental garrisons and troop movements to the British Commander in New York City, until his apparent role of British agent brought capture by incensed local settlers. Forever suspect by his neighbors, Crosby died without the obvious recognition of service, his achievements known only to the executive command of the Revolutionary Army.

Trivia: This was an attempt to correct an injustice over 160 years old - the true story of the spy, Enoch Crosby. First told in fiction by James Fenimore Cooper, as the adventure of one, Harvey Birch, Enoch Crosby's recognition as an outstanding patriot of the War for Independence comes late. This episode contradicts the Cooper story, and tells the true events, which was fictionalized by Cooper.

EPISODE #177   **"THE STOLEN GENERAL"**   Broadcast on March 5, 1940
    Starring: John Garfield as Colonel William Barton
    Ian MacAllister as soldier Readick
    Ted Jewett as the secretary
    Jeanette Nolan as Citizen Nolan
    Agnes Moorehead as Citizen Moorehead
    Kenneth Delmar as Hunt
    Ray Collins as Collins
    Alfred Shirley as Prescott
    Ian MacAllister as Coffin
    Elliott Reid as the third watch
    Ray Collins as the officer
    Ed Jerome as Wilcox
    Frank Readick as Austin
    Elliott Reid as Soldier Jewett
    Ed Jerome as Washington
    Alfred Shirley as second watch
    Frank Readick as Page
    Elliott Reid as the voice
    John McIntire as Overing
    Frank Readick as the aide
    Bill Pringle as Stanton
    Ted Jewett as the first watch
    John McIntire as Potter
    Elliott Reid as the sentry
    Elliott Reid as Turner
Based on a story by Marquis James, and adapted for *Cavalcade* by Robert Anderson, John Driscoll, Philo Higley, and Garrett Porter.
Produced and directed by Homer Fickett.

Thomas Chalmers is the announcer and Basil Ruysdael is the commercial announcer. Music composed and conducted by Donald Voorhees.

Story: In 1777, the new United States of America, on its first birthday hadn't established a routine of celebrations. Perhaps because things looked very dark for the colonies. The British fleet lay at anchor off Newport Island - Newport itself was held by the British Brigadier General Prescott. The capricious Colonel William Barton and a band of Rhode Island patriots decided to make a celebration that would long be remembered. With five whaleboats and a crew of seamen patriots, Barton kidnapped the British general from under the very guns of the British men-o'-war. The daring exploit brought renewed courage to all of New England, and in the words of General George Washington, "at an evil hour, a black cloud was lifted."

Trivia: This episode features cast games, as the titles of fictional citizens and soldiers had to be added (as often occurred for many scripts). Instead of making up names, however, citizens were given names from many of the supporting actors. Example: Agnes Moorehead played a small role of a citizen named Moorehead. Jeanette Nolan played the role of another female citizen in the same town, whose name was Nolan. Ray Collins played the role of citizen Collins. Elliott Reid played a soldier named Jewett (named after actor Ted Jewett) and Ian MacAllister played a soldier named Readick (named after actor Frank Readick). Listen to this episode for more humorous cast roles!

EPISODE #178   **"THE RAVEN WINS TEXAS"**   Broadcast on March 12, 1940
Script first written on February 2, 1940, revised on March 7 and 11, 1940.

Starring: Walter Huston as Sam Houston   John McIntire as Jackson
Ted Jewett as Tom   Elliott Reid as Clem
Ray Collins as Austin   Ted Jewett as Almonte
Ian MacAllister as the speaker   Ed Jerome as Santa Anna
Kenny Delmar as the delegate   Elliott Reid as the Southerland
John McIntire as Potter   Ray Collins as Martin
Kingsley Colton as Little Sam   Alfred Shirley as the Mexican
Jeanette Nolan as Peggy   Bill Pringle as Baker
Ian MacAllister as Smith   Elliott Reid as Brown
Kenny Delmar as White   Frank Readick as Hockley
Agnes Moorehead as Mrs. Dickinson

Based on the 1929 book "The Raven: A Biography of Sam Houston" by Marquis James, and adapted for *Cavalcade* by John Driscoll, _?_ Milward, and Garrett Porter.
Produced and directed by Homer Fickett.
Thomas Chalmers is the announcer and Basil Ruysdael is the commercial announcer. Music composed and conducted by Donald Voorhees.

Story: The continuation of the life story of the valiant and colorful Texas leader, Sam Houston. Houston now turns westward at the bidding of his friend, the President of the United States. Putting his good resolves behind him, Houston, along with a handful of desperate men fighting for freedom in sweep-plains of the west, turned sights to the Alamo. Houston's work in winning Mexican sovereignty from Mexico, making Texas an empire and a republic under his Presidency met with tragedy. The figure of Sam Houston fighting through to the end, finally securing its annexation into the United States, brought through the fulfillment of his dream for America.

Trivia: Several weeks ago, *The Cavalcade of America* presented the first half of Sam Houston's life story, adapted from Marquis James' Pulitzer Prize-winning novel, with Mr. Walter Huston playing the role of Houston, man of destiny. Although part one was presented in January, part two was never actually written; prepared for broadcast the week after. So the second part of this two-part presentation was dramatized a couple of months later. Incidentally, "Benedict Arnold" was originally scheduled for this date, but was pushed ahead three weeks. This second part presentation of Sam Houston's life was originally scheduled for March 19, but it was pushed ahead a week to accommodate Walter Huston's schedule.

EPISODE #179   **"JORDAN'S BANKS"**   Broadcast on March 19, 1940

Starring: Elliott Reid as Sam Davis
Ted Jewett as Fleming
John McIntire as the Chaplain
Kenny Delmar as Armstrong
Bill Pringle as the Chickasaw
Kenny Delmar as the aide
Ted Jewett as the sergeant
Frank Readick as Chase
Ian MacAllister as Wilson
Howard Smith as father
John McIntire as Ross
Ray Collins as Coleman
Ed Jerome as Porter
Ted Jewett as the voice
Howard Smith as the guard
Ed Jerome as Dodge
Jeanette Nolan as Millie
Kenny Delmar as Hobson
Agnes Moorehead as mother
Ray Collins as Coleman

Based on a story by Marquis James, and adapted for *Cavalcade* by John Driscoll, Margaret Lewerth, and Garrett Porter.
Produced and directed by Homer Fickett.
Thomas Chalmers is the announcer and Basil Ruysdael is the commercial announcer. Music composed and conducted by Donald Voorhees.
Story: Struggles and hatreds are soon forgotten in the forging of a nation, but the light of true heroism burns bright and out-lives the cause for which it perished. Rightly enough, no matter what the circumstances, the principles for which men live and die are remembered after them. This is the story of Sam Davis, a young Confederate spy, who gave his life for the ideals he cherished. Although the cause of the Confederacy perished, the spirit of Sam Davis lives on. The ideals for which he gave his life are principles of American character - loyalty to a promise, devotion to cause, and unselfish and sacred honor.

EPISODE #180   **"THE STORY OF JOHN FITCH"**   Broadcast on March 26, 1940

Starring: Thomas Mitchell as John Fitch
Elliott Reid as Johnson
Jeanette Nolan as Mrs. Whitby
Frank Readick as Jones
Ian MacAllister as Dr. Say
Jeanette Nolan as Mrs. Maitland
Bill Pringle as Isreal
Ray Collins as Voight
Agnes Moorehead as Nancy
Ted Jewett as Duncan
Ray Collins as the secretary
Ed Jerome as Vail
Ted Jewett as Brown
Kenny Delmar as Wells
Elliott Reid as Budd
Ted Jewett as Lowe
John McIntire as Franklin

Written for *Cavalcade* by John Driscoll and _?_ Sharp.
Produced and directed by Homer Fickett.
Thomas Chalmers is the announcer and Basil Ruysdael is the commercial announcer. Music composed and conducted by Donald Voorhees.
Story: The story of John Fitch, American pioneer in the invention of steam navigation, is like the story of so many inventors of the 18th century, fraught with continuing hard luck and misfortune. Despite the importance of his scientific achievement, he was to spend his life in a futile struggle for financial support in the development of his invention. Many times, he built a test steam packet, only to lose his boat through the blowing of a boiler, the breakdown of some minor piece of machinery and no money with which to repair the parts. So, while the great rivers of the West awaited only the perfecting of steam navigation to become the highways of modern progress, short-sighted eastern business men refused to invest in Fitch's contraptions. Broken-hearted, after a life-time of work and unremitting discouragements, Fitch died un-honored and impoverished.

EPISODE #181 "BENEDICT ARNOLD" Broadcast on April 2, 1940
Starring: Claude Rains as Benedict Arnold
Juano Hernandez as Punch
Jeanette Nolan as Hannah
Ian MacAllister as Walter
John McIntire as the speaker
Alfred Shirley as the servant
Elliott Reid as Andre
John McIntire as Washington
Agnes Moorehead as Peggy
Frank Readick as the Captain
Kenny Delmar as Cullin
Ray Collins as Reed
Ed Jerome as Brown
Ted Jewett as the Major
Kenny Delmar as Walker
Ted Jewett as York
Ed Jerome as Tallyrand
Bill Pringle as Matlack
Ian MacAllister as Timothy
Alfred Shirley as Clinton

Based on material suggested by Dr. Frank Monoghan, and adapted for *Cavalcade* by John Driscoll and _?_ Milward.
Produced and directed by Homer Fickett.
Thomas Chalmers is the announcer and Basil Ruysdael is the commercial announcer.
Music composed and conducted by Donald Voorhees.

Story: This the story of Benedict Arnold, able, peppery, impetuous general in the War of Freedom, tagged as traitor by generations of historians, defended by few. While people as we know them are never wholly good or bad, posterity demands of historians that they label their leading characters either one extreme or the other. In General Arnold a mixture of strength, weakness and temper created a most delicate balance. Many times one heroic action has redeemed for history an otherwise worthless career: Arnold's one fatal mistake wrote *finis* to his valuable and unremitting service to America.

Trivia: This broadcast was originally scheduled for February 13, 1940. For reasons unknown, the drama was pushed ahead for March 12, 1940. Again, the drama became rescheduled for this date.

EPISODE #182 "AMERICA SINGS: THE SONGS OF STEPHEN FOSTER" April 9, 1940
Revised on April 4, 5, and 8, 1940.
Starring: Agnes Moorehead as mother
Elliott Reid as Bones
John McIntire as Old Joe
Jeanette Nolan as the landlady
Frank Readick as Paw
Jeanette Nolan as Jeanie
Ed Jerome as the Interlocutor
Agnes Moorehead as Maw
Ed Jerome as the cop
Elliott Reid as Jim
Ray Collins as Cowan
Karl Swenson as Stephen Foster

Narrated by Channing Pollock.
Written for *Cavalcade* by John Driscoll, Robert M. Pollock, and Robert Tallman.
Produced and directed by Homer Fickett.
Thomas Chalmers is the announcer and Basil Ruysdael is the commercial announcer.
Music composed and conducted by Donald Voorhees.
Songs featured in the order of their appearance order: the 1864 song "Beautiful Dreamer," "Jeanie," the 1848 song "Oh, Suzanna," the 1853 song "Old Kentucky Home," the 1850 song "Camptown Races," the 1860 song "Old Black Joe," and "Swanee River."

Story: Although Stephen Collins Foster began his career as a bookkeeper, he soon was spending all his time and energy at song writing. This was his means of expression, and his whole life is told through his music. Before his death he composed the music and wrote the words of more than one hundred and twenty-five popular songs and melodies. This is Foster's life through the medium of his music, rather than by the usual dramatic presentations.

Channing Pollock: "Sometimes, I think the history of people is written in their music - not so much in the works of great composers as in songs that come from the souls of humble men and women. Tennyson said, 'The song that serves a nation's heart is in itself a deed,' and what deeds have echoed in, or been inspired by our country's melodies? Victor Herbert told me once that he thought no song survived that did not bring tears to the eyes or cause some human being to reach out for the touch of another."

EPISODE #183   **"DANIEL BOONE"**   Broadcast on April 16, 1940
Starring: John McIntire as Daniel Boone   Jeanette Nolan as Mrs. Boone
Sara Fussell as Becky   Ed Jerome as Harding
Kingsley Colton as Jimmy   Bill Pringle as Henderson
Agnes Moorehead as Rebecca   Frank Readick as Twitty
Ian MacAllister as Walker   Alfred Shirley as Hamilton
Ray Collins as Collins   Ted Jewett as Girty
Juano Hernandez as Blackfish   Kenny Delmar as the runner
Agnes Moorehead as Jemima   Elliott Reid as Flanders
Written for *Cavalcade* by John Driscoll and Garrett Porter.
Produced and directed by Homer Fickett.
Thomas Chalmers is the announcer and Basil Ruysdael is the commercial announcer.
Music composed and conducted by Donald Voorhees.
Story: It is impossible to imagine the history of America without the frontier. Though there were many millions of Americans, good, bad, brave, irresolute or daring, famous or anonymous, who chopped and fought and built ways from Plymouth Rock to Oregon, old Daniel Boone is the most famous of them all and one of our great American heroes. His deeds grew to legendary stature even during his lifetime; since his day they have become a true American saga.

Trivia: This episode was originally scheduled for broadcast on February 6, 1940. For reasons unknown, the script was later scheduled for broadcast on March 5, 1940. Again, it was pushed forward a few more weeks until this date.

More trivia: Note Ray Collins in the role of a fictitious "Collins."

EPISODE #184   **"ROBERT E. LEE"**   Broadcast on April 23, 1940
Starring: Philip Merivale as Robert E. Lee
Based on episodes from the four-volume, 1934-35 biography "R.E. Lee" by Dr. Douglas Southall Freeman, and adapted for *Cavalcade* by John Driscoll and Robert Tallman.
Produced by and directed by Homer Fickett.
Thomas Chalmers is the announcer and Basil Ruysdael is the commercial announcer.
Music composed and conducted by Donald Voorhees.
Story: Honoring the Confederacy's greatest general, and finest citizen, this drama stressed the personal nobility and moral courage rather than the military genius of the Southern hero. Robert E. Lee symbolized all that was noblest a struggle that was more than a war between States and more than a crusade for national union; rather a proud last stand of a great culture and a vanishing way of life.

Trivia: This broadcast originated from "The Mosque," in Richmond, Virginia, where the supporting actors from the Richmond Theatre Guild and local musicians participated in this broadcast. Only a couple of days before the broadcast, Philip Merivale paid a visit to hear stories of Civil War at the United Daughters of the Confederacy tea at home for Aged Confederate Women in Richmond.

More trivia: Ante-bellum dancers gave a performance on the stage after the broadcast. No sooner had the stage been cleared of musicians and sound effects props and microphones, when twenty-two sub-debs and their beaux took part in the dances, wearing costumes that were authentic replicas of ball dresses of 1860.

Even more trivia: Descendants of Robert L. Lee attended the initial East Coast performance, a couple of them played minor roles in the broadcast.

EPISODE #185   "THOMAS PAINE"   Broadcast on April 30, 1940
  Starring: Frank Readick as Tom Paine   Alfred Shirley as Goldsmith
  Jeanette Nolan as Mistress Trumbull   Jeanette Nolan as Meg
  Agnes Moorehead as Mrs. Crosby   Bill Pringle as Colburn
  John McIntire as Dr. Franklin   Elliott Reid as the aide
  John McIntire as Washington   Ted Jewett as Brainerd
  Ray Collins as Bates   Bill Pringle as Baker
  Ian McAllister as Morrison   John McIntire as Morrison
  John McIntire as Little   Ed Jerome as Kimball
  Elliott Reid as Reed   Kenny Delmar as Hawley
  Alfred Shirley as Harington   Alfred Shirley as Lafayette
  Bill Pringle as Lincoln   Ian MacAllister as Hamilton
  Ted Jewett as the announcer   Ian MacAllister as voice eight
  Alfred Shirley as voice seven   Ray Collins as Boston
  Ed Jerome as New York   Bill Pringle as Baltimore
  Ian MacAllister as Hancock   Ted Jewett as Jefferson
  Elliott Reid as Sam   Kenny Delmar as the sentry
  Elliott Reid as voice one   Ted Jewett as voice two
  John McIntire as voice three   Ray Collins as voice five
  Ed Jerome as voice four   Bill Pringle as voice six
Written for *Cavalcade* by John Driscoll and Garrett Porter.
Produced and directed by Homer Fickett.
Basil Ruysdael is the announcer.
Music composed and conducted by Donald Voorhees.
Story: America gave Thomas Paine the chance to be great, and Thomas Paine, more than almost any other man, gave America the will to be free. When Thomas Paine was thirty-seven years old, Benjamin Franklin suggested that he leave London and use the force and clarity of his writing in the new country of America. Thomas Jefferson said that Paine's plain-talk history of the American struggle, "Common Sense," created the Declaration of Independence. And Washington's bedraggled army, inspired by Paine's "Crisis," ceased deserting and won a victory over the Hessians at Trenton on Christmas Day 1776. For the mighty part his pen played in American independence, *Cavalcade* honors Paine.

Trivia: The original script title for this episode was "Thomas Paine in America," but it was decided long before the final draft of the script to shorten the title.

EPISODE #186   "NANCY HANKS"   Broadcast on May 7, 1940
  Starring: Agnes Moorehead as Nancy Hanks
  John McIntire as Tom Lincoln   Helen Lewis as Jinny
  Ted Jewett as Charley   Jeanette Nolan as Aunt Peggy
  Frank Readick as Old Sparrow   Elliott Reid as Dennis
  Frank Readick as Denton   Kingsley Colton as Abe Lincoln
  Sarah Fussell as the baby
Written for *Cavalcade* by John Driscoll, Homer Fickett, and Robert Tallman.
Produced and directed by Homer Fickett.
Basil Ruysdael is the announcer.
Music composed and conducted by Donald Voorhees.

Story: Abraham Lincoln paid tribute to his mother in words that have become immortal: "All that I am, or ever hope to become, I owe to my mother." Nancy Hanks, humble, unschooled mother of Abraham Lincoln, appeared to have a psychic knowledge of her son's great destiny. It was Nancy Hanks who persuaded her husband, Tom Lincoln, to give his son book learning. It was she who extracted a last promise from Tom Lincoln to permit young Abe to continue his education. And it was Nancy Hanks' Bible stories, recited to him in early childhood long before his meager schooling began, that Abraham Lincoln owed his literary style, lucid and Biblical.

Author's note: In researching this episode, I found a handwritten memo from S. Schumacher of the advertising department at 2503 Nemours with the following: "No record of contract with writer on 'Nancy Hanks.' Our records start with October 1940. The rights on this program read: No rights. Based on works of Carl Sandburg, published by Harcourt, Brace and Company'. "

EPISODE #187   **"ROGER WILLIAMS"**   Broadcast on May 14, 1940
Starring: Ray Collins as Roger Williams
Alfred Shirley as Governor Haynes
Jeanette Nolan as Anne Hutchinson
Bill Pringle as Winthrop
Ian MacAllister as Ryder
Juano Hernandez as Miantonomo
Ted Jewett as Canonicus
Agnes Moorehead as Mary
Ted Jewett as the Town Crier
Frank Readick as the coachman
Ted Jewett as Gorton
Alfred Shirley as Smith
Elliott Reid as the aide
Kenny Delmar as Wickes
Frank Readick as Harris
Elliott Reid as Arnold
John McIntire as Skelton
Ed Jerome as Dudley
Kenny Delmar as the Skipper
Written for *Cavalcade* by John Driscoll and Garrett Porter.
Produced and directed by Homer Fickett.
Basil Ruysdael is the announcer.
Music composed and conducted by Donald Voorhees.
Story: The guarantee that "Congress shall make no law respecting an establishment of religion or prohibiting the free exercise thereof," is one of America's proudest heritage. Roger Williams, apostle of soul liberty, whose beliefs ultimately found expression in the Constitution of the United States. Refusing to recant his heresies - that the authority of civil magistrates extended only to the bodies and outward state of man but not to his soul, and that the rightful owners of the land were the Indians - Roger Williams became a fugitive from the Massachusetts Bay Colony. His final triumph, a charter from the English Parliament, raised the Rhode Island and Providence Plantations to equality with the other New England colonies and secured for the apostle of religious freedom both liberty and peace.

EPISODE #188   **"JANE ADDAMS OF HULL HOUSE"**   Broadcast on May 21, 1940
Starring: Helen Hayes as Jane Addams
Written for *Cavalcade* by John Driscoll and Robert Tallman.
Produced and directed by Homer Fickett.
Basil Ruysdael is the announcer.
Music composed and conducted by Donald Voorhees.
Story: Jane Addams was born in a small town called Cedarville, forty miles south of Chicago's ugly Halsted Street, where she was to spend most of her life. As the daughter of that town's most respected citizen, she might have enjoyed a sheltered, luxurious life, married a rich man and avoided the painful sights and sounds that were to be her life in Hull House. Instead, she chose to establish in Chicago's worst slum a haven for the poor, the ignorant and the oppressed.

Trivia: Helen Hayes, radio's number two actress according to the Star of Stars Poll, although she was not a regular cast member of any program, returns in one of her brilliant roles for this broadcast, a dramatization of the life of Jane Addams. Coincident with the celebration of the fiftieth anniversary of Hull House, and the fiftieth anniversary of her death, famous social settlement which Jane Adams founded.

More Trivia: This broadcast originated from the Civic Auditorium in Milwaukee, Wisconsin.

EPISODE #189   **"SHOW BOAT"**   Broadcast on May 28, 1940
Starring the Ken Christie Choir.
Based on the Oscar Hammerstein II and Edna Ferber musical, and adapted for *Cavalcade* by John Driscoll and _?_ Sanford.
Produced and directed by Homer Fickett.
Basil Ruysdael is the announcer.
Music composed and conducted by Donald Voorhees.
Songs featured: "Make Believe," "Old Man River," a few segues to the "Show Boat" theme, "Streets of Cairo," "Why Do I Love You?" "Can't Help Lovin' That Man," and "After the Ball."
Story: On the night of December 27, 1927, a brilliant first-night audience filled the Ziegfeld Theatre to applaud the opening performance of "Show Boat" - a show destined to make theatrical history - a show that was to take its place in Americana as the great American operetta. The inspiration for the stage production was Edna Ferber's best selling novel of the same name, from which the libretto was fashioned by Oscar Hammerstein II. Jerome Kern composed the fine score. This musical drama provides us a colorful setting for a poignant story of those great days on the Mississippi.

EPISODE #190   **"JOHN SUTTER"**   Broadcast on June 4, 1940
Starring: Edwin Jerome as John Sutter
Gretchen Davidson as Mrs. Winters
Jeanette Nolan as Mrs. Wheeler
Alfred Shirley as Scotty
Jack Smart as the bartender
Ted Jewett as Chang
Bill Pringle as the Virginian
Gretchen Davidson as Mollie
Ray Collins as Sam
Jack Smart as the leader
Elliott Reid as Butch
Jack Smart as Don
Jack Smart as Jake
Kenny Delmar as Francisco
Jeanette Nolan as Carmencita
Ted Jewett as Horta
Kenny Delmar as Bill
Gretchen Davidson as Emily
Jeanette Nolan as Laura
Frank Readick as Marshall
Elliott Reid as Frank
Gretchen Davidson as Ellen
Ray Collins as Jack
Frank Readick as Si
Ray Collins as Jed
Kenny Delmar as Red
Kenny Delmar as Bowery
Elliott Reid as Alphonse
Alfred Shirley as Cockney
Ian MacAllister as the Yankee
John McIntire as Tinhorn
Bill Pringle as the judge
John McIntire as Roger
Ted Jewett as Dan
Ian MacAllister as Charley
Frank Readick as the Irishman
Frank Readick as Paolo
John McIntire as Alvarado
Ian MacAllister as Joe
Elliott Reid as Jeff
Agnes Moorehead as Anna
Jack Smart as the Governor
Ray Collins as Hank
Kenny Delmar as Ken
Agnes Moorehead as Gladys
Written for *Cavalcade* by John Driscoll, _?_ Harris, and Garrett Porter.
Produced and directed by Homer Fickett.
Basil Ruysdael is the announcer.

Music composed and conducted by Donald Voorhees.
Story: The great California gold discovery precipitated a clash between conflicting forms of wealth - mining and agriculture. Johann Augustus Sutter, the immigrant who left his tiny farm in Switzerland to realize his dream of vast lands, received, in California, a provisional land grant to an area equal to half of France. In the Sacramento River valley he made a fertile land of wheat fields, orchards and vineyards. Foreseeing the destiny of the United States, with dominion from Coast to Coast, John Sutter made his land rich to attract settlers to pave the way for California's entrance into the Union. But in 1848 gold was discovered near Sutter's sawmill. Greedy hordes swarmed over Sutter's fertile valley, leaving ruin in their wake. And Sutter's empire narrowed down to a small holding and a single farmhouse such as he had in Switzerland.

EPISODE #191 "VICTOR HERBERT" Broadcast on June 11, 1940

Starring: John McIntire as the narrator
Ray Collins as Theodore Roosevelt
Jeanette Nolan as Emma
Elliott Reid as the first voice
Ed Jerome as Bill

Jack Smart as Victor Herbert
Bill Pringle as the Cabby
Kenny Delmar as Orville
Ted Jewett as the second voice
Frank Readick as Paul Whiteman

Produced and directed by Homer Fickett.
Basil Ruysdael is the announcer.
Musical chorus under the direction of Ken Christie.
Music composed and conducted by Donald Voorhees.
Songs featured within the broadcast (listed in order of their appearance): The 1905 song "Kiss Me Again," a segue to "Mascot of the Troop," a few bars of "Falling in Love" was hummed, the 1910 song "Falling in Love" from *Naughty Marietta*, a segue to the "Italian Street Song," the song "Natoma" from 1910, "When You're Away," the 1940 song "It's a Great Day Tonight for the Irish," the 1917 song "Thine Alone," the 1903 song "March of the Toys," "Cuban Serenade," "Gypsy Sweetheart," "A Kiss in the Dark," the 1919 song "Indian Summer," and finally the 1898 composition "Gypsy Love Song."
Story: If Victor Herbert had had a lyric writer like Gilbert, of the English Gilbert and Sullivan team, he might well have founded an American Gilbert and Sullivan literature, because his facility and originality were equal to that of the great English operetta composer. Herbert was the first composer educated in the ultra-classic musical tradition of Europe to achieve national fame in the American operetta field, and sixteen years after his death, he still ranked as an outstanding composer of light opera. The scores of his more than forty operettas were typical of the first decade of the twentieth century - an era rich in the tradition of substantial comfort in living, graceful art and frothy entertainment.

EPISODE #192 "SUSAN B. ANTHONY" Broadcast on June 18, 1940

Starring: Cornelia Otis Skinner as Susan B. Anthony

Elliott Reid as the first Male Delegate
Agnes Moorehead as Victoria
Alfred Shirley as Chamberlain
Edwin Jerome as Selden
Ian MacAllister as the clerk
Kenny Delmar as Hall
Frank Readick as the porter
Gretchen Davidson as Mrs. Curtis
Edwin Jerome as Chairman
Helen Lewis as Mme. Chairman
Jeanette Nolan as Viola
Agnes Moorehead as Red
Helen Lewis as Gray

John McIntire as the second Male Delegate
Arlene Francis as Lady Aberdeen
Jeanette Nolan as the secretary
John McIntire as Judge Hart
Frank Readick as Marsh
Elliott Reid as the Barber
Kenny Delmar as the senator
Bill Pringle as Greeley
Arlene Francis as Mrs. Stanton
Gretchen Davidson as Annie
Ray Collins as Daniel Anthony
Elliott Reid as Blue
John McIntire as Green

Frank Readick as Black
Ian MacAllister as Brown
Jeanette Nolan as White
Dwight Weist as the narrator
Written for *Cavalcade* by John Driscoll, _?_ Eshenfelder, Garrett Porter, Robert Tallman
Produced and directed by Homer Fickett.
Basil Ruysdael is the announcer.
Music composed and conducted by Donald Voorhees.
Story: Twenty years of women's suffrage have almost eclipsed the bitter struggle for feminine civic rights which began to be articulate with Susan B. Anthony in 1845. Susan was not the repulsive-looking female that the irate males of her generation liked to represent her. Rather she was a handsome, becomingly-garbed, brilliant woman, with the kind of logic generally spoken of as masculine. The story of her sixty-year fight for women's rights and her intelligent devotion to the cause which was to enfranchise American women in 1920 is a tale that deserves greater emphasis than it has had in the annals of democratic progress.

EPISODE #193   **"WALTER REED"**   Broadcast on June 25, 1940
    Starring: John McIntire as Walter Reed
    Ian MacAllister as Dr. Carroll
    Edwin Jerome as Dr. Finlay
    Jack Smart as Howard
    Edwin Jerome as Lowe
    Jeanette Nolan as Fisher
    Jeanette Nolan as Miss Malone
    Bill Pringle as the Major
    Elliott Reid as Talcott
    Frank Readick as Emmett
    Kenny Delmar as Dr. Lazear
    Agnes Moorehead as Miss Brown
    Bill Pringle as General Wood
    Ted Jewett as O'Connor
    Ray Collins as Gorgas
    Elliott Reid as Fisher
    Ken Delmar as Blount
    Jack Smart as Rolfe
    Ted Jewett as Smith
    Dwight Weist as the narrator
Written for *Cavalcade* by John Driscoll, Garrett Porter, and Robert Tallman.
Produced and directed by Homer Fickett.
Basil Ruysdael is the announcer.
Music composed and conducted by Donald Voorhees.
Story: As a typical American boy, Walter Reed was highly educated. First at the University of Virginia, and later the Bellevue College Hospital and Johns Hopkins. After his education, Reed was called to Cuba to help fight a yellow fever epidemic at an American Army post. His experiments with the deadly yellow jack mosquito proved so conclusive that they opened the way to complete elimination of yellow fever, and so released the people of Panama and the Latin Americas from the terrible scourge of the tropics. Without this development, the Panama Canal could not have been built. In Washington, there stands the magnificent Walter Reed Hospital - a living memorial to this outstanding American doctor.

EPISODE #194   **"THE LOST COLONY"**   Broadcast on October 2, 1940
    Starring: Loretta Young as Eleanor Dare
    Kenneth Delmar as Manteo
    Ray Collins as Old Tom
    Ted Jewett as the courier
    Jeanette Nolan as Dame Coleman
    Edwin Jerome as the sentry
    Ted Jewett as the Captain
    Jeanette Nolan as Queen Elizabeth
    Edwin Jerome as Sir Walter Raleigh
    Ray Collins as Governor White
    Ted Jewett as Jonathan
    Alfred Shirley as Rev. Martin
    Kenneth Delmar as the messenger
    Kenneth Delmar as William
    Kenneth Delmar as the mate
    Karl Swenson as Captain Dare
    Ted Jewett as Herald
    John McIntire as John Borden
Written for *Cavalcade* by Paul Green.
Produced and directed by Homer Fickett.
Clayton Collyer is the commercial announcer and William Spargrove is the announcer.
Music composed and conducted by Donald Voorhees.

Story: The year 1584 was a troubled one for England. War with Spain was imminent, the fear of invasion by King Philip's Armada was a shadow over Scotland and the Isles. Sir Walter Raleigh persuaded Queen Elizabeth to give him two ships, ships which she really thought should be kept for the defense of Britain. We know that these bold adventurers organized the first white settlement on the American continent. We know that the long-feared war with Spain became a reality; the attempted invasion of Britain was launched, only to end in disaster for Philip's Armada.

EPISODE #195   "VALLEY FORGE"   Broadcast on October 9, 1940
    Starring: John McIntire as G. Washington   Alfred Shirley as Howe
    Edwin Jerome as the Washington   Kenny Delmar as Spad
    Ted Jewett as Mason   Ray Collins as Alcock
    Karl Swenson as Teague   Elliott Reid as Neil
    Edwin Jerome as Cutting   Ian Martin as Andre
    William Johnstone as Tench   Ted Jewett as Harvie
    Ian MacAllister as Conway   Bill Pringle as Folsom
    Sam Wanamaker as Sterling   Jeanette Nolan as Mary
    Jeanette Nolan as Betsy   Brad Barker is Rover (the dog)
Based on the 1934 play of the same name by Maxwell Anderson, and adapted for *Cavalcade* by Robert Tallman.
Produced and directed by Homer Fickett.
Clayton Collyer is the commercial announcer and William Spargrove is the announcer.
Music composed and conducted by Donald Voorhees.
The song "Yankee Doodle Dandy" was performed in this drama.
Story: During the bitter months of the bleak encampment many men began to think that it would be the final and crushing disaster to the American cause, but it was not the final disaster. It proved to be the end of disasters and the beginning of victory. Never had Washington's tiny army found itself in a more precarious position. Washington and his men had suffered three successive defeats. The British under General Howe had occupied Philadelphia, the national capitol. Washington settled his eleven thousand soldiers in winter headquarters at Valley Forge in December, 1777. The cold was intense, but Washington proved that he was the great leader of men. He was determined to keep the army in being to show that no disaster was enough to destroy it. He gave them the inspiration, the grim fortitude, the hope with which they again went forth in pursuit of the American dream of liberty.

Trivia: A *Cavalcade* broadcast is a dignified affair. Everyone, including the members of Don Voorhees' orchestra, wears evening clothes as a matter of course. Although, as an experiment, Maxwell Anderson's play "Valley Forge" was broadcast with the actors wearing the Colonial costumes of the drama's period. It was nice for the studio audience but certainly didn't mean a great deal to listeners. A Broadway theater, the Ritz, is used for the broadcasts and an audience of 1,200 people attend each one.

EPISODE #196   "THE PATHFINDER OF THE SEAS"   Broadcast on October 16, 1940
    Starring: Karl Swenson as Lt. Maury   Elliott Reid as the lookout
    Sam Wanamaker as Bos'n   Kenny Delmar as the sailor
    William Johnstone as Berryman   John McIntire as the secretary
    Ray Collins as Jackson   Ian MacAllister as Smith
    Ted Jewett as Yarnell   Edwin Jerome as Hubbard
    Jeanette Nolan as Ann   Kenny Delmar as the coachman
    Alfred Shirley as the Bell Announcer   Bill Pringle as Smythe
    William Johnstone as Laughlin   Alfred Shirley as Lord Packingham
    Produced and directed by Homer Fickett.
Clayton Collyer is the commercial announcer and William Spargrove is the announcer.

Music composed and conducted by Donald Voorhees.

Story: In the pilothouse of every ship that sails the seven seas the master mariner has a collection of charts, charts which hold for him priceless information; charts which tell him what he needs to know about the winds and the waves, the ocean currents, the pathways of the sea. And down in a corner of most of these charts, in very small type, is a legend which reads: "Founded upon the researches made in the early part of the 19th Century by Matthew Fontaine Maury, while serving as a lieutenant in the United States Navy." That legend today is printed on every pilot chart issued by the United States Hydrographic Office.

EPISODE #197 **"ANN RUTLEDGE AND LINCOLN"** Broadcast on October 23, 1940

Starring: Jeanette Nolan as Ann Rutledge Kenny Delmar as Armstrong
John McIntire as Abe Lincoln Kingsley Colton as Peter
Edwin Jerome as the doctor Ted Jewett as Mr. Winthrop
Ray Collins as Mr. Rutledge Karl Swenson as McNeil
Agnes Moorehead as mother
Written for *Cavalcade* by Norman Corwin.
Produced and directed by Homer Fickett.
Clayton Collyer is the commercial announcer and William Spargrove is the announcer.
Music composed and conducted by Donald Voorhees.

Norman Corwin: "In a little churchyard at New Salem, Illinois, sleeps a girl - a girl whose influence on a young store clerk helped to drive him along the hard road until he became one of the greatest Americans of them all, Abraham Lincoln. Ann Rutledge it was who inspired Lincoln to rise from the backwoods of Illinois to the place of greatness which is his today. The things she was, the feelings she had, her hopes and her fears - these are what our story is about."

EPISODE #198 **"THE RED DEATH"** Broadcast on October 30, 1940

Starring: Ed Jerome as Dr. Joe Goldberger Ted Jewett as the voice
Ray Collins as Doctor Horne Jeanette Nolan as Granny
Agnes Moorehead as Mary Elliott Reid as Elmer
William Johnstone as Owen Ted Jewett as the warden
Karl Swenson as Steve Kenny Delmar as Chimp
Sam Wanamaker as Joe Juano Hernandez as Sam
John McIntire as the governor Brad Barker supplied the animal voices
Narrated by George Coulouris.
Written for *Cavalcade* by Ruth Barth.
Produced and directed by Homer Fickett.
Clayton Collyer is the commercial announcer and William Spargrove is the announcer.
Music composed and conducted by Donald Voorhees.
Story: This is the story of an immigrant boy, raised on New York's east side, who was sent by the United States Public Health Service to investigate the "red death," the mysterious pellagra which had baffled science for two centuries. By unorthodox methods, this American scientist, Dr. Joseph Goldberger, found the cure, then the cause, for the disease. Pellagra, which was a familiar disease in other parts of the world for centuries began to appear in the United States about 1907. It reached alarming proportions, and Dr. Goldberger took charge of the investigation and eventually worked his way through to a brilliant victory over the "red death."

EPISODE #199 **"WILD BILL HICKOCK: THE LAST OF TWO GUN JUSTICE"**
Broadcast on November 6, 1940
Starring: Kenny Delmar as Wild Bill
Ray Collins as the Colonel
William Johnstone as the guard
John McIntire as Custer
Agnes Moorehead as Mrs. Brown
Edwin Jerome as Charles Martin
Agnes Moorehead as Calamity Jane
William Johnstone as Carl Mann
Karl Swenson as Charlie Rich
Juano Hernandez as the slave
Ted Jewett as Tompkins
Elliott Reid as the Corporal
Ted Jewett as the orderly
Bill Pringle as the mayor
Howard Smith as Readick
Ray Collins as Collins
John McIntire as Jess
Howard Smith as Hudson
Ann Sterrett as Bess
Jeanette Nolan as Sarah
Ed Jerome as McCanles
Brad Barker supplied the animal voices

Produced and directed by Homer Fickett.
Clayton Collyer is the commercial announcer and William Spargrove is the announcer. Music composed and conducted by Donald Voorhees.
Woody Guthrie is the vocal, who wrote an original ballad for this program, entitled "I Walked Out on the Streets of Lardeo."
Story: Hickok's adventures started when he was a mere lad in his home town, helping fugitive slaves to get to Canada and freedom. When he was only fifteen years old he ran away from home, fleeing punishment for a fatal brawl with a town bully. In "Bloody Kansas" in the 1850's he won his nickname of Wild Bill, single-handed stopping a riot. During the Civil War he performed valiant service for the Union Army as a spy behind the Confederate lines. As a symbol of that era, Hickok became a man on a tombstone which read: "A brave man, the victim of an assassin; J.B. Hickok, Wild Bill, aged 39 years, murdered by Jack McCall."

EPISODE #200 **"DR. FRANKLIN GOES TO COURT"** Broadcast on November 13, 1940
Starring: John McIntire as Ben Franklin
Alfred Shirley as Lord Howe
Ted Jewett as Morris
William Johnstone as Lackey
Edwin Jerome as the coachman
William Johnstone as the Ambassador
Agnes Moorehead as the first woman
Elliott Reid as Lafayette
Edwin Jerome as the Innkeeper
Ray Collins as John Adams
Sara Fussell as Bennie
Karl Swenson as Vergennes
Elliott Reid as the wig dresser
Jeanette Nolan as the second woman
George Coulouris as Louis
Kenny Delmar as Deane

Written for *Cavalcade* by Dr. Frank Monaghan.
Produced and directed by Homer Fickett.
William Spargrove is the announcer and Clayton Collyer is the commercial announcer.
Story: Dr. Franklin was the first American to achieve a world-wide reputation. Although he was an ardent American he was also a citizen of the world. A long life of distinguished achievement lay behind him. He felt, with some misgiving, that his career was near its end. When asked if he would serve as envoy to France he replied that his services could be worth but little - that he was like the end of a bolt of cloth on a merchant's shelf - "You may have me for what you will." His French mission represented the highest achievement of his life. This broadcast tells how Dr. Franklin went to court and came away with the treaties that ultimately resulted in the independence of the United States.

EPISODE # 201 **"THE FARMER TAKES A WIFE"** Broadcast on November 20, 1940
Starring: Nancy Kelly as Molly Larkins
Edwin Jerome as Mr. Fisher
Agnes Moorehead as Gammy Hennessy
Elliott Reid as Yazey Van Woorhis
Ray Collins as Gramp Riley
Howard Smith as Sam Weaver
Jeanette Nolan as Lucy Gurget
Karl Swenson as the Engineer

Kenny Delmar as Fortune Friendly	William Johnstone as Dan Harrow
Ted Jewett as Sol Tinker	John McIntire as Jotham Klore

Brad Barker supplied the voices for Jenny and Dobbin.
Based on the stage play by Frank B. Elser and Marc Connelly, and the novel *Rome Haul* by Walter D. Edmonds. Adapted for *Cavalcade* by Marc Connelly.
Produced and directed by Homer Fickett.
William Spargrove is the announcer and Clayton Collyer is the commercial announcer.
Story: For expansion demands resourcefulness and inventive genius. Railroads took the place of the Canal, did the same necessary work, but did it better. The destiny of the Canal had fulfilled itself; a picturesque era was over, but to a young America that era signified not only an early but a needful economic vitality in the development of a great Republic. To the "Canawlers," the Erie was the whole world.

Trivia: In 1935, Twentieth-Century Fox released a big-screen adaptation of *The Farmer Takes A Wife*, starring Henry Fonda in his first screen role. Later in 1953, Fox would remake the film as a musical, down-graded by critics as a flop.

EPISODE # 202   **"LIGHT IN THE HILLS"**   Broadcast on November 27, 1940

Starring:
Agnes Moorehead as Martha Berry	Elliott Reid as Robbie
William Johnstone as Secretary number one	Ann Sterrett as Mrs. White
Ted Jewett as Secretary number two	Howard Smith as the driver
Kenny Delmar as Casey	George Coulouris as Clark
Edwin Jerome as Williams	Kingsley Colton as David
John McIntire as Judge Wright	Virginia Routh as Elizabeth
Jeanette Nolan as the wife	Ray Collins as Roosevelt
Jeanette Nolan as Mammy	Howard Smith as Jeffrey
Karl Swenson as Mr. Berry	Sara Fussell as Sandy
Ronald Liss as Floyd	Warren Colston as Coolidge
William Johnstone as Aide	Kenny Delmar as the secretary

Written for *Cavalcade* by Frank Monaghan.
Produced and directed by Homer Fickett.
Floyd Mack is the announcer and Clayton Collyer is the commercial announcer.
Story: No man has more aptly characterized the contribution of Martha McChesney Berry to our nation than Theodore Roosevelt, who described her work as director of the Berry School For Mountain Children in Georgia as "the greatest practical work of American citizenship that has been done." A southern aristocratic lady, she is the symbol of humanity's noblest virtues: compassion and achievement. Quietly she had devoted a memorable lifetime to the betterment of her fellow human beings.

EPISODE # 203   **"THE BATTLE HYMN OF THE REPUBLIC"**   Aired on December 4, 1940
Written for *Cavalcade* by Alexander Woollcott, who was also star and narrator.
Produced and directed by Homer Fickett.
Richard Stark is the announcer and Clayton Collyer is the commercial announcer.
Original music score composed and conducted by Deems Taylor.
Features the 1862 song "The Battle Hymn of the Republic."
Story: It does not happen often, but when it does it shatters the apathy and the intolerance of millions. It happened to Julia Ward Howe. She had been writing poems and romances for years, but none of the were very good. But one day she visited an army camp near Washington D.C. There the things she saw and the things she heard began, almost unconsciously, to release the eloquent, but pent-up voice that was yearning for expression. That night she was in a tent, trying to sleep. But the events of the day had stirred her and sleep was impossible. The inner voice was beginning to speak. She had no light, but in the darkness of the tent she found paper and pencil and out came the words of the "Battle Hymn of the Republic."

Trivia: "The Battle Hymn of the Republic" was composed to the rhythm of the folk song "John Brown's Body," first published in *The Atlantic Monthly* in February of 1862.

EPISODE # 204   **"JOHN BROWN"**   Broadcast on December 11, 1940
    Starring: John McIntire as John Brown   George Coulouris as Stevens
    Kenny Delmar as Owen   Ted Jewett as the station master
    Karl Swenson as the operator   Howard Smith as Phelps
    William Johnstone as Robert E. Lee   Ed Jerome as Stuart
    Elliott Reid as Oliver   George Coulouris as Kagi
    Dwight Weist as Wise   Howard Smith as the jailer
    Kenny Delmar as the sheriff   Bill Pringle as the Judge
    Karl Swenson as the voice   Kenny Delmar as Poster
    Karl Swenson as Adolph   Charita Bauer as Annie
    Ray Collins as the storekeeper   Bill Adams as Abe Lincoln
    Juano Hernandez as James   Ed Jerome as Doyle
    Jeanette Nolan as Mrs. Doyle   Kenny Delmar as Salmon
    Agnes Moorehead as Mrs. Thompson   Ray Collins as Thompson
    Bill Pringle as the Innkeeper   Howard Smith as Tarver
    Produced and directed by Homer Fickett.
    Clayton Collyer is the commercial announcer.
    Story: A stirring drama of the pre-Civil War conflicts centering about the person of the fanatical John Brown, fiery abolitionist who took the law into his own hands to start a slave uprising by taking over the United States Armory. It was Brown who Lincoln once labeled as "the wrongest right man who ever lived."

    Trivia: Originally intended for this broadcast date was "The Big Stick," a biography on the life of Theodore Roosevelt, and Ray Collins starring in the lead. The script would later be retitled "Theodore Roosevelt, Man of Action," and broadcast on August 17, 1942 with Edward Arnold in the lead.

EPISODE # 205   **"THE UNDEFENDED BORDER"**   Broadcast on December 18, 1940
    Starring: Raymond Massey as the border voice
    John McIntire as the hunter   William Johnstone as Jean Baptiste
    Jeanette Nolan as Sally Forbes   Ray Collins as Bill Carter
    Karl Swenson as the settler   Bill Pringle as the negro
    Kenny Delmar as Rush   Robbin Cravin as Bagot
    Alfred Shirley as Jack   Sara Fussell as the boy
    Dwight Weist as John Rose   Ian Martin as MacEachern
    Ed Jerome as the official voice (Canadian)   Bill Pringle as the official voice (American)
    Ted Jewett as the Clerk   Brad Barker supplied the animal voices.
    Whispered voices (in order of appearance): Ray Collins, Dwight Weist, and Elliott Reid.
    Canadian voices were Ted Jewett, Karl Swenson, Ian Martin, and Dwight Weist;
    American voices were Elliott Reid, Ray Collins, William Johnstone and Clayton Collyer.
    Written for *Cavalcade* by Stephen Vincent Benet.
    Produced and directed by Homer Fickett.
    Richard Stark is the announcer, Clayton Collyer is the commercial announcer.
    Featuring the Ken Christie choir: The final hymn was sung in two different accents;
    Story: One of the great achievements of men of good will in the Western World is three thousand miles of water and land that separate the United States from the Dominion of Canada. This is the undefended border. It was an astonishing agreement our neighborly nations reached in 1817 whereby total disarmament of U.S. and Canadian fleets on the Great Lakes was accomplished and ended a program of disastrous naval rivalry.

Stephen Vincent Benet: "We wanted for some time to do the story of this long peace. With the idea in mind we called on Raymond Massey, the Canadian actor who made Abraham Lincoln live again for us, and talked with him about it. During a long and pleasant evening, with the fire crackling in the grate, he told many of the historical incidents of the border. It was partially his enthusiasm as a Canadian for the thing we wanted to do that made us resolve to do a *Cavalcade of America* show on it. While we had simply gone to him for aid in shaping our own ideas, it soon became apparent we should lose a great deal if we didn't employ his talent and enthusiasm in the dramatization."

Trivia: In shaping this, Mr. Massey had been of great aid. The final version heard on this broadcast might well be said to be a collaboration by Stephen Vincent Benet and Raymond Massey, with the *Cavalcade of America* furnishing the inspiration. Because of the context, this episode was broadcast by short-wave over three powerful stations which were heard regularly and clearly in South America. Those stations were WRCA and WNBI, operating out of Bound Brook, New Jersey, and Station WPIT operating out of Boston. For many years NBC had been short-waving some of its productions to South America during an hour of English broadcasts. Because this had been regularly established between 10 o'clock and 11 o'clock, this evening's broadcast was recorded and short-waved at 10 p.m., E.S.T.

EPISODE # 206   **"THE GREEN PASTURES"**   Broadcast on December 25, 1940
  Starring: Juano Hernandes as De Lawd   Tom Moseley as Mr. Deshee
  Dick Campbell as Cain the Sixth   Robert Johnson as the first boy
  Valentine Almaida as Myrtle   Orville Phillips as the second boy
  Mercedes Gilbert as the first cook   Juanita Hall as the second cook
  Muriel Rahn as Mammy Angel   Dodo Green as Gabriel
  Carrington Lewis as the choir leader   Richard Huey as the custard maker
  Christola Williams as Lady Angel   James Fuller as Adam
  Edna Thomas as Eve   Viola Dean as Zeba
  John Garth as Joshua   Alanzo Bozan as the gambler
  Gus Simons as Noah   Georgette Harvey as Noah's wife
  Emory Richardson as Isaac   Paul Floyd as Abraham
  Walter Whitfield as Aaron   Frank Wilson as Moses
  Paul Johnson as Corporal   James Fuller as Hezdrel
Muriel Rahn, Ken Renard, John Garth, and Frank Wilson are the unnamed voices.
The children were played by Robert Johnson, Orville Phillips, and Valentine Almaida.
Adapted for *Cavalcade* by Marc Connelly, from his famous 1930 Pulitzer Prize play.
Produced by Homer Fickett and directed by Marc Connelly.
Richard Stark is the announcer and Clayton Collyer is the commercial announcer.
Music effects furnished by the original Hall Johnson Choir; songs featured (in order of their appearance) was "A City Called Heaven," "Hallelujah!" "Turn You Round," "Dere's No Hiding Place," I'm Noways Weary and I'm Noways Tired," "A Blind Man Stood in De Middle of De Road," the 1932 song "Rise and Shine," "Hallelujah, King Jesus," and lastly a reprise of "A City Called Heaven."
Story: This is a simple, dynamic version of the Christian faith that is held by thousands of negroes in the deep South - the majority of whom could not read the Bible itself. They have a vast spiritual hunger - an unceasing urge to find the road to spiritual salvation. They have not (indeed, they could not) burdened themselves with the subtle distinctions of the theologians; they have taken the Old Testament and vaguely retold it in the everyday terms of their own lives. Instead of nectar and ambrosia they picture an unending series of fish frys throughout eternity - as well as "ten-cent seegars" for the adults.

Richard Stark: "It has been ten years since Marc Connelly found inspiration for 'The Green Pastures' in Roark Bradford's book, 'Ol' Man Adam an' His Chillun.' On the stage, and later on the screen, this play and music has brought exaltation and joy to millions of men, women and children, who found in it an expression of the overwhelming faith of the human spirit. We chose it because it is above the temporary madness that engrosses the earth."

Trivia: Marc Connelly wrote this play, using a series of brief southern sketches from Roark Bradford's "Ol' Man Adam an' His Chillun." Connelly co-directed a film version of his stage play in 1936 with William Keighley (who would later host *The Lux Radio Theatre*). It took a lot of guts on the part of the brothers Warner to make this movie in the face of planned boycotts by many southern theater owners. And Du Pont took those same guts for their latest *Cavalcade* presentation. The story featured an account of the Bible, according to Marc (Connelly that is), utilizing an all-black cast. The Hall Johnson Choir, who functioned as sort of a Greek Chorus to the action in the 1936 film, reprised many of the songs for this *Cavalcade* broadcast. It should also be noted that this was, historically, the first radio dramatization of Connelly's prize-winning play.

More trivia: The Hall Johnson Choir ensemble consisted of four children: Yvonne Stevens, Rudy Whittaker, Yvonne Bingley, and Paul Brown; seven men: Al Watts, Homer Tutt, Wardell Saunders, Hubert Brown, Ivan Sharp, Joseph Povton, and Earnest Adderley; and eight women: Alice Ramsay, Alberta Perkins, Elizabeth Burghardt, Susie Sutton, Frances Smith, Musa Williams, Thula Ortiz, and Trixie Smith.*

* There might have been one other woman in the chorus, as the list of singers featured one name erased from the original script. Possibility that one was unable to make the performance, or perhaps a misspelling and correction on the typist's part.

Marc Connelly: " 'The Green Pastures,' was an attempt to present certain aspects of a living religion in terms of its believers. The religion was that of thousands of Negroes in the deep South. With terrific spiritual hunger and the greatest humility these untutored black Christians - many of whom could not even read the book which was the treasure of their faith - have adapted the contents of the Bible to the consistencies of their everyday lives. In tribute to a people's simple act of faith and in the spirit of peace and good will on Christmas night, the *Cavalcade of America* presented 'The Green Pastures'."

EPISODE #207   **"WILL ROGERS"**   Broadcast on January 1, 1941

Starring: Cal Tinney as Will Rogers
John McIntire as Mr. Rogers
Peggy Riley as the first chorus girl
Jeanette Nolan as the second chorus girl
Agnes Moorehead as the fortune teller
William Johnstone as Edward
Karl Swenson as Wiley
Bill Pringle as Zack
William Johnstone as the American
Kenny Delmar as Texas Jack
Ray Collins as the agent
Ted Jewett as the doorman
Alfred Shirley as Equerry
Ted Jewett as the secretary
Elliott Reid as the attendant
Warren Colston as Coolidge
Edwin Jerome as Lederer
Peggy Riley as the girl
Ted Jewett as the Dutchman

Written for *Cavalcade* by Cal Tinney, friend and biographer of Will Rogers.
Produced and directed by Homer Fickett.
Richard Stark is the announcer, Clayton Collyer is the commercial announcer.
Story: Will Rogers was an appealing study in contradictions. He did not pose as an actor, yet he enriched the American stage and screen with some of the most memorable performances of his generation. Nothing he wrote could be exactly defined as literature, yet much of it will remain with time. Part Cherokee Indian, he dissipated the old wives'

notion that in the red man's blood there flows no humor. His ways were winning, his friends legion. A champion of clear, straight thinking in the face of sham and pretense, he has today two shrines. One is the stone and bronze monument standing on a wind-swept hill near his hometown in Claremore, Oklahoma. The other is in the hearts of his fellow men.

EPISODE #208 "MIGHTIER THAN THE SWORD" Broadcast on January 8, 1941
Starring: William Johnstone as Thomas Nast Edwin Jerome as Gillespie
Agnes Moorehead as Mrs. Nast Bill Pringle as Davis
Ted Jewett as the clerk Ed Jerome as the lieutenant
Dwight Weist as Harper Jeanette Nolan as Kate
John McIntire as "Boss" Tweed Howard Smith as Connolly
Ray Collins as Hall Karl Swenson as Sweeney
Elliott Reid as the secretary Alfred Shirley as MacAllister
Elliott Reid as the pressman Ted Jewett as Mike
Kenny Delmar as the captain Bill Pringle as the seaman
Howard Smith as the first mate Karl Swenson as Bos'n
Written for *Cavalcade* by Dr. Frank Monaghan.
Produced and directed by Homer Fickett.
Richard Stark is the announcer and Clayton Collyer is the commercial announcer.
Story: When Thomas Nast took to political satire in his cartoons, his influence was powerful. In the interests of civic honor he fashioned a series of cartoons which exposed the ill-famed "Boss" Tweed ring of political corruption in New York, clapped Tweed behind the bars and pointed the way for similar exposures, wherever needed, throughout the country. This work was regarded as the climax of Thomas Nast's career and his great contribution in behalf of decent government to the America of his times.

Dr. Frank Monaghan: "In the annals of American history the name of Thomas Nast will always be remembered as an example of honor and courage. His tremendous idealism, his belief in an impeccable morality for the community at large and his personal integrity both as a citizen and as one of the foremost cartoonists in American journalism remain as heroic facts to constitute him one of our nation's valued great."

EPISODE # 209 "AS A MAN THINKETH" Broadcast on January 15, 1941
Starring: Claude Rains as Thomas Cooper John McIntire as Rawle
Agnes Moorehead as Alice Cooper Ted Jewett as the bailiff
Alfred Shirley as Dr. Priestley Ray Collins as the foreman
William Johnstone as Thomas Jefferson Bill Pringle as Mason
Karl Swenson as Judge Buyers Ted Jewett as the clerk
Jeanette Nolan as Mrs. Henry Kenny Delmar as Gaoler
Ray Collins as the Aide Ray Collins as Taylor
Ted Jewett as Weaver Edwin Jerome as Chase
Karl Swenson as Miller
Produced and directed by Homer Fickett.
Richard Stark is the announcer and Clayton Collyer is the commercial announcer.
Story: In the struggle to maintain for Americans their right to free opinion as defined in the Constitution, the life of Thomas Cooper stands as a notable example. In the early days of our Republic when our statesman were frequently enmeshed in a tightening web of conflicting idealism and misunderstanding, Thomas Cooper so forcefully expressed his political convictions in a series of pamphlets that he tried for "seditious libel" and the outcome of that trial pointed the way towards the establishment of the permanent, personal guarantee of free expression not only to the Americans of his day, but to the Americans of ours.

EPISODE #210 **"WAIT FOR THE MORNING"** Broadcast on January 22, 1941
　　　　Starring: Anne Sterrett as Emily Dickinson
　　　　Also in the cast: Jeanette Nolan and John McIntire
　　　　Written for *Cavalcade* by Norman Rosten, based on the biography "The Life and
　　　　Mind of Emily Dickinson" by Genevieve Taggard.
　　　　Produced and directed by Homer Fickett.
　　　　Richard Stark is the announcer and Clayton Collyer is the commercial announcer.
　　　　Music composed and conducted by Don Voorhees.
　　　　Story: Practically none of Emily Dickinson's poetry appeared in publication during her
　　　　lifetime. Her fame, as one of America's major poets, began with the publication of
　　　　Poems some years after her death. To the literature of our nation this brooding New
　　　　England recluse had contributed a collection of lyrics that rank with the best of modern
　　　　poetry and have been recognized as a molding force in twentieth-century verse. While
　　　　it is both harsh and tender, her poetic philosophy reveals one of the most original and
　　　　exquisite minds of her generation. An iconoclast, she attacked traditional conception
　　　　enmeshing the poetry of her time.

　　　　Richard Stark: "To portray the role of Emily Dickinson we presented a talented young
　　　　actress from our *Cavalcade* players. Her name was Anne Sterrett and in this, her first
　　　　starring role, we wished her success."

EPISODE #211 **"DR. FRANKLIN TAKES IT EASY"** Broadcast on January 29, 1941
　　　　Starring: John McIntire as Ben Franklin　　Ed Jerome as Lathrop
　　　　Jeanette Nolan as Mrs. Liveright　　　　　Ray Collins as Parker
　　　　William Johnstone as Vail　　　　　　　　Ted Jewett as Cholmondoley
　　　　Karl Swenson as the son　　　　　　　　　Bob Readick as Tommy
　　　　Ronald Liss as Henry　　　　　　　　　　 Sarah Fussell as Deborah
　　　　Larry Robinson as Ben　　　　　　　　　　Agnes Moorehead as Mrs. Allen
　　　　Agnes Moorehead as Mrs. Martyn　　　　　 Gertrude Crippen as Polly
　　　　Written for *Cavalcade* by Erik Barnouw.
　　　　Produced and directed by Homer Fickett.
　　　　Richard Stark is the announcer and Clayton Collyer is the commercial announcer.
　　　　Music composed and conducted by Donald Voorhees.
　　　　Story: Ben Franklin was one of those rare people who are jacks of all trades and masters
　　　　of all. His versatility ranged from "Poor Richard's Almanac" to some of the wittiest
　　　　satire in American letters; from influencing an era in American statesmanship to
　　　　inventing the long pole with flexible "hands" at the end which storekeepers and
　　　　librarians use to reach objects on a high shelf. His brilliant mind immeasurably enriched
　　　　American life. The engaging side of Ben Franklin and his amazing inventive genius
　　　　was coupled with a new concept of the freedom to be won for the human spirit.

EPISODE #212 **"HENRY CLAY OF KENTUCKY"** Broadcast on February 5, 1941
　　　　Starring: Ray Collins as Henry Clay　　　Ed Jerome as Johnson
　　　　William Johnstone as Cass　　　　　　　 Karl Swenson as Calhoun
　　　　Juano Hernandez as Tom　　　　　　　　　 Ian MacAllister as Peabody
　　　　Ted Jewett as Chase　　　　　　　　　　　Bill Pringle as Seward
　　　　John McIntire as Webster　　　　　　　　 Anne Sterrett as Mrs. Webster
　　　　Edwin Jerome as Fillmore　　　　　　　　 Elliott Reid as the conductor
　　　　Jeanette Nolan as Martha　　　　　　　　 Elliott Reid as Mason
　　　　Agnes Moorehead as Lucretia　　　　　　　Brad Barker supplied the animal voices.
　　　　Written for *Cavalcade* by Garrett Porter.
　　　　Produced and directed by Homer Fickett.
　　　　Richard Stark is the announcer and Clayton Collyer is the commercial announcer.
　　　　Music composed and conducted by Donald Voorhees.

Story: He was known as "Prince Hal," "Harry of the West" and "The Old Coon." He was one of the immortal triumvirate of statesmen who dominated American foreign and domestic policy and the affairs of a rapidly expanding nation from the close of the War of 1812 until the beginning of the Civil War. This trio, although not one of them ever achieved the Presidency, labored all their lives to secure in the minds of our people the greatness of our country and to warn Americans of the futility and disaster of national disunion. They were Henry Clay, Daniel Webster and John C. Calhoun. This episode tells the story of Henry Clay's return from retirement to national politics as an old man. His last great effort - the compromise of 1850 - preserved our Union from a threat of disruption.

Trivia: The original title of this drama was "The Compromisers."

EPISODE #213   **"ABRAHAM LINCOLN: THE WAR YEARS"**   Broadcast February 12, 1941
Starring: Raymond Massey as Lincoln
Dick Van Patten as the little boy
Agnes Moorehead as Mary Lincoln
William Johnstone as Pinkerton
Ian MacAllaster as Jed
Leslie Sweeney as Jack
Jeanette Nolan as Ma
Marjorie Harf as the woman
Dick Van Patten as Tad
Kingsley Colton as Willie
George May as Chase
John Styles as Asa Trenchard
Jeanette Nolan as Mrs. Mountchessington
Andy Shaw as the first soldier
Elliott Reid as the first listener
John Styles as the third member
E. Keeling as the second member
Ted Jewett as the doctor
Andy Shaw as Welles
Hood Worthington as Cameron
Ted Jewett as the conductor
Karl Swenson as the voice
Ray Collins as Judd
John Styles as the servant
Elliott Reid as Pete
Frank Milano as Pa
Bob Roberts as the man
Ray Collins as the farmer
Elliott Reid as Robert
Rob Roberts as Seward
Karl Swenson as John W. Booth
Marjorie Harf as Augusta
Ted Jewett as the second soldier
Ian MacAllaster as the second listener
Ray Collins as the Army officer
Leslie Sweeney as the first member
William Johnstone as the chairman
Frank Milano as Bates
John Sacks as Blair

Adapted for *Cavalcade* by Robert E. Sherwood, from the 1940 novel of the same named by Carl Sandburg.
Produced and directed by Homer Fickett.
Richard Stark is the announcer and Clayton Collyer is the commercial announcer.
Music composed and conducted by Donald Voorhees.
Story: same as episode #174, broadcast on February 13, 1940

Trivia: This broadcast originated from "The Playhouse" in Wilmington, Delaware, home of the Du Pont Company. The supporting cast was, in addition to the *Cavalcade* players, eight members of the Little Theater Group of Wilmington, Delaware, local talents from within city limits. In honor of Lincoln's birthday, and in response to many letters from listeners, this encore presentation starred Raymond Massey, reprising last year's performance. "Abraham Lincoln: The War Years," written by Carl Sandburg - from which this drama was based - won the Pulitzer Prize in American History in 1940.

More trivia: In the roles of Tad and the little boy was a young radio actor named Dick Van Patten.

EPISODE #214 **"PLAIN MR. PRESIDENT"** Broadcast on February 19, 1941
Starring: John McIntire as WashingtonBill Pringle as the first voice
Ted Jewett as the second voiceEd Jerome as the third voice
Elliott Reid as the forth voiceKarl Swenson as Dr. Franklin
Agnes Moorehead as Mrs. MorrisTed Jewett as Mr. Morris
William Johnstone as HamiltonPaul Johnson as the servant
Juano Hernandez as SamRay Collins as Thomson
George Coulouris as HumphriesElliott Reid as the captain
Jeanette Nolan as MarthaPaul Johnson as Sam
Ted Jewett as the New EnglanderEd Jerome as the Marylander
Bill Pringle as the New YorkerTed Jewett as the Chancellor
Brad Barker supplied the animal voices.
Written for *Cavalcade* by Dwight Irving Cooke.
Produced and directed by Homer Fickett.
Richard Stark is the announcer and Clayton Collyer is the commercial announcer.
Music composed and conducted by Donald Voorhees.
Story: On April the sixteenth in the year 1789, a Virginia gentleman stepped into a coach and began the eight-day journey from Mount Vernon to New York. He was a tired gentleman, this traveler. He had served his country hard and truly, through pain and strife, through hunger and deprivations for eight terrible years. He had won, God knows, the right to peaceful, untroubled later life. But now in the peace-time spring of 1789 America needed him again. And so, George Washington was riding by coach - away from the box hedges of Mount Vernon, away from his private life. He was riding to save in peace the principles of government he had won in war.

Trivia: The original title of this script was "The Faith of George Washington."

EPISODE #215 **"EDGAR ALLAN POE"** Broadcast on February 26, 1941
Starring: Karl Swenson as Edgar Allan PoeCharita Bauer as Anna
William Johnstone as GrahamTed Jewett as Lee
Agnes Moorehead as Mrs. JonesKenny Delmar as Vern
Jeanette Nolan as Mrs. SmithEd Jerome as Latrob
John McIntire as BardRay Collins as Brown
Brad Barker supplied the animal voices.
Written for *Cavalcade* by Norman Rosten.
Produced and directed by Homer Fickett.
Richard Stark is the announcer and Clayton Collyer is the commercial announcer.
Music composed and conducted by Donald Voorhees.
Story: While our scientists, pioneers and statesmen were building a great and powerful nation in the material sense, America was not without that inner, intangible spirit that characterized the growth of our country in the world of literature. Literature may be said to be a people speaking their inmost thoughts in forms of acceptable cultural standards. America has been so interpreted by its great and acclaimed men and women of letters throughout the generations and one of her earliest and most profound voices belonged to a man whose life was shattered by disillusion and sorrow and tragedy, Edgar Allan Poe.

EPISODE #216 "VOICE IN THE WILDERNESS" Broadcast on March 5, 1941
  Starring: Henry Hull as William Penn   Elliott Reid as the Sentry
  Jeanette Nolan as Guli   John McIntire as the Recorder
  Alfred Shirley as Lord Mayor   Ian Martin as the foreman
  Karl Swenson as James   Kenny Delmar as Gaoler
  William Johnstone as Mead   Agnes Moorehead as Nell
  Ray Collins as Pepys   Ed Jerome as the Admiral
  George Couloris as Charles   Elliott Reid as Lackey
  Written for *Cavalcade* by Garrett Porter.
  Produced and directed by Homer Fickett.
  Richard Stark is the announcer; Clayton Collyer is the commercial announcer.
  Music composed and conducted by Donald Voorhees.
  Story: William Penn's "Holy Experiment" was a determined effort on the part of a group of people, calling themselves "Friends," to establish a colony of brotherly love in the New World. Under his gentle guidance and with his charitable appreciation of the problems of settlement in a virgin wilderness in whose silent, strange forests lurked Indian savages who might well have become hostile had not sympathy and understanding won them over to the colonists' side, the colonization of Pennsylvania was sensibly and prosperously achieved.

  Trivia: The original title of this script was "William Penn," later changed by the time the final draft of the script was written.

EPISODE #217 "BLACK RUST"   Broadcast on March 12, 1941
  Starring: William Johnstone as Mark Carleton   Ed Jerome as Petrov
  Stephen Schnabel as the lieutenant   Kenny Delmar as the peasant
  Agnes Moorehead as Ma Carleton   Elliott Reid as Jim
  Ray Collins as Pa Carleton   John McIntire as the secretary
  Ted Jewett as Jameson   Karl Swenson as Ole
  Ray Collins as the first miller   Ed Jerome as the second miller
  Ted Jewett as the third miller   Ted Jewett as the Aide
  Kenny Delmar as Mr. Swenson   Howard Smith as Burke
  Anne Sterrett as Mrs. Swenson   Stephen Schnabel as Pulaski
  Jeanette Nolan as Amanda
  Written for *Cavalcade* by Robert Tallman.
  Produced and directed by Homer Fickett.
  Richard Stark is the announcer and Clayton Collyer is the commercial announcer.
  Music composed and conducted by Donald Voorhees.
  Story: It started in the leaf of the young wheat, then attacked the stem. With frost the plant drooped and when the warm spring winds swept the prairies it snapped off dry and rotten at the soil line. Mark Carleton walked across the prairies, experimented, worked with the farmers. He learned about the marvelous wheat seeds used in the Russian Kubanka district. He went to Russia and brought back the conviction that if this wheat could be grown in America the plague of "Black Stem Rust" would be averted. This was an overwhelming problem and how it was solved by scientific accomplishment was a touch of genius by Mark Carleton.

EPISODE #218 "I SING A NEW WORLD"   Broadcast on March 19, 1941
  Starring: John McIntire as Walt Whitman   Karl Swenson as McAllister
  William Johnstone as the first Barker   Kenny Delmar as the man
  Pauline Preller as Madeleine   Elliott Reid as the second child
  William Johnstone as the first child   Ed Jerome as the bartender
  Jeanette Nolan as the lady Barker   Elliott Reid as Jimmy
  Ted Jewett as the second Barker   Jeanette Nolan as the girl

Agnes Moorehead as Mrs. Brown Howard Smith as Bill
Stephen Schnabel as Joe Peggy Riley as Sue
Kenny Delmar as the loudspeaker voice Ed Jerome as the third Barker
Written for *Cavalcade* by Robert Tallman.
Produced and directed by Homer Fickett.
Richard Stark is the announcer and Clayton Collyer is the commercial announcer.
Music score composed and conducted by Don Voorhees.
The 1854 song "I Dream of Jeanie With the Light Brown Hair" was performed.
Story: Towards the middle of the last century American literature was suddenly infused with a startling but heroic force of vitality that freshened its impact of power in the world of letters and endowed it with those qualities of grandeur and permanence it still retains today. The man who gave the literature of our century, this new force which struck strangely and compellingly into the poetry of Americans, and touched it with fire was Walt Whitman. For Walt Whitman sang of a New World. He put into immortal language the great and wonderful dreams that burn in the hearts of Americans, a poet of the people.

EPISODE #219 **"DOWN TO THE SEA"** Broadcast on March 26, 1941
Starring: William Johnstone as Herman Melville
Agnes Moorehead as Mrs. Shaw Karl Swenson as Portugee
Bill Pringle as Old Salt Peggy Riley as Fayaway
Ray Collins as Harper Ted Jewett as Russell
Peggy Riley as Ellen Kenny Delmar as the lookout
Ed Jerome as the first mate Alfred Shirley as Toby
Jeanette Nolan as Elizabeth John McIntire as Capt. Pease
Written for *Cavalcade* by Robert Tallman.
Produced and directed by Homer Fickett.
Richard Stark is the announcer and Clayton Collyer is the commercial announcer.
Music composed and conducted by Donald Voorhees.
Story: As the clarion accents of Walt Whitman's verse exalted the style and theme of American poetry, it was the stunning prose of Herman Melville that burst upon the literary currents of this nation and invigorated the stream of our literature not only for his, but ensuing generations. His masterpiece is known to readers in every land, "Moby Dick," a novel of the sea and the pursuit of a white whale that towers among civilization's imperishable legacies of art, of thought and of humanity. His relentless quest carried him from the 19th century New England of Transcendentalism and decadence to tremulous and exciting life in the islands of the south seas resulted in his creation of "Moby Dick," a triumph in American literature.

EPISODE #220 **"EDWIN BOOTH"** Broadcast on March 31, 1941
Starring: Paul Muni as Edwin Booth Elliott Reid as Wallace
William Johnstone as Riley Elliott Reid as Martin
Jeanette Nolan as the woman Bill Pringle as Patrick
John McIntire as Rivers Ted Jewett as Shields
William Johnstone as Taylor Ray Collins as Stanley
Karl Swenson as John Wilkes Ted Jewett as the voice
Anne Sterrett as Mary Jeanette Nolan as Laura
Agnes Moorehead as Elizabeth Ed Jerome as Scott
Kenny Delmar as Jones John McIntire as Junius
Alfred Shirley as Garries
Written for *Cavalcade* by Norman Rosten.
Produced and directed by Homer Fickett.
Richard Stark is the announcer and Clayton Collyer is the commercial announcer.
Music composed and conducted by Donald Voorhees.

Story: In the American theatre Edwin Booth fulfilled the Shakespearean admonitory analysis of an actor's art to the degree of transcendent immortality. His star has never set. His "Hamlet" still remains the ideal. Generations of other Hamlets have enriched our drama but Edwin Booth's retains that perfection untouchable by time or comparison while his other heroic roles are established traditions in the American theatre. Despite the horror of an infamous deed done by his brother John Wilkes Booth, the glory of Edwin is an eloquent legacy of honor and beauty to the nation.

EPISODE #221   **"ODE TO A NIGHTINGALE"**   Broadcast on April 7, 1941
   Starring: Agnes Moorehead as Frances   John McIntire as Audubon
   Peggy Riley as Fanny   Kenneth Delmar as Charles
   Kingsley Colton as John (boy)   Ted Jewett as Mathew
   Ken Delmar as Joshua   Jeanette Nolan as Georgiana
   William Johnstone as George   Elliott Reid as Tom
   Karl Swenson as John
   Written for *Cavalcade* by Maxwell Anderson.
   Produced and directed by Homer Fickett.
   Richard Stark is the announcer and Clayton Collyer is the commercial announcer.
   Music composed and conducted by Donald Voorhees.
   Story: Based on an authentic historical episode in the life of England's immortal poet. It is a little known fact that John Keats desired, at one time, to come to America to live but being unable to do so sent his brother in his place. As a symbol of concern, the mutual interests and the dual nature which marked the progress of the British and American people in the history of civilization.

   Trivia: Maxwell Anderson's original title of this script was "John Keats and America."

EPISODE #222   **"A PASSAGE TO GEORGIA"**   Broadcast on April 14, 1941
   Starring: Alfred Shirley as Gen. Oglethorpe   Anne Sterrett as the servant
   William Johnstone as the member   Ian Martin as George II
   Kenny Delmar as Stephens   Elliott Reid as Morrison
   William Johnstone as Flynt   Ian MacAllister as Johann
   Ian Martin as the servant   Ed Jerome as Adams
   Kenny Delmar as the speaker   Ed Jerome as Turnkey
   John McIntire as the warden   Elliott Reid as Delaney
   Ian MacAllister as the guard   Karl Swenson as Robert Castell
   Jeanette Nolan as Anne Castell   Agnes Moorehead as Eleanor
   Written for *Cavalcade* by Garrett Porter.
   Produced and directed by Homer Fickett.
   Ted Jewett is the announcer and Clayton Collyer is the commercial announcer.
   Music composed and conducted by Donald Voorhees.
   Story: After leaving Oxford, James Oglethorpe was a member of the House of Commons for more than a quarter of a century. He advocated legislative measures for the relief of debtor classes then prevalent in England, and it was this humane urge in his nature that led to his founding the Colony of Georgia. There his successful founding of Savannah, his alliance with the Indians, his safeguarding the colony against Spanish conquest and colonization secured Georgia and endowed it with the strength of purpose and character that led it, with twelve other colonies, to declare independence of the British Crown in 1776.

EPISODE #223 **"HENRY BERGH, FOUNDER OF THE A.S.P.C.A."** Aired April 21, 1941

    Starring: Stephen Schnabel as Sergei   Ted Jewett as the judge
    William Johnstone as Bonard   Kenny Delmar as Gerry
    Jeanette Nolan as the nurse   John McIntire as the lawyer
    Agnes Moorehead as Wheeler   Elliott Reid as the clerk
    Ian MacAllister as Hoffman   Ed Jerome as the driver
    John McIntire as Moujik   Karl Swenson as Berg
    Ted Jewett as the speaker   Elliott Reid as the helper

Narrated by Albert Payson Terhune, Brad Barker supplied the animal sounds.
Written for *Cavalcade* by Albert Payson Terhune.
Produced and directed by Homer Fickett.
Richard Stark is the announcer and Clayton Collyer is the commercial announcer.
Story: Moved by a spirit of noblest human charity, Henry Bergh is universally honored as the founder of the American Society for the Prevention of Cruelty to Animals. His original petition to the Legislature of the State of New York for the Society's charter included the names of some of the most wildest influential men of his time: Horace Greeley, George Bancroft, Peter Cooper and John Jacob Astor. It was in 1866 that his efforts were rewarded and the ASPCA under his presidency took its place among the varied and valuable institutions of American humanitarianism.

EPISODE #224 **"THE HEART AND THE FOUNTAIN"** Broadcast on April 28, 1941

    Starring: Madeleine Carroll as Margaret Fuller
    Jeanette Nolan as Matron   Peggy Riley as Molly
    Agnes Moorehead as Belle   Ed Jerome as Fairchild
    Bill Pringle as Dodgson   Kenny Delmar as McElrath
    Alfred Shirley as Carlyle   Ed Jerome as Monsignor
    Agnes Moorehead as Mrs. Carlyle   Elliott Reid as Orderly
    Stephen Schnabel as Mazzini   Karl Swenson as Ossoli
    John McIntire as the voice   Elliott Reid as Anderson
    Ted Jewett as Wilkins   John McIntire as Greeley
    Kenny Delmar as Thoreau   Ed Jerome as Ripley
    Ray Collins as Alcott   Ted Jewett as Hawthorne
    William Johnstone as Emerson   Bill Pringle as the doctor

Written for *Cavalcade* by Margaret Riley.
Produced and directed by Homer Fickett.
Richard Stark is the announcer and Clayton Collyer is the commercial announcer.
Music composed and conducted by Donald Voorhees.
Story: Margaret Fuller was a New Englander. She was the intellectual associate of the titanic leaders of American thought who radiated their molding opinion from 19th Century Boston. Emerson, Hawthorne, Lowell and Alcott welcomed her to their group. Horace Greeley, the great editor of the *New York Tribune*, recognizing in this woman a powerful talent, brought her to New York where her literary column paralleled Edgar Allan Poe's in absorbing, critical intensity. Following this period Greeley sent her to Europe as America's first woman foreign correspondent and her work in London and Italy as well as romance with an Italian nobleman brought Margaret Fuller to the heights of world recognition.

EPISODE #225   "THE TRIALS AND TRIUMPHS OF HORATIO ALGER"   May 5, 1941

Starring: Kenny Delmar as Horatio Alger
Kingsley Colton as Sonny
Sara Fussell as Wing
Agnes Moorehead as Mrs. Saunders
William Johnstone as Smith
Jeanette Nolan as Mrs. Matson
William Johnstone as O'Connor
Pauline Preller as Mrs. Stires
Pauline Preller as Mrs. Alger
Ray Collins as the story teller
Ronald Liss as Teddy
Jeanette Nolan as the nurse
Karl Swenson as Hugo
Jack Grimes as Mike
Ed Jerome as Rev. Smith
Ted Jewett as Loren
Peggy Riley as Patience
Kingsley Colton as Jim
Sara Fussell as Alger (age seven)
Jeanette Nolan as the Governess
John McIntire as Alger, Sr.
Jack Grimes as Jot
Agnes Moorehead as the nurse

Written for *Cavalcade* by Robert Tallman, based on material from "Horatio Alger, A Biography Without a Hero," by Herbert L. Mayes, originally published in 1928 by Macy-Masius, Inc.
Produced and directed by Homer Fickett.
Richard Stark is the announcer and Clayton Collyer is the commercial announcer.
Music composed and conducted by Donald Voorhees.
Story: Portrait of a writer, having little success artistically, nevertheless chronicled in a simple fashion books which revealed the process of a typically American characteristic in action - the will to success. If all the writings, all those novels of Horatio Alger were examined and a single moral extracted it would be that the indomitable will of an American is inherently capable of asserting itself against any odds, no matter how overwhelming. For Horatio Alger was telling the old American story, portraying the freedom of the individual in American society, proving the opportunities of democracy and instilling into the minds of millions of young readers - perhaps not too well, but certainly and inescapably - a sense of justice and equality.

EPISODE #226   "THEODOSIA BURR"   Broadcast on May 12, 1941

Starring: Anne Sterrett as Theodosia Burr
Alfred Shirley as Mr. Blennerhasset
Agnes Moorehead as Mrs. Blennerhasset
Ray Collins as the Foreman
Ed Jerome as Swartout
Elliott Reid as Pompey
William Johnstone as Hamilton
John McIntire as Jenkins
Elliott Reid as Cupid
Larry Robinson as Little Burr
Ted Jewett as the Marshall
Kenny Delmar as Alston
Gertrude Crippen as Mamselle
Karl Swenson as Aaron Burr

Written for *Cavalcade* of Robert Tallman.
Produced and directed by Homer Fickett.
Richard Stark is the announcer and Clayton Collyer is the commercial announcer.
Music composed and conducted by Donald Voorhees.
Story: Had Aaron Burr paid close counsel to his brilliant daughter, Theodosia, he might have become one of our Nation's greatest leaders. Educated in an atmosphere of patriotism and political idealism she had sat at the feet of a young Republic's statesmen planning the individual happiness and collective freedom for millions of Americans. But despite the fact of Theodosia's interest and valuable viewpoint Aaron Burr was an individual who thought and took no counsel other than his own. When, after her father's tragic duel with Alexander Hamilton and his ill-starred plan to create an empire in the southwest, when a nation turned against Aaron Burr, Theodosia stood by her father through hours of chaotic despair and by her efforts sought to account before history, for the lamentable mistakes of an American patriot strangely misguided by the current of his peculiar erratic genius.

EPISODE #227 "**DAVID CROCKETT**" Broadcast on May 19, 1941
    Starring: John McIntire as David Crockett Ray Collins as Bowie
    William Johnstone as the gunner   Ted Jewett as the messenger
    Bill Pringle as Travis   Elliott Reid as the first soldier
    William Johnstone as the second soldier   Ed Jerome as Paul Bunyan
    William Johnstone as man two   Elliott Reid as man one
    Elliott Reid as Lem   Ed Jerome as Arnold
    Ray Collins as Alexander   Kenny Delmar as the constable
    Agnes Moorehead as Sarah   Agnes Moorehead as Mrs. F.
    Ed Jerome as Finley   Karl Swenson as Daniel
    Peggy Riley as Polly   Larry Robinson as D. Crockett (as a boy)
    Bill Pringle as Pop   Kingsley Colton as Huck
    Juano Hernandez as John Henry
    Written for *Cavalcade* by Peter Lyon.
    Produced and directed by Homer Fickett.
    Richard Stark is the announcer and Clayton Collyer is the commercial announcer.
    Music composed and conducted by Donald Voorhees.
    Story: In order to gain admittance to the "Cloud Reserved for American Legends," Crockett tells his life story to other legends in Heaven. But Davy Crockett was more than a frontiersman. He served in the congress of the United States and aided in the establishment of our nation's laws. He was a humanitarian and a patriot of liberty and joined the Texans in proof of his devotion to the cause of freedom from tyranny. But above all Davy Crockett is one man whose deeds memorialize him in the legendary lore of our people. A short picturesque frontiersman who fought and died as the Alamo fell before the advancing columns of a Mexican Army under Santa Anna. The war which established the Texas Republic and gave the immortal cry, "Remember the Alamo" to the storied slogans of the unfolding history of America.

EPISODE #228 "**JOHNS HOPKINS**" Broadcast on May 26, 1941
    Starring: Karl Swenson as Johns Hopkins Kenny Delmar as Thomas
    William Johnstone as the lawyer   Ted Jewett as the town crier
    Pauline Preller as Hannah   Elliott Reid as Harold
    Charita Bauer as Mary   Kenny Delmar as George
    Ray Collins as Samuel   John McIntire as Gerard
    Ray Collins as Brown   Elliott Reid as Griffin
    William Johnstone as Arnold   Ted Jewett as Dulcy
    Agnes Moorehead as Elizabeth   Ed Jerome as the chairman
    Written for *Cavalcade* by Norman Rosten.
    Produced and directed by Homer Fickett.
    Richard Stark is the announcer and Clayton Collyer is the commercial announcer.
    Music composed and conducted by Donald Voorhees.
    Story: Johns Hopkins was a Quaker who was determined to amass a fortune. Little education was his, but through pluck and resourcefulness, he rose to become a leader of his times. He helped to build the Baltimore and Ohio Railroad and it was during an epidemic in Baltimore when the city's meager facilities were unable to cope with the ravages of disease that he discovered his great idea. It was an idea that brought health and happiness to his fellow citizens and aided in the development of scientific progress in America. His idea, today, is realized in one of our nation's famous and most distinguished medical centers, Johns Hopkins University in Baltimore, Maryland.

EPISODE #229   "THE WOMAN IN LINCOLN'S CABINET"   Broadcast on June 2, 1941
and "ANNA ELLA CARROLL: THE WOMAN IN LINCOLN'S CABINET"
Starring: Agnes Moorehead as Anna Ella Carroll
Kenny Delmar as the voice of conscience   Elliott Reid as the Sentry
Karl Swenson as Stanton   Ted Jewett as Scott
Ed Jerome as Abe Lincoln   Elliott Reid as the Aide
William Johnstone as Evans   Ray Collins as Johnstone
Bill Pringle as Halleck   John McIntire as Grant
John McIntire as Bower   Karl Swenson as the sergeant
Anne Sterrett as Mrs. Kelly   Elliott Reid as the hotel clerk
William Johnstone as Laughlin   Ray Collins as Bragg
Kenny Delmar as the story teller   Ted Jewett as the clerk
Bill Pringle as the speaker   Karl Swenson as the attendant
Based on material from the 1940 book "My Dear Lady" by Marjorie Barstow Greenbie, and adapted for *Cavalcade* by Robert Tallman.
Produced and directed by Homer Fickett.
Richard Stark is the announcer and Clayton Collyer is the commercial announcer.
Music composed and conducted by Donald Voorhees.
Story: It was during the Civil War that affairs of State called her to her unusual historical role. For it was during those thunderous years that President Lincoln sought her advice, so frequently and with such reliance upon her judgment that she became known as "the unofficial woman in Lincoln's Cabinet." Lincoln addressed her in the Presidential letters as "My Dear Lady." It was finally through her insistence that General U.S. Grant was appointed commander of the Northern Armies and the conflict thereby quickly ended. Her devotion to the cause of Union and Liberty is one of the most charming and powerful chapters in American history.

Trivia: There are two official script titles for this broadcast, both of which are listed above.

EPISODE #230   "YOUNG ANDREW JACKSON"   Broadcast on June 9, 1941
Starring: John McIntire as Andrew Jackson
Agnes Moorehead as Rachel   William Johnstone as Adam
Bill Pringle as Donelson   Ted Jewett as the speaker
Ed Jerome as Sevier   Kenny Delmar as the sheriff
Juano Hernandez as Black Wolf   Ed Jerome as the foreman
Karl Swenson as Smoot   Howard Smith as Blythe
William Johnstone as Tom   Ed Jerome as Silas
Ted Jewett as Jake   Ray Collins as Sorel
Karl Swenson as Sam Bowers   Kenny Delmar as Wibbles
Written for *Cavalcade* by Erik Barnouw and Robert Tallman.
Produced and directed by Homer Fickett.
Richard Stark is the announcer and Clayton Collyer is the commercial announcer.
Music composed and conducted by Donald Voorhees.
Story: One of the early rumblings of Secession in the United States was heard in South Carolina during the administration of Andrew Jackson. But the powerful voice of "Old Hickory" stilled the incipient tumult with the words, "The Union; it must and shall be preserved." Forthright, fiery, vigorous in mind and body was this dynamic President. Hero of Indian wars, the Battle of New Orleans and a waxing hot political career, Andrew Jackson was a mighty force in shaping the destiny of our Republic.

EPISODE #231 "ANNIE OAKLEY" Broadcast on June 16, 1941
Starring: Agnes Moorehead as Annie Oakley
Frank Readick as the American voice
William Johnstone as Wilhelm
Ed Jerome as Aide
Karl Swenson as Spieler
William Johnstone as the attendant
John McIntire as the Ringmaster
Agnes Young as Mrs. Shaw
Kenny Delmar as Biddle
Brad Barker supplied the animal voices
Ted Jewett as the Englishman
Ted Jewett as the Courtier
Agnes Young as Victoria
Kenny Delmar as the conductor
Elliott Reid as the stage manager
John McIntire as the doctor
Ray Collins as Frank
Karl Swenson as the referee
Elliott Reid as Elmer
Frank Readick as Mr. Shaw
Written for *Cavalcade* by Robert L. Richards.
Produced and directed by Homer Fickett.
Richard Stark is the announcer and Clayton Collyer is the commercial announcer.
Music composed and conducted by Donald Voorhees.
Story: One of America's best loved characters was Annie Oakley. She was acclaimed as the greatest woman marksman who ever drew a bead. It made no difference whether the target was large of small, stationary or movable, when Annie took aim there was no doubt that they'd have to replace the target. For in her travels throughout the world thousands of people came to see the crack marksmanship of Annie Oakley and were conquered by her simple, unaffected charm. From Queen Victoria to the humblest spectator high in the galleries, everyone rejoiced at her astonishing skill and through those years America grew to be proud of one of its most capable and winning daughters.

EPISODE #232 "JOEL CHANDLER HARRIS" Broadcast on June 23, 1941
Starring: Karl Swenson as Joel C. Harris
Agnes Moorehead as the second voice
Ed Jerome as Twain
Agnes Moorehead as Essy
Ray Collins as Howell
Juano Hernandez as Uncle Terrel
Junius Mathews as the brer rabbit
John McIntire as the narrator
Ray Collins as Roosevelt
Agnes Young as the first voice
Agnes Young as Mrs. Starke
Kenny Delmar as Mark
Ted Jewett as Sis Cow
Frank Readick as brer fox
Kenny Delmar as the librarian
Agnes Moorehead as the woman
Written for *Cavalcade* by Arthur Miller.
Produced and directed by Homer Fickett.
Richard Stark is the announcer and Clayton Collyer is the commercial announcer.
Music composed and conducted by Donald Voorhees.
Story: Sober, wise and judicious were the stately editorial columns of the Atlanta Constitution during the editorship of its famous and esteemed journalist, Joel Chandler Harris. Nevertheless, Joe Harris was not solely concerned with radiating forceful editorial opinion in one of our nation's great and distinguished newspapers. From the hills and backwoods of America's southland he gathered experiences and material from the dreams and lives of humble folk and translated their meaning and spirit into a rich American legacy, the stories beloved through generations in the name of "Uncle Remus."

EPISODE #233 "JEAN PIERRE BLANCHARD" Broadcast on June 30, 1941
Starring: Edwin Jerome as M. Blanchard
Larry Robinson as Everard, Jr.
Howard Smith as Mr. Griffith
Frank Readick as Mr. Bolton
Ray Collins as Dr. Rush
John McIntire as Trenton
Kenny Delmar as Taggard
Ted Jewett as Chester
Howard Smith as the driver
Agnes Young as Mrs. Griffith
Agnes Moorehead as Mrs. Bolton
Ted Jewett as the Aide
Frank Readick as Camden
Karl Swenson as Francois
Karl Swenson as Lancaster
Agnes Moorehead as Lady

Karl Swenson as Ternant
John McIntire as Washington
Kenny Delmar as Cist
Ray Collins as the Magistrate
Bill Pringle as Greene
Brad Barker supplied the animal voices
Written for *Cavalcade* by Garrett Porter.
Produced and directed by Homer Fickett.
Richard Stark is the announcer and Clayton Collyer is the commercial announcer.
Music composed and conducted by Donald Voorhees.
Story: The inventive genius that we like to think of as part of the American character has played a great part in the development of modern flight. The Wright Brothers are internationally famous. But more than a century before the Wrights' epic-making experiments, American entry into the air got off to an auspicious start in the balloon flight of Jean Pierre Blanchard. Ben Franklin had invited Blanchard, who had made the first balloon voyage across the English channel with a Doctor Jeffries of Boston in 1785, to "try America's air currents." Franklin promised Blanchard "an atmosphere favorable if not ideal for ballooning," as reckoned by the tug of a kite string. Blanchard's flight, made possible by the encouragement and support of Washington, Franklin and other American statesman, took place in 1796. In the enthusiasm of the great crowd of Americans who gathered from far and near to see Blanchard soar in his aeronaut up over Philadelphia across the Delaware River and land all of fifteen miles away, we may see the beginning of the great interest in aviation which today has made the skies of America a network of commerce.

EPISODE #234 "THE MYSTERY OF THE SPOTTED DEATH" Broadcast on July 7, 1941
Starring: John McIntire as the story teller
Bill Pringle as McClintic
Kenny Delmar as Roger
Ray Collins as Spencer
Edwin Jerome as the assistant
Frank Readick as Bill
Kenny Delmar as the janitor
Ted Jewett as Paul
Karl Swenson as Ricketts
Frank Readick as the man
Agnes Moorehead as the woman
Bill Pringle as the pioneer
Juano Hernandez as the Indian
Based on material from the book "Men Against Death" by Paul de Kruif, originally published in 1932 by Harcourt, Brace & Company, inc., and adapted for *Cavalcade* by Erik Barnouw.
Produced and directed by Homer Fickett.
Richard Stark is the announcer and Clayton Collyer is the commercial announcer.
Music composed and conducted by Donald Voorhees.
Story: In the spring of 1906 a young doctor from Chicago, Howard Ricketts, came to the Rockies on a hunting trip. He stayed to hunt far bigger game - the carrier of the virus responsible for spotted fever. Experiments with guinea pigs proved the criminal to be the wood tick, and Dr. Ricketts studied its life cycle until he could explain just why the spotted fever appeared only in the spring, being carried over from year to year by ticks living on the animals of the wooded hillsides. Impressed with the similarity between this disease and typhus fever, Dr. Ricketts went to Mexico to gather further data and while there encountered typhus and died, a martyr to science.

Trivia: The title of this episode was originally "The Mystery of the Rocky Mountain Spotted Fever," but was changed the week before broadcast.

EPISODE #235 "ANNE HUTCHINSON" Broadcast on July 14, 1941
Starring: Agnes Moorehead as Anne Hutchinson
Karl Swenson as Vane
William Johnstone as the Chief Elder
Ted Jewett as the town crier
Ray Collins as Coggeshall
Ted Jewett as Smithers
Kenny Delmar as Weems
Karl Swenson as one of the mob
Ed Jerome as one of the mob
Frank Readick as Smith

Pauline Preller as Charity
Pauline Preller as Mistress Haynes
Joan Tetzel as Jane
Agnes Young as Mistress Coddington
Kenny Delmar as Wheelwright
John McIntire as Winthrop

Agnes Young as Prudence
Peggy Riley as Priscilla
Bill Pringle as Peters
Larry Robinson as Edward
Ed Jerome as Cotton

Written for *Cavalcade* by Robert Tallman.
Produced and directed by Homer Fickett.
Richard Stark is the announcer and Clayton Collyer is the commercial announcer.
Music composed and conducted by Donald Voorhees.
Story: Because of her gentle kindness and immense intellectual power and because she underwent the trials and hardships of an outrageous misunderstanding in colonial America, Anne Hutchinson is remembered as one of our great pioneer heroines and leaders of the cause of free worship and rightfully deserves honor and recognition as one of the most brilliant and visionary women in our history. Extremely popular at first in the Colony, she provoked the stigma of heresy when during informal talks at her house she expressed the opinion that grace was more important to salvation than doing good works. The colonists turned against Anne Hutchinson for her expression of an inmost belief and the General Court sentenced her to banishment from Massachusetts. For the rest of her life she wandered in the American wilderness...

MR. LAMMOT DU PONT
PRESIDENT OF THE DU PONT COMPANY
AND
DR. C. M. A. STINE
VICE-PRESIDENT

will speak on the CAVALCADE OF AMERICA radio program Wednesday evening, October 13, on the occasion of the opening of the Du Pont exhibit, Better Things for Better Living... through Chemistry, at the Franklin Institute, Philadelphia.

The CAVALCADE OF AMERICA, recently voted "most worth-while family program" in a nation-wide poll conducted by the Women's National Radio Committee for the American Legion Auxiliary, has resumed its regular dramatizations, the story of William Penn being the subject of the October 13 broadcast. You are invited to tune in on this and future programs each Wednesday at 8 p.m. E.S.T. (9 p.m. P.S.T.; 10 p.m. M.S.T.) over a coast-to-coast Columbia Broadcasting System network.

EPISODE #236   "O. HENRY"   Broadcast on July 21, 1941

Starring: Karl Swenson as O. Henry
Kenny Delmar as Mickey
Agnes Young as Mrs. Smith
William Johnstone as O'Brien
Betty Garde as the Italian
Agnes Moorehead as the landlady
William Johnstone as the waiter
Ted Jewett as Mike
Kenny Delmar as Thomas
John McIntire as the paper editor

Betty Garde as Sally
Ed Jerome as the cop
John McIntire as Guy
Agnes Moorehead as Mrs. Lapedus
Ted Jewett as Jones
Agnes Young as Mrs. Arthur
Ted Jewett as the second waiter
Ed Jerome as Murphy
Frank Readick as Casey

Written for *Cavalcade* by Norman Rosten.
Produced and directed by Homer Fickett.
Richard Stark is the announcer and Clayton Collyer is the commercial announcer.
Music composed and conducted by Donald Voorhees.

Story: High ranking among the masters of the short story in world literature was William Sydney Porter who wrote under the famous pseudonym, "O. Henry." His contributions to American literature in the field of the short story carried on the tradition begun by Edgar Allan Poe and strengthened the notable opinion that in this branch of literary art, Americans have not been surpassed by writers of other nations and races. It can be asserted that we have not produced unparalleled novelists, dramatists and poets, but undeniably the writings of Edgar Allan Poe and O. Henry place the American short story second to none.

EPISODE #237   "CLIFFORD HOLLAND"   Broadcast on July 28, 1941

Starring: William Johnstone as Clifford Holland
Bill Pringle as the fat man
Agnes Moorehead as Mrs. O'Rourke
Ted Jewett as the jack operator
Juano Hernandez as Jim
Karl Swenson as Lev
John McIntire as McMartin
Bill Pringle as the cop

Ted Jewett as the doctor
Howard Smith as the new man
Ed Jerome as Ryan
John McIntire as the surveyor
Ted Jewett as the bartender
Ed Jerome as Pat
Kenny Delmar as O'Rourke
Karl Swenson as the interne

Written for *Cavalcade* by Robert Tallman.
Produced and directed by Homer Fickett.
Richard Stark is the announcer and Clayton Collyer is the commercial announcer.
Music composed and conducted by Donald Voorhees.

Story: One of the great scientific achievements of American ingenuity, enterprise and perseverance against odds, is the Holland Tunnel which links the states of New York and New Jersey by a subaqueous passageway, constructed beneath the waters of the Hudson River. It was completed at a cost of forty-eight million, a reduced expenditure from the original estimate of sixty-five million, and was hailed as one of the most remarkable engineering feats of the twentieth century. This triumph of science and industry was due to one man, Clifford Holland. Above all, Holland originated new methods to improve the safety of the sandhogs, which in turn, utilized his concern of the safety of his workmen.

Clayton Collyer: "We would like to express our appreciation to *Radio Daily* for the honor they have given *Cavalcade of America* in their first annual Harper and Brothers Award for outstanding writing in the radio field."

EPISODE #238   "JOSEPHINE BAKER"   Broadcast on August 4, 1941
　　　　　Starring: Agnes Moorehead as Doctor Baker　　　Florence Halop as Mrs. Ingram
　　　　　Adelaide Klein as Mrs. Bonelli　　　　　　　　　Agnes Young as Mrs. Smith
　　　　　William Johnstone as the Inspector　　　　　　　Betty Garde as Mary
　　　　　Ed Jerome as the cop　　　　　　　　　　　　　Kenny Delmar as the second cop
　　　　　Karl Swenson as the second commissioner　　　　Charita Bauer as Rose
　　　　　Adelaide Klein as Mrs. Rabinowitz　　　　　　　Florence Halop as Sophie
　　　　　Betty Garde as Mrs. Slattery　　　　　　　　　 Frank Readick as the janitor
　　　　　Kenny Delmar as Callahan　　　　　　　　　　　Ed Jerome as O'Malley
　　　　　John McIntire as the commissioner　　　　　　　Ted Jewett as the voice of Ad
　　　　　Agnes Young as Dr. Blackwell
　　　　　Based on the autobiography "Fighting for Life" by S. Josephine Baker, M.D., originally published in 1939 by Macmillan Company, adapted for *Cavalcade* by Robert Tallman. Produced and directed by Homer Fickett.
　　　　　Clayton Collyer is the announcer.
　　　　　Music composed and conducted by Donald Voorhees.
　　　　　Story: Public hygiene with emphasis on children's ailments induced through squalor and lack of medical attention was the great contribution of Dr. Baker to our civilization. Her career began when she entered the only medical school in the U.S. and sat at the feet of that famed pioneer of women doctors, Dr. Elizabeth Blackwell. After receiving her Medical Degree, Dr. Baker went to New York City and was appointed to the city Health Department. Here she came to know of the deplorable conditions that were taking their toll in child health. She instituted a series of clinics and through her efforts, health education for children was adopted in N.Y.'s public schools. Dr. Baker won national attention when she detected and captured an infected woman known as "Typhoid Mary," who notoriously and dangerously refused medical attention for this disease.

EPISODE #239   "RED LANTERNS ON ST. MICHAELS"   Broadcast on August 11, 1941
　　　　　Starring: Bill Johnstone as Perry White　　　　John McIntire as Beauregard
　　　　　Agnes Moorehead as Joan　　　　　　　　　　　Frank Readick as Phil
　　　　　Kenny Delmar as man one　　　　　　　　　　　Ted Jewett as man two
　　　　　Edwin Jerome as man three　　　　　　　　　　Howard Smith as the northern sailor
　　　　　Edwin Jerome as the second guard　　　　　　　Bill Pringle as the fourth man
　　　　　John McIntire as Fred　　　　　　　　　　　　 Bill Pringle as the lieutenant
　　　　　Howard Smith as the northern guard　　　　　　Howard Smith as the fifth man
　　　　　Agnes Moorehead as Joan　　　　　　　　　　　Ted Jewett as Jones
　　　　　Agnes Moorehead as Mrs. Whitehall　　　　　　 Kenny Delmar as March
　　　　　Based on the 1941 novel of the same name by Thornwall Jacobs, originally published by E.P. Dutton & Company, Inc., and adapted for *Cavalcade* by Erik Barnouw. Produced and directed by Homer Fickett.
　　　　　Carl Frank is the announcer and Clayton Collyer is the commercial announcer.
　　　　　Music composed and conducted by Donald Voorhees.
　　　　　Story: A heroic story of the South and its most dynamic and exciting city of Civil War days, Charleston, South Carolina. The despair that clouded the nation during the darkest days of the Civil War was deepest in Charleston. Here was the root. From here came the challenge to Unionism. If the Union was to prevail, Charleston must certainly be among those most abjectly crushed by Federal supremacy. Yet some of the noble spirit of reunion which followed the event at Appomattox is stressed. We see the young idealist - gentle, scientific and courageous Perry White - as the protagonist. His evolution from a youth fired by the high adventure of war which led him to perfect a crude submarine in order to break the Union naval blockade, then his despair, and finally his reborn faith in a united America at the termination of hostilities.

EPISODE #240 "STEPHEN ARNOLD DOUGLAS"   Broadcast on August 18, 1941
    Starring: Kenny Delmar as Stephen Douglas
    Bill Pringle as the Democrat
    Ian MacAllister as the supporter
    Agnes Moorehead as the abolitioness
    Edwin Jerome as Ninian
    Ted Jewett as McConnel
    Frank Readick as Herndon
    William Johnstone as Sheehan
    John McIntire as Abe Lincoln
    Frank Readick as the Republican
    Edwin Jerome as the Heckler
    Agnes Moorehead as Adele
    Ian MacAllister as Brown
    Pauline Preller as Mary
    Frank Readick as Jones
    Ian MacAllister as the voice
    Ted Jewett as Smith
    Bill Pringle as Miller

Written for *Cavalcade* by Garrett Porter, based on the 1934 book "Eve of Conflict" by George Fort Milton.
Produced and directed by Homer Fickett.
Carl Frank is the announcer and Clayton Collyer is the commercial announcer.
Music composed and conducted by Donald Voorhees.

Story: In their way, the debates of Lincoln and Douglas were more than forensic clashes in the tradition of political rhetoric that began with Demosthenes and continues to the present hour. Not in the intellectual serenity of an Athenian symposium nor in any dignified hall of state did these two orators wage vocal war over the political questions of their time. They carried the issues personally to the people. They spoke from wagons and often on nothing more pretentious than good rich Illinois fields. And in those people as always lay the ultimate resolution. Abraham Lincoln was elected President, and Stephen A. Douglas was rejected.

EPISODE #241 "SACAJAWEA"   Broadcast on August 25, 1941
    Starring: Jeanette Nolan as Sacajawea
    William Johnstone as Williams
    Carl Frank as the storyteller
    John McIntire as Clark
    Kenny Delmar as the soldier
    Frank Readick as Smith
    Karl Swenson as Simpson
    Ronny Liss as Baptiste
    Ted Jewett as Lewis
    Edwin Jerome as Charbonneau

Brad Barker supplied the animal sounds.
Written for *Cavalcade* by Robert L. Richards.
Produced and directed by Homer Fickett.
Carl Frank is the announcer and Clayton Collyer is the commercial announcer.

Story: The Lewis and Clark Expedition (1804-1806) was an epic in human achievement, the greatest exploration effort in American history. The success of that expedition was made possible by Sacajawea, "The Bird Woman," who thus became one of the most celebrated guides in the chronicles of our American past. Lewis and Clark employed Sacajawea as guides and interpreters. She was the only woman to accompany the tiny expedition. With her she took her newly-born son, Baptiste, strapped to her back, no woman was ever more patient, or brave or resourceful.

Historical Trivia: Historians have debated the time of Sacajawea's death. Some hold for 1812, while others maintain that she died at the Shoshone Agency in 1884. As wide as these dates may be, there still remains the debate. But there is no question of the many and great services she rendered the Lewis and Clark Expedition. Once a canoe containing the records of the expedition over-turned; Sacajawea, at the risk of her life, saved them. At another time she alone persuaded an Indian tribe not to massacre the expedition. Without her this great exploring effort would have become merely another lost expedition.

EPISODE #242 "**LEIF ERICSSON**" Broadcast on September 1, 1941

    Starring: Karl Swenson as Leif Ericson   Everett Sloane as the high priest
    John McIntire as Eric   Ed Jerome as Helji
    William Johnstone as Haki   Jeanette Nolan as Thorgunna
    Jeanette Nolan as Helja   Agnes Moorehead as Freyda
    Kenny Delmar as Finn   Ted Jewett as Pavo
    Frank Readick as Snorri

Written for *Cavalcade* by Norman Rosten.
Produced and directed by Homer Fickett.
Carl Frank is the announcer and Clayton Collyer is the commercial announcer.
Music composed and conducted by Donald Voorhees.
Story: Leif Ericsson was a Viking. He is believed to be the first European to have lived in the New World. The place he settled was called "Vineland," probably either Maine of Nova Scotia. He remained here throughout one winter. When his colonists finally returned by sail to the Norse stronghold of Greenland, they carried American soil, grain and tree specimens with them. Examine these several facts. Remember, they do not constitute either legend or mythology woven about the epic life of the Viking, Ericsson. They bring credence to the verdict of history: before Christopher Columbus, this Norse chieftain is known as the discoverer of America.

EPISODE #243 "**GERONIMO**" Broadcast on September 8, 1941

    Starring: Kenny Delmar as Leonard Anderson   Karl Swenson as the Indian
    John McIntire as Miles   Karl Swenson as Joplin
    Everett Sloane as Black Eagle   Ted Jewett as Adjutant
    Everett Sloane as the orderly   Frank Readick as Sarge
    William Johnstone as the soldier   Edwin Jerome as Geromino
    Jeanette Nolan as Eliza   Charita Bauer as Sarah
    William Johnstone as the operator   Ted Jewett as the Indian brave
    Everett Sloane as the second Indian brave

Written for *Cavalcade* by Peter Lyon.
Produced and directed by Homer Fickett.
Carl Frank is the announcer and Clayton Collyer is the commercial announcer.
Music composed and conducted by Donald Voorhees.
Story: General Miles was one of the most distinguished American soldiers of the 19th century. At the outbreak of the Civil War he gave up his business, raised a company of volunteers and entered the Army as a lieutenant in the 22nd Massachusetts regiment. He later joined the regular Army as a Colonel of infantry. During the next two decades he conducted many campaigns against the Indians and opened up vast areas of the West to settlement and to civilization. But among the last and most brilliant of his Indian campaigns was that which resulted in the surrender of Geromino, Natchez and the band of Apaches who had spread terror through great regions of the Southwest. But the tactical skill of Geromino and the dogged bravery of them all constituted a major problem for the best forces sent to apprehend them.

EPISODE #244 "**CITY OF ILLUSION**" Broadcast on September 15, 1941

    Starring: Agnes Moorehead as Eilley Bowers   Everett Sloane as the Preacher
    William Johnstone as Jed   Karl Swenson as Luff McCoy
    Ed Jerome as the bartender   Howard Smith as Sam Brown
    Betty Garde as Julia   John McIntire as MacKay
    Pauline Preller as Mrs. Gelhorn   Bill Pringle as the doctor
    Kenny Delmar as the voice of illusion   Jeanette Nolan as Louisa
    Karl Swenson as Constock   Frank Readick as Sandy
    William Johnstone as the coachman   Everett Sloane as Mr. Watson
    Pauline Preller as Angie   Jeanette Nolan as Matilda

Betty Garde as Abbie
Based on the 1941 novel of the same name by Vardis Fisher, and adapted for *Cavalcade* by Robert Tallman.
Produced and directed by Homer Fickett.
Carl Frank is the announcer and Clayton Collyer is the commercial announcer.
Music composed and conducted by Donald Voorhees.
Story: The day of the fabulous bonanza has gone. Only the ghost towns remain, shrouded memories of the gutted Comstock. But with the passing show that has colored and vitalized American history, the era when men were crazed with excitement and reckless dreams over a promised harvest of gold left a vivid, compelling and powerful mark on the course of the nation's destiny. Here we realize the age-old fact that seek for fortune as we may, there is something else to live for. There is something else that is more permanently beautiful than all the gold on earth.

Trivia: Although this episode was based on the Fisher novel, the title of the actual *Cavalcade* script was originally "The Story of the Comstock Silverlode." A few days before the actual broadcast, it was decided that "City of Illusion" had more apt appeal.

EPISODE #245   **"NATIVE LAND"**   **(PART ONE)**   Broadcast on September 22, 1941
Starring: Burgess Meredith narrates while Carl Sandburg reads from his own works.

Everett Sloan as the farmer	Larry Robinson as the child
Jeanette Nolan as the woman	Ted Jewett as the storekeeper
Carl Sandburg as Sandburg, Sr.	Larry Robinson as Carl Sandburg (age nine)
Kenny Delmar as Sandburg (young man)	William Johnstone as Jenkins
Frank Readick as Ed	Everett Sloane as the salesman
John McIntire as the second voice	Ed Jerome as the first voice
Everett Sloan as the third voice	Kenny Delmar as the fourth voice
Betty Garde as the working girl	Frank Readick as the newsboy
Ted Jewett as the commentator	Jeanette Nolan as the housewife
Betty Garde as the woman	Karl Swenson as the negro
William Johnstone as the gangster	Ted Jewett as the tough guy
Ed Jerome as the gambler	Betty Garde as the Texas woman
John McIntire as the old timer	Ted Jewett as the prosecutor
Frank Readick as the defendant	Karl Swenson as the attendant
Frank Readick as the man	Jeanette Nolan as the woman
William Johnstone as the pilot	

Written for *Cavalcade* by a staff of writers, including Robert L. Richards and Robert Tallman.
Material from the following, all written by Carl Sandburg, were obtained for this script: "Slabs of the Sunburnt West" originally published in 1922 by Harcourt, Brace and Company, Inc. "The People, Yes" originally published in 1936 by Harcourt, Brace and Company, Inc. "Abraham Lincoln: The War Years" originally published in 1939 by Harcourt, B & Comp., Inc. "The Corn Huskers" originally published in 1918 by Henry Holt and Company.
Produced and directed by Homer Fickett.
Carl Frank is the announcer and Clayton Collyer is the commercial announcer.
Music composed and conducted by Donald Voorhees.
Story: Modern America today moves fast. Momentous decisions, whose implications over-shadow any faced in the past, are clicking off like clockwork. Decisions will be made and executed by Americans through the processes of their traditional democracy while the actions of men long dead will be used as yardsticks. Events and men of past generations of Americans - our Revolution, our pioneers and frontiersman, the greatness and richness of our country, our men of letters, rich men, poor men, clowns and statesmen, appear in their proper roles as Americans act today.

Dr. Frank Monaghan: "For six years *Cavalcade of America* productions had presented great events and characters whose actions had paved the way for America, 1941. In a series of two broadcasts scheduled for September 22 and 29, *Cavalcade* planned to present a new type of production - two programs under the title 'Native Land.' Those programs showed how the tenuous thread of our relationship to the past had been kept alive, and how our ingrained heritage took us by the hand and lead us in the face of a dark future."

EPISODE #246 "**NATIVE LAND**" **(PART TWO)** Broadcast on September 29, 1941
Starring: Judith Anderson guests and Burgess Meredith narrates.

Agnes Moorehead as the woman	Betty Garde as the suburban wife
Charita Bauer as the practical girl	Jeanette Nolan as the worker's wife
Joan Tetzel as the young woman	Betty Garde as the Hell woman
Agnes Moorehead as the pioneer woman	Jeanette Nolan as Mrs. Brody
John McIntire as Simmons	Ed Jerome as Joe
Betty Garde as Mrs.	Kenny Delmar as Mr.
Agnes Moorehead as Cindy Lou	John McIntire as the lieutenant
Jeanette Nolan as the telephone	Joan Tetzel as the operator
Ed Jerome as the man	Kenny Delmar as the conductor
Jeanette Nolan as N.E. Mother	Elliott Reid as the boy
Betty Garde as Cathleen	Charita Bauer as Nora
Judith Anderson as Maurya	Elliott Reid as Bardley
John McIntire as the old man	Ed Jerome as Colan

Written for *Cavalcade* by a staff of writers, including Robert L. Richards and Robert Tallman.
Permission has been obtained for the use, within this script, of material from "Riders to the Sea," by John M. Synge, published in 1935 by The Modern Library, Inc.
Copyrighted material within the pages of the book by various authors were used in this script, from John M. Synge, John Quinn, Edward Synge and Francis Edmund Stephens, and L.F. Bassett.
Produced and directed by Homer Fickett.
Music composed and conducted by Donald Voorhees.
Story: The theme of this broadcast, the second half of a two-part presentation, was American women who played over the years in guiding the course of their nation and the part they are playing today. It told the heroism and self-sacrifice of women from the Revolutionary Wars to the present day, who have shaped the affairs of men and destiny of America.

Trivia: Judith Anderson played the feature role in an adaptation of "Native Land's" adaptation of "Clara Barton, Woman of Destiny," written by Blanche Colton Williams, the feature biography in the fall season of Lippincott Publications.

More Trivia: Originally planned for this broadcast as a highlight was a talk by Miss Alice Marble, World Champion Woman Tennis player and recently appointed U.S. Assistant Director of Civilian Defense in charge of National and Physical Training for Women, and it is known as the "Hale America" movement. She never made it to the program, and was not featured.

EPISODE #247 "**BOLIVAR, THE LIBERATOR**" Broadcast on October 6, 1941
Starring: Paul Muni as Bolivar
Adapted for *Cavalcade* by Robert Tallman, from an original story by Dudley Nichols.
Produced and directed by Homer Fickett.
Clayton Collyer is the announcer.
Music composed and conducted by Donald Voorhees.

Story: Bolivar was a military genius who led his people in revolt for twenty brilliant years, fought 500 battles and broke the grip of Spain over an area ten times the size of Spain. He liberated his people and fathered five republics, Columbia, Venezuela, Peru, Ecuador, and the country which took his name, Bolivia. He died over a hundred and fifty years ago, a lonely, broken man at age 47, believing that he had failed. But his memory is loved throughout the great America that stretches south of us to Cape Horn. As if he had lived yesterday, he lives in the hearts of his people as no man in North American history lives with us.

Trivia: *Radio Daily* magazine honored the *Cavalcade of America*, this week, in the first annual Harper and Brothers Award for outstanding writing in the radio field.

EPISODE #248   **"WATERS OF THE WILDERNESS"**   Broadcast on October 13, 1941
    Starring: Kay Francis as Teresa   Gale Gordon as Clark
    Gerald Mohr as Liard   Agnes Moorehead as Suzette
    Lou Merrill as Fernando   Bea Benadaret as Maria
    Jack Mather as Tom Pace   Gayne Whitman as the servant
    Bea Benadaret as the Indian woman   Pat McGeehan as the first homesteader
    Agnes Moorehead as female homesteader   Lou Merill as the first settler
    Jack Mather as the second settler   Jack Mather as the second homesteader
    Pat McGeehan as the third settler   Catherine Cragen as a supernumerary
    Grace Leonard as a supernumerary   Jerry Gale as a supernumerary
    Earle Ross as a supernumerary   Lou Merrill as voice one
    Jack Mather as voice two   Agnes Moorehead as voice three
    Pat McGeehan as voice four   Bea Benadaret as voice five
Based on the 1941 novel by Shirley Siefert, originally published by J.B. Lippincott Company, and adapted for *Cavalcade* by William Johnstone and Robert Richards. Produced and directed by Homer Fickett.
John Hiestand is the announcer and Gayne Whitman is the commercial announcer. Music composed and conducted by Robert Armbruster.
Story: The dramatic romance of the Mississippi Valley during the American Revolution. Two characters chiefly engage our attention. One is Teresa de Leyba, the soulful and vivacious young lady of old Spain. Perhaps you don't recognize the name. Then permit me to introduce the second - George Rogers Clark. And what have they to do with each other? That question is the inspiration of this broadcast. Clark was the brilliant soldier of the American Revolution, Teresa was the sister of Don Fernando de Leyba. See the connection now? **(HLYD)**

Trivia: William Johnstone, radio actor currently known for his role as Lamont Cranston, alias "The Shadow" during this broadcast, co-wrote the script for this episode, adapted from the Siefert novel of the same name.

Trivia: This was the first *Cavalcade* broadcast to originate from Hollywood, California instead of New York City. (Radio City, Hollywood to be exact.) Du Pont's radio agency decided on broadcasting from the West Coast not only for budget reasons, but to also present Hollywood stars whose hectic schedules forbid them from flying to the East Coast for a couple of radio presentations.

EPISODE #249   **"ALL THAT MONEY CAN BUY"**   Broadcast on October 20, 1941
    Starring: Edward Arnold as Daniel Webster   Jane Darwell as Ma Stone
    Walter Huston as Mr. Scratch   Earl Ross as Hawthrone
    Anne Shirley as Mary Stone   James Craig as Jabez Stone
    Wally Maher as the clerk   Lee Millar as the dog howls
    Sam Hearn, Phil Kramer, and Virgil Reimer were members of the jury.

Based on the 1937 prize winning short-story "The Devil and Daniel Webster" by Stephen Vincent Benet, and adapted for *Cavalcade* by Howard Teichmann.
Produced and directed by Homer Fickett.
John Hiestand is the announcer and Gayne Whitman is the commercial announcer.
Music composed and conducted by Robert Armbruster.
Story: The scene is laid in New Hampshire where Daniel Webster has really never died. His character, his moral strength, his eloquence still reverberates through the Green Hills and permeates the lives of the natives. Seemingly, the Devil is with us always in New Hampshire and elsewhere. Jabez Stone, an earthy, calculating individual, is the New England Dr. Faustus, a man who sells his soul for a mess of pottage, glittering coins of gold, a fine house, mortgages, earthly power. But it is only for seven years and then comes the reckoning. With an impeccable legal contract, Mr. Scratch (the Devil himself) comes to claim Jabez Stone, or rather what is left of Jabez Stone. Fortunately, Jabez retains Mr. Webster to defend him before the strangest jury ever assembled. Do not be alarmed for Jabez Stone is relieved of the contract and is returned to his old self - but in saving Mr. Stone, Senator Webster bases his speech to the jury on the spiritual birthright which belongs to us all. The debate of the century on the problem of the redemption of a man's soul from materialism that always threatens to engulf the best of us. **(HLYD)**

Trivia: In 1941, RKO released *All That Money Can Buy* (a.k.a. *The Devil and Daniel Webster*), a film that established Edward Arnold in the role of Daniel Webster. Arnold would later reprise his film role in other radio dramatizations of this same story, on such programs as *This is My Best* in 1945. For this broadcast, Walter Huston reprised his screen role of Mr. Scratch, alias Lucifer, as did Jane Darwell as Ma Stone, James Craig as Jabez Stone, and Anne Shirley as Mary Stone. Bernard Herrmann's music score in the 1941 film won an Academy Award. The film was not a box office success, losing $53,000 on its first run.

The premiere was held early in October in New York City, under the same name, *All That Money Can Buy*. The title of the original story by poet Stephen Vincent Benet was "The Devil and Daniel Webster." Both titles are equally effective; each highly expressive of the theme of the story.

More trivia: Actress Simone Simon, who played the role of Belle Dee in the movie, was originally signed to reprise her film role in this broadcast, as did the others. But her foreign accent made it difficult to reflect over the microphone, and she was unable to star in the broadcast with the rest of the cast.

EPISODE #250   "**CAPTAIN PAUL**"   Broadcast on October 27, 1941
   Starring: Claude Rains as Captain Paul   Karl Swenson as Jack
   Betty Garde as the landlady   Jeanette Nolan as Catherine
   Frank Readick as Jackson   Kenny Delmar as the English Mate
   Ted Jewett as the English Captain   John McIntire as Dr. Franklin
   Kenny Delmar as the captain   William Johnstone as the commander
   Horace Braham as Captain White   Edwin Jerome as the father
   Anne Sterrett as Dorothea
Based on the 1941 book of the same name by Commander Edward Ellsberg and Lucy Buck Ellsberg, and adapted for *Cavalcade* by John Driscoll and Arthur Miller.
Produced and directed by Homer Fickett.
Clayton Collyer is the announcer.
Music composed and conducted by Don Voorhees.
Story: Like unnumbered thousands who have contributed mightily to the building of the nation, John Paul Jones was not a native-born American. He adopted a nation which, after many years and many trials, formally claimed him as her own. Like millions of

other Americans, native and adopted, he was of humble birth. When he was twelve years old, he was apprenticed to a ship's captain who took him on a journey to Virginia. He served as a mate on several slave ships - until finally he became disgusted with the traffic and resigned. Soon we find him in Philadelphia assisting in the earliest efforts of the struggling Continental Congress. The new United States had virtually no Navy, not a single ship worthy of a place in a battle fleet, and certainly no funds or credit with which to purchase any. So John found a ship, acquired a crew, and created a tradition.

EPISODE #251 "ONE FOOT IN HEAVEN" Broadcast on November 3, 1941

Starring: Florence Eldridge as mother   Fredric March as father
Betty Garde as Mrs. Thurston   Virginia Routh as Sister Carrie
Elliott Reid as Hartzell   Karl Swenson as Haskins
Jeanette Nolan as Sister Betty   Jeanette Nolan as Mrs. Sandow
John McIntire as Thurston   Kenny Delmar as John
Frank Readick as Potter   Gertrude Crippen as Mrs. Appleby
Edwin Jerome as Doc   Frank Readick as McAfee

The Reverend Doctor Norman Vincent Peale, of the Marble Collegiate Church in New York City makes a brief appearance at the end of the program.
Based on the 1941 screenplay by Casey Robinson and the biography of the same name by Hartzell Spence. Adapted for the *Cavalcade* radio program by Jean Holloway.
Produced and directed by Homer Fickett.
Clayton Collyer is the announcer.
Music composed and conducted by Don Voorhees.
Story: There is now more virtue in the growing of a beat than in the bleatings of a sophisticated *bistro*. We are returning to a more normal, a simpler life. No person in recent literature better exemplifies this simple, vital living than the Reverend William H. Spence, a Methodist parson of Iowa. We know of no better recent picture of Christianity in action. Parson Spence had both feet planted on good American earth - that rich soil of Iowa - and still had one foot in Heaven. Parson Spence was the antithesis of Elmer Gantry. Spence was the normal, vital clergyman.

Trivia: Warner Brothers released *One Foot in Heaven* in 1941, a film that received critical acclaim as well as an Academy Award nomination for Best Picture of the Year. Fredric March reprised his film role for this *Cavalcade* broadcast, and March's real-life wife Florence Eldridge played the role of Hope Morris Spence, the film role Martha Scott starred in the movie. Rev. Norman Vincent Peale, who was the technical advisor of the film, was also technical advisor of this broadcast, to add authenticity to the production.

EPISODE #252 "DRUMS ALONG THE MOHAWK" Broadcast on November 10, 1941

Starring: Henry Fonda as Gil   Jeanette Nolan as Lana
Betty Garde as Widow McKlennar   Edwin Jerome as Blue Back
Ted Jewett as the voice of war   John McIntire as Adam Buckley
Karl Swenson as Peter Tasch   Kenneth Delmar as Silas Kane
Frank Readick as Loring Kvczh   Edwin Jerome as the officer

Based on the 1939 screen play by Lamar Trotti and Sonya Levien, and the novel by Walter Dumaux Edmonds. Adapted for *Cavalcade* by Howard Teichmann.
Produced and directed by Homer Fickett.
Clayton Collyer is the announcer.
Music composed and conducted by Donald Voorhees.
Story: The historic Mohawk Valley, a land of turbulence and love against which back ground sets a typical pioneer, Gil Martin. Martin and his wife built a small log cabin home, only to lose it to the marauding Indians. Homeless, Martin sets out to help the militia rid the land of each and every Mohawk on American soil - even if it costs him his life.

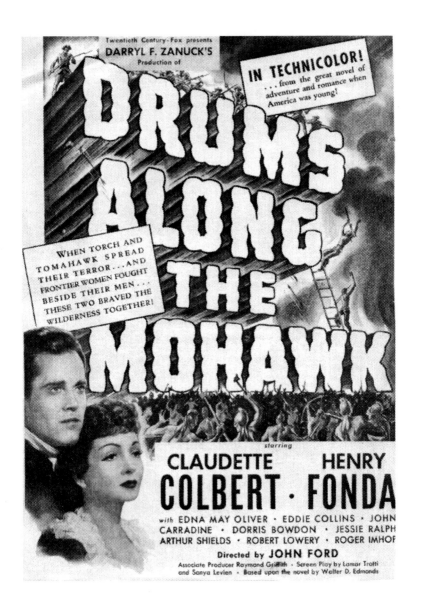

Movie poster advertising Twentieth-Century Fox's *Drums Along the Mohawk*. Henry Fonda reprised his film role for the November 10, 1941 *Cavalcade of America* broadcast.

Henry Fonda: "It's a personal satisfaction for me to work on the *Cavalcade of America* and I'd like to pay my respects to the *Cavalcade* players, with a particular 'thank you' to Jeanette Nolan who played opposite me. I've always admired Du Pont for the inspiration this program brings each week and naturally, I am happy to have been part of it."

Trivia: Fonda reprised his role of Gil Martin from the 1939 film released by Twentieth-Century Fox, the first color film directed by John Ford. In order to create the authenticity of the film, Ford reportedly had a prop man chase down more than a hundred flintlocks in Ethiopia, where they had been used in combat in the mid-thirties, used by Ethiopian soldiers trying to repel Mussolini's invading armies. More than 200,000 feet of lumber had to be transported into the area where a giant fort had to be built for the picture!

EPISODE # 253   **"THEY DIED WITH THEIR BOOTS ON"**   Broadcast November 17, 1941
Starring: Errol Flynn as General Custer   John McIntire as the officer
Jeanette Nolan as Libby   Ed Jerome as California Joe
Kenny Delmar as Roberts   Frank Readick as Sharp
Ed Jerome as Crazy Horse   Karl Swenson as Taipe
John McIntire as Grant   Buster Wiles as the secretary
Ed Jerome as the conductor   Elliott Reid as the sergeant-at-arms
Karl Swenson as the third reporter   Kenny Delmar as the second reporter
Ted Jewett as the first reporter   Elliott Reid as the boy
Based on the 1942 screenplay by Wally Klein and Aeneas MacKenzie, and adapted for *Cavalcade* by Robert Tallman.
Produced and directed by Homer Fickett.
Clayton Collyer is the announcer.
Music composed and conducted by Don Voorhees.
Story: The name of General Custer at once calls to mind one of the most dramatic moments of American History - Custer's Last Stand, or more accurately the massacre of Custer and 264 of his men at the Battle of the Little Big Horn on June 25, 1876. Custer served during the Civil War with conspicuous bravery. After the war he saw extensive service against the Indians in the west. Long before his last expedition he had acquired both experience and fame as an expert Indian fighter, especially with the Seventh U.S. Calvary. The circumstances which sent him against the Sioux were curious and tragic. Through the stupidity of two of his officers, Custer was not reinforced in time to prevent the famous disaster.

Trivia: Three days after this broadcast, on November 20, 1947, Raoul Walsh's *They Died With Their Boots On*, starring Errol Flynn, Olivia deHavilland, and Arthur Kennedy, opened at the Strand. Woody Herman and his orchestra were on stage. This movie was the eighth and final film Flynn and deHavilland starred in, the film everyone in Hollywood said would eventually be made, and with Flynn born for the role of Custer. With thousands of extras and with only sixteen Sioux Indians, director Walsh managed to capture battle scenes rarely accomplished in Hollywood.

Errol Flynn: "I don't think I'll ever forget shooting that battle scene. You know it made me kind of nervous working with those Indians. You see they were real Sioux from the Dakota reservation, the actual descendants of the braves who fought the original battle. I kept remembering I was dressed like General Custer, and had my fingers crossed hoping they'd remember I wasn't really Custer. It's been a busy week for me - finishing the picture in Hollywood and then flying on to New York for this radio version."

Movie trivia: Jack Warner's stomach ulcers were in a fret when the budget soared over $2 million, and dozens of stuntman were injured every day. So many that the studio sent a field hospital up to the location site where the battle scenes were being filmed. Three men died during filming, one fell from a horse and broke his neck, another stuntman had a heart attack. The third, actor Jack Budlong, insisted on using a real saber to lead a cavalry attack across a bridge supposedly under artillery fire. As Budlong dashed forward with his men, an explosive charge beneath the bridge went off prematurely and blew the actor and his horse upward. The saber came down point upward, wedged in some splintered wood of the bridge, and Budlong fell on top of it, running himself through For the *Cavalcade* performance, no one was in any danger of dying over the air.

EPISODE #254   "SO RED THE ROSE"   Broadcast on November 24, 1941

Starring: Joan Bennett as Valette
Edwin Jerome as Malcolm
Juano Hernandez as William
Elliott Reid as Edward
John McIntire as Higby
Ted Jewett as the first soldier
Kenny Delmar as Stope

Jeanette Nolan as Sally
Karl Swenson as Duncan
Kenny Delmar as Pendleton
Elliott Reid as Mason
Ed Jerome as the second soldier
Frank Readick as the yankee

Based on the novel by Stark Young, and the screenplay by Laurence Stallings, Edwin Justus Mayer and Maxwell Anderson. Adapted for *Cavalcade* by William Dorsey Blake and Robert Tallman.
Produced and directed by Homer Fickett.
Clayton Collyer is the announcer.
Music composed and conducted by Don Voorhees.
Story: The story of the deep South of the days before and during the Civil War. It resolves around the McGehees of Montrose and a related family, the Bedfords of Portobello, among the wealthiest of all the great planters of Mississippi. These men and women presented the finest elements of that gracious civilization of the old South. Into their midst there suddenly came the Civil War - disrupting and scattering families - disrupting and altering the very civilization of which they were conspicuous members.

Robert Tallman: "In preparing our radio play we [William Blake and Tallman] tried to emphasize the spirit of the novel - and both critics and the general public acclaim this, Mr. Young's work, as something that seems directly and abundantly from the heart - a thing laden with beauty and tenderness and understanding. No author had been more successful in recapturing the spirit of the old South and few have realized so well the tragedy of the great conflict in terms of both individuals and family groups. The war had its romantic interludes and it was these that make up some of the finest episodes in our script, 'So Red the Rose'."

Trivia: Bennett played the role of Vallette Bedford, the role Margaret Sullavan starred in the 1935 Paramont picture. This was the first major sound film to deal with the Civil War's efforts on the Southern family. It preceded *Gone With the Wind* by four years, and Margaret Mitchell's novel by a year. The success of *Gone With the Wind* kept all of the major motion picture studios from making any Civil War movies, fearing that the audience would compare and box office receipts would fall. In the example of *So Red the Rose*, they were right.

EPISODE #255   "CIMARRON"   Broadcast on December 1, 1941
        Starring: Irene Dunne as Sabra Cravatt   Gale Gordon as Yancey Cravatt
        Paula Winslow as Mrs. Venable   Jerry Hausner as Cim
        Jack Mather as Grat Nolan   Howard McNear as Lon Yountis
        Dorothy Scott as Mrs. Wyatt   Howard McNear as Copy Desk
        Paula Winslow as Miss Winslow   Lou Merrill as Mr. Oakes
        Barbara Jean Wong as the boy
Based on the novel by Edna Ferber, and adapted for *Cavalcade* by Paul Franklin and Robert Tallman.
Produced and directed by Homer Fickett.
John Hiestand is the announcer and Gayne Whitman is the commercial announcer.
Music composed and conducted by Robert Armbruster.
Story: The dramatic interweaving of the destinies of two determined and dynamic individuals against the dramatic background of Oklahoma. It is Oklahoma from the days of "The Great Run of 1889" through the colorful Indian difficulties, the discovery of oil, the growth of boom cities, to the present. With colorful characters, with faultless pace and color, the incredible story of the development of the most incredible period and region of the development of the most incredible period and region of American History. The story of Cimarron is a true and startling chapter of America. **(HLYD)**

     Trivia: Irene Dunne reprised her film role of Sabra Cravat from the 1931 RKO film of the same name. *Cimarron* had the largest budget the studio ever committed to a film up to that point, $1,433,000. Though it received across-the-board raves, it lost money, more than half a million. Dunne won an Oscar nomination as best supporting actress, and the film itself won an Oscar for Best Film, Best Adaptation and Best Set Decoration. *Cimarron* was remade in 1960, due to the reputation the 1931 film received, considered the best western made until the mid-fifties when *Shane*, *Red River*, and *High Noon* captivated the audiences.

EPISODE #256   "MEN IN WHITE"   Broadcast on December 8, 1941
        Starring: Franchot Tone as Dr. Ferguson   Betty Garde as Miss Barker
        John McIntire as Dr. Hochberg   Frank Readick as Dr. Gordon
        Frank Readick as Dr. Gordon   Frank Readick as Shorty
        Elliott Reid as Pete   Arlene Francis as Laura
        Jeanette Nolan as Barbara   Elliott Reid as the Orderly
        Ted Jewett as Dr. Wren   Pauline Preller as Miss Barnes
        Sara Fussell as Dorothy   Karl Swenson as Dr. Cunningham
        Kenny Delmar as Mr. Smith   Peggy Riley as Mrs. Smith
Based on the Pulitzer-prize winning play by Sidney Kingsley, and adapted for *Cavalcade* by Robert Tallman.
Produced and directed by Homer Fickett.
Clayton Collyer is the announcer.
Music composed and conducted by Don Voorhees.
Story: Dr. Ferguson is a promising young surgeon serving an internship in a hospital of which Dr. Hochberg is the chief of the surgical staff. Dr. Hochberg is a kindly and elderly doctor who is devoted to the progress of medicine and who wishes to have Dr. Ferguson continue his medical researches in Vienna. But Ferguson is interested not only in medicine, he is also in love with Miss Laura Hudson, and she is not so greatly interested in medical research. She wants Ferguson to settle down in marriage and a "nice, comfortable practice." Two careers offer themselves to Dr. Ferguson - an easy, worldly success. . . or devotion to medical science. Who shall win, Dr. Hochberg or Miss Hudson?

Trivia: "Men in White" was first produced at the Broadcast Theatre in New York City in September 1933. It was instantly acclaimed by both critics and the general public. It was the first conspicuous success of a youthful and brilliant dramatist, Mr. Sidney Kingsley, who had graduated only a few years before from Cornell University and its fine department of drama. "Men in White" received a Pulitzer Prize and was quickly and effectively translated into the medium of the motion pictures. Clark Gable starred as Dr. Ferguson in the 1934 MGM film of the same name. Jean Hersholt, who played Dr. Hochberg in the same film, also was currently playing another doctor, Dr. Christian, on radio for more than fifteen years. "Men in White," however, remains one of the best American plays of a decade of good plays.

History fans take note: The date of this broadcast is an important date in American history. Before and after this broadcast, NBC announcers read the latest bulletins concerning the bombing of Pearl Harbor.

EPISODE #257 **"THE GREAT MAN VOTES"** Broadcast on December 15, 1941
Starring: Ray Collins and Orson Welles
Based on a story by Gordon Malherbe Hillman, adapted for *Cavalcade* by Peter Lyon.
Produced and directed by Homer Fickett.
John Hiestand is the announcer and Gayne Whitman is the narrator.
Music composed and conducted by Robert Armbruster.
Story: In America the ballot has remained free and powerful. This charming and effective demonstration of the power and the sanctity of that high privilege: the right to vote. Here, a school teacher has fallen upon unhappy days. He has become a night watchman - fallen in his own esteem and in that of his neighbors. Suddenly it is discovered that he is the sole voter in a vital city precinct. The politicians rush in to flatter and cajole him. But the old basic integrity is still there: in spite of lavish adulation and of coercion he goes to the voting booth and casts his ballot in the good American fashion. The Great Man votes as he pleases. **(HLYD)**

Dr. Frank Monaghan: "This week all America is celebrating the birthday of a most precious heritage of our democratic form of government. It is a solemn and a momentous celebration, for it was just one hundred and fifty years ago that the first ten amendments to the Federal Constitution were ratified. These amendments contain what is popularly known as our national 'Bill of Rights.' Some of the framers of the original Constitution maintained that such an additional statement of the basic freedoms of religion, press, speech and assembly was not necessary. But the good American instinct to have things stated in clear and unmistakable terms prevailed; and these important amendments came into being."

Trivia: In 1939, RKO released a big-screen version of the Hillman story with Lionel Barrymore in the lead role. Barrymore's real-life health cast him perfectly as an alcoholic college professor who earns his self-respect when his two children create a situation in which their father's lone vote will decide who the town's next mayor will be.

Orson Welles: "This week in America we are celebrating the one hundred and fiftieth anniversary of our charter of human liberties - the Bill of Rights. And so we have chosen as our story that truly fine RKO picture *The Great Man Votes*. It is the story of a little man - a little man who, while destiny smiled, became a Great Man, because of his country, and the liberties and rights he has in his country. And because he understood the full value of those liberties and rights, in terms of human dignity and human hopes."

Trivia: Orson Welles reprised this drama on other radio programs, such as the *Gulf Screen Guild Theater*.

EPISODE #258 "THE GREEN PASTURES" Broadcast on December 22, 1941
Starring: Juano Hernandez as De Lawd
Adapted for *Cavalcade* by Marc Connelly, from is 1930 Pulitzer Prize winning play.
Produced by Homer Fickett and directed by Marc Connelly.
Clayton Collyer is the announcer.
Music furnished by the original Hall Johnson Choir.
Music composed and conducted by Don Voorhees.
Songs featured throughout the performance: "Rise and Shine," "Hallelujah, King Jesus," "Turn You 'Round," "Dere's No Hiding Place," "I'm Noways Weary and I'm Noways Tired," "A Blind Man Stood on De Middle of De Road," and lastly the Choir hums "A City Called Heaven."
Story: This is a simple, dynamic version of the Christian faith that is held by thousands of negroes in the deep South - the majority of whom could not read the Bible itself. They have a vast spiritual hunger - an unceasing urge to find the road to spiritual salvation. They have not (indeed, they could not) burdened themselves with the subtle distinctions of the theologians; they have taken the Old Testament and vaguely retold it in the everyday terms of their own lives. Instead of nectar and ambrosia they picture an unending series of fish frys throughout eternity - as well as "ten-cent seegars" for the adults.

Dr. Frank Monaghan: "This moving drama - one of the finest from the pen of Marc Connelly - won the Pulitzer Prize as the best play of the year; many thousands witnessed it during a long and successful run on the stage; many more thousands have read the original material by Roark Bradford which Mr. Connelly adapted for the theatre. *Cavalcade* was the first to sense the fine radio possibilities of 'The Green Pastures' It was first presented by the *Cavalcade of America* on a Christmas evening of 1940. The enthusiastic response of the listening public confirmed our belief that there are few, if any, plays more effective or appropriate for the season."

Trivia: Marc Connelly's radio writing included a number of religious scripts on *The Eternal Light*, a Sunday-afternoon program during the late forties into the sixties.

EPISODE #259 "THE GORGEOUS HUSSEY" Broadcast on December 29, 1841
Starring: Paulette Goddard as Peggy   Karl Swenson as Randolph
Frank Readick as Timberlake   Ted Jewett as the butler
Jeanette Nolan as Mrs. Jackson   John McIntire as Jackson
Elliott Reid as the porter   Betty Garde as Mrs. Calhoun
Kenny Delmar as the aide   Jeanette Nolan as Mrs. Cabot
Arlene Francis as Mrs. Beale   Ed Jerome as Mr. Calhoun
Kenny Delmar as Van Buren   Ted Jewett as the voice of the press
Elliott Reid as Bos'n
Based on the novel of the same name by Samuel Hopkins Adams, and adapted for *Cavalcade* by Robert Tallman.
Produced and directed by Homer Fickett.
Clayton Collyer is the announcer.
Music composed and conducted by Don Voorhees.
Story: "The Gorgeous Hussy" was Peggy Eaton, wife of Senator Eaton of Tennessee, who later became the secretary of War in the Cabinet of President Andrew Jackson. It was her love for Senator Eaton, her turbulent vitality, and her courage that created what all America knew and discussed as "The Eaton Affair" during 1829 and in the years that followed. The story of the beautiful tavern keeper's daughter Peggy Eaton, wife of Senator Eaton of Tennessee. She was a favorite of President Andrew Jackson, who was determined to have her accepted socially in Washington. Calhoun objected and the resultant warfare has far reaching political consequences.

Trivia: Paulette Goddard starred as Peggy O'Neal Eaton, the role Joan Crawford played in the 1936 MGM film. The film had lots of facets of a little-known woman in U.S. history, and was a box office disappointment. This was the first radio presentation of the work that received wide and enthusiastic acclaim in the world of books and of the movies.

EPISODE #260   "VALLEY FORGE"   Broadcast on January 5, 1942
>   Starring: Lionel Barrymore as Washington   Erik Rolf as Stirling
>   Elliott Lewis as Tench   James Eagles as Neil
>   Jack Mather as Varnum   Gerald Mohr as Lafayette
>   Arthur Q. Bryan as Rafe   Norman Field as Harvie
>   Gordon Wallace as Folsom   Earl Ross as Alcock
>   Joe Du Val as Marty   Vernon Steele as Howe
>   Based on the 1934 play of the same name by Maxwell Anderson, and adapted for *Cavalcade* by Robert L. Richards.
>   Produced and directed by Homer Fickett.
>   John Hiestand is the announcer and Gayne Whitman is the commercial announcer.
>   Music composed and conducted by Robert Armbruster.
>   Story: During the bitter months of the bleak encampment many men began to think that it would be the final and crushing disaster to the American cause, but it was not the final disaster. It proved to be the end of disasters and the beginning of victory. Never had Washington's tiny army found itself in a more precarious position. Washington and his men had suffered three successive defeats. The British under General Howe had occupied Philadelphia, the national capitol. Washington settled his eleven thousand soldiers in winter headquarters at Valley Forge in December, 1777. The cold was intense, but Washington proved that he was the great leader of men. He was determined to keep the army in being to show that no disaster was large enough to destroy it. He gave them the inspiration, the grim fortitude, the hope with which they again went forth in pursuit of the American dream of liberty. **(HLYD)**

>   **Trivia:** "Valley Forge" was performed numerous times on other radio programs - three times on the *Cavalcade of America*. Others programs that featured an adaptation of Anderson's stage play were *The Eternal Light* and the *Texaco Star Theater*.

EPISODE #261   "THE GENTLEMAN FROM PARIS"   Broadcast on January 12, 1942
>   Starring: Charles Boyer as Lafayette   Sharon Douglas as Marie Antoinette
>   Pat McGeehan as Provence   Howard McNear as De Kalb
>   Howard McNear as Henri   Pat McGeehan as the soldier
>   Mary Shipp as the peasant girl   Charles Penman as the first sentry
>   Eric Rolfe as the second sentry   Charles Penman as the captain
>   Gayne Whitman as the sailor   Elliott Lewis as Tench
>   William Farnum as Washington
>   Written for *Cavalcade* by Robert Tallman.
>   Produced and directed by Homer Fickett.
>   John Hiestand is the announcer and Gayne Whitman is the commercial announcer.
>   Music composed and conducted by Robert Armbruster.
>   Story: Lafayette is the best-known Frenchman in the history of the United States. At the close of the American Revolution thousands of American soldiers and officers knew him affectionately as "The Marquis." His reputation has persisted and it is just that it should, for it is based upon a solid historical foundation. At a time when France was ruled by a small group of noble families, Lafayette was the first person of high distinction to side openly with the American patriots. Although the King forbade him to leave France,

(cont'd)

Lafayette escaped and sailed to the New World. But in Philadelphia he met a cold reception, for the Continental Congress had been plagued by a series of European adventurers who had flocked to America to carve out new careers and fortunes. Lafayette generously offered to serve as a volunteer and at his own expense. This Congress could hardly decline. **(HLYD)**

EPISODE #262   **"AN AMERICAN IS BORN"**   Broadcast on January 19, 1942
Starring: Bette Davis as Marta Kroft   Raymond Edward Johnson as Karl Kroft
Originally written for another radio program by Arch Oboler, based on a story by Fanya Foss and Peter Packer.
Produced and directed by Arch Oboler.
Clayton Collyer is the announcer.
The original musical score was by Gordon Jenkins and the orchestra was under the direction of Donald Voorhees.
Story: A small group of people cross the Mexican border yearning for the liberty which is America and await the time they can come to the country under the quota. More specifically, it is the story of Karl and Marta who willingly met many trials in order that their child might be born an American.

Trivia: Bette Davis was Arch Oboler's favorite actress, and Davis could be counted on for any special or broadcast Oboler wrote and directed. Davis appeared in numerous Oboler productions, even when the pay was for scale. Among some of the Oboler series she was heard on, *Treasury Star Parade*, *Arch Oboler's Plays* and *Plays for Americans*.

Bette Davis: "Arch Oboler wrote this play more than a year ago - and then just a few days ago I read an item in my newspaper about a lady named Mrs. Lloyd B. Turner, wife of an American oil man in Venezuela. A few years ago, she started on a three thousand mile journey home to Houston, Texas - to make sure her child would be born in the United States. That to me is evidence of a great faith. First - she had faith that her child would be a boy, and that he could become President of the United States. As a matter of fact (laughs) it turned out to be a girl!"

Dr. Frank Monaghan: "To many millions in Europe, America beckons forth as an earthly paradise because it is a land of freedom. They know the bitter taste of despotism, the heavy load of misery. Mr. Oboler has taken a small group of these unhappy men and women who yearn for the liberty which is America. They are across the border in Mexico awaiting the time when they can come to America under the quota."

Trivia: Ear-phoned Oboler, NBC's ace author/producer/director, saw to it during this broadcast that a falling tree *really* sounded like a falling tree. Oboler, a radio pioneer in his own name, cooperated in the Hollywood Radio City "Sound Perspective" experiments. In this instance he saw to it that a real tree and real twigs, branches and undergrowth were collected for this one sound effect, a massive pile of two and a half feet, and flattened by two sound men.

EPISODE #263   **"TOMORROW AND TOMORROW"**   Broadcast on January 26, 1942
Starring: Madeleine Carroll as Eve Redman
Based on the stage play by Philip Barry, and adapted for *Cavalcade* by Peter Lyon.
Produced and directed by Homer Fickett.
John Hiestand is the announcer and Gayne Whitman is the commercial announcer.
Music composed and conducted by Robert Armbruster.

(cont'd)

Story: This is the crux of the intensely human drama that reminds us that tomorrow is the child of today. Eve Redman has a conventional husband, a comfortable home and a child. But she falls in love with a brilliant young doctor, Nicholas Hay. Dr. Hay is about to return to London and to his care of bomb-shocked children. Shall Eve give up the responsibility of her home and child and go with Dr. Hay? Shall she sacrifice the future to enjoy today or will she remain loyal to the promise of tomorrow as represented by her infant son? The hope of the future is vested in the children of today. **(HLYD)**

Trivia: Paramount filmed a big-screen version of this film in 1932, with Ruth Chatterton in the lead role of Eve Redman. Barry's drama didn't adapt to the screen successfully as his other plays such as *The Philadelphia Story* (1940). "Tomorrow and Tomorrow" was dramatized over the radio before, back in late 1938 on *The Texaco Star Theater*.

EPISODE #264   **"CAPTAINS OF THE CLOUDS"**   Broadcast on February 2, 1942
    Starring: James Cagney as Brian MacLean   Alan Hale as Tiny Murphy
    Reginald Denny as the commanding officer   Dennis Morgan as Johnny Dutton
Based on the 1942 screenplay by Arthur T. Horman, Richard Macaulay, and Norman Reilly Raine, and adapted for *Cavalcade* by Robert Tallman.
Produced and directed by Homer Fickett.
John Hiestand is the announcer and Gayne Whitman is the commercial.
Music composed and conducted by Robert Armbruster.
Story: "Bush-Pilots" are the hardy aviators of northern Canada - courageous and skillful men who fly freight and medical supplies to the remote outposts of North America. When the war bursts upon Canada, Brian and two fellow "Bush-Pilots" fly their "jalopies" to a R.C.A.F. base and present themselves for immediate fighting service. They became snarled in red tape; are finally told they are too old for active fighting service but are accepted as instructors. They are soon "washed out" as instructors because they fly by instinct and not by rules. Brian MacLean and his surviving comrades during a sudden emergency, are permitted to ferry an unarmed bomber to England. Over the Atlantic a Messerschmidt attacks the squadron and begins to shoot down the defenseless bombers. Brian MacLean always wanted to get a Messerschmidt. He crashes his own plane into the enemy - losing his own life - but saving the squadron so that it might go on to continue the great fight. **(HLYD)**

Trivia: Cagney reprised his film role of Brian MacLean in this *Cavalcade* adaptation of the 1942 Warner Brothers film, which was also Cagney's first Technicolor film. The film was to open in New York on February 12th. Morgan reprised his screen role of Johnny Dutton, Alan Hale as Tiny Murphy, and Reginald Denny as a Commanding Officer.

Dr. Frank Monaghan: "Tonight the *Cavalcade of America* presents an epic story of heroism in the clouds - that weird and startling battlefield in which a new destiny for mankind is being written. As in many recent *Cavalcade* programs this radio drama is a preview of what we believe will be one of the best motion pictures of the year, Warner Brothers' *Captains in the Clouds*, starring James Cagney. Tonight, on the *Cavalcade of America*, Mr. Cagney plays the starring role of Brian MacLean, the dashing 'bush-pilot' you will shortly see on the screen."

EPISODE #265   "**ABRAHAM LINCOLN: THE WAR YEARS**"   Broadcast February 9, 1942

    Starring: Raymond Massey as Lincoln   Kingsley Colton as Willie
    William Johnstone as Seward   Kenny Delmar as Cameron
    Alfred Shirley as Blair   Ed Jerome as Welles
    John McIntire as Bates   Bill Pringle as the doctor
    Elliott Reid as the first listener   Kenny Delmar as the second listener
    William Johnstone as the first soldier   Ted Jewett as the second soldier
    Betty Garde as Mrs. Mountchestington   Peggy Riley as Augusta
    Kenny Delmar as Asa Trenchard   Karl Swenson as John W. Booth
    Ted Jewett as Chase   Elliott Reid as Robert
    Larry Robinson as Tad   Jeanette Nolan as Mary Todd Lincoln
    Alfred Shirley as Pinkerton   Ted Jewett as the servant
    Ed Jerome as Judd   Elliott Reid as Jed
    Kenny Delmar as Pete   Ted Jewett as Jack
    Karl Swenson as the father   Betty Garde as the mother
    Larry Robinson as the little boy   Ed Jerome as the man
    Peggy Riley as the woman   Bill Pringle as the farmer
    Karl Swenson as the voice   Ted Jewett as the conductor
    Based on the 1940 novel of the same name by Carl Sandburg, and adapted for *Cavalcade* by Robert E. Sherwood.
    Produced and directed by Homer Fickett.
    John McIntire and Clayton Collyer are the announcers.
    Music composed and conducted by Donald Voorhees.
    Story: same as episode #174, broadcast on February 13, 1940

Trivia: This was a repeat performance - the third to be exact - of two previous presentations that received high critical acclaim. Almost immediately after the first broadcast on February 13, 1940, the listening audience brought forth a flood of commendation. The Institute for Education by radio at the Ohio State University honored *Cavalcade* with its first award ever granted a commercial program. The Lincoln program was repeated in Wilmington, Delaware on February 12, 1941. Now, for a third (and what was to be the final) time, and a high sense of gratification, *Cavalcade of America* presented that popular tribute to the memory of a truly great American.

EPISODE #266   "**THE DARK ANGEL**"   Broadcast on February 16, 1942

    Starring: Merle Oberon as Kitty   Jeanette Nolan as Shannon
    Karl Swenson as Alan   William Johnstone as Gerald
    Ted Jewett as the first soldier   Kenny Delmar as the second soldier
    Betty Garde as Ann   John McIntire as Tanner
    Kenny Delmar as the voice
    Based on Guy Bolton's stage play, and adapted for *Cavalcade* by Norman Rosten.
    Produced and directed by Homer Fickett.
    Clayton Collyer is the announcer.
    Music composed and conducted by Donald Voorhees.
    Story: The basic motivation of the story is old . . . quite old, yet it is ever new. It is a story of love. More specifically, it is the story of the love of two men for a girl and of the rendering and overwhelming love for one of them. Alan, Gerard and Kitty, were childhood playmates. Both Alan and Gerald love Kitty; Kitty is fond of Gerald; she loves Alan. The war comes. Both Alan and Gerald are surgeons in the Army. They are home on leave. Alan and Kitty plan to be married at once, but before that happens the leave is canceled, and Alan and Gerald return to active duty. While in service Alan goes blind. Now he knows that he should not marry Kitty. He disappears and goes into a hospital under an assumed name. Believing that Alan is dead, Kitty agrees to marry Gerald. Meanwhile, in the hospital where Alan is slowly recovering his sight, the

authorities discover that their patient has been there under an assumed name. And Alan's nurse reads an item in the newspaper announcing the coming marriage of Gerald and Kitty. Alan's doctor communicates with Gerald. Both Gerald and Kitty rush to the hospital. Alan, informed of their impending visit, prepares to receive them. He also carefully prepares to conceal the fact that he is blind.

Trivia: Oberon reprised her 1935 screen performance of Kitty in this adaptation of the Samuel Goldwyn film that won Oberon an Academy Award nomination for Best Actress. (Oberon lost to Bette Davis for *Dangerous*.) Goldwyn had produced another filmed version of this story previously in 1925 with Ronald Colman.

P.S. And Alan and Kitty lived happily ever after.

EPISODE #267   "**ARROWSMITH**"   Broadcast on February 23, 1942
Starring: Tyrone Power as Dr. Martin Arrowsmith
Lurene Tuttle as Leora	Gail Patrick as Yeska
Harry Bartel as Norton	Howard McNear as Dunziger
Dix Davis as Willie	Lou Merrill as Gottlieb
Earl Ross as the governor	Howard McNear as Stokes
Wally Maher as Drake	Bea Benedaret as Carrie
Earl Ross as the native	Jean Vandepyle as the secretary
Wally Maher as reporter one	Harry Bartel as reporter two

Walt Snow, Richard Wallace, Catherine Cragen, Jack Mather, and Harry Saz were Superintendents.
Based on the 1925 novel by Sinclair Lewis, and adapted for *Cavalcade* by Margaret Lewerth.
Produced and directed by Homer Fickett.
John Hiestand is the announcer and Gayne Whitman is the commercial announcer.
Music composed and conducted by Robert Armbruster.
Story: Dr. Arrowsmith was a young doctor who was possessed by a reverent desire to bring scientific knowledge to the rescue of an ailing humanity. That urge is strong within him, but there is something else that is more compelling. He yearns to do research work - to discover new and useful truths. But Dr. Arrowsmith has a wife, and he must earn a living. He begins his practice in a small community in South Dakota. He has few patients but many difficulties. Conflict is inevitable when Dr. Arrowsmith's scientific ideas come into clash with entrenched local interests bolstered by ignorance and simple quackery. Then comes an offer of a research position in a laboratory under the direction of his old teacher, Dr. Max Gottlieb. He accepts and plunges into the work he loves best. This struggle during which his wife dies (a victim of the plague) provides the tense drama fighting fear and ignorance and apathy. **(HLYD)**

EPISODE #268   "**ACCENT ON YOUTH**"   Broadcast on March 2, 1942
Starring: Walter Pidgeon as Stephen Gaye	Ellen Drew as Linda
Kenny Delmar as Flogdell	Karl Swenson as Dickie
Arlene Francis as Genevieve	Kenny Delmar as Detective

Based on the play by Samson Raphaelson, adapted for *Cavalcade* by Robert Tallman.
Produced and directed by Homer Fickett.
Clayton Collyer is the announcer.
Music composed and conducted by Donald Voorhees.
Story: This drama resolves around three age-old elements: youth, age and love. The basic conflict is between youthful love and the love of mature middle age. Many a brilliant author has placed the accent on the wrong word just as did Stephen Gaye when he submerged his personal life in his career as a playwright. How he is made to discover the error and how the accent is finally shifted is the absorbing theme of one of the most

successful plays in a decade of the American theatre. Stephen reads with his secretary a script of a new play based upon an elderly man who falls in love with a young girl. he finally decides that it is all impossible nonsense - that it could never happen. He determines to junk it. Then real people enter and begin to simplify and complicate Gaye's life. Through them he learns what was wrong with both his play and himself.

Trivia: Herbert Marshall and Sylvia Sidney starred in the 1935 Paramont release, remade years later under the titles *But Not For Me* and *Mr. Music*.

EPISODE #269   **"WAIT FOR THE MORNING"**   Broadcast on March 9, 1942
Starring: Madeleine Carroll as Emily Dickinson   Karl Swenson as father
Charita Bauer as her Vinnie Dickinson   William Johnstone as George
Written for *Cavalcade* by Norman Rosten, based on the biography "The Life and Mind of Emily Dickinson" by Genevieve Taggard.
Produced and directed by Homer Fickett.
Clayton Collyer is the announcer.
Music composed and conducted by Donald Voorhees.
Story: same as episode #210, broadcast on January 22, 1941

Madeleine Carroll: "I like to think that when you applauded me so graciously tonight that mixed up in your applause there was just a little of 'we're glad to see you back again on the *Cavalcade* stage.' I know it makes me very happy to be playing for you a second time this season with the *Cavalcade* players. And so thank you again, everybody."

Trivia: This episode was a repeat performance of a previous script, a last minute solution because the script originally planned, "The Age of Innocence," was tossed on the shelf only days before broadcast.

EPISODE #270   **"DEAR BRUTUS"**   Broadcast on March 16, 1942
Starring: Fredric March as Dearth   Kenny Delmar as the narrator
Betty Garde as Alice   Karl Swenson as Matey
Jeanette Nolan as Mrs. Coade   John McIntire as Coade
Charita Bauer as Margaret
Based on the stage play by James M. Barrie, adapted for *Cavalcade* by Robert Tallman.
Produced and directed by Homer Fickett.
Clayton Collyer is the announcer.
Music composed and conducted by Donald Voorhees.
Story: Next to "Peter Pan," "Dear Brutus" is the most beloved of all the plays of Sir James Matthew Barrie. Ageless in theme, it has its roots in a mystery as ancient and universal as humanity itself. For Barrie had the compassionate wit to know that in the folk tales and myths of our forefathers, we can find the deepest and most secret wishes of ourselves. Barrie has chosen an English country home as the locale for his play. It could be any place, anywhere and anytime. Universal in theme, it is the story of a man, who on an enchanted midsummer's eve, dared to look - and in so doing lived, for one enchanted hour, his life as it might have been. And when he had, he knew, as William Shakespeare had expressed it long before him: "The fault, dear Brutus, is not in our stars - but in ourselves - that we are underlings."

On the next page: A sample of the flyers passed out to the audience attending the stage performances. Paul Lukas on "Passport to Freedom," the first episode of the 1946 - 47 season.

PAUL LUKAS

BACK ON THE AIR!

DU PONT CAVALCADE OF AMERICA

presents

PAUL LUKAS *in*

"*Passport to Freedom*"

MONDAY EVENING, AUGUST 26, 1946

NATIONAL BROADCASTING COMPANY
Coast to Coast Network

BETTER THINGS FOR BETTER

EPISODE #271   "**ANGELS ON HORSEBACK**"   Broadcast on March 23, 1942
Starring: Myrna Loy as Dr. Mary Breckenridge
Also in the cast: Kenny Delmar and William Johnstone
Written for *Cavalcade* by Robert Tallman.
Produced and directed by Homer Fickett.
Clayton Collyer is the announcer.
Music composed and conducted by Donald Voorhees.
Story: Up the steep trails and along the ridges of the mountains of Kentucky ride nurses on horseback carrying medical care and education to the people whose high, and inaccessible, homeland has been called the last frontier of America. Using this great background for a fictional story, this drama presented a woman and two men whose love involved their careers in this public service. Those familiar with the courageous and generous work of Dr. Mary Breckenridge in creating and developing the Frontier Nursing Service, know the risks that are part of the daily routine along the treacherous mountain trails and the flowing of torrential mountain streams, where one misstep means a plunge to certain death. This tale involves lovely Jane Eaton, who has given up an idle life in New York society to join the frontier service, and two men - both doctors and both in love with her.

EPISODE #272   "**THE SILENT HEART**"   Broadcast on March 30, 1942

Starring: Ingrid Bergman as Jenny Lind   Kenny Delmar as Clerk
William Johnstone as Whitman   Edwin Jerome as Webster
Ted Jewett as Greeley   Karl Swenson as Joseph
Ted Jewett as the call boy   Edgar Vincent as the sailor
John McIntire as P.T.   Jeanette Nolan as the queen
Ted Jewett as the voice   William Johnstone as Otto
Edgar Vincent as Hans   Betty Garde as Anna

Written for *Cavalcade* by Norman Rosten, based on research by Carl Carmer.
Produced and directed by Homer Fickett.
Clayton Collyer is the announcer and Kenny Delmar is the narrator.
Music composed and conducted by Donald Voorhees.
Featuring the Ken Christie Singers. Elizabeth Mulliner sings Bergman's role of Jenny Lind, singing the 1813 song "Last Rose of Summer."
Story: Few artists until modern times achieved the universal acclaim that came in the middle of the last century to a young singer, who, overnight, won the heart of a younger America and who is forever remembered as the Swedish nightingale. Though the story of her fame is familiar to most, including her debut at the Old Castle Garden on the Battery in New York, with the great Barnum for her manager, and with the town's celebrities bidding for seats, the details of her love story gave her career a new interest. For while the world threw its heart at the feet of the great singer there was one heart that was missing, and it was the only one that Jenny Lind cared about. All the others could hardly make up for its absence.

Trivia: This *Cavalcade* broadcast was based on unpublished material brought to light by Carl Carmer while doing research for his current best-selling novel "Genesee Fever."

EPISODE #273   "YELLOW JACK"   Broadcast on April 6, 1942
Starring: Tyrone Power as Major Walter Reed

Ted Jewett as Gorgas	Karl Swenson as Finlay
Betty Garde as nurse Collins	Jeanette Nolan as nurse Martin
Karl Swenson as voice one	Ed Jerome as voice two
Kenny Delmar as voice three	Ted Jewett as voice four
Ian Martin as Lazear	Bill Pringle as the Tory
William Johnstone as Carroll	Edwin Jerome as Gramonte
John McIntire as O'Hara	Kenny Delmar as McClelland
Paul Stewart as Busch	Frank Readick as Brinkerhoff

Adapted for *Cavalcade* by Peter Lyon, based on the stage play of the same name by Sidney Howard.
Produced and directed by Homer Fickett.
Clayton Collyer is the announcer.
Music composed and conducted by Donald Voorhees.
Story: Until a few men risked their lives in scientific experiment, while Dr. Walter Reed and his associates peered into the miasmic mystery which surrounded the disease, epidemics of the plague had ravaged great cities in the United States and year after year had spread terror in the land. No one knew where it came from, or how it moved from place to place. They did not know that the buzz of a certain mosquito held the fatal warning of the rattlesnake. How Dr. Reed, working with previous experiments, pieced together the evidence and tracked down Yellow Jack, is not only one of the greatest detective stories of science, but a record of imperishable gallantry - notable alike for its historical significance and its dramatic intensity.

EPISODE #274   "A CONTINENTAL UNIFORM"   Broadcast on April 13, 1942

Starring: Basil Rathbone as General Arnold	Eric Rolfe as the Aide
Rosemary De Camp as Peggy	Lou Merrill as the surgeon
Gale Gordon as George Washington	Elliott Lewis as the story teller
Gerald Mohr as Tallyrand	Hans Conried as York
Lou Merrill as the servant	Gale Gordon as Hamilton
Eric Rolfe as the major	Hans Conried as Andre
Elliott Lewis as Punch	Gerald Mohr as Captain Pell

Written for *Cavalcade* by Robert Tallman.
Produced and directed by Homer Fickett.
John Hiestand is the announcer and Gayne Whitman is the commercial announcer.
Music composed and conducted by Robert Armbruster.
Story: As military commander of Philadelphia, Benedict Arnold tried to control the merchants and came into sharp contact with the civil authorities. His expenses soon surpassed the resources of a slender purse. He fell in love with Peggy Shippen who had many Tory contacts. Here begins the disintegration of a bold patriot who now is frustrated, harassed by debts and in love with a glamorous woman of dubious allegiance. Slowly the plan of treason begins to form; slowly it is perfected with all the skill and cunning once devoted to the patriot cause. Then, on the eve of success, a minor mistake betrays the whole plan. Arnold escapes, but became the most despised of Americans. Even the men who had seduced him in his loyalty did not trust him. In the bitter, melancholy years that followed, Benedict Arnold meditated on all the real things he had lost. And, as he lay dying, he called for his old Continental uniform, "I want to die in my old uniform, Peggy. May God forgive me for putting on any other." **(HLYD)**

On the next page: Two newspaper advertisements of classic *Cavalcade* episodes.

DU PONT
Cavalcade
of America

presents

PAT O'BRIEN

in

"200,000 Flyers"

MONDAY EVENING
OCTOBER 1, 1945

NATIONAL BROADCASTING COMPANY

Coast to Coast Network

8.00-8.30 .... E.T.   9.30-10.00 .... M.T.
7.00-7.30 .... C.T.   8.30- 9.00 .... P.T.

Consult Your Local Radio Timetable

Originating from Hollywood

DU PONT
Cavalcade
of America

presents

IDA LUPINO

in

"Nellie Was A Lady"

MONDAY EVENING
SEPTEMBER 17, 1945

NATIONAL BROADCASTING COMPANY

Coast to Coast Network

8.00-8.30 .... E.T.   9.30-10.00 .... M.T.
7.00-7.30 .... C.T.   8.30- 9.00 .... P.T.

Consult Your Local Radio Timetable

Originating from Hollywood

EPISODE #275 **"IN THIS CRISIS"** Broadcast on April 20, 1942

Starring: Claude Rains as Tom Paine
Agnes Moorehead as Mme. Bonneville
Don Costello as Smythe
Eric Rolfe as the attendant
Gavin Gordon as the second minister
Gale Gordon as the fourth minister
Eric Rolfe as Aitken
John Lake as Greene
Elliott Lewis as the sergeant
Elliott Lewis as the voice
Ray Collins as the stranger
John Mather as Hughes
Hans Conried as the first minister
Elliott Lewis as the third minister
John Mather as the printer
Gale Gordon as Washington
Hans Conried as Marsden

Written for *Cavalcade* by Robert L. Richards.
Produced and directed by Homer Fickett.
John Hiestand is the announcer and Gayne Whitman is the commercial announcer.
Music composed and conducted by Robert Armbruster.
Story: Now and then a man embodies an idea so completely that his name is forever connected with it and becomes, in fact, a sort of symbol of the principle he lived for. Such a man was Thomas Paine - friend of Washington and Franklin and builders of the American concept of freedom. His ideas were the explosive that set off the shot 'heard round the world. His words had the challenging rattle of a drum call to arms; his phrases were the piercing war scream of the fife. His was a mind mobilized for freedom, and when his mall, dark dynamic figure streaked across the Colonial skies to rouse patriots and to comfort the Commander at Valley Forge, he spoke, to borrow Emerson's phrase, "in words as hard as cannonballs." **(HLYD)**

EPISODE #276 **"THIS SIDE OF HADES"** Broadcast on April 27, 1942

Starring: Loretta Young as Molly Pitcher
Karl Swenson as John
Jeanette Nolan as Mrs. Irvine
John McIntire as George Washington
William Johnstone as Anderson
Ted Jewett as the Colonel
Paul Stewart as the orderly
Ed Jerome as Irvine
Betty Garde as Beulah
William Johnstone as the sentry
Paul Stewart as Smith
Ed Jerome as Jones
Bill Pringle as the Captain

Written for *Cavalcade* by Robert Tallman, based on research by Carl Carmer.
Produced and directed by Homer Fickett.
Clayton Collyer is the announcer.
Music composed and conducted by Donald Voorhees.
Story: Molly was the robust, earthy daughter of John George Ludwig, a German immigrant farmer who settled before the Revolution in eastern Pennsylvania. She was untutored and unlettered - a daughter of menial toil. She married John Hays, a neighborhood barber. Her husband enlisted in the army for a year - and when that was over he re-enlisted in Colonel William Irvine's 7th Pennsylvania Regiment. She went off to war with her husband - and cooked and washed and mended uniforms and nursed the sick. Then came the Battle of Monmouth - June 28, 1778 - the hottest day of a hot summer. Soldiers literally died of thirst. Molly ran back and forth from the front lines to a distant well with her pitcher of water. When her husband fell exhausted by his cannon an officer ordered that the gun be removed, but Molly discarded her pitcher and took over the cannon - firing it with even greater effect than her husband. Soldiers called her "Sergeant Molly" or "Major Molly," but she never received any commission. She was content to be plain "Molly Pitcher."

EPISODE #277 **"THE PRINTER WAS A LADY"** Broadcast on May 4, 1942
    Starring: Lynn Fontaine as Anne Royall   Kenny Delmar as Simms
    Larry Robinson as the newsboy   Bill Pringle as George
    Frank Readick as Sec. Eaton   Ted Jewett as the clerk
    John McIntire as President Jackson   Paul Stewart as Coxe
    Ed Jerome as the Congressman   Dwight Weist as the judge
    Bill Pringle as the printer   Ed Jerome as Swann
    Jeanette Nolan as Sally   Bill Pringle as the fireman
    William Johnstone as Grey   Paul Stewart as Johnson
Written for *Cavalcade* by Robert L. Richards.
Produced and directed by Homer Fickett.
Clayton Collyer is the announcer.
Music composed and conducted by Donald Voorhees.
Story: She was born in squalor and ignorance in Maryland in 1769, growing up in the wilderness. She met, worked for and finally married a cultivated gentleman, a distinguished soldier, William Royall. When he died she was defrauded of her estate and at the age of 55 she found herself penniless. But for Anne Royall life only began at 55. She borrowed a few dollars and began to travel and to write. She was amusing and shrewd and caustic. But, more important, she was brave and honest. After she had traveled throughout the United States she settled down in the Washington of Andrew Jackson. There she established a newspaper (of which she was proprietor, editor, printer, reporter and newsboy). It never had a large circulation, but it had an immense influence. Anne Royall was a national figure, fighting intolerance, corruption, selfish monopolies.

Homer Fickett: "The ample budget allowed practically free rein in choice of players. To us, sufficient proof of this was when *Cavalcade* lured Alfred Lunt for his initial radio appearance and at another time ["The Printer Was a Lady"], we secured his wife Lynn Fontaine for her microphone debut. The idea behind casting seems to be that of deciding exactly who, from all the ranks of fine performers, will be able to enact the part to perfection."

EPISODE #278 **"A TOOTH FOR PAUL REVERE"** Broadcast on May 11, 1942
    Starring: Raymond Massey as Lige Butterwick   Peggy Riley as Mrs. Prichard
    Jeanette Nolan as Hannah   Kenny Delmar as Eben
    Frank Readick as Barber Joe   Ted Jewett as Beckett
    Larry Robinson as Peter   Kenny Delmar as the boat man
    Ed Jerome as the patrol man   Betty Garde as Mrs. Moorehead
    William Johnstone as the small voice   Paul Stewart as Weller
    Jeanette Nolan as the boat woman   Betty Garde as the deaf woman
    William Johnstone as the mason   Frank Readick as the sentry
    Ted Jewett as Kirk   Ed Jerome as the barkeep
    John McIntire as Woodbury   Larry Robinson as William
    John McIntire as the windblown voice   Peggy Riley as the girl
    Karl Swenson as Paul Revere   Ed Jerome as the patrol man
Brad Barker supplied the animal voices, including the horses.
Written for *Cavalcade* by Stephen Vincent Benet, based on his 1937 stage play.
Produced and directed by Homer Fickett.
Clayton Collyer is the announcer.
Music composed and conducted by Donald Voorhees.
Story: With an imagination as inventive as it is true, with rare humor and deep understanding of such material, we look back on a great historical event. As inheritors of the liberties won when the "embattled farmers" stood at Concord bridge and fired the shot heard 'round the world we know what they fought for and why we cherish it, and fight now to preserve it. We look now, into the heart of one of those farmers and tell the

tale of Lige Butterwick, who went to see a celebrated silversmith in Boston about getting his tooth fixed, and who remained to join that silversmith - a man named Paul Revere - at Lexington.

EPISODE #279   "**REMEMBER THE DAY**"   Broadcast on May 18, 1942
    Starring: Claudette Colbert as Nora Trinnell
    Gale Gordon as Dewey (as a man)   Erik Rolf as Mr. Steele
    Elliott Lewis as Dan Hopkins   Janet Beecher as Mrs. Roberts
    Louise Erickson as the girl   Conrad Binyon as the boy
    Herb Vigran as the bellboy   Jack Mather as Stokes
    Tommy Cook as Dewey (as a boy)   Jack Mather as the porter
    Written for *Cavalcade* by George Barraud.
    Produced and directed by Homer Fickett.
John Hiestand is the announcer and Gayne Whitman is the commercial announcer.
Music composed and conducted by Robert Armbruster.
Story: In the lives of most men, they say, there are three women of powerful influence - mother, wife, and school teacher. This drama lets us see in the figure of its classroom heroine one of the true molders of America and how she shaped the course of one great destiny. In the true spirit and intent of the high purpose of those who educate the nation's youth, through their precepts created in each generation the America of the future. There is a noble calling, and a tremendous responsibility and in the story of one such teacher, and a great man who remembered the day of his schooling, with tenderness and gratitude, *Cavalcade* touches the mainsprings of enlightened democracy. **(HLYD)**

EPISODE #280   "**YOUNG TOM JEFFERSON**"   Broadcast on May 25, 1942
    Starring: Tyrone Power as Tom Jefferson   William Farnum as Dr. Franklin
    Jack Mather as John Adams   Gale Gordon as Peter
    Clarence Muse as Jed   Joe Latham as the farmer
    Georgia Backus as the hostess   Hans Conried as the governor
    Jack Mather as the Sgt-at-Arms   Erik Rolf as the judge
    Don Costello as the clerk   Norman Field as the host
    Don Costello as the Captain   Georgia Backus as Martha
    Ray Collins as Henry   Erik Rolf as the chair
    Gale Gordon as the doctor   Bob Mauch as the soldier
    Hans Conried as the Chaplain   Elliott Lewis as the narrator
    Written for *Cavalcade* by Robert L. Richards.
    Produced and directed by Homer Fickett.
John Hiestand is the announcer and Gayne Whitman is the commercial announcer.
Music composed and conducted by Robert Armbruster.
Story: Among the men who have done significant things in our nation's history is Thomas Jefferson. Among the great documents of our American past is the Declaration of Independence. That immortal statement was first conceived as a charter of hope. In it are some things which are calmly stated as accepted facts. It was young Tom Jefferson who wrote that Declaration. John Adams gave him a little assistance, and Dr. Franklin helped him with a phrase here and there. But it was basically the thought, the language, the rhetoric of a freckled young man from Virginia. **(HLYD)**

Trivia: For Tyrone Power, this was one of his last radio broadcasts before joining the Navy, co-starring with William Farnum. Although Farnum played numerous supporting roles on *Cavalcade*, Farnum had often appeared with Ty's father in a handful of Hollywood films.

EPISODE #281   "**CLARA BARTON**"   Broadcast on June 1, 1942

Starring: Madeleine Carroll as Clara Barton
Bill Pringle as Senator Z
Kenny Delmar as the narrator
Everett Sloane as Jim
Jeanette Nolan as Ann
Everett Sloane as Stanton's Secretary
Jimmy McCallion as Jimmy
John McIntire as Wilson
Ed Jerome as Senator X
Ted Jewett as the orderly
Bill Pringle as the waiter
Ed Jerome as Senator Y
Frank Readick as the cabby
Karl Swenson as Stanton
Paul Stewart as Hay
Ted Jewett as the secretary

Written for *Cavalcade* by Robert Tallman.
Produced and directed by Homer Fickett.
Clayton Collyer is the announcer.
Music composed and conducted by Donald Voorhees.

Story: After ten years of teaching school, Clara Barton found herself in Washington at the time of the Civil War. Following the Battle of Bull Run, she was heartily depressed by the stories she heard about the suffering of the soldiers caused by a lack of supplies. Here was a problem - she at once had an answer. She simply advertised in a newspaper and supplies came pouring in. In July 1862, she received permission to visit the sick and wounded near the battle lines. She was highly interested in securing and distributing supplies. For four years after the war, she directed the extensive search for missing soldiers. A great humanitarian she was, and will always be remembered.

EPISODE #282   "**THE COLOSSUS OF PANAMA**"   Broadcast on June 8, 1942

Starring: Walter Huston as William Crawford Gorgas
Written for *Cavalcade* by Robert Tallman.
Produced and directed by Homer Fickett.
Clayton Collyer is the announcer.
Music composed and conducted by Donald Voorhees.

Story: In 1904, William Crawford Gorgas was sent to Panama, where he encountered a mass of administrative stupidly and official apathy that was almost worse than yellow fever itself. Under the leadership of President Roosevelt, the U.S. was determined to build a canal in an attempt to create an all-water passage from the Atlantic to the Pacific. The engineers believed that money spent on killing mosquitoes was a waste - and they were too often supported by the politicians back home. It was Gorgas, never daunted, who fought against the ignorance and blundering. He won his long battle and the Canal Zone was freed of yellow fever. And with that victory the canal was made possible.

EPISODE #283   "**THE LADY AND THE FLAG**"   Broadcast on June 15, 1942

Starring: Paulette Goddard as Betsy Ross
Arlene Francis as Martha
Paul Stewart as Robert Morris
Adelaide Klein as Olivia
Alan Bunce as Green
Kenny Delmar as Arthur
Will Geer as Griscom
Karl Swenson as John
Frank Readick as the soldier
Ed Jerome as Washington
Anne Sterrett as Mary
Stefan Schnabel as the second soldier
Agnes Young as Marie
Ted Jewett as the minister
Ian Martin as Austin
Alan Bunce as Roger

Written for *Cavalcade* by Norman Rosten.
Produced and directed by Homer Fickett.
Clayton Collyer is the announcer.
Music composed and conducted by Donald Voorhees.

Story: Betsy Griscom's parents objected to her proposed marriage to John Ross, a clergyman's son. Betsy and John promptly eloped. They opened an upholstery shop on Arch Street in Philadelphia and lived in modest quarters on the second floor. John was later killed in the war, leaving Betsy a widow. Sadness crept in, until one day, came her moment in history. General George Washington, Robert Morris, and General Ross (her brother-in-law) came into her shop and asked it she could and was willing to make a flag of the new United States. They produced rough drawings which contained stars with six points. Betsy suggested stars with five points and quickly showed them how such stars could be cut with a single clip of the scissors. And the rest as they say . . . is history.

EPISODE #284   **"THE BATTLE OF THE OVENS"**   Broadcast on June 22, 1942
Starring: Jean Hersholt as Christopher Ludwick
Written for *Cavalcade* by Arthur Miller.
Produced and directed by Homer Fickett.
Clayton Collyer is the announcer.
Music composed and conducted by Donald Voorhees.
Story: As men measure prestige and reputation, Ludwick had never even entered the reckoning. He had come from Germany to America and had settled in Philadelphia. He was a baker, a good baker and an honest baker. He lived humbly and industriously. But when the American Revolution began he was an old man, far too old for active military service. Ludwick was determined to do his part. He persisted and finally became the Superintendent of Bakers in the Continental Army. Ludwick knew bread and he knew that an army must have bread. Realizing the final stake of victory, Ludwick performed a contribution unlike any.

Arthur Miller: "The American nation had never raised a monument to Christopher Ludwick; no city had ever named a street or a boulevard for him; no biographer had ever troubled to put his story within the cover of a book. His name was unknown even to persons otherwise informed of the details of our national history. The historian must confess that there are not many available details on the career of Ludwick, but the facts that we did have provided the basis of a dramatic and appropriate story."

EPISODE #285   **"HYMN FROM THE NIGHT"**   Broadcast on June 29, 1942
Starring: Helen Hayes as Julia W. Howe   Ed Jerome as Sumner
Ted Jewett as Breckenrdge   Frank Readick as Parker
Adelaide Klein as Mrs. Brown   Ed Jerome as Abe Lincoln
Frank Readick as the voice of Secession   Bill Pringle as Brooks
Ted Jewett as the voice of the Union   Will Geer as Brown
Adelaide Klein as Agnes   Karl Swenson as Charles
Ted Donaldson as Sammy   Frank Readick as Marshall
Kenny Delmar is the narrator.
Written for *Cavalcade* by Robert Tallman.
Produced and directed by Homer Fickett.
Clayton Collyer is the announcer.
Music composed and conducted by Donald Voorhees.
Story: It does not happen often, but when it does, it shatters the apathy and the intolerance of millions. It happened to Julia Ward Howe. She had been writing poems and romances for years, but none of the were very good. But one day she visited an army camp near Washington D.C. There the things she saw and the things she heard began, almost unconsciously, to release the eloquent, but pent-up voice that was yearning for expression. That night she was in a tent trying to sleep. But the events of the day had stirred her and sleep was impossible. The inner voice was beginning to speak. She had no light, but in the darkness of the tent she found paper and pencil and out came the words of the "Battle Hymn of the Republic," all composed to the rhythm of "John Brown's Body."

EPISODE #286 "**THE GENTLEMAN FROM THE ISLANDS**" Broadcast on July 6, 1942
    Starring: Alfred Lunt as Alexander Hamilton
    Ed Jerome as Van Ness   Frank Readick as Cheetham
    Ted Jewett as the Secretary   Kenny Delmar as Hosack
    Ted Jewett as the attendant   Karl Swenson as Barr
    Karl Swenson as Swarthout   Will Geer as Pendleton
    James McCallion as James   Arlene Francis as Betsy
    Written for *Cavalcade* by Robert Tallman.
    Produced and directed by Homer Fickett.
    Clayton Collyer is the announcer.
    Music composed and conducted by Donald Voorhees.
    Story: Soon after Aaron Burr became Vice President of the United States, Alexander Hamilton took a disliking toward the man. Hamilton even helped elect Thomas Jefferson. Burr ran for Governor of New York in 1804. Hamilton again opposed him. This time Burr lost the election. Angry, Aaron Burr challenged Hamilton to a duel. On July 11, 1804, the men faced each other with pistols in Weehawken, New Jersey. Burr fatally wounded Hamilton with one shot. A New York coroner's inquest "found a verdict of willful murder by Aaron Burr, Vice President of the United States."

    Trivia: This was Alfred Lunt's first radio appearance. He would later guest on two other *Cavalcade* broadcasts.

EPISODE #287 "**MAN OF IRON**" Broadcast on July 13, 1942
    Starring: Dean Jagger as Lt. Worden   Ted Jewett as the helmsman
    William Johnstone as Ericcson   James McCallion as Bos'n
    William Johnstone as the mate   Karl Swenson as Stanton
    James McCallion as Greene   Bill Pringle as the Captain
    Ian Martin as the attaché   Frank Readick as the telegrapher
    Paul Stewart as Helmsman   Ted Jewett as the sailor
    Frank Readick as the commodore   Ed Jerome as Abe Lincoln
    Arnold Moss as Fox   Arlene Francis as Olivia
    Paul Stewart as the first officer   Kenny Delmar as the narrator
    Written for *Cavalcade* by Robert L. Richards and Robert Tallman.
    Produced and directed by Homer Fickett.
    Clayton Collyer is the announcer.
    Music composed and conducted by Donald Voorhees.
    Story: When the Civil War broke out the Federal Government learned, to its great dismay, that the Confederates were building an iron-clad ship, the Merrimac, which promised to sweep the Union Navy from the seas. John Ericsson, one of the greatest inventors of the nineteenth century, came forward and offered to build, in the incredibly short period of one hundred days, a vessel that would destroy the Merrimac. Ericsson's "Cheesebox on a Raft" appeared and engaged the new menace in successful battle. Ericsson had introduced a basic new principle of naval warfare to the world.

LISTEN
*every Tuesday Evening
to the "Cavalcade of America"*
Consult your local radio time table

EPISODE #288 "**THE WILD YOUNG MAN**" Broadcast on July 20, 1942
 Starring: Dean Jagger as Stephen Decatur
 Written for *Cavalcade* by Peter Lyon.
 Produced and directed by Homer Fickett.
 Clayton Collyer is the announcer.
 Music composed and conducted by Donald Voorhees.
 Story: In November of 1803, Stephen Decatur was in the Mediterranean commanding the *Enterprise*, a small boat of twelve guns. Affairs between the United States and the Barbary pirates were reaching a breaking point. For years we had paid these pirates annual tribute so that they would not molest American ships. Even Great Britain, undisputed mistress of the seas, paid tribute to the Barbary pirates and did not contest their local supremacy. Stephen Decatur captured a ship and proposed that he sail into the harbor of Tripoli, under the very guns of the forts - and destroy the *Philadelphia*, an American ship captured by the Tripolitans. With a handful of men he did what Lord Nelson declared was "the most bold and daring act of the age."

EPISODE #289 "**MAN OF DESIGN**" Broadcast on July 27, 1942
 Starring: Karl Swenson as Eli Whitney
 Paul Stewart as Brown
 Frank Readick as man two
 Charita Bauer as Henrietta
 Ed Jerome as Goodrich
 William Johnstone as Jefferson
 Paul Stewart as man three
 Paul Stewart as workman two
 William Johnstone as voice one
 Frank Readick as Cushing
 Frank Readick as Matthew
 Ted Jewett as man one
 Everett Sloane as Townsend
 Will Geer as Edwards
 Ted Jewett as the barkeep
 Everett Sloane as Adams
 Ian Martin as Gansevoort
 Kenny Delmar as workman two
 Will Geer as voice two
 Kenny Delmar as North
 Written for *Cavalcade* by Peter Lyon.
 Produced and directed by Homer Fickett.
 Clayton Collyer is the announcer.
 Music composed and conducted by Donald Voorhees.
 Story: Eli Whitney devoted his time to his ideas - which produced the cotton gin and later, in the North, the idea of interchangeable parts, in the production of munitions and the tools of war. The story of Eli Whitney, the man who gave us the idea of "mass production." It was simply the assembling of accurately prepared separate parts to form a perfect whole. In its time this was a most revolutionary idea; in our time it is the most dominant idea. The firm basis of victory in the field of naval and military operations.

Homer Fickett: "Before Pearl Harbor we showed a preference for stories glorifying the history of America. But since the war, we have modified our policy and now do many modern plays, or historical connotation. Recently we did a show on Eli Whitney. Now you would think that we built the script about his invention of the cotton gin. But we didn't. We showed that Whitney was really the inventor of today's assembly line."

EPISODE #290 "**THIS OUR EXILE**" Broadcast on August 3, 1942
 Starring: Madeleine Carroll as Evangeline
 Frank Readick as voice one
 Everett Sloane as voice four
 Betty Garde as Anna
 Kenny Delmar as the man
 Everett Sloane as the narrator
 Paul Stewart as Clement
 Kenny Delmar as Priest
 Ed Jerome as Basil
 Kenny Delmar as voice three
 Ted Jewett as voice two
 Ed Jerome as Fiddler
 Paul Stewart as the guide
 Betty Garde as the nurse
 Ted Jewett as Harold
 Will Geer as Benedict
 Karl Swenson as Gabriel
 Frank Readick as the leader

Based on the drama "Evangeline" by Henry Wadsworth Longfellow, and adapted for *Cavalcade* by Norman Rosten.
Produced and directed by Homer Fickett.
Clayton Collyer is the announcer.
Music composed and conducted by Donald Voorhees.
Story: The separation of a beautiful Arcadian girl, Evangeline, from her beloved Gabriel was but one tragic incident of the thousands that arose from the exile of the Arcadians in 1755. This forcible parting of the two lovers has long been considered by novelists and poets alike to be a classic example of the tragedy of parted lovers. As long ago as 1840, Nathaniel Hawthorne first thought of using it as a basis for a novel, but he gave it to a friend, Henry Wadsworth Longfellow, who made of it one of the great narrative poems of the English language. What one of us does not know at least the opening stanza of Longfellow's immortal poem, Evangeline?

EPISODE #291   "I, MARY WASHINGTON"   Broadcast on August 10, 1942
Starring: Madeleine Carroll as Mary Washington   Ted Jewett as the doctor
Larry Robinson as George the second   Sarah Fussell as the baby
Karl Swenson as George Washington   Betty Garde as Ella
Ed Jerome as Augustine   Kenny Delmar as the narrator
Written for *Cavalcade* by Robert Tallman.
Produced and directed by Homer Fickett.
Clayton Collyer is the announcer.
Music composed and conducted by Donald Voorhees.
Story: Mary Ball was pretty and gay and rapidly caught the attention of local swains. But she was determined to wait until the right man appeared. He appeared in the person of Augustine Washington and in 1730 they were married and moved to Westmoreland in Western Virginia. Here Augustine and Mary carved a small fortune out of the wilderness. And George Washington was born in 1732. Augustine had had sons by a previous marriage. When their father died, according to the custom of the day, Augustine left almost all of his property to the sons by the first marriage. Mary Washington was left very little, and poor George had to fend for himself.

EPISODE #292   "THEODORE ROOSEVELT, MAN OF ACTION"   August 17, 1942
Starring: Edward Arnold as Theodore Roosevelt
Written for *Cavalcade* by Robert L. Richards and Robert Tallman.
Produced and directed by Homer Fickett.
Clayton Collyer is the announcer.
Music composed and conducted by Donald Voorhees.
Story: America was founding an empire and from it all emerged a young fighter named Teddy Roosevelt, battling his way up through the political hurly-burly of his native New York. Charging up San Juan Hill at the head of his famous Rough Riders to capture the hearts and imaginations of his countrymen. In the election of 1900 a grateful nation made him its Vice President. Less than a year later, on September 14, 1901, President McKinley died at the hand of an assassin and Rough Rider Roosevelt became the 26th President of the United States. And a soldier and man of action he was.

Trivia: The title previously given to this episode was "The Big Stick," and later "Theodore Roosevelt." However, by the time the final draft of this script came into being, it was lengthened to "Theodore Roosevelt, Man of Action."

EPISODE #293   "THE GIANT IN THE MEADOW"   Broadcast on August 24, 1942
Starring: Ralph Bellamy as Theobald Smith

Based on material from the book "Microbe Hunters" by Paul de Kruif, originally published in 1926 by Harcourt, Brace & Company. Adapted for *Cavalcade* by Milton Geiger and Robert Tallman.
Produced and directed by Homer Fickett.
Clayton Collyer is the announcer.
Music composed and conducted by Donald Voorhees.
Story: When he graduated from Cornell in 1881, Dr. Theobald Smith was determined to study medicine. Two years later he graduated as a doctor. Fascinated by the high adventure of discovery, the how and the why of things, he joined the Bureau of Animal Industry of the United States Department of Agriculture. At this time the disease called "The Texas Fever" was wiping out vast herds of cattle. Unless it could be controlled it threatened to destroy the entire cattle industry of America. After many disappointments and failures he finally proved that the disease was carried by a tick. This brilliant discovery that insects can and do carry disease not only made it possible to control The Texas Fever, but it opened up the great new field of scientific speculation and research.

EPISODE #294   **"PROPHET WITHOUT HONOR"**   Broadcast on August 31, 1942
Starring: Charles Laughton as Homer Lea
Written for *Cavalcade* by Robert Tallman, based on material submitted by Joshua B. Powers.
Produced and directed by Homer Fickett.
Clayton Collyer is the announcer.
Music composed and conducted by Donald Voorhees.
Story: In 1909, Homer Lea published a small but dynamic book entitled "The Valor of Ignorance." He hoped that intelligent Americans would read it and would profit from it. A few persons did read it. Some readers were simply puzzled; others, equally puzzled, denounced both the book and the author. Various peace societies said that it was war-mongering. Lea had demonstrated the menace of Japan to the United States and explained, with military precision, how she would attack. Three years later, on his death bed, he finished "The Day of the Saxon," a startling prediction of the menace of Japan to the British Empire.

Trivia: Du Pont was authorized by Joshua B. Powers, the originator of this story, to print and distribute copies of this script to schools, colleges, and similar institutions, but not to be used for commercial purposes.

EPISODE #295   **"SOLDIER OF A FREE PRESS"**   Broadcast on September 7, 1942
Starring: Claude Rains
Written for *Cavalcade* by Peter Lyon, _?_ Wilson, and _?_ Lerner.
Produced and directed by Homer Fickett.
Clayton Collyer is the announcer.
Music composed and conducted by Donald Voorhees.
Story: Perhaps it would be more accurate to call Richard Harding Davis America's first modern newspaper correspondent. He was a man of polished wit and of urbane tastes; he was a master of the vivid phrase and of the dramatic situation. His sense of news values was superb; his search for the picturesque was constant. For the American public, Davis was the first correspondent whose name was intimately associated with a war. During the Spanish-American War some readers did not know quite whether Davis was reporting the war or fighting the war. In truth, he was doing both. For in the attack of the Rough Riders on San Juan Hill, Davis discarded his notes, picked up the rifle of a wounded American soldier and plunged into the battle.

Trivia: The original title of this original radio script was "Soldier of Fortune."

EPISODE #296 (UNTITLED) Broadcast on September 14, 1942
This broadcast consisted of no drama, but of a speech by the former U.S. Ambassador to Japan, the Honorable Joseph C. Grew on the occasion of awarding the Army-Navy E Award at the Remington Arms Plant in Bridgeport, Connecticut.
First heard was C.K. Davis, President of the Remington Arms Company, who introduced the former Senator from Connecticut, the Honorable Frederic C. Walcott, who introduced Ambassador Grew.
Produced and directed by Homer Fickett.
Clayton Collyer is the announcer.
Opening and closing theme was composed and conducted by Donald Voorhees.

Clayton Collyer: "The Du Pont Company turned over its regular program to its affiliated company, Remington Arms, in order that [the listeners] may hear in the living *Cavalcade of America* - a man who knew more about Japan than perhaps any other American, the honorable Joseph Clark Grew, former United States Ambassador to Japan."

Trivia: Mr. Grew spoke from Bridgeport, Connecticut, home of the Remington Arms Company, where he was the principal guest of honor at ceremonies marking the award of the joint Army-Navy "E for Excellence" to the workers of Remington Arms for their outstanding achievement in the war cause. Broadcast via remote from the Hotel Stratfield in Bridgeport, Connecticut - however Clayton Collyer and Voorhees and his orchestra originated from New York.

Trivia: The episode "Eagle to Britain" was originally scheduled for this date, but the thrilling story of the ferrying of a great bomber from America to the battles in the skies was postponed, so that Joseph Grew was able to give his speech. A copy of this inspiring talk was made available in pamphlet form. A free copy was sent to any listener who addressed a note of a post card to the Radio Section at Du Pont, in Wilmington, Delaware.

EPISODE #297 "EAGLE TO BRITAIN" Broadcast on September 21, 1942
Starring: Kenny Delmar
Written for *Cavalcade* by Milton Geiger and Peter Lyon.
Produced and directed by Homer Fickett.
Clayton Collyer is the announcer.
Music composed and conducted by Donald Voorhees.
Story: Your introduction to the Ferry Command, that high bridge above ocean and cloud that is the Air Transport Command. Four men in a bomber - pilot, flight engineer, navigator and radio man - these are the men who guide these precious planes thousands of miles to the battle line by day and by night, through rain, fog and ice. Here you'll learn how it feels to step into a bomber on a chill and foggy night in North America's flying outposts - as they point the nose of the plane eastward over the turbulent Atlantic.

EPISODE #298 "JUAREZ" Broadcast on September 28, 1942
a.k.a. "THUNDER FROM THE MOUNTAIN"
Starring: Orson Welles as Juarez
Ted Jewett as Bernal
Stephen Schnabel as Joe
Karl Swenson as Saligny
Alfred Shirley as the second soldier
Arlene Francis as Margarita
Stephen Schnabel as Don Manuel
Frank Readick as Felipe
Kenny Delmar as Louis
Paul Stewart as Comonfort
Kenny Delmar as Diego
Ed Jerome as Ortega
Will Geer as the Texan
Karl Swenson as the father
Ed Jerome as Santa Anna
Paul Stewart as the fourth Ambassador

Karl Swenson as the second Ambassador   Alfred Shirley as the third Ambassador
Ted Jewett as the first Ambassador   Ed Jerome as the voice
Based on a 1942 book "Juarez, Hero of Mexico" by Nina Brown Baker and adapted for *Cavalcade* by Arthur Miller.
Produced and directed by Homer Fickett.
Clayton Collyer is the announcer.
Music composed and conducted by Donald Voorhees.
Story: Seventy-five years ago on June 19th, as the light of dawn broke over the peak of Mount Popocatapetal, death by rifle fire was administered to Ferdinand Maximilian, last Emperor of Mexico. With it came liberty to a nation. More than any other one man was responsible. He was Benito Juarez. Juarez has many things in common with an American we all cherish and love. The sixteenth President of the United States. Morals and wisdom ages with Juarez, and when the country goes in turmoil, it is Juarez that the people need more than anything else.

Trivia: Orson Welles was originally scheduled to star in a new original drama entitled "The Man Who Wouldn't Be President." The script, however, was pre-empted, broadcast months later with Edward Arnold in the lead. Instead, Welles starred in this drama about Benito Juarez, a hero of Mexico and fighter of freedom.

Trivia: This episode features two "official" script titles, both of which are listed above.

EPISODE #299   "**I WAS MARRIED ON BATAAN**"   Broadcast on October 5, 1942
Starring: Madeleine Carroll as Lt. Engel   Betty Garde as Sally
Arlene Francis as Betty   Peggy Riley as Grace
Ed Jerome as the Chaplain   Peggy Riley as the chief nurse
Frank Readick as the Captain   Karl Swenson as the second doctor
Karl Swenson as the officer   Clayton Collyer as the soldier
Ted Jewett as Johns   Ed Jerome as the first doctor
Frank Readick as Adams   Kenny Delmar as Emanuel
Written for *Cavalcade* by Arthur Miller, based on an article in a 1942 issue of *American Magazine*, published by the Crowell-Collier Publishing Company.
Produced and directed by Homer Fickett.
Clayton Collyer is the announcer.
Music composed and conducted by Donald Voorhees.
Story: The true story of an Army nurse who served her country through the tragic and heroic days of the fall of Manila, and through the horrors of Bataan and Corregidor. Here she met and fell in love with Lt. Emanuel Engel, Jr., and was married to him on a jungle battlefield. For a wedding march they had the ceaseless rumble of guns. They had six hours of honeymoon before Lt. Engel returned to duty at Mariveles. When the remainder of the American force withdrew to Corregidor for their last stand, she left her husband on Bataan and had not seen or heard of him since. The War Department simply recorded him as "missing in action."

EPISODE #300   "**ADMIRAL OF THE OCEAN SEA**"   Broadcast on October 12, 1942
Starring: Orson Welles as the narrator   Frank Readick as the mate
Sara Fussell as the girl   Ted Jewett as the professor
Karl Swenson as Christopher Columbus   Frank Readick as Thomas
Stephen Schnabel as the guest   Kenny Delmar as Jose
Everett Sloane as Indian Joe
There were numerous unnamed voices throughout the drama, those who played those minor roles were: Karl Swenson, Ian Martin, Ed Jerome, Everett Sloane, Stephen Schnabel, Frank Readick, Ted Jewett, and Kenny Delmar.

Written for *Cavalcade* by Norris Houghton and Robert Meltzer, based upon Professor Eliot Morrison's "Admiral of the Ocean Sea," written in 1942.
Produced and directed by Homer Fickett.
Clayton Collyer is the announcer.
Music composed by Ardon Cornwell and conducted by Donald Voorhees.
Story: The world into which Christopher Columbus was born was a small world indeed. Europe had been pretty well explored and settled, but even the best informed geographers knew very little of the greater part of Asia or of Africa. They did not even suspect the existence of the Americas nor of the great continent of Australia. But it is not correct to think that these men believed that the world was flat and that beyond the horizon was a point at which men and ships would drop as if from the edge of a table top. Men pondered the problem - they had the idea, but they lacked the courage . . . with the exception of Columbus.

Kenny Delmar: "You see, Orson was Orson in everything he did. And he came on to *The March of Time*, which was one of my programs and he came on to *Cavalcade* by Du Pont. And I got to know him and I got to admire him and I don't know of anybody that could come into a theater or room and immediately fires were off - it would be like fireworks went off . . . he had that kind of magic."

EPISODE #301   "**THAT THEY MIGHT LIVE**"   Broadcast on October 19, 1942
Starring: Madeleine Carroll as Marie Zakshefska
Written for *Cavalcade* by Norman Rosten, based on an original idea by Jane Douglas.
Produced and directed by Homer Fickett.
Clayton Collyer is the announcer.
Music composed by Ardon Cornwell and conducted by Donald Voorhees.
Story: America was still a raw, young country when - nearly a hundred years ago - Marie Zakshefska stepped off an immigrant boat. She was 23 then. Maria sought in the Land of the Free what Europe had denied her - the right to practice medicine. No chance did she find to heal the sick and suffering until she was helped by Elizabeth Blackwell. This pioneer woman was also a leader in the fight for women's rights. Through her influence Marie Zakshefska at last got the chance to practice medicine in America. How she finally achieved her own hospital and medical school, originated a nurses' training school at this hospital, and became New England's greatest woman physician are told.

EPISODE #302   "**IN THE BEST TRADITION**"   Broadcast on October 26, 1942
Starring: Orson Welles
Written for *Cavalcade* by Peter Lyon. Permission had been obtained for use within the script of the Carl Sandburg text for the "Road to Victory" Exhibition, shown at the Museum of Modern Art.
Also featured an address by Rear Admiral W.H.P. Blandy, USN.
Produced and directed by Homer Fickett.
Clayton Collyer is the announcer.
Music composed by Ardon Cornwell and conducted by Donald Voorhees.
Story: America was peaceful and prosperous in 1826 when John Adolphus Dahlgren joined the Navy. But ahead lay that "irrepressible conflict" which would bring on our Civil War. America needed great leaders to preserve the Union. Abe Lincoln was one who stepped forward, Ulysses Grant another. And John Dahlgren was to lead the way for America on a crucial naval front. While men and institutions had to be replaced by those which better answered our needs, he was busy revolutionizing our instruments of naval warfare.

Orson Welles: "Every now and then, an American is awarded the Navy Cross. It doesn't happen often - a Navy Cross is an honor that means something. And when a man does get one, his citation sounds something like this: Such severe damage was inflicted on the flight decks of the Japanese carriers that they were effectively put out of action. His courage and inspiring leadership in the face of great danger and very large opposition were in the face of great danger and very large opposition were in keeping with the finest traditions of the United States Naval Service. For this *Cavalcade* presentation, we thought we'd like to talk about our Navy and its traditions."

Trivia: Since tomorrow was Navy Day, and in observance to the one hundredth anniversary of the Navy Ordnance, it was a double privilege for Du Pont to bring the listeners this radio drama, "In the Best Tradition." In addition to the life story of John Dahlgren, we had the privilege of hearing Rear Admiral W.H.P. Blandy, currently our Chief of the Bureau of Naval Ordnance, who had recently returned from the Pacific Theatre of War.

More Trivia: Admiral W.H.P. Blandy's address was broadcast via remote pick up from Lake Minnetonka in Minneapolis. In the event of facilities break-down, an alternate page was submitted within Clayton Collyer's script. Thankfully, he did not have to utilize it. Enclosed is the following that was on the substituted page. Collyer: "Ladies and Gentlemen, due to facilities conditions over which we have no control, we are unable to pick up Admiral W.H.P. Blandy from Minneapolis. However, we do have the talk he had prepared and we will read it to you at this time." At which time, a copy of the speech would have been read by Collyer. Instead, Collyer announced the planned introduction: "Ladies and gentlemen, it is now *Cavalcade*'s privilege to present to you the Chief of our Navy's Bureau or Ordnance, Rear Admiral W.H.P. Blandy." This shows just how prepared and detailed Du Pont was in preparing their scripts for broadcast.

EPISODE #303   "**TOWARD A FARTHER STAR**"   Broadcast on November 2, 1942
Starring: Madeleine Carroll as Amelia Earhart   Frank Readick as Johnny
Written for *Cavalcade* by Arthur Miller and Addy Richton, based on material from the 1942 book "Soaring Wings" by George Palmer Putnam.
Produced and directed by Homer Fickett.
Clayton Collyer is the announcer.
Music composed by Ardon Cornwell and conducted by Donald Voorhees.
Story: Learning to fly was easy for Miss Earhart, for she was a born aviatrix. Her greatest difficulty came after she had mastered the art. Aviation was, comparatively speaking, in its infancy and when she sought to get work as a commercial pilot, she found herself face to face with an apparently insurmountable hurdle; women were not wanted in commercial aviation. Flying was a man's job. How this blonde spite of a girl proved that women could fly as well as men, and how she helped to blaze the trails of modern aviation is told in this exciting and thrilling saga.

EPISODE #304   "**TORPEDO LANE**"   Broadcast on November 9, 1942
Starring: Dean Jagger as the narrator, Ed Jerome as Mike, and Ann Thomas as Helen
Written for *Cavalcade* by Stuart Hawkins, based on a story by Frederick Painton.
Produced and directed by Homer Fickett.
Clayton Collyer is the announcer.
Music composed by Ardon Cornwell and conducted by Donald Voorhees.
Story: A tanker is torpedoed without warning. Men dive beneath the flaming sea and come up splashing. The lookout man on a cargo vessel has become a sentry against submarines. Boat drill is now a means of saving seconds to save lives. Facing dangers like the Murmansk Passage - that hell of bombs, torpedoes, sinking and death - our

merchant seamen stick at their jobs to write one of the most glorious chapters yet in American Maritime history. These Merchant Seamen knew the war was their job. Our men in uniform and their arms had to be transported to far-flung battlefronts of the United Nations. Our allies had to be supplied. This a story of these present-day heroes of the Merchant Marine - men without benefit of glamour or acclaim who go quickly about their business of sailing cargo vessels across dangerous seas.

Trivia: With the opening scene in the New York Headquarters of the National Maritime Union, Du Pont originally intended for Alan Ladd to play the lead role. Because of conflicting schedules in Hollywood, Ladd was unable to attend the performance. Dean Jagger took his place.

EPISODE #305   "**ALASKA UNDER ARMS**"   Broadcast on November 16, 1942

Starring: Arlene Francis as the narrator
Frank Readick as Japanese one
Everett Sloane as Japanese three
Ted Jewett as Japanese two
Ed Jerome as Alaskan one
Will Geer as Alaskan two
Karl Swenson as Alaskan three
Chester Stratton as another Japanese
Stephen Schnabel as Wollschlager
Ed Jerome as the Chief
Kenny Delmar as the first Senator
Frank Readick as the second Senator
Everett Sloane as the third Senator
Ted Jewett as the Colonel
Karl Swenson as the first man
Stephen Schnabel as the second man
Jimmy McCallion as Stan
Frank Readick as Gus
Will Geer as the third man
Kenny Delmar as the fourth man
Betty Garde as the woman
Ed Jerome as the Sergeant
Karl Swenson as Buckner
Betty Garde as the woman's voice
Everett Sloane as the man's voice
Ted Jewett as the announcer
Kenny Delmar as the lieutenant
Chester Stratton as the second officer
Jimmy McCallion as the flight leader
Ted Jewett as the first officer
Ed Jerome as the third officer
Will Geer as the Speaker
Kenny Delmar as the Congressman
Ted Jewett as Pease
Jimmy McCallion as Kennicott
Ed Jerome as Henry
Chester Stratton as Gulliver
Karl Swenson as servant two
Stephen Schnabel as servant one
Everett Sloane as voice three
Ted Jewett as voice one
Betty Garde as voice two
Will Geer as Sourdough
Ed Jerome as Mitchell
Juano Hernandez as man two
Jimmy McCallion as man one

Written for *Cavalcade* by Peter Lyon, based on the recent 1942 book "Alaska Under Arms" by Jean Potter.
Produced and directed by Homer Fickett.
Clayton Collyer is the announcer.
Music composed by Ardon Cornwell and conducted by Donald Voorhees.

Story: When the United States purchased the vast territory of Alaska from Russia in 1867, it was virtually an unknown land. Few officials in Washington knew what they were buying; the American public was profoundly unaware of what Alaska was and why it is being acquired. It was promptly dubbed "Seward's Folly" and was made the butt of ignorant jokesters. The American public has quickly come to know something about Alaska - potentially one of the richest regions on Earth. It is rich, little known and sparsely settled. There were a few men who first realized its possibilities and who glimpsed the future. And in spite of public apathy and ignorance, they were able to consummate the purchase they helped, in a very real sense, to shape the future of the North American continent.

EPISODE #306 "**FEAST FROM THE HARVEST**"   Broadcast on November 23, 1942
  Starring: Louis Bromfield as the narrator
  Kenny Delmar as the Spirit of Edward
  Will Geer as the Spirit of Jonathan
  Betty Garde as the Spirit of Sapphira
  Agnes Young as the Spirit of Maria
  Jimmy McCallion as Henry
  Everett Sloane as the Spirit of John
  Ed Jerome as the Spirit of Benjamin
  Sarah Fussell as Sapphira
  Will Geer as Jonathan
  Karl Swenson as the Caller
  Everett Sloane as Rev. Simpson
  Charita Bauer as Mary
  Agnes Young as Maria
  Frank Readick as Ezekiel
  Ted Jewett as Ezra
  Written for *Cavalcade* by Louis Bromfield.
  Produced and directed by Homer Fickett.
  Clayton Collyer and Junius Matthews are the announcers.
  Music composed by Ardon Cornwell and conducted by Donald Voorhees.
  Story: This is the harvest of the Pilgrims from the stony soils around Plymouth Rock. This is the harvest of women who farmed while their men fought our Revolutionary War. This is the harvest of the homesteader who won his free land in the Civil War. On this Thanksgiving, ordinary Americans - people who live close to the soil in which our history is rooted - people who send their sons to die for the land to which the struggle of their forefathers brought freedom - people who know the deepest meaning of thanksgiving in their harvest of Food for Victory.

EPISODE #307 "**SISTER KENNY**"   Broadcast on November 30, 1942
  Starring: Madeleine Carroll as Sister Kenny
  Betty Garde as Mrs. Kenny
  Alfred Shirley as another M.D.
  Kenny Delmar as Jerry
  Larry Robinson as Danny
  Will Geer as the voice
  Betty Garde as the nurse
  Karl Swenson as Dr. Pohl
  Frank Readick as the questioner
  Karl Swenson as Celinto
  Alfred Shirley as McDonnell
  Adelaide Klein as Mrs. Morgan
  Frank Readick as Harry
  Kenny Delmar as Crawford
  Everett Sloane as Dr. Knapp
  Ed Jerome as Dr. Cole
  Ted Jewett as the premier
  Written for *Cavalcade* by Norris Houghton, based on a story by Sister Kenny.
  Produced and directed by Homer Fickett.
  Clayton Collyer is the announcer.
  Music composed by Ardon Cornwell and conducted by Donald Voorhees.
  Story: Elizabeth Kenny has amazed the world - and she has, for the first time in history, given hope where there was none. Miss Kenny came to the United States in 1940, after thirty years of battling Infantile Paralysis in hospitals and clinics deliberation, the Medical Advisory Committee of the National Foundation for Infantile Paralysis endorsed her self-discovered treatment. Today, doctors, nurses and technicians from every corner of America are being trained in the Kenny Method. For clinical evidence has definitely shown that with the Kenny treatment it is now possible, in a high percentage of cases, to prevent the tragic consequences of polio.

  Trivia: Sister Kenny appears on the program, after the drama, speaking via remote from Minneapolis.

  More trivia: The title of this script was originally "Sister Kenny - Savior of Youth."

EPISODE #308   "THE ROAD TO VICTORY"   Broadcast on December 7, 1942
Starring: Carl Sandburg in a drama that probably featured the largest cast/character list of all:

Everett Sloane as the narrator	Karl Swenson as the first reporter
Will Geer as the pioneer	Will Geer as the first man
Dwight Weist as the second man	Will Geer as the hog caller
Frank Readick as the judge	Carl Frank as the first farmer
Kenny Delmar as the second farmer	Dwight Weist as Adolph Hitler
Kenny Delmar as the second reporter	Frank Readick as Nomura
Ted Jewett as Kurusu	Will Geer as the third farmer
Adelaide Klein as the wife	Edwin Jerome as the third man
Frank Readick as the recruiting officer	Betty Garde as the mother
Sarah Fussell as Ruthy	Agnes Young as the grandmother
Adelaide Klein as Mrs. Brown	Dwight Weist as Mr. Somers
Larry Robinson as Johnny	Agnes Young as the lady
Adelaide Klein as Shirley	Ann Thomas as Rosie
Ed Jerome as Salesman	Betty Garde as the stenographer
Agnes Young as Gertie	Jimmy McCallion as Jerry
Everett Sloane as Robert	Will Geer as Albert
Dwight Weist as William	Karl Swenson as the Japanese voice
Kenny Delmar as the Riveter	Frank Readick as Joe
Karl Swenson as the fourth farmer	Agnes Young as the fourth farmer's wife
Ann Thomas as Mary	Carl Frank as Tom
Betty Garde as the girl	Kenny Delmar as Bill
Ted Jewett as the helper	Dwight Weist as the checker
Will Geer as Mack	Everett Sloane as Bob
Edwin Jerome as the officer	

There is also a count of twenty-six numerous voices of unnamed characters all played by various performers listed above.
Based on the following works by Carl Sandburg: "The People, Yes" published in 1936 by Harcourt, Brace & Company, Inc., "Smoke and Steel" published in 1920 by Harcourt, Brace & Company, Inc., and "Road to Victory" published in 1942 by the Museum of Modern Art.
Written for *Cavalcade* by Norman Rosten.
Produced and directed by Homer Fickett.
Clayton Collyer is the announcer.
Music composed by Ardon Cornwell and conducted by Donald Voorhees.
A vocal number is sung by the Delta Rhythm Boys.
Story: The Japanese envoys laughed and joked in Washington as news of Pearl Harbor reached their ears. To their masters in Berlin and Tokyo they reported only the "soft" voices of an American people unaware of danger. Flushed with easy victories, the Axis didn't even hear what happened here in the sudden hush after the news came through. Pearl Harbor made up millions of minds in a flash. The voices of Americans roared back united. Theirs were the shouts of pioneers who rolled back the vast silence of the wilderness before them, the songs of freedom which rose above the clamor of building new cities, new railroads, new steel mills . . the yells of fighting men who defeated tyranny and slavery many times before this. Carl Sandburg had listened carefully to the voices of America during the past year and he plays our own voices back to us.

Clayton Collyer: "Carl Sandburg has traveled the road along with the American people, speaking with their voices and interpreting their silences. On December seventh, the anniversary of the day of infamy and awakening, we paused to celebrate the road builders and those traveling along the road."

EPISODE #309 "**THE MAN WHO WOULDN'T BE PRESIDENT**" Aired December 14, 1942
Starring: Edward Arnold, William Farnum, Joseph Kearns, and Agnes Moorehead
Written for *Cavalcade* by Hector Chevigny.
Produced and directed by Homer Fickett.
John Hiestand is the announcer.
Music composed and conducted by Robert Armbruster.
Story: Daniel Webster was a solid man. He could fight, and when he fought it was for peace. In the first half of the last century, he fought for compromise between the parties to the "irrepressible conflict" called the Civil War. But he could not stem the tide which brought it on. On another front he fought hard and won. His untiring effort and devotion to the cause of peace resulted in the famous Webster-Ashburton Treaty which wiped out many old causes of fiction between America and England. It laid the basis for the firm friendship and unity so vital today for the two nations who face a common enemy. Did Webster know the vital importance of his work? Listen to his plea before a hostile Senate! But when you find out why he wouldn't be president, then you'll know the full measure of his devotion to the nation. **(HLYD)**

Trivia: This script was originally scheduled for broadcast back in October with Orson Welles in the lead, however the script was postponed and later broadcast on this date.

EPISODE #310 "**A CHILD IS BORN**" Broadcast on December 21, 1942
Starring: Lynn Fontaine and Alfred Lunt
Karl Swenson as the soldier   Carl Frank as the narrator
Ted Jewett as the first voice   Everett Sloane as the prefect
Ann Thomas as Sarah   Charita Bauer as Leah
Kenny Delmar as Joseph   Frank Readick as Dismas
Written for *Cavalcade* by Stephen Vincent Benet.
Produced and directed by Homer Fickett.
Clayton Collyer is the announcer.
Also features vocalist Elizabeth Mulliner.
Features music sung by Ken Christie's chorus.
Songs: "A Shepherd's Carol," and "Come, All Ye Faithful."
Original score composed by Ardon Cornwell and under the direction of Don Voorhees.
Story: The scene is an inn whose keeper loves the chink of money, loves it too well - the good sound thumping coin. For this he will make any compromise with the world. His wife, who has lost her only child, prepares the sauces for a banquet, for the perfect has taken over the entire inn for a great celebration. The wife trembles with an inner joy, for she feels that a "something begins. Something is full of change and sparking stars. Something is loosed that changes all the world." As she works two who strangers come to the door seeking shelter from the bitter cold. But there are no rooms. She takes pity on them and sends them to a stable - and goes back to her work. Outside the inn there appear singing shepherds and kings and great lords - their eyes shining with good news.

Homer Fickett: "Oftentimes *Cavalcade*'s dramas were written by top money authors such as Robert Sherwood, Carl Sandburg, Maxwell Anderson, and Stephen Vincent Benet, who happened to be working on *Cavalcade*'s Easter program when he became fatally ill. Benet's 'A Child is Born' was originally written for this program."

EPISODE #311 "**THE EAGLE'S NEST**" Broadcast on December 28, 1942
Starring: Paul Muni as Garibaldi   Paul Muni as Liguri
Ted Jewett as the Colonel   Karl Swenson as the beggar
Everett Sloane as Marino   Junius Mathews as the parrot
Kenny Delmar as the innkeeper   Betty Garde as Anita
Carl Frank as Antonio   Ted Jewett as Pepe

Will Geer as Whitman
Edwin Jerome as Alberto
Frank Readick as Sears
Kenny Delmar as the German guard
Larry Robinson as Johnny
Karl Swenson as the messenger
Edwin Jerome as Alfredo

Adapted for *Cavalcade* by Arthur Miller, from on an original story by Konrad Bercovici.
Produced and directed by Homer Fickett.
Clayton Collyer is the announcer.
Music composed by Ardon Cornwell and conducted by Donald Voorhees.
Story: Garibaldi was the George Washington of Italy, and this is his struggle to cast off the alien yoke. Some eighty years ago it was other foreign invaders, notably the Austrians, who oppressed the Italian people. After having lived in America, he declared to one of his American friends: "The sympathy which comes to me from free men, citizens of a great nation, like yourselves, gives me courage for my task in the cause of Liberty and Progress. I regard today the American people at the sole arbiter of questions of humanity, amid the universal thralldom of the soul and intellect. Please express these my sentiments to your countrymen . . ."

EPISODE #312   **"BETWEEN THEM BOTH"**   Broadcast on January 4, 1943
   Starring: Nancy Kelly as Florrie
   Virginia Rauth as the salesgirl
   Carl Frank as Dave
   Frank Readick as Andrews
   Agnes Young as Emmy
   Kenny Delmar as the lieutenant
   Will Geer as the first soldier
   Karl Swenson as the wounded soldier
   Betty Garde as Mildred
   Everett Sloane as Nick
   Ted Jewett as the man
   Ed Jerome as John
   Jackie Kelk as Buddy
   Ted Jewett as the sergeant
   Frank Readick as the second soldier
   Ann Sterrett as Betty

Written for *Cavalcade* by Kay Van Riper.
Produced and directed by Homer Fickett.
Clayton Collyer is the announcer.
Music composed by Ardon Cornwell and conducted by Donald Voorhees.
Story: At the breakfast table of the Fraser family, who live in a small stucco house near a great airplane factory. John Fraser, the father, is a railroad engineer. Buddy, the young son, is an expert mechanic. Each is working hard in the war effort, each is mindful and proud of Beth, the older daughter of the family, who is serving as a nurse in the Solomon Islands. But there is another daughter, Florrie, who works, when she feels like working, in the plane factory. She is careless, selfish and defiant. One day news comes that Beth has been killed by shrapnel while nursing the wounded under fire. This marks the beginning of a series of startling changes.

EPISODE #313   **"DIARY ON A PIG BOAT"**   Broadcast on January 11, 1943
   Starring: Edwin Jerome as Lt. Com. T. H. Haase
   Frank Readick as Red Franklin
   Ted Jewett as Wash
   Ted Jewett as the log/narrator
   Karl Swenson as Lt. Meade
   Will Geer as Gallagher
   Jackie Kelk as Thompson
   Carl Frank as Boyd
   Ken Delmar as Ensign Waller
   Everett Sloane as the narrator

This broadcast included a short talk by a real Navy Sub commander, Lt. Com. Willard A. Saunder.
Based on an original 1942 *Saturday Evening Post* story by Frederick C. Painton, and adapted for *Cavalcade* by Stuart Hawkins.
Produced and directed by Homer Fickett.
Clayton Collyer is the announcer.
Music composed by Ardon Cornwell and conducted by Donald Voorhees.
Story: Perhaps the average American - perhaps even the well-informed American - thinks that the Germans have a virtual monopoly of successful under-sea warfare of that

they are masters in the building of these warships of the deep. This is not distinctly true. Americans were experimenting with submarines a hundred years before there was a Germany - even the old Germany of the Kaiser Wilhelm. But, when the final history of the war can be told, there will be no more a thrilling story than the saga of the United States Submarine, of the "pig boat," as their crews affectionately term them. While the full factual story cannot be told we can get a typical and authentic glimpse of an American submarine in action against the Japanese.

Trivia: *Cavalcade* prides itself upon the accuracy of its programs. This script was shown to the commander of an American submarine which had recently returned from a successful mission off the coast of Japan. After reading it carefully he said: "There is only one change that I could possibly suggest. When we are down at the bottom and being blasted by enemy depth bombs the men address me as 'Skipper' instead of 'Captain'." So the script writer, Stuart Hawkins, changed "Captain" to "Skipper."

EPISODE #314 "**SOLDIERS OF THE TIDE**" Broadcast on January 18, 1943
    Starring: Dennis Morgan as Peters   Ted Jewett as the narrator
    Edwin Jerome as the Colonel   Karl Swenson as Blair
    Everett Sloane as Lon   Frank Readick as F-X
    Kenny Delmar as Rudy
    Written for *Cavalcade* by Peter Lyon.
    Produced and directed by Homer Fickett.
    Clayton Collyer is the announcer.
    Music composed by Ardon Cornwell and conducted by Donald Voorhees.
Story: For a long and agonizing time there seemed no end to the crushing victories of the little men of Japan. America, recovering from the first shocks of their blows, poured men and equipment across the vast Pacific to transform a retreat into the beginnings of victory. That change came on a tiny island called Guadalcanal in a group of islands known as the Solomons. There, the United States Marines landed and seized an almost-completed Japanese air field, now known as Henderson Field, from which American bombers and fighter planes daily pound the Japanese. This is that story - the successful battle for the control of the Matanikau River.

EPISODE #315 "**THE FLYING TIGERS**" Broadcast on January 25, 1943
    Starring: Ralph Bellamy as Al Fisher   Kenny Delmar as Randy
    Karl Swenson as Norrie   Everett Sloane as Joe
    Ted Jewett as Tokyo   Frank Readick as Smitty
    Carl Frank as Gordon   Will Geer as Harry
    Karl Swenson as Wang Fong   Everett Sloane as Lee Kim
    Kenny Delmar as Chang Lum   Will Geer as Chan Loy
    Lee Ya-Ching as Lao Ming   Ted Jewett as the man
    Edwin Jerome as the doctor
Based on the 1942 screenplay by Kenneth Gamet and Barry Trivers, and material from the book of the same name by Robert Whelan. Adapted for *Cavalcade* by Robert Sloane.
    Produced and directed by Homer Fickett.
    Clayton Collyer is the announcer.
    Music composed by Ardon Cornwell and conducted by Donald Voorhees.
Story: The world has moved so swiftly and there have been many important events to record that many fewer Americans are aware of the exploits of the small group of Americans, who went to the assistance of the small group of Americans who went to the assistance of China in her bitter struggle against Japanese aggression. Officially they were known as "The American Volunteer Group"; popularly they were, and are, known as "The Flying Tigers." There were not many of them; their equipment and supplies

were meager and insufficient; the fields from which they operated were inadequate. But no air force ten times larger ever operated with such deadly efficiency. They were a terror to the Japanese pilots who had long bombed defenseless Chinese with impunity.

Trivia: John Wayne starred in the 1942 Republic Pictures release of the same name, Wayne's first war film. Ralph Bellamy played the part of Jim Gordon, the role Wayne starred in the year before.

EPISODE #316   **"TO THE SHORES OF TRIPOLI"**   Broadcast on February 1, 1943
Starring: Joseph Cotten as General Eaton
Written for *Cavalcade* by Peter Lyon, based on research done by author Carl Carmer.
Produced and directed by Homer Fickett.
Clayton Collyer is the announcer.
Music composed by Ardon Cornwell and conducted by Donald Voorhees.
Story: The extraordinary exploits of an expedition that one hundred and thirty-seven years ago set out from Egypt and finally raised the American flag in triumph on the shores of Tripoli. The expedition was led by a bold, swash-buckling Connecticut Yankee, General William Eaton. The U.S. had been blackmailed and victimized by the predatory rulers of the Barbary States who demanded (and long received) tribute to permit the safe passage of American ships in 1801. They declared war against the U.S. Eaton, who as Consul to Tunis had become familiar with pirate politics, came to Washington and suggested a plan to invade Tripoli and bring Pasha Yussuf to terms. The story of General Eaton's conquest of Derna is one of the strangest and most brilliant in American history. It was the first glowing example of what has become an American axiom, "The Marines have landed and the situation is well in hand."

EPISODES #317   **"THE PERFECT TRIBUTE"**   Broadcast on February 8, 1943
Starring: Edwin Jerome as Abe Lincoln   Frank Readick as the eyewitness
Carl Frank as Stanton   Ted Jewett as Stevens
Everett Sloane as Hay   Karl Swenson as Chase
Will Geer as Saunders   Kenny Delmar as Seward
Carl Frank as Blair   Ted Jewett as the lieutenant
Everett Sloane as Wills   Ted Jewett as the voice
Carl Frank as the chairman   Everett Sloane as the secretary
Kenny Delmar as Everett   Karl Swenson as Carter
Based on the story of the same name by Mary Raymond Shipman Andrews, originally published in 1906 by Charles Scribner's Sons (it was the third printing in 1943 that was used and brought to Hayes' attention) and adapted for *Cavalcade* by Raphael Hayes.
Produced and directed by Homer Fickett.
Clayton Collyer is the announcer.
Music composed by Ardon Cornwell and conducted by Donald Voorhees.
Story: President Lincoln was on a train bound for Gettysburg to speak at the ceremonies which would mark the dedication of a national cemetery. He was tired and worn. He had little time to think about a speech, but Lincoln took pen in hand, as the train rolled along to Gettysburg. The next day at the ceremonies Edward Everett delivered an oration that lasted for almost two hours. When he finished there was thunderous applause. Lincoln then spoke for almost two minutes. Before many of his audience realized that he had begun to speak, he had already finished. There was only a ripple of applause. It seemed that Lincoln had failed. Back in Washington he received mixed opinions and reports. Lincoln, while going on a walk, was nearly knocked down by a lad named Warrington Blair - whose brother, a Confederate captain, was dying in a nearby prison hospital. Lincoln, learning that the captain wants to draw a will, pretends that he is a simple lawyer and goes to the hospital. It is from the dying officer that Lincoln received "the perfect tribute."

EPISODE #318 "WAR COMES TO DR. MORGAN"   Broadcast on February 15, 1943

    Starring: Elliott Nugent as Dr. Morgan   Arlene Francis as Anne
    Frank Readick as Corporal   Kenny Delmar as the sergeant
    Adelaide Klein as Ella Barnes   Virginia Rauth as Emily
    Barbara Weeks as Mrs. Judson   Will Geer as Henry Grant
    Karl Swenson as Amos   Edwin Jerome as Dr. Altman
    Barbara Weeks as the maid

Written for *Cavalcade* by Kay Van Riper.
Produced and directed by Homer Fickett.
Clayton Collyer is the announcer.
Music composed by Ardon Cornwell and conducted by Donald Voorhees.

Story: "In Europe, medicine is less science and more art; in America, it is more science and less art." But Dr. Jim Morgan of Pineville and Dr. Paul Moreau of Paris are men who use both to serve mankind. Dr. Jim is a "family doctor." He loves his small town. He loves a girl named Ann. He loves them all so much that he feels that he must leave them. His "family" becomes the fighting men of Guadalcanal. Jim persuades Dr. Paul Moreau to come and care for the people of Pineville in Jim's absence. Dr. Moreau brings more than great skill. He also brings great understanding. How the two men together overcame old prejudices in the society matrons and farmers of the small town and how Dr. Paul helped Ann to understand are highlights of this war drama.

EPISODE #319 "THE PLOT TO KIDNAP WASHINGTON"   Broadcast February 22, 1943

    Starring: Edmund Gwenn as Hercules Mulligan   Ed Jerome as the first man
    Adelaide Klein as Molly   Frank Readick as second man
    Kenny Delmar as Alexander Hamilton   Karl Swenson as the third man
    William Geer as Greene   Carl Frank as the fourth man
    Ian Martin as Major Fleming   Ian Martin as the fifth man
    Juano Hernandez as Cato   Frank Readick as Asa
    Alfred Shirley as Col. Stuart   Karl Swenson as the officer
    Barbara Weeks as Mrs. Dawson   Kenny Delmar as the first officer
    Carl Frank as the second officer   Ted Jewitt as the jailer
    Ted Jewett as the bartender

Written for *Cavalcade* by Janet and Joseph Ruscoll, based off of copyrighted material by Carl Carmer from 1943.
Produced and directed by Homer Fickett.
Clayton Collyer is the announcer.
Music composed by Ardon Cornwell and conducted by Donald Voorhees.

Story: Espionage has played an important part in every great war. The American public is reasonably aware of the role of spies in the Civil War and in World War I. Your introduction to Mr. Hercules Mulligan, a patriotic tailor who remained in New York City during its occupation by the enemy, and who served his country in devious and dangerous ways. Mulligan did a thriving business in supplying uniforms for the officers of the King; he also did a dangerous business in supplying the patriots with valuable information gleaned from his officer customers. To operate effectively he had to pretend that he was an ardent Tory - an attitude which provoked the anger of his old Whig friends. At last his activities were suspected and he was thrown into jail by his enemy.

Trivia: The original title of this drama was "A Plot to Kidnap General Washington."

EPISODE #320   "THE DIARY OF A SABOTEUR"   Broadcast on March 1, 1943
Starring: Mildred Natwick as Mrs. Abbott   Joseph Schildkraut as Karl Ritter
Ted Jewett as the Nazi   Carl Frank as Charley
Virginia Routh as Priscilla   Karl Swenson as Clem
Kenny Delmar as Max   Edwin Jerome as Fred
Stephen Schnabel   Will Geer as the first FBI Agent
Howard Smith as the second FBI agent   Howard Smith as voice four
Ed Jerome as voice three   Will Geer as voice one
Barbara Weeks as voice two   Frank Readick as the FBI voice
Kenny Delmar as the band leader   Ted Jewett as the clerk
Karl Swenson as the page   Virginia Routh as the secretary
Stephen Schnabel as Van Voss
Based on the 1943 book "Sabotage" by Michael Sayers and Albert E. Kahn, and adapted for *Cavalcade* by Peter Lyon.
Produced and directed by Homer Fickett.
Clayton Collyer is the announcer.
Music composed by Ardon Cornwell and conducted by Donald Voorhees.
Story: From the earliest days of the Nazi power in Germany a vast army of highly trained and technical experts under the Psychological Laboratory of the Nazi Third Reich in Berlin has been waging a secret war against America by planting seeds of dissension wherever there was fertile soil. Through the efforts of secret agents posing as uninterested persons in all walks of life, dissension has been created among races and creeds. Distrust in democracy and the American way of life has been carefully planned with diabolical cunning. Rumors and lies have been spread with great calculation. Well meaning organizations with an abhorrence of war have been made the unintentional disseminators of propaganda calculated to divide our country and strengthen the Reich.

Trivia: In the recently published best selling book "Sabotage," by Michael Sayers and Albert E. Kahn, the machinations of the Psychological Laboratory of the Nazi Third Reich had been exposed. Although the people in this radio play was fictitious, the facts were real.

EPISODE #321   "THE EIGHTEENTH CAPTAIN"   Broadcast on March 8, 1943
Starring: Ralph Bellamy as John Paul Jones   Ted Jewett as the first voice
Carl Frank as the second voice   Will Geer as Adams
Kenny Delmar as Hewes   Ed Jerome as Morris
Carl Frank as Hancock   Alfred Shirley as Pearson
Will Geer as Dale   Kenny Delmar as Simpson
Barbara Weeks as the countess   Bill Pringle as Franklin
Frank Readick as Saltonstall   Clayton Collyer as the narrator
Based on the 1943 book "John Paul Jones, Fighter for Freedom and Glory" by Lincoln Lorenz, and adapted for *Cavalcade* by Stuart Hawkins.
Produced and directed by Homer Fickett.
Clayton Collyer is the announcer.
Music composed by Ardon Cornwell and conducted by Donald Voorhees.
Story: The romantic story of John Paul Jones is ever old and ever new. It is old because his audacious exploits were the most brilliant episodes of an American Navy that was then only in the making. The Navy in the days of John Paul Jones had no past, but he clearly saw that it was destined to a mighty future. His story is as new as tomorrow morning's watch - whatever it be on an American man-of-war in the Mediterranean or in the Solomons or in the North Atlantic. For today the Navy, carrying the battle to the most grim alliance of enemies in our history, is living up to the tradition established by Captain Jones.

Trivia: This broadcast was based upon many recently-discovered facts which was soon to appear in a biography, "John Paul Jones, Fighter for Freedom and Glory," written by Lincoln Lorenz and was to be published a month later by the United States Naval Institute in Annapolis, Maryland.

EPISODE #322   "A CASE FOR THE F.B.I."   Broadcast on March 15, 1943
Starring: Edward G. Robinson as McVane
Sara Fussell as the baby
Virginia Routh as Miss Meade
Karl Swenson as Stevenson
Everett Sloane as Esterbrook
Ted Jewett as the radio
Karl Swenson as Kleeman
Carl Frank as Green
Frank Readick as Marlow
Kenny Delmar as Murphy
Barbara Weeks as Mrs. Hendrick
Carl Frank as Dolan
Ted Jewett as Bradley
Will Geer as Gray
Ed Jerome as Hendrick
Based on an actual case file from the F.B.I., adapted for *Cavalcade* by Stuart Hawkins. Produced and directed by Homer Fickett.
Clayton Collyer is the announcer.
Music composed by Ardon Cornwell and conducted by Donald Voorhees.
Story: In 1908, the U.S. Federal Bureau of Investigation was founded as the permanent investigative force of the Department of Justice. And those beginnings bore little resemblance to the F.B.I. that we now know. It is not until the reorganization of 1924 that it began to acquire its present form and characteristics - especially the services of a group of highly trained, non-political agents. The case which *Cavalcade* dramatizes is an attempted extortion and a threatened murder. The only clues were two tiny bits of metallic dust. And from the laboratory of the F.B.I. begins the strange quest which *Cavalcade* presented - with the approval and cooperation of the Federal Bureau of Investigation.

Trivia: A message from J. Edgar Hoover about wartime juvenile delinquency was read.

More trivia: *Cavalcade of America* was privileged to present a drama taken from the actual records of the F.B.I. All the names used on the program were fictitious, but the incidents and the procedure was authentic.

EPISODE #323   "LIFETIDE"   Broadcast on March 22, 1943.
Starring: Alfred Lunt as Dr. Bethune
Ted Jewett as the clerk
Stephen Schnabel as the Spanish Peasant
Ian Martin as McCauley
Will Geer as Jenkins
Adelaide Klein as girl
Ed Jerome as Gomez
Barbara Weeks as Manolita
Kenny Delmar as the commandant
Karl Swenson as the orderly
Barbara Weeks as the Chinese nurse
Carl Frank as the Chinese soldier
Adelaide Klein as the old woman
Ed Jerome as the first peasant
Frank Readick as the narrator
Will Geer as Fisher
Kenny Delmar as Barnwell
Ted Jewett as Lin Man
Ian Martin as the first doctor
Karl Swenson as the second doctor
Ed Jerome as the chairman
Adelaide Klein as mother
Kenny Delmar as father
Virginia Rauth as the nurse
Sara Fussell as Yvette
Paul Stewart as the first storm trooper
Stephen Schnabel as the third peasant
Stephen Schnabel as the third storm trooper
Paul Stewart as the second peasant
Based on the 1943 biography "Doctor Bethune" by Ted Allan, and adapted for *Cavalcade* by Robert Tallman.
Produced and directed by Homer Fickett.
Clayton Collyer is the announcer.

Music composed by Ardon Cornwell and conducted by Donald Voorhees.
Story: The unusual story of Dr. Norman Bethune, one of earth's talented and courageous men. He saw the threat of Axis aggression long before it was apparent to the informed publics of the democracies. He not only saw it, but he determined to do something about it. So the Spanish Civil War, in which Hitler and Mussolini held a dress rehearsal for World War II, found him tending the Loyalist wounded. And in China Dr. Bethune served in field inspired services that Dr. Bethune finally lost his life - devoted to the service of humanity against Fascist aggression. During his battlefield experiences he contributed notably to the development of mobile blood banks, by means of which the lives of many thousands of soldiers have been saved - and through the continuing struggle the lives of hundreds of thousands of fighting men will be preserved.

Trivia: After dramatizing the story of Dr. Norman Bethune's contributions to the development of mobile blood banks, *Cavalcade* presented as guest speaker Major General James Carre Magee, Surgeon General of the United States Army.

EPISODE #324   **"THE COOK ON THE P-T BOAT WRITES HOME"**   March 29, 1943
Starring: William Bendix as Joe Caldwell   Everett Sloane as Saunders
Virginia Rauth as the waitress   Kenny Delmar as Nick
Frank Readick as Ed Betts   Kenny Delmar as Jablowski
Will Geer as the torpedo man   Howard Smith as MacKey
Everett Sloane as the ensign   Jackie Kelk as the radioman
Ian Martin as the second radio man   Ian Martin as the Quartermaster
Ted Jewett as the third radio man   Ted Jewett as Paul Betts
Karl Swenson as Hanson   Ed Jerome as the commander
Carl Frank as Gilling   Ann Thomas as Sally
Written for *Cavalcade* by Frank Gabrielson.
Produced and directed by Homer Fickett.
Clayton Collyer is the announcer.
Music composed by Ardon Cornwell and conducted by Donald Voorhees.
Story: A comedy melodrama based upon the exploits of the crew of an un-named "P-T Boat" based in the Solomon Islands. It is told in the form of a letter written home by Joe Caldwell, Seamen Second Class and "P-T" Cook First Class par excellence. Two of the three motors of the boat were actually out of commission and two members of the small crew were immobilized in a Navy hospital when Lt. Gilling, the commanding officer, received orders that every boat must join the squadron in patrol off Guadalcanal - in readiness against an expected Japanese attack. Joe was only dreaming of the post-war world before the action began - especially what place might be best for him to establish a restaurant - but when it ended Joe had at least one answer to his problem - even if it was not the best one.

Trivia: The original title of this script was "The P-T Cook Writes Home."

VINCENT PRICE and RICHARD WHORF
in A RACE FOR LENNIE
MONDAY EVENING   JANUARY 29, 1945

EPISODE #325   **"SUBMARINE ASTERN"**   Broadcast on April 5, 1943

    Starring: Ray Milland as Dan Harper   Frank Readick as Sparks
    William Johnstone as the ensign   Ed Jerome as the Captain
    Carl Frank as the helmsman   Frank Readick as Adams
    Will Geer as Flanders   Karl Swenson as Larson
    Carl Frank as Hedeman   Ted Jewett as the voice
    Stephen Schnabel as the German Captain   Stephen Schnabel as Cookie
    Jackie Kelk as Jimmy   Ted Jewett as Les
    Everett Sloane as Skip   Will Geer as Bosun
    Barbara Weeks as Pat   Karl Swenson as O-D
    William Johnstone as Phil   Virginia Routh as Doris
    Written for *Cavalcade* by David Harmon.
    Produced and directed by Homer Fickett.
    Clayton Collyer is the announcer.
    Music composed by Ardon Cornwell and conducted by Donald Voorhees.
    Story: Older than the Republic itself is the United States Coast Guard. As the Revenue Cutter Service, it began in 1790, patrolling our coast for the enforcement of custom laws and the armed protection of the sea coast. In 1915 Congress combined it with the Life Saving Service to make the efficient peacetime Coast Guard Patrol, under the direction of the Treasury Department. Five months before Pearl Harbor, in July 1941, Congress again acted and placed the Coast Guard under the Navy Department. To its multitudinous peacetime duties, such vital functions as convoy duty, protecting the landing of troops and anti-submarine patrol were added. Not only along our own shores, but as far afield as the Solomon Islands, the Coast Guard boys are now on duty.

    Trivia: This broadcast included an interview with a sailor from the "Campbell," Chief Gunner's Mate George H. Corston.

EPISODE #326   **"THE LENGTHENING SHADOW"**   Broadcast on April 12, 1943

    Starring: Fredric March as Thomas Jefferson   Carl Frank as James Madison
    Virginia Routh as Mme. Helvetius   Ian Martin as Mazzei
    Barbara Weeks as Mme. De Tesse   William Johnstone as Lafayette
    Ted Jewett as the secretary   Karl Swenson as Hamilton
    Will Geer as another secretary   Ed Jerome as G. Washington
    Arlene Francis as Martha Randolf   Alfred Shirley as Abbe Gerra
    Charita Bauer as Ellen Coolidge   Frank Readick as the narrator.
    Frank Readick as John Hancock   Ian Martin as another secretary
    Will Geer as John Adams   Karl Swenson as Livingston
    Everett Sloane as Dr. Franklin   Carl Frank as Patrick Henry
    Ted Jewett as Edmund Pendleton   Ed Jerome as George Wythe
    William Johnstone as Dabney Carr   Alfred Shirley as John Page
    Written for *Cavalcade* by Margaret Burening.
    Produced and directed by Homer Fickett.
    Clayton Collyer is the announcer.
    Music composed by Ardon Cornwell and conducted by Donald Voorhees.
    Story: In his long career Jefferson held many distinguished posts; he had been governor of Virginia; minister to France; Secretary of State under Washington; and twice President of the United States. Yet when he devised the inscription for his tombstone he chose to mention only three things; that he was the author of the Declaration of Independence, author of the Virginia statute for religious freedom and father of the University of Virginia. The "Four Freedoms" of our time and the lofty aspirations of the United Nations are merely less eloquent amplifications of sentiments which Thomas Jefferson first phrased for the inspiration and the guidance of generations of Americans who have followed and profited from his labors and his high vision.

Trivia: According to an NBC Press release of April 12, 1943, The dedication of the Jefferson Memorial marked the beginning of a vast series of official Jefferson celebrations throughout the nation. April 13 of this month marked the two hundredth anniversary of the birth of Thomas Jefferson. On the afternoon of the thirteenth, the President of the United States formally dedicated the impressive Jefferson Memorial in Washington. On the eve of this momentous anniversary, an episode marking this celebration, *Cavalcade* presented this drama about Thomas Jefferson.

EPISODE #327   **"LISTEN FOR THE SOUND OF WINGS"**   Broadcast on April 19, 1943

Starring: Paul Lukas as Pastor Niemoeller   Karl Swenson as Von Ribbentrop
Ed Jerome as Gestapo one   Will Geer as Gestapo two
Stephen Schnabel as the guard   Frank Readick as the old man
Carl Frank as the prisoner   Virginia Routh as the secretary
Ed Jerome as Himmler   Jackie Kelk as Frank
Barbara Weeks as Frau Hesler   Ted Jewett as the orderly
Dwight Weist as Adolph Hitler   Everett Sloane as Rudloff
Kenny Delmar as the narrator

Written for *Cavalcade* by Arthur Miller, based on material published in 1942 from Fleming H. Revell Company.
Produced and directed by Homer Fickett.
Clayton Collyer is the announcer.
Music composed by Ardon Cornwell and conducted by Donald Voorhees.

Story: Pastor Niemoeller was one of the millions whom Hitler hoodwinked in his diabolical quest for power. And Niemoeller, like countless others in Germany and throughout the world, must accept a share of the responsibility in assisting Hitler to power. Niemoeller was duped by Hitler's promises and publicly urged his election. Then, when Hitler firmly held the reins of government, the mask was cast aside and the treachery became transparent. Some openly protested against this fraudulence; they were liquidated. Others refused to associate themselves with the new regime; they were cast into concentration camps so that their bodies might be broken and their spirits crushed. Niemoeller, sustained by his high courage and his belief in the freedom of the Church, had not faltered in his faith.

EPISODE #328   **"SOLDIERS IN HIGH BOOTS"**   Broadcast on April 26, 1943

Starring: Jon Hall as Smitty   Joe Granby as Medico
Frank Nelson as the Texan   Reed Hadley as the farmer
Wally Maher as Mac   Frank Graham as the jumpmaster
Bob Bruce as the captain   Jim Bannon as the officer
Hal Gerard as the C.O.   Hans Conried as Olaf
Frank Graham as the navigator.

Written for *Cavalcade* by Peter Lyon.
Produced and directed by Homer Fickett.
John Hiestand is the announcer, and Gayne Whitman is the commercial announcer.
Music composed and conducted by Robert Armstrong.

Story: Paratroops are being used in larger and larger numbers for Commando raids from the air - for sabotage and intelligence activities as well as for actual invasion. Before the war, the Russians had demonstrated the possibilities of these troops and had trained large numbers of them. But the Russians did not conceive the idea. It was our own Dr. Benjamin Franklin who thought of it many years ago. When the first balloon experiments were being made in Paris in the 1780's, canny Dr. Franklin began to speculate upon the future use of such machines in time of war. He said that if these simple, crude machines were built by the thousands and if each of them carried but one of two soldiers, these fighting men could then be dropped behind enemy lines to demolish and destroy the enemy. **(HLYD)**

EPISODE #329   "**SOLDIERS IN GREASEPAINT**"   Broadcast on May 3, 1943
Starring: Kay Francis, Mitzi Mayfair, and Martha Raye as themselves

Wally Maher as Bob	Frank Graham as the hotel man
Hans Conried as Charlie	Bob Bruce as the Corporal
Hal Gerard as the soldier	Eustace Wyatt as the guardsman
Virginia Gordon as the nurse	Sheila Sheldon as the princess
Joseph Kearns as the colonel	Frank Nelson as the another soldier
Wally Maher as another soldier	Frank Graham as the paratrooper
Bob Bruce as the Sergeant	Hans Conried as another soldier
Hal Gerard as another soldier	Joe Granby as the commanding officer

Written for *Cavalcade* by George Corey.
Produced and directed by Homer Fickett.
Jim Bannon is the announcer, and Georgia Backus is the commercial announcer.
Music composed and conducted by Robert Armbruster.
Story: Theatre folk have long been famous for being able to take it. In the best traditions of show-land: personal sorrow, poor health, or difficult environments are merely spurs to better performances. It's not strange then, that the global struggle now being carried on by our armed services should supply the soldiers for new adventures in theatrical history. This is the dramatic tale of the first "live" U.S.O. Camp Show to visit the American battle lines. It's the account of four gallant ladies, stars of the stage and screen, who left their comfortable Hollywood homes, to serve without pay, in the British isles and along the North African battlefront. The story is particularly thrilling because it is factual.
(HLYD)

Trivia: There were four Hollywood stars originally scheduled for this broadcast, Kay Francis, Carole Landis, Mitzi Mayfair, and Martha Raye. Only Landis was unable to make the broadcast, which consisted of re-enactments of scenes of the skits with which they entertained the boys abroad.

EPISODE #330   "**FAT GIRL**"   Broadcast on May 10, 1943

Starring: Edward Arnold as Capt. Phillips	Hans Conried as Firth
Frank Graham as Brown	Bob Bruce as Verbrugge
Leo Cleary as the first sailor	Edwin Mills as the second sailor
Bob Bruce as the third sailor	John Lake as Wilson
Leo Cleary as Mack	Edwin Mills as Saunders
Bob Bruce as Dowd	Eric Rolfe as the voice on the loudspeaker
Wally Maher as Bratt	Frank Graham as Joe
Edwin Mills as Fred	Eric Rolfe as Paul
Hal Gerard as Don	John Lake as Maloney
Bill Sloan as the signalman	Hans Conried as the skipper

Based on a story of the same name by Isabel Leighton and Charles Rawlings, published in 1943 by the Curtis Publishing Company, and adapted for *Cavalcade* by Paul Peters.
Produced and directed by Homer Fickett.
Jim Bannon is the announcer and Gayne Whitman is the commercial announcer.
Music composed and conducted by Robert Armbruster.
Story: In the years that our Navy had been fighting the Japanese in the Pacific, there had been many glorious and dramatic battles, but certainly none more gallant than the story of the U.S.S. Neosho, an auxiliary oilier, attached to the Pacific Fleet. An ugly duckling among the Navy's flashing destroyers and imposing battleships, her overgrown tanker lines, her eighteen-knot cruising speed and her 150,000-barrel fuel tanks were the butt of every joke the men on the glamour battle-wagons could think of. "Wet nurse," "floating gas stations" and "fat girl" were some of the more polite taunts they tossed toward her hard-working crew as she heaved alongside the fighting ships, took it all good naturedly and came into her own, first at Pearl Harbor and later, in the Coral Sea.   **(HLYD)**

Trivia: This broadcast originated from Hollywood. The Captain of the ship appears on the show to thank his crew.

More trivia: For those wanting to know who the voices were in the closing cut-in, Georgia Backus was the wife, Pinky Parker was husband, and Noel Mills was daughter.

EPISODE #331   "**NURSES UNDER SEALED ORDERS**"   Broadcast on May 17, 1943
Starring: Geraldine Fitzgerald
Written for *Cavalcade* by Arthur Arent.
Produced and directed by Homer Fickett.
Clayton Collyer is the announcer.
Music composed by Ardon Cornwell and conducted by Donald Voorhees.
Story: The Nurses Corps has been an integral part of the Army since 1901 and all nurses have entered the Army as commissioned officers since 1920. Fever-stricken soldiers returning from the Spanish-American War were the first to receive the care of American Red Cross Nurses who were admitted to the Army hospitals by order of President McKinley. The American Red Cross procures all Army nurses for War Service and at the beginning of 1943, there were approximately 20,000 nurses in the Army with the rank of Second Lieutenant, every one of them volunteers. The drama presented concerns four nurses of Bataan, who underwent the ninety-eight days of ceaseless attack at the rocky fortress commanding the entrance to Manila Bay.

EPISODE #332   "**PHARMACIST'S MATE, FIRST CLASS**"   Broadcast on May 24, 1943
Starring: Alfred Drake as Brick
Ted Jewett as voice one
Carl Frank as the announcer
Ted Jewett as the Annunciator
Carl Frank as Dashiell
William Johnstone as voice four
Florence Halop as Polly
William Johnstone as Downes
Frank Readick as Snodgrass
Will Geer as Bradley
Michael O'Shea as Eddie
Jackie Kelk as voice two
Frank Readick as Farrell
Karl Swenson as the skipper
Will Geer as voice three
Ed Jerome as Dr. Brand
Jackie Kelk as Bud
Karl Swenson as Brown
Ed Jerome as McQueen
Written for *Cavalcade* by Stuart Hawkins.
Produced and directed by Homer Fickett.
Clayton Collyer is the announcer.
Music composed by Ardon Cornwell and conducted by Donald Voorhees.
Story: Young Eddie Cochrane's first assignment was a submarine on duty in waters much nearer Tokyo than Pearl Harbor. His first case, acute appendicitis. A pharmacist's mate is not expected to be a surgeon. But factual records of two such operations successfully performed aboard a submarine submerged in enemy waters of the Pacific illustrate that the youths trained by the Navy can do things that experts might consider impossible. Actual details of one of these operations - retractors fashioned from spoons, a tea strainer for an ether cone - is dramatized. The do-it-anyway spirit of the Navy will always find a way.

Trivia: The pharmacist's mate who actually did the surgery is interviewed after the story.

EPISODE #333   "MR. LINCOLN'S WIFE"   Broadcast on May 31, 1943
Starring: Helen Hayes as Mary Todd Lincoln

Sara Fussell as Tad	Frank Readick as voice two
Betty Garde as voice one	Carl Frank as voice three
Virginia Rauth as the nurse	Will Geer as the judge
Arlene Francis as Kate Chase	Agnes Young as the maid
Alfred Shirley as the policeman	Ed Jerome as voice four
Frank Readick as Ben Helm	Karl Swenson as Stoddard
Larry Robinson as Roberte	Ted Jewett as the fourth man
Skippy Homier as Willie	Virginia Rauth as the second woman
Sara Fussell as Pierre	Arlene Francis as the first woman
Carl Frank as the third man	Will Geer as the second man
Ed Jerome as the first man	Agnes Young as Emilie
Betty Garde as Lizzie	Ed Jerome as the doctor

Based on the 1943 book of the same name by Polly Anne Colver Harris, and adapted for *Cavalcade* by Victor Wolfson.
Produced and directed by Homer Fickett.
Clayton Collyer is the announcer.
Music composed by Ardon Cornwell and conducted by Donald Voorhees.

Story: Mary Todd's formal education was topped off with four years at an exclusive French boarding school and a term at a famous Lexington, Kentucky, educational institution. Her sister, Elizabeth, had married the son of Gov. Edwards of Illinois, and was living in Springfield, Illinois. Mary visited her sister frequently and it was there she met Abraham Lincoln. Theirs was a tempestuous courtship. After one estrangement which lasted several months, they were married in Springfield on November 4, 1842. Her years in the White House were a long succession of unhappiness and she was the victim of the most vicious sort of gossip. Her seventeen years of widowhood were tragic beyond belief. The shot which killed her husband toppled her from her proud position to humiliation and obscurity. She died in the house where she had become engaged to Lincoln, on July 16, 1882.

Trivia: The script title to this drama was originally "Mary Todd, Widow of Abraham Lincoln."

Jean Arthur in the Cavalcade play, "Journey Among the Lost."

EPISODE #334 "**THE ENEMY IS LISTENING**"   Broadcast on June 7, 1943
   Starring: Everett Sloane as Mr. X
   Jackie Kelk as Pinky
   Karl Swenson as Bill
   Agnes Young as Mrs. march
   Frank Readick as the first driver
   C.A. Krumschmidt as Mark
   Will Geer as the voice
   Mary Francis Heflin as Sally
   Joan Tetzel as Janie
   Arlene Francis as the second man
   Ted Jewett as the conductor

   Ed Jerome as Mr. March
   Betty Garde as Annie
   Will Geer as the milkman
   Ted Jewett as the second driver
   Paul Stewart as the man
   Frank Readick as Stevenson
   Carl Frank as the second man
   Ted Jewett as the doorman
   Everett Sloane as Smith
   Doris Nolan as the first man

   Written for *Cavalcade* by Mignon G. Eberhart.
   Produced and directed by Homer Fickett.
   Clayton Collyer is the announcer.
   Music composed by Ardon Cornwell and conducted by Donald Voorhees.
   Story: Axis agents are everywhere! Their schools have been training spies and saboteurs for years. Enemy agents want to know all about movements of troops, ships, raw materials, and finished supplies. It isn't likely that the person sitting beside you in a train . . . the telephone user in the booth next to yours is a spy, but the words they overhear, repeated in an ever-widening circle, might eventually reach enemy agents. Your rumor, added to many others, can very easily form a complete picture which will do America and the other Allies incalculable damage. This is a fictional story, of course, but a perfect example of how "a slip of the lip can sink a ship."

   Trivia: Mignon Eberhart, famous writer of mystery articles and magazine stories, had chosen this subject and this program (*Cavalcade*) as her first radio script.

EPISODE #335 "**MAKE WAY FOR THE LADY**"   Broadcast on June 14, 1943
   Starring: Madeleine Carroll as Mary Putnam Jacobi
   Arlene Francis as Sara
   Frank Readick as the chairman
   Stephen Schnabel as Jacobi
   Everett Sloane as Laron
   Ted Jewett as the voice
   Paul Stewart as the second professor
   Virginia Routh as Mme. Garnier
   Carl Frank as the secretary
   Skip Homeier as the boy
   Agnes Young as the mother
   Jackie Kelk as Haven
   Barbara Weeks as Mrs. Kelley
   Virginia Routh as Mrs. Frank
   Carl Frank as Kelley
   Paul Stewart as Frank

   Sarah Fussell as Jane
   Paul Stewart as Harper
   Ian Martin as the citizen
   William Johnstone as Jacques
   Ian Martin as the first professor
   Everett Sloane as the minister
   Barbara Weeks as the landlady
   Ted Jewett as Rau
   Frank Readick as Saunders
   Ed Jerome as George Putnam
   Will Geer as the sentry
   Arlene Francis as Mrs. Ferner
   Agnes Young as Mrs. Mullen
   Ed Jerome as Ferner
   Will Geer as Mullen

   Written for *Cavalcade* by Sidney Alexander.
   Produced and directed by Homer Fickett.
   Clayton Collyer is the announcer.
   Music composed by Ardon Cornwell and conducted by Donald Voorhees.
   Story: Since the days when Mary Putnam argued and cajoled for long months to gain admittance as a student to the Ecole de Medecine in Paris, the goal of all medical students of her time, women in medicine and the very field have come a long way. But then, in the middle of the nineteenth century, it was almost unheard of for a woman to seek any such independent career. Mary Putnam had what it took, however, in

perseverance and talent, and won her goal not only as a doctor, but in many other fields of feminine endeavor. In addition, she was active almost wherever feminine movements for advancements flourished, and her reputation and ability did a great deal towards the ultimate success of many of these causes.

EPISODE #336   "**THE UNSINKABLE MARBLEHEAD**"   Broadcast on June 21, 1943

    Starring: Dean Jagger as Captain Robinson *and* the narrator

Arlene Francis as the first woman	Virginia Routh as second woman
Sara Fussell as the boy	Will Geer as Will
Arlene Francis as Mrs. J.C. Clump	Everett Sloane as Blake
Carl Frank as Corpsman O'Shea	Edwin Jerome as Foreman
Ted Jewett as Bos'n Mate	Frank Readick as Jonesy
Jackie Kelk as the kid	Frank Readick as Sparks
Paul Stewart as Bracken	Ed Jerome as Knox
Will Geer as the doctor	Ted Jewett as Liang
Ian Martin as Goggins	Dwight Weist as the messenger
Carl Frank as the helmsman	Alfred Shirley as the fire control
Everett Sloane as the gunnery	Dwight Weist as Van Bergen
Paul Stewart as the man at sky control	Ian Martin as the lookout
Alfred Shirley as the man in the engine Room	

Written for *Cavalcade* by Charles K. Freeman.
Produced and directed by Homer Fickett.
Clayton Collyer is the announcer.
Music composed by Ardon Cornwell and conducted by Donald Voorhees.
Story: Ten thousand miles through enemy infested water, her rudder jammed, steering by her engines, reported sunk time after time, the U.S.S. Marblehead steamed into an American port not long ago with flags flying and her crew lined up proudly on her deck. The U.S.S. Marblehead was commissioned as a cruiser on September 9, 1924. Naval jack of all trades, cruisers are used to convoy duty, to run down commerce raiders of the enemy, provide an escort for aircraft carriers, to cover landing operations, and fight enemy cruisers. Relative speed is their principle attribute. They are fast, but capable of steaming long distances at moderate speed with convoys. They pack a wallop of the hit-and-run variety. Cruisers are vulnerable, since they are large enough to be a good target, but lightly armored as a rule.

EPISODE #337   "**SKY NURSEMAID**"   Broadcast on June 28, 1943

Starring: Maureen O'Sullivan as Jean Owens	Carl Frank as the driver
Frank Readick as Stevens	Jackie Kelk as Jimmie
Edwin Jerome as Cummings	Karl Swenson as Jenkins
Will Geer as the stretcher bearer	Virginia Routh as Edna
Everett Sloane as Bill	Will Geer as Freddie
Arlene Francis as Irene	Ted Jewett as the voice

Written for *Cavalcade* by Sue Taylor White.
Produced and directed by Homer Fickett.
Clayton Collyer is the announcer.
Music composed by Ardon Cornwell and conducted by Donald Voorhees.
Story: Air Evacuation Transport planes fly through dangers made more hazardous by the condition of the patients they carry. Most of the time when they carry wounded, they cannot dive or take to high altitudes to escape pursuing enemy craft. The condition of the wounded makes level flight imperative . . . and the skill of the pilot must carry them through. The Army personnel who man these planes are among the unsung heroes of the war. This is an exciting dramatization of a true incident of the courageous Air Evacuation Transport Service.

EPISODE #338 "LISTEN TO THE PEOPLE" Broadcast on July 5, 1943
    Starring: Ethel Barrymore as the narrator   Ted Jewett as the second American
    Carl Frank as the first American   Everett Sloane as the old man
    Will Geer as WPA   Carl Frank as Smith
    Stephen Schnabel as Moeller   Barbara Weeks as the woman
    Ed Jerome as Brown   Will Geer as the farmer
    Norman Lloyd as the Totalitarian   Alfred Shirley as the colonel
    Karl Swenson as the Conservative   Frank Readick as the radical
The script was written by Stephen Vincent Benet, who adapted from is 1941 poem.
An epilogue by Carl Sandburg is read by Ethel Barrymore.
Produced and directed by Homer Fickett.
Clayton Collyer is the announcer.
Music composed by Ardon Cornwell and conducted by Donald Voorhees.
Story: On this day when the American re-dedicates himself to those things for which America stands, "Listen to the People" sounded like a prophetic warning and we hear it in retrospect. This is Independence Day, fourth of July, the day we mean to keep. Whatever happens and whatever falls out of a sky grown strange, this is a firecracker day for sunburnt kids. The day of the parade, slam-banging down the street. The girls who giggle and the boys who push, all of them there and all of them a nation.

Carl Sandburg: "Stephen Vincent Benet's writings reflected a profound love and understanding of America. From coast to coast and border to border he knew his country, her people, and her cities, towns and villages. On July 4, 1941, 'Listen to the People' was first broadcast . . . when the clouds of war were still on a distant horizon. Last summer he said 'I shall not write a long narrative poem about this war.' Such poetry, he added, would come from men under 20. 'I haven't been in it,' he said, 'I won't have had the experience to write about it.' Yet this great epic poem, 'Listen to the People,' is one of the most understanding statements of our aims in this struggle."

Trivia: Beginning with this broadcast, actor Norman Lloyd began playing small supporting roles, all unbilled throughout the broadcasts. . . sometimes playing more than one role!

More Trivia: Stephen Vincent Benet died on April 4 of this year. At the time of his death he was engaged in writing an Easter script for *Cavalcade*. The last words he wrote were "I am the Resurrection . . ."

Ethel Barrymore: "Stephen Benet was a whimsical man and it would have pleased him to know that a radio play he wrote goes marching on like 'John Brown's Body'."

"SIGN HERE, PLEASE"
Starring KEENAN WYNN
with BOB BAILEY
MONDAY EVENING   MARCH 19, 1945

EPISODE #339 "**SOLDIER OF THE CLOTH**"   Broadcast on July 12, 1943
Starring: Ralph Bellamy as "Padre" Reardon *and* the narrator
Everett Sloane as the doctor   Norman Lloyd as Casey
William Sloane as King   Jackie Kelk as Chris
Frank Readick as Dakin   Carl Frank as Roberts
Will Geer as Tim   Karl Swenson as the singer
Everett Sloane as the corpsman   Norman Lloyd as Lacey
Everett Sloane as the Japanese   Ted Jewett as Hank
Will Geer as Blake   Karl Swenson as the Sergeant
Carl Frank as Frank   Frank Readick as Runt
Written for *Cavalcade* by Milton Wayne.
Produced and directed by Homer Fickett.
Clayton Collyer is the announcer.
Music composed by Ardon Cornwell and conducted by Donald Voorhees.
Story: The first chaplain in the United States Army was Reverend John Hurt, of Virginia, appointed "chaplain to the forces" by General Washington during the Revolution. Since then, chaplains have been in every war in which America was engaged. In proportion to their numbers, chaplains in WWI suffered heavier casualties than did members of any other branch of the Armed Services. They were making the same record in the second World War. In one of the first American soldier's graves in North Africa lies the body of a chaplain, the Reverend Clement Falter in civilian life, killed while landing with his regiment at Casablanca. Two chaplains were decorated for bravery under fire within two months after the North African landing. Clergymen are exempt from the draft, and they all serve by their own choice - a link between the boys in service and the folks back home. This episode told the actual experience one of our brave chaplains at Guadalcanal, his spiritual service, and his complete disregard for personal safety in the very thick of battle.

Trivia: The radio editor of *The Cleveland Plain Dealer* was the latest critic to date to speak a word of praise about *Cavalcade*. His comment on the 13th of July: "The major weakness with the radio drama this past season was its lack of top-flight scripts. Except in a very few instances, the best dramatic plays offered were, as usual, borrowed from Hollywood . . . the top originals, I think were written for *Cavalcade of America* . . ."

More trivia: Students from the New York University's Summer Radio Workshop added to their practical experiences in radio when they attended rehearsals of "Soldier of the Cloth" on July 9.

EPISODE #340 "**THE SCHOOLHOUSE AT THE FRONT**"   Broadcast on July 19, 1943
Starring: George Tobias as George Annas   Virginia Routh as the operator
Stephen Schnabel as Kimishivski   Carl Frank as the third soldier
Stephen Schnabel as the second soldier   Jackie Kelk as the first soldier
Ted Jewett as Zysbyk   Will Geer as Tolliver
Frank Readick as Smith   Ed Jerome as Ruga
Everett Sloane as Poppov   Norman Lloyd as Lesan
Ted Jewett as Foo   Carl Frank as Barbuti
Karl Swenson as Deming   Carl Frank as voice one
Frank Readick as voice two   Will Geer as voice three
Arlene Francis as the woman   Jackie Kelk as voice four
Edwin Jerome as the referee   Sara Fussell as Mary
Norman Lloyd as Goldie   Arlene Francis as the waitress
William Johnstone as Proctor   Everett Sloane as Adams
Written for *Cavalcade* by Frank Gabrielson.
Produced and directed by Homer Fickett.

Clayton Collyer is the announcer.
Music composed by Ardon Cornwell and conducted by Donald Voorhees.
Story: Each new soldier entering the U.S. Army is classified according to his trade or other experience, and is further classified according to his I.Q. If his score is 110 or more out of a possible 161, he is tested for highly technical instruction or Specialized College Training of Officer Candidate's School. Since the United States is the melting pot of the world, it is not surprising to learn that thousands of the men inducted into our fighting forces are illiterates. Special Training Units have been set up all over the country in camps to teach these men the rudimentary elements of education before they can become fighting men and to equip them for a better civilian life after the war is over. This is the story of ten of these Functional Illiterates, George Annas and nine of his companions. George, a wrestler, was physically capable of annihilating the enemy, but woefully lacking the three R's. This is how he was made not only a brawny, but a brainier fighting man - in a schoolhouse set up in one of our Army training units.

EPISODE #341 "**DIAMONDS AT WAR**" Broadcast on July 26, 1943
Starring: Charles Colburn as Mr. Leffingwell
Karl Swenson as Steward
Arlene Francis as Patricia
Ted Jewett as the cop
Stephen Schnabel as Schmidt
Everett Sloane as Sir Roger
Frank Readick as Barker
Carl Frank as the driver
Ed Jerome as Karl
Based on the 1943 book "They Deal in Death" by Robert Terrall, and adapted for *Cavalcade* by Peter Lyon.
Produced and directed by Homer Fickett.
Clayton Collyer is the announcer.
Music composed by Ardon Cornwell and conducted by Donald Voorhees.
Story: During the second World War, the United Nations controlled the sources of supply of about 95% of the world's diamonds. Under the mass production of war equipment, and the desperate urgency for utmost speed, this happy fact gave us a substantial advantage over the Axis in the production of war material. Once, diamond tools of one sort or another had been employed chiefly to grind down mill wheels and drill holes in false teeth, of all things. During the war they helped to turn out the tanks and bombers, the jeeps and submarines that were operating wherever our boys and our Allies were fighting. The Axis failed to get as large a stock of diamonds as they had hoped for when they invaded Belgium and Holland. The position of Japan may be guessed from the fact that a few weeks before Pearl Harbor, Japanese were arrested in Los Angeles for attempting to smuggle industrial diamonds out of the country. This is the story of the world's diamond center, one short block of Forty-seventh Street in New York, and the murderous lengths to which the Axis powers would go to steal diamonds.

THE DU PONT "CAVALCADE OF AMERICA" PROGRAM has received citations from . . .

Women's National Radio Committee • Institute for Education by Radio • George Foster Peabody Award • Youthbuilders, Inc. • Women's Press Club • Radio Committee of the United Parents Association • Radio Guide Phi Beta Radio Award Club • Club Women of Cleveland • Creative Art Fellowship, Visalia, Calif. • The Billboard Annual Radio Editors Poll Radio Daily Poll • Motion Picture Daily Fame Poll • Cleveland Plain Dealer Poll • National Headquarters of the American Red Cross Pasadena Junior College, Calif. • Milwaukee Journal Poll • Boston Herald Radio Poll • Des Moines Tribune Annual Radio Poll • Freedoms Foundation Award • Screen Guide Magazine Award

EPISODE #342   "NINE MEN AGAINST THE ARCTIC"   Broadcast on August 2, 1943
    Starring: Dean Jagger as Captain Monteverde   Frank Readick as Spencer
    Everett Sloane as O'Hara   Carl Frank as Tucciarone
    William Johnstone as Howarth   Ted Jewett as Wedel
    Will Geer as Best   Karl Swenson as Tetley
    Ed Jerome as Demorest   Carl Frank as Prichard
    Stephen Schnabel as Balchen   Ted Jewett as Spina
    Karl Swenson as Puryear   Norman Lloyd is the narrator
    Written for *Cavalcade* by Paul Peters.
    Produced and directed by Homer Fickett.
    Clayton Collyer is the announcer.
    Music composed by Ardon Cornwell and conducted by Donald Voorhees.
    Story: Nine men, ferrying one of our B-17 Flying Fortresses across Greenland's icy wastes, made a crash landing. The story of their rescue after five months of unbelievable privations makes as thrilling a drama as has come the war. Time after time rescue attempts failed. So difficult were the weather conditions that on one rescue attempt, Captain J.G. Moe, of the Air Transport Command, and Jimmy Wade, a pilot, who crashed less than an hour's flying time away from the marooned men, spent nearly four months reaching the Continent. Fortunately they were taken in by Eskimos they were lucky enough to meet near the scene of their crash. Col. Brent Balchen, the Norwegian-American pilot, who finally achieved the rescue, has been on many a Polar Expedition with Admiral Byrd, Sir Hubert Wilkins and Lincoln Ellsworth. In March 1931, he was one of three pilots comprising a search expedition off the Newfoundland Coast while engaged in movie work. All of the movie people aboard were saved.

EPISODE #343   "SHORT CUT TO TOKYO"   Broadcast on August 9, 1943
    Starring: Ralph Bellamy as Mr. Ford   Norman Lloyd as Joe
    Frank Readick as Wally   Edwin Jerome as Buckner
    Everett Sloane as Senator   Ted Jewett as the Jap officer
    Will Geer as Mike   Ted Jewett as Jake
    Stephen Schnabel as Gus   Ted Jewett as the voice filter
    William Johnstone as Smitty   Florence Halop as Rose
    Carl Frank as Broler   William Johnstone as Chaplain
    Will Geer as Hank   Stephen Schnabel as George
    Frank Readick as the sergeant   Everett Sloane as Sammy
    Carl Frank as the Squadron Commander   Norman Lloyd as Butch
    Edwin Jerome as the Jap pilot
    Based on the 1943 book by Corey Ford, and adapted for *Cavalcade* by Isabel Leighton.
    Produced and directed by Homer Fickett.
    Clayton Collyer is the announcer.
    Music composed by Ardon Cornwell and conducted by Donald Voorhees.
    Story: The Aleutian Islands have been described as a string of barren, rocky, treeless islands, sketching like stepping stones from Asia to North America. The Japanese thought they could use the same stepping stones to reach the American Continent. America's enemies had long recognized the importance of the Aleutians, during the years when most of us were regarding them as wasteland. For instance . . . back in the Thirties Japan planned a good-will flight from Tokyo to Washington . . . asked permission to station a few observers on the Aleutians to see the flight. We consented and groups of Japanese were landed on the Islands. The plane in Tokyo developed a series of engine troubles and the summer was over before they seemed to be remedied. Japan then explained it was too late in the season to make the flight - and picked up their Aleutian observers who had spent the entire summer on the island - making use of their time in a fashion that later set the tale of this broadcast.

Trivia: Scores of companies and individuals wrote letters as a result of this story, near the close of spring. The people who responded were keenly interested in learning more about the WIPS - Women In Production Service - the patriotic organization founded by the women workers of the Du Pont Company's Spruance Rayon Plant near Richmond, Virginia. The firms inquiring about the WIPS organization were: The Glenn L. Martin Co., RCA Victor Division of RCA, The Clotex Corporation, Lockheed Aircraft Corporation, Thomas A. Edison, Inc., General Electric Co., Vega Aircraft Corporation, Grumman Aircraft Engineering Corporation, Curtiss-Wright Corporation, Goodyear Aircraft Corporation, Western Electric Company, and the United States Rubber Comp.

Trivia: An adaptation of this book was dramatized two months later on another radio program, *Words at War*, on October 19, 1943.

Trivia: There are certain segments in this broadcast in which a harmonica was heard playing in the background. Michael Chimes, a professional harmonica player, was hired for those segments heard in the broadcast.

EPISODE #344   "**THE MAJOR AND THE MULES**"   Broadcast on August 16, 1943
Starring: Warren William as Colonel Polifka
Carl Frank as Doc   Ed Jerome as Kenny
William Johnstone as Harry   Will Geer as the Sergeant
Frank Readick as Fred   Ted Jewett as the soldier
Everett Sloane as the Australian   Norman Lloyd as the Colonel
Written for *Cavalcade* by Robert Tallman and Milton Wayne.
Produced and directed by Homer Fickett.
Clayton Collyer is the announcer.
Music composed by Ardon Cornwell and conducted by Donald Voorhees.
Story: Business in mules is good . . . a strange by-product of war times. In addition to the demands of the Army for mules, farmers throughout the country were buying them to use in place of impossible-to-get farm machinery. Mules were plodding through African mud. They were also working in the Southern war theatre . . . and before the animals could go to war they were put through several months of rigorous conditioning and training. When they joined the Army, they had to come up to certain specifications. In 1787 the King of Spain presented George Washington with a jack which was used for breeding purposes at Mount Vernon. This broadcast focuses attention on mules in a different fashion, when the weekly radio series presented a dramatization of a true incident in the South Pacific.

EPISODE #345   "**THE WEAPON THAT SAVES LIVES**"   Broadcast on August 23, 1943
Starring: Edmund Lowe as the narrator   Barbara Weeks as Mme. Trefouel
Everett Sloane as Paracelsus   William Johnstone as Domagk
Karl Swenson as the assistant   Carl Frank as the voice one
Will Geer as Ewins   Ted Jewett as Phillips
Karl Swenson as the voice on the phone   Mike O'Day as Tom
Frank Readick as Red   Ed Jerome as Marshall
Stephen Schnabel as Robin   Everett Sloane as Ehrlich
Ed Jerome as the professor   Stephen Schnabel as Gelmo
Carl Frank as voice two   Norman Lloyd as voice three
Will Geer as the voice of the Professor   Sara Fussell as Alice
Norman Lloyd as Perkin   Ted Jewett as Hofmann
Written for *Cavalcade* by Arthur Arent.
Produced and directed by Homer Fickett.
Clayton Collyer is the announcer.
Music composed by Ardon Cornwell and conducted by Donald Voorhees.

Story: Sulfa, the miracle medicine, the savior of uncounted lives, won a sweeping victory at Pearl Harbor. In the hospitals there, after that infamous December seventh, doctors saw badly wounded men who looked and felt well. Men who, in the light of past experiences, should have died were recovering, eager to get back in the fight. Doctors found an absence of infection in wounds, mildness of post-operative reactions and swift, clean healing of wounds. Sulfa drugs, plus good organization that gave the wounded prompt attention, performed this miracle. This is the dramatic discovery of this life-saving drug, and the men who spent their lives experimenting with sulfa - spent years trying to perfect it - so that today's humanity might have its miracle-working benefits.

EPISODE #346 "DEAR FUNNY FACE" Broadcast on August 30, 1943

Starring: Wendy Barrie as Jean
Everett Sloane as Chris
Will Geer as the Seabee
Virginia Routh as the operator
Barbara Weeks as Mrs. Bleeker

Alfred Drake as Larry
Frank Readick as the boy
Ted Jewett as the second boy
Ed Jerome as the commander

Written for *Cavalcade* by Paul Peters.
Produced and directed by Homer Fickett.
Clayton Collyer is the announcer.
Music composed by Ardon Cornwell and conducted by Donald Voorhees.

Story: Their emblem was a busy bee in a sailor hat, firing a tommy-gun and carrying a wrench and hammer. Their slogan was "We Fight For What We Build." Their work carried them right up to the battle fronts. They were the Navy Seabees, the Construction Battalion of fighting builders in the war. In this dramatization, you'll hear the trials and tribulations, and feel the glorious spirit, of our Seabees in his letters to his wife he left behind him and whom he always addresses as "Dear Funny Face." You'll hear his dramatic story of the Seabees building roadways for troops, hangars for our airplanes, and you'll almost smell the smoke of the battle as they start work before it clears away.

Trivia: Paul Peters originally entitled this script "A Story of the Navy Seabees," however the title was later changed by the time the final draft came about.

EPISODE #347 "DOUBLE PLAY" Broadcast on September 6, 1943

Starring: Brian Donlevy as Lt. Steve Yancey
Hans Conried as the doctor
Hal Gerard as the orderly
Gayne Whitman as the first base umpire
Georgia Backus as Sandra
Wally Maher as the voice
Frank Graham as the junior officer

Kent Smith as Lt. Steve Yancey
Virginia Gordon as the nurse
Hal Gerard as 2nd base umpire
Eddie Marr as Jones
Eddie Marr as the radio voice
William Johnstone as Johnny

Based on a recent 1943 *Saturday Evening Post* story of the same name by Jacland Marmur, and adapted for *Cavalcade* by Isabel Leighton.
Produced and directed by Homer Fickett.
Jim Bannon is the announcer and Gayne Whitman is the commercial announcer
Music composed and conducted by Robert Armbruster.

Story: Down at the Naval Academy at Annapolis, in the ward-rooms of the fleet and at land bases from the Panama Canal to Guadalcanal, they still talk about the great baseball team the Academy had a certain year in the thirties. Midshipman Harry Yancey played first. His brother, Steve - a year younger - had hoped to be a first-sacker, but his arms were too short; he had to content himself with a berth at short-stop. On second was a chap named Jones. And the three of them rang up more double plays than even the Yankees. Yancey to Jones to Yancey, became a legend at the Academy - almost as well known as the famous Tinker to Evers to Chance play. **(HLYD)**

Trivia: As an important step in the new fall line-up for *Cavalcade*, the plan was to have the September series of shows originating from Hollywood. This move of the program to the West Coast was in line with current plans to present top-ranking stars each week on *Cavalcade*. Wartime transportation problems would be eliminated when the program moved to Hollywood. Big name stars such as Gary Cooper, Cary Grant, James Cagney, Ingrid Bergman and Ginger Rogers would be available to take the leading roles in *Cavalcade* dramatizations of history-in-the-making in a world now at war. This was the first episode originating from Hollywood.

More Trivia: This *Cavalcade* script was written by Isabel Leighton, well known short story writer and author of numerous articles for the *Saturday Evening Post, Liberty*, and other national magazines. An authority on Naval subjects, Miss Leighton was at her best when writing stories of the sea.

EPISODE #348   "**IRON CAMELS**"   Broadcast on September 13, 1943
    Starring: Pat O'Brien as Colonel Carey   Wally Maher as Collins
    Herb Vigran as voice two   Jack Edwards, Sr. as voice one
    Herb Vigran as the courier   William Johnstone as Roul
    Howard McNear as Blackburn   Jack Edwards, Sr. as the sergeant
    Elliott Reid as Smith   Ted Von Eltz as the General
    Frank Graham supplied all of the remaining small voices heard throughout.
    Written for *Cavalcade* by Robert L. Richards and Sue Taylor White. Based on actual records of the Army Transportation Corps.
    Produced and directed by Homer Fickett.
    Jim Bannon is the announcer and Gayne Whitman is the commercial announcer.
    Music composed and conducted by Robert Armbruster.
    Story: Old Timers in the business say railroading is either in your blood or it isn't. Railroading isn't an acquitted taste - you're born with it or you never have it. At eighteen, Steve was studying civil engineering with railroading as his goal. After Pearl Harbor Steve enlisted in the Transportation Corps of the Army Service Forces. And in Tunisia, as a Lt.-Col. commanding a Railroad Battalion, Steve learned what railroading under fire really was. Later, a day came in the Battle of Tunisia when the tables were turned. Rommel's famed Africa Korps was retreating. The Army Transportation Corps really hit its stride laying new tracks to bring troops, ammunition and supplies. **(HLYD)**

    Trivia: The original title of this drama was "Iron Camels in Africa."

EPISODE #349   "**THE VENGEANCE OF TORPEDO 8**"   Broadcast on September 20, 1943
    Starring: Randolph Scott as Lt. Harold Larsen, U.S.N.
    Wally Maher as Ernest   Theodore Von Eltz as Sparks
    Theodore Von Eltz as the Captain   William Johnstone as Frenchy
    Joseph Kearns as Taurman   Georgia Backus as Missy
    Joseph Kearns as the conductor   Lois Corbett as the operator
    Marjorie Davies as Birmingham Operator   Elliott Reid as the ship operator
    Hal Gerard as the petty officer   Jack Edwards, Sr. as the Admiral
    Frank Graham as the narrator
    Based on the book "Torpedo 8" by Ira Wolfert, originally published in 1943 by the Houghton Mifflin Company, and adapted for *Cavalcade* by Robert L. Richards and Milton Wayne.
    Produced and directed by Homer Fickett.
    Jim Bannon is the announcer and Gayne Whitman is the commercial announcer.
    Music composed and conducted by Robert Armbruster.
    Story: The Navy in its official communiqué on the career of the aircraft carrier "Hornet" paid high tribute to the courage of Torpedo Squadron 8. It was revealed that one of their

most heroic attacks took place when they took off in search of a Japanese force of four aircraft carriers reported to be more than 150 miles away. Torpedo Squadron 8 pressed straight on to the target despite the fact that they had become separated from their escorting fighters and in spite of the Jap Zeros swarming around them, inflicted their torpedo hits. This is a special tribute to these heroic men. **(HLYD)**

Trivia: Joel McCrea was originally signed up to star on the broadcast of September 20th - the story of the famous U.S. Navy Squadron. Originally entitled "Torpedo Eight," the bill collected by Squadron members for the beath of their comrades over Midway accounted for two Jap carriers, a transport and a heavy cruiser.

EPISODE #350   "**THE HATED HERO OF 1776**"   Broadcast on September 27, 1943
Starring: Basil Rathbone as Thomas Paine   Ruth Warrick as Irene
William Johnstone as Jackson   Elliott Reid as Jamie
Vernon Steele as Roberdeau   Frank Graham as the narrator
Carleton Young as the servant   Wally Maher as Ben
Based on the 1943 book "Citizen Tom Paine" by Howard Fast, and adapted for *Cavalcade* by Raphael Hayes and Robert L. Richards.
Produced and directed by Homer Fickett.
Jim Bannon is the announcer and Gayne Whitman is the commercial announcer.
Music composed and conducted by Robert Armbruster.
Story: It has frequently been said that it was Tom Paine who fired Washington with the ardor that made him the commander of our Revolutionary Army, and certainly there is no American who does not remember the memorable words with which he began his immortal "Crisis." The story we get involved in will deal with Jefferson's attempt as President, to bring Paine back to his native land after long years of exile. You will hear of the abuse heaped on Paine when he was writing and shouting for freedom in the coffee houses of Philadelphia. Rabble-rouser, drunkard and a blasphemous man were a few of the epithets thrown at him, but he, perhaps more than any other man, used his pen and voice to help effect American Independence. **(HLYD)**

Trivia: Beginning with this broadcast, *Cavalcade* took to the air over sixty-three additional stations. This meant that in addition to the sixty-two stations on which the program was then being heard, there would be many new stations through-out the country on which radio listeners may tune in to the Du Pont program locally.

EPISODE #351   "**CONTINUE UNLOADING**"   Broadcast on October 4, 1943
Starring: John Garfield as Bill Forsyth   Wally Maher as Giovanni
William Johnstone as Lt. Williamson   Frank Graham as the Captain
Joseph Kearns as the Ranger Officer   Tyler McVey as the CPO
Herb Vigran as the first Coast Guardsman   Elliott Reid as the soldier
Joseph Kearns as Gunner one   Tyler McVey as Gunner two
Howard McNear as the second Coast Guardsman
Written for *Cavalcade* by Stanley Young.
Produced and directed by Homer Fickett.
Jim Bannon is the announcer and Gayne Whitman is the commercial announcer.
Music composed and conducted by Robert Armbruster.
Story: The U.S. Coast Guard has so many and varied war-time duties, it would take a catalogue to list them all. Convoy escorting, rescues, capture of enemies, evacuation of civilians, landing of men and supplies are only a few. This is the story of the invasion force in history, and the gallant part played in the Sicilian landing by the U.S. Coast Guard. General Patton bet Admiral Kirk it would take eight days to unload, but in 72 hours, men, tanks, munitions, fuel, food were ashore. Combat Photographer's Mate Bill Forsyth was supposed to get pictures of the Coast Guard in action, but before he knew it,

he had rescued a wounded buddy, and was right in the thick of the landing operations, lugging supplies to shore and grabbing pictures where and when he could. **(HLYD)**

Homer Fickett: "New York being 'the radio home' of the program, *Cavalcade* draws on theatrical talent for its stellar parts, or summons Hollywood scintillates willing to travel back to Manhattan. Of course more stars are available in Hollywood - that was the reason we came out here to put on broadcasts."

EPISODE #352   "BOB HOPE REPORTS"   Broadcast on October 11, 1943
   Starring: Bob Hope as himself   Elliott Reid as the Steward
   Virginia Gordon as the girl   Wally Maher as the voice
   Jack Mather as the Captain   Howard McNear as Doc A
   William Johnstone as Doc B   Georgia Backus as the nurse
   Frank Graham as Charlie   Paul Hilton as the boy
   William Johnstone as Flier two   Tom Collins as Flier one
   Eddie Marr as the soldier   Frank Graham as the General
   Tom Collins as voice A   Jack Mather as voice B
   Howard McNear as voice one   Wally Maher as voice two
   Eddie Marr as Brook   Georgia Backus as the mother
   Beverly Brown as the operator
   Written for *Cavalcade* by Glenn Wheaton.
   Produced and directed by Homer Fickett.
   Jim Bannon is the announcer and Gayne Whitman is the commercial announcer.
   Music composed and conducted specially for this broadcast by Robert Armbruster.
   Story: Hope covered about 250 camps and hospital shows in eleven weeks. He rested from camp shows by bobbing up in hospitals, dropping in on ack-ack crews, sloshing across rain-swept heaths to entertain soldiers on maneuvers. Hope's gags got around so fast he had to keep changing them and he and scriptwriter Hal Block ground out new ones in bumpy transits, or in hotel rooms long past midnight. This a dramatization of this history-making entertainment junket. **(HLYD)**

Trivia: In commemoration of *Cavalcade's* eight years on radio, this anniversary program marked the beginning of its ninth year on the air. Bob Hope, the comedian who had recently staged a smashing entertainment offensive for Johnny Doughboy over-seas, gave a first-hand report through Army camps in England, Africa, Sicily and Iceland. Sidelights of Hope's performances on ammunition dumps, army trucks, plane wings, gas-lit recreation halls and open roads under shellfire formed the basis of the script, written by Glenn Wheaton, scripter who prepared the weekly short-wave program *Command Performance*.

More trivia: After a schedule so strenuous that it might well have broken the proverbial back of anyone else, Hope gave his shows to nearly a half-million soldiers, British as well as Americans. "It was the greatest thing that ever happened to me," Hope said upon his return. "I wouldn't have missed it for the world." Hope gave the overseas troops the Hollywood lowdown. "They're drafting all the leading men in Hollywood," he said. "When you walk down the street, instead of saying 'What do you know, Joe?' you say, 'When do you go Joe?' You know, if it keeps up, most of the leading men next season will be on the adrenaline side. Can you imagine Hedy Lamarr waiting to be kissed while Lewis Stone plugs in his heating pad?"

More trivia: *Time* magazine devoted the front cover and several pages of it's September issue to the saga of one of the most unusual events of the war, the record-breaking tour of Bob Hope through the battlefields and camps of England and Sicily to entertain our boys overseas.

More trivia: To show their genuine appreciation of his appearances, doughboys bombarded him with countless gifts: captured daggers, Lugers and dirks, and a Mussolini medal awarded to a fertile Italian mother of eight children.

EPISODE #353 "**THE GENERAL WORE CALICO**" Broadcast on October 18, 1943
    Starring: Jane Darwell as Mother Bickerdyke
    Richard LeGrande as Reverend Beecher
    Hans Conried as Lieutenant Butterfield
    William Johnstone as the ninth soldier
    Stan Farrar as the eighth soldier
    Herb Virgran as the second soldier
    William Griffis as the second man
    Hal Gerard as the third soldier
    Richard LeGrande as the fifth soldier
    Wally Maher as the fourth soldier
    Hans Conried as the second doctor
    Jack Edwards, Jr. as Harry
    Harry Bartell as the aide
    Frank Graham as General Grant
    Wally Maher as John Mather
    Stan Farrar as the conductor
    Hal Gerard as the first man
    Georgia Backus as Mrs. Webb
    Jack Edwards, Jr. as the boy
    William Johnstone as the doctor
    Herb Vigran as Andrew
    Harry Bartell as the sixth soldier
    Bill Griffis as the seventh soldier
    Written for *Cavalcade* by Paul Peters.
    Produced and directed by Homer Fickett.
    Jim Bannon is the announcer and Gayne Whitman is the commercial announcer.
    Music composed and conducted by Robert Armbruster.
    Story: When the Civil War broke out, there were no organizations like the Red Cross, the USO, and other voluntary groups such as we have today to minister to the fighting men's needs. Shortly after the war started, the U.S. Sanitary Commission was founded, motivated by a "simple desire and resolute determination to secure for men who have enlisted in this war - that care which it is the duty of the nation to give them." Mary Bickerdyke, a widow of Galesburg, Illinois, and a woman of indomitable determination and spirit, was a member of that first voluntary group. **(HLYD)**

    Trivia: This *Cavalcade* broadcast presents Jane Darwell, herself a direct descendent of Andrew Jackson, and an Academy Award winner, in this interesting drama presented an unusual achievement in a special salute to all of the American women currently engaged in war work.

EPISODE #354 "**TAKE HER DOWN!**" Broadcast on October 25, 1943
    Starring: Robert Young as Commander Gilmore
    Georgia Backus as Hilda
    Frank Graham as Wilson
    William Johnstone as Davis
    Tyler McVey as Wagner
    Hans Conried as Arnie
    Wally Maher as McCabe
    Jack Edwards, Jr. as Doug
    Bob Bruce as Jack
    Harry Bartell as Red
    William Griffis supplied all of the extra voices
    Written for *Cavalcade* by Norman Rosten and Robert L. Richards.
    Produced and directed by Homer Fickett.
    Jim Bannon is the announcer and Gayne Whitman is the commercial announcer.
    Music composed and conducted by Robert Armbruster.
    Story: same as episode #407, broadcast on October 30, 1944
    (HLYD)

    Trivia: A few weeks before this broadcast, the U.S.S. Gilmore was christened at a West Coast port, by the widow of Commander Howard Gilmore. In recognition of Navy Day, October 27, and as a tribute to one of the immortal heroes of all time, a stirring dramatization of submarine Commander Gilmore, U.S.N., whose command "Take Her Down," meant the sacrifice of his life.

EPISODE #355   "**BURMA SURGEON**"   Broadcast on November 1, 1943
    Starring: George Brent as Dr. Gordon Seagrave   Eddie Marr as Hsu Llan
    Eustace Wyatt as Non - Comm.   Frank Graham as the officer
    Barbara Jean Wong as Koi   Eddie Marr as the sentry
    Wally Maher as Stilwell   Georgia Backus as Tiny
    Hans Conried as Simpson   Bill Johnstone as the headman
    Lucille Meredith as Ehla   Bill Johnstone as the radio man

Based on the book of the same name by Gordon S. Seagrave, Lt. Colonel, Medical Corps, U.S. Army Forces in China, India, Burma, originally published in 1943 by W.W. Norton & Comp., Inc., adapted for *Cavalcade* by Milton Wayne and Robert L. Richards. Produced and directed by Homer Fickett.

Jim Bannon is the announcer and Gayne Whitman is the commercial announcer.

Music composed and conducted by Robert Armbruster.

Story: When he was five, young Gordon Seagrave had a bad case of hero worship. The object of his admiration was a great two-fisted Irishman who told him tales of high adventure as a member of the Irish Constabulary, the Royal Northwest Mounted Police and of how he had side-stepped death dozens of times in the jungles of Burma. Then, to cap the climax, this demi-god had swung a chair over his head with his teeth and drunk a glass of water standing on his head. "Who is he?" young Gordon asked his mother. "A medical missionary from Nmkhan in the Shan States of Burma," was the answer. Then and there Gordon Seagrave announced that he, too, would be a medical missionary to Burma. **(HLYD)**

EPISODE #356   "**JOE DYER ENDS A WAR**"   Broadcast on November 8, 1943
    Starring: James Craig as Joe Dyer   Beulah Bondi as Mrs. Dyer
    Conrad Binyon as Cy   Wally Maher as the first man
    Joseph Kearns as Josh   Hans Conried as the first settler
    Joe Forte as the second man   Joe DuVal as the third man
    Bob Bruce as the second settler   William Johnstone as the governor
    Joe Forte as the first counselor   Joe DuVal as the second counselor
    Eustace Wyatt as the third counselor   Bob Bruce as Willis
    Hans Conried as the judge   Frank Graham as the first voice
    Wally Maher as the second voice   Eustace Wyatt as the third voice
    William Johnstone as the fourth voice   Joseph Kearns as the fifth voice
    Frank Graham as the narrator

Written for *Cavalcade* by Robert L. Richards and Victor Wolfson.

Produced and directed by Homer Fickett.

Jim Bannon is the announcer and Gayne Whitman is the commercial announcer.

Music composed and conducted by Robert Armstrong.

Story: In the beginning there was America but no Americans - only Pennsylvanians, New Yorkers, Virginians, Georgians. The conflicting interests of the colonies were a barrier to national unity which, at best, was a far-off ideal. Only the vague, unproved idea of freedom - held the newly-liberated colonies together. And among the conflicting interests of the several colonies were their boundaries. The original grants and charters had been loosely drawn. Frequently two or even more colonies laid claim to the same lands, and with equal justice. A classic case was the dispute between Pennsylvania and Connecticut. Both colonies, by right of charter, claimed lands along the Susquehanna. When families from Conn. attempted to settle there, irate Pennsylvanians burned their houses, arrested them for trespassing. Civil war seemed imminent, for had not such boundary disputes, since time immemorial, been settled by wars? **(HLYD)**

Trivia: Gayne Whitman saluted women in the Du Pont work force during this episode.

More Trivia: The original title of this drama was "The Trenton Trial."

EPISODE #357   "12 DESPERATE MILES"   Broadcast on November 15, 1943

Starring: Edward Arnold as the Captain
William Griffis as Bill
William Johnstone as the Admiral
Hans Conried as Drake
William Johnstone as Chris
Wally Maher as Pete
Harry Bartell as the Helmsman
Eustace Wyatt as the British General
Harry Lang as Padula
Frank Graham as the colonel
Bob Bruce as the Major
Bob Bruce as the Sheriff
Harry Bartell as Marschak
Hans Conried as Mario
Joseph Kearns as Bixby

Based on the 1943 *Saturday Evening Post* article by Bertram A. Fowler, and adapted for *Cavalcade* by Isabel Leighton and Milton Wayne.
Produced and directed by Homer Fickett.
Jim Bannon is the announcer and Gayne Whitman is the commercial announcer.
Music composed and conducted by Robert Armbruster.
Story: The vast Allied armada carrying troops, planes, tanks and guns was soon to converge on North Africa, to seize the Axis-Vichy-held south flank of the Mediterranean. There had to be an umbrella of planes over the landing operations. But there was only one field from which the umbrella of planes could be raised. It was a field that could be taken, but only if gasoline, supplies and ammunition could be landed twelve miles up the tortuous, unnavigable Sebu River, a stream so shallow that the Navy despaired of finding a ship that could make the trip. Then someone remembered the Contessa - gallant and willing but salt-caked, rust-stained, "held together with spit and prayer," to quote her captain, with little between her and the junk heap except a job that no other ship could do. Then, with sealed orders, the Contessa sailed on a blind date with destiny. **(HYLD)**

EPISODE #358   "SOLDIERS OF THE SOIL"   Broadcast on November 22, 1943

Starring: Russell Hayden as John Landis
Fay Helm as Mrs. Landis
Georgia Backus as Grace Landis
Joel Davis as John Landis (age seven)
Lila Webb as Mrs. Eldridge
* Stars the movie cast.
Carroll Nye as David Landis
Will Wright as Samuel Landis
Frank Graham as Richard Landis
Dix Davis as Joey
William Johnstone as the preacher

Based on the 1943 screenplay, and adapted for *Cavalcade* by Stuart Hawkins and Robert L. Richards.
Produced and directed by Homer Fickett.
Jim Bannon is the announcer and Gayne Whitman is the commercial announcer.
Music composed and conducted by Robert Armbruster.
Story: This is the tale of how one farmer, John Landis, found his answer to the duty-call of his country when his older brother David, a marine, came home blind from the battle front. The drama portrays a generation of life on the Landis family's farm, the whole broad sweep of agriculture in its relation to war needs for food and fiber. David's return from the war with a handicap caused John to resolve to put on his brother's uniform and get into the fight "with a gun in his hands." But blind David finds the answer for John in John's own life story, which is one of sacrifice and courage, and in the farm itself. He persuades John to stay on the farm, to use his skill and knowledge in keeping his acres in production. **(HLYD)**

Trivia: As a tribute to the all-important role the farmer was playing in the war, the Du Pont Company had sponsored a stirring motion picture, *Soldiers of the Soil*, produced by a Hollywood studio with a splendid cast of featured players. Although the film had just been released, this broadcast was a highlight of the fall season. Prints of the this new film was available in 16 mm and 35 mm - 38 minutes running time - could be attained through the film laboratories of the State Agriculture Extension Service or the Vocational and Educational Training Service.

EPISODE #359   "THE WISE MAD GENERAL"   Broadcast on November 29, 1943
   Starring: Warner Baxter as General Wayne   Lloyd Nolan as David Herbert
   Georgia Backus as Ann   Billy Roy as Jeremy
   William Johnstone as the second soldier   Harry Bartell as Greene
   Hans Conried as the first soldier   Frank Graham as Craik
   Harry Bartell as the third soldier   Wally Maher as Cooper
   William Johnstone as Reed   Hans Conried as Maloney
   Howard McNear as Bolen   Jay Novello as Mason
   Jack Edwards, Sr. as Colonel Butler   Frank Graham as Captain Bettin
   Howard McNear as Lt. Crane   Jack Edwards, Sr. as Bowzar
   Based on the book "Mutiny in January" by Carl Van Doren, originally published in 1943 by Viking Press, and adapted for *Cavalcade* by Milton Wayne.
   Produced and directed by Homer Fickett.
   Jim Bannon is the announcer and Gayne Whitman is the commercial announcer.
   Music composed and conducted by Robert Armbruster.
   Story: "The Wise Mad General" takes its title from the deep tolerance, the profound understanding and rich sympathy of the Revolutionary officer whom America remembers best as Mad Anthony Wayne. Its heroes, however, are common soldiers of the Revolution, unsung, forgotten men - hungry, cold - who fought the war in ragged, scanty uniforms on empty stomachs. The villains of the play are an ungrateful, indifferent citizenry and their faithless public servants who neglected to provide their army with the essentials of war - men who offered only pennies in voting supplies of ammunition and clothing and food to the men who were fighting the battle for America's freedom.
   (HLYD)

EPISODE #360   "NAVY DOCTOR"   Broadcast on December 6, 1943
   Starring: Brian Donlevy as Dr. Flower   Everett Sloane as the narrator
   Will Geer as Willis   Frank Readick as Cutler
   Ted Jewett as the loudspeaker   Edward Jerome as Captain Greenman
   Fred Utall as Dr. Brown   Owen Jordan as the operator
   Ted Jewett as Becker   Owen Jordan as Wagner
   Paul Stewart as the wounded man   Paul Stewart as Morrow
   Frank Readick as the sailor   Owen Jordan as the signalman
   Paul Stewart as the officer
   Written for *Cavalcade* by Paul Peters, based on the experiences of Comm. Charles F. Fowler.
   Produced and directed by Paul Stewart.
   Carl Frank is the announcer and Clayton Collyer is the commercial spokesman.
   Music composed by Ardon Cornwell and conducted by Donald Voorhees.
   Story: Seventeen years ago, Dr. Charles F. Fowler finished medical school and hung his shingle on a battleship. For seventeen years, in his sick bay on destroyer, cruiser or battle wagon, he tended the ills of men of the sea. His official title is Medical Officer, but in the hearts of men of his ship who call him, with affection and complete lack of awe, "Doc" or "Surge," he holds a very special place. Even in peacetime a medical officer's post is no simple job. He must sometimes operate in heavy storms. But in wartime, with shells exploding, fires raging, the Navy doctor goes about his work with an efficiency and an unswerving devotion to duty that has made him time and again a true Naval hero.

Homer Fickett: "When it is on its home stage, *Cavalcade* had its own stock company to carry all of the supporting roles. The cream of the crop was when we introduced such now well-knowns as Agnes Moorehead, Orson Welles, Ray Collins, and Nancy Kelly. Welles was just another actor when he first came to me and asked for a part on our show."

EPISODE #361   "CHECK YOUR HEART AT HOME"   Broadcast on December 13, 1943
Starring: Shirley Booth as Jennifer Prescott, A.P.C.

Ned Weaver as Mark	Helen Claire as Peg
Ed Jerome as R.C. Executive	Alfred Shirley as Steward
Helen Claire as Polly	Peg La Centra as Carrie
Elaine Kent as Alice	Norman Lloyd as the photographer
Ted Jewett as the first soldier	Frank Readick as the second soldier
Owen Jordan as the third soldier	Adelaide Klein as the nurse
Paul Stewart as the fourth soldier	Will Geer as Joe
Will Geer as the fifth soldier	Paul Stewart as the Sergeant
Ted Jewett as the Lieutenant	Owen Jordan as the voice
Frank Readick as George	Ed Jerome as Captain
Norman Lloyd as the second voice	Owen Jordan as the Corporal

Based on material from the 1943 book "They Sent Me to Iceland" by Jane Goodell, and adapted for *Cavalcade* by Milton Wayne.
Produced and directed by Paul Stewart.
Carl Frank is the announcer and Clayton Collyer is the commercial spokesman.
Music composed by Ardon Cornwell and conducted by Donald Voorhees.
Story: The Red Cross nurses and recreation workers on that bleak, desolate outpost of the North Atlantic call themselves the F.B.I. - the Forgotten Babes of Iceland. There the days are an endless chain of monotony - bad weather, bad roads, terrific winds and an unvarying diet of tinned meat and dehydrated potatoes. For the men of the Army stationed there, it is one of the toughest assignments in the service. Nothing ever happens . . . their only job is to see that nothing ever does. And so, when the first party of Red Cross recreation workers arrived in Iceland to set up canteens, club rooms and a program of recreation and entertainment, the men were jubilant. The people at home had not forgotten them. Something was going to happen at last.

Trivia: Ballad singer Burl Ives plays a minor role in this broadcast, that of a man named Lenny.

More Trivia: Rita Hayworth was originally scheduled to star in the lead role of Jennifer.

EPISODE #362   "A CHILD IS BORN"   Broadcast on December 20, 1943

Starring: Helen Hayes as the Innkeeper's wife	Philip Merivale as the Innkeeper
Norman Lloyd as the soldier	Ted Jewett as the voice
Ed Jerome as the Prefect	Ann Thomas as Sarah
Charita Bauer as Leah	Karl Swenson as Joseph
Frank Readick as Dismas	

Based on the biblical story from the book of Matthew, and adapted for *Cavalcade* by Stephen Vincent Benet.
Produced and directed by Paul Stewart.
Carl Frank is the announcer.
The special music for this broadcast was composed by Ardon Cornwell and conducted under the direction of Donald Voorhees.
The song "O Come, All Ye Faithful" was sung by a chorus in the background.
Story: The play is the old, old story of Christ's birth in Bethlehem of Judea, and yet the story is timeless; the place - anywhere. Herod is Herod; he is any tyrant and all of them. He is all tyrants who would grind humanity like dry wheat between the stones. The innkeeper is the innkeeper of long ago who had no room for Mary and Joseph. And yet he is all mankind who, in a thousand small ways . . . by careless, appeasing compromise . . . loses his freedom "by not caring, not daring to go beyond the ragged edge of

fortitude." His wife is womankind that senses "something is loosed to change a shaken world" every time a child is born.

Trivia: Stephen Vincent Benet's reverent and inspiring play was written for *Cavalcade* the year before. Because it related to a war torn world, the timeless story of the Christmas birth in Judea was performed again. William Rose Benet, brother of the late Stephen Vincent Benet introduced the drama.

EPISODE #363   "U-BOAT PRISONER"   Broadcast on December 27, 1943
   Starring: Richard Arlen as Archie Gibbs   Ned Weaver as the narrator
   Roland Winters as the first German sailor   Frank Readick as the Irishman
   Norman Lloyd as the voice   Roland Winters as the first seaman
   Peter Capell as Lt. Zimmer   Stephan Schnabel as the 2nd German officer
   Jack MacBryde as the third seaman   Mandel Kramer as Cue
   Frank Readick as the fourth seaman   Norman Lloyd as the second seaman
   Ted Jewett as the first German officer   Ted Jewett as Tex
   Jack MacBryde as the second officer   Ed Jerome as the third German sailor
   Ed Jerome as the dispatcher   Mandel Kramer as the second German sailor
   Lousi Saas as the Foreign Language announcer

Freely adapted from the book of the same name by Archie Gibbs, originally published in 1943 by Houghton Mifflin Company. Adapted for *Cavalcade* by Arthur Arent. Produced and directed by Paul Stewart.
Carl Frank is the announcer and Clayton Collyer is the commercial spokesman.
Music composed by Ardon Cornwell and conducted by Donald Voorhees.
Story: Archie Gibbs was waiting for something to pick him up - and for the second time in twenty-four hours. Being torpedoed was getting to be a monotonous routine. Before he knew it Archie Gibbs was rolling on the foredeck of a German submarine and looking into the muzzle of a .38 revolver. Day and night were one to Archie Gibbs aboard the submarine. There was little to do but listen to the radio. And as they listened, Gibbs found what he needed to sustain him, come what might. The German sailors were dialing for something, dialing endlessly but never finding what they sought. But at last they found it. Long and clear the signal came in, and you could have knocked Archie Gibbs over with a pin-cushion. For what he heard was "Deep in the Heart of Texas!" and the German sailors were clapping in approved American fashion at just the proper times. Then and there Archie Gibbs ceased to be scared. Suddenly he knew just what he'd say to the officers when they questioned him. If America could write the kind of songs all the world wanted to sing - well, that was just the medicine Archie Gibbs needed.

EPISODE #364   "BULLSEYE FOR SAMMY"   Broadcast on January 3, 1944
   Starring: Jackie Kelk as Sammy Brine   Alfred Drake as Lt. Alfred Hefler
   Ned Weaver as the narrator   Will Geer as Jenks
   John Thomas as Ensign James   Ted Jewett as the lookout
   Ted Jewett as the Chief Petty Officer   Norman Lloyd as the yeoman
   Agnes Young as the telephone operator   Agnes Young as Maw
   Floyd Beeckley as the quarter master   Floyd Beeckley as the voice
   Frank Readick as Sparks   Frank Readick as the cook
   Martin Wolfson as the voice on the ship   Ed Jerome as the Admiral's voice
   Martin Wolfson as the voice on Bullhorn   Ed Jerome as Commander McDaniel
Written for *Cavalcade* by Arthur Arent and Laurence Schwab.
Produced and directed by Paul Stewart.
Carl Frank is the announcer and Clayton Collyer is the commercial spokesman.
Music composed by Ardon Cornwell and conducted by Donald Voorhees.
Story: Sammy Brine went into the Navy with a chip on his shoulder. Chances are that he'll leave it with those same shoulders decorated with the epaulets of an officer. That's

what the Navy does for lads like Sammy. The skipper sized Sammy up right about the first time he saw him. "Raised on a beer bottle in a cinder patch in Jersey. He's had to eat a lot of dirt on the way up. He's bound to spit out some. They can build a ship in seventy-two days now. It takes longer to make a man, but that's what the Navy'll do before we get though with him." The skipper was right; the Navy did. Here is the story of Sammy Brine and his "poisonal" war against the Axis.

EPISODE #365 "**HERE IS YOUR WAR**" Broadcast on January 10, 1944

    Starring: Jackie Gleason as Ernie Pyle   Jack Edwards, Sr. as the voice (Military)
    William Griffis as soldier one   Howard McNear as soldier two
    William Johnstone as soldier three   Charlie Lung as soldier four
    Joe DuVal as the Major   Eddie Marr as soldier A
    Wally Maher as soldier B   Harry Bartell as Jackson
    Pinto Colvig as the Arab boy   Charlie Lung as soldier D
    Frank Graham as soldier C   Howard McNear as soldier E
    William Griffis as the pilot   Frank Graham as the second pilot
    Eddie Marr as the third pilot   Jack Edwards, Jr. as the operations officer

Based on the 1943 book of the same title by Ernie Pyle, originally published by Henry Holt and Company, Inc., and adapted for *Cavalcade* by Stanley Young.
Produced and directed by Homer Fickett.
Jim Bannon is the announcer and Gayne Whitman is the commercial spokesman.
Music composed and conducted by Robert Armbruster.
Story: In the unforgettable style which has made Ernie Pyle a welcome daily guest in millions of American homes, this crack correspondent takes us from transport to foxhole to bomber hop - through a dozen situations that alternately brought tears of laughter and of sorrow. But there was the feeling of being in on something big - of actually witnessing a shot-by-shot close-up of the war as history unfolds it. To get the real news of the war, the feel and the flavor of the life which the American soldier leads, to learn what the men of the army are thinking and talking and griping about, Ernie Pyle lived their life - right on the battle line. He found that life at the front consists of danger in spurts, laughs, tragedies and perpetual discomfort. But he found it worthwhile. **(HLYD)**

    Trivia: An adaptation of this novel was dramatized two months before on another radio program, *Words at War*, on November 2, 1943.

EPISODE #366 "**TERRENCE O'TOOLE, M.P.**" Broadcast on January 17, 1944

    Starring: George Murphy as Terrence O'Toole   Dick Ryan as Lieutenant
    William Johnstone as Kappa   Jeanette Nolan as Bridget
    Franklin Parker as the Major   Wally Maher as Raker
    Eddie Marr as the Sergeant   George Neise as Kalinsky
    William Griffis as Newmark   Robert Bruce as Callen
    James Nusser as Blount   Charlie Lung as Miller
    Tyler McVey as the first two voices   Ken Christy as voice three

Written for *Cavalcade* by Milton Wayne.
Produced and directed by Homer Fickett.
Jim Bannon is the announcer and Gayne Whitman is the commercial spokesman.
Music composed and conducted by Robert Armbruster.
Story: Cops were poison to old man Flanagan. And, probably because he had once had a brush with an M.P. as a doughboy back in '17, the Army Military Police were an object of his special and personal scorn. This was bad news to Terrence O'Toole who was engaged to Molly Flanagan, for Terrence was an M.P., and Molly, alas, was so timid that she was afraid of her own shadow - to say nothing of her father's two hundred pound bulk. Of course, it was true that Terrence hadn't asked to be an M.P.; he wanted action. "And action it is you'll be gettin'," the burly sergeant promised, as Terrence entrained for

the Army's new Military Police School at Fort Custer, Michigan. And action? This drama is packed with action as Terrence's life was after he landed in North Africa, and his first combat mission. **(HLYD)**

EPISODE #367 "**THE DOCTOR SHOOTS A CANNON**" Broadcast on January 24, 1944
Starring: Preston Foster as Captain Eric G. Hakansen, Director of the Institute
Otto Kruger as Dr. Gordon B. Fauley   Gene Lockhart as Dr. Andrew C. Ivy
Written for *Cavalcade* by Paul Peters and Robert Tallman.
Produced and directed by Homer Fickett.
Jim Bannon is the announcer and Gayne Whitman is the commercial spokesman.
Music composed and conducted by Robert Armbruster.
Story: A lone Nazi flyer, his motors spitting in distress, swooped out of the Mediterranean sky. In the tense moment before he disappeared in a plume of smoke into the sea, with suicidal fury he released a bomb on the prow of an American destroyer. The craft was shaken as if by giant hands. Two decks below - a hundred feet from the exploding bomb - a Navy chaplain felt a sudden, searing pain. A wave of unimaginable heat enveloped him - a heat so intense that it blistered the paint of the passageway. Here was a new problem - flashburn - a challenge to the skill and ingenuity of the men who were working three thousand miles away in the Navy's great Medical Research Institute at Bethesda, Maryland, just outside of Washington. This tells how one Navy Captain and two Navy scientists developed a protective cream - known by its formula number, "M-70" - which sent men into battle looking like soldiers in greasepaint. **(HLYD)**

EPISODE #368   "**THE SAILOR TAKES A WIFE**"   Broadcast on January 31, 1944
Starring: Dick Powell as Barry Arthur   Ona Munson as Kathy
Frank Graham as the narrator   Robert Bruce as Buck
Eddie Marr as the voice   George Neise as the seaman
Franklyn Parker as the cook   Herbert Lytton as the doctor
Franklyn Parker as the commandant   William Johnstone as the leader
Wally Maher as Fingers   Tyler McVey as the man
Eddie Marr as the officer   Herbert Lytton as the Captain
John McIntire as Pop
Written for *Cavalcade* by Allan E. Sloane.
Produced and directed by Homer Fickett.
Jim Bannon is the announcer and Gayne Whitman is the commercial spokesman.
Music composed and conducted by Robert Armbruster.
Story: Barry Arthur was a young newspaper city editor who usually saw eye to eye with Kathy, his star feature writer. But when Kathy wanted to do a story on the Merchant Marine, editor Barry was full of scorn. "A bunch of guys in turtle neck sweaters who raise Cain in water-front dives - row with the navy and land in the clink! Forget it." But that was before a lot of mixed emotions - jilted love, duty, patriotism, to say nothing of an Irish temper and bad eyes - steered Barry himself into the Merchant Marine. Barry found out that those men in turtle neck sweaters were real men doing a job the equal in danger and toughness of any in the armed services. **(HLYD)**

Kenny Delmar: "Jeanette Nolan and John McIntire, her husband - the two of them - they were like the Munt and Fontan of the radio business. They would go away. . . they had a very beautiful ranch in Montana and they would go away but whenever they came back they were sought after with such unbelievable intensity for their work. They were working the minute they arrived back in New York. But I think Jeanette was *the* most diversified and most intense of all actresses I worked with. . . Jeanette could do fifteen and even more characters and do them all in perfection."

EPISODE #369 "**PROLOGUE TO GLORY**" Broadcast on February 7, 1944
    Starring: Raymond Massey as Lincoln   Everett Sloane as Offut
    Ed Jerome as Tom Lincoln   Agnes Young as Sarah
    Ted Osborne as Emory   Norman Lloyd as Bert
    Ted de Corsia as Dave   Ted Jewett as Squire
    Evelyn Varden as Aunt Polly   Charita Bauer as Ann
    Ted Osborne as the chairman   Norman Lloyd as Onstott
    Nell Harrison as Granny   Bill Adams as the narrator
Based on the 1936 play of the same name by Ellsworth Prouty Conkle, and adapted for *Cavalcade* by Arthur Arent and Robert Tallman.
Produced and directed by Paul Stewart.
Roland Winters is the announcer, and Clayton Collyer is the commercial announcer.
Music composed by Ardon Cornwell and conducted by Donald Voorhees.
Story: Here is the Lincoln that few men know - the lank, rugged young man whose giant frame reminded one citizen of New Salem of "the ground plan for a long horse." And here is the picture of Abe Lincoln against the homespun background of a frontier town - the story, full of rich and unexpected humor, of a young man trying to find out where he fitted into the scheme of things. Here we meet his father, Tom Lincoln, a freedom loving American and strong individualist who felt it was time to be moving on to new fields when the day came he could hear the sound of his nearest neighbor's shotgun. Some of Lincoln's most enduring characteristics take on new significance when seen against the background of his early life. We also meet Ann Rutledge and understand perhaps for the first time her tremendous influence upon his life and entire career.

EPISODE #370 "**G.I. VALENTINE**" Broadcast on February 14, 1944
    Starring: Frances Langford as herself   Tony Romano as himself
    June Lockhart as the Red Cross Girl   Ed Penney as Thomaselli
    Frank Graham as the Official   Janet Logan as the Stenographer
    Jeanette Nolan as the Nurse   William Griffis as the first soldier
    William Johnstone as the second soldier   John W. Bailey, Jr. as the third soldier
    Wally Maher as the officer   Franklin Parker as the Colonel
    Frank Graham as Eddie Riggs   Lurene Tuttle as Wac Green
    Jeanette Nolan as Wac Ryan   Janet Logan as Wac Hopton
    Georgia Backus as Mrs. Hotchkiss   William Johnstone as the Chaplain
Written for *Cavalcade* by Frank Gabrielson.
Produced and directed by Homer Fickett.
Jim Bannon is the announcer and Gayne Whitman is the commercial spokesman.
Music composed and conducted by Robert Armbruster.
Story: Frances Langford reports with sympathy and deep understanding a woman' view of our men at the front. It's a tender and thrilling story about the G.I. Joes in foxholes and mud and about their wives and sweethearts and families back home . . . and about the babies they have never seen. This play told what women on these fronts were doing to help win the war; women in England and Africa and Italy - civilians and service women. **(HLYD)**

Trivia: Frances Langford presented a song entitled "Please Don't Cry," that she publicly announced may be the song of war, a ballad written by a youngster in England, with words he could sing but that didn't say what he wanted them to when he put them in a letter. Langford had recently been named one of the ten outstanding women of 1943 in recognition of her unselfish efforts in entertaining the men overseas.

EPISODE #371   "THE PURPLE HEART COMES TO FREE MEADOWS"   Feb. 21, 1944

Starring: Wendy Barrie as Jill
Dick Foran as Sharky
Agnes Young as Miss Thompson
Parker Fennelly as the Reverend
Everett Sloane as Orange-Ade
Parker Fennelly as the voice
Wendy Barrie as the girl
Norman Lloyd as the orderly
Guy Kibbee as Uncle Caleb
Eva Condon as Mrs. Tyler
Everett Sloane as Champney
Ted Jewett as the conductor
Ted Jewett as Gus
Dick Foran as the soldier
Norman Lloyd as Buddy
Ed Jerome as General Washington

Written for *Cavalcade* by Halsted Welles.
Produced and directed by Paul Stewart.
Roland Winters is the announcer and Clayton Collyer is the commercial announcer.
Music composed by Ardon Cornwell and conducted by Donald Voorhees.

Story: The significance and brave tradition of the Purple Heart decoration are familiar to many soldiers and civilians, but what is not generally known is that George Washington personally awarded the first Purple Heart to a wounded soldier in the Revolutionary War. Since that day so many years ago this decoration has remained a symbol of courage in battle and an acknowledgment of a soldier's service to his country. Concerning this week's drama, we meet Uncle Benny who is on his way to meet his boy, Sharky, a sergeant, who is coming back from the Arctic Circle on the 2:11 train. Sharky is coming home with the Purple Heart and Uncle Benny is getting Free Meadows to give a party. But Sharky is fed up with civilian questions and doesn't want to talk about the war. Most of all he doesn't want to talk to a lot of folks at a big party.

EPISODE #372   "JUNIOR ANGEL"   Broadcast on February 28, 1944

Starring: Jane Darwell as Miss Boyle
Agnes Young as Mrs. Johnson
Nell Harrison as the patient
Marilyn Erskine as Claire
Vera Allen as the mother
Ed Jerome as the father
Virginia Weidler as Ruthie
Charita Bauer as Marion
Pat Ryan as Jean
Mary Francis Heflin as Patsy
Chester Stratton as Billy
Mary Francis Heflin as the nurse

Written for *Cavalcade* by Peter Lyon.
Produced and directed by Paul Stewart.
Roland Winters is the announcer and Clayton Collyer is the commercial announcer.
Music composed by Ardon Cornwell and conducted by Donald Voorhees.

Story: When young America sets its heart on doing something there's usually action and there is likely to be fireworks. Ruthie Crawford was a fourteen year old girl in an average American family. The war hadn't touched her very deeply, even when her brother went away, but it did catch up with her in what she would have described as "a slightly tremendous fashion" when the very special boy next door went off to camp. So, very suddenly the war was brought home to Ruthie, and she realized that she wanted very much to so something, to be a part of all that was going on in the world. The result was that Ruthie volunteered as a Student's Aide in the local hospital. She volunteered to do after school and on weekends a lot of the odd jobs around a hospital that need so desperately to be done - things that the overworked nurses and the depleted hospital staff didn't have time to do. Ruthie's friends followed her example and soon all the girls were lending a hand.

Trivia: Virginia Weidler played the lead role of Ruthie, a young girl who does good for her fellow man. Jane Darwell starred in a supporting role, that of Miss Boyle. Although Darwell was more popular of the two Hollywood stars, Darwell was a last minute addition, not originally intended to appear on the program. Some convenient opportunity and timing occurred a few days before broadcast, which allowed *Cavalcade* to feature Darwell - even if it was a supporting role.

EPISODE #373   "ODYSSEY TO FREEDOM"   Broadcast on March 6, 1944
    Starring: Brian Donlevy as Edward Kowalski, A.M.M. 2/c - U.S.N.
    Frank Graham as Wladyslaw   Eddie Marr as Thaddeus
    Robert Bruce as Casimir   Franklin Parker as Jan
    Forrest Lewis as Joseph   John McIntire as the Consul
    William Griffis as the Vice-Consul Forrest Lewis as the Kommandant
    William Griffis as Holzmann   Albert Van Antwerp as Mansard
    Frank Graham as the underground agent   Harry Lang as the Frenchman
    Hal Gerard as Gendarme   John McIntire as the jailer
    Arthur Q. Bryan as the guard   Jack Bailey as the driver
    Tyler McVey as the man   Tyler McVey as voice one
    Robert Bruce as voice two
    Written for *Cavalcade* by Isabel Leighton and Milton Wayne.
    Produced and directed by Jack Zoller.
    Jim Bannon is the announcer and Gayne Whitman is the commercial spokesman.
    Music composed and conducted by Robert Armbruster.
    Story: A stirring and intensely moving story of an American who was pursued by the Gestapo through half of Europe . . . a man whose courage and resolve and love of freedom were so strong that in spite of almost unbelievable obstacles and hardship he was able to escape twice from German concentration camps. This man, Edward Kowalski, born in America, returned to Poland with his family when he was a youngster. He was at a Naval College when the war broke and his destroyer was sunk. Kowalski managed to get to England on a fishing boat and when a Free Polish regiment was formed he fought with them through the bloody days of Dunkerque. While trying to escape to Switzerland he and his comrades were captured and taken to a German labor camp. From then on the recital of his adventures is an amazing and true report of haunting fear brought to an end finally by his escape to the United States. **(HLYD)**

EPISODE #374   "SONG FROM SPOKANE"   Broadcast on March 13, 1944
    Starring: Patrice Munsel as herself   Jessie Royce Landis as the mother
    Edwin Jerome as Grant Sherwood   Ted Jewett as the announcer
    Jackie Kelk as Pete   Charita Bauer as the girl
    Santos Ortega as the father   Jackie Kelk as the boy's voice
    Hester Sondergaard as Madame   Ted Jewett as the fencing teacher
    Stephen Schnabel as the actor   Hester Sondergaard as Signora
    Stephen Schnabel as the professor
    Written for *Cavalcade* by Halsted Welles.
    Produced and directed by Paul Stewart.
    Roland Winters is the announcer and Clayton Collyer is the commercial announcer.
    Music composed by Ardon Cornwell and conducted by Donald Voorhees.
    Features the song "I'll Never Smile Again."
    Story: It wasn't so very many years ago that great and successful singers were almost exclusively an imported commodity. Like the best wines and the latest fashions, the great singers - the supposed "best" in every cultural art - had to come from across the sea. At the very least, successful artists must have studied abroad; the American artist, for some unknown reason, received scant attention. This is the exciting story of Patrice Munsel - a little girl taking singing lessons way out in Spokane, Washington - who in a few short years reached the Mecca of her chosen profession - the Metropolitan Opera. Patrice's success story may sound incredible to some, but others will find in it living proof that the rewards of hard work and persistency coupled with talent are greater than they ever were.

    Trivia: George Albee was the Du Pont News Reporter during the intermission.

EPISODE #375   "G.I. CIRCUIT"   Broadcast on March 20, 1944

Starring: Joe E. Brown as the narrator
Ann Southern as Lily Valentine
William Griffis as soldier two
Tyler McVey as soldier three
Robert Latting as soldier four
Will Wright as soldier five
William Griffis as soldier six
Wally Maher as Sergeant two
Jack Edwards, Jr. as Sergeant one
Tom Holland as soldier one
Wally Maher as Lloyd
Arthur Q. Bryan as the cook
Will Wright as Wolfson
Robert Latting as voice seven
Robert Clarke as voice one
Tom Holland as voice two
Franklin Parker as voice three
Tyler McVey as voice four
Jack Edwards, Jr. as voice five
Arthur Q. Bryan as voice six
Diana Gayle as Evelyn
Eddie Marr as Walsh
Robert Clarke as the boy
Polly Connell as the nurse
Franklin Parker as the doctor
Frank Graham as Higby
Written for *Cavalcade* by Paul Peters.
Produced and directed by Homer Fickett.
Jim Bannon is the announcer and Gayne Whitman is the commercial spokesman.
Music composed and conducted by Robert Armbruster.
Story: American knows the great job U.S.O. Camp Show units are doing in entertaining our servicemen all over the world. It knows, too, that the nation's stars of stage, screen and radio have been giving their time unselfishly in making personal appearances with these traveling groups. But America doesn't know the full story of the little people - the unsung small time vaudevillians and performers who make up the largest percentage of personnel in U.S.O. shows. There's excitement and gaiety and tenderness in the story of the unknown who work in mud and sand and heat and cold to bring a little happiness and remembrance of home to the boys in the foxholes. **(HLYD)**

Trivia: Joe E. Brown knows show business and its people. He's lived with them and worked with them; and he knows the heartaches and the dreams of every trouper who hopes some day to get into the big time. And Joe E. Brown knows what it's like to travel with a U.S.O. show, because he's been around the world and made hundreds of appearances before our men at the fighting fronts. He's acquainted with the war in a very personal fashion, too, for he had lost a son.

More Trivia: A Tap Dancer and an Accordionist was featured for this broadcast.

WEATHER IS A WEAPON
Starring
DANA ANDREWS
MONDAY EVENING   **MAY 14, 1945**

EPISODE #376 "SO SORRY - NO MERCY" Broadcast on March 27, 1944
Starring: Pat O'Brien as Royal Arch Gunnison
Frank Graham as the Jap voice II Charlie Lung as the Japanese officer
Wally Maher as the Jap voice one Georgia Backus as the American woman
Jack Edwards, Jr. as the captain Albert Van Antwerp as voice one
Herb Lytton as voice two Jack Edwards, Jr. as voice three
Frank Graham as voice four Barbara Jean Wong as the little girl
Irene Tedrow as Mrs. Gunnison Alex Havier as Sancho
Robert Bruce as the Jap soldier Eddie Marr as the Jap General
Eric Snowden as Twiller Georgia Backus as the woman's voice
Written for *Cavalcade* by Joseph Russell and Stanley Young.
Produced and directed by Homer Fickett.
Jim Bannon is the announcer and Gayne Whitman is the commercial spokesman.
Music composed and conducted by Robert Armbruster.
Story: The speed with which history is made in these times gives added interest to the stories of those individuals who have been privileged to live history in the making. One such person is Royal Arch Gunnison, famous newspaper correspondent and radio commentator, who recently returned to the United States on the "Gripsholm" after eighteen months in a Japanese prison camp. Back in America, Gunnison was assigned to the Far East and from that time on he made a first-hand study of the entire Pacific area. He became convinced that Japan was preparing to strike at the Occidental nations. Gunnison was in Manila when the Japanese attacked and the recent release of the story of the inhuman treatment of the Bataan prisoners by the Japanese makes the account of his own experiences all the more timely and significant. **(HLYD)**

Trivia: Royal Arch Gunnison appears in the program, and speaks after the drama, with words of encouragement to people still under the domination of the Japs. "Hold out," he says, "we are coming back!" Japan was not the first of the Axis nations to deal roughly with Gunnison. In 1934 he was thrown out of Germany for exposing to the world the secret of German rearmament plans. The man who threw him out was Rudolph Hess.

EPISODE #377 "AMBULANCE DRIVER, MIDDLE EAST" Broadcast on April 3, 1944
Starring: Alan Ladd as William Prescott Leo Cleary as the Colonel
Lal C. Mehra as the sheik Pat Sylvester as the woman
John McIntire as the merchant Jack Edwards, Jr. as the native
Barbara Jean Wong as the child Charlie Lung as Sgt. Cockney
Cy Kendall as Bedouin Vendor Wally Maher as Joe
Tom Collins as the lieutenant
Written for *Cavalcade* by Arthur Arent and Paul Franklin.
Produced and directed by Homer Fickett.
Jim Bannon is the announcer and Gayne Whitman is the commercial spokesman.
Music composed and conducted by Robert Armbruster.
Story: In the sultry of 1914 Kaiser Wilhelm's Prussians advanced to the River Marne, only to experience one of the classic defeats of military history. A French army had been rushed to the front in taxicabs and busses, and the grim parade of wounded made it necessary to commandeer all sorts of vehicles to serve as makeshift ambulances. Among the men who offered to drive them were a number of young Americans who were working in Paris, and this friendly gesture to a nation in distress resulted in a lasting attachment. By the end of the war the American Field Service had been formed and 2,500 men in the volunteer ambulance unit were salvaging lives from Flanders to the Balkans. This is the story of William Prescott of the AFS serving with the British Army in the Middle East. And entire division is threatened with smallpox that has been traced to one tribe of Bedouins who were the carriers of the disease. Prescott was assigned the

highly dangerous mission of hunting down the elusive and unfriendly Bedouins and inoculating them with the serum that would control the epidemic. **(HLYD)**

EPISODE #378   "THE FIRST COMMANDO"   Broadcast on April 10, 1944
    Starring: Alfred Drake as Flint   Everett Sloane as Gen. Francis Marion
    House Jameson as Harry   Ted Jewett as the soldier
    Geoffrey Bryant as the lieutenant   Janet Fox as Mrs. Crofts
    Ed Jerome as the sergeant   Ed Jerome as James
    Ronny Liss as Spidle   Frank Pacelli as the third Marine
    Geoffrey Bryant as the first Marine   Harry Bellaver as the second Marine
    Written for *Cavalcade* by Alan Lomax and Peter Lyon.
Produced and directed by Jack Zoller.
Roland Winters is the announcer and Clayton Collyer is the commercial announcer.
Music composed by Ardon Cornwell and conducted by Donald Voorhees.
Story: In the early days of the war, the world began to hear of brilliantly executed punitive raids against the enemy in occupied territories. Sudden, sharp, deadly blows dealt to the invaders by small groups of men who attacked by night . . . accomplished their mission . . . and returned swiftly into the night. Then the world heard more and more of these amazing bands of fighting men . . . from many countries and under many names. From England came stories of the deeds of the Commandos. From Russia - stories of the Guerrillas. From the U.S., stories of the Marine Raiders, of the Army Rangers. But such bands of fighting men, and their methods of fighting, are not new in the history of the war. They are the latest of a long tradition . . . a tradition that began in America, with American soldiers, more than 170 years ago. These are the events of these first Commandos, of their General, Francis Marion, and of the ingenuity and courage of this band as it fought its part of a war in the swamps of South Carolina.

    Trivia: This story is told with singing transitions.

EPISODE #379   "A MASK FOR JEFFERSON"   Broadcast on April 17, 1944
    Starring: Walter Huston as Thomas Jefferson   Hal Gerard as Monsieur "C"
    Frank Graham as the narrator   George Sorel as the servant
    Ian Wolfe as Browere   Georgia Backus as Patsy (older)
    Janet Waldo as Patsy (younger)   Frank Graham as the voice
    Hans Conried as Lafayette   Charlie Lung as Monsieur "A"
    Albert Van Antwerp as Monsieur "B"   George Niese as the third citizen
    Virginia Gregg as the second citizen   Albert VanAntwerp as 1st citizen
    Franklin Parker as Coachman   Herb Rawlinson as Montmorin
    Written for *Cavalcade* by Arthur Arent.
Produced and directed by Homer Fickett.
Jim Bannon is the announcer and Gayne Whitman is the commercial spokesman.
Music composed and conducted by Robert Armbruster.
Story: This drama is a play within a play. When we first meet Jefferson he is an old man, 82, and an American artist is making a plaster "life mask" of the great man's features. Jefferson nearly suffocates while he is under the mask and it is then that he recalls the almost forgotten incident during his stay in Paris so long ago. Although Jefferson thought that posterity would never remember the time in his stormy life when he brought American ideas of democracy to France, and this drama is proof that posterity has not forgotten. The year was 1783. Jefferson was in Paris as the American Ambassador to France. While there he was visited by Lafayette and other famous Frenchmen who sought his advice and ideas on democracy and how France should be governed. **(HLYD)**

EPISODE #380 "THE STORY OF PENICILLIN"   Broadcast on April 24, 1944
    Starring: George Coulouris as the narrator   George Coulouris as Dr. John Florey
    Herbert Rawlinson as Dr. Alexander Fleming   Irene Tedrow as woman one
    Joe Forte as Ecclesiasticus   Georgia Backus as woman two
    Forrest Lewis as Dr. Graham   Forrest Lewis as Pasteur
    Charlie Lung as Alfie (Lancashire)   Frank Graham as Chain
    Joe Forte as Abraham   James Nusser as voice one
    Eddie Marr as voice two   George Neise as voice three
    Irene Tedrow as the nurse   Bob Jellison as the soldier
    Written for *Cavalcade* by Morton Wishengrad.
    Produced and directed by Homer Fickett.
    Jim Bannon is the announcer and Gayne Whitman is the commercial spokesman.
    Music composed and conducted by Robert Armbruster.
    Story: It might be said that penicillin was born as a result of WWII. In the decade of the thirties, the sulfonamides were the popular anti-bacterial agents. They were powerful and there was still much to learn about them - new treatments, new refinements, new appellations. But in England, a bacteriologist, Dr. Alexander Fleming, was carrying on research in a new field. He was greatly concerned with studying the properties of a strange green fungus which was very similar to the common bread mold. Fleming's experiments were not applied until after Dunkirk, when British hospitals were filling with the dead and dying. The sulfa drugs were saving thousands. . . but they were helpless against some infections. A more powerful anti-bacterial agent was needed immediately. **(HLYD)**

EPISODE #381 "THE ADVENTURES OF MARK TWAIN"   Broadcast on May 1, 1944
    Starring: Fredric March as Mark Twain   Agnes Young as Mrs. Clemens
    Skip Homeier as Sam (Twain as a boy)   Staats Cotsworth as Orion
    John Thomas as the voice   Howard Smith as Higgins
    Ed Jerome as Bixby   George Mitchell as the leadsman
    John Thomas as Langdon   Agnes Young as Dowager
    George Mitchell as the elderly man   Ed Jerome as the elderly gentleman
    Betty Worth as Livy   Humphrey Davis as Pond
    Ted Jewett as the English Scholar
    Based on the 1944 screenplay by Harry Chandlee and Alan LeMay (which in turn was based on an adaptation by LeMay and Harold M. Sherman of biographical material owned by the Mark Twain Company), adapted for *Cavalcade* by Paul Peters.
    Produced and directed by Jack Zoller.
    Ronald Winters is the announcer and Clayton Collyer is the comm. announcer. Music composed by Ardon Cornwell and conducted by Donald Voorhees.
    Story: Sam Clemens was born in the little town of Hannibal, Missouri. He became a world famous lecturer and humorist as "Mark Twain." As a young boy Sam tried to follow his mother's wish that he learn the printing trade, but the Mississippi River was in his blood. He wrote when he left home, "I have to simply try for the river, because I know I'll never be happy in my life if I don't." Sam reveled in the

Advertisement for same drama, on the same day, but different program!

Mississippi mud for years and even became one of the best steamboat pilots on the river - until one day he saw the picture of a girl. From that day on he was imbued with an ambition new to him.

Trivia: Warner Brothers was promoting their biographical film on the life of Mark Twain to great extent. Not only was a flawless performance given from March for his role of Twain, but the true story of how he developed his name is also described in detail. In one scene, when March is attempting to steer a riverboat through the fog-bound waters he hears a black deckhand, after throwing out a weight from the bow to determine the depth of water ahead, shout back: "Mark the twain (twine - the rope tied about the weight) . . . (feet)." And here is born the *nom de plume* of one of America's finest writers and humorists, Samuel Clemens / Mark Twain.

More trivia: One the same evening, only hours before, the same drama was presented on another radio program, which also starred March in the role of Twain.

EPISODE #382   **"AUTOBIOGRAPHY OF AN ANGEL"**   Broadcast on May 8, 1944
Starring: Helen Hayes as Ann Norris
Written for *Cavalcade* by Lisa Barrett Brew and Peter Lyon.
Produced and directed by Jack Zoller.
Ronald Winters is the announcer and Clayton Collyer is the commercial announcer.
Music composed by Ardon Cornwell and conducted by Donald Voorhees.
Story: When Ann Norris was a small girl, she decided that she was going to be a nurse. She wanted to dress up all in white like an angel and make everybody well and happy. She'd be a crisp, efficient woman curing all ills in the daytime and then be a beautiful wisp of a lady at night. And perhaps she'd get a job as a nurse on an ocean liner and meet a handsome man who was ill - and she'd make him well and they'd fall in love and marry and live happily ever after. And one day Ann Norris became a nurse, but it wasn't as she had imagined it would be when she was a child. It was work - hard work - particularly when she became Lieutenant Ann Norris, Red Cross nurse. The nurses followed the big show - the big battles of this war in Africa and Sicily and Italy.

EPISODE #383   **"THE BLESSINGS OF LIBERTY"**   Broadcast on May 15, 1944
Starring: John Garfield as Pvt. Jim Hunter, U.S. Army
Francis X. Bushman as Mr. Hunter   Georgia Backus as Mrs. Hunter
Bob Jellison as Lou   Tom Holland as Al
Frank Graham as Tony   Conrad Binyon as Jim (age ten)
Paul Hilton as Tom (age ten)   Franklin Parker as man one
Francis X. Bushman as man two   Forrest Lewis as Steve
Dick Ryan as Mr. Jameson   Howard McNear as Davis
Francis X. Bushman as Noonan   Adelaide Klein as Mrs. Krieg
Griff Barnett as Prudy   Janet Waldo as Mary
Howard McNear as the speaker   Franklin Parker as the chairman
Dick Ryan as the voice
Written for *Cavalcade* by Sylvia Richards and Robert L. Richards.
Produced and directed by Homer Fickett.
Jim Bannon is the announcer and Gayne Whitman is the commercial announcer.
Music composed and conducted by Robert Armbruster.
Story: The story of the men and deeds that give life - bone and blood - to the words of our freedom. Principally it concerns Private Jim Hunter, twenty-five years old and from the town of Adams, Indiana. Jim with his company is in a farm house on the Anzio beachhead in Italy, waiting in the dawn for the hour of attack. As the soldiers wait they talk of many things - the kind of talk that keeps them from thinking of what they will soon have to do. Jim Hunter finds a copy of the World Almanac that some other

soldiers have left behind and as he idly thumbs through it he reads aloud a passage from the Constitution of the United States . . . **(HLYD)**

Trivia: Gene Kelly was originally scheduled to play the lead role of Private Jim Hunter.

EPISODE #384   "A SHIP TO REMEMBER"   Broadcast on May 22, 1944
    Starring: John Hodiak as Bill   Eddie Marr as Joe
    Preston Foster as the narrator   Frank Graham as the chief
    Robert Bruce as sailor one   Harry Bartell as sailor two
    William Griffis as sailor three   Charlie Lung as the executive officer
    Herb Rawlinson as the Captain   Harry Bartell as the Quartermaster
    William Griffis as the Lieutenant   Tyler McVey as voice one and two
    Tom Holland as the Yeoman   Charlie Lung as the officer
    Robert Bruce as Bull-Horn   Frank Graham as the man
Based on the 1943 book of the same name by Alexander P. Griffin, and adapted for *Cavalcade* by Edith Somner.
Produced and directed by Homer Fickett.
Jim Bannon is the announcer and Gayne Whitman is the commercial announcer.
Music composed and conducted by Robert Armbruster.
Story: The Hornet started her shakedown cruise the day after Christmas, 1941 - just fifteen days after Pearl Harbor. She has her first crew aboard, the crew who were to make her their home until her death a year later. Bill and Joe, two enlisted sailors, were a part of her crew, a part of the men who made her more than a ship - made her in some way a composite of all the lives of the men who sailed on her. The saga of the Hornet through the eyes of Joe and Bill tells how the ship's crew felt that their ship had helped to bomb Tokyo when the Hornet carried Jimmy Doolittle and his heroic men and planes to and within flying distance of Japan's capitol. **(HLYD)**

EPISODE #385   "SING A WAR SONG"   Broadcast on May 29, 1944
    Starring: Kay Armen, Ray Block, the Golden Gate Quartet, and Deems Taylor
    Deems Taylor is the narrator.
Written for *Cavalcade* by Peter Lyon.
Produced and directed by Jack Zoller.
Roland Winters is the announcer and Ted Pearson is the commercial announcer.
Music for this program was under the supervision of Donald Voorhees and his orchestra of 28 men, Ray Block and a chorus of 24 voices and the Golden Gate Quartet, and directed by Donald Bryan.
Songs sung and performed in order of their appearance: "Elmer's Tune," "Praise the Lord and Pass the Ammunition," "Rosie the Riveter," "Don't Forget to Say No, Baby," "This is the Army, Mr. Jones," "One More Mile to Go," "One Little Wac," "Milkman, Keep Those Bottles Quiet," and "When the Yanks Go Marching In."
Story: On Saturday evening, December 6, 1941, America was a nation at peace. On that particular day the two songs that most of America was singing and listening to were "Tonight We Love" and "Elmer's Tune." Less than twenty-four hours later, we were a nation at war. In the days and weeks and months that followed, Americans set about doing the work at hand, with grimness and determination. But through those dark, tense days the American people were singing. The American people were singing as they trooped into the factories and the training camps.

Deems Taylor: "Maybe it was you who said that one of the troubles with this war was that nobody had written a good song for it yet. Maybe, if you did say that, you were one of the people that said the same thing in the last war. The fact is, of course, that we have dozens of war songs. . . tonight, on the *Cavalcade of America*, we are counting some of these songs over again. . . "

Trivia: In commemoration of Memorial Day, a program of current war songs which are part of the lives of the men and women of the Armed Forces and of the home front. The lyrics and music weave a story of spirit and courage. They depict a nation and its people that can still sing as they fight their way to victory.

EPISODE #386   **"TREASON"**   Broadcast on June 5, 1944
   Starring: Joseph Cotten as Matthew Clarkson   Dorothy Lovett as Sally
   Richard Whorf as Benedict Arnold   Joe Forte as the clerk
   Frank Graham as Major Franks   Lurene Tuttle as Peggy
   Albert Van Antwerp as George Washington   Howard McNear as Reed
   Written for *Cavalcade* by Robert Gessner, from his 1944 novel of the same name.
   Produced and directed by Homer Fickett.
   Jim Bannon is the announcer and Gayne Whitman is the commercial announcer.
   Music composed and conducted by Robert Armbruster.
   Story: George Washington, during the early days of the Revolutionary War, considered him the young nation's most valuable general. In fact, the dashing Benedict Arnold was a one-man army, wheeling his horse as though it were a hound between his legs - here, there, everywhere rallying his troops and fighting the Hessians to a standstill. Almost single-handed he whipped a ragged, dispirited, victory-hungry American militia into a successful fighting machine and by trouncing the enemy at Saratoga, saved the Army and, perhaps, even the new republic from crushing defeat. We're concerned now with a young American soldier, the G.I. soldier of his day, and the way he came to realize the true nature of his hero, Benedict Arnold. **(HLYD)**

EPISODE #387   **"MY FIGHTING CONGREGATION"**   Broadcast on June 12, 1944
   Starring: Brian Donlevy as the Chaplain   Wally Maher as Sgt. Ed MacGowan
   Frank Graham as Jim   Harry Bartell as Joe
   Bob Jellison as Anzovino   Robert Bruce as the voice
   Eddie Marr as the cook   Harry Lang as the captain
   Jack Edwards, Jr. as Larry   Tom Holland as Bill
   Based on the 1943 book of the same name by Chaplain William Taggart and Christopher Cross, and adapted for *Cavalcade* by Sylvia Berger.
   Produced and directed by Homer Fickett.
   Jim Bannon is the announcer and Gayne Whitman is the commercial announcer.
   Music composed and conducted by Robert Armbruster.
   Story: You don't exactly shoot down Zeros with a prayer book, but a lot of G.I.'s in ornery, unpleasant spots wherever there's mean fighting going on around the globe are convinced their chaplains are doing their share in the war. All the way from the buck private up they stream in and out of the chaplain's tent bringing him their troubles. . . Case in point: one of those chaplains - William C. Taggart of the nineteenth Bombardment Group of the U.S. Army. A man who went into battle without a gun and won the love and admiration that all men have for a good fighter. It is men like Chaplain Taggart who, without the weapons of war, fight as gallantly in their own way as the young heroes who fly the bombers and man the guns. **(HLYD)**

Trivia: The Army Chief of Chaplains, Brig. General William R. Arnold, spoke from via remote from Washington.

More Trivia: This episode was originally scheduled to star two Hollywood actors, Brian Donlevy and Robert Walker. For reasons unknown, Walker was unable to attend, so radio actor Wally Maher took over Walker's role of Sgt. Ed MacGowan.

EPISODE #388 **"TOKYO SPEARHEAD"** Broadcast on June 19, 1944
Starring: Richard Conte and Stuart Erwin
Based on the 1944 diary by Sgt. Paul Lutsens, and adapted for *Cavalcade* by Bernard Feins and Russell Hughes.
Produced and directed by Homer Fickett.
Jim Bannon is the announcer and Gayne Whitman is the commercial announcer.
Music composed and conducted by Robert Armbruster.
Story: A group of soldiers from Michigan find themselves in the New Guinea jungles, trying to cross nearly impassable mountains. **(HLYD)**

Trivia: Kevin O'Shea was originally scheduled to co-star with Richard Conte.

More trivia: Gene Kelly was originally scheduled to star before Conte, O'Shea, and Erwin.

EPISODE #389 **"WHAT PRICE FREEDOM?"** Broadcast on June 26, 1944
Starring: Herbert Marshall as Robert Morris

Jane Drennan as Mary	Sarah Berner as Sally
Shirley Mitchell as the housewife	Frank Graham as John
Victor Rodman as Hancock	Dick Ryan as the farmer
William Griffis as Griffin	Dix Davis as the boy
Albert Van Antwerp as Jay	Bob Jellison as the soldier
Herb Rawlinson as Babcock	Bob Jellison as the president
Victor Rodman as voice one	Dick Ryan as voice two
Frank Graham as voice three	William Griffis as the courier
Albert Van Antwerp as Washington	Dix Davis as the drummer

Written for *Cavalcade* by Halsted Welles.
Produced and directed by Homer Fickett.
Jim Bannon is the announcer and Gayne Whitman is the commercial announcer.
Music composed and conducted by Robert Armbruster.
Story: In the early days of the Republic, Congress was faced with a tremendous problem in raising the money necessary to finance and supply General Washington's armies. The citizens were slow to pay their taxes and slower to lend their money to a government that seemed to offer little in the way of security for their hard-earned dollars. Half of the time the soldiers didn't get paid at all. Many patriots kept on fighting without pay but many others deserted. It was just such a situation as this that Congress called on Robert Morris, wealthy ship-owner and land-owner, to serve as Superintendent of Finances. Morris begged, cajoled, used force and gradually got enough money together to pay the troops and buy the necessary supplies. . . raised to meet the cost of freedom. **(HLYD)**

Trivia: *Cavalcade*'s special guest this evening is Secretary of the Treasury Henry A. Morgenthau, Jr. as speaker, who brought the radio audience an important message about the need for yet more money to win the war.

More Trivia: Walter Pidgeon was originally scheduled to star in this episode, Herbert Marshall took his place instead.

EPISODE #390 **"MY FRIEND McNAIR"** Broadcast on July 3, 1944
Starring: Jose Ferrer as Andrew McNair   Everett Sloane as Joe Grogan
Barbara Weeks as Connie   Jack Manning as Bull
Paula Victor as Girl   Ted Jewett as the soldier
Based on a story by Tammy Carter, and adapted for *Cavalcade* by Leonard Spiegergass.
Produced and directed by Jack Zoller.
Ronald Winters is the announcer and Ted Pearson is the commercial spokesman.

Music composed by Ardon Cornwell and conducted by Donald Voorhees.
Story: When the early American patriots inscribed on the Liberty Bell the words: "Proclaim liberty throughout the land unto all the inhabitants thereof" it became more than a bell - it became a spirit in metal and a striving in steel that has quickened the hearts of men everywhere who have fought in the cause of freedom. The sound of this bell has been heard on the Island of Malta, at Stalingrad and on the beaches of Frances - wherever men are fighting and dying for the rights without which life would be unbearable. This is the story of two brave men, different as night and day, yet thrown together in the strange comradeship which war brings. One of the men, McNair, knew what he was fighting for, and the other man, Joe, was to learn - for the Bell still rings.

EPISODE #391   "**FROM EMPORIA, KANSAS**"   Broadcast on July 10, 1944
   Starring: Parker Fennelly as the neighbor   Frank Readick as William White
   Eva Condon as the woman   Everett Sloane as McClure
   Barbara Weeks as Mary   Ed Jerome as George
   Staats Cotsworth as the cop   Morgan Farley as Caspari
   Barbara Weeks as Sallie   Morgan Farley as the printer
   Jack Manning as voice three   Stacy Harris as voice two
   Staats Cotsworth as voice one   Eva Condon as the wife
   Written for *Cavalcade* by Peter Lyon.
   Produced and directed by Jack Zoller.
Ronald Winters is the announcer and Ted Pearson is the commercial spokesman.
Music composed by Ardon Cornwell and conducted by Donald Voorhees.
Story: When William Allen White became famous as editor of "The Emporia Gazette," one of the many important offers he had was to become associated with one of the nation's biggest magazines. But he turned it down, because he liked living in Emporia, Kansas. That was the Will White who believed it was his royal American privilege to live and die in a country town, to run a country newspaper, to say what he pleased when he pleased, how he pleased and to whom he pleased.

EPISODE #392   "**BOOMERANG**"   Broadcast on July 17, 1944
   Starring: Frank Lovejoy as Kennedy   Everett Sloane as Miller
   Ted Jewett as the Japanese announcer   Staats Cotsworth as the four striper
   Ted Jewett as the talker   Jack Manning as Myers
   Ed Jerome as the Admiral   Leon Janney as Adams
   Jack Manning as Bull   George Mitchell as the lookout
   Leon Janney as Marston   Dwight Weist as Andrews
   Dwight Weist as the engine room voice   George Mitchell as the skipper
Based on the 1944 novel of the same name by Commander William C. Chambliss, and adapted for *Cavalcade* by Paul Peters.
Produced and directed by Jack Zoller.
Ronald Winters is the announcer and Ted Pearson is the commercial spokesman.
Music composed by Ardon Cornwell and conducted by Donald Voorhees.
Story: In November 1943, the Tokyo radio announced the sinking of the Japanese destroyer Hokaidokaze in the South Pacific with the loss of all hands. That was a very strange announcement coming from Japan for the Japanese Navy wasn't given to proclaiming to the world how its fleet is being whittled down ship by ship - and for an official announcer to mention a specific vessel by name, that was unheard of. But the truth of the matter was that the Imperial Admiralty sighed with relief when the Hokaidokaze slid to the bottom of the ocean, for the ship had become a menace to Japan. Her very existence on the surface of the water was a slap in the face of the Land of the Rising Sun - a land that takes its slaps in the face very seriously. The fantastic tale of this Japanese destroyer that was captured by Americans is dramatized.

EPISODE #393 "LOVELY LADY" Broadcast on July 24, 1944
Starring: Ted De Corsia as Minelli
Larry Haines as the aide
Ted Jewett as the other aide
Will Geer as Patterson
Everett Sloane as the Engineer Colonel
Ed Jerome as the General
Martin Wolfson as the Captain
Staats Cotsworth as Marlowe
Ed Begley as the Courier
Dwight Weist as the narrator

There were three voices in this episode, one-liner only, played by three of the above cast members.
Written for *Cavalcade* by Julian Blaustein and Daniel Taradash.
Produced and directed by Jack Zoller.
Roland Winters is the announcer and Ted Pearson is the commercial announcer.
Music composed by Ardon Cornwell and conducted by Donald Voorhees.
Story: During the invasion of Sicily, American soldiers of one division were pursuing Germans who were retreating along a narrow and precipitous mountain trail. In their advance the G.I.'s came to an enormous chasm which was created when the enemy had blown a huge section of the road into the sea. Apparently the division faced an insurmountable obstacle, but the Germans hadn't reckoned the spirit of Americans like Private Minelli whose pride and joy was a bulldozer which he called "Lovely Lady." And so, under the direction of Minelli, the men put on a display of one type of power the Germans hadn't figured on - work power compounded of teamwork, ingenuity and sweat. When they overcame that insurmountable obstacle, they just about changed the course of an entire campaign.

EPISODE #394 "THE CONQUEST OF QUININE" Broadcast on July 31, 1944
Starring: House Jameson as the narrator
John Moore as Hoffman
Sarah Fussell as Alice
Ed Jerome as Viceroy
Ted Jewett as the professor
John Griggs as Strecker
John Griggs as Schuleman
Martin Blaine as Woodward
Roland Winters as the second Frenchman
Neil Fitzgerald as the Scotsman
Neil Fitzgerald as the Englishman
Ed Jerome as Pasteur
Everett Sloane as Perkin
Peg La Centra as the Countess
Everett Sloane as De Vega
Donald Randolph as the scientist
Roland Winters as Rabe
Ted Jewett as Mietzch
Jack Manning as Doering
Martin Blaine as the first Frenchman
Donald Randolph as the German
Guy Sorel as Pelletier

Written for *Cavalcade* by Arthur Arent.
Produced and directed by Jack Zoller.
Roland Winters is the announcer and Ted Pearson is the commercial announcer.
Music composed by Ardon Cornwell and conducted by Donald Voorhees.
Story: Millions of men, women and children have died of malaria and for centuries it seemed as though the search for a cure would be forever fruitless. Then in the early part of the seventeenth century the dying wife of the Spanish Viceroy in Lima, Peru, received a potion made from the bark of a native tree and miraculously recovered from malaria. Little was known of the chemical composition of the bark of the chichona tree - or what gave it its wonderful effectiveness, and it was not until 1820 that two young French scientists isolated a drug from the cinchona bark and named it "quinine." So great was the need for an abundant, cheap supply of this life-saving drug that in 1850 the Society of Pharmacy of France offered a prize of four thousand francs to the scientist who could discover a means of preparing quinine synthetically. Scientists all over the world responded to this urgent call but, although their research continually probed the unknown in countless experiments, the years rolled on and when the present war broke out a synthetic quinine was still only a dream. Two American scientists, Robert B. Woodward and William E. Doering, finally succeeded where so many had failed.

EPISODE #395 "A WALK IN THE SUN"   Broadcast on August 7, 1944
    Starring: Larry Haines as Tyne   Frank Lovejoy as the narrator
    Ted Jewett as Hoskins   Jack Manning as Arch
    Staats Cotsworth as Halverson   Everett Sloane as Porter
    Jack Manning as McWilliams   Ken Lynch as Rivera
    Owen Jordan as Freedman   Warren Parker as Ward
    Everett Sloane as Joe   Owen Jordan as the motorcycle rider
    Staats Cotsworth as Trasker
Based on the 1944 book of the same name by Harry Brown, and adapted for *Cavalcade* by Milton Wayne.
Produced and directed by Jack Zoller.
Roland Winters is the announcer and Ted Pearson is the commercial announcer.
Music composed by Ardon Cornwell and conducted by Donald Voorhees.
Story: At a distance the men in any given army all look pretty much alike and, furthermore, they seem to act and think as a unit. But when you get a close-up of just a portion of that army, you realize that an army is composed of individuals. This is the story of the men in one of those small army groups, an infantry platoon, which in the invasion of Italy was given the job of capturing an enemy-held farm-house after the troops had landed in the dark of night on the Italian shore. And its story of the way those men talked and fought and died in four hours of action.

EPISODE #396 "THE GALS THEY LEFT BEHIND"   Broadcast on August 14, 1944
    Starring: Shirley Booth as Jo Sullivan   Helen Claire as Taffy Smith
    Parker Fennelly as Rod Cluff   Patsy O'Shea as Eloise
    Brad Barker as Rosie
Based on the 1944 book of the same name by Margaret Shea, and adapted for *Cavalcade* by Edith Somner.
Produced and directed by Jack Zoller.
Roland Winters is the announcer and Ted Pearson is the commercial announcer.
Music composed by Ardon Cornwell and conducted by Donald Voorhees.
King Ross supplied the harmonica music for the song "Auld Lang Syne."
This episode also features the song "Oh, You Beautiful Doll."
Story: Jo Sullivan and Taffy Smith were wartime casualties as far as a happy home life was concerned. Their husbands in service had gone overseas and, like so many other women, their life was a lonely one. But Jo and Taffy decided to combat loneliness by working a Maine farm which Jo's aunt had left her. Jo remembered the farm as being wonderful. But her comment on returning to the farm was "I remember it always smelled of gingerbread and piccalilli and geraniums, with a little spicy dash of cow and clover floating in the from the barn . . . now, it just smells." Not only that, but the house was lopsided and the beds were lumpy. There was no one to help with the work. A muskrat was dead in the well and the farm was a million miles, more or less, from civilization. But these two girls were determined to make their own way on the farm.

EPISODE #397 "THE STORY OF CANINE JOE"   Broadcast on August 21, 1944
    Starring: Everett Sloane as Potts   Warren Parker as Henry
    Warren Parker as Hennessy   Ed Jerome as Wilson
    Ed Jerome as the doctor   Ted Jewett as the officer
    Ted Jewett as the loud speaker   Larry Haines as Mac
    George Mitchell as the sergeant   Brad Barker as Canine Joe
    Peg La Centra as Susan
Written for *Cavalcade* by Arthur Miller.
Produced and directed by Jack Zoller.
Roland Winters is the announcer and Ted Pearson is the commercial announcer.
Music composed by Ardon Cornwell and conducted by Donald Voorhees.

Story: Trained dogs play an important part in the war today, just as they have in other wars through the centuries. History does not tell of the first appearance of dogs on the field of battle. The reason is simple enough - dogs were following men to war long before their masters had learned to write history with anything except chisel and hammer on the dark stone walls of caves. Vivid eyewitness accounts of WWII came to us from men in all branches of service, but the K-9 Corps has never had its own G.I. spokesman. This is the story of a K-9 warrior - a collie named "Joe." Based on factual reports of the part played by dogs in the war, this is the story of "Joe" as told by his trainer, Private Pottsy of the United States Army.

EPISODE #398   "YANKEE FROM OLYMPUS"   Broadcast on August 28, 1944
    Starring: Karl Swenson as Wendell Holmes   Sidney Smith as Shattuck
    Everett Sloane as Brandeis   Ted Jewett as Bailiff
    Ed Jerome as the messenger   Evelyn Varden as Mrs. Holmes
    Ted Jewett as Butler   Horace Braham as Dr. Holmes
    Betty Caine as Fanny   Everett Sloane as John Holmes
Based on the 1944 book of the same name by Katherine Drinker Bowen, and adapted for *Cavalcade* by Isaiah Lee.
Produced and directed by Jack Zoller.
Roland Winters is the announcer and Ted Pearson is the commercial announcer.
Music composed by Ardon Cornwell and conducted by Donald Voorhees.
Story: Oliver Wendell Holmes' father had high hopes for his brilliant son, but he never wanted the boy to be a lawyer. "The law," Holmes, Senior remarked, "is the refuge of the dull-witted and the fossil-brained." He wanted his son to be a great man and it was his opinion that no lawyer could be a great man. The words of the elder Holmes sound strange in the light of American history, for Oliver Wendell Holmes became famed for his legal brilliance, his wisdom and his biting wit. Furthermore, because of the originality and independence of thought contained in his legal opinions, Holmes became known throughout the length and breadth of the country as "The Great Dissenter."

EPISODE #399   "WHAT MAKES A HERO?"   Broadcast on September 4, 1944
    Starring: Richard Widmark as James Slayton   Staats Cotsworth as Tanner
    Larry Haines as Al   Jack Manning as the man
    Everett Sloane as the third sergeant   George Mitchell as Captain
    Larry Fletcher as the first sergeant   Jack Arnold as the art
    Warren Parker as the medical officer   Warren Parker as 2nd sergeant
    Jack Manning and Williams   Larry Haines as Corporal
Written for *Cavalcade* by Bernard Feins and Russell Hughes.
Produced and directed by Jack Zoller.
Roland Winters is the announcer and Ted Pearson is the commercial announcer.
Music composed by Ardon Cornwell and conducted by Donald Voorhees.
Story: Very often, people are inclined to forget that a man's size is not necessarily a measure of his capabilities. There is a tendacy to be impressed by size, to expect big things of big people, and overlook the kind of bigness that a little man may carry with him. But if ever anyone achieved bigness, it was certainly Jim Slaton who, back in the early part of 1941, was a taxi-driver in Gulfport, Mississippi. Jim didn't wait to be drafted. When the Japs raided Pearl Harbor, he went straight off to enlist. The first time they rejected him because of his height and weight. But Jim was determined. He gained the weight and the Army agreed to take him. When the chance came at last to prove himself in battle, Jim Slaton's exploits earned him the Congressional Medal of Honor, the British Military Medal, *and* the Soviet Order of the Patriotic War, Second Class.

EPISODE #400 "THE DOCTOR GETS THE ANSWER" Broadcast on September 11, 1944
    Starring: Donald Buka as Doug Bennett   Ed Jerome as the Medical Doctor
    Everett Sloane as the officer   Frank Lovejoy as Shorty
    Guy Sorel as the Frenchman   Frank Lovejoy as the drillmaster
    Hester Sondergaard as the French woman   Martin Blaine as the soldier
    Ethel Everett as nurse   Everett Sloane as the British man
    Written for *Cavalcade* by Peter Lyon.
    Produced and directed by Paul Stewart.
Roland Winters is the announcer and Ted Pearson as the commercial announcer.
Music composed and conducted by Donald Voorhees.
Story: Sgt. Doug Bennett was a waist gunner in a Flying Fortress that was shot down over Germany shortly before D-Day. Bennett managed to escape to France where he was picked up by the British invasion forces and shipped back to England. There, at a base hospital, the doctor in charge reviewed Bennett's condition: "Bullet wound in his upper left forearm - infected. Severe shock. Mild Malnutrition. Traumatic neurosis." In other words, Bennett had suffered a psychic wound as well as a physical one. He had begun to exhibit signs of mental shock and it was decided to send him back to the United States for further treatment. Although primarily the story of young Doug Bennett's experiences, this drama is, in a larger sense, a view of the vast rehabilitation program that was set up for the treatment of men wounded in mind and the body.

EPISODE #401 "HYMN FROM THE NIGHT" Broadcast on September 18, 1944
    Starring: Rosalind Russell as Julia Howe   Frank Graham as the narrator
    Howard McNear as Marshall   Ian Wolfe as Howe
    Lillian Randolph as Agnes   John McIntire as Brown
    Leo Cleary as Senator Brooks   Howard McNear as Senator Sumner
    Franklin Parker as Senator Breckenridge   Frank Graham as Judge Parker
    Jeanette Nolan as Mrs. Brown   John McIntire as Abe Lincoln
    Leo Cleary as the voice of Secession   Franklin Parker as the voice of the Union
    Written for *Cavalcade* by Robert Tallman.
    Produced and directed by Jack Zoller.
Walter Huston is the host and Gayne Whitman is the announcer.
Music composed and conducted by Robert Armbruster.
Story: For years Julia Ward Howe had been enjoying moderate success as a writer of poems and light romances. After America was suddenly thrust into civil war, she felt she was doing nothing that was equal to the problems around her. She had always been strongly against slavery but had never been able to fully express the great emotion surging within her. In Washington during the war she visited an army camp and later, sitting at her hotel window, she watched wagon-loads of wounded pass beneath. At last the voice that had been pent up so long began to speak. She wrote the words that poured forth and set them to tune of "John's Brown Body." **(HLYD)**

Trivia: This is the first episode of the tenth season, and the first episode with Walter Huston as host, who would go on to host the program for the most of the season.

EPISODE #402 "LIFETIDE" Broadcast on September 25, 1944
    Starring: Walter Pidgeon as Dr. Bethune   Dick Ryan as Fisher
    Howard McNear as doctor two   Bob Bruce as doctor one
    Wally Maher as Father   Norma Jean Nilsson as Yvette
    Bea Benaderet as the girl   Tom Holland as Spanish Peasant
    John McIntire as Gomez   Bea Benaderet as the Chinese Nurse
    Albert Van Antwerp as peasant one   Barbara Jean Wong as the nurse
    John McIntire as the orderly   Bob Jellison as the other orderly
    Eddie Marr as Chinese Soldier   Charlie Lung as peasant three

　　　　　Tom Holland as peasant two 　　　Georgia Backus as the old woman
　　　　　Howard McNear as the Commandant 　Lurene Tuttle as Manolita
　　　　　Wally Maher as McCauley 　　　　　Eddie Marr as the storm-trooper
　　　　　Lurene Tuttle as the nurse 　　　　Georgia Backus as the mother
　　　　　Herbert Rawlinson as the chairman 　Charlie Lung as Lin Nan
　　　　　Frank Graham is the narrator.
　　　Based on the material from the 1943 publication "Doctor Bethune" by Ted Allen, and adapted for *Cavalcade* by Robert Tallman.
　　　Produced and directed by Jack Zoller.
　　　Walter Huston is the host and Gayne Whitman is the announcer.
　　　Music composed and conducted by Robert Armbruster.
　　　Story: The lives of many thousands of soldiers on the fighting fronts today are being served because of men like Doctor Bethune, who pioneered the development of the mobile blood bank. When in the 1930's Dr. Bethune saw the threat of a war that would eventually touch America's shores, he went to Spain to help cure for the loyalist wounded and to teach them the miraculous life-saving properties of blood plasma. When his work was done there, he went to China. He worked in field hospitals and directly behind the front lines. There Dr. Bethune found it hard to convince people that plasma would mitigate some of the horrors of the war. But Norman Bethune was tough and, before he lost his life at the front, he succeeded in making the whole world aware of the benefits of blood plasma. **(HLYD)**

EPISODE #403　**"VOICE ON THE STAIRS"**　Broadcast on October 2, 1944
　　　　　Starring: Edward G. Robinson as Tom Paine 　George Couloris as the stranger
　　　　　Lurene Tuttle as Mrs. Bonneville 　　　　　　Charlie Lung as Smythe
　　　　　Bob Jellison as the sergeant 　　　　　　　Wally Maher as Hughes
　　　　　Herbert Rawlinson as the second minister 　Frank Graham as Marsden
　　　　　Howard McNear as the third minister 　　　Howard McNear as Greene
　　　　　John McIntire as the first minister 　　　　John McIntire as Washington
　　　　　Herbert Rawlinson as Aitkin 　　　　　　　Wally Maher as the printer
　　　　　Frank Graham as the fourth minister 　　　Dick Ryan as the attendant
　　　　　Written for *Cavalcade* by Robert L. Richards.
　　　　　Produced and directed by Jack Zoller.
　　　Walter Huston is the host and Gayne Whitman is the announcer.
　　　Music composed and conducted by Robert Armbruster.
　　　Story: Were Thomas Paine here today, he would tell of a voice which spoke to him, questioning the right of some men to enslave others. He would say that this voice sent him - an impoverished English tax collector - to seek a better way of life in America and made him rise from the position of an obscure Philadelphia magazine editor to leader in spurring the colonies on to winning their freedom. Thomas Paine's inspired writings burned the word "Independence" on the people's hearts - and in the nation's grave crisis he wrote words which, more than a century and a half later, still have the power to give the American people hope and confidence... **(HLYD)**

　　　　Historical Trivia: Not many history books record this fact, but Thomas Payne, famous pamphleteer during the American Revolution, was originally a corset maker.

EPISODE #404　**"VALLEY FORGE"**　Broadcast on October 9, 1944
　　　　　Starring: Walter Huston as General Washington 　Bob Jellison as Alcock
　　　　　Herbert Rawlinson as Howe 　　　　　　　　　　Pinky Parker as Marty
　　　　　John McIntire as voice one 　　　　　　　　　 Tom Holland as voice two
　　　　　Frank Graham as voice three 　　　　　　　　　Pinky Parker as voice four
　　　　　Albert Van Antwerp as voice five 　　　　　　 Boyd Davis as Harvie
　　　　　Wally Maher as Folsom 　　　　　　　　　　　　Ernest Whitman as Rafe

Frank Graham as Lafayette Tom Holland as Neil
Albert Van Antwerp as Stirling John McIntire as Tench
Based on the 1934 play of the same name by Maxwell Anderson, and adapted for *Cavalcade* by Robert L. Tallman.
Walter Huston is the host and Gayne Whitman is the announcer.
Music composed and conducted by Robert Armbruster.
Story: During the bitter months of the bleak encampment many men began to think that it would be the final and crushing disaster to the American cause, but it was not the final disaster. It proved to be the end of disasters and the beginning of victory. Never had Washington's tiny army found itself in a more precarious position. Washington and his men had suffered three successive defeats. The British under General Howe had occupied Philadelphia, the national capitol. Washington settled his eleven thousand soldiers in winter headquarters at Valley Forge in December, 1777. The cold was intense, but Washington proved that he was the great leader of men. He was determined to keep the army in being to show that no disaster was enough to destroy it. He gave them the inspiration, the grim fortitude, the hope with which they again went forth in pursuit of the American dream of liberty. **(HLYD)**

EPISODE #405   "REPORT FROM THE PACIFIC"   Broadcast on October 16, 1944
Starring: Jerry Collonna, Bob Hope, Patty Thomas, and Frances Langford as themselves
Tom Holland as voice one John McIntire as Reyes
Tyler McVey as the dentist Frank Martin as Ferguson
Frank Graham as Blue Water Tom Holland as voice three
Eddie Marr as voice four Dorothy Lovett as the Red Cross Girl
Bob Jellison as voice five Tyler McVey as Gus
Richard Crenna as Wally Franklin Parker as voice six
Bob Jellison as Maurie Eddie Marr as voice two
John McIntire as man one Frank Martin as man two
Tyler McVey as man three Bob Jellison as man four
Franklin Parker as voice eight Barney Dean as Barney
Frank Martin as Slim Eddie Marr as voice seven
Frank Graham as the narrator Tom Holland as Doc
Richard Crenna as the soldier
The writer of this script is unknown, but there is a good possibility that Bob Hope himself actually wrote the script. It has copyright 1943, by Bob Hope Productions. Produced and directed by Jack Zoller.
Walter Huston is the host and Gayne Whitman is the announcer.
Music composed and conducted by Robert Armbruster.
Story: Bob Hope and his South Pacific partners, songstress Frances Langford and comedian Jerry Collonna, brings us highlights of their amazing experiences from their latest U.S.O. tour through the jungles and islands of the South Pacific. The American people received these great civilian-soldiers enthusiastically, and were so grateful for the straight link they provided with their boys overseas. Bob Hope is essentially a "showman." He's at his best when he's singing his songs and cracking his jokes that mean home and heart to millions of service boys. **(HLYD)**

Trivia: "I was born with a sense of timing and coordination," said Bob Hope, who as a master of the gag and the art of ad-libbing has become the world's number one comedian. Star of stage, screen and radio, this inimitable showman has also produced two best sellers, "They've Got Me Covered" and the recent "I Never Left Home," a sparkling account of what he saw and did on his first overseas U.S.O. entertainment junket to Europe and Africa. In 1941, he was awarded an Oscar for his "contribution to humanity" in giving a record-breaking 562 benefits in two years.

EPISODE #406   "THE GIRL LINCOLN LOVED"   Broadcast on October 23, 1944
    Starring: Joan Fontaine as Anne   John McIntire as Abe Lincoln
    Jeanette Nolan as Mother   Tom Holland as McNeil
    Albert Van Antwerp as Mr. Rutledge   Franklin Parker as Mr. Winthrop
    Lou Merrill as Armstrong   Tommy Bernard as Peter
    Herbert Rawlinson as the doctor
    Written for *Cavalcade* by Norman Corwin.
    Produced and directed by Jack Zoller.
    Walter Huston is the host and narrator, and Gayne Whitman is the announcer.
    Music composed and conducted by Robert Armbruster.
    Story: same as episode #197, broadcast on October 23, 1940   **(HLYD)**

EPISODE #407   "TAKE HER DOWN"   Broadcast on October 30, 1944
    Starring: Clark Gable as Commander Gilmore   John McIntire as Arnie
    Lou Merrill as Davis   Tyler McVey as Wagner
    Jack Edwards, Jr. as Doug   Frank Graham as Wilson
    Ed McDonald as McCabe   Georgia Backus as Hilda
    Bob Bruce as Jack   Harry Bartell as Red
    Written for *Cavalcade* by Norman Rosten and Robert L. Richards.
    Produced and directed by Jack Zoller.
    Walter Huston is the host and Gayne Whitman is the announcer.
    Music composed and conducted by Robert Armbruster.
    Story: The submarine which Commander Howard Gilmore was commanding had come upon a Jap ship off Rabaul. It tried to ram Gilmore's sub, but the Commander outwitted the Jap skipper and rammed the enemy ship instead which, listing heavily, opened fire with a 50-caliber machine gun. Seriously wounded on the deck of his sub, Gilmore was unable to reach the conning tower. At the cost of his life, he gave the immortal command, "Take Her Down."   **(HLYD)**

    Trivia: This was Clark Gable's first radio appearance since he was released from active duty. Having left the United States Army Air Forces with the rank of Major, Gable was the proud possessor of the Air Medal for his service as gunner and photographer in bombing attacks over Europe. Tickets for this broadcast were at a premium and those lucky enough to rate them were very happy folks - until the show went on the air. Clark played the role of a submarine officer and in order to create the reality of a man in a submarine (complete with echoed voice), Gable spent most of the program speaking from off-stage in an isolation booth. The audience left the performance feeling gypped over the fact that they did not get to see as much of their star as they were informed before-hand. Numerous attendants wrote to complain to Du Pont over the matter - too many to be ignored.

EPISODE #408   "JANE ADDAMS OF HULL HOUSE"   Scheduled for November 6, 1944
    Starring: Loretta Young as Jane Addams
    Written for *Cavalcade* by Robert Tallman.
    Produced and directed by Jack Zoller.
    Walter Huston is the host and Gayne Whitman is the announcer.
    Music composed and conducted by Robert Armbruster.
    Story: Even as a child when she walked with her father through the slums of her own town, Jane Addams was terribly affected by the suffering she saw and had glowing ambitions to devote her life to helping them. But never had she seen anything like the pitiful squalor of Halsted Street and she knew then that she would never be happy seeing such injustice and doing nothing about it. She knew it meant hard work, that it wouldn't be easy for one woman to break through the prejudice of a world of men. It meant giving up some of the other things she wanted in life . . . even the one man she wanted to marry.

Trivia: This script was not broadcast, as the time slot was sold to the National Independent Committee for Roosevelt and Truman. The election speeches, the Republican/Democratic special, also pre-empted other radio programs that evening. The reason I continue numbering the episodes using this episode as #408 instead of labeling the next episode #408 is because Du Pont actually numbered their scripts and pamphlets with official "Episode numbers." To keep precise, this episode is numbered.

EPISODE #409   "THE LAZIEST MAN IN THE WORLD"   Broadcast on November 13, 1944
  Starring: Charles Laughton as Ben Franklin   Elinor Taylor as Deborah
  Dix Davis as Henry   Bill Roy as Ben
  Delie Ellis as Polly   Anne Stone as Mrs. M.
  Tommy Cook as Tommy   Anne Stone as Mrs. L.
  Jean Vanderpyle as Mrs. Allen   Boyd Davis as Parker
  John McIntire as Lathrop   David Hughes as the son
  Harry Powers as the glass player   Frank Graham as Vail
  Written for *Cavalcade* by Erik Barnouw.
  Produced and directed by Jack Zoller.
  Walter Huston is the host and Gayne Whitman is the announcer.
  Music composed and conducted by Robert Armbruster.
  Musical glasses performed by Harry Powers.
  Story: Benjamin Franklin, a jack-of-all trades and master of all, whose brilliant mind and inventive genius so enriched our national life that generation after generation has honored him. Ben Franklin in his later years, from the depths of his armchair, wrote long letters to friends and answered his granddaughter's many questions about his life. We see him going back through the years to explain to little Deborah why he calls himself "the laziest man in the world," how he came to invent some of the many labor-saving devices - the chair that unfolds into a stepladder, the harmonica, the stove, bifocal spectacles, and the lightning rod. Each of these was calculated to free man from drudgery, to make extra hands for him - arms that could reach everywhere to give him freedom and power to make a better world. **(HLYD)**

EPISODE # 410   "THE ADMIRAL"   Broadcast on November 20, 1944
  Starring: Robert Montgomery as Dewey   Charlie Lung as the first sailor
  Tom Holland as the second sailor   Lou Merrill as Spaulding
  Howard McNear as the third sailor   Bob Cole as the forth sailor
  John McIntire as Gridley   Robert Clarke as the fifth sailor
  Tom Holland as the German Lt.   Lou Merrill as Von Dietrich
  Robert Clarke as Winder   Frank Graham as Brumby
  Frank Graham as Thuman   John McIntire as Prince Henry
  Charlie Lung as Yasui   Howard McNear as Buck
  Bob Cole as Caldwell   Herb Rawlinson as Chichester
  Written for *Cavalcade* by Arthur Arent, based on the book of the same name by Laurin H. Healy and Louis Kutner.
  Produced and directed by Jack Zoller.
  Walter Huston is the host and Gayne Whitman is the announcer.
  Music composed and conducted by Robert Armbruster.
  Story: The role of Admiral George Dewey, America's first crusader for a powerful navy, one that would secure not only the greatness of our country but would also help to maintain world peace. When General MacArthur and Admirals Kinclaid and Halsey moved into the Philippines this past October to fight one of the greatest naval battles of history, the spirit of Admiral Dewey was high on the bridge of the biggest battle-wagon, watching the Jap ships disappear under the deep waters off Leyte and Luzon. George Dewey was one of the truly great men of naval history. **(HLYD)**

Trivia: In 1939, Robert Montgomery was in England making a picture when WWII broke out. He joined the American Field Service in France the following spring and drove an ambulance under fire in twenty-four hour shifts until that country fell. In June of 1941, after his return to America, he went on active duty with the U.S. Navy and took part in the daring raid at Kula Bay. As a writer, he realized his ambition when *Collier's* printed his memorable "Letter to a German Hero," which vented his white-hot anger against the Nazis. Recently released from active duty, this was Montgomery's first radio appearance since he was released from active duty.

EPISODE #411   "WITNESS FOR THE PEOPLE"   Broadcast on November 27, 1944
    Starring: Fay Bainter as Anne Royall   Ray Collins as Andrew Jackson
    Tommy Bernard as the newsboy   Frank Graham as Eaton
    Herb Rawlinson as the congressman   Joe DuVal as the printer
    Jeanette Nolan as Sally   Lou Merrill as Grey
    Gerald Keene as Johnson   John McIntire as Simms
    Lou Merrill as the clerk   Herb Rawlinson as the Judge
    Joe Du Val as Coxe   Howard McNear as Swann
    Gerald Keene as the Foreman
    Written for *Cavalcade* by Robert L. Richards.
    Produced and directed by Jack Zoller.
    Walter Huston is the host and Gayne Whitman is the announcer.
    Music composed and conducted by Robert Armbruster.   **(HLYD)**
Story: It wasn't until Anne Royall was penniless and widowed at 55 that she decided to make a career for herself as a writer. So, borrowing a few dollars, she began to travel and to write. After she had seen the United States, she settled down in the Washington of Andrew Jackson. There, she established a newspaper for the purpose of crusading against the intolerance and corruption that she saw existing in America. The circulation of the paper was never large, but it's influence became so great that repeated attempts were made to suppress her fierce accusations. However, Anne was determined that freedom of speech should continue in America, fighting to the last to uphold her beliefs.

EPISODE #412   "DOUGHNUT GIRL"   Broadcast on December 4, 1944
    Starring: Lana Turner as Pat Holland   Bob Cole as the soldier
    Frank Martin as the southern Lieutenant   John McIntire as man one
    Peg La Centra as Anne   Bob Jellison as the soldier
    John McIntire as Lt. Grilley   Frank Graham as Bill
    Harry Bartell as Tony   Bob Cole as man two
    Frank Martin as man three   Tom Holland as Rip
    Virginia Curley as the woman   Walter Huston as the narrator
    Ad libs supplied by Polly Connell, Mary Brown, and Catherine Cragen.
    Written for *Cavalcade* by Edith Somner.
    Produced and directed by Jack Zoller.
    Walter Huston is the host and Gayne Whitman is the announcer.
    Music composed and conducted by Robert Armbruster.
Story: Pat, a Red Cross recreation worker, soon learned that recreation work on New Guinea included far more than merely looking pretty and passing out doughnuts. For one thing, the men under-doing the daily hardships and risks of modern war were much more interested in talking about the folks back home than in romance. And canteen work didn't just mean being a good listener, but included such things as scrubbing floors and whipping up hundreds of sandwiches at a moment's notice. Most amazing of all, was the fact that, instead of Pat inspiring the men who fought and died shoulder to shoulder, it was these same men who gave Pat the will to go on working - and hoping. Their courage and their sacrifice changed Pat Holland from a carefree young girl to a mature and selfless woman.   **(HLYD)**

Trivia: The dramatization of Pat Holland's life on New Guinea is based upon factual material supplied by Annette Robbins, an American Red Cross Recreation worker, recently returned from this theatre of operations. The story is a tribute to the fortitude and spirit of countless "Clubmobile Girls," whose work on every fighting front forms one of the proudest chapters in the history of the American Red Cross.

EPISODE #413   **"THE CONQUEST OF PAIN"**   Broadcast on December 11, 1944
   Starring: Brian Donlevy as the narrator
   Dorothy Lovett as the nurse
   John McIntire as voice one
   Fred Howard as Raymond Lully
   Herb Rawlinson as Joseph Priestley
   Tyler McVey as Ivan
   Tyler McVey as Dr. Crawford Long
   Frank Graham as Horace Wells
   Paul McVey as Cooley
   Herb Rawlinson as Jackson
   Jeanette Nolan as Elizabeth
   Howard McNear as Dr. John C. Warren
   Boyd Davis as the other patient
   Boyd Davis as the doctor
   Paul McVey as the Surgeon
   Frank Graham as the patient
   Tyler McVey as Paracelsus
   Howard McNear as Humphrey Davy
   Jeanette Nolan as the girl
   Pinky Parker as Jim
   Dorothy Lovett as the wife
   Fred Howard as Riggs
   John McIntire as William Morton
   Boyd Davis as Eben
   Paul McVey as voice two

Written for *Cavalcade* by Morton Wishengrad.
Produced and directed by Jack Zoller.
Walter Huston is the host and Gayne Whitman is the announcer.
Music composed and conducted by Robert Armbruster.

Story: Eight men discovered anesthesia - eight men whose lives spanned seven centuries. Ramond Lully, a thirteenth century alchemist found a white, sweetish fluid which he called vitriol. Two centuries later, Paracelsus, physician extraordinary, rediscovered the white fluid, fed it to his chickens and his chickens fell asleep. Joseph Priestly discovered nitrous oxide in the 18th century England. Public opinion prevented Priestly from experimenting with his new discovery, just as it stiffed Humphrey Davy, Michael Faraday, and Dr. Crawford Long. But exactly one hundred years ago from today a New England dentist named Horace Wells performed an experiment which initiated a new era in the history of anesthesia. Wells inhaled nitrous oxide gas and then had one of his wisdom teeth extracted. Just as he had expected, he felt "not so much as a pin prick" and this success crystallized his plan to win public recognition for the wonderful pain killer. **(HLYD)**

Trivia: Brian Donlevy's kaleidoscopic career includes such things as being a bugler in Pershing's expedition to Mexico at the age of fourteen; three years of World War combat duty as a Lafayette Escadrille pilot; a year's training at Annapolis; a job as a collar and cigarette ad model. He scored his first screen success as a Frisco thug in "Barbary Coast," but his ability went unrecognized until "The Great McGinty" established him as a top-flight star. Donlevy was the narrator for this broadcast.

EPISODE #414 "DOCTOR IN CRINOLINE" Broadcast on December 18, 1944
Starring: Loretta Young as Dr. Blackwell
Barbara Lee Benton as the child
John McIntire as Dwyer
Jeanette Nolan as Kitty
Georgia Backus as Aunt Barbara
Lou Merrill as Field
Herbert Rawlinson as Hale
Mary Jane Croft as Miss Waller
Herbert Rawlinson as Gilpin
Eleanor Taylor as Mary Jean
John McIntire as Collins
Dick Ryan as Mr. Webster
Mary Jane Croft as Emily
Fred Howard as Dr. Lee
Peg La Centra as Laura Dawson
Howard McNear as Smith
Frank Graham as the reporter
Dick Ryan as Mr. Elwell
Bea Benaderet as Mrs. Elder
Howard McNear as Benedict
Lou Merrill as the director
Bea Benaderet as Cornelia

Written for *Cavalcade* by Merrill Dennison, based on the book "The First Woman Doctor" by Rachel Baker.
Produced and directed by Jack Zoller.
Walter Huston is the host and Gayne Whitman is the announcer.
Music composed and conducted by Robert Armbruster.
Story: In an era famed for its conservative attitude toward women, Elizabeth Blackwell became the first woman doctor, the founder of the first women's hospital and medical school and the first advocate of preventive medicine. She also established the first training school for nurses and pioneered for home nursing and out-patient care. All this was accomplished in the face of tremendous obstacles which she overcame by sheer force of will and unflagging perseverance. In 1899, Elizabeth Blackwell's name had achieved a permanent place on the roster of famous and brilliant pioneers whose struggles against the wilderness of prejudice and ignorance created our modern civilization. **(HLYD)**

Trivia: The original title for this script on the first draft was "The First Woman Doctor." The title was changed by the second to final draft, "America's First Woman Physician." The final draft (the "as broadcast" script) featured one final title change, "Doctor in Crinoline."

EPISODE #415 "AMERICA FOR CHRISTMAS" Broadcast on December 25, 1944
Starring: Walter Huston as the Emcee
Dick Ryan as G.I. one
Bob Jellison as G.I. two
Tom Holland as G.I. three
Dick Ryan as the storekeeper
John McNear as the peddler
Howard McNear as the man in Maryland
Griff Barnette as Ed, the Mid-Western
Pinky Parker as man one from Arkansas
Paul McVey as Sarge from the Army
Lou Merrill as the farmer from Idaho
Tom Holland as the young man
Frank Graham as the narrator
Polly Connell as Marilyn
Herb Lytton as the Californian
Griff Barnette as Minster in New England
Paul McVey as the Farmer in New England
Pinky Parker as Ben
Lou Merrill as the West Virginian
Herb Lytton as Bob, the Mid-Western
Bob Jellison as man two from Arkansas
Howard McNear as Arkansas Legislator
Frank Graham as the Texan
John McIntire as the Old Fellow (Texan)

Based on material from "A Treasury of American Folklore" by A.L. Botkins, and adapted for *Cavalcade* by Peter Lyon.
Produced and directed by Jack Zoller.
Gayne Whitman is the announcer.
Music composed by Woody Guthrie and conducted by Robert Armbruster.
Music arranged by Earle Robinson, and the Sportsmen Quartet sings songs.
Songs: "Stormalong," segue to "Hard Travelin'," segue to the 1940 song "Wabash Cannonball," the 1851 song "Arkansas Traveler" and the 1860 song "Street of Laredo."

Story: A Christmas show is being given on a small Pacific Island by a group of itinerant USO camp show performers. The master of ceremonies is an old vaudeville trouper, hard-bitten, sentimental - a magnificent showman. He and his small troupe face an audience which is at once the most critical and most appreciative in all their long theatrical experience. It is an audience of home-sick GIs - men who remember other and different Christmases, when palm trees were merely stage props in "sarong" movies, rather than grim reminders of the loneliness and isolation which is war.

Trivia: Du Pont hired a guest soloist for this broadcast, an authority on American Folk music and the composer of Ballad for Americans - Earle Robinson.

EPISODE #416   "WESTWARD THE WOMEN"   Broadcast on January 1, 1945
Starring: Ann Harding as Abigail
John McIntire as Ben
Charlie Lung as the Captain
Verna Felton as Mrs. Jones (second part)
Bob Jellison as the driver
Fred Howard as Mr. Herbert
Katherine Kerry as Mrs. Fairchild
Barbara Eiler as girl (2nd part)
John McIntire as Joe (second part)
Bob Jellison as Clyde, (second part)
Griff Barnette as Hank (second part)
Lila Webb as the 2nd woman (second part)
Herb Rawlinson as Steele
Katherine Kerry as timid lady (second part)
Charlie Lung as Lemuel (second part)
Lou Merrill as Smith (second part)
Frank Graham as Prentice (second part)
Peg La Centra as Betty (second part)
Frank Graham as Hill
Dick Ryan as Davis (second part)
Lila Webb as Annie, the farmer's wife
Lou Merrill as Beasley, Annie's husband
Tommy Bernard as Clyde, the little boy
Griff Barnette as the sheriff
Leg La Centra as Mrs. Cain
Leone Ledoux as the sound of the baby cry
Dick Ryan as Mr. Perkins
Verna Felton as Mrs. Perkins
Barbara Eiler as Delia, Mrs. Cain's daughter
Based on the 1944 book of the same name by Nancy Wilson Ross, and adapted for *Cavalcade* by Turner Bullock.
Produced and directed by Jack Zoller.
Walter Huston is the host and Gayne Whitman is the announcer.
Music composed and conducted by Robert Armbruster.
Story: Abigail Duniway learned about the lot of women at an early age when she witnessed her mother's trials on the long journey west. Later, as a married woman, Abigail met her own misfortunes with typical determination. When her husband lost his farm, she decided to open a store in Portland, Oregon. She ran into opposition and prejudice, but despite the disapproval of both men and women, she managed to keep her millinery shop going and even made a profit. Many women came to buy because her stock was good, and many came to get advice and help. Not content with winning her own independence, Abigail began to help other women win theirs. In the face of every obstacle, she continued to stump Oregon countryside on behalf of women's rights and even spoke in saloons for lack of a better meeting place. **(HLYD)**

Trivia: Barbara Eiler, who played the role of Delia, Mrs. Cain's daughter, later played the role of Babs, Chester Riley's daughter on the radio comedy *The Life of Riley*.

EPISODE #417   "NAME, RANK, SERIAL NUMBER"   Broadcast on January 8, 1945
Starring: William Holden as the narrator
Forrest Lewis as Captain Ruening
Kent Smith as Major Von Bentz
John McIntire as the Red Cross man
Sgt. James W. Seay as Captain Spencer
John Beal as Lieutenant Williams
Trude Burk as the nurse
Paul Theodore as Sergeant Cole
Paul Theodore as pilot three
Herb Lytton as the voice
Frank Graham as Voldrig
Sgt. Charles D. Tannen
Herb Lytton as Kraly
Pat McVey as pilot one

John McIntire as the officer		Frank Graham as pilot two
Corporal John Arthur Kennedy as Sergeant Mason
Based on the United States AAF training film "Resisting Enemy Interrogation" by Harold Medford, and adapted for *Cavalcade* by Ben Kagen.
Produced and directed by Jack Zoller.
Walter Huston is the host and Gayne Whitman is the announcer.
Music composed and conducted by Robert Armbruster.
Story: Few people realize how much information can be gained from a single chance remark made by a prisoner of war. Although every flier knows that he must never give more than name, rank and serial number, if he is captured, the enemy is often clever enough to obtain more information. A "friendly" chat . . . a few leading questions are the enemy's weapons. Seemingly insignificant pieces of information, such as the name of a man's home town may lead to the discovery of a future allied operation, for all such fragments of knowledge are put together by enemy intelligence to form a coherent whole. One by one, four men of an American bomber crew, unknowingly divulge bits of information which Captain Ruening of the German intelligence pieces together. **(HLYD)**

Trivia: William Holden was listed as Lt. Bill Holden for this broadcast, and the supporting cast included many of the AAF personnel. Others billed were Sgt. John Beal and Private Kent Smith.

EPISODE #418 "IMMORTAL WIFE" Broadcast on January 15, 1945
    Starring: Ida Lupino as Jessie		Herbert Rawlinson as General Scott
    John McIntire as Nicollet		Frank Graham as John
    Jane Morgan as Mother		Fred Howard as the minister
    Ann Stone as Mrs. Scott		Ann Stone as Elise
    Jean Van Derpyl as Mary		Griff Barnett as Father
Based on the 1944 book of the same name by Irving Stone, and adapted for *Cavalcade* by Halsted Welles.
Produced and directed by Jack Zoller.
Walter Huston is the host and Gayne Whitman is the announcer.
Music composed and conducted by Robert Armbruster.
Story: When she was seventeen, Jessie Benton married young Lieutenant Fremont and, together, they helped mold one of the most important periods in American history. Strengthened and encouraged by his wife, Fremont opened the fabulously rich west to land-hungry settlers and, almost single-handed, he brought about the annexation of California to the United States during the Mexican War. Together, John and Jessie Fremont went through glory and disgrace, affluence and poverty, international fame and complete obscurity. Fremont rose from lieutenancy to be a world-famous general and world-famous explorer . . . was court marshaled for following secret orders . . . discovered a gold mine . . . lost it . . . at one time was offered the nominations of both the Democratic and Republican parties for President of the United States! Through it all, his wife stood at his side, giving him the encouragement and help he needed. **(HLYD)**

EPISODE #419 "PENNY FANCY" Broadcast on January 22, 1945
    Starring: Claire Trevor as Phillips		Herbert Rawlinson as Dr. Larkin
    John McIntire as Dr. Parry		Tommy Cook as Tommy
    Cathy Lewis as the nurse		Jeanette Nolan as Miss Cree
    Noreen Gamill as the supervisor		Lois Corbett as Miss Caswell
    Mary Jane Croft as Miss Cameron		Peg La Centra as Miss Malloy
    Mary Jane Croft as Mrs. Sanders		Cathy Lewis as Margaret
    Frank Graham as Mr. Aikins		Eric Snowden as Jack
    Tommy Cook as the voice		Peg La Centra as Gwen
    Noreen Gamill as Mrs. Fry		Lois Corbett as Joan

Dick Ryan as Mr. O'Brien   Jeanette Nolan as Mrs. Hale
Written for *Cavalcade* by Hubert Chain.
Produced and directed by Jack Zoller.
Walter Huston is the host and Gayne Whitman is the announcer.
Music composed and conducted by Robert Armbruster.
Story: In 1941, at the height of the blitz, Great Britain rocked under the hurtling explosives of the Luftwaffe and tried desperately to rearm and prepare for the invasion which was expected momentarily. At this crucial time, word came from Bristol of a growing number of typhoid fever cases. Hospitals were packed, doctors were overworked, trained personnel was gone, and all the normal public health machinery was disrupted. Unless soon checked, a typhoid epidemic might paralyze the nation. Into the emergency went six American Public Health Nurses, led by Elizabeth Phillips. They had been sent to England with the Harvard Field Hospital Unit and had seen six of their sister nurses lose their lives when their ship was torpedoed. **(HLYD)**

Trivia: On January 26th, the nation celebrated National Public Health Nursing Day and *Cavalcade*'s play dramatized the important service rendered by the nurses to be honored on that day. Fay Bainter had originally signed to play the lead role of Elizabeth Phillips, but had to back out days before broadcast.

DU PONT INVITES YOU TO TUNE IN TO
Cavalcade of America Broadcast
MONDAY EVENING, MARCH 10, 1947

★

FULL PROGRAM DETAILS AND LIST OF COAST-TO-COAST RADIO STATIONS ATTACHED

★

The message about "Delsterol" "D"-Activated Animal Sterol will be heard by Du Pont's vast radio audience at the conclusion of the broadcast.

EPISODE #420 **"A RACE FOR LENNIE"** Broadcast on January 29, 1945
Starring: Vincent Price as Dr. Frederick Grant Banting
Richard Whorf as Dr. Charles H. Best   Earl Keen as Dr. Jones
Frank Graham as the voice   John McIntire as the doctor
Dorothy Lovett as Mother   Tommy Bernard as Lennie
Earle Ross as McLeod   Earl Keen as the voice of the barking dog
Pinky Parker as Dr. Robinson   Bob Jellison as the dealer
Written for *Cavalcade* by Morton Wishengrad.
Produced and directed by Jack Zoller.
Walter Huston is the host and Gayne Whitman is the announcer.
Music composed and conducted by Robert Armbruster.
Story: Diabetes had long been known to medical men, but it was only little by little that knowledge about it accumulated. In 1921, when two young Canadian scientists, Frederick Grant Banting, a surgeon, and Charles H. Best, a physiologist, took up the search, this much was known - that the disease made the human body unable to use properly the food energy it received, especially sugars, a major source of energy. With this established, it was logical that if a hormone could be restored to the body by artificial methods, diabetes could be relieved. Banting and Best propounded the theory that it would be possible to isolate an enzyme - free hormone tissue from the pancreas and make an extract from that tissue. Hampered by lack of funds, often discouraged by failure, eating and sleeping in their laboratory, they went ahead unceasingly. And as they worked, they raced against the swiftest, surest opponent known to man . . . death - from diabetes that was coming not only to a small boy, Lennie, wasting away under his mother's eyes, but also to thousands of diabetics throughout the world. **(HLYD)**

Jack Zoller: "I have to tell you about one particular broadcast. A little girl who had listened to a broadcast entitled 'A Race for Lennie,' about the dangers of diabetes, recognized some of the symptoms given as her own. The child told her mother and was taken to a doctor who confirmed the child's judgment. The mother later wrote to the program and said that the disease, because it had been recognized so soon, was checked."

EPISODE #421 **"THE ROAD TO BERLIN"** Broadcast on February 5, 1945
Starring: Bing Crosby, Jeannie Darrell, Joe Dirita, and Darlene Garner
Written for *Cavalcade* by Glenn Wheaten.
Produced and directed by Jack Zoller.
Gayne Whitman is the announcer.
Music composed and conducted by Robert Armbruster.
Songs featured are "Blue of the Night," the 1942 song "White Christmas," the 1933 song "Easter Parade," the 1929 melody "Pagan Love Song" is performed on an accordion, and the 1944 song "Shoo Shoo Baby."
Story: To the fund of stories about Bing Crosby several were recently added when he went on an eight weeks' tour of England and France to entertain American soldiers. Playing to audiences ranging from 400 to 15,000 three times a day, he brought pleasure to all - from Generals to enlisted men - as he sang the songs they wanted most. Crosby blocked the traffic in London singing from a balcony, broadcast to Germany from Paris, and played all over France to the accompaniment of applause, planes, and artillery fire. It is said that the Germans called him "Der Bingle," and once he almost had a chance to find out firsthand whether or not this is true when he and a companion by mistake entered a town which was still held by enemy forces. **(HLYD)**

Trivia: Originally titled "U.S.O. Anniversary," and later retitled "Bing Crosby and the Anniversary of the U.S.O." this broadcast presented Bing Crosby re-creating his trip to Europe. Today is the Fourth Anniversary of the United Service Organizations.

EPISODE #422 **"THE MAN WHO TAUGHT LINCOLN"** Broadcast on February 12, 1945
Starring: Walter Huston as Mentor Graham   John McIntire as Abe Lincoln
Victor Rodman as the officer   Frank Graham as the attendant
Griff Barnette as Hawkins   Joel Davis as the boy
Barbara Lee Benton as Almira   Pat Lowery as Minerva
Jeanette Nolan as Sarah   Beverly Barnes as Ann
Pat Lowery as the girl
Based on the 1944 book "Mentor Graham" by Duncan and Nickols, and adapted for *Cavalcade* by Bernard Reines.
Produced and directed by Jack Zoller.
Walter Huston is the host and Gayne Whitman is the announcer.
Music composed and conducted by Robert Armbruster.
Story: Your introduction to Mentor Graham, a rural school teacher, a man who would have been completely forgotten had he not taken the trouble to encourage and teach a raw-boned young frontiersman and help him through the most difficult period of his life ... Abraham Lincoln. Mentor was not much older than Abe, and they had been born into neighboring families in Kentucky. Because Abe showed a desire for learning, Mentor took him into his school to teach him the rudiments of "readin, 'ritin, and 'rithmetic." To Mentor came the satisfaction of seeing his work completed, and his pupil obtain the highest honor in the nation, for Mentor Graham was an honored guest on the speaker's platform when Abe was inaugurated President of the United States. **(HLYD)**

Trivia: On the 135th anniversary of Abraham Lincoln's birth, *Cavalcade* presented a story of a little-known man who had a great influence on the life of the future president. This was the last episode to be hosted by Walter Huston.

EPISODE #423 **"WASHINGTON AND THE TRAITOR"** Broadcast on February 19, 1945
Starring: Herbert Marshall as General Washington   Verne Smith as the narrator
Paul Theodore as Captain Drake   Forrest Lewis as Lafayette
John McIntire as General Knox   Paul Marion as Captain Shaw
Herbert Rawlinson as Col. Lamb   Griff Barnette as the doctor
Lurene Tuttle as Peggy   Joseph Kearns as Col. Varick
Frank Graham as Major Franks   Tom Holland as Col. McHenry
Howard McNear as Hamilton
Written for *Cavalcade* by Arthur Arent, from material submitted by Carl Van Doren.
Produced and directed by Jack Zoller.
Gayne Whitman is the announcer.
Music composed and conducted by Robert Armbruster.
Story: In the fall of 1780, the war for freedom had been dragging on for four years. Valley Forge was past; Saratoga and Trenton had been won; the ill-equipped American volunteers had learned that they could beat their polished professional opponents. Victory was on the horizon. Then a more dangerous enemy appeared, treason by one of their own countrymen. General Benedict Arnold was plotting to deliver the forts at West point to the opposing forces. Success of the scheme would have cut the American armies in two and almost surely would have brought quick and total defeat. On the very day the traitors were about to put their plan to action, almost on the same hour, the American commander-in-chief, General Washington, visited West Point on a routine tour of inspection. The plot was discovered. **(HLYD)**

Trivia: Marking the birthday of the father of our country, *Cavalcade* presented Herbert Marshall in the lead role of George Washington. The title of this script was originally "The Crisis - A Day in Washington's Life."

EPISODE #424 "FLIGHT NURSE" Broadcast on February 26, 1945
    Starring: Marsha Hunt as Pat   Marjorie Reynolds as Ski
    John McIntire as the surgeon   Tom Holland as the medic
    Frank Martin as the pilot   Harry Bartell as soldier one
    Howard McNear as soldier two   Lee Milar as soldier three
    David Ellis as soldier four   Frank Graham as the marine
    Howard McNear as surgeon two   John McIntire as the co-pilot
    Written for *Cavalcade* by Peter Lyon and Charles Rabiner.
    Produced and directed by Jack Zoller.
    Gayne Whitman is the announcer and narrator.
    Music composed and conducted by Robert Armbruster.
    Story: A young American Flight Nurse named Pat Thompson was abroad a ship which roared off a newly-won Philippine landing strip with its load of wounded on the way to Guam. For her, the fear of Japanese planes unexpectedly bursting from the clouds with their rain of lead and death, was about to be an unpleasant memory rather than a daily reality. For Pat had handed in her resignation and planned to go back to regular army nursing. Her "last" trip promised to be uneventful until the navigator reported a Pacific storm ahead. To attempt to fly over the disturbed area might dangerously affect the wounded, but there was no choice. Then enemy planes loomed in the distance, apparently preparing to attack . . . **(HLYD)**

EPISODE #425 "BERNADINE, I LOVE YOU" Broadcast on March 5, 1945
    Starring: William Bendix as Irving Breckenridge
    Written for *Cavalcade* by Arthur Miller.
    Produced and directed by Jack Zoller.
    Gayne Whitman is the announcer.
    Music composed and conducted by Robert Armbruster.
    Story: Irving Breckenridge was the most cheerful man in his paratroop company. Through the campaigns in Africa, Sicily, and Italy, he was always ready with a wisecrack, a joke, or a tune on his harmonica when the going was toughest. Next to letters from home, Irving was the best morale-builder in the company. Suddenly he became despondent. The wisecracks stopped as did the music from his harmonica, and the spirits of the whole outfit fell with his. Irving had not heard from his young wife at home in months, though he had been writing to her regularly . . . with the help of his friends who penned the letters for him. He was convinced that she no longer loved him. Something had to be done. So Irving took his problem to the Red Cross Field Representative and asked him to find out what was wrong at home. **(HLYD)**

    Trivia: This broadcast marked the opening of the 1945 Red Cross War Fund Drive.

EPISODE #426 "SEVEN IRON MEN" Broadcast on March 12, 1945
    Starring: Walter Brennan and Richard Whorf
    Based on the book "Seven Iron Men" by Paul de Kruif, published by Harcourt Brace & Co., Inc., and the Curtis Publishing Company in 1929. Adapted for *Cavalcade* by Merrill Denison.
    Produced and directed by Jack Zoller.
    Gayne Whitman is the announcer.
    Music composed and conducted by Robert Armbruster.
    Story: In Northern Minnesota, deep in the forests that surround Lake Superior, looms a fabulous mountain of almost pure iron. It is the richest body of iron ore in the world - the famous Mesabi Range. The story of the discovery of that range, and the story of the search made by the Merritt Boys is dramatized. Theirs was a search that took a lifetime and every cent they had. The family was made up seven sons of Lew Merrit, a seasoned pioneer of the Northwest. Lew was convinced that there was iron in the territory and

when he grew old and moved away, he left his sons there, pledged to hunt for the iron until they found it. Headed by Lon, the Merritts kept that pledge. The rode, paddled, and walked thousands of miles prospecting until that eventful day . . . **(HLYD)**

EPISODE #427   **"SIGN HERE, PLEASE"**   Broadcast on March 19, 1945
    Starring: Burgess Meredith as Jimminy D. Peters   Bob Bailey as Hal
    Earle Ross as Bayers   Jeanette Nolan as the nurse
    Jeanette Nolan as the woman whimpers   Frank Graham as the voice
    Ed MacDonald as the Navy Captain   Howard McNear as the Admiral
    John McIntire as the General   Leone Ledoux as the baby cry
    Earle Ross as the signalman   John McIntire as voice on phone
    Howard McNear as the captain   Benny Rubin as Stinky
    Frank Graham as Harvard
    Written for *Cavalcade* by Philip Lewis.
    Produced and directed by Jack Zoller.
    Gayne Whitman is the announcer.
    Music composed and conducted by Robert Armbruster.
    Story: "Our ship, gentlemen . . . a noble craft, the latest model, with all improvements including an anchor. We call this model an LST. That stands for 'Let's Sink Together'." Thus were three brand new young sailors on the Navy Amphibious Command introduced to their first ship. And if they were somewhat surprised and dubious, they weren't the only ones; for it was in the early days of the war and the Amphibious Command had just been created. The three young sailors who had such a dubious introduction to their ship - Hal, Stink, and Harvard - found that their introduction had come from a man who never let his lack of knowledge standing the way of conversation. He was their shipmate Jimminy D. Peters. Together they went through seven invasions in the Pacific, delivering their cargo safely every time. All of it took place under bombardment - not always by Jap guns, but always by the rapid fire tongue of Jimminy Peters. **(HLYD)**

    Trivia: Gayne Whitman makes a blooper at the very start of the program.

    More trivia: *Cavalcade* presented the dramatic story of the men who first landed invasion supplies on Pacific shores to commemorate the third anniversary of the Navy Amphibious Command.

    More Trivia: Keenan Wynn was originally signed to star in the lead role of Jimminy D. Peters, Burgess Meredith took his place.

EPISODE #428   **"GRANDPA AND THE STATUE"**   Broadcast on March 26, 1945
    Starring: Charles Laughton as Monaghan   Arthur Shields as Sheean
    David Ellis as young Monaghan   Frank Graham as August
    Dickie Meyers as George   Conrad Binyon as Charley
    Tom Bernard as the child Monaghan   Joey Pennario as Jack
    Bobby Larson as Mike   Joel Davis as Joe
    John McIntire as Alf   Anne Stone as the girl
    Frank Graham as the man   David Ellis as Meg's voice
    John McIntire as the vet
    Written for *Cavalcade* by Arthur Miller.
    Produced and directed by Jack Zoller.
    Gayne Whitman is the announcer.
    Music composed and conducted by Robert Armbruster.
    Story: Back in 1887, people all over the United States were contributing dimes to build a base for the newly-donated Statue of Liberty. Butler Street, Brooklyn, was all subscribed, with the single exception of Mr. Monaghan, the stingiest man on the block.

So a neighbor went to call on him. And that's how it all began. Monaghan wasn't going to put up any dime for a statue he'd never seen. He didn't believe there was one anyway. When shown the sections of the statue lying in the warehouse, he still wasn't going to contribute because to his way of thinking it was all broken. What's more the tablet in her hand should have said "Welcome All," not "July 4, 1776." The neighbor retired in defeat. The statue was erected - in spite of Grandpa Monaghan. But one day, years later, Grandpa went out with the kids in the neighborhood to see the statue. There he found out what the statue stood for in the hearts of the people in America. **(HLYD)**

Trivia: America's number one pin-up girl, the Statue of Liberty, celebrated her 59th birthday this year. Charles Laughton, who was well remembered for his portrayal of the sadistic Captain Bligh in "Mutiny on the Bounty," rewrote many of his lines from the original script.

EPISODE #429 "MY WAYWARD PARENTS" Broadcast on April 2, 1945
    Starring: Anne Baxter as Laura   Brian Donlevy as Irvin S. Cobb
    Lurene Tuttle as Elizabeth   Peg La Centra as Nell
    Fred Howard as George   Frank Graham as the editor
    Harry Lang as the bartender   Dawn Bender as young Elizabeth
Based on the book of the same title by Elizabeth Cobb, as published by Bobbs-Merrill in 1945. Adapted for *Cavalcade* by Phyllis Parker.
Produced and directed by Jack Zoller.
Gayne Whitman is the announcer.
Music composed and conducted by Robert Armbruster.
Story: "There isn't anyone like you, anywhere," said a young wife to her husband once, and urged him on to prove it to the world. She was right, for the young wife was Laura Cobb and her unique husband was Irvin S. Cobb, who did prove to be one of the greatest American story tellers and humorists of all time. Cobb began as managing editor of the daily paper in Paducah, Kentucky, and rose to be a first-rate newspaper man. But still he wasn't satisfied. And neither was Laura. He wanted to write fiction, yet was afraid he wouldn't make enough at it to support his family. Laura encouraged him to take the chance. He quit his job and created the first of the "Judge Priest" stories which were to make him famous. **(HLYD)**

EPISODE #430 "ROBINSON CRUSOE, USN" Broadcast on April 9, 1945
    Starring: Chester Morris as George Tweed   David Ellis as Vincente
    Frank Graham as Joe   Dorothy Scott as Josefa
    Raymond Lawrence as Antonio   Eddy Fields as the Commander
    Henry Russell as the Ensign   Charlie Lung as Manuel
    Frank Graham as Krump   Eddy Fields as Francisco
    Charlie Lung as the Japanese   Conchita Nagsayo as the boy
    Lou Crosby as Tyson
Based on the book of the same by George Ray Tweed and Blake Clark, and adapted for *Cavalcade* by Morton Wishengrad.
Produced and directed by Jack Zoller.
Gayne Whitman is the announcer.
Music composed and conducted by Robert Armbruster.
Story: On December 10, 1941, the evil tide of Japanese power which was sweeping through the Pacific engulfed the last American defense on the island outpost of Guam. Few managed to escape, but George Tweed and his friend Tyson were among them. But the Japanese had a list of all who escaped and the hunt was on. Aided by friendly natives, the Americans who had escaped - six in all - met, and then separated for to continue their flight in pairs lessened the danger of discovery. Although the natives continued to help them whenever they could, the Japanese hunted four of them down

with savage tenacity and killed them. Then Tyson and Tweed decided to split up. Finally Tyson was caught and murdered. Tweed was alone, the last American on Guam. For months Tweed was constantly on the move, constantly pursued. Finally, a native led him to an almost inaccessible cave high in a cliff overlooking the sea. There he waited for deliverance . . . or death. **(HLYD)**

EPISODE #431 **"DOCTORA IN MEXICO"** Broadcast on April 16, 1945
    Starring: Irene Dunne as Doctora   Jay Novello as Garcia
    Fred Shields as Lopez   Ann Tobin as Antonia
    Harry Lang as Fernando   Pat McGeehan as Gonzalez
    Carlton Kadell as Jim   Martha Wentworth as Dona Pancha
    Bob Bruce as George   Francis X. Bushman as Papa
Based on the book of the same title by Olive Floyd, as published by G.P. Putnam's Sons in 1944. Adapted for *Cavalcade* by Arthur Arent.
Produced and directed by Jack Zoller.
Frank Graham is the announcer and Gayne Whitman is the commercial spokesman.
Music composed and conducted by Robert Armbruster.
Story: From the beginning, Dr. K.N. Dale had to fight ignorance and prejudice, as well as disease. Many of her fellow physicians had nothing but suspicion and hatred for her. Many time the peons in the small villages where she practiced were incited against her. But she refused to be discouraged. Katherine Neel Dale eventually married her girlhood sweetheart, who came to Mexico as a missionary, and together they carried on their work, caring for the souls and bodies of the people of their adopted country. From miles around ailing men, women and children would come to the "Senora Doctora." Most of them were too poor to pay anything more than an egg or some vegetables. But Dr. Dale was interested in helping them, not in making money. This policy, however, so antagonized some of the local physicians that finally they ordered her to leave and threatened her when she refused. **(HLYD)**

EPISODE #432 **"WEAPON: 4-H"** Broadcast on April 23, 1945
    Starring: Skip Homeier as Ted   Virginia Weidler as Ann
    Nanette Vallon as Eleanor   Henry Russell as Harris
    Hal Gerard as the doctor   Griff Barnette as the square dance caller
    Lee Millar as Dave   Verna Felton as Mrs. Martin
    Griff Barnette as Mr. Martin   Harry Lang as voices of the duck and cow
Written for *Cavalcade* by Peter Lyon.
Produced and directed by Jack Zoller.
Frank Graham is the announcer and Gayne Whitman is the commercial spokesman.
Music composed and conducted by Robert Armbruster.
Story: As 4-H Club members Ann and Dave had as their motto, "Feed a Fighter in '45," and they were working hard to raise their quota of food. They had problems enough but still another presented itself when friend Ted arrived, fresh from the city. Ted was supposed to help them out with the work, but he was more of a hindrance. He didn't know a furrow from a harrow - and didn't care; he regarded a cow as a poor substitute for a malted milk shaker. A complete liability, he was instrumental in almost wrecking the youngster's whole food-raising program. This is the work and the spirit of fun behind the important wartime food-raising programs of Americas. **(HLYD)**

Trivia: Skippy Homeier, co-star of this *Cavalcade* broadcast, achieved stage fame for his role of the Nazi-indoctrinated youngster in "Tomorrow the World" and was signed by MGM to re-enact this role on the screen. Listeners would remember him in a number of previous *Cavalcade* roles, one of which was the young Mark Twain in "From Emporia, Kansas." Before that, he was featured once as the young Lincoln and again as Tad Lincoln. The original title of this drama was "Come Green Up Time."

WEAPON 4-H
Starring VIRGINIA WEIDLER and SKIPPY HOMEIER

MONDAY EVENING   APRIL 23, 1945

EPISODE #433 **"THE PHILIPPINES NEVER SURRENDERED"** Broadcast April 30, 1945
    Starring: Edward G. Robinson as Edward Kuder   Frank Graham as the Japanese
    Martha Wentworth as Maruki   Alex Havier as the worker
    Charlie Lung as the Japanese Captain   Ivan Green as the radio man
    Hal Dawson as General MacArthur   Fred Shields as the Colonel
    Pedro de Cordoba as Pandangaman   David Ellis as Manalao
    Sidney Miller as the voice on the short-wave   Sidney Miller as Moro
    Based on a series of articles by Edward Kuder and Peter Martin, which originally appeared in the 1944 issues of *The Saturday Evening Post*. Adapted for *Cavalcade* by Arthur Miller.
    Produced and directed by Jack Zoller.
    Frank Graham is the announcer and Gayne Whitman is the commercial spokesman. Music composed and conducted by Robert Armbruster.
    Story: For twenty years Kuder, an American, had been Superintendent of Schools in the sleepy town of Dansalan on Mindanao. When the Japanese approached Dansalan, instead of leaving with the out-numbered American forces, Kuder chose to go into the hills to live with the natives and to encourage them to fight the Japanese. It was a hard job, and it was a dangerous one. Kuder was constantly hunted by the enemy. Also, he had trouble convincing some of the natives they should not believe the Japanese propaganda, but rather should fight against the new order. Gradually his work began to bear fruit. **(HLYD)**

    Trivia: Lamont Du Pont read a message about the United Nations.

EPISODE #434 **"ARTIST TO THE WOUNDED"** Broadcast on May 7, 1945
    Starring: Geraldine Fitzgerald as Ann Jordan   David Ellis as Dave
    Virginia Gordon as nurse two   Joe Worthy as Harry
    Howard McNear as the doctor   Bill Christy as Soldier three
    Dave Roberts as Soldier four   Anne Stone as Helen
    Paul Theodore as Soldier two   Tom Holland as Soldier one
    Dorothy Scott as the nurse   Ed MacDonnell as the cynic
    Bill Christy as the messenger
    Written for *Cavalcade* by Bernard Reines.
    Produced and directed by Jack Zoller.
    Frank Graham is the announcer and Gayne Whitman is the commercial spokesman. Music composed and conducted by Robert Armbruster.

Story: Successful in her work, Ann was fairly contended drawing fashionable gowns, until her fiancé was reported missing in action in Germany. Then her career lost its fascination. She felt the need of giving even more time to the war effort . . doing the thing she could do best. So she turned to volunteer work with one of the least-known of the USO's many services, Camp Shows "Hospital Sketching Program." Ann was frightened when she made her first visit to the hospital wards and began sketching portraits of the wounded. But she soon found most of the men easy to work with - ready to laugh with her, secretly pleased with the results of her sketching. Then one day as she watched a convoy of wounded arriving at the hospital, she was rewarded by the sight of a face she had carried in her heart for many months. **(HLYD)**

EPISODE #435   **"WEATHER IS A WEAPON"**   Broadcast on May 14, 1945
Starring: Dana Andrews
Written for *Cavalcade* by Charles Rabiner.
Produced and directed by Jack Zoller.
Frank Graham is the announcer and Gayne Whitman is the commercial spokesman.
Music composed and conducted by Robert Armbruster.
Story: December, 1944 . . . Europe . . . the Allied armies which had been beating the Germans back across the continent suddenly found themselves reeling before sledgehammer attacks. The Germans had broken through at Bastogne! In spite of desperate fighting, our armies were being forced to retreat. Their air forces were grounded because of unbroken bad weather and the Germans had taken stunning advantage of this stroke of bad luck to push the attack. Unless the bombers, fighters, and observers could get into the air again, the Allied armies might be cut to ribbons and thrust into the sea. Army Air Forces Weather Service, which has played a little-known but highly important part in the job of out-guessing and out-fighting the enemy. As this story shows, the Battle of the Bulge proved to the world once more that weather is a weapon. **(HLYD)**

EPISODE #436   **"HOW TO BUILD PARADISE"**   Broadcast on May 21, 1945

Starring: Robert Young as Captain Parsons	Dave Ellis as Holly
Harry Bartell as Merritt	Jay Novello as Davis
Harry Bartell as the radio voice	Bill Hudson as Peters
Sidney Miller as Lupe	Jay Novello as Tiave
David Ellis as Jim	Bill Hudson as Greey
Carlton Ka Dell as Jones	Sidney Miller as Bart
Bob Cole as Bill	Herbert Rawlinson as Goodman

Based on the book "Mob 3" by Captain Robert P. Parsons, as originally published by Bobbs-Merrill Company in 1945. Adapted for *Cavalcade* by Philip Lewis.
Produced and directed by Jack Zoller.
Frank Graham is the announcer and Gayne Whitman is the commercial spokesman.
Music composed and conducted by Robert Armbruster.
Story: In the early days of the Pacific war, when our Navy was beginning to expand, several doctors of a Navy Mobile Unit were set ashore on a small island somewhere in the Pacific to face one of the biggest problems of their lives. Their job was to superintend the building of a modern hospital in the mire of the jungle. A hospital to care for the men wounded in the surrounding fighting areas. Captain Robert P. Parsons led and encouraged the small group as it battered its way through a maze of natural obstacles. Because of a constant downpour of rain, mud was everywhere. Then a hurricane struck the island - a hurricane of energy - with the arrival of a contingent of Seabees! Demons for work, they had laid foundations for buildings within a few hours and in less than eight weeks, when the first ship arrived, the hospital stood ready to receive its wounded. **(HLYD)**

EPISODE #437 **"RECON PILOT"** Broadcast on May 28, 1945
  Starring: William Holden
  Based on the AAF Army training film "Reconnaissance Pilot" by Sgt. Guy Trosper, and adapted for *Cavalcade* by Sgt. Harold Medford, who was Technical Sergeant at the time. Produced and directed by Jack Zoller.
  Frank Graham is the announcer and Gayne Whitman is the commercial spokesman.
  Music composed and conducted by Robert Armbruster.
  Story: Packy was a young American flyer who wanted to shoot Japs more than anything else on Earth after his father was killed, fighting against them in the early days of the Pacific Campaign. He worked hard to fit himself for the job and became a good flier, best in his class - a "hot pilot" as the Air Force terms it. He could almost make that P-38 talk. Ready and eager for his assignment as a combat flier, Packy was assigned, instead, to flying reconnaissance ships armed with nothing more deadly than an aerial camera. Packy hated it. He thought that being a "Photo Joe" was dull and monotonous and, moreover, he doubted that his work was very important. Then one day something happened . . . **(HLYD)**

  Trivia: Harold Medford was a radio script writer who contributed to numerous programs during the early forties. *Suspense* and *The Whistler* were but a few. When the war came, Medford lent his writing talents in the service, and later returned to radio writing when the war came to a close. Medford eventually turned to screen-writing for television shows and feature-length movies such as *Tales of Tomorrow* and *The Window* (1948).

  More Trivia: Actor William Holden has the distinction of being the first Hollywood actor to participate in combat during WWII. Lieutenant Holden was remembered for his appearance on another *Cavalcade* broadcast, also based on an Army Air Forces Training Film, "Name, Rank, and Serial Number." He played, also, in the original film, as he did in the film on which this broadcast was based.

EPISODE #438 **"THE LIEUTENANTS COME HOME"** Broadcast on June 4, 1945
  Starring: Bob Bailey as Lt. Carlton Rouh   Marjorie Reynolds as Phyllis Rowand
  Verne Smith as the staccato voice   Lou Crosby as Wally
  Margaret Brayton as the operator   Verne Smith as the medic
  Victor Rodman as the Major   Dave Ellis as Frank
  Jack Grimes as the voice of the pigeon   Sidney Miller as Polanski
  Leo Cleary as voice three   Herman Waldman as voice two
  Sidney Miller as voice one   Leo Cleary as the Sergeant
  Written for *Cavalcade* by Arthur Arents.
  Produced and directed by Jack Zoller.
  Frank Graham is the announcer and Gayne Whitman is the commercial spokesman.
  Music composed and conducted by Robert Armbruster.
  Story: Carlton Rouh and Phyllis Rowand had been high school sweethearts. Engaged to be married, they postponed taking the step - as did many young couples - when the war interrupted their lives. Phyllis joined the USA Nurse Corps, while Carlton went into the Marines as a private. Both were sent overseas and, strangely, they met in Australia. But they could not be seen together because of the difference in their ranks. Dodging MP's constantly, they often managed to meet on a 24-hour pass. The solution was for Carlton to get his commission. And he got his commission - the hard way. In 1944 Peleiu was invaded and Carlton was seriously wounded when he threw himself on a grenade in an attempt to protect his men. For his act he won a recommendation for the Congressional Medal of Honor. **(HLYD)**

  Trivia: The original title of this drama was "The Second Lieutenants Came Home."

EPISODE #439 "THE LAW WEST OF THE PECOS" Broadcast on June 11, 1945
    Starring: Walter Brennan as Judge Roy Bean   Lou Crosby as the Ranger
    Barton Yarborough as Black Bart   Hal Gerard as Gambler
    Griff Barnette as the second voice   Howard McNear as Pancho
    Howard McNear as the executive   Bob Brice as the worker
    Pinky Barker as the cowboy   Harry Lang as Torres
    Jack Edwards, Jr. as the bandit
Written for *Cavalcade* by William E. Robinson.
Produced and directed by Jack Zoller.
Frank Graham is the announcer and Gayne Whitman is the commercial spokesman.
Music composed and conducted by Robert Armbruster.
Story: Ruthless killings and mob violence were everyday occurrences in Vinnegarron, Texas, in the 1880's. There was no legal authority - no law officers. The man who shot first was right. Vinnegarron was the lawless Old West at its worst. Into this maelstrom came Roy Bean. Nominally a business man, he had planned to set up a store but he soon decided that law and order were more important. So he appointed himself judge and proceeded to enforce his own law. With a shabby copy of "The Revisited Statutes of Texas, 1879" in his hip pocket and a pair of guns in his holsters, he set out to bring justice and some sort of order to the vast plains of West Texas. Not always did he act according to the exact letter of the law, but he was what the country needed. **(HLYD)**

Trivia: About a year after this broadcast, circa early 1946, Walter Brennan reprised his *Cavalcade* performance of Judge Roy Bean for an experimental radio pilot entitled *Law West of Pecos*. Scripted by William E. Robinson, this second broadcast featured the continuing adventures of Judge Roy Bean, and his adventures in the wild west. The script for the pilot was not the same dramatized on *Cavalcade*. This second one involved Judge Bean battling wits against the Pecos Kid, played by Lou Crosby. Wilbur Hatch composed and conducted the music for the pilot broadcast, and Ford Pearson was the announcer. Broadcast in early to mid-1946, the pilot never picked up a sponsor, and so the proposed western never came to be.

EPISODE #440 "PARTY LINE" Broadcast on June 18, 1945
    Starring: Verna Felton as Mrs. Dexter   Agnes Moorehead as Elmira
    Jane Morgan as Mrs. Maxwell   Mary Jane Croft as Louise
    Norma Jean Nilsson as Lousie (child)   Henry Blair as Kenneth
    Virginia Sale as Mrs. Hogg   Mary Jane Croft as Mrs. Meyers
    Victor Rodman as Mr. Benson   Virginia Sale as Mary
Based on the 1945 story of the same name by Louise Baker, and adapted for *Cavalcade* by Sylvia Berger.
Produced and directed by Jack Zoller.
Frank Graham is the announcer and Gayne Whitman is the commercial spokesman.
Music composed and conducted by Robert Armbruster.
Story: Miss Elmira held forth in those days in the town of Mayfield as queen of the telephone system. Miss Elmira knew everything that was going on in town - what the butcher had today, where the doctor was and where he was going next, who was having his hair cut and how much the new baby weighed. What's more, Miss Elmira took an active part in affairs about town when she thought her help was needed. Her self-assigned duties included protecting the homes of the sick from unnecessary calls, reassuring anxious wives and mothers, and giving advice on cooking and dress making. But her biggest job was snaring a husband for the town's spinster, a mild and colorless school teacher who hadn't had a caller in fifteen years. **(HLYD)**

EPISODE #441 **"DDT"** Broadcast on June 25, 1945

Starring: Richard Whorf as Squires
Maybelle Prindaville as Maria
Barbara Lee Benton as Angelina
Lew Lauria as the Corporal
Joseph Agnello as Bonomi
Frank Martin as Jacobson
George Sorel as voice one
George Sorel as Pietro
Don Orlando as Rizzo
Hal Dawson as the Major
Dick Hogan as the Sergeant
Jay Novello as De Georgio
Frank Martin as voice two
Ramsey Hill as Nicolo

Written for *Cavalcade* by Charles Rabiner.
Produced and directed by Jack Zoller.
Frank Graham is the announcer and Gayne Whitman is the commercial spokesman.
Music composed and conducted by Robert Armbruster.
Story: For untold centuries typhus has been one of mankind's greatest enemies. Epidemics of this dreaded disease have swept the world - irrespective of race, color or social status - leaving countless thousands of dead behind. Disease of one kind or another has skulled in the shadow of war, feeding and growing on poverty and starvation, causing more death and misery than the battlefield. When American troops landed in Italy, our medical officers knew what danger threatened. They had come armed with a new weapon which was thought to be effective but which was yet untried and unproved - dichlor-diphenyl-trichloroethane - a white powder familiarly known as DDT. **(HLYD)**

Trivia: Originally titled "DDT - the Powder of Life," this broadcast featured Du Pont's spokesman telling how the company worked on to develop and produce DDT for the Army. This was the final episode of the season.

EPISODE #442 **"ASSIGNMENT FOR THE PROF"** Broadcast on August 27, 1945

Starring: Burgess Meredith as Prof. Harold Moffet   Irene Tedrow as Mrs. Moffet
Others in the cast include Leo Cleary, George Sorel, Theodore Von Eltz, Bill Green, Eric Snowden, and John Brown
Written for *Cavalcade* by Bernard Feins and Russell Hughes.
Produced and directed by Jack Zoller.
Frank Graham is the announcer and Gayne Whitman is the commercial spokesman.
Music composed and conducted by Robert Armbruster.
Story: No one was much surprised when Prof. Harold Muffet walked out of his classroom one day and just disappeared. He was a mild little man and though he wasn't really absent-minded, he did forget things once in a while. So everyone supposed he'd gone off for a vacation and had forgotten to announce his departure. Some weeks later the professor was back again - lecturing to his geology class on shell heaps in America. He didn't say much about his absence because he couldn't, so no one knew - not even Sally, his wife - that he had been one of the most dangerous and important secret missions of the war. **(HLYD)**

Trivia: The program begins with a bulletin from Manila about the U.S. occupation of Japan. For any nit-pickers out there: the actual script title featured the abbreviation of "Professor" in the actual script, as listed above, not the full word.

On the next page: Two *Cavalcade* advertisements seen in magazines and newspapers.

presents

BURGESS MEREDITH

in

"The Rain Fakers"

MONDAY, DECEMBER 30, 1946

NATIONAL BROADCASTING COMPANY
COAST TO COAST NETWORK

8.00-8.30	E.T.	9.30-10.00	M.T.
7.00-7.30	C.T.	8.30- 9.00	P.T.

DU PONT CAVALCADE OF AMERICA

presents

SHIRLEY BOOTH

in

"The Woman on Lime Rock"

MONDAY, JANUARY 6, 1947

NATIONAL BROADCASTING COMPANY
COAST TO COAST NETWORK

8.00-8.30	E.T.	9.30-10.00	M.T.
7.00-7.30	C.T.	8.30- 9.00	P.T.

EPISODE #443   "CARGO OVER BURMA"   Broadcast on September 3, 1945
Starring: Richard Conte and Michael O'Shea
Written by for *Cavalcade* by Sergeant Jack Denove.
Produced and directed by Jack Zoller.
Tom Collins is the announcer and Gayne Whitman is the commercial spokesman.
Music composed and conducted by Robert Armbruster.
Story: Hauling freight from one place to another doesn't sound very exciting, but it does have its moments, as any veteran truck-driver will testify. Consider the possibilities, then, for the men of the Combat Cargo Flyers as they hauled freight over some of the worst mountains in the world (and enemy territory at that). With their travel hampered by everything from monsoons to Zeros and their freight including such dangerous items as high explosives and rebellious Jap prisoners. That was all in the day's work for the men of the Combat Cargo Flyers. Their job was to deliver the goods, no matter what, and things like storms and bullets were not allowed to interfere.   **(HLYD)**

Trivia: Sgt. Jack Denove, of the 15th Combat Cargo Squadron and the 4th Combat Cargo Group, wrote this script, based on true events he experienced overseas, thus making it an authentic story.

EPISODE #444   "SAWDUST UNDERGROUND"   Broadcast on September 10, 1945
Starring: Bob Bailey, Nanette Balon, Ramsey Hill and John Hodiak
Written for *Cavalcade* by Walter Reilly and Leonard Spigelgass.
Produced and directed by Jack Zoller.
Tom Collins is the announcer and Gayne Whitman is the commercial spokesman.
Music composed and conducted by Robert Armbruster.
The song "The Hutsut Song" was performed in this broadcast.
Story: The two men were strange individuals. A patrol of the American armies advancing on Paris had picked then up, and now the question was what to do with them. They claimed they were Americans who had escaped from the Germans but it was small wonder that the commanding officer, before whom they stood cast, an amused though skeptical eye on them. After all, who would expect a pair of Americans to appear - one bedecked in an orange clown suit with black pompoms, the other in green tights with purple spangles? The CO was puzzled. He thought he'd seen everything. Was all this, he wondered, a clever trick, a bit of ingenious enemy strategy? His doubts were removed when he'd heard their story. The tale was so fantastic it had to be true.   **(HLYD)**

EPISODE #445   "NELLIE WAS A LADY"   Broadcast on September 17, 1945
Starring: Agnes Moorehead as Nellie Bly
Written for *Cavalcade* by Turner Bullock.
Produced and directed by Jack Zoller.
Tom Collins is the announcer and Gayne Whitman is the commercial spokesman.
Music composed and conducted by Robert Armbruster.
Story: By the year 1888 women were beginning to emerge timidly from their time-honored "place in the home," to carve their niches in genteel businesses, but a woman who aspired to be a newspaper reporter was daring, indeed. Despite prejudices and keen male competition, one woman - a certain Nellie Bly who had the appearance of a gentle dove and the energy of a hungry tiger - led the way and talked herself into a position on the "New York World." Nellie made up her mind at the very beginning that typing up daily recipes and writing colorful accounts of weddings were not in her line. So she set out to unearth some of the most sensational stories of the day. She begged on the street, she went up in a balloon, she took the job as a maid, hunted mashers, interviewed murderers and even had herself committed to an insane asylum. Nellie Bly became a name to be reckoned with not only in New York, but all over the world.   **(HLYD)**

EPISODE #446 "THE BATTLE TO STAY ALIVE"   Broadcast on September 24, 1945
Starring: Robert Young
Written for *Cavalcade* by Arthur Arent, based on "The Conquest of Epidemic Disease" by C. E. Winslow.
Produced and directed by Jack Zoller.
Tom Collins is the announcer and Gayne Whitman is the commercial spokesman.
Music composed and conducted by Robert Armbruster.
Story: When one thinks of the practice of medicine today, one thinks of great gleaming hospitals, of highly trained doctors, of marvelous drugs and other miracles of healing. It is an almost incredulous thought that not so very long ago, even the most learned men believed that sickness was caused by evil spirits. "Thou art contaminated by demons!" they would say to the suffering - and then leave them to die alone. Gradually, men began to learn about diseases and how they spread. They began studying courses. They learned the three major sources of epidemics and they took action. Instead of abandoning the infected to wander aimlessly, spreading their disease, doctors began to isolate their cases and to give them diligent treatment. This is the story of the conquest of epidemic disease. **(HLYD)**

EPISODE #447 "200,000 FLYERS"   Broadcast on October 1, 1945
Starring: Pat O'Brien
Written for *Cavalcade* by Willard Wiener, based on his book of the same name.
Produced and directed by Jack Zoller.
Tom Collins is the announcer and Gayne Whitman is the commercial spokesman.
Music composed and conducted by Robert Armbruster.
A band plays "Hail, Hail, the Gang's All Here" during this broadcast.
Story: Few people realize that a mere six years ago the United States Air Force was seventh in size, not first as it was during World War II. Compared with the armies Axis, we had but a handful of planes and only a few hundred airmen were being trained each year. True, the assembly lines of American factories turned them out in unbelievable numbers but that is only part of the story. How about trained men back to fly those planes? That was what a few far-sighted young men back in 1939 wondered - men who proved they had the courage and wisdom to accomplish a task of incalculable value in winning the war. This is the true story of how our nation, inspired and directed by a few, accomplished the amazing job of increasing its trained airmen from five hundred to over one hundred thousand a year - and in record time. **(HLYD)**

EPISODE #448 "THE SPY ON KILOCYCLES"   Broadcast on October 8, 1945
Starring: Henry Fonda
Written for *Cavalcade* by Bernard Feins and Russell Hughes.
Produced and directed by Jack Zoller.
Tom Collins is the announcer and Gayne Whitman is the commercial spokesman.
Music composed and conducted by Robert Armbruster.
Story: Early in the war, Government agents started work on one of the most thrilling and vital cases of their careers. In the vicinity of Dorchester, Mass., a transmitter was being illegally operated, sending valuable information to the Nazis. The spy might pave the way for a sabotage movement and had to be caught - and promptly. Relentlessly, the authorities tracked down every clue, but they got nowhere. The spy was too clever - his messages, short and snappy, gave little on which to go. This also made it difficult for the government men to pin-point the location of the transmitter. They were baffled. One day an American girl, vacationing, found an odd piece of metal on the beach. Her curiosity aroused, she turned it over to the authorities, was thanked politely, and heard no more about it. . . **(HLYD)**

Trivia: Starring in this *Cavalcade* broadcast was Henry Fonda, whose appearance was his first professional one since his return to civilian life. He had recently been released from the Navy after three years of distinctive service.

EPISODE #449 "CHILDREN, THIS IS YOUR FATHER" Broadcast on October 15, 1945
Starring: Loretta Young as Mrs. Lester   Gale Gordon as Lt. Sam Lester
Marlene Aames as Karen   Tommy Bernard as Mickey
Written for *Cavalcade* by Priscilla Kent.
Produced and directed by Jack Zoller.
Tom Collins is the announcer and Gayne Whitman is the commercial spokesman.
Music composed and conducted by Robert Armbruster.
Story: When Lt. Sam Lester came home from the war, he found that things had changed mightily around his house. Home just wasn't the same. After being away for four years, he found that his children had almost forgotten him as he really was, and had built up a too-flattering picture of him as a hero. Although he had done a hard and useful job in the supply corps, it had not been glamorous work and here were his children believing that he had almost wiped out the whole German army single-handed. And what's more, they wanted souvenirs to proved it! **(HLYD)**

EPISODE #450 "JOHNNY COMES HOME" Broadcast on October 22, 1945
Starring: Robert Walker as Johnny   Marsha Hunt as Jane
Howard McNear as Charlie   Jerry Hausner as Les
Ken Peters as the Sergeant   Louise Erickson as Susie
Sidney Miller as the tailor   Charles Carroll as Thorwald
Ken Peters as Al   Jerry Hausner as Art
Sidney Miller as Larry
Written for *Cavalcade* by Norman Barnes and Philip Gelb.
Produced and directed by Jack Zoller.
Tom Collins is the announcer and Gayne Whitman is the commercial spokesman.
Music composed and conducted by Robert Armbruster.
The song "Johnny Comes Marching Home" is performed in this broadcast.
Story: These are glad days. They are days that will be long remembered for the dreams and cherished wishes of millions of men and women are coming true at last. Johnny is coming home. Every day now, all over the nation, tens of thousands of our fighting men are living the day they have dreamed of for so long. They are coming back to the towns and homes and people they love. But these are trying days, too. Problems of readjustment, problems of re-employment, problems of personal relations arise to greet the jubilant young man with his discharge papers. This is the story about Johnny Adams who comes home to a tweed suit and a green striped necktie after four years of olive drab and finds life complicated by many things. Sometimes tender, sometimes humorous, it is a very important story about a typical young American, his girl and his future. **(HLYD)**

Trivia: Robert Walker and Susan Peters were originally scheduled to star in this broadcast, however, during the week before broadcast, Peters had to back down. Marsha Hunt took her place.

EPISODE #451 "MY SON JOHN" Broadcast on October 29, 1945
Starring: Humphrey Bogart, Alan Reed as Zirk, and Jerry Hausner as Johnny
Based on the 1945 book "USS Seawolf" by Gerold Frank, James D. Horan and J.M. Eckberg.
Adapted for *Cavalcade* by Philip Lewis.
Produced and directed by Jack Zoller.
Tom Collins is the announcer and Gayne Whitman is the commercial spokesman.
Music composed and conducted by Robert Armbruster.

Story: For countless centuries men who sailed the seas have been superstitious. When John Dayman came aboard the "U.S.S. Seawolf" and the ship's luck changed, the whole crew believed that Dayman was a Jinx. The title of Jinx seemed justified, too, because the "U.S.S. Seawolf," which had been formerly one of the most successful submarines in the fleet, began having very bad luck. As her torpedoes missed target after target, enemy depth charges churned the waters around her. With an unwavering certainty, the crew members declared Dayman the cause of their ill-fortune and swore to get him off the ship, one way or another. **(HLYD)**

Jack Zoller: "Humphrey Bogart was on one *Cavalcade* show, cast as a submarine sailor in war action. He complained bitterly that his lines were too Rover Boy - I think that's what he called it - for him. Well, we asked the writer to change the lines so that Humphrey could sound real tough and everybody was made very happy. For the actors, we try to be reasonable."

Trivia: The title of this script was originally "U.S.S. Seawolf."

EPISODE #452 **"THE BUILDERS OF THE BRIDGE"** Broadcast on November 5, 1945
Starring: Claire Trevor as Emily Roebling   Frank Graham as Washington Roebling
Based on the biography of the same title by D.B. Steinman, originally published by Harcourt, Brace & Company, Inc. in 1945. Adapted for *Cavalcade* by Priscilla Kent.
Produced and directed by Jack Zoller.
Tom Collins is the announcer and Gayne Whitman is the commercial spokesman.
Music composed and conducted by Robert Armbruster.
Story: In the days after the greatest war in the history of the world, our thoughts turn again naturally but awkwardly to creating and building. This is the story of such men, two engineers, father and son, and the younger man's wife, Emily, each of whom had the genius and courage to build the greatest bridge of their day. One man gave his life, the other his strength, that the bridge might be built. And Emily gave as much, if not more than either. For almost fifteen years they worked on their great bridge, this gleaming span across New York's East River - the Brooklyn Bridge. **(HLYD)**

EPISODE #453 **"A SAILOR WHO HAD TO HAVE A HORSE"** Aired November 12, 1945
Starring: Mary Jane Croft, Harry Jackson, Joseph Julian, Eddie Marr, Sidney Miller, Horace Murphy, Victor Rodman, James Stewart, and Herb Vigran
Based on the short story of the same title by Gretta Palmer, as originally published in a 1945 issue of *Reader's Digest*, and adapted for *Cavalcade* by Bernard Feins and Russell Hughes.
Produced and directed by Jack Zoller.
Tom Collins is the announcer and Gayne Whitman is the commercial spokesman.
Music composed and conducted by Robert Armbruster.
Story: Many seamen, famous and otherwise, have set out in ships to find strange things, frequently against the advice of all the people who were supposed to know. Case in point: Mr. Vance Corman, a modern sailor, who faced as much ridicule as Columbus and Ponce de Leon, who was simply looking for a horse. And no special kind either - no winged horse, no horse of gold - just a plain everyday riding horse. Being a practical man, Vance carried just a saddle. But the trouble was that Vance was a sailor in the U.S. Navy, engaged in fighting a global war, and finding a horse on a battleship was quite a job. But Vance was determined. And while he did his job as a sailor all over the world, he hung on to that saddle and kept looking. He just had to find a horse. **(HLYD)**

Trivia: James Stewart, starring as Vance on this broadcast, had just been released from the Army Air Forces with the rank of Colonel.

More trivia: During the second performance, the West Coast broadcast, the cast ran a little late because of a laugh spread. Instead of a lengthy allocation, James Stewart said a two sentence speech about the victory loan drive. "Ladies and Gentlemen, I was going to make a little speech about the Victory Loan Drive, but we are running a little short of time. I just want to remind you to buy lots of Victory Bonds. Thanks a lot. Goodnight." During the previous East Coast broadcast, Stewart gave a half-page speech about the bond drive.

EPISODE #454   "I COUNT THE DAYS"   Broadcast on November 19, 1945
    Starring: Signe Hasso as Johanna   Elliott Lewis as Steve
    Written for *Cavalcade* by Bernard Victor Dryer.
    Produced and directed by Jack Zoller.
    Tom Collins is the announcer and Gayne Whitman is the commercial spokesman.
    Music composed and conducted by Robert Armbruster.
    A Dutch folk song was played on a guitar.
    Story: For more than a decade, stories have been coming out of Europe - stories of hate and fear, greed and evil, destruction and death. They were stories that told of the growing sickness of a continent and the despair of its people. But now the source of that sickness has been destroyed by fire, and from the rubble of ruined cities and towns are coming new stories that are alive with hope. Such a play is this one, a tale of a young woman who suffered through the worst of the terrible years, almost losing her will to live and a task she must perform. Suddenly she found a new hope for tomorrow, a way of helping to prevent the recurrence of such a catastrophe.   **(HLYD)**

EPISODE #455   "TRAVELLER TO ARKANSAS"   Broadcast on November 26, 1945
    Starring: Lloyd Nolan as Pop Pilarski and Sam Edwards as Arky
    Written for *Cavalcade* by Charles Rabiner.
    Produced and directed by Jack Zoller.
    Tom Collins is the announcer and Gayne Whitman is the commercial spokesman.
    Music composed and conducted by Robert Armbruster.
    Story: "Pop" Pilarski was the roughest, toughest sergeant in the Ordnance outfit. He had all the kindliness and consideration of any angry rhinoceros, and was about as lovable as a booby trap. But for some odd reason, a private from Arkansas took a liking to the sergeant. Instead of pleasing "Pop," the boy's admiration of him just made him fume. Being disliked seemed to make him happy. Things weren't improved one bit by Arky's knocking "Pop" out either. Of course he had a good reason, but that cut no ice with "Pop." Nobody could slug him and get away with it. "Just wait till we get out of combat area," he bellowed, "I'll have him transferred! I'll have him court marshaled! I'll have him shot! I'll murder him myself!" He did nothing of the sort.   **(HLYD)**

EPISODE #456   "DIRECTION HOME"   Broadcast on December 3, 1945
    Starring: Thomas Mitchell as Jerry Sweeney   Howard Duff as Everett
    Mary Jane Croft as Eve
    Written for *Cavalcade* by Bernard Feins and Russell Hughes.
    Produced and directed by Jack Zoller.
    Tom Collins is the announcer and Gayne Whitman is the commercial spokesman.
    Music composed and conducted by Robert Armbruster.
    Technical information about the use of radar was furnished by the U.S. Army Signal Corps.
    Story: All men who help win a war, cannot be fighters. But the men who don't fight are often subject to criticism. That's how is was with Everett Matthews, a young man who stayed home to work on one of the greatest weapons of the war. Eve Sweeney, the girl who was in love with Everett, was proud of her fiancé and his work. But her father heartily disliked Everett because he wasn't in uniform. How a young man could stay

home and sit behind a frosted glass door when the world was trembling on the brink of disaster was more than Mr. Sweeney could understand. Eve and Everett had about reconciled themselves to the parental wrath, when Jerry Sweeney faced a crisis which was to make him forever thankful for his new son-in-law. This is the story of a stubborn Irishman, of a boy and a girl, and of the great magic eye . . . radar. **(HLYD)**

EPISODE #457   **"BIG BOY BLUE"**   Broadcast on December 10, 1945
Starring: Henry Fonda as Eugene Field
Written for *Cavalcade* by Gerald Holland.
Produced and directed by Jack Zoller.
Tom Collins is the announcer and Gayne Whitman is the commercial spokesman.
Music composed and conducted by Robert Armbruster.
Story: Every once in a while a man is born who is so natural and human that the people around him think he's peculiar - a little eccentric even. And like many good things, his worth and charm are appreciated only after the passing of time. There was such a man in America. He earned his living as a newspaper reporter but his city editors often shook their heads and wondered why they even hired him. His prospective father-in-law had to be forcefully persuaded to accept him as his daughter's husband. This man was Eugene Field. Eugene had a lot of fun just living. He loved to fly kites with children, play jokes on stuffed shirts, wear carpet slippers to the office, and write sentimental verses. Poetry that has endeared him to generations of children. **(HLYD)**

Trivia: Du Pont had made a public announcement the week before that Lee Bowman and Marsha Hunt were to star in this play about that charming humorous writer of verses, Eugene Field. Apparently they were scheduled to star in this drama, but instead, Henry Fonda took the role.

EPISODE #458   **"THE MAGNIFICENT MEDDLER"**   Broadcast on December 17, 1945
Starring: George Sanders as Dr. Benjamin Rush
Written for *Cavalcade* by Lee Schoen, based on the book "Benjamin Rush" by Nathan Goodman, as originally published by the University of Pennsylvania Press in 1934.
Produced and directed by Jack Zoller.
Tom Collins is the announcer and Gayne Whitman is the commercial spokesman.
Music composed and conducted by Robert Armbruster.
Story: "Let him have sunlight and fresh air. Don't let anyone annoy him." And thus began an experiment with insanity. People said it would fail, said it was dangerous, and some threatened the doctor, but he was determined to have his way. He felt sure the "meddling" of which he was accused would pay off in human lives. This doctor was Benjamin Rush, a prominent Philadelphia physician. In 1789, scornful of opposition, he began his work to save the mentally ill from treatment worse than that of criminals. He risked his reputation to show that mental illness could be helped and sometimes cured. Today, countless thousands owe their lives and happiness to the work of Dr. Rush, also known as "The Magnificent Meddler." **(HLYD)**

EPISODE #459   **"NAMES ON THE LAND"**   Broadcast on December 24, 1945
Starring: Frank Morgan
Based on the 1945 book of the same name by George R. Stewart, and adapted for *Cavalcade* by Peter and Jane Lyon.
Produced and directed by Jack Zoller.
Tom Collins is the announcer and Gayne Whitman is the commercial spokesman.
Music composed and conducted by Robert Armbruster.
Includes the song "Wright Sonovox."
Story: From every corner of the World, servicemen have returned to the home towns they love. They are Boston and San Francisco, Tamps and St. Louis, Corpus Christi and

Minneapolis. But there are also a thousand other towns that you never heard of, towns with odd names in every country of every state of the Union. Each of them is home for some American service man or woman. This is a mythical tour of fascinating American towns you've probably never heard of, towns with names that are odd, historical, funny, beautiful or memorable, towns that are America at peace -at Christmas. **(HLYD)**

EPISODE #460 **"TEN IN TEXAS"** Broadcast on December 31, 1945
Starring: Walter Brennan
Written for *Cavalcade* by Walter "Hank" Richards, based on an article entitled "The Ranch That Changed the West" by Lewis Nordyke from a 1945 issue of *Reader's Digest*.
Produced and directed by Jack Zoller.
Tom Collins is the announcer and Gayne Whitman is the commercial spokesman.
Music composed and conducted by Robert Armbruster.
Story: Out of the great State of Texas have come many tall tales, but none more fascinating than this authentic tale of the famed and fabulous XIT Ranch. With three million acres of land making up this vast cattle empire, the ranch wasn't just big, it was immense - larger than the whole state of Rhode Island. It was thirty miles wide, and 250 miles long. When the owners set out to fence it, they put up two thousand miles of fence and they counted their cattle by the tens of thousands. Naturally, the problem involved in opening up such a ranch were tremendous. The story of the rise of the XIT and the lasting impression the ranch made on the territory of Texas is one of the most colorful stories of the Old West. **(HLYD)**

EPISODE #461 **"BUILD ME STRAIGHT"** Broadcast on January 7, 1946
Starring: Joseph Cotten as Donald McKay   Claire Trevor as Albenia McKay
Written for *Cavalcade* by Phyllis Parker.
Produced and directed by Jack Zoller.
Tom Collins is the announcer and Gayne Whitman is the commercial spokesman.
Music composed and conducted by Robert Armbruster.
Story: As a younger man, Donald McKay dreamed of building great new ships, bigger and faster than any the world had ever seen. He wanted to build them swift and sleek, with slim lines and towering masts that would carry acres of sail and send ships flying over the seas. As always, the doubters declared loudly that nobody could build ships such as he planned. "Why you can't hold that much timber together!" But Donald and his courageous wife went ahead and built ships which astonished the world. McKay's "Clipper Ships" helped make America the leading maritime nation of the world. Then, McKay started work on his biggest dream, the largest ship afloat - "The Sovereign of the Seas." She was tremendous, and the whole nation awaited her launching. **(HLYD)**

EPISODE #462 **"VENTURE IN SILK HAT"** Broadcast on January 14, 1946
Starring: Howard Duff, and Franchot Tone as James J. Andrews
Based on the 1944 story "Railroad Avenue" by Freeman H. Hubbard, and adapted for *Cavalcade* by Norris Houghton.
Produced and directed by Jack Zoller.
Tom Collins is the announcer and Gayne Whitman is the commercial spokesman.
Music composed and conducted by Robert Armbruster.
Story: The O.S.S. has turned out many unsung heroes whose fantastic adventures will in time be fully known and praised. And yet it is doubtful that any of these modern adventurers have undertaken tasks stranger than the one attempted by a courageous agent of the Union Army. During the Civil War, one of the most colorful and intrepid secret agents was a man named James J. Andrews. After accomplishing an impressive number of dangerous missions for the North, he undertook the biggest and most hazardous job of his career. Andrews, attired in a frock coat and a silk hat, set out with his small group of agents to take over the wreck of an entire railroad. **(HLYD)**

EPISODE #463 **"THE CAMELS ARE COMING"** Broadcast on January 21, 1946
  Starring: Francis X. Bushman, Laraine Day, Jerry Hausner, Fred Howard, Joel McCrea,
  Horace Murphy, Sarah Selby, Dink Trout, and Cora Witherspoon
  Written for *Cavalcade* by David Lesan.
  Produced and directed by Jack Zoller.
  Tom Collins is the announcer and Gayne Whitman is the commercial spokesman.
  Music composed and conducted by Robert Armbruster.
  Story: Indianola was a rough town in 1856, and there wasn't much that could happen
  that would startle the hardy Texas citizens. Tequila-swigging cavalrymen, stampedes,
  tornadoes, and sudden attacks by murderous Commanche Indians were all in the day's
  work. One thing only awed Indianola, and that was the pageant put on every year by the
  wife of the commanding officer of the Fourth Cavalry. Each year Mrs. Crane staged a
  remarkable version of the story of "Ali Baba and the Forty Thieves," and the town wasn't
  the same for months before and after. Strong men trembled at the thought of Ali Baba.
  But this year, a young Zoological professor, fired with the spirit of research, brought with
  him, right across the respectable Texas landscape, eleven of the biggest, ugliest beasts
  that the natives had ever seen - "real live camels from Araybiuh!" **(HLYD)**

  Trivia: Marsha Hunt was originally scheduled to co-star with Joel McCrea, who did not
  attend this broadcast.

EPISODE #464 **"COMMENCEMENT IN KHAKI"** Broadcast on January 28, 1946
  Starring: Dana Andrews as Corporal Johnson   Nancy Kelly as the lovely WAC
  Eddie Marr as Sime   Gale Gordon as Captain Waters
  Written for *Cavalcade* by Harry Granick.
  Produced and directed by Jack Zoller.
  Tom Collins is the announcer and Gayne Whitman is the commercial spokesman.
  Music composed and conducted by Robert Armbruster.
  Story: "You started this, now you finish it. Tell the captain anything you like. Tell him
  I died. Tell him it was all a short circuit in your infantile, flat-headed, cotton-brained
  model of a numskull! Tell him anything, you king-sized moron! I won't do it!" And
  that was how Corporal Pete Johnson reacted when he found that his old pal Sime had
  "sold him down the river." Everything had been fine in Pete's life, until Sime got him
  mixed up in one of the most hectic, yet pleasurable experiences of his Army career,
  involving a post as instructor of public speaking in Camp Kilmer's new Army College
  and, among other things, a lovely WAC. **(HLYD)**

EPISODE #465 **"CHILDREN OF OL' MAN RIVER"** Broadcast on February 4, 1946
  Starring: John Hodiak as the showboat man   Janet Blair as Josephine Costello
  Others in the cast: Tommy Bernard, Don Brodie, Francis X. Bushman, Joseph Du Val,
  Louise Erickson, Horace Murphy, Herbert Rawlinson, Richard Ryan, Cora Witherspoon
  Based on the 1936 autobiography by Billy Bryant, and adapted for *Cavalcade* by Walter
  "Hank" Richards.
  Produced and directed by Jack Zoller.
  Tom Collins is the announcer and Gayne Whitman is the commercial spokesman.
  Music composed and conducted by Robert Armbruster.
  Story: For generations, the mighty Mississippi has symbolized to Americans romance
  and adventure. Folks who lived on the river always had a gay and colorful aura about
  them. And of the people who lived on and loved the muddy river, none were more
  romantic than those who ran the famous showboats. The stories they told, the songs they
  sung, the dance routines their button shoes clicked out, constitute a lively chapter in our
  country's history. **(HLYD)**

Trivia: This *Cavalcade* broadcast presented the story of a showboat team - "The Four Bryants," whose craft covered the Mississippi river from one end to the other. The dramatization was taken from the book of the same name, written by one of the original Bryants, Billy.

EPISODE #466   **"REMEMBERED DAY"**   Broadcast on February 11, 1946
   Starring: Walter Pidgeon as Abraham Lincoln   Georgia Backus as Elizabeth
   Also in the cast: Griff Barnett, Tommy Bernard, Henry Blair, David Ellis, Alan Hewitt, Sam Hill, and Jay Novello
   Written for *Cavalcade* by John H. Sachs and Milton Wayne.
   Produced and directed by Jack Zoller.
   Tom Collins is the announcer and Gayne Whitman is the commercial spokesman.
   Music composed and conducted by Robert Armbruster.
   Story: The small Pennsylvania town was crowded with people who were filled with the trouble and sorrow that had overcome the entire nation. These were dark days in November, 1863. Among the throngs in the town were hundreds of prisoners, scores of wounded and dying. Although a great battle had been fought and won, there could be no jubilation for the cost had been too great. Then into the town came the man who bore the full weight of the nation's troubles, who symbolized the suffering of the whole country. The President. There he met another man, a soldier who was fighting on the opposite side against all that the President stood for. Their meeting dramatized the whole terrible conflict. **(HLYD)**

Trivia: This script originally featured two titles, only because a decision could not be made as to which was the best of the two. Even the title page of the scripts said "Remembered Day" or "Abe Lincoln's Answer." Before broadcast time, however, the former of the two won by a flip of the coin!

EPISODE #467   **"YOUNG MAJOR WASHINGTON"**   Broadcast on February 18, 1946
   Starring: Gregory Peck as George Washington
   Also in the cast: Hal K. Dawson, Jerry Hausner, Ramsey Hill, Raymond Lawrence, Edwin Max, Howard McNear, George Sorel, Roland Varno, and Stan Waxman
   Written for *Cavalcade* by Robert Kanigher.
   Produced and directed by Jack Zoller.
   Tom Collins is the announcer and Gayne Whitman is the commercial spokesman.
   Music composed and conducted by Robert Armbruster.
   Story: When we think of George Washington, we usually think of him as the Commander of the Continental Armies or as the first President of the United States, placid, dignified, aristocratic in appearance. It is hard to imagine him involved in fantastic and dangerous adventures. And yet, his exploits as a young man were amazing. As result and daring as the best hero of romantic fiction, he combated 1,000 miles of wilderness, just before the French and Indian war, on a mission so packed with hair-raising adventure, it made most Western movies seem pale by comparison. **(HLYD)**

   Note: An all-male cast.

EPISODE #468   **"STAR IN THE WEST"**   Broadcast on February 25, 1946
   Starring: Ida Lupino as Nancy Hormer   William Johnstone as Paul Hormer
   Francis X. Bushman as Dale   Lillian Randolph as Mirabelle
   Earl Smith as Jeb
   Others in the cast: Ed Max, Margaret Brayton, Ruth Perrot and Franklin Parker.
   Written for *Cavalcade* by Bernard Reines.
   Produced and directed by Jack Zoller.
   Tom Collins is the announcer and Gayne Whitman is the commercial spokesman.

Music composed and conducted by Robert Armbruster.
Story: Just a hundred years ago this week an independent nation was annexed to the United States. It was a big and prosperous nation, larger than many in Europe, with a proud history and a vigorous citizenry . . . the Republic of Texas. This is the story of two ordinary people, Nancy and Paul Hormer, who helped to build Texas, a young couple who worked and dreamed and suffered when the new state was growing out of prairie land. But because they were confident of the future greatness of Texas, they fought against obstacles proudly and gladly. **(HLYD)**

Trivia: A program in honor of the 100th anniversary of Texas Statehood.

EPISODE #469 **"THE CASE OF THE TREMENDOUS TRIFLE"** Broadcast March 4, 1946
Starring: Brian Donlevy as Edwin L. Drake   Betty Arnold as Laura
Horace Murphy as Uncle Billy
Written for *Cavalcade* by Bernard Feins.
Produced and directed by Jack Zoller.
Tom Collins is the announcer and Gayne Whitman is the commercial spokesman.
Music composed and conducted by Robert Armbruster.
Story: For years, Uncle Billy Smith had been the best dog-gone brine well driller in Titusville. In fact, not only in Titusville, but in all of Pennsylvania. He boasted that his record was perfect; he'd never brought in a tainted well. When he drilled into the Pennsylvania soil for brine to make salt, he always found it, and he was proud of his infallibility. But one day in 1868, he received a rude shock. A well dressed and very impressive looking stranger came to town, hunted up Uncle Billy, and made him a handsome offer to drill another well. What shocked Uncle Billy was that the stranger wanted the one thing he had always avoided. The stranger was a tainted well! What these two men accomplished changed the history of the entire world. **(HLYD)**

EPISODE #470 **"THE DOCTOR WITH HOPE IN HIS HANDS"** Broadcast March 11, 1946
Starring: Edward G. Robinson as Dr. Harvey Cushing
Ian Wolfe as Charles   Ann Tobin as Miss A.
Also featuring: James Eagles, Jerry Hausner, Ramsey Hill, William Johnstone, Edwin Max, Howard McNear, Sidney Miller, Jack Moyles, and Guy Sorel
Written for *Cavalcade* by Bernard Victor Dryer.
Produced and directed by Jack Zoller.
Tom Collins is the announcer and Gayne Whitman is the commercial spokesman.
Music composed and conducted by Robert Armbruster.
Story: Dr. Harvey Cushing was an American physician and surgeon, one of the world's greatest brain surgeons. He won fame for his achievements in neurosurgery and for experimental work on the brain, nervous system, and pituitary gland. As a result of Cushing's work, neurological surgery became a respected medical subspecialty, which many of the recent advancements in brain surgery are now based. **(HLYD)**

EPISODE #471 **"ALASKAN BUSH PILOT"** Broadcast on March 18, 1946
Starring: Dick Foran as Mac   Gale Page as Mrs. Mac Narney
Also starring: Francis X. Bushman, Howard McNear, Elliott Lewis, Bill Johnstone, Tommy Bernard, and Ann Tobin
Written for *Cavalcade* by Harold Franklin and Bernard Feins.
Produced and directed by Jack Zoller.
Tom Collins is the announcer and Gayne Whitman is the commercial spokesman.
Music composed and conducted by Robert Armbruster.
Story: In Washington not long ago, a Major in the Surplus Property Division of the Air Corps received a routine assignment to check up on a man, known as Mac, who had asked to buy two of the government's cargo planes. The assignment took him to Alaska

and into the kitchen of Mac's home where his wife was operating a two-way radio set in contact with her "bush pilot" husband. Almost every day, she relayed to him calls for rescue from the stranded, calls for quick deliveries of commodities. The Air Corps representative, in investigating the duties of this pilot, found himself involved in one of the most amazing businesses he'd ever heard of. A "bush" pilot, it seemed, had to combing all the better traits of an eagle, a donkey, a bookkeeper, a business man - and a knowledge of baby delivering helped, too. **(HLYD)**

Trivia: Dick Foran was originally scheduled to co-star with Claire Trevor in this broadcast, however, Trevor had to back down due to a busy schedule, and so Gale Page took her place.

EPISODE #472 **"THE GENERAL'S WIFE"** Broadcast on March 25, 1946
    Starring: William Johnstone as Zachary Taylor
    Agnes Moorehead as Margaret Mackall Smith
Based on an original story by Kate and Howard Phillips, and adapted for *Cavalcade* by Priscilla Kent.
Produced and directed by Jack Zoller.
Tom Collins is the announcer and Gayne Whitman is the commercial spokesman.
Music composed and conducted by Robert Armbruster.
Story: One summer evening, back in 1810, a lovely young lady sat on her front porch, waiting for a young soldier to call. She was charming, spirited and well bred. What's more, she knew exactly what she wanted - this young lieutenant in the U.S. Army whom she was planning to marry or know the reason why. And when Lieutenant Zachary Taylor strode up the path to the house, he walked into a tender relationship that lasted for 40 years through life's troubles and adventures and ended in the White House. **(HLYD)**

EPISODE #473 **"WHEN CUPID WAS A PUP"** Broadcast on April 1, 1946
    Starring: Cornel Wilde as Dick   Sam Hill as Bobbie
    Griff Barnett as Larson   Jerry Hausner as Ed
    Elliott Lewis as Carl   Earl Keen as Oscar
    Don Brodie as one of the seals   Leo Cleary as the other seal
    Starring: Griff Barnett, Jerry Hausner, Sam Hill, Elliott Lewis, and Cornel Wilde
Based on an original story by Richard English, originally published by the Curtis Publishing Company, and adapted for *Cavalcade* by Bernard Feins and Harold Franklin.
Produced and directed by Jack Zoller.
Tom Collins is the announcer and Gayne Whitman is the commercial spokesman.
Music composed and conducted by Robert Armbruster.
Story: The Farallone Islands are bleak, barren piles of stone twenty-six miles from the San Francisco shore. A lone lighthouse - nothing more - sits high upon the rocks. A job as a lighthouse keeper there attracted Max who had just returned from the Okinawan beach-heads and wanted to get away from everything and everybody. Max accepted the position, prepared to be quietly content just helping the head lighthouse keeper and watching the ocean. But before long complications set in, chiefly for two reasons. One was the lighthouse keeper's daughter, a beautiful daughter, a beautiful girl named Jackie, and the other was a rather retarded but lovable little seal called Oscar. Max had also to contend with Jackie's jealous and bullying boy friend, and Oscar's general ignorance of the facts of life. Max even had to teach the seal to swim! **(HLYD)**

On the next page: A copy of a poster that appeared on poster boards and walls on and near the La Salle High School in Niagara Falls, New York.

Cavalcade of America

presents

Robert Montgomery with Anita Louise

in

"Incident at Niagara"

broadcast from
La Salle High School Auditorium
Niagara Falls, N. Y.

MONDAY EVENING
Sept. 27, NBC Network

EPISODE #474 **"CIRCUS DAY"** Broadcast on April 8, 1946
Starring: Griff Barnett as Cheyenne Charlie
Others in the cast: Tommy Bernard, Margaret Brayton, Francis X. Bushman, Jack Carrington, Ted Donaldson, Jerry Hausner, Rosemary Kelly, Anne Revere, Dick Ryan
Written for *Cavalcade* by Sigmund Miller.
Produced and directed by Jack Zoller.
Tom Collins is the announcer and Gayne Whitman is the commercial spokesman.
Music composed and conducted by Robert Armbruster.
Story: One of the big days in the life of almost every young American is the day the circus rolls into town with its parades and blaring bands, gay wagons and roaring animals, striking costumes and last but not least - peanuts and pink lemonade. This is a recreation of the coming of the circus to a small town. From the arrival at dawn to the departure at midnight, the carnival spirit filled the town with movement and excitement, made all hearts beat faster, and brought new life to the countryside for miles around. For one whole day, the activities of every household centered around going to the circus. But with the Hopkins family, the day was made unusually complicated by affairs involving eggs, ice skates, and broken hearts. **(HLYD)**

EPISODE #475 **"THE GREAT McGRAW"** Broadcast on April 15, 1946
Starring: Pat O'Brien as John J. McGraw
Sam Edwards as voice two
Sidney Miller as Merkle
Bob Bruce as Harry Cross (reporter)
Dick Ryan as the umpire
Ken Peters as Donlin
Herman Waldman as Red
Ken Peters as Cris
Byron Kane as Evers
Harry Lang as fan one
Dick Ryan as voice one
Byron Kane as voice three
Harry Lang as Freedman
Sidney Miller as the writer
Bill Martell as Larry
Sam Edwards as Mel Ott
Tom Graham as Fogel
Herman Waldman as Rog
Tim Graham as O'Day
Stan Waxman as fan two
William Johnstone is the narrator.
Adapted for *Cavalcade* by Peter Lyon, from the 1944 book "McGraw of the Giants" by Frank Graham.
Produced and directed by Jack Zoller.
Tom Collins is the announcer and Gayne Whitman is the commercial spokesman.
Music composed and conducted by Robert Armbruster.
Story: "Shaddap! I'm the boss of this club." And so he was. The speaker was a man who was to have a tremendous influence on the history of big league baseball - John J. McGraw - the mighty "Muggsy." With a hair-trigger temper and an iron will, he was a colorful and difficult man, but he soon whipped the New York Giants into shape. He had to battle everyone from his own players to the umpire and the spectators to get his way, but he usually got it. The result was that McGraw developed some of the finest players in history, and the Giants won pennant after pennant. **(HLYD)**

EPISODE #476 **"MEET ARTIE GREENGROIN"** Broadcast on April 22, 1946
Starring: William Bendix as Artie Greengroin
William Johnstone as the Captain
Francis X. Bushman as the Colonel
Peter Leeds as the Lieutenant
Eddie Marr as the Supply Sergeant
John Brown as Sergeant Glump
Peter Leeds as the co-pilot
Paula Winslowe as Gwen
Howard McNear as the pilot
Howard McNear as the Sergeant
Sidney Miller as Charlie
Jerry Hausner as Sidney
Based on the book "Artie Greengroin, P.F.C." by Harry Brown, originally published in 1945 by Alfred A. Knopf. Adapted for *Cavalcade* by Arthur Arent.
Produced and directed by Jack Zoller.
Tom Collins is the announcer and Gayne Whitman is the commercial spokesman.

Music composed and conducted by Robert Armbruster.
Story: There may have been worse soldiers in the American army than Pfc. Artie Greengroin, but it's doubtful. He seemed to have a genius for getting out of work and into trouble. His only joys seemed to be griping, boosting his beloved Brooklyn, and courting the gorgeous Gwendolyn, an English girl who "don't speak English too good. More the way them English speak it." But Artie's troubles really began when he tangled with a very tough sergeant named Glump, who not only took an instant dislike to Artie, but what was worse, a definite liking for Gwendolyn. The resulting complications involved revenge, the guardhouse, bloodthirsty plots, German fighter planes, and a very angry Colonel O'Crock. **(HLYD)**

Trivia: Although Artie was a fantastic character, it should stand to be corrected that Artie was a fictional G.I. whose hilarious adventures in England appeared in *Yank*, the Army Weekly. Artie never lived - on land nor sea nor in the air - but his roots went deep, and the G.I.'s in the European Theatre of Operations understood him - and approved.

EPISODE #477 "THIRST WITHOUT END" Broadcast on April 29, 1946
Starring: James Cagney as Robert   Will Wright as the Sergeant
Bea Benadaret as Elaine   Conrad Binyon as Freddie
Tommy Bernard as Jackie   George Sorel as Olson
William Johnstone as Palmer   Virginia Gregg as Dorothy
Written for *Cavalcade* by Henry Denker.
Produced and directed by Jack Zoller.
Tom Collins is the announcer and Gayne Whitman is the commercial spokesman.
Music composed and conducted by Robert Armbruster.
Story: Bob Corbin had a good job, a lovely wife, and a fine son - everything that a promising young man could ask for. Then, almost before he knew it - Bob had become an alcoholic. During a period of stress, he began to drink for relaxation. Suddenly realizing that the habit was governing his life, that he was neglecting his work and his family, he tried in vain to stop. His efforts were half-hearted until he became involved in an accident which threatened to stamp him as a hit-and-run driver as well as an alcoholic. In desperation, Bob turned to "Alcoholics Anonymous." Because of his desire to be cured, the members were able to lend him a helping hand. This is just one story of the many unfortunate people who suffer from "thirst without end." **(HLYD)**

Jack Zoller: "We once used Jimmy Cagney - but he happened to be just a little bit nervous. In fact, so nervous that he dropped a page of his script. Do you now what that means in a radio show? I'll never forget those few seconds of deadly silence! Then the young radio actress playing with him came right to his rescue, she just shoved her own script in front of his eyes and pointed to the right place with her finger. Meanwhile she reached down and scooped up the sheet he had dropped. That girl knew her business."

EPISODE #478 "THE UNSINKABLE MRS. BROWN" Broadcast on May 6, 1946
Starring: Helen Hayes as Molly Brown   Cameron Prud'Homme as Johnny
Based on the 1933 story of the same name from the book "Timberline" by Gene Fowler, and adapted for *Cavalcade* by David Lesan.
Produced and directed by Jack Zoller.
Ted Pearson is the commercial spokesman and Dwight Weist is the announcer.
Music composed by Ardon Cornwell and conducted by Donald Voorhees.
Story: Once upon a time, a young girl with red hair lived in a mining town in Colorado. She was poor and not too educated, but she was a charming person, and people though it a shame when she married a prospector who hadn't a dime. But after their marriage, her husband found a silver mine worth twenty-five million dollars! The little girl with red

hair was one of the richest women in America. She went from the mining shack to a mansion and on to the royal palaces of Europe. She had a beautiful singing voice and a knack for making friends. Her amazing life was filled with adventures and triumphs and tragedies, but she found her most exciting adventure amidst a shipwreck in the middle of the Atlantic Ocean. Her name was Molly Brown.

Trivia: The book on which this episode was based on, written by Gene Fowler, was later made into a Broadway musical entitled "The Unsinkable Molly Brown," and later a movie in 1964 with Debbie Reynolds in the lead.

EPISODE #479   **"STORM"**   Broadcast on May 13, 1946
   Starring: John Beal and Dane Clark
   Based on the 1941 book of the same name by George Stewart, and adapted for *Cavalcade* by Milton Wayne.
   Produced and directed by Jack Zoller.
   Ted Pearson is the commercial spokesman and Dwight Weist is the announcer.
   Music composed by Ardon Cornwell and conducted by Donald Voorhees.
   Story: Out of the desolate wastes of Siberia flowed a great river of frigid air. It swept down across the mountains and plains of China and out over the tossing waters of the Pacific. It moved smoothly and quickly ahead until suddenly the mass of cold air became a storm. Across thousands of miles of ocean it traveled, growing stronger and more powerful, until finally the headlines of California newspapers screamed "Rain Predicted!" On the Continent people waited, hoping and fearing. Although rain was desperately needed, no one dared foretell how much damage the storm might do, how many lives it might take as it tore across our Western plains. Then, the storm roared in from the ocean and struck the mountainous coast with tremendous power . . .

   Trivia: Louis Calhern was originally scheduled to play the role Dane Clark performed.

EPISODE #480   **"THE PETTICOAT JURY"**   Broadcast on May 20, 1946
   Starring: Jean Arthur as Miss Prescott   Robert Haag as Royce Emery
   Others in the cast included Jim Boles, Milton Herman, Wilda Hinkel, Ed Jerome, Ted Jewitt, Bess MacCammon, Ted Osborne, Cameron Prud'Homme, and Sidney Slon
   Written for *Cavalcade* by Joseph Cochran.
   Produced and directed by Jack Zoller.
   Ted Pearson is the commercial spokesman and Dwight Weist is the announcer.
   Music composed by Ardon Cornwell and conducted by Donald Voorhees.
   Story: When Miss Euphemia Prescott left Boston to teach school in the wide open spaces of the West, she was prepared for a different sort of life. She had heard much of the great new land of opportunity and she was prepared to live there and like it. But when she arrived at her new home, she was rudely shocked for it was a lawless community, when a man's rightness and worth were judged by his speed and accuracy with a six-shooter. Euphemia had lived all her life in staid and civilized nineteenth century Boston, and this new land confused and disgusted her. She decided to go back immediately, but something happened . . . and Miss Euphemia Prescott decided to stay on and bring law and order to the town, no matter how she had to do it.

   Trivia: *Cavalcade* brought Jean Arthur to the radio waves, in one of her rare radio performances.

EPISODE #481 **"SPIN A SILVER DOLLAR"** Broadcast on May 27, 1946
Starring: Carl Frank, Helen Hayes, Juano Hernandez, Wilda Hinkel, Cameron Prud'Homme, Sidney Slon, and Edith Tachna
Based on incidents from the book of the same name by Alberta Hannum, originally published by Viking Press in 1944. Adapted for *Cavalcade* by Robert Cenedella.
Produced and directed by Jack Zoller.
Ted Pearson is the commercial spokesman and Dwight Weist is the announcer.
Music composed by Ardon Cornwell and conducted by Donald Voorhees.
Story: The lives led by Bill and Sally Lipincott who operate "Wide Ruins," a Navajo trading post in Arizona.

Trivia: A romantic institution of the past, a symbol of Victorian luxury, elegance, and adventure entitled "The Old Fall River Line" was originally scheduled for this week. For reasons unknown, the script was not broadcast, and was shelved until September of the next season when it was finally dramatized on *Cavalcade of America*.

EPISODE #482 **"I GUESS IT'S HERE TO STAY"** Broadcast on June 3, 1946
Starring: Lois Volkman, Frank Behrens, Horace Braham, Edwin Bruce, Nancy Douglas, Ted Jewitt, Jack Manning, Cameron Prud'Homme, Everett Sloane, Sidney Slon, and Gladys Thornton
Written for *Cavalcade* by Arthur Arent.
Produced and directed by Jack Zoller.
Ted Pearson is the commercial spokesman and Dwight Weist is the announcer.
Music composed by Ardon Cornwell and conducted by Donald Voorhees.
Story: Historically, fifty years ago this week, the first horse-less carriage made its sputtering appearance in Detroit. Charles B. King's remarkable machine unleashed the fury of its 3 h.p. engine and attained the breathtaking speed of six miles per hour. This story takes us back to those early days of motoring. Because these victories were more often balky than not, many a motoring party returned to its starting point through the kindness of a farmer and his team. The old family doctor shook had head and proclaimed that the human body was never meant to travel at more than ten miles per hour. Against this nostalgic background of dusters and goggles, you'll capture the comedy and pathos, the courage and daring of these pioneers of the first motorcars fifty years ago.

EPISODE #483 **"MY FRESHMAN HUSBAND"** Broadcast on June 10, 1946
Starring: Geraldine Fitzgerald as Jane   Richard Widmark as Russ Spencer
Others in the cast included Lois Volkman, Jack Grimes, Alan Hewitt, Ed Jerome, Jack Manning, and Cameron Prud'Homme
Written for *Cavalcade* by Priscilla Kent.
Produced and directed by Jack Zoller.
Ted Pearson is the commercial spokesman and Dwight Weist is the announcer.
Music composed by Ardon Cornwell and conducted by Donald Voorhees.
Story: When young Russ Spencer returned home from the war, he found his life pretty complicated - what with a wife and a new baby and earning a living and all. It seemed like the best thing for him to do was to settle down in his old job and be happy with what he had. Then Jane decided that what he really should do was go to college on the G.I. Bill of Rights. There he could learn to be what he really wanted, a newspaper man. Russ was astounded. "Me! Go to college? I'm too old to be starting college. I'm twenty-five!" But Jane had her way, and off they went, to battle with insufficient money, tough studies, exams, the housing situation, and baby raising. It was a hectic Freshman year for Russ and Jane.

Trivia: Geraldine Fitzgerald appeared on this *Cavalcade* broadcast, compliments of her vacation. While she was in New York on a holiday, director Zoller inquired if she would be interested in interrupting her vacation to appear for the radio microphones. She accepted.

EPISODE #484   **"ALGERIAN ADVENTURE"**   Broadcast on June 17, 1946
Starring: George Murphy as Noah
Others in the cast included Ted Osborne, Dan Ocko, Milton Herman, Bob Dryden, Frank Behrens, Ed Jerome, and Rolf Sedan.
Written for *Cavalcade* by Russell Hughes.
Produced and directed by Jack Zoller.
Ted Pearson is the commercial spokesman and Dwight Weist is the announcer.
Music composed by Ardon Cornwell and conducted by Donald Voorhees.
Story: In 1812 the new United States of America, a struggling little nation with doubtful prestige among other countries, was at war with England, the most powerful nation in the world at that time. Many believed that our embryonic nation would be decisively beaten and she might well have been had not a few outstanding minds such as the young scholar, Noah, been put to task. When attacks by the Barbary Pirates in the Mediterranean became out of hand, Noah was sent to consul to Algiers. As U.S. representative of the court of one of the cruelest tyrants in Africa, he had neither ships nor men nor adequate money to back him up. But he had a calm, calculating, ingenious mind and had to rely solely on his wits to accomplish his mission - that of convincing the Beys of Tunis and Algiers of the value of American friendship and, in addition, freeing some of his countrymen from slavery.

EPISODE #485   **"THE CRUISE OF THE CASHLOT"**   Broadcast on June 24, 1946
Starring: Cameron Andrews, Ed Jerome, Adelaide Klein, Everett Sloane, Agnes Young
Based on a story from the 1934 book "Mostly Canallers" by Walter D. Edmonds, and adapted for *Cavalcade* by Priscilla Kent.
Produced and directed by Jack Zoller.
Ted Pearson is the commercial spokesman and Dwight Weist is the announcer.
Music composed by Ardon Cornwell and conducted by Donald Voorhees.
Starring: Back in the old days, there was a redoubtful sailor named Ben Meeker, or "Captain" Ben Meeker, as he preferred to be called because he was the owner and captain of a barge on the Erie Canal. Captain Ben liked to think of himself as a bold adventurer. He feared but one person, his wife Emmy. He would have had a lot more fun it hadn't been for Emmy who was always insisting that he do things the safe and sensible way. One day, Emmy had to leave the barge for a few days and Captain Ben and his assistant, Henry, were on their own. Immediately they became involved in an adventure as fantastic as it was funny. No one would have believed that the quiet Erie Canal had been the scene of such hilarious escapades, the least of which was Captain Ben's personal fight with a whale. . . one of the biggest fish stories ever told.

EPISODE #486   **"PASSPORT TO FREEDOM"**   Broadcast on August 26, 1946
Starring: Paul Lukas as Martin Slezan
Lucille Meredith as Maria
Barney Phillips as Joe Sampson
William Conrad as Mr. Cardwell
Frances Robinson as Helen
Sidney Miller as radio commentator two
Jack Kruschen as radio commentator one
William Johnstone as Conductor
Jack Lloyd as Stani
Sam Edwards as boy two

Jack Kruschen as the examiner
Earle Ross as Jan *and* Ben
Jerry Hausner as Newsy
Jack Lloyd as the candidate
Bernice Barrett as Diana
Sam Edwards as Fred
Irene Tedrow as Sophie
William Conrad as the man
Sidney Miller as boy one
George Sorel as the policeman

William Johnstone as the official Barney Phillips as policeman
Written for *Cavalcade* by Priscilla Kent.
Bud Hiestand is the commercial spokesman and Dwight Weist is the announcer.
Music composed and conducted by Robert Armbruster.
Story: When Martin Slezan came to the U.S. to visit, he was convinced that this country was a nation of slaves, where the workers had no rights, no freedoms, and almost no property. He was convinced that everything and everybody was run for the exclusive benefit of a few "Capitalistic Bosses," who grew rich while the masses of people starved. That was what he had been taught by the government propaganda in his own country. Naturally, he was startled when he began looking around. He found that the masses of people lived a greatly different life from what he had imagined. **(HLYD)**

EPISODE #487   "**WITH CRADLE AND CLOCK**"   Broadcast on September 2, 1946
Starring: Herbert Marshall as Dr. Jonathan Kent   Byron Kane as the servant
Mary Jane Croft as Margaret *and* the maid   Ira Groselle as the captain
Byron Kane as the husband   Eric Snowden as Bosun
Martha Wentworth as Grandma   Dorothy Scott as Hetje
Ramsey Hill as Lourens   Gloria Gordon as mother
Lurene Tuttle as Janet   Eric Snowden as the driver
Ken Peters as Bayard   Francis X. Bushman as the mayor
Based on the 1946 novel of the same name by Knud Stowman, and adapted for *Cavalcade* by Bernard Victor Dryer.
Produced and directed by Jack Zoller.
Gayne Whitman is the commercial spokesman and Bud Hiestand is the announcer.
Music composed and conducted by Robert Armbruster.
Story: In 1702 when New York was a small town and the populace easily scandalized, Dr. Johnathan Kent stepped off a ship from England and announced his intent to set up practice and to handle maternity cases! It was unheard of. Nobody but the midwives ever helped expectant mothers. The man must be mad. But Dr. Kent was determined. He himself had been an orphan because of the mistakes of a midwife had killed his mother. There were prejudices to fight and many disappointments to suffer but finally Dr. Kent had a chance to prove his skill. America gave the young doctor his opportunity as it has to so many. This is the life of America's first obstetrician. **(HLYD)**

Trivia: The role of the captain was played by a radio actor name Ira Groselle. . . which was actually an alias for film actor Jeff Chandler.

EPISODE #488   "**DANGER: WOMEN AT WORK**"   Broadcast on September 9, 1946
Starring: Fay Bainter as Josephine Clarke   Howard Duff as the narrator
Junius Matthews as Sam   Pinky Parker as Bill
June Foray as Mary Ann   Anne Whitfield as Katy
Tom Bernard as Tom   Horace Murphy as Sprague
Fred Howard as Edwards   Ken Christy as Collins
Pinky Parker as the counterman   Fred Howard as Registrar
William Conrad as Red   William Johnstone as Gus
Ken Christy as Mitchell   William Conrad as Lockwood
Virginia Gregg as Katy (age 25)   Virginia Gregg as Mrs. Palmer
Written for *Cavalcade* by Doris Frankel.
Produced and directed by Jack Zoller.
Gayne Whitman is the commercial spokesman and Bud Hiestand is the announcer.
Music composed and conducted by Robert Armbruster.
Story: This was a tribute to American truck drivers, and the story of a woman truck driver, Josephine Clark. She was one of the hundred of truck drivers who helped keep the empires and corporations of the country alive. **(HLYD)**

Trivia: June Foray's voice has been used in numerous radio and television programs, as well as movies. She supplied the voice for Rocky and Natasha on *The Bullwinkle Show*, and the green which in numerous Bugs Bunny cartoons. Remember the voice of the killer doll named "Talky Tina" on that one *Twilight Zone* episode?

More Trivia: Although Fay Bainter was scheduled to appear on this broadcast, the original script entitled "Cross Creek," based on Margaret Kinnan Rawling's book of the same title, was originally planned for dramatization. "Cross Creek" was scrapped and replaced with "Danger: Women at Work." Fay Bainter optioned for the different role.

EPISODE #489   "GENERAL BENJAMIN FRANKLIN"   Broadcast on September 16, 1946
  Starring: Charles Laughton as Benjamin Franklin   Joseph Kearns as Morris
  Kathleen Lockhart as Debby Franklin   Howard Duff as the soldier
  Raymond Lawrence as the Adjutant   Junius Matthews as the man
  Jay Novello as soldier two   George Zucco as Braddock
  Jay Novello as the secretary   Raymond Lawrence as the aide
  Howard Duff as the lieutenant   Junius Matthews as Beatty
  William Johnstone as McLaughlin
  Written for *Cavalcade* by Zachary Metz.
  Produced and directed by Jack Zoller.
  Gayne Whitman is the commercial spokesman and Bud Hiestand is the announcer.
  Music composed and conducted by Robert Armbruster.
  Story: In 1775 the bustling city of Philadelphia was the center of culture in the new world. Pressing close upon it was the Indian wilderness, a wilderness once subdued but now again teaming with danger. The French with their Indian allies had been pushing through the frontier. The red-coated regiments which the British King had sent to face the enemy had been vanquished. Such were the conditions in Philadelphia - and in the terrified countryside about it - when Dr. Benjamin Franklin, publisher, philosopher, scientist, statesman and honored prophet of the new age decided that now was no longer the time for mincing of words; it was a time for action.   **(HLYD)**

EPISODE #490   "THE OLD FALL RIVER LINE"   Broadcast on September 23, 1946
  Starring: Mary Jane Croft, Brian Donlevy, Carl Frank, Jerry Hausner, Bill Johnstone, Sidney Miller, Ken Peters, Clayton Post, Herbert Rawlinson, and Theodore Von Eltz
  Based on research made available through the courtesy of the Old Fall River Line for almost half a century. The script writer remains unknown.
  Produced and directed by Jack Zoller.
  Gayne Whitman is the commercial spokesman and Bud Hiestand is the announcer.
  Music composed and conducted by Robert Armbruster.
  Story: When our great grandfathers were boys, the railroads of America were symbols of speed, but the symbols of luxury and romance and commerce were the steamboats. The "floating palaces" of the Mississippi were famous throughout the nation. Running from Fall River, Mass., through Long Island Sound to New York, its great white ships made the overnight run from Boston and New York for almost a century. They were the last word in luxury, complete with velvet and silver, crystal and mahogany. Hundreds of canaries sang in the grand salon. To Americans everywhere these ships meant gaiety and adventure. And they meant progress, too, for they contributed much to building modern America.   **(HLYD)**

Trivia: This episode was scripted the season before, and was originally intended to be broadcast on May 27, 1946. It was pre-empted until the following season, now broadcast after all these months.

EPISODE #491 "ONE WAGON WESTWARD"   Broadcast on September 30, 1946
Starring: Skip Homeier as John Sager   Hugh Studebaker as Henry Sager
Leora Thatcher as Naomi Sager   Horace Murphy as Clem
Theodore Von Eltz as the doctor   Barbara Benton as Catherine
Tommy Bernard as Frank   Griff Barnett as Captain Shaw
Noreen Gammill as Mrs. Whitman   Theodore Von Eltz as Dr. Whitman
Written for *Cavalcade* by Ruth Woodman.
Produced and directed by Jack Zoller.
Gayne Whitman is the commercial spokesman and Bud Hiestand is the announcer.
Music composed and conducted by Robert Armbruster.
Story: A century ago America was a young nation expanding to the West as far as the Pacific Ocean. It was the time of the covered wagons, of courage and high adventure. Many episodes from those long Westward journeys are recounted today with pride, but few stories are as dramatic as that of little Johnny Sager. The Sager family, typical of the thousands of energetic Americans who built up the West, left Missouri to find a new home in Oregon and to help open a new land of opportunity for others. Death left the six children parent-less, but, led and inspired by young Johnny, they met disease and privation . . . and kept going. **(HLYD)**

EPISODE #492 "THAT THEY MIGHT LIVE"   Broadcast on October 7, 1946
Starring: Robert Young as Dr. Jackson   Jane Morgan as the mother
Ken Christy as Jim Tolan   Rosemary Kelly as Mrs. Harmon
Anne O'Neal as Mrs. Watkins   Maybelle Prindaville as Dr. Ellen Patterson
Based on the autobiography of Dr. Chevalier Jackson, originally published in 1938 by the MacMillan Company. Adapted for *Cavalcade* by Milton Wayne.
Produced and directed by Jack Zoller.
Gayne Whitman is the commercial spokesman and Bud Hiestand is the announcer.
Music composed and conducted by Robert Armbruster.
Story: The life of Dr. Chevalier Jackson and how his invention of the bronchoscope brought relief to thousands of suffering people. **(HLYD)**

Jack Zoller: "Most interest is generated by the medical subjects dramatized. The story of the man who invented the bronchoscope, in which the fact was stressed that a baby should never be allowed to play with anything smaller than its fist, resulted in many letters from mothers who wrote in appreciation of this warning."

EPISODE #493 "THE HICKORY TREE"   Broadcast on October 14, 1946
Starring: Agnes Moorehead as Elizabeth Jackson   Walter Tetley as Andrew Jackson
Conrad Binyon as Robbie   Bill Johnstone as MacPherson
Herb Butterfield as Colden   Hans Conried as Rawden
Gayne Whitman is the announcer.
Written for *Cavalcade* by Henry Walsh.
Produced and directed by Jack Zoller.
Gayne Whitman is the commercial spokesman and Bud Hiestand is the announcer.
Music composed and conducted by Robert Armbruster.
Story: The mother and her two sons were having supper when a knock came at the door. They seized their rifles, preparing to fight for their lives, for the Waxhaw country of North Carolina was a savage wilderness in 1779. Only shortly before they had fought off a band of marauders. Fortunately this time their visitor was a friend and, though welcomed by the widow and her sons, he brought news that started Elizabeth Jackson off on the greatest adventure of her life. Elizabeth started out on a dangerous mission on which she set an inspiring example of American courage, self-sacrifice and patriotism. **(HLYD)**

EPISODE #494 "MR. CONYNGHAM SWEEPS THE SEAS" Broadcast on October 21, 1946
    Starring: Douglas Fairbanks, Jr. as Gustavus Conyngham

Alec Harford as Ratcher	Carl Harbord as Borney
George Zucco as Allstyn	William Johnstone as Harding
Wally Maher as Brigg	Ramsey Hill as Neaulaire
Herb Rawlinson as the Mayor	Jay Novello as the agent
Frederick Worlock as the Admiral	Herb Rawlinson as the Sergeant
Ramsey Hill as the Warden	Jay Novello as the guard
Alec Harford as guard two	Carl Harbord as Williams

    Written for *Cavalcade* by Russell S. Hughes.
    Produced and directed by Jack Zoller.
    Gayne Whitman is the commercial spokesman and Bud Hiestand is the announcer.
    Music composed and conducted by Robert Armbruster.
    Story: The true events of how Gustavus Conyngham, American sailor during the Revolution, harassed and fought the entire mighty, British Navy with one patched-up, twelve-gun American vessel. **(HLYD)**

EPISODE #495 "FLYING TIGERS FLY AGAIN" Broadcast on October 28, 1946

Starring: George Murphy as Bob	Jerry Hausner as Catfish
William Johnstone as Link	Ken Peters as the messenger
Barney Phillips as Bart	Harry Lang as Rossie
Stan Waxman as the voice	Joe Du Val as Mosher
Adriene Marden as the waitress	Gavin Gordon as Tower
Ken Peters as Jorgensen	

    Written for *Cavalcade* by Daisy Amoury.
    Gayne Whitman is the announcer.
    Produced and directed by Jack Zoller.
    Gayne Whitman is the commercial spokesman and Bud Hiestand is the announcer.
    Music composed and conducted by Robert Armbruster.
    Story: When Joe and Duke and Bob were flying China skies as members of the famous crew, "Flying Tigers," they dreamed of going home to a business of their own. Instead of wanting to get back on the ground and stay there, they formulated plans for starting their own airline! Their buddies laughed at them. How could they raise that kind of money? Gravely, Joe offered to bet his limit that within a year after peace, these particular Flying Tigers would be flying again. His limit was a nickel. The "indomitable three" soon discovered that running their own airline was perhaps more peaceful than combat flying but not much easier. Having worked out the problem of securing financial backing, they were confronted next with the task of getting sufficient planes and crews . . . and business! **(HLYD)**

    Trivia: Bob Prescott, president and founder of The Flying Tigers appears in this broadcast.

EPISODE #496 "AN HONORABLE TITAN" Broadcast on November 4, 1946

Starring: Robert Young as Adolph Ochs	Griff Barnett as Wise
Herb Butterfield as MacGowan	Janet Scott as the woman
Frances Chaney as Effie	Ken Christy as the conductor
William Johnstone as Miller	Walter Tetley as the newsboy
Ken Christy as Trask	Griff Barnett as the alderman
William Johnstone as the man	Herb Butterfield as Wallach

    Based on the 1946 book of the same name by Gerald W. Johnson, and adapted for *Cavalcade* by Sylvia Berger.
    Produced and directed by Jack Zoller.
    Gayne Whitman is the commercial spokesman and Bud Hiestand is the announcer.

Music composed and conducted by Robert Armbruster.
Story: When the little office boy of the Knoxville "Chronicle" had his salary raised to the grand total of one dollar and a half a week, he was deliriously happy. He had made his first step up in the newspaper world. But few could have guessed at that time that the eleven-year-old boy would someday be one of the greatest and most honored publishers in the world. This is the story of Adolph Ochs who started publishing his first paper with a capital of twelve and a half dollars (and that borrowed) and who is, today, best known by the reputation of the paper he built to greatness - the "New York Times."

EPISODE #497   "COUNTRY LAWYER"   Broadcast on November 11, 1946
  Starring: Edward Arnold as the lawyer   Eddie Firestone, Jr. as David
  Herb Butterfield as Silas   Jane Morgan as Mrs. Haverstraw
  Anne O'Neal as Agatha   Myra Marsh as Mother
  Ken Christy as Johnson
Based on material from the 1939 book of the same name by Bellamy Partridge, and adapted for *Cavalcade* by Henry Denker.
Produced and directed by Jack Zoller.
Gayne Whitman is the commercial spokesman and Bud Hiestand is the announcer.
Music composed and conducted by Robert Armbruster.
Story: Mr. Adams, a shrewd small-town country lawyer, teaches his seventeen year old son the values and responsibilities of working his own law firm. Spending a few days with his father, Dave witnesses his father save a marriage, and prevent a con artist with getting away with a cruel scam to an old woman - and in the process, Mr. Adams teaches the con the true value of American justice. **(HLYD)**

Trivia: It seems that *Cavalcade* could not make up their mind of what to broadcast on this date. Their first intention was a story celebrating the hundredth anniversary of Thomas Alva Edison. After having already made a public announcement, *Cavalcade* decided to broadcast a drama entitled "Wings to Freedom," with John Hodiak in the lead. This second proposal was pre-empted (later broadcast as "Wings to Glory") and days before broadcast, "Country Lawyer" was presented.

EPISODE #498   "THE PINKERTON MAN"   Broadcast on November 18, 1946
  Starring: Lee Bowman as Pinkerton   Griff Barnett as Evans
  Wally Maher as Arthur   Lois Corbet as Holley
  William Johnstone as Collins   Sara Selby as Edna
  Pinky Parker as the storekeeper   Griff Barnett as man one
  Pinky Parker as man two
Written for *Cavalcade* by Russell S. Hughes.
Produced and directed by Jack Zoller.
Gayne Whitman is the commercial spokesman and Bud Hiestand is the announcer.
Music composed and conducted by Robert Armbruster.
Story: In 1850, Allan Pinkerton, an American detective, established one of the first detective agencies in the United States. He first won fame for exposing the activities of a band of counterfeiters. In 1861, Pinkerton guarded Abraham Lincoln as he journeyed from Springfield, Ill., to Washington D.C., to be inaugurated as President. His accomplishments also include smashing several Western gangs. His earliest "Wild West" case ended with the capture of the Reno brothers, a gang of train robbers. **(HLYD)**

Trivia: Wally Maher was accidentally credited as "Walter Maher" in this broadcast.

EPISODE #499 **"PARADE"** Broadcast on November 25, 1946
        Starring: Jean Hersholt as Peter Verek   Virginia Gregg as Alice
        Leora Thatcher as the Salvation Army Lassie   Jerry Mann as Clement
        Bob Bruce as the Salvation Army Captain   Bob Bruce as the voice
        Milton Herman as the drunkard   Jane Webb as the woman
        Jerry Hausner as Victor (age 21)   Jane Webb as Dorothy
        Tommy Bernard as Victor (as a boy)   Milton Herman as the Judge
        Written for *Cavalcade* by Priscilla Kent.
        Produced and directed by Jack Zoller.
Gayne Whitman is the commercial spokesman and Bud Hiestand is the announcer.
Music composed and conducted by Robert Armbruster.
Story: Peter Verek is not a famous man. Historically, he'll never be known as a patriot, a dreamer or a man of religion, but the qualities embodied in each were very much a part of his character. No biographer will ever immortalize him, yet the unassuming life of Peter Verek is rich with nobility and quiet dignity. There is a difference between greatness and fame. Thirty years ago, Peter came to America with a dream. He dreamed of a small white house - his symbol of happiness and security. Before long he married a pretty girl who helped him plan for the day when the house would become a reality. It wasn't easy to provide a living for his wife and children and still put aside money from his small wages. During an era that was dark with the shadows of two wars and a depression, Peter, like many another good American, worked hard to achieve his modest aim - a decent home for himself and his loved ones. **(HLYD)**

EPISODE #500 **"MOTHER OF FREEDOM"** Broadcast on December 2, 1946
        Starring: Ann Harding as Anna Zenger   William Conrad as John Zenger
        Joseph Kearns as Harrison   Stanley Waxman as Hamilton
        Francis X. Bushman as the Governor
Based on the 1946 book "Anna Zenger" by Kent Cooper, and adapted for *Cavalcade* by Philip Lewis.
Produced and directed by Jack Zoller.
Gayne Whitman is the commercial spokesman and Bud Hiestand is the announcer.
Music composed and conducted by Robert Armbruster.
Story: Anna Zenger, forsook the wealthy "acceptable" men of her world to marry an unschooled printer. One of the men she had scorned was Francis Harrison, urbane, power-mad adviser to the autocratic Governor of the colony. Harrison would stop at nothing to preserve the unassailable strength of his political position or bring to her knees the one woman who had ever dared to reject him. Despite her perilous position, Anna inspired her husband to greater skill in his trade and daring use of his talents. In a colony where the only newspaper was subservient to the wishes of the Governor, Anna and John Zenger raised a voice of protest against the injustices of their day. In doing so, they risked their lives and their happiness. **(HLYD)**

On the next page: Two advertisements to classic *Cavalcade* broadcasts.

Cavalcade of America

presents

JOSEPH COTTEN
and
CLAIRE TREVOR

in

"Build Me Straight"

**MONDAY EVENING
JANUARY 7, 1946**

NATIONAL BROADCASTING COMPANY
Coast to Coast Network

8.00-8.30 .... E.T. 8.30- 9.00 .... P.T.
7.00-7.30 .... C.T. 9.30-10.00 .... M.T.

Consult Your Local Radio Timetable

Originating from Hollywood

DU PONT Cavalcade of America

presents

HELEN HAYES

in

"The Unsinkable Mrs. Brown"

**MONDAY EVENING
MAY 6, 1946**

NATIONAL BROADCASTING COMPANY
Coast to Coast Network

Consult Your Local Radio Timetable

EPISODE #501 **"WINGS TO GLORY"** Broadcast on December 9, 1946
    Starring: John Hodiak as John   Herb Butterfield as Father
    Ken Christy as the grocer   Anne O'Neal as the gossipist
    Eddie Firestone, Jr. as Jim   Ken Christy as the doctor
    Dawn Bender as Jane
    Written for *Cavalcade* by Walter "Hank" Richards.
    Produced and directed by Jack Zoller.
    Bud Hiestand as the announcer and Gayne Whitman as the commercial spokesman.
    Music composed and conducted by Robert Armbruster.
    Story: Since man first looked above him and saw the birds in flight, he has dreamed of flying. Throughout the ages failure after failure seemed to prove that man was an earthbound creature. Then came a man with a thought which was, in 1883, very foolish. Because John Joseph Montgomery was the kind of American who didn't like the word "impossible," he firmly believed he could fly - not as other men had risen above the ground by inflating balloons with light gasses, but as a bird soars, with wings. His own sister, injuring her back in attempting to save his experiment, was told that would never walk again, and the blame was placed on "that fool" Montgomery. As a most ardent enthusiast, John's sister made a bargain with the young inventor. If he could fly, she could walk. **(HLYD)**

    Trivia: Originally entitled "Wings To Freedom," this episode was intended for broadcast back on November 11, 1946, with John Hodiak in the lead. Hodiak did manage to make the performance, at this later date.

EPISODE #502 **"THAT POWELL GIRL"** Broadcast on December 16, 1946
    Starring: Peggy Ann Garner as Maud Powell
    Also in the cast: Herb Butterfield, Tom Collins, Gloria Gordon and William Johnstone
    Written for *Cavalcade* by Lester Davis.
    Produced and directed by Jack Zoller.
    Bud Hiestand as the announcer and Gayne Whitman as the commercial spokesman.
    Music composed and conducted by Robert Armbruster.
    Story: The world of music in the late nineteenth century was still a man's world. In Aurora, Illinois a young girl's destiny was limited to the arts and crafts that became a young lady who would some day settle down to raise a family. For young Maud Powell, such plans for her future were a handicap. She knew she had the talent to become a great musical artist. As Maud progressed from piano to violin, from simple melodies to intricate concert compositions, her teachers and parents realized that there was more than mere skill in her playing. **(HLYD)**

    Trivia: The original title of this script was "A Little Singing - A Little Sewing."

EPISODE #503 **"THE DU PONT CHORUS"** Broadcast on December 23, 1946
    Under the direction of Daniel W. Boyer in a program of Christmas Carols.
    Bill H. Hamilton as the announcer and emcee.
    Broadcast from the stage of "The Playhouse" in Wilmington, Delaware.
    Accompanists are Virginia B. Williams and Eleanor B. Edge.
    Mr. Walter S. Carpenter, Jr., President of the Du Pont company spoke during intermission.

    On the next page: a reproduction of a cover from one of the Du Pont flyers that was handed out to the audience attending the broadcast. Inside the flyer were photos of the announcer, director, producer, and speech maker. A schedule of the songs sung was also listed inside. Lastly, a special Christmas message from Du Pont.

DU PONT CAVALCADE OF AMERICA

presents

The Du Pont Chorus

broadcasting from the

PLAYHOUSE THEATRE

MONDAY, DECEMBER 23, 1946

NATIONAL BROADCASTING COMPANY
COAST TO COAST NETWORK

8.00-8.30	E.T.	9.30-10.00	M.T.
7.00-7.30	C.T.	8.30- 9.00	P.T.

ORIGINATING IN WILMINGTON, DEL. - BROADCAST No. 503

BETTER THINGS FOR BETTER LIVING . . . THROUGH CHEMISTRY

Songs sung and performed in consecutive order: "Silent Night," "Deck the Halls," the French carol "Come With Torches," Miss Lois Kadel of the Wilmington Chemical Dept. sung a solo of "When the Crimson Sun," the 16th century French carol "Sing We Noel" arranged by Harvey Gaul, the Australian "As Lately We Watched" sung solo by Dr. Carl Sweitzer of the Experimental Station at Wilmington and arranged by Wayne Howorth, Nobel Cain's "De New Born Babe" sung by soloist Mr. J. Clark Gonzalez of the Chambers Works at Pennsgrove, New Jersey, the fourteenth century Latin composition "In Dulci Jubilo," "Joy to the World," F. Melius Christiansen's "Beautiful Savior" sung by soloist Miss Nettie Hitch of the Fabrics and Finishes Department, Alan Clifford of the Experimental Station sings a solo of Pietro A. Yon's "Gesu Bambino," and finally a reprise of "Silent Night."

Trivia: Before the on-air broadcast, the viewing audience attending the broadcast was treated with a three-song warm up by the chorus: Johann Sebastian Bach's "All Men Now Sing Rejoice," the folk-tune of Bohemia entitled "The Angels and Shepherds" arranged by Clarence Dickenson, and "The Carol of the Bells."

More Trivia: The Du Pont Chorus consisted of the following: Gladys Law, Ann Boles, Frances Edwards, Eleanor Edge, Elizabeth McDonough, Elizabeth Long, Dorothy Hanway, Elizabeth Klimuc, Kathryn Kane, Ruth McFarlane, Ruth Breslin, Evelyn Sparre, Jean Lee, Esther Garver, Ruth Phelps, Ruth Price, Marion Perse, Beverly Price, Sarah Freedman, June White, Margaret Cupp, Virginia Baureithel, Lois Kadel, Edith Churchman, Mildred Daub, Lucille Williams, Caroline Swetland, Doris Huck, Suzanne Myers, Elva Wells, Catherine Curren, Lois Foster, William Groundland, Carl Schweitzer, Richard Lindsey, Raymond Fisher, John Mitchell, H.W. Jacobson, Howard Berg, Paul Pinkney, Pauline Winter, Katherine Rupert, William Ulmer, Harry Eatough, John Ludlow, A.J. Hill, Jr, Benjamin Hurd, Eleanor Wells, H.W. Arnold, Frederick Johnston, R.K. Weaver, Esther Savage, Katherine Clements, John Henderson, John Gregg, Maurice Ward, Eugene Evers, Willis Brondyke, George Smith, R.A. Jackson, Mathilda Ernst, William -------y *, Kathryn Hutson, Carlotta Jester, Marguerite George, Mary Ellen Moore, Eunice Thawley, Lois Rineer, Virginia Williams, Olive Foraker, Mary Wolf, Mary Edna Sincock, Henrietta Trower, Doris Barlow, Verna Edmonds, Irene Smiley, Nettie Hitch, Emily Brown, Irene Feaster, Helen Pierce, Jean Beckerle, Margaret Hennis, Christine Cox, Dora Mae Way, Pearl Fox, Gertrude Berg, Regina Nixon, Ernestine Hays, May Curley, Anne Thomas, Melba Johns, Ellen Garcelon, Lillian McCall, Esther Evans, Rose Kracsun, Gertrude Hannigan, Veronica Chadick, Doria Nicholls, Jean Hollingsworth, Nell Coope, Evelyn Baird, Caroline R. Frazer, E. Lucille Manning, Julia Scout, Anne Burrows, Ann Lenderking, June Bramble, Margaret Feltz, Bernice Wilkinson, Cora Strother, Katherine Bigelow, M. Elizabeth Merritt, Betty Beyer, Eleanor Neumayer, Elizabeth Hackett, Esther McQuay, Evelyn Mcknik, Catherine Hauger, Francis E. Smith, Perc Morrow, Thomas Williams, Donald Swing, William Mooney, Aubrey Norton, Gordon Danielson, Adolph Friz, Paul B. Landing, W.J.P. Calder, John M. Thompson, T.F. Killheffer, J. Clark Gonzalez, Lynne Ulich, Harold Unruh, Carl Denison, James D. MacAlister, Donald Gerrish, Jacob Wantz, Eric Loges, David Gurton, J. Harold King, F.H. Brinley, Ralph Dorn, and Theodore Kuehn.

* author's note: I was unable to read the last name as the original document was damaged.

EPISODE #504 **"THE RAIN FAKERS"** Broadcast on December 30, 1946
    Starring: Burgess Meredith as Walter   Ted Jewitt as the Colonel
    Vicki Vola as Jane   Edgar Stehli as the Professor
    Cameron Prud'Homme as McDonald   Alan Hewitt as Brown
    Written for *Cavalcade* by Frank Gabrielson.
    Produced and directed by Jack Zoller.
    Ted Pearson is the announcer and Gayne Whitman is the commercial spokesman.
    Music composed by Ardon Cornwell and conducted by Donald Voorhees.
    Story: One summer not long ago, Walt, a local weatherman, could offer little hope of relief from a drought that was threatening the local crops. In desperation, the Farmer's Association decided to call in the "famous" Colonel Dazian. Even though Walt knew that Dazian was a fake, he had to admit that the Colonel had had remarkable success in other towns. With a spiel full of hocus pocus and an impressive array of cannon and "radio-magnetic" equipment, the Colonel claimed he could bring rain to the farmer's parched fields. The farm folk stood in awe of him and loudly denounced Walter for doubting the Colonel's claims. Even Walter's girl ignored him when he angrily censored their hero. Determined to expose Dazian, Walt used scientific knowledge, some smart deductive reasoning and not a little deception. In succeeding, he did far more than outwit another swindler.

    Trivia: The original title of this script was "Forecast for Tomorrow."

EPISODE #505 **"THE WOMAN ON LIME ROCK"** Broadcast on January 6, 1947
    Starring: Shirley Booth as Ida Lewis   Edgar Stehli as General Sherman
    Cameron Prud'Homme as Captain Lewis   Les Tremayne as Will Carver
    Richard Keith as the doctor   Agnes Young as Fannie
    Alan Hewitt as Jaquith
    Written for *Cavalcade* by Ruth Woodman.
    Produced and directed by Jack Zoller.
    Ted Pearson is the announcer and Gayne Whitman is the commercial announcer.
    Music composed by Ardon Cornwell and conducted by Donald Voorhees.
    Story: Captain Hosea Lewis planned on being a lighthouse keeper all his life. One day in the fall of 1858, his daughter, Ida, was summoned to the island to learn that her father would never be able to realize his ambition. Rather than relinquish their post, the two Lewises maintained their vigil over the Newport harbor, together. Hosea drew upon his years of experience and passed his wisdom on to his daughter. Her willing hands accomplished the tasks that his were unable to perform. At length, the role of lightkeeper fell to Ida alone. As the years passed, her unflagging devotion to her service brought fame and recognition, for Ida Lewis more than once displayed heroism in the face of danger and loyalty to the seafaring men who depended upon her for safe passage to port.

    Trivia: Shirley Booth is a well known and highly respected actress in New York theatrical and radio circles. On the stage, she has been seen in such productions as "Land's End," "Hollywood Pinafore," "Tomorrow the World" and "My Sister Eileen." She created the original Miss Duffy role heard on the popular *Duffy's Tavern* radio program.

EPISODE #506 "THE PRAIRIE BURNER" Broadcast on January 13, 1947
    Starring: Louis Allbritton as Mary   Ralph Bellamy as Cyrus Halliday
    Ted De Corsia as Coulter   Edwin Jerome as Windy
    Joseph Boland as Pete   Cameron Andrews as Jake
    Walter Kinsella as Mike   Ted Osborn as Cutplug
    Written for *Cavalcade* by Henry Walsh.
    Produced and directed by Jack Zoller.
Ted Pearson is the announcer and Gayne Whitman is the commercial spokesman. Music composed by Ardon Cornwell and composed by Donald Voorhees.
Story: In 1867, a young railroad engineer named Cyrus Halliday wanted to bring railroad service to a whole new section of the United States. He planned to link the already busy rail hub of Topeka, Kansas, with the growing center of Santa Fe, New Mexico. There were two problems confronting Cyrus. The first was money. He found it impossible to convince investors of the potentialities of the railroad line he proposed. The second problem was purely local. Sam Coulter was a powerful and unscrupulous cattleman embittered by one bout with the railroads in another part of the country. Although Sam would admit it only reluctantly, the railroad that he feared and fought proved its worth in a time of great need.

EPISODE #507 "BUILDER OF THE SOO" Broadcast on January 20, 1947
    Starring: William Holden as Charles Harvey   Marsha Hunt as Katie
    Bess McCameron as Mrs. Burroughs   Bob Dryden as Dr. Lash
    House Jameson as Moris   Cameron Prud'Homme as Ira
    Written for *Cavalcade* by Paul Peters.
    Produced and directed by Jack Zoller.
Ted Pearson is the announcer, and Gayne Whitman is the commercial announcer. Music composed by Ardon Cornwell and conducted by Donald Voorhees.
Story: In 1852, Charles Harvey, a traveling salesman, arrived at Sault Ste. Marie, Michigan, with an idea concerning a canal. Here, on the shores of Lake Superior, iron ore and copper had been discovered in great quantity, but bulk transportation by ships was impossible between this rich source and the factories a thousand miles to the east because of a single mile of unnavigable river rapids. In the sparsely settled frontier town, Harvey found that few people held any hope for a canal through the isthmus to open up the potentialities of the Great Lakes area. A girl named Katie Bingham was the only person who encouraged Harvey's interest and growing enthusiasm for the project. Though experts claimed it would take at least ten years to build the "Soo" Canal, the young salesman requested permission from the Michigan State University to undertake construction of a waterway in just 2 years. In order to accomplish this task, Harvey and Katie relied on a last-minute improvisation that defied traditional engineering methods.

EPISODE #508 "A CHANCE FOR JIMMY" Broadcast on January 27, 1947
    Starring: Basil Rathbone as Dr. Bacon   David Anderson as Jimmie
    Carl Frank as Jimmie's father   Alice Youngman as Jimmie's mother
    House Jameson as doctor one   Clyde North as doctor two
    Alan Hewitt as doctor three
    Written for *Cavalcade* by Erik Barnouw.
    Produced and directed by Jack Zoller.
Ted Pearson is the announcer and Gayne Whitman is the commercial announcer. Music composed by Ardon Cornwell and conducted by Donald Voorhees.
Story: Typhlitis. Eighty years before, this word struck fear into the heart of many a parent with a sick child. Doctors did their best with the little knowledge they had, but generally all attempts at treatment failed. During the Civil War, a young doctor in Boston named Francis Henry Brown came to realize this fact in the course of the many examinations he made of recruits for the Union Army. He determined to devote his life's

work to the health of the young. As his work progressed, Brown became increasingly dissatisfied with the diagnosis and treatment of many children's ills, particularly typhlitis. To better study and treat sick children, Brown established a children's hospital in Boston, the first of its kind in this country.

Trivia: Basil Rathbone was also the star of a radio program, *Scotland Yard's Inspector Burke*, which was broadcast on the same evening as *Cavalcade*. This prompted Rathbone to leap from one stage to another studio throughout the evening.

More trivia: The title of this script was originally "The Children's Hospital."

EPISODE #509 **"THE MAGNIFICENT FAILURE"** Broadcast on February 3, 1947
   Starring: Burgess Meredith as Josiah White   Alice Reinhart as Elizabeth
   Martin Wolfson as Danvers   Charles Penman as Smith
   Cameron Andrews as Jake   Alan Hewitt as Howell
   Based on the 1946 book "Josiah White" by Eleanor Morton, and adapted for *Cavalcade* by Philip Lewis.
   Produced and directed by Jack Zoller.
   Ted Pearson is the announcer, and Gayne Whitman is the commercial announcer.
   Music composed by Ardon Cornwell and conducted by Donald Voorhees.
   Story: At the end of the eighteenth century, America had just completed a bitter struggle for freedom from European governments. Politically, we were independent, but because ours was primarily an agricultural nation, we found ourselves still inextricably bound to our former rulers . . . economically. One Josiah White felt so keenly about this defect in our system that his quick brain was ever imagining new ways of doing things. Unfortunately, plan after plan of his fell short of success and he came to be known as a "fool." Josiah realized that nearly every one of his failures could be blamed on the absence of good, cheap fuel. Wood was fine for kitchen stoves but industry needed something that would burn at a higher temperature and cost less than English coal. At last Josiah decided to utilize a "black stone" that he knew was better in all ways than what was then being imported.

EPISODE #510 **"THE VOICE OF THE WIZARD"** Broadcast on February 10, 1947
   Starring: Dane Clark as Thomas Edison   Donna Reed as Mary
   Alan Hewitt as the manager   Bob Dryden as Kruesi
   Jack Manning as Fred   John Sylvester as George
   Chester Stratton as the reporter
   Written for *Cavalcade* by Erik Barnouw.
   Produced and directed by Jack Zoller.
   Ted Pearson is the announcer and Gayne Whitman is the commercial spokesman.
   Music composed by Ardon Cornwell and conducted by Donald Voorhees.
   Story: Mr. Gridley was furious. When he came into his telegraph office, he found that young Tom Edison was loafing on the job, eating sandwiches and reading a volume of the encyclopedia marked "Egg to Fub." What's more, his work was being done by a machine! Naturally, Mr. Gridley fired Edison. But young Edison was due to surprise a great many more people before he was through. His machines that talked and pictures that moved opened up whole new worlds for millions of people. More important, he brought the people of different nations closer together and his contributions to the art of communication made tremendous changes in the lives of the whole human race.

   Trivia: *Cavalcade* commemorates the 100th anniversary of Thomas Edison's birth with this broadcast. Mickey Rooney was originally scheduled to star in the lead role of Edison.

EPISODE #511 "MAN AGAINST THE MOUNTAIN"   Broadcast on February 17, 1947
    Starring: Chester Morris as Gustave Marsh   William Johnstone as Tom
    Virginia Gregg as Elizabeth   Martha Wentworth as Aunt Hitty
    Barney Phillips as Oscar   Byron Kane as Bert
    Byron Kane as the voice one   Victor Rodman as Abbott
    Dick Ryan as Luis   Dick Ryan as Campbell
    Jerry Hausner as voice two
    Written for *Cavalcade* by Ruth Woodman.
    Produced and directed by Jack Zoller.
    Bud Hiestand is the announcer and Gayne Whitman is the commercial spokesman.
    Music composed and conducted by Robert Armbruster.
    Story: In 1903, Lone Pine, California was an obscure town nestled close to the base of Mount Whitney, the highest mountain in the United States. Gustave Marsh, one of the inhabitants of Lone Pine, had looked up at Whitney's eastern slope for many years and each time felt that the greatness of this mountain was being wasted. There, he thought, on the summit was an ideal site for an observatory. Its great height would allow an astronomer to study the stars and planets unhampered by low-lying clouds or the generally murky sea-level atmosphere. Gustave knew the hardships involved in realizing such an ambition - blazing a trail up the yet untravelled eastern slope, constructing the trail itself and finally, contacting a group of scientists with an interest in his plan. But he was confident it could be done. **(HLYD)**

EPISODE #512 "ABIGAIL OPENS THE WHITE HOUSE"   Broadcast on February 24, 1947
    Starring: John McIntire, and Ida Lupino as Abigail Adams
    Written for *Cavalcade* by Priscilla Kent.
    Produced and directed by Jack Zoller.
    Bud Hiestand is the announcer and Gayne Whitman is the commercial spokesman.
    Music composed and conducted by Robert Armbruster.
    The song "Rallying 'Round Our Liberty" was featured.
    Story: When George Washington declined to run for a third term, his place at the head of our nation was taken by John Adams. Adams found that this infant country had little faith in his administration. His severest critic was the brilliant and popular Alexander Hamilton, the man who voiced a demand for war when Adams received an insulting ultimatum from the French government. Abigail Adams knew the difficulties her husband faced and determined to spare him every needless worry. It was Abigail who convinced Adams that peace with the French was worth at least one more diplomatic gesture. This is the story of Abigail Adams, wife of our second President and mother of our sixth, a unique woman in American history. **(HLYD)**

EPISODE #513 "MR. PULLMAN'S PALACE CAR"   Broadcast on March 3, 1947
    Starring: Robert Young as George M. Pullman   William Johnstone as Aldrich
    Fred Howard as Rainey   Georgia Backus as Mrs. Aldrich
    John McIntire as Williams   Jeanette Nolan as Mrs. Edwards
    Written for *Cavalcade* by Paul Peters.
    Produced and directed by Jack Zoller.
    Bud Hiestand is the announcer and Gayne Whitman is the commercial spokesman.
    Music composed and conducted by Robert Armbruster.
    Story: Back in 1855, a few railroads could offer you the comforts of a "sleeping car." For fifty cents, you could stretch out on a bare wooden plank for a night's rest. You didn't even have to take your boots off. Most travelers preferred to suffer sitting up on the hard benches of the regular coaches. Then along came George Mortimer Pullman with the astounding idea that proper accommodations could make train travel actually enjoyable. He presented rough sketches of his new type of railroad car to Joel Aldrich, president of the Chicago and Alton Railroad. Aldrich let Pullman borrow his master car

builder, Shield Williams, and encouraged the use of one of his old sheds as their workshop. When the special car was finished it was, indeed, the height of luxury with its plush seats, upper and lower berths, washrooms and of all wonders - sheets on the beds! **(HLYD)**

EPISODE #514 **"THE STIRRING BLOOD"** Broadcast on March 10, 1947
    Starring: Lee Bowman as Dave Evans   Una Merkel as Opal
    Ken Christy as the editor   Herb Butterfield as Dr. Karl Landsteiner
    Jerry Hausner as Robert   Bob Bailey as Alexander Wiener
    Hugh Thomas as Gordon   Stan Waxman as Levine
    Ann Tobin as the nurse
Written for *Cavalcade* by Sigmund Miller and Halsted Welles.
Produced and directed by Jack Zoller.
Bud Hiestand is the announcer and Gayne Whitman is the commercial spokesman.
Music composed and conducted by Robert Armbruster.
Story: In 1900, blood was blood. If a doctor called for a transfusion, the patient received blood from the most convenient donor. Occasionally, a transfusion didn't "take" and the patient died. Strangely enough, the same donor's blood would save one man one day and kill another the next. Dr. Karl Landsteiner was determined to discover the reason for this mysterious behavior of blood. But it soon became apparent that even his great step forward had not made the transfusion one hundred percent reliable. . . Alexander Wiener noted that even though transfusions were being administered according to Landsteiner's recommendations, there were still rare cases where repeated transfusions were dangerous. These two men combined their findings to learn yet another fact about blood that would help prevent unnecessary deaths. **(HLYD)**

Trivia: This broadcast, dramatizing the story of the discovery of the mysterious Rh factor in human blood, received the largest amount of requests from listeners during this season, asking for a repeat performance. Their requests were granted a few months later.

EPISODE #515 **"THE MAN WITH GREEN FINGERS"** Broadcast on March 17, 1947
    Starring: Lionel Barrymore as Luther Burbank   Henry Blair as Tad
    Constance Crowder as Mrs. Brenner   Joseph Kearns as Williams
    Herb Butterfield as George   Nanette Valar as the woman
    Francis X. Bushman as the Judge   Joseph Kearns as the man
    Bob Bailey as the conductor   Bob Bailey as Tad (age 41)
    Janet Scott as Merle
Written for *Cavalcade* by Russell S. Hughes.
Produced and directed by Jack Zoller.
Bud Hiestand is the announcer and Gayne Whitman is the commercial spokesman.
Music composed and conducted by Robert Armbruster.
Story: Around the turn of the century, a small boy named Tad wandered into one of the most wonderful gardens in all California and stood, transfixed, as he watched and listened to the owner, Luther Burbank. Slowly, Tad learned that Luther had published a catalog to tell the world about the new plants he had developed and that something the plant wizard had said in that catalog had caused many people to turn against him. Distrusted and shunned, Burbank was prepared to leave the garden - following a failure at a public meeting. Just when it appeared that this horticultural genius was about to meet physical violence from his own townspeople, he made a discovery about human nature that meant as much to him as any successful experiment with plants. **(HLYD)**

Trivia: Actor, artist and composer, Barrymore was also something of a horticulturist himself and had raised prize winning Indian corn and sub-tropical plants in his garden.

Story: Around the turn of the century, a small boy named Tad wandered into one of the most wonderful gardens in all California and stood, transfixed, as he watched and listened to the owner, Luther Burbank. Slowly, Tad learned that Luther had published a catalog to tell the world about the new plants he had developed and that something the plant wizard had said in that catalog had caused many people to turn against him. Distrusted and shunned, Burbank was prepared to leave the garden - following a failure at a public meeting. Just when it appeared that this horticultural genius was about to meet physical violence from his own townspeople, he made a discovery about human nature that meant as much to him as any successful experiment with plants. **(HLYD)**

Trivia: Actor, artist and composer, Barrymore was also something of a horticulturist himself and had raised prize winning Indian corn and sub-tropical plants in his garden.

EPISODE #516 **"THE MAN WHO STEPPED ASIDE"** Broadcast on March 24, 1947
    Starring: Thomas Mitchell as William Seward   John McIntire as Abe Lincoln
    Written for *Cavalcade* by Philo Higley.
    Produced and directed by Jack Zoller.
    Bud Hiestand is the announcer and Gayne Whitman is the commercial spokesman.
    Music composed and conducted by Robert Armbruster.
    Story: When President Lincoln took office, he called upon William Seward to serve as Secretary of State. Seward had been generally considered the most likely presidential candidate before the Chicago convention had nominated Lincoln. In the stormy months preceding the Civil War, there was a marked lack of unity in the Lincoln Cabinet. The Secretary of State was reputed to hold sway over Lincoln and control his major decisions, and it was no secret that Seward disagreed violently with many of the President's policies. Suddenly, the seceding states made a clever political overture towards Great Britain. Seward planned to oppose their strategy with strong action, but Lincoln had an entirely different approach to the situation. The lack of agreement between these two powerful men not only threatened to delay the end of the war between the states but it menaced also our hard-won international position. **(HLYD)**

EPISODE #517 **"KANSAS MARSHALL"** Broadcast on March 31, 1947
    Starring: Henry Fonda as Wyatt Earp   Jerry Hausner as Billy
    John McIntire as Peshaur   Herb Butterfield as the Mayor
    Horace Murphy played a minor role as well.
    Based on the book "Frontier Marshal" by Stewart N. Lake, and adapted for *Cavalcade* by Maurey Robinson and Russell S. Hughes.
    Produced and directed by Jack Zoller.
    Bud Hiestand is the announcer and Gayne Whitman is the commercial spokesman.
    Music composed and conducted by Robert Armbruster.
    Ozie Waters was the singing cowboy.
    Story: When men asked Wyatt Earp what his name was, they often laughed at his answer. They would remark, "What's the matter, Mister? Got the hiccups?" But when this quiet, cool-eyed man with the odd name drew out his six-shooter, they stopped laughing. Even the most hard-bitten criminal of the lawless western frontier respected Wyatt. Marksmanship alone did not qualify a man for the perilous job of town marshall back in the 1870's. It took courage and continuous devotion to an unpleasant duty. In Tombstone, Arizona, Wyatt met a problem that called for more than courage, more than skill, and more than his fanatic devotion to duty. He discovered that truly civilized community conditions can not be maintained by a single man and his guns. **(HLYD)**

Trivia: In 1939, Randolph Scott starred as Wyatt Earp in the film "Frontier Marshall," based on the book of the same name by Stewart N. Lake. It was this same book that was used for the basis of this radio script. During the week of this broadcast, Henry Fonda

EPISODE #518   "THE SKIPPER FROM STONINGTON"   Broadcast on April 7, 1947
   Starring: Dana Andrews as Richard Loper   Anita Louise as Mardie
   Norman Field as Tam   Gloria Gordon as Mrs. Spooner
   Stan Waxman as Marcy
   Adapted for *Cavalcade* by Stuart Hawkins, based on the 1946 book of the same name.
   Produced and directed by Jack Zoller.
   Bud Hiestand is the announcer and Gayne Whitman is the commercial spokesman.
   Music composed and conducted by Robert Armbruster.
   Story: The life of Richard Loper, the ship builder and sea captain who designed the first wooden ship with iron braces. At a critical period in American history, Loper never had the chance to go whaling, but his name will live on in history as a great ship builder. **(HLYD)**

EPISODE #519   "THE PEANUT VENDOR"   Broadcast on April 14, 1947
   Starring: Don Ameche as Amadeo Obici   Jay Novello as Mario
   Norma Kendall as Louise   Bobby Santon as young Amadeo
   Herb Butterfield as John Hance   Milton Herman as Billy
   Written for *Cavalcade* by Priscilla Kent.
   Produced and directed by Jack Zoller.
   Bud Hiestand is the announcer and Gayne Whitman is the commercial spokesman.
   Music composed and conducted by Robert Armbruster.
   Story: Amadeo Obici was hungry. On the last lap of a long journey from his native Italy to Pennsylvania, where his uncle awaited him, a kindly station-master gave the boy some peanuts. Amadeo never forgot how good they tasted. In fact, it wasn't long after he'd made his home with his uncle that he decided to roast and sell peanuts for a living. He soon discovered that he had a competitor named Louise. Amadeo ended the rivalry by forming a partnership, and Mr. and Mrs. Obici became famous in Wilkes-Barre for their high business standards. But the little business had a rocky road. In order to expand their plant and improve their purchasing and marketing methods, they approached a southern banker for a large loan. . . which has become a nation-wide business which we know today as Planter's Peanuts. **(HLYD)**

   Trivia: Don Ameche was currently heard on his own radio program, *Drene*. The Du Pont Company took the opportunity after the broadcast to acknowledge nationally that station KFI in Los Angeles was celebrating it's 25th anniversary.

EPISODE #520   "THE DOCTOR AND THE PRESIDENT"   Broadcast on April 21, 1947
   Starring: Douglas Fairbanks, Jr. as Dr. Waterhouse
   Maureen O'Sullivan as Eliza   George Zucco as Uncle
   William Johnstone as President Jefferson Henry Blair as Danny
   Written for *Cavalcade* by Robert Wallsten, dramatized with the cooperation of Princeton University Press which was publishing "The Papers of Thomas Jefferson" under a grant from *The New York Times*.
   Produced and directed by Jack Zoller.
   Bud Hiestand is the announcer and Gayne Whitman is the commercial spokesman.
   Music composed and conducted by Robert Armbruster.
   Story: We of the 20th Century have never seen the scourge of smallpox sweep through our land. Dr. Benjamin Waterhouse did have to witness these tragic occurrences. Worse, he had to stand by helplessly, knowing all the while that he had the knowledge and technique that could stamp out this plague. Held powerless by both his townspeople and the medical profession itself, Dr. Waterhouse turned his sights to Washington D.C. In the hopes of finding a man of action to whom people would listen, he called on Thomas Jefferson. He found our president not only willing and able to assist him, but also ready with a scientific plan of his own for proving Waterhouse's method. **(HLYD)**

EPISODE #521 "**FRONTIER WIDOW**"   Broadcast on April 28, 1947
Starring: Anne Baxter as Ann Robertson   John McIntire as John Cockrill
Horace Murphy as Lem   William Johnstone as the Captain
Nanette Vallon as the woman   William Johnstone as Thomas
Ed Max as the Indian Chief
Written for *Cavalcade* by Agnes Eckhardt and Priscilla Kent.
Produced and directed by Jack Zoller.
Bud Hiestand is the announcer and Gayne Whitman is the commercial spokesman.
Music composed and conducted by Robert Armbruster.
Story: When Ann Robertson's husband was killed by the Indians, she and her three young daughters joined a small pioneer band that was preparing to leave Fort Caswell for the Cumberland Bluffs in the Territory of Tennessee. She felt certain she could earn her place with the settlers by teaching their children and helping the other women, but she had to reckon with John Cockrill. As one of the leaders of the expedition, he did not believe that pioneer settlements needed education or that a widow with children should undertake such a dangerous journey. A surprise Indian attack gave Ann a chance to prove she was more of a help than a hindrance to the colony. **(HLYD)**

Trivia: This drama was originally scheduled for an April 14 broadcast.

EPISODE #522   "**THE SCHOOL FOR MEN**"   Broadcast on May 5, 1947
Starring: Gregory Peck as Jim Davenport   Bob Bailey as Jerry
Betty Lou Gerson as Agnes
Others in the cast included: Ken Christy, Virginia Gregg, Elliott Reid, Frances Heffin and Peggy Webber.
Written for *Cavalcade* by Philip Lewis.
Produced and directed by Jack Zoller.
Bud Hiestand is the announcer and Gayne Whitman is the commercial spokesman.
Music composed and conducted by Robert Armbruster.
Story: Young Jerry Davenport knew all about the FBI and had a certain amount of respect for their wonderful record, but he felt quite certain that test tubes and microscopes would never replace a well-founded reputation for sheer courage. Jerry's brother, Jim, was also a policeman who believed that bravery was essential. He believed, too, in the knowledge taught him by the FBI school he had attended in Washington D.C. The course had proved to him that a school-trained guardian of the law stood a better chance of seeing a criminal to justice than a policeman who learned his job the hard way. Jim had a chance to help his brother and prove his point when a local murder had the police force baffled. With the willingness cooperation of FBI headquarters the ruthless murderer was finally trapped by a thread and a pocket knife. **(HLYD)**

Trivia: For this date, *Cavalcade* originally intended to dramatize the story of Gifford Pinchot, one of America's most avid soil conservationists. The drama was entitled "Man of the Forest," and a little more than a week before this date, the script was put aside and inadvertently never broadcast.

EPISODE #523   "**PAGE ONE**"   Broadcast on May 12, 1947
Starring: John Hodiak as Joseph Pulitzer   Jack Kruschen as Udo
Written for *Cavalcade* by Charles K. Freeman.
Produced and directed by Jack Zoller.
Bud Hiestand is the announcer and Gayne Whitman is the commercial spokesman.
Music composed and conducted by Robert Armbruster.
Story: A year after he had joined Lincoln's forces because he believed that his newly-adopted country was in danger, young Joseph Pulitzer found himself out of the army and

without a job. In this state he was an ideal target for an opportunist who promised him employment, collected five dollars to "cover transportation," and disappeared. Pulitzer's description of the swindle to a newspaper reporter was so lucid, so detailed and so well-phrased that he was encouraged to write the story himself. The article helped Pulitzer to become a staff writer for the paper and thereafter, his rise in the newspaper world was a rapid one. **(HLYD)**

EPISODE #524   "WITNESS BY MOONLIGHT"   Broadcast on May 19, 1947
  Starring: Joseph Cotten as Abe Lincoln   Ted Osborn as Watkins
  Earl George as Fullerton   Bob Dryden as Allen
  Irene Hubbard as Aunt Hannah   House Jameson as the Judge
  Lawson Zerbe as Duff   Bob Haag as Billy
  George Petrie as Johnson
  Written for *Cavalcade* by Henry W. Denker, based on a story in *The Lincoln Reader* by Paul M. Angle, published by the Rutgers University Press.
  Produced and directed by Jack Zoller.
  Bill H. Hamilton is the announcer and Gayne Whitman is the commercial spokesman.
  Music composed by Ardon Cornwell and conducted by Donald Bryan.
  Story: Lincoln and Herndon, attorneys-at-law, in closing their ledgers, were puzzled by an item, "one book - fifty cents." Then the lawyer who was about to become president recalled the expenditure. It had, indeed, been a small price to pay for a life . . . In defending young Duff Armstrong against a framed murder charge, Lincoln learned that the prosecution was hinging everything upon the testimony of one witness who claimed he had seen the victim murdered and that he possessed the weapon Armstong had used. Shrewdly, Lincoln proceeded to attack the witness's story, producing finally his "trump card" - the fifty-cent book.

  Trivia: This *Cavalcade* performance originated from Newark, New Jersey. In the studio audience in the Mosque Theatre in Newark as special guests were Du Pont men and women from eight Du Pont plants in modern New Jersey.

EPISODE #525   "UNDER THE BIG TOP"   Broadcast on May 26, 1947
  Starring: Robert Young as John E. Kenna
  Others in the cast included: Roy Atwell, Bob Dryden, Sarah Fussell, Richard Hogue, Frank Milano, Neil O'Mally, Nancy Sheridan and William Wyatt
  Written for *Cavalcade* by Erik Barnouw.
  Produced and directed by Jack Zoller.
  Bill H. Hamilton is the announcer and Gayne Whitman is the commercial spokesman.
  Music performed by The Charleston Symphony Orchestra, conducted by Antonio Modarelli.
  Story: Congressman John Kenna discovered, much to his dismay, that not many others shared his belief that Charleston should be made the capitol of West Virginia. Wherever he campaigned, he found that other speakers championing other cities had preceded him. But his worst competition was a circus which seemed to travel on his heels and drew his springtime audiences from him as the "Pied Piper." Then the tide turned. Kenna and Lolow, a circus clown whom he met, combined their talents in a hair-raising, death-defying act that brought the voters to the polls in swarms and wrote a fascinating chapter in the history of one of our greatest states.

  Trivia: Nancy Kenna Morton, the granddaughter of Congressman Kenna appears in the drama, which was broadcast from Charleston, West Virginia. In the studio audience as special guests were more than 3,500 Du Pont Men and Women, employees from neighboring plants.

EPISODE #526 "THE STIRRING BLOOD"   Broadcast on June 2, 1947
    Starring: Lee Bowman as Dave Evans   Una Merkel as Opal
    Ken Christy as the editor   Jerry Hausner as Robert
    Herb Butterfield as Landsteiner   Elliott Reid as Wiener
    Hugh Thomas as Gordon   Stan Waxman as Levine
    Ann Tobin as the nurse   Howard McNear as Stetson
    Written for *Cavalcade* by Sigmund Miller and Halsted Welles.
    Produced and directed by Jack Zoller.
    Bud Hiestand is the announcer and Gayne Whitman is the commercial spokesman.
    Music composed and conducted by Robert Armbruster.
    Story: Same as episode #514, broadcast on March 10, 1947. **(HLYD)**

    Trivia: Because of the unusual interest in the dramatic story of the discovery of the mysterious Rh factor in human blood, as evidenced by the many requests received from listeners [which held the record this season], *Cavalcade* decided to repeat the drama.

EPISODE #527 "A LADY OF DISTINCTION"   Broadcast on June 9, 1947
    Starring: Ida Lupino as M. Carey Thomas   Jeanette Nolan as the mother
    Norman Field as the father   Peg La Centra as Anna
    Howard McNear as Mr. Rockefeller
    Others in the cast included: Stanley Farrar, Junius Matthews, Jack Kruschen, David Ellis, and Edith Tachna.
    Written for *Cavalcade* by Doris Frankel.
    Produced and directed by Jack Zoller.
    Bud Hiestand is the announcer and Gayne Whitman is the commercial spokesman.
    Music composed and conducted by Robert Armbruster.
    Story: Even at the romantic age of eighteen, lovely Carey Thomas was not preoccupied with thoughts of marriage and a home. Instead, she was far more interested in proving that the woman of 1877 had a mind as good as any man's. She enrolled as the first woman student at Johns Hopkins University, but she soon discovered that several of the faculty did not welcome a woman in their classes and, what was worse, did not consider her eligible for a degree. Determined to continue her studies, she went to Europe and later returned home with academic honors that far exceeded her own expectations.
    M. Carey Thomas had won her case. **(HLYD)**

EPISODE #528 "WOMAN ALONE"   Broadcast on June 16, 1947
    Starring: Virginia Bruce as Alice Evans
    Also in the cast: Herb Butterfield, Fred Howard, Eddie Marr, Sidney Miller, Howard Smith, Helen Spring, Luis Van Rooten, and Nanette Vallon.
    Written for *Cavalcade* by Bernard Victor Dryer.
    Produced and directed by Jack Zoller.
    Gayne Whitman was the commercial spokesman and Bud Hiestand was the announcer.
    Music composed and conducted by Robert Armbruster.
    Story: When Alice Evans was a young girl on her father's farm, she saw a heifer lose her calf before her time. The same night, a neighboring wife lost her baby in the same manner. Years later, when Alice became a bacteriologist in a government laboratory, she began to believe that the two deaths she had witnessed earlier were more than coincidental. Further study revealed a marked similarity between the germs that killed the calf and germs that sometimes caused undulant fever in human beings. Alice prepared a scientific paper which she presented before the Society of American Bacteriologists, but found the results of her research received little attention. Few doctors and few dairies would accept such untested evidence. Directly challenged by a famous scientist, Alice determined to prove her theory by an unusual method. The work of years depended upon one experiment . . . **(HLYD)**

Trivia: Jane Wyman was originally scheduled to star in this broadcast, but unfortunately, had to back out of her commitment. Virginia Bruce substituted.

EPISODE #529   **"THE IRON HORSE"**   Broadcast on August 18, 1947
Starring: Robert Young as Peter Cooper   Walter Brennan as Harris
Cast #1: Joseph Bell, Barbara Eiler, Jerry Hausner and Peggy Webber
Cast #2: William Johnstone, Tish Payne, Sarah Jane Wells, Francis X. Bushman
Written for *Cavalcade* by Erik Barnouw.
Produced and directed by Jack Zoller.
Frank Bingman is the announcer and Gayne Whitman is the commercial spokesman.
Music composed and conducted by Robert Armbruster.
Story: Peter Cooper experiments with the steam engine and makes the railroad practical. The famous race of the "Tom Thumb" is dramatized. Cooper's experimental steam engine made it possible for the completion of the Erie Canal.   **(HLYD)**

What the -? The cast for this episode is not for certain. Although a few of the voices on the actual recording of this broadcast match a couple of names listed above, there is incoherent information regarding this broadcast. Robert Young and Walter Brennan are definite casts. Cast list #1 came from the actual script, while Cast list #2 originated from an actual photo of the morning rehearsals.

EPISODE #530   **"THE RED STOCKINGS"**   Broadcast on August 25, 1947
Starring: John Hodiak as Albert Spalding   Mary Jane Croft as Sarah
Fred Howard as Jones   Gale Gordon as the Judge
Jane Morgan as the mother   Gerald Mohr as Growley
Written for *Cavalcade* by Lucy Kennedy, based on the book "America's National Game" by Albert Spalding, originally published in 1911 by the American Sports Publishing, Company.
Produced and directed by Jack Zoller.
Frank Bingman is the announcer and Gayne Whitman is the commercial spokesman.
Music composed and conducted by Robert Armbruster.
Story: Shortly after young Albert Spalding was made captain and pitcher for the famous Boston "Red Stockings" baseball team, he discovered two problems that were hindering the growth of American baseball. For one, most of the bats and balls were so poorly made that they lasted only a few games and thousands of youngsters who wanted to learn how to play just couldn't afford to keep buying new equipment. Secondly, the so-called "amateur" players of his day were often supported by crooked gamblers. Spalding set out to rectify both these evils, using his own standards of skill and fair play as a springboard. His faith in these standards and the effect they could have on the nation's youth helped to make baseball, in the ball park and on the sandlot, the great American pastime.   **(HLYD)**

EPISODE #531   **"MISSION TO CUBA"**   Broadcast on September 1, 1947
Starring: Lee Bowman as Lt. Andrew Rowan
Herb Butterfield as Major Wagner
Nestor Piava as General Garcia
Based on an 1898 essay by Elbert Hubbard, and the book by Lt. Andrew S. Rowan, both of which are entitled "A Message for Garcia," and adapted for *Cavalcade* by Halsted Welles.
Cavalcade by Halsted Welles.
Produced and directed by Jack Zoller.
Frank Bingman is the announcer and Gayne Whitman is the commercial spokesman.
Music composed and conducted by Robert Armbruster.

Story: Lt. Andrew Rowan accepted one of the toughest assignments ever handed out by our Military Intelligence. His was the task of bringing a message from the United States Government to General Garcia, leader of the Cuban rebels, just before the then imminent Spanish-American War. Rowan had never been to Cuba; he did not speak the language of the country and he was to proceed without any idea as to the whereabouts of the rebels, and without identifying credentials in case of arrest. **(HLYD)**

Trivia: This story was filmed and released by Twentieth-Century Fox in 1936 with Wallace Beery, John Boles and Barbara Stanwyck in the leads, under the title "A Message to Garcia." For that filmed historical adventure, it took four screenwriters to complete the script. (It only took one to write the script for *Cavalcade*.)

EPISODE #532   **"KITCHEN SCIENTIST"**   Broadcast on September 8, 1947
  Starring: Ida Lupino as Fannie Farmer   Dorothy Scott as Emma
  Janet Scott as Mrs. F-----   Paula Winslow as Jane
  Paula Winslow as Maggie   Alan Reed as Father
  Bob Bailey as George   Joseph Bell as Dr. Maynard
  Howard McNear as the manager   Fay Baker as the woman
  Joseph Bell as the principal   Howard McNear as MacIntyre
  Fay Baker as Mrs. Shaw   Charles Seel as Joslin
  Bob Bailey as Dr. Chapman
  Produced and directed by Jack Zoller.
  Written for *Cavalcade* by Helen Hersfeld and Priscilla Kent.
  Frank Bingman is the announcer and Gayne Whitman is the commercial spokesman.
  Music composed and conducted by Robert Armbruster.
  Story: As a girl, Fannie Farmer didn't like to cook. A light-hearted and beautiful girl, her interests inclined towards dancing and ice skating with her wide circle of friends in Boston. When one of these ice skating parties resulted in acute over-exposure and consequent paralysis of her legs, Fannie felt certain that she had an empty life to look forward to. But as her fine spirit returned, she became enthusiastic over the idea of a career and enrolled at the Boston Cooking School. Her ambition and courage took her to the top of that famous institution and today her well-known cookbooks are almost required reading for every bride and her volumes specializing in diets and recipes for invalids are referred to in hospitals and homes all over the world. **(HLYD)**

EPISODE #533   **"RETURN TO GLORY"**   Broadcast on September 15, 1947
  Starring: Lionel Barrymore as John Q. Adams   Jane Morgan as Louisa Adams
  Written for *Cavalcade* by Garrett Porter.
  Produced and directed by Jack Zoller.
  Frank Bingman is the announcer and Gayne Whitman is the commercial spokesman.
  Music composed and conducted by Robert Armbruster.
  Story: When John Quincy Adams' term as President ended he thought he had reached the end of his long career as a statesman. A few years later, he was asked to run for Congress. He accepted and was elected. In Congress, as in the White House earlier, his refusals to compromise his political principals made him extremely unpopular. Viewed with particular disfavor was the belief he held that it was his duty as a public servant to present whatever petitions were forwarded to him, regardless of their apparent value or his opinion of them. Soon, however, he found himself the victim of a gag rule, designed to silence these bills forever. Adams, then advanced in years and physically weakened, launched a bitter and relentless attack on the gag rule because he knew it could lead to what he feared most . . . Union without Liberty. **(HLYD)**

EPISODE #534 **"THE GIRL WHO RAN FOR PRESIDENT"** Broadcast September 22, 1947
Starring: Virginia Bruce as Belva Lockwood   Alan Reed as Grover Cleveland
Adapted for *Cavalcade* by Ruth Adams Knight and Halsted Welles. Based on the 1947 book of the same name by Laura Kerr, just published the week before this broadcast by Thomas Nelson & Sons.
Produced and directed by Jack Zoller.
Frank Bingman is the announcer and Gayne Whitman is the commercial spokesman.
Music composed and conducted by Robert Armbruster.
Story: When Belva Lockwood's husband was badly hurt in an accident, she applied to the local school supervisor for a position as a teacher. Her excellent background readily qualified her for the job, but she discovered that the salary of women teachers was fixed far below that of the men. Determined to end this and other penalties upon being a woman, Belva Lockwood later went to the nation's capitol and organized the Equal Rights Association. She and her followers concentrated their big attack on the national vote, which was limited to men only. To call attention to this injustice, she accepted a nomination to run for the President of the United States. **(HLYD)**

EPISODE #535 **"BIG BOY"** Broadcast on September 29, 1947
Starring: Brian Donlevy as Babe Ruth   Sidney Miller as the peanuts and popcorn
Milton Herman as the cold drinks   Alan Reed as the man
Jimmy Ogg as the boy   Tommy Bernard as Babe Ruth (as a boy)
Henry Blair as the friend   Milton Herman as the Italian
Howard McNear as Mathias   Gale Gordon as Dunn
Fred Howard as Barrow   Tommy Bernard as kid two
Jimmy Ogg as kid one   Fred Howard as the doctor
Joseph Bell as father   Ann Tobin as the nurse
Henry Blair as Johnny   Howard McNear as Huggins
Gale Gordon as the catcher   Alan Reed as the umpire
Joseph Bell as the voice   Sidney Miller as the sports announcer
Written for *Cavalcade* by Brice Disque, Jr.
Produced and directed by Jack Zoller.
Frank Bingman is the announcer and Gayne Whitman is the commercial spokesman.
Music composed and conducted by Robert Armbruster.
Story: George Herman Ruth first discovered his pitching arm when he was eight years old. A few days later, he became the mainstay of the baseball team at St. Mary's industrial School for Boys where he had made a fast friend of his coach, Brother Mathias. When his star player was eighteen and ready to graduate, Brother Mathias cautioned him against the many pitfalls of swift success and in the years that followed, Ruth never forgot this early lesson. His hard, clean sportsmanship on the diamond and his friendly manner in private life won him millions of fans, particularly among the youngsters. One of these fans was a small boy who was dangerously ill in a hospital. Babe Ruth made a solemn promise to that boy. **(HLYD)**

Trivia: Brian Donlevy, who plays "the Babe" on this *Cavalcade* broadcast, is not only a baseball fan but a great admirer of Ruth. When word reached Donlevy that *Cavalcade* intended to do a drama on the life of Babe Ruth, he rejected Du Pont's offer to play Eliphalet Remington and offered to play Babe Ruth instead.

EPISODE #536 "OF SUCH IS THE KINGDOM"   Broadcast on October 6, 1947
    Starring: Henry Fonda as Jim West   Betty Lou Gerson as Marion
    William Roy as Joe   Howard McNear as Theodore Roosevelt
    Written for *Cavalcade* by Theodore R. Nathan.
    Produced and directed by Jack Zoller.
    Frank Bingman is the announcer and Gayne Whitman is the commercial spokesman. Music composed and conducted by Robert Armbruster.
    Story: Young Jimmy West couldn't attend high school on Fridays because that was the day he ran the laundry at the city orphanage where he lived. During the rest of the week, we worked part time at a bicycle shop so that when he finished school he would have enough money to pay his tuition at the National University Law School. One of his first cases as a lawyer was the defense of a young boy unjustly accused of stealing. West was shocked to find that a child was subjected to the same legal action accorded hardened criminals. He brought this grave problem to the attention to Teddy Roosevelt who accepted his suggestion to establish children's courts. West then turned towards a cause which was nearest his heart and, once again, found he had the President's enthusiastic support. **(HLYD)**

EPISODE #537 "THE FORGE"   Broadcast on October 13, 1947
    Starring: Ronald Reagan as Eliphalet Remington   Barbara Fuller as Abigail
    Others in the cast include Alan Reed and Howard McNear
    Written for *Cavalcade* by Joseph Cochran
    Produced and directed by Jack Zoller.
    Frank Bingman is the announcer and Gayne Whitman is the commercial spokesman. Music composed and conducted by Robert Armbruster.
    Story: Eliphalet Remington didn't have enough money to buy a new rifle but he did have his father's forge and his own high standards of workmanship. So he spent weeks carefully machining the parts of a gun (as carefully as though he were sharpening fine silver pieces for his mother). His gun completed, Remington entered a nearby target-shooting contest and found himself scheduled to shoot against the state champion, who owned one of the most expensive rifles made. Eliphalet Remington didn't win the match but he did win something that soon proved far more important. **(HLYD)**

EPISODE #538 "THE OATH"   Broadcast on October 20, 1947
    Starring: June Duprez as Abigail Fillmore   William Powell as Millard Fillmore
    Written for *Cavalcade* by Erik Barnouw.
    Produced and directed by Jack Zoller.
    Bill H. Hamilton was the announcer and Gayne Whitman is the commercial spokesman. Music composed by Ardon Cornwell and conducted by Max Miller.
    Story: Millard Fillmore was the second Vice President of the United States to inherit the nation's highest office, assumed the Presidency after the death of Zachary Tyler. Soon after Fillmore took office, he heated Senate debates between slavery and antislavery forces. The Compromise of 1850, which he helped achieve, had been opposed by President Taylor because of its concessions to the South. But when Taylor died, Fillmore urged passage of the compromise and quickly signed it into law.

    Trivia: This broadcast originated from Buffalo, New York. During the closing credits, the east coast broadcast featured Hamilton saying "On last Monday's Cavalcade, our play 'The Forge' was written by Joseph Cochran." Apparently it was forgotten during last week's east coast broadcast. On the west coast, this announcement was not made.

EPISODE #539 **"THE ADMIRAL WHO HAD NO NAME"** Broadcast on October 27, 1947
Starring: Robert Montgomery as John Paul Jones   House Jameson as Wylie Jones
Written for *Cavalcade* by Russell S. Hughes.
Produced and directed by Jack Zoller.
Bill H. Hamilton is the announcer and Gayne Whitman is the commercial spokesman.
Music composed by Ardon Cornwell and conducted by Donald Bryan.
Story: Because young, outspoken John Paul had made so many political enemies during his stay in the far West Indies, he knew he could never expect anything resembling a "fair trial" for killing a man while putting down a mutiny on his own ship. So he made his escape to America, where he met Wylie Jones, a wealthy plantation owner who offered him friendship. At first, Paul was suspicious but, in time, the two became fast friends. A loyal British subject, Paul was dismayed to learn that Wylie Jones was among those who were organizing a revolt against the British rule of the Colonies. Circumstances soon forced Paul to choose between friendship in a new country and loyalty to his native land, a difficult decision for John Paul Jones.

Trivia: In celebration that today is Navy day.

EPISODE #540 **"THE FLAME"** Broadcast on November 3, 1947
Starring: Helen Hayes as Carrie Chapman Catt
Written for *Cavalcade* by Robert Cendella, based on certain incidents from the book "Carrie Chapman Catt" by Mary Gray Peck, originally published in 1944 by H.W. Wilson, Company.
Produced and directed by Jack Zoller.
Bill H. Hamilton was the announcer and Gayne Whitman is the commercial spokesman.
Music composed by Ardon Cornwell and conducted by Donald Bryan.
Story: When Carrie Chapman Catt was only twenty-four years old she was superintendent of schools in Mason City, Iowa. Despite her success in the field of education, Carrie was dissatisfied and soon determined to devote her life to the then-unpopular cause of Women's Suffrage. Carrie traveled through twenty states giving lectures and helping women organize for their rights. After more than thirteen years in her chosen work, Carrie succeeded Susan B. Anthony as president of the Women's Suffrage Association. In this capacity she faced a crisis in her career. One state, and one state alone, stood between failure and the successful ratification of suffrage.

Trivia: The star of this broadcast, Helen Hayes, the "First Lady of the Theater," was one of New York's busiest women these days. On Broadway she was currently starring in the long-run hit, "Happy Birthday." In addition, she was giving lavishly of her time and efforts to many worthy causes, among them being the "Show of Shows" which was presented on October 30 at Madison Square Gardens for the New York University Medical Center.

More Trivia: The original title for this drama was "The Better Part."

More Trivia: Helen Hayes' real-life daughter, Mary MacArthur, played a role in this episode.

EPISODE #541 **"THE UNNATURAL DEATH"** Broadcast on November 10, 1947
Starring: Lee Bowman as Dr. Bailey Ashford   Frank Behrens as Colonel
Frank Behrens as Manz   Jim Goss as the General
Estrela Diaz as Maria   Joe Di Santis as Don Miguel
George Tiplady as Scotty   James McCallion as the Sergeant
Juano Hernandez as Pepe   Juano Hernandez as Angelita
Pami Hernandez as Angelita   Pami Hernandez as the patient

John Harper as the aid man   John Harper as the runner

Written for *Cavalcade* by Bernard Victor Dryer, based on the book "Soldier in Science" by Bailey K. Ashford, originally published in 1934 by William Marrow & Company, Inc. Produced and directed by Jack Zoller.

Bill H. Hamilton is the announcer and Gayne Whitman is the commercial spokesman. Music composed Ardon Cornwell and conducted by Donald Bryan.

Story: The Spanish-American War was over, but there was little peace on the newly-occupied island of Puerto Rico. Despite attempts to curb a disease known as "la muerte natural," the death rate among the civilians soared . . . and the blame fell upon the American Army Forces. Captain Bailey Ashford, Medical Corps, was ordered to stop the dread malady from spreading. Although Ashford's test hospital kept his busy during the day, he worked long hours at night in his laboratory trying to find a cure for the mysterious disease. He tried prescribing a new diet, but to no avail. Then, a routine study of a microscope slide led him to a new and promising diagnosis.

EPISODE #542   **"HURRY UP' YOST"**   Broadcast on November 17, 1947

Starring: Thomas Mitchell as Fielding Yost
Grace Keddy as Mrs. Yost
Cameron Prud'Homme as the first old timer
Cameron Prud'Homme as Baird
John Alexander as Schultz
Lyle Sudrow as the Buffalo player
George Petrie as the Stanford Coach
Bob Dryden as voice two
Elliott Reid as the Oosterbaan

Bill Stern as himself
Ted Osborn as the Professor
George Petrie as the reporter
John Alexander as the doctor
Lyle Sudrow as Heston
Ted Osborn as the conductor
John Harper as voice one
Elliott Reid as Summerville
Lois Volkman as the baby cry

Written for *Cavalcade* by Arthur Arent.
Produced and directed by Jack Zoller.
Bill H. Hamilton is the announcer and Gayne Whitman as the commercial spokesman. Music composed by Ardon Cornwell and conducted by Donald Bryan.
The band pays the 1936 song "The Victors" and the 1927 song "Varsity."

Story: On Fielding H. Yost's first day as football coach at the University of Michigan in 1901, he discovered that the university had over two thousand male students but the turnout for the football team was a mere fifteen or twenty men. Yost decided then and there that the new motto at Michigan was "Athletics for all." Each year made him more certain that the may to make his motto a reality was to make football pay. The key to Yost's plan was a huge stadium that would seat at least 75,000 spectators. He knew it was up to him to show the college and the state that his idea was not a waste of time and money, and he was willing to risk his own health and football reputation to prove that a wide and varied college athletic program is essential to the general health and physical well-being of our country's vitally important man power.

Jack Zoller: "In that broadcast, Mitchell was playing Coach Yost of Michigan. He was portrayed grabbing informally in his own home kitchen with a member of his football squad, explaining some new positions. The script had him calling out to his wife, "What'll I use for a football to show what I mean?" Instead he yelled, "What'll I use for a baseball?" (laughs) It was just a slip but a bad one."

Bill Stern: "Thomas Mitchell was a joy to work with during the rehearsals. Between the east and west coast performances I didn't spend as much time. He was on a split-second schedule as I recall. As soon as the first performance was over - his last line as a matter of fact - Mitchell rushed out to the Booth Theater for his leading role in the Broadway stage hit, 'An Inspector Calls'. I wish I had the chance to know him better. He joked around on the stage more often than reading his lines seriously."

Trivia: Miss Janet Graves, Managing Editor of *Screen Guide Magazine* appeared after the drama to present *Cavalcade* with an award for "its vital contribution to our national life."

EPISODE #543   **"US PILGRIMS"**   Broadcast on November 24, 1947
    Starring: George Tobias as Baaraczek   George Tobias as the Boss Pilgrim
    Mercedes McCambridge as Miss Haskell   Ralph Bell as Bauer
    Ralph Bell as Joe   Mildred Clinton as Mrs. Hanson
    Mildred Clinton as Mrs. Joe   Murray Forbes as Benny
    Peter Capell as the officer   Dan Ocko as Chief of Friendly Indians
    Rolly Bester as Mrs. Benny   Louis Sorrin as the extra
    Written for *Cavalcade* by Frank Gabrielson.
    Produced and directed by Jack Zoller.
    Bill H. Hamilton is the announcer and Gayne Whitman as the commercial spokesman.
    Music composed by Ardon Cornwell and conducted by Donald Bryan.
    Story: Mr. Baaraczek tells the story of the first Thanksgiving with unconscious humor and a deep pride in his adopted country. Some of the details may become confused in his version of the old familiar story, but few historians have caught the spirit of freedom that prodded Boss Pilgrim and his friends. His account of the voyage and the landing is strangely flavored with his own personal enjoyment of Thanksgiving.

EPISODE #544   **"TOWARDS THE HORIZON"**   Broadcast on December 1, 1947
    Starring: Van Heflin as John Powell   Lois Volkman as Lucy
    Everett Sloane as Walter   Cameron Prud'Homme as the doctor
    Maurice Franklin as the President   Jeanne Tatum as Emma
    Bob Dryden as Bill Dunn   Larry Robinson as Hawkins
    Cameron Prud'Homme as Sumner   Brad Barker as the dog
    Jack Manning as Hall   Everett Sloane as Howland one
    Bob Dryden as Howland two   Maurice Franklin as the voice
    Written for *Cavalcade* by Halsted Welles, from an original radio story by Dan Hammerman.
    Produced and directed by Jack Zoller.
    Bill H. Hamilton is the announcer and Gayne Whitman is the commercial spokesman.
    Music composed and conducted by Donald Bryan, Tom Scott was the cowboy singer.
    Story: In 1869, John Wesley Powell led a 900-mile expedition down the Colorado River through the Grand Canyon. The first to trace the course of this turbulent river, the six-man party made the hazardous trip successfully in 97 days. During the journey, Powell saw how the Colorado and other great rivers could be diverted to irrigate the dry, useless deserts that comprised nearly two-fifths of our land. After he returned, he toured the country advocating an irrigation project for the great West, but years went by with no sign of national legislation to put his recommendations into effect. Then the tide turned and at last Powell saw the work of a lifetime help turn vast uninhabitable areas into rich, fertile farmland.

EPISODE #545   **"DIAMONDS IN THE SKY"**   Broadcast on December 8, 1947
    Starring: Kathleen Lockhart as Maria Mitchell   June Lockhart as Gladys
    Gene Lockhart as Mr. Moats   Bill Adams as Dr. Sanderson
    Ethel Owen as Mrs. Remson   Gladys Thornton as Mrs. Moats
    Neill O'Malley as Coachman
    Written for *Cavalcade* by Luther Davis.
    Produced and directed by Jack Zoller.
    Bill H. Hamilton is the announcer and Gayne Whitman is the commercial spokesman.
    Music composed by Ardon Cornwell and conducted by Donald Bryan.

Story: Maria Mitchell has been described as America's first great woman scientist. President Lincoln referred to this 19th century astronomer as "an important natural resource." Miss Mitchell, however, was more than a famous scientist and astronomer. In her own dynamic way, she was also a noted educator at a time when it was "improper" for young women to learn much more than how to cook, sew and play light music for their future husbands. A few daring families did allow their daughters to study the arts and sciences. In the interest of these students, Maria Mitchell joined the faculty of Vassar College. To help one girl get permission to join her classes, Maria donned an apron and carried her fight right into the very kitchen of an unsympathetic father!

EPISODE #546   "THE DAY THEY GAVE BABIES AWAY"   Broadcast December 15, 1947
    Starring: Claude Jarman, Jr. as Robbie   Natalie Core as Mrs. Eunsen
    Jack Hartley as Swede   Sarah Fussell as Jimmie
    Cameron Prud'Homme as Mike   David Anderson as Kirk
    Lois Volkman as Annabelle   Lois Volkman as Jane
    Cameron Prud'Homme as Dr. Delbert   Judy Lockser as Elizabeth
    Eda Heineman as Mrs. Runyon   Grant Richards as Mr. Tyler
    David Anderson as Howard, Jr.   Natalie Core as Mrs. Tyler
    Jack Hartley as Mr. Stevens   Irene Hubbard as Mrs. Stevens
    Grant Richards as the fisherman   Eda Heineman as Mrs. Clarey
Adapted for *Cavalcade* by Frank Gabrielson, based on the 1947 book by Dale Eunsen. Produced and directed by Jack Zoller.
Bill H. Hamilton was the commercial spokesman and Ted Pearson was the announcer. Music composed by Ardon Cornwell and conducted by Donald Bryan; "Little Town of Bethlehem" was sung by a few members of the cast near the end of the drama.
Story: One day in 1868, a 12 year-old boy took over his father's place at the head of the family. And although his widowed mother's health was failing, young Robert, on weekdays, went to school in order to finish the sixth grade as his father would have wanted. On Saturdays he worked as a cook's helper at a lumber camp. The money he earned helped feed and clothe his five younger brothers and sisters. A few days before Christmas, Robbie's mother died of typhoid fever. Before she passed away, she told her eldest son to find the other children good homes, a different home for every child.

Trivia: The author of the story, Dale Eunsen, was fiction editor of *Cosmopolitan* magazine, and spoke after the drama. His comment, "I had a particular reason for writing this story and wanting you [the listening audience] to hear it. Robbie was my father."

EPISODE #547   **"THE DU PONT CHORUS"**   Broadcast on December 22, 1947
    J. Margaret Feltz is the Soprano Soloist and J. Clark Gonzalez as the Tenor Soloist.
    Virginia B. Williams and Eleanor Edge are accompanists.
    Branson Frey played the organ.
    Broadcasting from "The Playhouse" from Wilmington, Delaware.
    Walter S. Carpenter, Jr., President of the Du Pont Company was guest speaker.
    Daniel W. Boyer is director, Bill H. Hamilton is the announcer.
    Songs in order of broadcast: "Silent Night," "Carol of the Bells" (arranged by Peter J. Wilhousky), "God Rest You Merry Gentlemen," "When the Crimson Sun," "Praise Him Ye Stars of Light" (an arrangement by R. Deane Shure based on an old Welsh tune, "Hyfrodol" by Pritchard), "Lo! How A Rose E're Blooming" (an early Italian Christmas carol written by M. Praetorius and arranged by C. Albert Scholin), "Away in a Manger," the 1819 song "Angels from the Realms of Glory" composed by James Montgomery set to music by Henry Smart, Adolphe Adam's "O Holy Night" (arranged by W.W. Gilcrist), "O Come, All Ye Faithful," "All Men Now Sing Rejoice" (one of J.S. Bach's greatest), "Lullaby on Christmas Eve," and "Deck the Halls."

Trivia: This festive presentation originated from Wilmington, Delaware. Walters S. Carpenter, Jr. was the speaker. [Newspapers list Walters and Frey] This was the second annual music program of carols, no drama being presented.

To give you an idea of how much went into production for each annual Christmas carol program, the following is a list of people in the DuPont Chorus: Virginia Williams, Nettie M. Hitch, Doris Barlow, Perc Morrow, Robert K. Weaver, Thomas Williams, Irene Feaster, Irene Smiley, Gertrude Hannigan, J. Margaret Feltz, Mildred I. Mason, Rose A. Kracsun, George Roy Tully, Harmer B. Colvin, Donald V. Swing, Janet E. Koehler, Margaret Palfrey, Elizabeth Hackett, Marguerite George, Julia Scout, May E. Curley, Lillian McCall, Esther E. Evans, J. Clark Gonzalez, Adolph Friz, Donald I. Gerrish, Ellen K. Anderson, Edith Churchman, Lucille Manning, Kathryn Kane, Janice Sutter, Elva Wells, Dorothy Hanway, Elizabeth Klimuc, Katherine Clements, Marion Perse, Jessica Reed, Lois Weber, Frances Edwards, Carl Denison, Carl E. King, Richard Lindsey, Celeste Martin, Jean Hitt, S. Elizabeth Long, Ruth Phelps, Kathryn King, Carl E. Schweitzer, Fred L. Johnston, William Groundland, Ruth Beslin, Mary McMonagle, Lucille Williams, Sara Freedman, Margaret Geesey, Emily G. Krantz, Dorotha Redman, Suzanne Myers, Helen G. Pierce, Katherine Bigelow, Roger A. Hines, William Brondyke, Thomas Legg, Emily D. Brown, Lois G. Rineer, Catherine Hauger, Christine Cox, Margaret V. Wren, Elizabeth McDonough, Irma Husheback, Arthur J. Hill, George Tabet, John Mitchell, Jr., Raymond Fisher, Cora M. Strother, Irene Stones, Esther S. McQuay, J. Hollingsworth, William Ulmer, W.J.P. Calder, Harold W. Arnold, Fredric A. Wonn, Harry Eatough, Howard F. Berg, John Henderson, Hubert Simerson, Stanley O. Shaw, Jacob F. Wantz, R. Carter W. Jones, Eugene Evers, T.F. Killheffer, John L. Ludlow, Thomas C. Steen, Conrad L. Hoover, E.P. Meibohm, Paul S. Pinkney, Thomas A. Ford, Robert MacDonald, George L. Smith, John C. Coates, Walter Foraker, Jr., Jane Magowan and Theodore Kuehn.

EPISODE #548 **"POWHATAN'S DAUGHTER"** Broadcast on December 29, 1947
Starring: Joan Caulfield as Pocahontas Ian Martin as Smith
Dan Ocko as Powhatan Lamont Johnson as the warrior
Ted Osborn as Archer Edgar Stehli as Ratcliffe
Douglas Parhirst as Hunt House Jameson as Guard
Cathleen Cordell as Mrs. Horton Ted Osborn as the Captain
House Jameson as Sir Thomas Lamont Johnson as Rolfe
Douglas Parhirst as the driver
Written for *Cavalcade* by Priscilla Kent.
Produced and directed by Jack Zoller.
Bill H. Hamilton was the commercial spokesman and Ted Pearson was the announcer.
Music composed by Ardon Cornwell and conducted by Donald Bryan.
Story: The Colony of Jamestown, settled by the English, was kept alive by an Indian girl who showed the colonists the ways of the new world, who brought them food, and who did everything she could to keep peace between the settlers and her father's tribe. When incident after incident caused ill feeling between the Indians and the settlers, Pocohantas asked her husband to allow her to accompany him to England and present a peace plan before the King. At length she won the chance to put her daring proposal into action.

EPISODE #549 **"THE JUSTICE AND THE LADY"** Broadcast on January 5, 1948
Starring: Basil Rathbone as Oliver W. Holmes Dorothy Gish as Fanny Holmes
Cathleen Cordell as Debby Agnes Young as Mary
Cameron Andrews as Jim Jack Lloyd as Poe
Bob Dryden as the butler Lon Clark as Roosevelt
Cathleen Cordell as Mrs. Roosevelt Lon Clark as Stanley
Bob Dryden as Irving Lyle Sudrow as Shelton

Donald Bain supplied the animal sounds.
Written for *Cavalcade* by Virginia Radcliffe, based on selected material from the 1943 - 1944 book "Yankee From Olympus" by Catherine Drinker Bowen.
Produced and directed by Jack Zoller.
Bill H. Hamilton was the commercial spokesman and Ted Pearson was the announcer.
Music composed by Ardon Cornwell and conducted by Donald Bryan.
Story: "A great man must have an urchin at the edge of his triumph . . . to tell him his crown is on crooked!" Justice Oliver Wendell Holmes had his urchin. The name was Mrs. Holmes. When the Justice came home tired and irritable from a day in Court, his wife would sparkle him back to his normal good spirits. When he howled with rage over a misplaced book, she would leave on his desk a note that might read: "I am a very old man. I have had many troubles, most of which never happened." Throughout both their long and eventful lives, they were the perfect partners.

EPISODE #550 "THE CONSCIENCE OF BLACK DAN'L"   Broadcast on January 12, 1948
    Starring: Thomas Mitchell as Daniel Webster   Ted Osborn as Whig
    Barbara Weeks as Caroline   Delmar Neutzman as the voice
    Warren Parker as Whig two   Rod Henderson as Wingroom
    Rod Henderson as the man   Warren Parker as John
    Delmar Neutzman as the voice
Written for *Cavalcade* by Russell S. Hughes.
Produced and directed by Jack Zoller.
Bill H. Hamilton was the commercial spokesman and Ted Pearson was the announcer.
Music composed by Ardon Cornwell and conducted by Donald Bryan.
Story: Daniel Webster was a loyal and prominent member of the Whig party and he held high hopes of being their nominee for the office of President in 1840. The Whigs, however, chose a more conservative and less controversial candidate, General Harrison. "Black Dan'l" was highly disappointed, but in the interest of his party and his country he accepted the position of Secretary of State that Harrison offered him. When Harrison died in office, and Tyler became President, an important decision Webster made all but ruined his political career. Then eight years later, he was asked to serve in the Senate to help make the Whigs defeat the Clay Compromise. He entered the Senate chamber prepared to do the bidding of the party that could yet make him President.

EPISODE #551   "SHERIFF TEDDY"   Broadcast on January 19, 1948
    Starring: Joel McCrea as Teddy Roosevelt   Grace Albert as the housekeeper
    Charlie Eggleston as the Western conductor   Jim Boles as Dutch
    Joe Latham as Dynamite   Charlie Eggleston as Sutherland
    Charles Penman as Jake   Lon Clark as Packard
    Grace Albert as Shirley Belle   Larry Robinson as Frankie
Written for *Cavalcade* by Halsted Welles.
Produced and directed by Jack Zoller.
Bill H. Hamilton was the commercial spokesman and Ted Pearson was the announcer.
Music composed by Ardon Cornwell and conducted by Donald Bryan.
Story: When Teddy Roosevelt was twenty-five, his doctor ordered him to quit his political life and go out West for a complete rest. The party bosses in Albany agreed with the doctor, for secretly they had felt that the young reformer had been "washed up" for quite some time as far as politics were concerned. Teddy went West, but he found little rest. He soon realized that the Badlands were owned by outlaws and rustlers. There were few laws, and no one to enforce them. Eventually, the young tenderfoot found himself faced with the alternative of playing a crooked game and getting along as best he could or leaving town before he was invited to a "necktie party." Roosevelt risked his life in making a decision and mapping out a plan of action.

Trivia: The original title of the Teddy Roosevelt drama was "The Four-Eyed Sheriff."

EPISODE #552   **"THE PERFECT UNION"**   Broadcast on January 26, 1948
    Starring: Robert Taylor as John Marshall   Ogden Miles as Charles
    Lyle Sudrow as Tom   Rosemary Rice as Eliza
    Gay Seabrook as Jane   Ginger Jones as Martha
    Alfred Shirley as Ambler   Patricia Ryan as Mary Ambler
    Mary Hull as the shopkeeper   Ed Jerome as Patrick Henry
    Written for *Cavalcade* by Virginia Radcliffe.
    Produced and directed by Jack Zoller.
    Bill H. Hamilton was the commercial spokesman and Ted Pearson was the announcer.
    Music composed by Ardon Cornwell and conducted by Donald Bryan.
    Story: While John Marshall was studying law at William and Mary College after the Revolutionary War, he fell in love with Mary Ambler. Even before he met her, he made a wager that he would win her to his way of thinking, in both matrimony and politics. Winning Mary Ambler to matrimony was not too difficult. Then, Marshall was elected to the House of Delegates, and his views of the proposed Constitution seemed alarming to his wife. Nevertheless, John was firm in his belief that only by a strong unity of the states could true freedom and liberty be guaranteed. One the eve of the Virginia Convention for ratification of the Constitution, John's wife was critically ill. He knew that his presence at the meeting could help effect the passage of the bill. But he wanted to be sure that his wife wished him to leave her to attend the convention.

EPISODE #553   **"GOOD MORNING, MISS TYCKMAN"**   Broadcast on February 2, 1948
    Starring: Helen Hayes as Miss Tyckman   Ethel Browning as the mother
    Sarah Fussell as Harold   Edwin Bruce as John
    Gladys Thornton as Miss Henry   Peter Griffiths as Edward
    Lois Volkman as Jennie   Ethel Browning as the secretary
    Ed Jerome as Mr. Kraft   Lois Volkman as Helen
    Staats Cotsworth as Charles Oram   Joseph Bell as Grant
    House Jameson is narrator.
    Written for *Cavalcade* by Frank Gabrielson.
    Produced and directed by Jack Zoller.
    Bill H. Hamilton was the commercial spokesman and Ted Pearson was the announcer.
    Music composed by Ardon Cornwell and conducted by Donald Bryan.
    Story: Joanna Tyckman taught seventh grade. She'd been teaching for some thirty-eight years and could remember in detail the personalities and achievements of many earlier students. One of them had distinguished himself as an international statesman, and she was as proud of his record as it if had been her own. One day there was a crucial moment in Joanna Tyckman's life. She knew that the school's principal was leaving as soon as a replacement could be found. She would have been honored to take his place, but she would never have asked to be recommended for the position. Someone else was made principal and it was then for the first time that Miss Tyckman wondered whether or not all her efforts had been worthwhile. She found an encouraging answer when a visitor paid a surprise call.

    Trivia: The original title of this script was "The Teacher."

EPISODE #554   **"MR. LINCOLN GOES TO THE PLAY"**   Broadcast on February 9, 1948
    Starring: Robert Young as Abe Lincoln   Joe Di Santis as John Wilkes Booth
    Cameron Prud'Homme as Edwin Stanton   Alice Reinheart as Mary Todd Lincoln
    Charles Penman as U.S. Grant   Ted Osborn as Paine
    Sidney Slon as John   Juano Hernandez as Willie
    Joseph Bell as Hess   Sidney Smith as Fate

Written for *Cavalcade* by Russell S. Hughes.
Produced and directed by Jack Zoller.
Bill H. Hamilton was the commercial spokesman and Ted Pearson was the announcer.
Music composed by Ardon Cornwell and conducted by Donald Bryan.
Story: Mary Lincoln was eager to go to the theater. She felt that her husband needed some relaxation from his arduous duties as President. Influenced by an alarming dream and advised against such a conspicuous public appearance so soon after the end of the war, Lincoln attempted to postpone her plans. During the few days that preceded the performance, arrangements were changed many times. Finally, the Lincolns definitely decided against attending the theater. Then, several hours before the opening curtain, circumstances made them reverse their decision. This is the true tale of the fateful events that led to Abraham Lincoln's tragic visit to Ford's Theater on the night of April 14.

EPISODE #555   **"THE ALERTING OF MR. POMERANTZ"**   Broadcast February 16, 1948
    Starring: Paul Muni as Mr. Pomerantz   Mildred Clinton as Vera
    Nat Polen as Dave   Charlotte Keen as the woman
    Bob Dryden as the superintendent   Nat Polen as the newsboy
    Ralph Bell as Dr. Shankman   Joseph Bell as Huebner
Written for *Cavalcade* by Paul Peters, based on the short story of the same name by Berton Rouche, originally published in a 1948 issue of *The New Yorker Magazine*.
Produced and directed by Jack Zoller.
Bill H. Hamilton was the commercial spokesman and Ted Pearson was the announcer.
Music composed by Ardon Cornwell and conducted by Donald Bryan.
Story: Not long ago, a new type of fever broke out and suddenly in a medium-sized American suburb. It was spreading quickly and threatening to become an epidemic. Local doctors and the U.S. Public Health Service set to work immediately, and found unexpected aid from a Polish-American exterminator named Charlie Pomerantz. Pomerantz knew his job. Certain that he knew what was causing the spread of the mystery fever, he rushed to Washington with his theory. It made good sense and he was asked to return to the infected area and set up a field laboratory. This is how modern scientific methods and a hunch defeated a dangerous enemy to the health of our country.

    Trivia: The real Charlie Pomerantz appeared after the drama.

EPISODE #556   **"THIS WAY TO TOMORROW"**   Broadcast on February 23, 1948
    Starring: Paul Lukas as Michael Pupin   Jack Manning as Tom
    Jack Manning as Fellow   George Petrie as Jerry
    George Petrie as Bully   William Redfield as the boy
    William Redfield as the student   Ted de Corsia as man one
    Ted de Corsia as the vendor   Alan Devitt as man two
    Alan Devitt as the voice   Grace Albert as Elaine
    Elizabeth Watts as Mrs. Garrity
Written for *Cavalcade* by Robert Cenedella.
Produced and directed by Jack Zoller.
Ted Pearson is the announcer and Bill H. Hamilton is the commercial spokesman.
Music composed by Ardon Cornwell and conducted by Donald Bryan.
Story: Michael Pupin, an immigrant boy, had no steady job, but he earned money by following the horse-drawn coal carts through the streets of New York. When the driver dumped the coal in front of people's houses, Pupin would request the job of hauling the coal into the cellar. One of his coal customers was so impressed by Pupin's ambition and willingness to work that he hired him on the spot for a regular job in a factory. With his new wages, Pupin was able to enter and to work his way through Columbia University. Many years after his graduation he returned to become a professor at that institution.

Trivia: In an effort to capture Pupin's character, Lukas visited the Columbia University offices and laboratory of the great inventor, which have been preserved almost unchanged since Pupin's death in 1935. Dean George B. Pegram, head of Columbia's Graduate Faculties and one of America's leading Physicists, who was a colleague of Pupin, elaborated on passages in Pupin's book for the benefit of Mr. Lukas.

EPISODE #557 "THE BLACK DUSTER" Broadcast on March 1, 1948
Starring: Cornel Wilde as young Dave Hammer   Irene Hubbard as Ma Hammer
Cameron Prud'Homme as Pa Hammer   Rosemary Rice as Darlene
Jim Goss as Elmer   Lyle Sudrow as John
George Petrie as Al   Charles Eggleston as Joe
Charles Eggleston as Bill   Cameron Andrews as George
Written for *Cavalcade* by Virginia Radcliffe.
Produced and directed by Jack Zoller.
Ted Pearson is the announcer and Bill H. Hamilton is the commercial spokesman.
Music composed by Ardon Cornwell and conducted by Donald Bryan.
Story: Pa Hammer's wheat farm near Babylon Springs, Texas, was in pretty bad shape. It wasn't Pa's fault. He'd done his best, but the drought had dried out all his land and the land around him. It didn't take much of a wind to stir up a "Black Duster"... a dust storm that blew away good soil and made the area all but uninhabitable. Pa's son Dave came back from the University full of new ideas for the farm. They were good ideas, but they were new. Despite his father's opposition, Dave went ahead with his plan to save the soil. He and a few others pooled their tractors, their gasoline and their manpower to do some contour plowing. Pa Hammer learned a new respect for the help that science can offer to the men who provide our nation and the world with food.

EPISODE #558 "NO GREATER LOVE" Broadcast on March 8, 1948
Starring: Dorothy McGuire as Clara Maass   Lyle Sudrow as Steve
Judy Parrish as Bertha   Joseph Bell as Dr. Franklin
Ray Johnson as Juan   Edwin Jerome as Dr. Finlay
Raymond E. Johnson as the Surgeon General   John Raby as Dr. Carroll
Written for *Cavalcade* by Virginia Radcliffe.
Produced and directed by Jack Zoller.
Ted Pearson is the announcer and Bill H. Hamilton is the commercial spokesman.
Music composed by Ardon Cornwell and conducted by Donald Bryan.
Story: Clara Maass, an American Army nurse in Cuba in 1900, was one of many men and women who were trying to stop the mounting toll of death caused by yellow fever. One celebrated Cuban doctor championed the theory that the fever was spread by a mosquito. Clara Maass was among the few people who listened to him, for she believed passionately that without a proven theory or a cure she could do little for the patients who lay dying in her wards. One patient in particular - a Steve Dolan of the Sanitation Commission - she would gladly have given her life to save. Then something happened to make Clara volunteer to take the bite of an infected mosquito...

EPISODE #559 "PAGING MISS ELLEN" Broadcast on March 15, 1948
Starring: Geraldine Fitzgerald as Ellen Swallow   Clayton Collyer as Prof. Richards
Raymond Edward Johnson as Prof. Andrews   Alan Devitt as Dr. Runkle
Jerry Hausner as Sims   Ted Osborn as Prof. Ordway
Alan Hewitt as Herbert   Cameron Andrews as Cabby
Margaret Draper as Katy   Margaret Draper as the girl
Written for *Cavalcade* by Priscilla Kent and Virginia Radcliffe.
Produced and directed by Jack Zoller.
Ted Pearson is the announcer and Bill H. Hamilton is the commercial spokesman.
Music composed by Ardon Cornwell and conducted by Donald Bryan.

Story: Ellen H. Swallow worked hard in her father's grocery store, not only taking orders behind the counter but making deliveries as well. Boston of 1860 looked outward at this "unladylike" activity. But Ellen was earning money for a purpose. Her purpose was fulfilled only with the opening of Vassar College nearby - and Ellen was accepted. From there, Ellen entered the Mass. Institute of Technology as the first female student. With her Bachelor of Science Degree, she was offered the opportunity to help establish the first laboratory designed to give women scientific training. She served there without pay and without title for many years. Ellen took the chance of a lifetime to show educators and America at large that women could do much to help make science not only part of learning but part of living.

Raymond Edward Johnson: "They were night shows. It was a whole new audience and a wider audience... of course the afternoon audiences [daytime soap operas] was a woman's audience. And that was a night show. Of course we - the actors - always sought them because they [night shows] paid more and they sounded more important. Whether they were or not - that depends upon the money that was earned by the agencies. But that's what it was. The afternoon was the ladies' audience and the *Cavalcade* were big shows and scary shows because they were live and boy... you'd better be right. There was more money of the table."

EPISODE #560   **"THE PRESIDENT AND THE DOCTOR"**   Broadcast on March 22, 1948
Starring: Thomas Mitchell as Dr. Sam Bard   Ted Osborn as James Madison
Basil Rathbone as President George Washington   Earl George as Quincy
Raymond E. Johnson as Col. Alexander Hamilton   Dick Keith as the man
Anne Seymour as Martha Washington   Earl George as Zabulan Pace
Joseph Bell as Sam Fraunces   Dick Keith as Jason
Written for *Cavalcade* by Welbourn Kelley.
Produced and directed by Jack Zoller.
Ted Pearson is the announcer and Bill H. Hamilton is the commercial spokesman.
Music composed by Ardon Cornwell and conducted by Donald Bryan.
Story: George Washington was inaugurated as first President of the United States on March 4, 1789. Only three months later he lay gravely ill at a time when the success of our new government depended on his steady guidance. A Dr. Samuel Bard, considered the finest doctor in the capitol city - then New York - was called and following an operation, the patient began a slow but steady recovery. The President was confined to his bed for such a long period that soon rumors spread throughout the young Republic that Washington was failing or had actually died. To quell the rumor and to quiet all doubts and fears, President Washington made a brave decision, the results of which nearly meant his death.

Trivia: The original title of this script was "The Ride."

EPISODE #561   **"ROSES IN THE RAIN"**   Broadcast on March 29, 1948
Starring: Ralph Bellamy as Cleveland   Joan Caulfield as Frances
Agnes Young as the housemother   Jerry Hausner as the boy
George Petrie as the reporter   Ethel Owen as mother
Ed Jerome as Webb   Gladys Thornton as Celia
Bob Dryden as the man (American)   Burton Mallory as Whitney
Bob Dryden as the Frenchman   Ed Jerome as the Italian
Burton Mallory as the voice in Washington
Written for *Cavalcade* by Virginia Radcliffe.
Produced and directed by Jack Zoller.
Ted Pearson is the announcer and Bill H. Hamilton is the commercial spokesman.
Music composed by Ardon Cornwell and conducted by Donald Bryan.

Story: When Frances Folsom was attending Wells College, she had an attentive suitor who sent her roses regularly, but whom the beautiful student refused to take seriously. She even forgot a date with him on the very evening he asked her to become his wife. The year was 1885. The suitor was Grover Cleveland - then President of the United States. Frances Folsom's mother, in an effort to dissuade her from accepting the President, took her daughter to Europe to visit. In their absence, the courtship became the talk of the nation. Gossipy women and political enemies alike took the news and shaped it to their liking. Out of the noise and confusion came Frances' answer.

EPISODE #562   "WOMAN OF STEEL"   Broadcast on April 5, 1948
Starring: Helen Hayes as Rebecca Lukens   Cameron Prud'Homme as Solomon
Everett Sloane as Enos   Ted de Corsia as Shadrach
Based on an original story by Lucy Kennedy, and adapted for *Cavalcade* by Philip Lewis.
Produced and directed by Jack Zoller.
Ted Pearson is the announcer and Bill H. Hamilton is the commercial spokesman.
Music composed by Ardon Cornwell and conducted by Donald Bryan.
Story: Rebecca Lukens lived in an era when it was thought no woman could manage a business successfully. When the death of her husband in 1825 left her as sole owner of an iron works, she was told that pig iron and petticoats didn't mix. Her mill superintendent gave orders to close. The mill fires began to go out. Suddenly Rebecca felt that her husband's dream of the value of iron in industry was too precious to let die. So she set to work filling an order for iron plates for the first ironclad steamboat in America.

EPISODE #563   "THE MAN WHO TOOK THE FREEDOM TRAIN"   Aired April 12, 1948
Starring: Eddie Albert as Eddie Bullock   Shirley Booth as Marge
Written for *Cavalcade* by Frank Gabrielson.
Produced and directed by Jack Zoller.
Bill H. Hamilton was the commercial spokesman and Ted Pearson was the announcer.
Music composed by Ardon Cornwell and conducted by Donald Bryan.
Story: If it had not been Washington at Valley Forge or Lincoln at Gettysburg, the world would not long remember either place. If Eddie Bullock's brother had not landed with the Marines on Iwo Jima, he would not have died - but then, Iwo Jima might still be in Japanese hands. Eddie Bullock was afraid of visiting the Freedom Train because it would take his lunch hour; afraid of his boss; afraid of getting married; afraid of going into business for himself. One day on the Freedom Train with his girl, Marge, he suddenly realized what the world would be like if other men in other times had been afraid to push ahead - to work and strive and sacrifice.

Jack Zoller: "Most of our *Cavalcade* stories deal with the experiences of actual people. Sometimes, however, it has been found more effective to create a fictional character who is representative of a group. One example was the 'Freedom Train' story. The fictional character was a young man, discouraged with the problems of modern life, who visited the Freedom Train. In a dream sequence, the Train takes off with him on a rapid trip through history. When he awakens [near the end of the drama], he realizes what a sad place America would be if our fore-fathers had been as easily discouraged as himself."

On the following page: A full-size movie poster displayed on walls and bulletin-boards across the New Brunswick region, including the campus of Rutgers University. Tickets were very high for both performances (East Coast and West Coast), and Paul Lukas took time before each broadcast to answer questions the student audience asked about Hollywood, *Cavalcade*, and Lukas' personal life.

Cavalcade of America

presents

PAUL LUKAS
ANN RUTHERFORD
JACKIE COOPER

in

"WINNER TAKES LIFE"

(The dramatic story of Dr. Waksman's development of streptomycin — science's new weapon against disease)

broadcast from

RUTGERS UNIVERSITY

The State University of New Jersey

New Brunswick, New Jersey

**MONDAY EVENING
APRIL 19
NBC NETWORK**

EPISODE #564 "WINNER TAKES LIFE" Broadcast on April 19, 1948
    Starring: Paul Lukas as Dr. Waksman   Ann Rutherford as Julie
    Jackie Cooper as John   Lyle Sudrow as the Colonel
    Joseph Bell as the Major   Betty Alexander as Miss Bugie
    Betty Alexander as the nurse   Lyle Sudrow as Al
    House Jameson as the narrator   Neill O'Malley as the General
    Written for *Cavalcade* by Bernard Victor Dryer.
    Produced and directed by Jack Zoller.
Ted Pearson is the announcer and Bill H. Hamilton is the commercial spokesman.
Music composed by Ardon Cornwell and conducted by Donald Bryan.
Story: This is the dramatic story of a twentieth-century pioneer and his achievements in extending the frontiers of medical knowledge. Dr. Selman A. Waksman is the pioneer, and like so many other American pioneers he came here as an immigrant to search for what he wanted in life. His was a search for knowledge, rather than wealth. And in achieving his goal, he gave medical science another powerful weapon for its never-ending fight against disease. Scientists knew that there is a constant battle going on in the soil between microbes - some of them harmful, some beneficial. But Dr. Waksman wanted to know more. He believed that if he knew enough about these soil microbes, he could harness them to fight deadly disease germs in the human system.

Trivia: This broadcast originated from the campus of Rutgers University, The State University of New Jersey, located in New Brunswick, New Jersey. The audience attending the broadcast was not open to the public like the majority of the other broadcasts. The seats were limited and offered to Du Pont employees and their families in nearby plants.

Bernard Victor Dryer: "I think 'Winner Takes Life' was one of the most interesting episodes, because people know a great deal about penicillin and the new miracle drugs which are being produced, and streptomycin had a particularly interesting story because of the way Dr. Waksman up at the Rutgers University went about discovering. Regardless of what the listeners may think, we were actually very lucky to get Paul Lukas to play the part. He is a great actor and I think it was a very good show."

EPISODE #565 "LEE OF VIRGINIA" Broadcast on April 26, 1948
    Starring: Leo G. Carroll as Robert E. Lee
    Written for *Cavalcade* by Virginia Radcliffe.
    Produced and directed by Jack Zoller.
Bill H. Hamilton was the commercial spokesman and Ted Pearson was the announcer.
Music composed by Ardon Cornwell and conducted by Donald Bryan.
Len Sterling was the ballad singer, who sang an original ballad for this drama.
Starring: The war between the states had ended, and General Robert E. Lee turned his face homeward. Concerned over the future of young soldiers who had given up everything to follow him through the tragic days of the war, General Lee was not displeased when offered the presidency of Washington College at Lexington, Virginia. He hesitated only for fear association of his name with the college would cause hostile feeling in northern states. But Lee assumed the presidency of the great institution now known as Washington and Lee University. This is his successful battle on behalf of his young countrymen.

Trivia: There are some documents "suggesting" that Thomas Mitchell was originally slated for the role of Robert E. Lee, however there was no definite documentation.

EPISODE #566 "THUNDER ON THE HUDSON"   Broadcast on May 3, 1948
   Starring: Robert Mitchum as Washington Irving, and Julie Haydon
   Written for *Cavalcade* by Russell S. Hughes and Virginia Radcliffe.
   Produced and directed by Jack Zoller.
   Ted Pearson is the announcer and Bill H. Hamilton as the commercial spokesman.
   Music composed by Ardon Cornwell and conducted by Donald Bryan.
   Story: Washington Irving tried hard to become a lawyer, but somehow he couldn't keep his legal presentations dry and serious. This upset the head of his firm, disturbed his parents, and worried his fiancee. Humor in a court of law was unthinkable. Irving wondered how long he could continue this career. On leisurely drives in the carriage with his fiancee, he would tease her with long tales about imaginary characters who lived in the hills and made thunder . . . and slept for twenty years. Matilda loved to listen to his stories and urged him to put pen to paper, to make the legendary history of New York State live and breath. This meant giving up his career as a lawyer which he did gladly. For Americans, young and old, have been delighted in the droll characters - Ichabod Crane, Rip Van Winkle, the Headless Horseman and others.

EPISODE #567 "VILLAGE DOCTOR"   Broadcast on May 10, 1948
   Starring: Melvyn Douglas as Dr. Archie Sudan
   Written for *Cavalcade* by Russell S. Hughes.
   Produced and directed by Jack Zoller.
   Ted Pearson is the announcer and Bill H. Hamilton as the commercial spokesman.
   Music composed by Ardon Cornwell and conducted by Donald Bryan.
   Story: Archie Sedan worked hard at medical research and teaching. His vacation plans were delayed many times, but one day he decided to go fishing. No sooner had he reached the mountainous region of Colorado in search of its trout streams than local settlers began coming to him for help. He gave up his research career and moved permanently in Colorado. For over twenty years, through winter snow, spring rain and mud, and summer heat, he ministered to the people and taught them the fundamentals of good health.

EPISODE #568 "QUEEN OF HEARTBREAK TRAIL"   Broadcast on May 17, 1948
   Starring: Irene Dunne as Harriet   Ed Begley as the sailor
   Bob Dryden as Little Joe   Don Douglas as Big Pete
   Ted de Corsia as Steve   Milt Herman as Collier
   Earl George as Black Jack   Edwin Bruce as Danny
   Ed Begley as Mac   Bob Dryden as the first man
   Don Douglas as the conductor   Ted de Corsia as the Captain
   Milt Herman as the first miner   Earl George as the second miner
   Written for *Cavalcade* by Arthur Arent and Paul Peters, derived in part from an article by Barrett Willoughby, which appeared in a 1930 issue of *The American Magazine*.
   Produced and directed by Jack Zoller.
   Ted Pearson is the announcer and Bill H. Hamilton as the commercial spokesman.
   Music composed by Ardon Cornwell and conducted by Donald Bryan.
   Story: The "Gold Rush" was on in the Klondike. Perhaps the most unlikely of the new arrivals to the rip-roaring town of Skagway in 1897 was a widowed mother of four, Harriet Pullen. Hired as cook to a large mining camp at three dollars a day, she found her "kitchen" was a tent which her predecessor had left in a hopeless mess. Somehow she managed to cook her first meal, topped off with delicious apple pie - a touch of home to the lonely miners - and her first battle was won. Still, she could not support her children on this salary. Even the extra money from apple pies made at night wasn't enough. So she sent for her beloved horse. It was then that Harriet Pullen became Queen of Heartbreak Trail. She was the first and only woman to run a pack train over the most difficult stretch of trail in the country.

EPISODE #569 **"THE ENLIGHTENED PROFESSOR"** Broadcast on May 24, 1948
Starring: Gale Gordon and Franchot Tone
Written for *Cavalcade* by Robert Anderson and Bernard Victor Dryer, based on the biography "Benjamin Silliman: Pathfinder in American Science" by John F. Fulton and Elizabeth Thomson, originally published in 1947 by Henry Schuman, Inc.
Produced and directed by Jack Zoller.
Ted Pearson is the announcer and Bill H. Hamilton as the commercial spokesman.
Music composed by Ardon Cornwell and conducted by Donald Bryan.
Story: Benjamin Stillman was an American pioneer in chemistry and geology. When he was selected as first professor of science at Yale in 1802, many protested against placing this "alchemists' art" in the same academic category with Latin and Greek. Benjamin knew no more about natural phenomena than his contemporaries but he could envision the vast possibilities science presented, and he hoped to learn along with his students. Installed in a weird basement room in one of the college buildings, he discovered there was no equipment available for his experiments. How he procured the necessary supplies, attracted the students to this new field of study, and eventually established the first Chair in Chemistry in the U.S. provides an interesting sidelight on our scientific background.

Bernard Victor Dryer: "I started out as a reporter, not a radio writer, actually. Then I worked on a radio show called *The Human Adventure*, which the Columbia Broadcasting System and the University of Chicago tried to dramatize scientific research. I think people liked it because at the end of 1940 they gave it a Peabody Award. I think it was a good program and when *Cavalcade* came about, I did a number of programs dramatizing scientific research for them. 'The Unnatural Death,' 'Winner Takes Life,' and 'The Doctor with Hope in his Hands.' 'The Enlightened Professor' was my fourth and last contribution to the program."

Trivia: Bernard Victor Dryer originally entitled his script "The Professor," but changed the title a week before broadcast.

EPISODE #570 **"WHO WALK ALONE"** Broadcast on May 31, 1948
Starring: MacDonald Carey as Ned Langford   Louis Calhern as Gen. Leonard Wood
Written for *Cavalcade* by Virginia Radcliffe and Milton Wayne, based on material from the book of the same name by Perry Burgess, published in 1940.
Produced and directed by Jack Zoller.
Bill H. Hamilton was the commercial spokesman and Ted Pearson was the announcer.
Music composed Ardon Cornwell and conducted by Donald Bryan.
Story: When Ned Langford discovered he had contracted leprosy while campaigning in the Philippines during the Spanish-American War, he was in despair. This dread disease had such superstitious connotations that Ned thought he would be an outcast, severed forever from friendly human companionship and happiness. The one man Ned felt he could trust with his terrifying secret was General Leonard Wood, whom he had met during the war. General Wood was a doctor as well as a soldier, and he gave Ned the spirit and courage to seek a new future at the leper colony on Culion in the Philippines. This is the moving story of Ned's victory over loneliness and despair. It is also, in part, the story of Gen. Leonard Wood, who initiated the long fight against leprosy and sacrificed his life and career in the interest of his country.

EPISODE #571 **"THE LAST FRONTIER"** Broadcast on June 7, 1948
  Starring: Ray Milland as Remington   Shirley Mitchell as Eva
  Juano Hernandez as One Horse   Bob Dryden as Shorty
  Cameron Prud'Homme as the Old Timer   Ralph Nelson as the Art Critic
  Ralph Nelson as the Lieutenant
Based on the book "Frederic Remington - Artist of the Old West" by Harold McCracken, originally published in 1948 by J.B. Lippincott Company. Adapted for *Cavalcade* by Arthur Arent.
Produced and directed by Jack Zoller.
Ted Pearson is the announcer and Bill H. Hamilton is the commercial spokesman.
Music composed Ardon Cornwell and conducted by Donald Bryan.
Story: Frederic Remington was not the sort of artist to sit and dream of the pictures he wanted to paint. His pictures had to be realistic in every detail. Fascinated by the rugged beauty of the West, he took extended trips into the dangerous Indian country of the Dakotas to record America's "Last Frontier." Living with cowhands and traveling with the U.S. Cavalry as they chased warring Indians, he secured the sketches on which to base his authentic and picturesque art of the far West. Often, he would risk his life on expeditions to check the proper detail of line or color for his canvas.

  Trivia: Hollywood versatile Ray Milland, was once a member of the British Household Cavalry.

EPISODE #572 **"CHAUTAUGUA FABLE"** Broadcast on June 14, 1948
  Starring: William Powell as father Carver   Agnes Young as the mother Carver
  Rosemary Rice as Martha   Donald Hastings as Dewey Craver
Written for *Cavalcade* by Frank Gabrielson.
Produced and directed by Jack Zoller.
Ted Pearson is the announcer and Bill H. Hamilton is the commercial spokesman.
Music composed Ardon Cornwell and conducted by Donald Bryan.
Story: In the days of the horse and buggy, one of the bright spots in the lives of people living in small communities was the Chautaugua. For months before and after the arrival of the big tent and its attractions, Chautaugua was the talk of the countryside. It was the only opportunity for many farmers and townspeople to enjoy the cultural entertainment we take for granted. There were lectures for mother, political speeches for father, magicians and shows for the children, band concerts and singing for everyone. When the Carver family went to Chautaugua there was a very special added attraction - William Jennings Bryan was the principal speaker.

EPISODE #573 **"SKYLARK SONG"** Broadcast on June 21, 1948
  Starring: Lucille Ball as Grace Moore
Based on material from the 1944 autobiography "You're Only Human Once" by Grace Moore, and adapted for *Cavalcade* by Virginia Radcliffe.
Produced and directed by Jack Zoller.
Ted Pearson is the announcer and Bill H. Hamilton is the commercial spokesman.
Music composed Ardon Cornwell and conducted by Donald Bryan.
Marjorie Brett and Marjorie Hammill are the vocalists.
Story: Grace Moore had always dreamed of being a great singer. When her father took her to the Music Academy in Washington, D.C., during the winter of 1917, she revolved to make music her life. At the Academy she worked unceasingly to improve her voice. After long months of practice, she decided to go to New York and get a job on the stage, despite the horrified protests of her parents. She was unsuccessful at first in securing a role on the stage, she failed miserably in her first audition at the Met. But this beautiful young girl fought and struggled and studied. She overcame each obstacle as it presented itself until finally she became one of America's great singing stars.

Trivia: Marjorie Brett sings the role of Grace Moore. Gene Tierney was originally signed for the role of Grace Moore for this episode.

EPISODE #574   **"THE COMMON GLORY"**   Broadcast on June 28, 1948
Starring: Basil Rathbone as Thomas Jefferson   John Raby as Fred
Margaret Draper as Eileen   Jo Boland as Matthew
Cathleen Cordell as Pocohontas   Cathleen Cordell as Patty
Horace Braham as Burton   House Jameson as Smith
Delmar Nuetzman as Death   Delmar Nuetzman as the voice
Based on the 1948 Williamsburg Festival-Drama (play) of the same name by Paul Green, and adapted for *Cavalcade* by Erik Barnouw.
Produced and directed by Jack Zoller.
Ted Pearson is the announcer and Bill H. Hamilton is the commercial spokesman.
Music composed Ardon Cornwell and conducted by Donald Bryan.
Story: To freedom-loving Americans everywhere, the fundamental principle of "life, liberty and the pursuit of happiness" is an expression of our way of life . . . a precious heritage of democracy handed down by our fathers. Thomas Jefferson, who wrote those words, knew well the faith and sacrifice necessary to establish this philosophy. This challenging story tells about the dark and anxious days of the Revolutionary War when the new nation's very existence was in doubt. Weary and dispirited, Thomas Jefferson's lost hope when the British invaded Virginia, but a sudden turn of events gave him the courage to go on.

Trivia: Basil Rathbone, who appeared in "The Heiress" on the New York stage, had to be rushed off to the opening curtain of the stage drama as soon as *Cavalcade* came to a close. Although Rathbone played the role of Thomas Jefferson for *Cavalcade*, his costume did not even match the time period of the radio performance as he needed to be ready for the evening's performance.

EPISODE #575   **"THE EXILED HEART"**   Broadcast on July 5, 1948
Starring: Rosemary De Camp as Louisa M. Alcott   Elliott Reid as Laddie
Alice Reinheart as Anna
Written for *Cavalcade* by Virginia Radcliffe.
Produced and directed by Jack Zoller.
Ted Pearson is the announcer and Bill H. Hamilton is the commercial spokesman.
Music composed Ardon Cornwell and conducted by Donald Bryan.
Story: Louisa M. Alcott's father was a philosopher and a dreamer who never understood the necessity for budgets and money so Louisa took it upon herself to support the family. On one occasion she was given the opportunity to visit Europe as a sailing companion to an invalid friend. While in France she met a young Polish musician, the only man she had ever loved. His name was Laddie, short for Ladislaus Wisniewski. He urged her to write "Little Women" and she included him in the story as the boy next door. Deeply as they loved each other, Louisa felt she could not abandon her family and Laddie could not give up his dream of freeing Poland. Wisely they made their choice between dreams and reality.

Trivia: "The Exiled Heart" was not the script intended to be broadcast on this date. *Cavalcade* originally scheduled Juano Hernandez in a drama entitled "The Burning Bush," a courageous story of Booker T. Washington. But Hernandez had to back out, due to prior commitments. Quickly pulling a script meant for a later broadcast, Du Pont hired Rosemary De Camp, an expert dialectician who appeared on numerous radio shows, most notably *Dr. Christian*. In Hollywood, De Camp was known as the "girl with a hundred faces." As for the "Burning Bush" script, Hernandez kept his promise months later in November of 1948 - a new season later!

EPISODE #576 "BREAK THE NEWS" Broadcast on July 12, 1948

 Starring: John Lund as Riggs   Bob Dryden as Bennett
 Craig McDonnell as the Portland Operator   Howard Smith as Hale
 Bob Dryden as the New Haven Operator   Don Douglas as Jones
 Howard Smith as the farmer   Craig McDonnell as Connally
 Don Douglas as the lineman   James McCallion as Eddie
 James McCallion as the messenger   Parker Fennelly as Kelby
 John Seymour as Ralph   Ted de Corsia as Craig
 Ted de Corsia as the Boston Operator   Cameron Prud'Homme as the editor

The role of "1948" was played by Cameron Prud'Homme.
Written for *Cavalcade* by Arthur Arent.
Produced and directed by Jack Zoller.
Ted Pearson is the announcer and Bill H. Hamilton is the commercial spokesman.
Music composed Ardon Cornwell and conducted by Donald Bryan.
Story: Exactly one hundred years ago, representatives of six competitive newspapers met around a table in the offices of *The New York Sun*. Worried by the rapidly rising and already staggering cost of obtaining the news, they decided to band together. In this historic meeting, the Associated Press was born. Led by a band of daring and resourceful newsmen, the infant service quickly proved itself. Scoring in its first year a scoop of national interest on the nomination of Zachary Taylor for President, A.P. correspondents swiftly followed with a series of spectacular operations. They traveled anywhere, covering fires and floods, murders, elections . . . anything that was news. In a few short years they built an institution world famous for its accuracy and integrity. This is the story of the early days when the Associated Press was fighting for recognition.

 Trivia: With this broadcast, *Cavalcade* completed its current series. The program would return to the air on Monday, September 13 with more inspiring plays about the men and women who by their courage, enterprise and resourcefulness have contributed to the building of this great nation.

EPISODE #577 "GETTYSBURG" Broadcast on September 13, 1948

 Starring: Dick Powell as the voice   Bryan Raeburn as Sally
 Jimmie McCallion as the baby cry   Jimmie McCallion as John
 Donald Hastings as Billy   Les Damon as Haskell
 Horace Braham as Col. Lyon-Fremantle   Joan Lorring as Cornelia
 Danny Harris as the younger brother   Stefan Schnabel as Captain Shreibert
 Delmar Neutzman as Abe Lincoln   Delmar Neutzman as the husband
 Dennis King, Jr. as the friend

Based on the book of the same title by Earl Schenck Miers and Richard Brown, originally published in 1948 by the Trustees of Rutgers College and Rutgers University Press in New Brunswick, New Jersey. Adapted for *Cavalcade* by Halsted Welles.
Produced and directed by Jack Zoller.
Ted Pearson is the announcer and Bill H. Hamilton is the commercial spokesman.
Music composed Ardon Cornwell and conducted by Donald Bryan.
Story: An emotion-charged story of valiant men and women who helped carry through the war that welded a nation together. Portrayed with rare compassion and understanding, it tells the story of people who played parts too small for history to record. A housewife trapped in a farmhouse on the field of battle . . . a young Confederate soldier dreaming of a pretty girl he had chanced to see . . . a beautiful young girl who had left the peace and comfort of her home to share in the horror and suffering of war . . . and a little boy, who almost became a murderer! These are the people behind the battle scenes who will live again to thrill and inspire you in this memorable drama.

EPISODE #578 "THE PROUD WAY" Broadcast on September 20, 1948
Starring: Laraine Day as Varina Howell   House Jameson as Jefferson Davis
Ginger Jones as Mary Bradford   Lyle Sudrow as Young Joe
Don Douglas as Uncle Joe   Maurice Ellis as James
Howard Smith as the voice   Brad Barker supplied the animal voices.
Based on portions of the novel of the same title by Shirley Seifert, originally published in 1948 by Lippincott. Adapted for *Cavalcade* by Virginia Radcliffe.
Produced and directed by Jack Zoller.
Bill H. Hamilton was the commercial spokesman and Ted Pearson was the announcer. Music composed by Ardon Cornwell and conducted by Donald Brian.
Story: Lovely, seventeen-year-old Varina Howell wasn't one to pass up a challenge. Even the kind she encountered on her holiday visit to a Mississippi plantation. Proud and headstrong, she had risked her life to ride the fiery stallion, Sultan. Then she met his silent and bitter master, Jefferson Davis, who lived alone and on his dark plantation brooding over the memory of his bride. Attracted by his somber charm, Varina resolved to make him love her. She tricked him into bringing her to Brierfield, his gloomy plantation which had heard no laughter in eight years. Varina risked her happiness and even her life to meet the challenge of rebuilding a man's broken spirit. She fought to bring Jefferson Davis back from his past . . . to meet his destiny.

"Incident at Niagara" is the exciting story of a man who stopped a war before it started

EPISODE #579   "INCIDENT AT NIAGARA"   Broadcast on September 27, 1948
Starring: Anita Louise as Mary McDermott
Robert Montgomery as Jeremy Hallett
Written for *Cavalcade* by Virginia Radcliffe and Peter Ruric.
Produced and directed by Jack Zoller.
Bill H. Hamilton was the commercial spokesman and Ted Pearson was the announcer. Music composed Ardon Cornwell and conducted by Donald Bryan.
Story: The exciting story of a man who stopped a war before it started. A group of unscrupulous men seized strategic Navy Island in the year 1837. They hoped that from this vantage point on Niagara River, above the famous Falls, they could stir up malcontents on both sides of the United States-Canadian border. Their objective was to annex a portion of Canadian territory - a course that could only lead to war. Into these troubled waters sailed the steamer "Caroline," with First Mate Jeremy Hallett. Jeremy wasn't thinking of war. His thoughts were on his sweetheart, Mary, who was waiting for him, and the dress he was bringing her. A dress he hoped she'd wear as a wedding gown. Then Jeremy found out that his cargo contained arms and ammunition for the rebels. Jeremy didn't intend to "feed a war." He refused to unload his deadly cargo.

Trivia: This broadcast originated from the La Salle High School Auditorium in Niagara Falls, New York.

EPISODE #580 "ACTION AT SANTIAGO" Broadcast on October 4, 1948
    Starring: John Dall
    Robert Trout narrates.
    Written for *Cavalcade* by Arthur Arent.
    Produced and directed by Jack Zoller.
    Bill H. Hamilton was the commercial spokesman and Ted Pearson was the announcer.
    Music composed by Ardon Cornwell and conducted by Donald Bryan.
    Story: One of the most exciting, daring, and typically American plans ever executed by our Navy was the bottling up of the Spanish Fleet in Santiago Harbor during the Spanish-American War. Seven men were needed to scuttle the Merrimac at the entrance to the harbor . . . two thousand volunteered. These men knew that the people of the nation were counting on them to prevent the Spanish Fleet from bombarding the Eastern Seaboard. They also knew that their chance of surviving the ordeal was one out of ten.
    Trivia: Robert Trout was a member of the NBC news staff and had covered such important events as the coronation of King George VI and D-Day.

EPISODE #581 "HOME TO THE HERMITAGE" Broadcast on October 11, 1948
    Starring: Walter Pidgeon as Andrew Jackson   Fay Bainter as Rachel Jackson
    Written for *Cavalcade* by Virginia Radcliffe and Peter Ruric. Adapted from the novel "Home to the Hermitage" by Alfred Lelan Crabb, originally published in 1948 by The Bobbs-Merrill Company.
    Produced and directed by Jack Zoller.
    Bill H. Hamilton was commercial spokesman and Ted Pearson was the announcer.
    Music composed Ardon Cornwell and conducted by Donald Bryan.
    Story: The beautiful and historic home of Andrew Jackson is one of the nation's most revered patriotic shrines. The original Hermitage was made of logs. Then came the first brick Hermitage, completed around 1819. In 1831, Jackson remodeled the structure, adding two wings and a mass of columns in the front. Three years later fire demolished the building. It was, once again, rebuilt and refurnished. It is this establishment you see today when you visit The Hermitage - and this is that story.

    Trivia: This program originated from The Chattanooga Memorial Auditorium in Chattanooga, Tennessee, to inaugurate the formal opening of the new Du Pont nylon plant.

EPISODE #582 "THE DARKEST HOUR" Broadcast on October 18, 1948
    Starring: Burt Lancaster as Jack Jouett
    Adapted for *Cavalcade* by Russell Hughes, from an incident in 1948 publication "Jefferson, The Virginian" by Dumas Malone, published by Little Brown and Company.
    Produced and directed by Jack Zoller.
    Bill H. Hamilton was the commercial spokesman and Ted Pearson was the announcer.
    Music composed by Ardon Cornwell and conducted by Donald Bryan.
    Story: In the dark days of the Revolutionary War, following the invasion of Virginia, the colonies were so disheartened that one more blow would have convinced many that they were fighting against insurmountable odds. Realizing this, the British conceived a bold and daring scheme that might have ended the war in a single stroke. They planned to take prisoner the man who was the heart of the Revolution - the man who wrote the American Declaration of Independence - Thomas Jefferson. If it had not been for the quick thinking of Jack Jouett, a captain in the American forces, all the years of struggle might have been for naught.

EPISODE #583 "BRYANT'S STATION"   Broadcast on October 25, 1948
Starring: Irene Dunne as Jemima Johnson   Chuck Webster as Captain Gregg
Suggested by a chapter entitled "Jemima Johnson," in the book "Women in American History" by Grace Humphrey, originally published in 1919 by the Bobbs-Merrill Company. Adapted for *Cavalcade* by Frank Gabrielson.
Produced and directed by Jack Zoller.
Bill H. Hamilton was the commercial spokesman and Ted Pearson was the announcer. Music composed Ardon Cornwell and conducted by Donald Bryan.
Story: 1782 in Bryan's Station, as in most of the tiny outposts along the Kentucky Frontier, grim preparations are being rushed . . . guns are being readied and powder that the savage Wyandottes are ready for the warpath. To Jemima Johnson, the threat of the Wyandottes brings a special terror. For it is rumored that Simon Girty, the hated and merciless white renegade, will lead the war party - the same Simon Girty who twelve years before has sworn to have revenge when she told him she was to marry another man.

EPISODE #584 "THE BLUE COCKADE"   Broadcast on November 1, 1948
Starring: Linda Darnell as Temperance Wick   John Hodiak as George Mitchell
Arthur Vinton as Wayne   Arthur Vinton as the man
Jim Goss as Chester   Katherine Raht as the mother
Katherine Raht as the woman   Elliott Reid as Newton
Donald Buka as the Aide   Donald Buka as Roger Goode
Written for *Cavalcade* by Robert Cenedella.
Produced and directed by Jack Zoller.
Bill H. Hamilton was the commercial spokesman and Ted Pearson was the announcer. Music composed by Ardon Cornwell and conducted by Donald Bryan.
Story: During the long, cold winter of 1780, the Continental Congress found it necessary to offer a cash bonus to new recruits. None, however, was provided for the battle-hardened veterans of four years' service. Angered by this treatment, some of the Pennsylvania Line troops serving under General "Mad Anthony" Wayne deserted and prepared to march to Philadelphia to present their demands to Congress. Along the way they met Tempke Wick, a courageous farm girl. George, the leader, explained the cause of their desertion. She believed however that no individual grievance was as important as the cause for which the war was being fought, and revealed the mutineer's plan to General Wayne.

EPISODE #585 "GARDEN KEY"   Broadcast on November 8, 1948
Starring: Paul Muni as Dr. Jonathan Mudd   Alan Hewitt as the Prosecutor
Larry Robinson as Herold   Ted Osborn as the Major
Arnold Moss as John W. Booth   Alan Hewitt as the clerk
Ted Osborn as voice two   Arnold Moss as voice three
Agnes Young as Mrs. Mudd   Les Damon as Lovett
Bill Zuckert as the Sergeant   Dick Sanders as the Judge
Ralph Bell as voice one
Written for *Cavalcade* by Arthur Arent.
Produced and directed by Jack Zoller.
Bill H. Hamilton was the commercial spokesman and Ted Pearson was the announcer. Music composed by Ardon Cornwell and conducted by Donald Bryan.
Story: It was 1865, and a grief-stricken Nation mourned its lost leader, Abe Lincoln. In a grim Military Tribunal, hard-faced officers listened as Dr. Samuel Mudd swore he had no idea the man brought to him with a broken leg was John Wilkes Booth, Lincoln's assassin. The Nation demanded quick vengeance, and Dr. Mudd, found guilty of conspiracy in the plot on Lincoln's life, was sentenced to spend the rest of his life on Garden Key, a desolate island prison. Shunned even by the thieves and murderers there, Dr. Mudd lived in solitary confinement, broken in spirit and body.

EPISODE #586 "THE BURNING BUSH" Broadcast on November 15, 1948
Starring: Juano Hernandez as Booker T. Washington
Herbert Coleman as Booker (small child)   Albert Harris as Booker (older child)
Amanda Randolph as mother   Agnes Young as Mrs. Ruffner
Billy Greaves as Ernest   Billy Greaves as Fred
Viola Dean as Miss Mackie   Viola Dean as Elsie
Richard Gordon as General Armstrong   Alonzo Dean as Clyde
Alonzo Dean as the man   Pauline Myers as Carrie
Bertha Powell as Hattie
Based on material in the autobiography "Up From Slavery" by Booker T. Washington, and adapted for *Cavalcade* by Frank Gabrielson.
Produced and directed by Jack Zoller.
Bill H. Hamilton was the commercial spokesman and Ted Pearson was the announcer.
Music composed by Ardon Cornwell and conducted by Donald Bryan.
Story: Born in slavery and reared in poverty, young Booker T. Washington realized at an early age that education was the only means by which his people could enjoy their newly found freedom. For his own education, he worked anywhere, doing anything . . . meanwhile studying at night and at odd hours until finally he graduated from Hampton Institute. Then he began what was to be his life's work. Throwing himself into the fight to improve conditions for his race, he envisioned a great vocational school for Negroes. Traveling the country, he lectured to raise money, worked in the fields and in the classroom, and managed to create the institution that is now Tuskegee - a school which will stand forever as a monument to the genius and courage of this great American.

Trivia: Wanting to meet George Tobias, Juano Hernandez paid a visit during the rehearsals of *Cavalcade*, while in costume from his Broadway stage play "Set My People Free," which he was starring in.

EPISODE #587 "US PILGRIMS" Broadcast on November 22, 1948
Starring: George Tobias as Baaraczek   George Tobias as the Boss Pilgrim
Bess Johnson as Miss Haskell   Ralph Bell as Joe
Ralph Bell as Bauer   Rolly Bester as Mrs. Benny
Dan Ocko as Chief of Friendly Indians   Peter Cappell as the officer
Mildred Clinton as Mrs. Hanson   Mildred Clinton as Mrs. Joe
Murray Forbes as Benny
Written for *Cavalcade* by Frank Gabrielson.
Produced and directed by Jack Zoller.
Bill H. Hamilton was the commercial spokesman and Ted Pearson was the announcer.
Music composed by Ardon Cornwell and conducted by Donald Bryan.
Story: Same as episode # 543, broadcast on November 24, 1947.

Trivia: After last year's presentation of "Us Pilgrims," a huge number of letters were mailed to Du Pont and it became increasingly aware that this drama was well received. In appreciation to the many letters, Du Pont offered a rebroadcast of this drama.

EPISODE #588 "THE BETRAYAL" Broadcast on November 29, 1948
Starring: Dorothy McGuire as Peggy Shippen   Alan Hewitt as Benedict Arnold
Written for *Cavalcade* by Halsted Welles.
Produced and directed by Jack Zoller.
Bill H. Hamilton is the commercial spokesman and Ted Pearson is the announcer.
Music composed by Ardon Cornwell and conducted by Donald Bryan.
Story: The youngest and most beautiful of the four Shippen daughters Peggy dreamed great dreams. In the handsome and arrogant General Benedict Arnold, hero of Saratoga and Military Governor of Philadelphia, she found not only love, but the opportunity to

fulfill her hopes. Despite her family's objections, Peggy married Arnold. And, knowing that fame and wealth could come to them if they would hand over to the British the plans for West Point, Peggy was a willing tool for her husband in this - one of the most dangerous intrigues in American history.

Trivia: This drama, "The Betrayal," was originally scheduled for broadcast on October 25, 1948, with Irene Dunne in the lead role of Peggy Shippen.

EPISODE #589   **"OLIVER WENDELL HOLMES MacLANAHAN"**   December 6, 1948
Starring: Pat O'Brien as Oliver W. Holmes
Grace Keddy as Kate MacLanahan
Written for *Cavalcade* by Frank Gabrielson.
Produced and directed by Jack Zoller.
Bill H. Hamilton was the commercial spokesman and Ted Pearson was the announcer.
Music composed by Ardon Cornwell and conducted by Donald Bryan.
Story: As the time grew nearer for the birth of their first child, Dennis MacLanahan grew frantic with worry. The thought of the terrible fever which was taking the lives of so many mothers in Boston that year of 1843 made him sick with apprehension, and life without Kate, his pretty wife, would be unthinkable. No one, not even the doctors, knew what caused child-bed fever. But Dennis felt that Mother Moore, the community's kindhearted midwife, had something to do with it! He was determined that she should not touch Kate. He decided, despite the outraged protests of Kate's parents, that she should have a doctor. He appealed to Boston's most famous doctor, Oliver Wendell Holmes; and the little doctor began the work which led to the discovery of the cause of the fever - a discovery which has resulted in saving the lives of untold thousands of mothers and babies.

EPISODE #590   **"FAMILY CIRCLE"**   Broadcast on December 13, 1948
Starring: Cornelia Otis Skinner as the narrator   Patricia Ryan as Maud Durbin
Douglas Fairbanks, Jr. as Otis Skinner
Based on the book "Family Circle" by Cornelia Otis Skinner, originally published by Houghton-Mifflin Company in 1948. Adapted for *Cavalcade* by Virginia Radcliffe
Produced and directed by Jack Zoller.
Bill H. Hamilton is the commercial spokesman and Ted Pearson is the announcer.
Music composed by Ardon Cornwell and conducted by Donald Bryan.
Story: His mind filled with plans for a theatrical troupe of his own, Otis Skinner felt he has no time for girls . . . especially for ingenues like Maud Durbin. But when his dreams were ready to become a reality, the wise and kindly actress, Mme. Modjeska, persuaded him to take Maud with him as his leading lady. With high hopes the troupe started out. And as the days quickly passed, the young star and his leading lady fell deeply in love. Married at the close of one tour, they took to the road again, and were completely happy despite the days without money or food, and dingy hotel rooms, and the shabby theaters. Being together, sharing the hopes and heartaches that made up their theatrical world, was the most important thing in their lives.

EPISODE #591   **"THE DU PONT CHORUS"**   Broadcast on December 20, 1948
J. Clark Gonzalez was Tenor Soloist, Eleanor Edge was accompanist.
Bill Hamilton is the announcer and emcee.
Theodore F. Killheffer was president of the Du Pont Chorus.
Mr. Crawford H. Greenewalt, president of the Du Pont Company spoke during intermission.
Under the direction of Frank J. Clark, Jr.
Broadcast from "The Playhouse" in Wilmington, Delaware.

Songs sung and performed in consecutive order: "Break Forth O Beauteous Heavenly Light," the English carol "The Gloucestershire Wassail," the sixteenth century French carol "Shepherds All Shepherds," "Sing We All Noel," the Moravian carol "Hark Now O Shepherds," "Glory to God in the Highest," soloist Mr. J. Clark Gonzalez of the Du Pont Chambers Works in Penns Grove, New Jersey sings "O Holy Night," "The Carol of the Bells," "The Shepherds Story," "O Come All Ye Faithful," and in closing the humming of "Break Forth O Beauteous Heavenly Light."

Trivia: Frank J. Clark, Jr. holds degrees in music from the Westminister Choir College and Columbia University. While a student he sang in Carnegie Hall, under the direction of Toscanini, with the NBC Symphony Orchestra, and under John Barbirolli with the New York Philharmonic. He has also studied choral direction and radio technique with Fred Waring.

Trivia: The Du Pont Christmas Chorus included: Elva Wells, Marion Perse, Jane B. Phillips, Frances E. Mulrine, Elizabeth McDonough, Carlotta J. Toner, G. Katherine King, Anne E. Burrows, Irene Smiley, Elizabeth S. Hayes, Josepha K. Killheffer, Verna E. Edmonds, Caroline R. Frazer, Lee Krantz, Esther S. McQuay, E. Lucille Manning, Alice L. Coleman, Celeste Martin, Emily Dunn, Ruth E. Williamson, mary Ellen Moore, Thelma S. Tully, Rose A. Kracsun, Jane Magowan, Doris M. Evans, Esther Evans, Elizabeth A. Hackett, Margaret E. Palfrey, Edith E. Churchman, Doris M. Huck, Mildred I. Mason, Pearl Rose, Gertrude E. Berg, Charlotte Ryder, Irma Hushebeck, Jean H. Kay, Betty A. Abbott, Ruth M. Dallin, Ruth Phelps, Marian J. Fister, Betty Holder, Carolyn B. Swetland, Gertrude Hannigan, Dorothy Hanway, Elizabeth Klimuc, Jean E. Hollingsworth, Virginia B. Williams, Dorotha G. Redman, Louise R. Schucher, Janet Koehler, Ellen K. Anderson, Joan P. Bayer, Walter B. Foraker, John C. Coates, J.N. Hunsberger, Thomas Legg, William S. Groundland, George A. Tabet, Adolph Friz, Eric Loges, Isabelle McCandless, Jessica A. Reed, L. Irene Feaster, Eleanor R. Vandegrift, Paul D. Kohl, Roger J. Barnhart, Margaret T. Geesey, Sarah Freedman, Bernice Wilkinson, May E. Curley, Marian F. Phillips, Frances L. Moore, Theodore W. Kuehn, R.N. McDonald, I.D. Roche, James B. Brooks, George L. Smith, George R. Tully, John M. Thompson, E.P. Meibohm, J.C. Lehr, Francis E. Smith, Donald I. Gerrish, Willis F. Brondyke, Kathryn M. Kane, John Mitchell, R.F. McCartney, G.M. Whitman, John L. Ludlow, Theodore F. Killheffer, Roger A. Hines, Richard Bryson, Thomas W. Charles, Harry Eatough, John L. Scott, Thomas N. Williams, J. Clark Gonzalez, Perc Morrow, Carl Schweitzer, Harold W. Arnold, Stanley D. Shaw, W.J.P. Calder, Conrad L. Hoover, John Henderson, Doris J. Barlow, Ruth Breslin, Rose T. Canfield, Margaret V. Wren, Robert K. Weaver, Ruth L. Shipley, W.A. Shearer, Jr., Lois G. Rineer, Carl King, Eugenia Hitt, Eugene Evers, Eleanor Edge, and A. Wallace Copeland.

EPISODE #592 **"THE INDIGO GIRL"** Broadcast on December 27, 1948
Starring: Gene Tierney as Eliza Lucas   Staats Cotsworth as Charles Pinckney
Bob Dryden as Pierre Obin
Produced and directed by Jack Zoller.
Written for *Cavalcade* by Paul Peters and Virginia Radcliffe.
Bill H. Hamilton was the commercial spokesman and Ted Pearson was the announcer.
Music composed by Ardon Cornwell and conducted by Donald Bryan.
Story: In 1741, the French in Haiti were growing prosperous making dye, while the planters in the Colony of South Carolina were failing. Hoping to find a new crop for the Colony, Colonel Lucas brought an overseer named Cromwell from the West Indies to see if Indigo could be successfully grown in America. When Colonel Lucas left his young daughter, Eliza, in charge of the plantation, she was not satisfied with Cromwell's progress, and hired Pierre Obin to assist him. Then things began to happen! Cromwell denounced Pierre as a runaway convict and during a fight, Pierre stabbed Cromwell.

EPISODE #593 "THE GIFT OF JOHNNY APPLESEED"   Broadcast on January 3, 1949
        Starring: John Lund as Link Barren   Elaine Rost as Sally Greenup
Based on the short story "Autumn Rains Were the Curtains" in Walter Havighurst's book "Land of Promise," originally published by The MacMillan Company in 1947. Adapted for *Cavalcade* by Russell S. Hughes.
Produced and directed by Jack Zoller.
Bill H. Hamilton was the commercial spokesman and Ted Pearson was the announcer. Music composed by Ardon Cornwell and conducted by Donald Bryan.
Story: Dreaming of a place of his own, Link Barren turned West to wild, unsettled Illinois - with its vast stretches of unbelievably rich black soil. Passing through Ohio he paused at the farm of Fleming Greenup, and there fell in love with honey-haired Sally Greenup. But Sally, while deeply attracted to Link, had often heard of heartaches and toil which pioneer women endured. Her parents reminded her of the easy life offered by Ike Hyar, owner of the richest farm in the district. Knowing he had only his love and ambition to offer Sally, Link decided to leave. Enter Jonathan Chapman, the gentle, kindly man known as Johnny Appleseed. Through his sympathy and understanding, Johnny Appleseed offered Sally and Link the precious gifts of courage and truth, and faith in the future.

EPISODE #594 "EXPERIMENT AT MONTICELLO"   Broadcast on January 10, 1949
        Starring: Rex Harrison as Thomas Jefferson
        Joan Lorring as Sally   Ed Jerome as Corcoran
        Cathleen Cordell as Patsy   Elliott Reid as Druce
        Cathleen Cordell as Mrs. Reynolds   Ed Jerome as Trimble
        Extras in the cast: Anna Maude Morath, Mae Questal, Mike Garrin, John Harper, Bert Cowlan, Dorothy Storm.
Written for *Cavalcade* by Arthur Arent.
Produced and directed by Jack Zoller.
Bill H. Hamilton was the commercial spokesman and Ted Pearson was the announcer. Music composed by Ardon Cornwell and conducted by Donald Bryan.
Story: Smallpox was becoming epidemic in 1801, and there seemed to be little that could stop it. In Boston, Dr. Benjamin Waterhouse advanced his theory of vaccination to control the disease, but only a few people, among them Thomas Jefferson, sided with him. When Sally Corcoran, pretty young daughter of Monticello's overseer, arranged a meeting between Jefferson and her friend, John Druce, Jefferson asked the young medical student his opinion of vaccination. John, whose experience was limited to the teaching of his professors, termed Waterhouse a fraud. But smallpox had reached Monticello, and Jefferson offered himself not only to be vaccinated, but to inoculate any person on his plantation - including his slaves and servants - with Dr. Waterhouse's serum.

Trivia: Stage and screen star Rex Harrison, who played Thomas Jefferson in this, his first (and only) *Cavalcade* performance, appeared on the radio stage in the costume of a character from another century. Harrison was currently appearing on the Broadway stage as King Henry VIII in "Anne of the Thousand Days," had to rush from the broadcast directly to the stage of the theatre in order to make the opening curtain. This made it imperative that he don his costume and make-up before coming on the Longacre Theatre for *Cavalcade of America*.

More trivia: Mae Questal, the voice of the original Betty Boop, played a small role in this broadcast.

EPISODE #595 **"SECRET OPERATION"** Broadcast on January 17, 1949
    Starring: John Payne as Erdmann   Vivian Barry as the nurse
    Ethel Owen as the housekeeper   House Jameson as Bryant
    Les Damon as O'Reilly   Lyle Sudrow as the sailor
    Jim Goss as Cleveland   Joseph Bell as Janeway
    George Petrie as the reporter   Norman Rose as the narrator
    Written for *Cavalcade* by Morton Wishengrad.
    Produced and directed by Jack Zoller.
Bill H. Hamilton was the commercial spokesman and Ted Pearson was the announcer.
Music composed by Ardon Cornwell and conducted by Donald Bryan.
Story: One June night in 1893, Dr. John Erdmann received a mysterious summons to assist in a secret operation. He was told nothing about it - only a messenger would call for him and that the operation was of great importance. Absolute secrecy was imperative. The patient turned out to be Grover Cleveland, newly inaugurated, and facing possible death by cancer. The nation was facing a crucial period and news of the President's condition could have led to widespread panic.

Trivia: The real eighty-five-year-old Dr. Erdmann appeared on the program after the drama. Dr. John F. Erdmann assisted in supervising the script in which John Payne played him in "Secret Operation." Erdmann also attended the rehearsals.

EPISODE #596 **"THE QUEEN'S HANDMAID"** Broadcast on January 24, 1949
    Starring: Madeleine Carroll as Marie Therese   Guy Sorel as Jean
    Stefan Schnabel as Talon   Leonard Sherer as Aristide
    Horace Braham as voice one   Horace Braham as Robert
    Walter Black as voice two
Based on material contained in the book "I Thee Wed" by Gilbert W. Gabriel, and adapted for *Cavalcade* by Virginia Radcliffe.
Produced and directed by John Zoller.
Bill H. Hamilton was the commercial spokesman and Ted Pearson was the announcer.
Music composed by Ardon Cornwell and conducted by Donald Bryan.
Story: In the winter of 1793, a strange new colony called "Azilum" grew out of the Pennsylvania wilderness. Here a group of émigrés from the French Revolution had settled to build a new court for their queen, Marie Antoinette. The dream was shared by Marie Haussier, former handmaid to the queen. The Governor of Azilum, Monsieur Talon, noticing Marie's resemblance to Marie Antoinette, tricked the girl into impersonating the queen. He hoped this masquerade would sufficiently impress a visiting American so he could arrange a loan. A large ball was held and Marie played her part well. Suddenly Marie learns that the Queen was dead . . .

Trivia: Gilbert W. Gabriel, the author of which this episode was adapted from, appeared at rehearsal and autographed a copy of his book for Madeleine Carroll.

EPISODE #597 **"ONE LAST ROMANCE"** Broadcast on January 31, 1949
    Starring: Walter Hampden as Benjamin Franklin   Una O'Connor as Abigail
    Craig McDonnell as the salty voice   Joan Lorring as Elizabeth
    Staats Cotsworth as Stephen   Michael Alexander as the seaman
Based on a passage in the 1939 book "America's Old Masters" by James Thomas Flexner, and adapted for *Cavalcade* by Halsted Welles.
Produced and directed by John Zoller.
Bill H. Hamilton was the commercial spokesman and Ted Pearson was the announcer.
Music composed by Ardon Cornwell and conducted by Donald Bryan.
Story: The story of how Benjamin Franklin played Cupid for the intended bride of America's first great artist, Benjamin West, and his lover, imprisoned by an evil brother.

EPISODE #598   "THE STORE THAT WINKED OUT"   Broadcast on February 7, 1949
    Starring: Zachary Scott as Abe Lincoln   Lyle Sudrow as Bill Berry
    Based on the 1947 book "Berry and Lincoln, Frontier Merchants: The Store that Winked Out" by Zarel C. Spears and Robert S. Barton. Adapted for *Cavalcade* by Arthur Arent. Produced and directed by John Zoller.
    Bill H. Hamilton was the commercial spokesman and Ted Pearson was the announcer.
    Music composed by Ardon Cornwell and conducted by Donald Bryan.
    The original ballad "The Store Winked Out" was written by Virginia Radcliffe and sung by Jimmy Atkins.
    Story: When Abe Lincoln was defeated for the Illinois State Legislature, he was determined to try again. But in the meantime, he wanted to earn money for a set of law books, and was persuaded to take a partnership in Bill Berry's general store. Among the traits which Abe had was his deep sympathy for everyone's problems, and worthless inventories grew - the business slackened. It became apparent that the store was a failure and they must sell out. One day, as they were cleaning up, they unpacked for the first time a barrel of goods which Abe had purchased from an immigrant pioneer. At the bottom, soiled but useable, was a complete set of law books. And Lincoln began his study of law behind a counter in a store that was almost forgotten and soon "winked out."

    Trivia: Ann Rutledge (great grand-niece of Lincoln's wife) actually plays the part of Ann Rutledge.

EPISODE #599   "A VALENTINE FOR SOPHIA"   Broadcast on February 14, 1949
    Starring: Glenn Ford as Nathaniel Hawthorne   Patricia Ryan was Sophia
    Alice Rineheart as Liz   Also in the cast: Muriel Kirkman
    Based on material from the book "Nathaniel Hawthorne" by Randall Stewart, originally published in 1948 by Yale University Press. Adapted for *Cavalcade* by Virginia Radcliffe
    Produced and directed by John Zoller.
    Bill H. Hamilton was the commercial spokesman and Ted Pearson was the announcer.
    Music composed by Ardon Cornwell and conducted by Donald Bryan.
    Story: After ten years of discouragement, Nathaniel Hawthorne was angrily feeding his "Twice Told Tales" to the fireplace when he learned that a publisher was interested. The book, which he quickly rewrote, gained for Hawthorne recognition as an author, but little financial return. Among the admires of the book was Hawthorne's lovely neighbor, Sophia Peabody, with whom the author fell deeply in love. But with the little money from his writing, the two could not marry. Hard at work, Nathaniel had little time for his writing. But his work brought him, for the first time, into contact with a new kind of America - the men of the docks and ships. From them, he gained a background for his later writing.

EPISODE #600   "THE UNHEROIC HERO"   Broadcast on February 21, 1949
    Starring: Douglas Fairbanks, Jr. as Robert Stobo   Ian Martin as Robertson
    Harold Dyrenforth as Van Braam   Dan Ocko as the Indian
    Ian Martin as the second officer   Lamont Johnson as Washington
    Dan Ocko as the Sentry   Guy Sorel as the guard
    House Jameson as the first officer   Murray Forbes as first servant
    Bob Dryden as the Official's voice   Bob Dryden as 1st French Officer
    Murray Forbes as the Frenchman   Guy Sorel as 2nd French Officer
    Suggest by an incident in "Young Washington, Volume One" by Douglas Southall Freeman, originally published in 1948 by Charles Scribner's Sons. Adapted for *Cavalcade* by Halsted Welles.
    Produced and directed by John Zoller.

Bill H. Hamilton was the commercial spokesman and Ted Pearson was the announcer.
Music composed by Ardon Cornwell and conducted by Donald Bryan.
Story: When the young Virginian Robert Stobo signed to serve under Major George Washington, he regarded the mission as a "lark." But the few "friendly" skirmishes he had envisioned turned into a real battle, and Washington and his command were defeated at the hands of the French and Indians. Stobo was sent as a hostage to Fort Duqusne, and while there promised Washington to spy on the defenses of the French. So, at great personal danger, he made rough plans of the Fort and bribed an Indian to take them to Washington. The mission was successful, but news of it leaked out; and the French sentenced Stobo to death as a spy.

EPISODE #601   **"PINK LACE"**   Broadcast on February 28, 1949
Starring: Janet Blair as Pauline Cushman   Staats Cotsworth as McNairy
Written for *Cavalcade* by Virginia Radcliffe.
Produced and directed by Jack Zoller.
Bill Hamilton was the commercial spokesman and Ted Pearson was the announcer.
Music was composed by Ardon Cornwell and conducted by Donald Bryan.
Story: During the War Between the States, actress Pauline Cushman interrupted her career to do special espionage work which she believed might help save the Union. By openly declaring herself for the South, she was free to move around gathering information. Although warned never to write anything which might incriminate her, Miss Cushman copied the key to the secret Confederate code which she hid in the pink lace of her petticoat. She was arrested as a spy by the South, but escaped to the Union lines. For her bravery and patriotism, Pauline Cushman was formally commissioned a Major in the Calvary of the United States Army. Her uniform varied from other officer' in but one detail - instead of the customary stock there was a proud jabot of pink lace.

Trivia: This episode technically has two titles. The official script title was "Pink Lace," but before hand, it was originally entitled "The Girl in the Pink Lace." At the beginning of the broadcast, announcer Ted Pearson announces the drama as the "The Girl in the Pink Lace."

More trivia: Madeleine Carroll was originally scheduled to star as Pauline Cushman, she was unable to attend. Janet Blair signed up for the role.

EPISODE #602   **"JOURNEY AMONG THE LOST"**   Broadcast on March 7, 1949
Starring: Jean Arthur as Dorthea Lynd Dix
Based on "Dorothea Dix, Forgotten Samaritan" by Helen E. Marshall, originally published by the University of North Carolina Press in 1937, and adapted for *Cavalcade* by Morton Wishengrad.
Produced and directed by Jack Zoller.
Bill Hamilton was the commercial spokesman and Ted Pearson was the announcer.
Music was composed by Ardon Cornwell and conducted by Donald Bryan.
Story: In the year 1841, a soft-voiced woman dressed in cashmere made a journey among the lost - the mentally ill who were confined to prisons and almshouses. Appalled at the treatment these people were receiving, Dorthea Dix spent her time and money to make a study of conditions under which these unfortunates existed in Massachusetts. In her notebooks, the bleak record accumulated - a record of unrelieved horror. When it was completed, she was ready to present her story to the Massachusetts legislature. Her battle was rewarding. In 1843, the Massachusetts legislature voted to remove the indigent insane and the mentally ill from the almshouses and the prisons, and care for them in public hospitals - the first such hospitals in America.

EPISODE #603 **"MY HUNT AFTER THE CAPTAIN"** Broadcast on March 14, 1949
Starring: Conrad Nagel as Dr. Holmes Conrad Nagel as Wendell
Cecil Roy as the woman Ian Martin as the boy (age 24)
James McCallion as the Sergeant Cecil Roy as the messenger
Ian Martin as the conductor Donny Harris as Frank
Rosemary Rice as Jonesy Arthur Waitland as Dudley
Ivor Francis as the boy (age 16) Rod Hendrickson as the conductor (age 24)
Rod Hendrickson as the driver Ivor Francis as the Corporal
Written for *Cavalcade* by Arthur Arent.
Produced and directed by Jack Zoller.
Bill Hamilton was the commercial spokesman and Ted Pearson was the announcer.
Music was composed by Ardon Cornwell and conducted by Donald Bryan.
Story: Trains going toward the battle areas were crowded with worried, tense looking civilians. They were men looking for their wounded sons - men like Dr. Oliver Wendell Holmes of Boston. When his search had ended, the little doctor went home, put pen to paper and revealed his love for his son in the now famous anecdote. It was a loved that proved inarticulate when the two men were face to face - a love Dr. Holmes expressed in this quotation from the Bible, "For this our son and brother was dead and is alive again, and was lost and is found."

Trivia: In 1862, an article in *The Atlantic Monthly* touched the hearts of a nation at war. It was the simple, moving story of a father searching for his soldier-son - an anxious search that led even to the battlefield. A script based on that article was originally scheduled for this date. "A Letter from Europe," about the French-born Albert Gallatin who with President John Adams and Thomas Jefferson, helped avert an international crisis - was originally scheduled for the broadcast of March 14. For reasons unknown, this story was pre-empted a week.

More trivia: William Eythe did not have to be flown from the west coast, as he was currently starring on Broadway in the musical revue, "Lend and Ear," which he was also co-producing. Conrad Nagel was recently star of the stage play "For Love or Money."

EPISODE #604 **"LETTER FROM EUROPE"** Broadcast on March 21, 1949
Starring: Charles Boyer as Albert Gallatin Barbara Weeks as Hannah
Ethel Owen as the woman Ethel Owen as Mrs. Harwood
Joseph Bell as the Massachusetts man Scott Tennyson as Janney
Scott Tennyson as the courier House Jameson as Thomas Jefferson
Alan Hewitt as the chairman Robert Dryden as the voice one
Arnold Moss as voice two Alan Hewitt as the chairman
Robert Dryden as the butler Arnold Moss as John Adams
Written for *Cavalcade* by Russell Hughes.
Produced and directed by Jack Zoller.
Bill Hamilton was the commercial spokesman and Ted Pearson was the announcer.
Music was composed by Ardon Cornwell and conducted by Donald Bryan.
Story: In 1798, when war with France seemed inevitable, a small group of men marshaled themselves against it. Among those opposing the clash was European-born Albert Gallatin. Gallatin feared a conflict would destroy the young nation. He believed, with President Adams and Thomas Jefferson, that the dispute could be settled peaceably by sending envoys to France. But those who feared loss of national honor more than loss of freedom branded Gallatin a French sympathizer. When those he loved were hurt by these bitter attacks, Gallatin lost heart for the flight. Then a letter from a cousin in Europe reaffirmed for him the universal need for freedom, and gave him renewed courage. Gallatin won his fight, and went on to become Secretary of the Treasury under President Jefferson, and United States Ambassador to France and England.

EPISODE #605 **"BOY WANTED"** Broadcast on March 28, 1949
    Starring: Virginia Bruce as Miss Ransome   Allen Shea as Rudy Petersen
Written for *Cavalcade* by Frank Gabrielson.
Produced and directed by Jack Zoller.
Bill Hamilton was the commercial spokesman and Ted Pearson was the announcer.
Music was composed by Ardon Cornwell and conducted by Donald Bryan.
Story: When police and neighbors heard a child's frightened cries, they found Rudy Petersen alone and afraid. The boy's grandmother, with whom he lived, was dead. There was affection and understanding for Rudy at the Children's Shelter where he was taken. But Miss Ransome, head of the Shelter, knew that Rudy particularly needed the love and attention of parents. She found such parents in the Hawleys, a middle-aged couple who desperately wanted a child. Rudy and Mrs. Hawley got along fine from the start. But the boy was antagonistic to Mr. Hawley. It took time, patience and the understanding aid of Miss Ransome to work out this conflict.

EPISODE #606 **"CITIZEN MAMA"** Broadcast on April 4, 1949
    Starring: Irene Dunne as Mama   Rosemary Rice as Katrin
    Carl Frank as Papa   Iris Mann as Dagmar
    Donald Hastings as Nels   Alice Yourman as Aunt Jenny
    Arnold Robertson as Uncle Chris   Bob Dryden as the clerk
    House Jameson as Examier
Based on the 1943 novel "Mama's Bank Account" by Kathryn Forbes, and adapted for *Cavalcade* by Frank Gabrielson.
Produced and directed by Jack Zoller.
Bill Hamilton was the commercial spokesman and Ted Pearson was the announcer.
Music was composed by Ardon Cornwell and conducted by Donald Bryan.
Story: Told through the eyes of Katrin, a Norwegian family's tribulations, trials and triumphs are dramatized as they immigrated to America. Mama is the heartwarming core of the story as she is the central character, mother and inspiration to all.

Trivia: This program originates from Buffalo, New York, celebrating the 25th anniversary of cellophane. Irene Dunne reprised her role as Mama from the 1948 RKO film *I Remember Mama*. This was later mounted as a major Broadway production by Richard Rodgers and Oscar Hammerstein II.

Rosemary Rice: "Iris Mann played Dagmar for the first three television episodes of *I Remember Mama*. I recently did a re-enactment of "Citizen Mama" for a convention, the one with Irene Dunne in the lead. I have a copy of that script and it was the same script used in the re-enactment. I remember working with Robert Taylor on one broadcast, William Powell on another. I loved the one Jackie Cooper as I also listened to a recording of that episode - I absolutely loved that one. But *Cavalcade* was one of my favorite programs among others - *Studio One* and *Screen Director's Playhouse*."

EPISODE #607 **"DINNER AT BELMONT"** Broadcast on April 11, 1949
    Starring: Janet Blair as Ida Foster   Margery Maude as Mrs. Polk
    Les Damon as Gale Thurston   Ed Jerome as Berrien Lindsley
    Ted Osborn as General Johnson   James McCallion as the Corporal
    James Monks as Jupiter   Joan Shea as Adelicia
    Bob Dryden as the soldier
Based on the 1942 novel by A.L. Crabbe, adapted for *Cavalcade* by Virginia Radcliffe.
Produced and directed by Jack Zoller.
Bill Hamilton was the commercial spokesman and Ted Pearson was the announcer.
Music was composed by Ardon Cornwell and conducted by Donald Bryan.

Story: During the Civil War, Sarah Polk, the widow of President Polk, found herself in an awkward position. Although her family ties and her friends were Southern, she stood for the Union. Sarah believed the Nation could again be welded when the war was over. But it would demand mutual interests and understanding. It would be a task for the young people of both North and South - like Gale Thurston and Ida Foster. Sarah understood the clash of loyalties between these two, and helped reweave their romance . . . a romance that symbolized to her the need for all young Americans to unite and erase the scars left by the war. Her courage and faith helped lay the cornerstone for a strong, united America.

EPISODE #608 "HONEST JOHN GAMINSKI AND THE THIRTEEN UNCLE SAMS"
Broadcast on April 18, 1949
Starring: Oscar Homolka as Honest John
Ed Jerome as Haller
Lyle Sudrow as Joe
Pat O'Malley as Contractor
John Gibson as Stevie
Marilyn Erskine as Mary
Bill Adams as Uncle Sam one
Earl George as Uncle Sam two
Written for *Cavalcade* by Frank Gabrielson.
Produced and directed by Jack Zoller.
Bill Hamilton was the commercial spokesman and Ted Pearson was the announcer.
Music was composed by Ardon Cornwell and conducted by Donald Bryan.
Story: Honest John Gaminski, politician, didn't take reporter Joe Laurel's accusations too seriously. Honest John ran the party machine, and didn't see anything wrong with hiring twelve "live" Uncle Sams to swing an election. But Honest John had reckoned without the visit from the thirteenth Uncle Sam. In a dream, Uncle Sam took John back to the politician's childhood days of hunger and despair in a foreign land . . . through a life in an America that greed and selfishness could have made real. John was forcibly reminded that the American way of life was based on freedom - a freedom by the people which, to survive, must truly serve the people. Will Honest John awaken to serve his country and community?

EPISODE #609 "LADY ON A MISSION" Broadcast on April 25, 1949
Starring: Dorothy McGuire as Elizabeth
House Jameson as James
Mildred Clinton as Felicite
Bob Dryden as the coachman
Staats Cotsworth as Legroux
Bernard Grant as Carnot
Stefan Schnabel as the guard
Luis Van Rooten as the ring leader
Based on a chapter from the book "First Ladies" by Mary Ormsbee Whitton, as originally published by Hastings House in 1948. Adapted for *Cavalcade* by Margaret Lewerth.
Produced and directed by Jack Zoller.
Bill Hamilton was the commercial spokesman and Ted Pearson was the announcer.
Music was composed by Ardon Cornwell and conducted by Donald Bryan.
Story: Paris, 1794: hatred and terror followed in the wake of the Revolution. The prisons were filled. One of those accused of being a traitor was Madame Lafayette, wife of America's great friend, the Marquis de Lafayette. America was shocked, but our Ambassador to France, James Monroe, was helpless. To plead to the Committee of Public Safety for release would mean the loss of prestige for America, and might further harm Madame Lafayette's position. Then the Ambassador's lovely wife, Elizabeth Monroe, suggested a daring scheme. If the people of France became aware of America's concern for Madame Lafayette, the Committee might hesitate to carry out plans for her execution. To make her country's position clear, Elizabeth Monroe, in the face of grave personal danger, called upon Madame Lafayette at the prison. The scheme worked. Madame Lafayette was released, and American diplomacy gained new stature.

Trivia: The original title of this script was "Mission Accomplished."

EPISODE #610 **"WHEN WE'RE GREEN WE GROW"** Broadcast on May 2, 1949
    Starring: Jane Darwell as Ma Logan   Helen Claire as Miss Jennie
    Judy Lockser as Clover   Iris Mann as Blossom
    Larry Robinson as Luke   Bill Adams as Sam
    Cecile Roy as the baby   Donald Hastings as Charlie
    Chuck Webster as the man   Staats Cotsworth as Mr. Kibbee
Dorothy Storm, Betty Brensca, and Jim Goss as extras.
Adapted for *Cavalcade* by Virginia Radcliffe, based on the book of the same name by Jane S. McKimmon, which was originally published by the University of North Carolina Press in 1945.
Produced and directed by Jack Zoller.
Bill Hamilton was the commercial spokesman and Ted Pearson was the announcer.
Music was composed by Ardon Cornwell and conducted by Donald Voorhees.
Story: "People are just like the land. When there is no hope, they are gray and barren. But when they're green, they grow." And so it was with Ma Logan. A farmer's wife, each day brought drudgery, and Ma couldn't remember when she'd been young. It really was quite an event when a buggy broke down in the road near the Logan farm. Ma had her first visitor in three years. Better still, to find out it was Jane McKimmon, the new "Home Demonstration Agent." With her coming, a new life began for the Logans. "Miss Jennie" taught the Logan girls to earn money by selling tomatoes they grew and canned. She showed Ma how to make a new hat. But most of all, "Miss Jennie" brought them hope.

Trivia: Eighty-one year old Jennie McKimmon spoke over the microphone after the drama. Jane Darwell played another "Ma" on the big screen, as "Ma Joad" in *The Grapes of Wrath* (1940).

EPISODE #611 **"HEARD 'ROUND THE WORLD"** Broadcast on May 9, 1949
    Starring: Donald Crisp as Judge Henry French   House Jameson as Emerson
    Ian Martin as Patrick   Elliott Reid as Dan
    Alice Yourman as Mother   Eric Dressler as Mr. Alcott
    Ginger Jones as May   Barbara Townsend as Louisa
Others in the cast: Alfred de la Fueute, Larry Robinson, Irene Hubbard, Jerry Solars, and Michael Alexander.
Written for *Cavalcade* by Halsted Welles, based on two publications. One was the 1947 book "Journey Into Fame" by Margaret French Cresson of Harvard College. The second was the story "Concord, American Town" by Townsend Scudder.
Produced and directed by Jack Zoller.
Bill Hamilton was the commercial spokesman and Ted Pearson was the announcer.
Music composed by Ardon Cornwell and conducted by Donald Voorhees.
Story: April 19, 1875 promised to be a big day in the life of Judge Henry French of Concord. A statue created by the Judge's son was to be dedicated. There would be speeches by Ralph Waldo Emerson, the editor of *The Atlantic Monthly*, and President Grant. The eve of the great event was cold, windy and rainy. The judge worried about the statue. He was proud of it, proud of his son. Suppose the wind blew it over? Suppose it should be damaged before the unveiling? The judge had to find out. Standing before the shrouded monument, the old man recalled the events that had shaped the career of his son, Daniel. He remembered the shy, sensitive boy who was to be honored when the statue was unveiled. But for all his pride, the Judge never dreamed how symbolic that statue would become . . . how important would be the statue of the Minute Men. Nor did he know that a few years later his son, Daniel Chester French, would create another great work: the seated, brooding figure in the Lincoln Memorial.

From "The House Near Little Dock Street," a *Cavalcade of America* broadcast starring Ginger Rogers.

Trivia: The daughter of Daniel Chester French appears after the story and tells an anecdote about her father.

EPISODE #612   **"THE HOUSE NEAR LITTLE DOCK STREET"**   Broadcast May 16, 1949

Starring: Ginger Rogers as Lydia Darrah   Guy Sorel as Lord Sorel
Richard Newton as Lt. Newton   Horace Braham as Patterson
Edgar Stehli as Banks   Scott Tennyson as Philip
Alan Hewitt as the Major   Iris Mann as Susanna
Richard Newton as Sentry   Scott Tennyson as Jennings
Guy Sorel as the ordley   Vinton Hayworth as Col. Craig
Walter Black as Sgt. Black   Alan Hewitt as Sgt. Alan
Written for *Cavalcade* by Margaret Lewerth.
Produced and directed by Jack Zoller.
Bill Hamilton was the commercial spokesman and Ted Pearson was the announcer.
Music composed by Ardon Cornwell and conducted by Donald Voorhees.
Story: During the winter of 1777, a small group of Washington's men were camped near Philadelphia at Whitemarsh. In British-occupied Philadelphia, troops were comfortably billeted in citizen's homes. Mrs. Lydia Darrah was the unwilling hostess to colonel Robert Patterson, Adjutant to General Howe. One night Col. Patterson called a meeting of his staff. He ordered the Darrah household to their rooms. But Lydia, suspecting an impending British action, listened in on the discussion. When she learned that the British planned a surprise attack on the troops at Whitemarsh, she knew she must move quickly to warn the Continentals.

Trivia: This *Cavalcade* episode brought together Hollywood actress Ginger Rogers and New-York-based radio actor Vinton Hayworth. Believe-it-or-not, Vinton was Ginger Rogers' uncle (Rogers' mother and Hayworth's wife were sisters). To add confusion to the Hayworth name, Vinton was Rita Hayworth's mother's brother!

EPISODE #613   **"WOMAN WITH A SWORD"**   Broadcast on May 23, 1949

Starring: Madeleine Carroll as Anna Ella Carroll   Charles Webster as the voice
Ray Johnson as Judge Lemuel Evans   Ted Osborn as Senator Wade
Alice Reinheart as Virgie Stewart   John Grigg as Mr. Ashton
Amanda Randolph as Millie   Ed Jerome as Abraham Lincoln
Ted Osborn as the driver   Charles Webster as Stanton
John Grigg as John W. Booth
Adapted for *Cavalcade* by Virginia Radcliffe, from incidents in the novel of the same name by Hollister Noble, as originally published by Doubleday and Company in 1948.
Produced and directed by Jack Zoller.
Bill Hamilton was the commercial spokesman and Ted Pearson was the announcer.
Music composed by Ardon Cornwell and conducted by Donald Voorhees.
Story: Anna Carroll was a brilliant constitutional lawyer. In the dark days of the Civil War, President Lincoln asked her to evaluate the Northern strategy. She discredited the plans for an attack along the Mississippi. Instead she proposed the "Tennessee Plan" which General Grant carried through to victory. Later, when the war ended, Anna Carroll learned that the man she loved, a Southern soldier, had been killed in the campaign she had planned. Carroll found she could be useful once again when President Lincoln asked her to help build a peaceful, united America. The President planned to make public her part in winning the war, and to ask Congress to repay her for her services and the personal funds she had spent. An assassin's bullet interfered, and Anna became a woman without plans, without love, without the recognition she deserved.

EPISODE #614 "**THE RELUCTANT REBEL**"   Broadcast on May 30, 1949
    Starring: Robert Cummings as Adam Corlear   Ed Jerome as Duane
    Fran Lafferty as Delight   Agnes Young as Mrs. Delaplace
    Bob Dryden as Buck   John Gibson as Baker
    Ross Martin as the landlord   John Griggs as Ethan Allen
    Byron Kane as Olin   John Gibson as Grant
    Ross Martin as the lieutenant   Bob Dryden as voice one
    Byron Kane as voice two

Adapted for *Cavalcade* by Arthur Arent, based on the book of the same name by Frederick F. Van de Water, originally published by Duell, Sloan and Pierce in 1948. Produced and directed by Jack Zoller.
Bill Hamilton was the commercial spokesman and Ted Pearson was the announcer.
Music composed by Ardon Cornwell and conducted by Donald Voorhees.
Story: Strangers were viewed with suspicion in New England just prior to the Revolutionary War. The Vermont territory had been given to both New York and New Hampshire under conflicting grants, and the settlers were determined to fight for their homes. Adam Corlear, who had inherited some of the disputed land, went to Bennington to investigate. His interest was first captured by young Delight Royden. And Ethan Allen, leader of the "Green Mountain Boys," convinced Adam of the New Hampshiremen's rights. When Delight's home was burned by renegade New Yorkers, she fled with an English friend to British-held Fort Ticonderoga for protection. But tension was mounting between America and England, and Delight became a virtual prisoner. Forgetting personal interests, Allen saw an opportunity not only to rescue Delight, but to aid America by taking the weakly defended Fort. Adam joined the plan, which freed Delight and brought the Fort into American hands.

EPISODE #615 "**THE RETURN OF THE LODGER**"   Broadcast on June 6, 1949
    Starring: Richard Widmark as Jacob Riis   Ian Martin as Ted Roosevelt
    Charles Penman as the Sergeant   Charles Penman as the voice
    Walter Kinsells as Mulleavy and Ferry   Edgar Stehli as the watchman
    Bill Zuckert as the cop   Art Kohl as the tramp
    Stefan Schnabel as Dutch   Brad Barker as the puppy

Written for *Cavalcade* by Morton Wishengrad.
Produced and directed by Jack Zoller.
Bill Hamilton was the commercial spokesman and Ted Pearson was the announcer.
Music composed by Ardon Cornwell and conducted by Donald Voorhees.
Story: On a bleak, wet night in 1896, two wayfarers visited a police lodging house near the docks in New York City. Here shelter was offered indiscriminately to thieves, blackguards, and even children. The place was a school of crime and a nursery of vice. The sight of the sleeping men and children brought to one of the men sharp, painful memories of a night twenty-five years earlier. A lonely, homeless boy, Jacob Riis had asked for shelter in this same filthy, disease-ridden lodging house. What happened to him that night made him determined to wipe out such conditions. The other man viewed the scene with horror and rising anger. He heard his friend's story of brutal treatment at the hands of the men in charge. A few days later, as Police Commissioner of the city of New York, Theodore Roosevelt gave the orders that closed forever the police lodging rooms. Together Roosevelt and Riis went on to extend social reforms in the crowded tenements, the courts and schools.

Trivia: The original title of this script - before the actual broadcast - was "Night in a Lodging House." Richard Widmark, who has the starring role in this broadcast, was a popular supporting actor on *Cavalcade* a few short years ago.

EPISODE #616 "**FOOTLIGHTS ON THE FRONTIER**" Broadcast on June 13, 1949
Starring: Walter Hampden as Joe Jefferson
Staats Cotsworth as the voice of father
John Griggs as Featherstone
Patricia Hosley as Rosalind
Mary Lou Foster as the young lady
Ivan Cury as Jefferson (child)
Agnes Young as Joe's mother
John Griggs as Jikes
Patricia Hosley as Betsy
Written for *Cavalcade* by Frank Gabrielson.
Produced and directed by Jack Zoller.
Bill Hamilton was the commercial spokesman and Ted Pearson was the announcer.
Music composed by Ardon Cornwell and conducted by Donald Voorhees.
Story: Springfield, Illinois, with the legislature in session, was an ideal location for a family of show people who wanted their own theatre, and decided to invest their few dollars and all of their efforts into building a theatre. Only one thing threatened a successful opening: the ingenue's bad old. Ten-year-old Joe decided to solve this problem by auditioning local girls for an understudy. His plans backfired when he criticized the performance of a local daughter, and the Council rescinded the theatre permit. Heartbroken, young Joe told his troubles to a tall stranger, who successfully pleaded the case to the City Council. The "friend in need" was a struggling young lawyer named Abe Lincoln. The boy was Joe Jefferson, later to become one of the great actors of the American theatre.

Trivia: Walter Hampden's Shakespearean roles have made him well known to theatre audience. Eleven-year-old Ivan Cury had been acting little more than a year, but was already becoming well known to radio listeners.

EPISODE #617 "**RIDIN' SHOTGUN**" Broadcast on June 20, 1949
Starring: Ralph Bellamy as Scott
Arthur Kohl as Red
Scott Tennyson as Charlie
Ivan Cury as the boy
Cameron Andrews as the bartender
Jeanette Nolan as Dixie
Bob Dryden as Billings
Jeanette Nolan as Blackburn
Arthur Kohl as Dobbs
Brad Barker as the voice of the dog
Bob Dryden as Nichols
Don Douglas as Shipley
Scott Tennyson as the guard
Cameron Andrews as the doctor
Written for *Cavalcade* by Arthur Arent, suggested by episodes in "The Black Hills" by Robert J. Casey, originally published by Bobbs-Merrill in 1949.
Produced and directed by Jack Zoller.
Bill Hamilton was the commercial spokesman and Ted Pearson was the announcer.
Music composed by Ardon Cornwell and conducted by Donald Voorhees.
Story: The Wells Fargo Company was an early American express and banking organization. Henry Wells and William G. Fargo founded the company in 1852. But transportation of goods, merchandise and money had to be done inefficiently, often at a loss from the thieves and murders on the stage trails. The Blackburn Gang was one such group, and they looted almost every stage coach carrying money. This is the story of how one Scott Davis of Deadwood, South Dakota, rode shotgun on the coach carrying the Wells Fargo gold and finally captured the Blackburn Gang.

Trivia: The broadcast of June 20, 1949 was originally scheduled to be the final broadcast of the season, and the closing drama was to be "The Homecoming of Sou Chan." During the set-ups for this broadcast, Fred Allen offered to make an appearance if they could reschedule the drama for the week after. Du Pont's agency agreed and a script sitting on the shelf waiting for dramatization was performed instead. The "Homecoming" script was pre-empted for the week after, making the broadcast of June 27 the final of the season.

EPISODE #618   "THE HOMECOMING OF SOU CHAN"   Broadcast on June 27, 1949
  Starring: Kenny Delmar as Sou Chan   Guy Repp as Tom
  Edgar Stehli as Pin Chan Moe   Cameron Andrews as Dr. Sung Wong
  Ted Osborn as Mr. Livingstone Fu   Rolly Bester as Mrs. MacKenzie
  Art Kohl as customer Arthur Wi   John Gibson as the policeman
  Guy Repp as the second brother   Kim Chan as the first brother
  John Gibson as Reilly   Richard Gordon as father
  Vivian Barry as Viola   Alan Shay as Stanley
  Dick Gordon as Mr. MacKenzie   Kim Chan as the waiter
  Special guest appearance by Fred Allen.
  Written for *Cavalcade* by Frank Gabrielson.
  Produced and directed by Jack Zoller.
  Bill Hamilton was the commercial spokesman and Ted Pearson was the announcer.
  Music composed by Ardon Cornwell and conducted by Donald Voorhees.
  Story: When Sou Chan arrived in America, he had only one dream. That one day he would return to his home in China - a millionaire. He worked very hard and saved every penny. Soon he had five hundred dollars. But then his cousin, Pin Chan, needed an expensive operation. Sou gave him the five hundred dollars as a New Year's gift. Starting again, Sou cooked in a lumber camp, worked as a house-boy, and even sold rattlesnakes for rattlesnake wine. By 1939 he had worked his way East and had forty-eight hundred dollars saved. With the money he bought a restaurant. Business was good, but not good enough. When the bank demanded fifteen hundred dollars, Sou was unable to meet his obligations. Things looked desperate. But then Sou Chan's customer's and friends came to the rescue.

  Trivia: Kenny Delmar, who was a regular player on *Cavalcade* several years ago, was best known for his portrayal of Senator Claghorn on *The Fred Allen Show*. The real Sou Chan appears after the story. One of Sou Chan's regular customers, Fred Allen, appears at the end of the broadcast to congratulate him. This was the last show of the season.

  More trivia: Rolly Bester, who plays the Chinese Marriage Broker in this broadcast, has played Chinese accents on numerous radio programs previous. Almost two years later she would play Mother Wong in the *Cavalcade* episode, "Chinese Daughter." She had also played the daughter of Charlie Chan on the radio series of the same name. She appeared frequently on *Mr. District Attorney*, *The Fat Man*, *The Shadow*, *Big Story*, and was currently heard as Mrs. Antonio, the landlady, on *Pepper Young's Family*.

EPISODE #619   "WIRE TO THE WEST"   Broadcast on August 30, 1949
  Starring: Raymond Massey as Hiram Sibley   Parker Fennelly as the operator
  Cameron Prud'Homme as Judge Selden   Abby Lewis as Emmie
  Lauretta Fillbrandt as Elizabeth Sibley   Michael O'Day as the boy
  Raymond Edward Johnson as Kittleheim   House Jameson as Cornell
  Arthur Kohl as Morris   Scott Tennyson as Mann
  Michael O'Shay as Bill   Arthur Kohl as Creighton
  Scott Tennyson as the operator   James Goss as Brigham Young
  Raymond Edward Johnson as Judge Field   James Goss as the voice
  Written for *Cavalcade* by Irve Tunick.
  Produced by Roger Pryor and directed by Jack Zoller.
  Bill Hamilton was the commercial spokesman and Ted Pearson was the announcer.
  Music composed by Ardon Cornwell and conducted by Donald Voorhees.

(cont'd)

Story: Over a hundred years ago there was chaos in the infant telegraph industry. Service was bad, rates high, business unprofitable. Hiram Sibley was a man of vision. He saw that the industry needed coordination to better serve the public, and he went to work, buying up and merging the fifty separate telegraph companies. The name he gave to his new organization was Western Union.

Trivia: This was the first broadcast of the fifteenth season, being broadcast on a new day . . . Tuesday. However, NBC's complete West Coast network facilities was not available to broadcast *Cavalcade* until the end of Daylight Savings Time. This broadcast - and the next three shows - were not heard in the West. On September 27, Mountain and Pacific Coast stations joined the rest of the NBC network in presenting *Cavalcade* to the entire nation.

More trivia: Miss Alice E. Byrnes, a schoolteacher, recently purchased four shares of Du Pont stock. As she says, she had a small amount of extra money available and wanted to invest it so that it would be earning a return until she might have some special use for it. Much to Miss Byrnes' surprise, she turned out to be the company's 100,000th stockholder. The next thing she knew, she received an invitation to visit Mr. Crawford H. Greenewalt, President of the Company, and to make a tour of several Du Pont plants as a guest of the Company. With her sister, Marian, Miss Byrnes had just this week returned from visiting plants in several states - stopping off to pay a sight-seeing visit to Washington D.C., which she has never seen. She also visited the Du Pont Company's home office in Wilmington, Delaware, and the Du Pont Exhibit on the boardwalk at Atlantic City. Miss Myrnes' visit to *Cavalcade* was the climax of her trip. She was not only guest on the program, but was interviewed by announcer Bill Hamilton.

EPISODE #620 **"LAY THAT MUSKET DOWN"** Broadcast on September 6, 1949
Starring: Paul Henreid as Christopher Ludwick   Leon Askin as the soldier
Edwin Jerome as George Washington   Bob Dryden as Karl
Stefan Schnabel as Hessian   Peter Cappel as Oberst
Arnold Robertson as Max   Max Wessels as Singer
Based on a passage from the 1946 book, "Lost Men of American History" by Stewart H. Holbrook, and adapted for *Cavalcade* by Russell Hughes.
Produced by Roger Pryor and directed by Jack Zoller.
Bill Hamilton was the commercial spokesman and Ted Pearson was the announcer.
Music composed by Ardon Cornwell and conducted by Donald Voorhees.
Story: Christopher Ludwick, a Philadelphia baker, wanted to serve his country. He had come to America from the Herman state of Hesse-Darmstadt some twenty years before, and he and his family had prospered. Now, during the Revolutionary War, he had a plan through which he might show his gratitude to his adopted land. Ludwick got Washington's approval of his plan. Posing as a deserter from the Continental Army, he slipped through the British lines to the Hessian camp on Staten Island. There he hoped to promote desertion among his former countrymen who were mercenaries serving the British. He was, however, spotted by British officers and forced to disclose of Washington's troops. Without powder the British could not attack Washington. So, as Ludwick made his own escape, he blew up the enemy's arsenal.

EPISODE #621 "JOE PALMER'S BEARD" Broadcast on September 13, 1949

    Starring: Brian Donlevy as Joe Palmer
    Cameron Andrews as Jed
    Donald Rose as Tommy
    Scott Tennyson as Trask
    Arnold Robertson as the jailer
    Agnes Young as Nancy
    James Goss as Wilson
    Bill Adams as Williams
    John Seymour as the Judge
    Arthur Kohl as the voice

Based on a passage from the 1946 book "Lost Men of American History" by Stewart H. Holbrook, and adapted for *Cavalcade* by George Faulkner.
Produced by Roger Pryor and directed by Jack Zoller.
Bill Hamilton was the commercial spokesman and Ted Pearson was the announcer.
Music composed by Ardon Cornwell and conducted by Donald Voorhees.
Story: Joseph Palmer of Fitchburg, Massachusetts, wore a beard: a fine, full, red beard. In the year of 1830 there was no law against a man wearing chin whiskers, but no American male who wished to be considered sane, upright and respectable did so. When Tommy Palmer was tormented by his playmates about his father's beard, Joe decided to shave it off. That was the day, however, that the local authorities demanded the removal of the "indecent" whiskers. Now, Palmer was not really a stubborn man, and his beard was not as important to him as were his wife and son - but keeping those whiskers became a matter of principle. When the local judge threatened a jail sentence, Palmer chose to go to prison rather than shave off his beard. Palmer wrote to a newspaper editor. Soon the story appeared in papers throughout the country. Journalists accused the New England court of making mockery of American justice and individual liberty. The Fitchburg officials gave way to the pressure of public opinion, and when they released their prisoner, Joe Palmer still wore his beard, a flaming symbol of liberty.

EPISODE #622 "TROUBLESOME JANE" Broadcast on September 20, 1949

    Starring: Ruth Hussey as Jane Swisshelm
    Ross Martin as Henry
    Bob Dryden as Perkins
    Klock Ryder as Si
    Rod Hendrickson as Sam
    Wilda Hinkle as the farm woman
    Kenny Delmar as Captain Seeley
    Helen Gerald as Elizabeth
    Anthony Randall as Imbrie
    Sarah Fussell as Josie
    Joseph Bell as the farmer
    Maurice Ellis as Moses

Jeff Britton, Donald W. Keyes, Salem Ludwig, and John Harper as the townspeople.
Written for *Cavalcade* by Luther Davis, suggested by an article in Margaret Ferrand Thorp's book "Female Persuasion" and by Jane Swisshelm's autobiography, originally published by the Yale University Press in 1949.
Produced by Roger Pryor and directed by Jack Zoller.
Bill Hamilton was the commercial spokesman and Ted Pearson was the announcer.
Music composed by Ardon Cornwell and conducted by Donald Voorhees.
Story: In the middle 1800's, when most women stayed home and kept house, Jane Swisshelm owned and published her own anti-slavery newspaper. As a columnist, her political articles in the *New York Tribune* had made her internationally famous. When Jane arrived in St. Cloud, Minnesota on a visit, she found that slave labor was being brought into the free territory. It wasn't long before she began publishing an abolitionist paper, "The St. Cloud Visitor." The chief object of her attacks was Captain Seeley, a local politician who was growing quite wealthy on slave labor. He used threats to quiet her criticisms of him. When she refused to be frightened, Seeley sent his ruffians to destroy some of the newspaper's printing equipment. Then the townspeople got into the act - but on whose side?

Trivia: John Nesbitt appears at the end to promote his next week's appearance.

EPISODE #623 **"THE IMMORTAL BLACKSMITH"** Broadcast on September 27, 1949
  Starring: John Nesbitt as the narrator   John Griggs as Tom Davenport
  Jean Gillespie as Emily Davenport   Joseph Bell as Professor Helms
  Parker Fennelly as Oliver Davenport   William Podmore as Prof. Stanton
  Scott Tennyson as the first customer   Cameron Andrews as the second customer
  Written for *Cavalcade* by John Nesbitt.
  Produced by Roger Pryor and directed by Jack Zoller.
  Bill Hamilton was the commercial spokesman and Ted Pearson was the announcer.
  Music composed by Ardon Cornwell and conducted by Donald Voorhees.
  Story: In the little town of Brandon, Vermont, over a hundred years ago, there lived a blacksmith named Tom Davenport. Tom had a small business, a patient wife Emily, and a flair for tinkering with contraptions of one sort or another. One day Tom came home with an apparatus for which he had traded much of his worldly goods - a magnetic contrivance of wires and jumping sparks and jars of acid. It seemed to have no earthly use whatever. Tom became absorbed with the contraption. He neglected blacksmithing. Through weeks and months and years of toil, he groped his way toward the incredible marvel of the electric motor. Tom's discovery attracted great attention, but American industry was not yet ready to use it. They stand as pioneers whose dreams helped to pave the way for an industrial and prosperous America.

EPISODE #624 **"THE LADY BECOMES A GOVERNOR"** Broadcast on October 4, 1949
  Starring: Dorothy McGuire as Margaret   Peter Capell as the guard
  Staats Cotsworth as Judson   Vinton Hayworth as Calvert
  Sarah Burton as Kathryn   Richard Newton as Geoffrey
  Guy Spaul as Stanton   John Stanley as Peters
  Malcolm Keen as the officer   Richard Gordon as the chairman
  Richard Newton as one of the soldiers   Michael Alexander as the other soldier
  Malcolm Keen as the Governor
  Based on the book "Mistress Brent" by Lucy M. Thurston, and adapted for *Cavalcade* by Margaret Lewerth.
  Produced by Roger Pryor and directed by Jack Zoller.
  Bill Hamilton was the commercial spokesman and Ted Pearson was the announcer.
  Music composed by Ardon Cornwell and conducted by Donald Voorhees.
  Story: When Leonard Calvert, third Lord Baltimore, was governor of the colony of Maryland, women had few rights. For example, no unmarried woman could own property for more than seven years. Lady Margaret Brent, young, beautiful and unmarried, seemed likely to become a victim of this law. Her unscrupulous brother-in-law, Captain Rogers, was enforcing it to gain the farmland she had captured from the wilderness. When a rebellion broke out in Maryland, Margaret suggested that Virginia soldiers be brought in. During the fighting, Calvert contracted a fatal disease. Just before he died, he handed his governor's seal to Margaret, whom he loved and trusted. She later appeared before the Assembly to fight for her plantation. So convincing were her pleas that not only were her rights upheld, but she became the first woman to hold a seat in the Maryland assembly.

EPISODE #625 **"THIS LITTLE PLOT OF GROUND"** Broadcast on October 11, 1949
  Starring: Cornel Wilde as Ralph Waldo Emerson   Ethel Owen as Aunt Mary
  Jean Gillespie as Ellen Louisa Tucker   Eric Dressler as the doctor
  Written for *Cavalcade* by Halsted Welles, based on portions in the 1949 book "Ralph Waldo Emerson" by Ralph Rusk.
  Produced by Roger Pryor and directed by Jack Zoller.
  Bill Hamilton was the commercial spokesman and Ted Pearson was the announcer.
  Music composed by Ardon Cornwell and conducted by Donald Voorhees.

Story: In the early part of the eighteenth century, young Ralph Waldo Emerson was preparing to follow his brothers and his father into the Ministry. For years, under the stern guidance of his Aunt Mary, he dedicated his time, talents and hopes to the Church. Yet he lacked confidence. Emerson doubted his ability to match the brilliance and energy of his father and brothers. Then Emerson met and fell in love with Ellen Louisa Tucker. She was lovely and understanding, but incurably ill. Despite his Aunt's objections, Emerson persuaded Ellen to marry him, and accepted a post as pastor of a Boston church. Ellen gave Emerson the confidence and faith he had lacked. His sermons achieved new vigor, and by having the courage to speak his own mind, Emerson became one of our great American leaders of thought.

Trivia: For many years the Du Pont Company has operated on the belief that all personal injuries can be prevented. Now a new world's-best no-injury record had been won by the Du Pont plant at Martinsville, Virginia - twenty-one million man-hours - nearly seven years - with no lost-time injuries. This broke a five-year record held by another Du Pont plant at Seaford, Delaware. During this broadcast, Mr. Ned H. Dearborn, President of the National Safety Council, presented a special award to Mr. Don Hartford, manager of the Martinsville plant. The bronze plaque was permanently placed in the plant as a reminder that injuries *can* be prevented. The National Safety Council had also voted to the Du Pont Company its awards for Distinguished Service to Safety for the years 1945 through 1948. Du Pont had previously won this award for the years 1942, 1943, and 1944.

More trivia: Cornel Wilde held the "Award of Honor" certificate presented to Du Pont by the National Safety Council on *Cavalcade*. That evening the award was accepted on behalf of the company by H.L. Miner.

EPISODE #626 **"REMEMBER ANNA ZENGER"** Broadcast on October 18, 1949
Starring: Rosalind Russell as Anna Zenger Peter Capell as John Zenger
Arthur Maitland as Andrew Hamilton Barry Thompson as the foreman
Barry Thompson as Harrison William Podmore as Morris
Neil Fitzgerald as the tax collector Ed Jerome as Cosby
William Podmore as Alexander James McCallion as Bradley
Berry Kroeger as Delancey Neil Fitzgerald as the voice
Adapted for *Cavalcade* by Morton Wishengrad, from the book "Anna Zenger" by Kent Cooper, which was originally published by Farrar Straus in 1946.
Produced by Roger Pryor and directed by Jack Zoller.
Bill Hamilton was the commercial spokesman and Ted Pearson was the announcer.
Music composed by Ardon Cornwell and conducted by Donald Voorhees.
Story: In America of 1720, certain men from the Old World saw themselves as rulers of the New. They stopped at nothing to build and safeguard their power. Among these men were the Governor of the Colony of New York and his power-mad adviser. Newspapers were powerless. If they spoke in protest the presses were destroyed or the editors jailed. But an unschooled printer named Peter Zenger, and his wife, Anna, dared to oppose the corrupt practices in the New York Colony. Although Peter could not find the words to say what he felt, Anna could and did. When Peter printed her articles under his own name, he was quickly arrested. Anna continued to fight. She appealed to one of the leading lawyers of the time to defend her husband.

Trivia: Rosalind Russell was currently appearing in *The Velvet Touch*, the first release of Independent Artists, a new company of which she was co-owner. Russell appeared in co-operation and agreement that a pitch was made at the end of the program about the new movie.

More trivia: Script writer Philip Lewis wrote the first draft of this script, originally entitled "Anna Zenger," but when Morton Wishengrad wrote the second draft, the script varied so much that the original plot was almost unrecognizable, and Wishengrad received the script credit.

EPISODE #627   **"LIFE LINE"**   Broadcast on October 25, 1949
Starring: Dane Clark as Bob Forrest   Peggy Lobbin as Lula
Michael O'Day as the voice   George Petrie as Tucker
Les Damon as Kindler   Cameron Prud'Homme as Frodle
Bill Smith as Landru   Phil Sterling as Phillips
Written for *Cavalcade* by Margaret Lewerth and Irve Tunick.
Produced by Roger Pryor and directed by Jack Zoller.
Bill Hamilton was the commercial spokesman and Ted Pearson was the announcer.
Music composed by Ardon Cornwell and conducted by Donald Voorhees.
Story: Bob Forrest, a veteran of the Coast Guard, wanted to go into business for himself. Some friends told him that in the America of 1946 there was no opportunity for a small business. But Bob didn't feel that way. He was young and he had an idea, and he believed that America would give him the chance he needed. While in the Coast Guard, he had discovered that on the bottom of Puget Sound lay thousands of logs, an underwater forest. Bob got a contract with a large pulp company, which agreed to buy all the good logs he could salvage. Largely on the strength of this contract, the bank granted him a loan to buy his equipment, and then he went to work. It was tough going at first; the work was hard, and dangerous. But Bob stuck to it. He salvaged his equipment from the bottom of the Sound, and in the past year and a half, his company had salvaged nearly $75,000 worth of lumber.

Trivia: The real Bob Forrest made an appearance after the drama.

EPISODE #628   **"STRIKE A BLOW FOR LIBERTY"**   Broadcast on November 1, 1949
Starring: Tyrone Power by Thomas Forty   Arthur Kohl as Asa
Staats Cotsworth as Rivington   Barry Thompson as Delancey
Peter Capell as O'Keefe   George Petrie as the soldier
Arnold Robertson as the guard   Bill Smith as Weed
Marilyn Erskine as Ellen   George Petrie as Tallmadge
Arnold Robertson as man one   Arthur Kohl as man two
Adapted for *Cavalcade* by Arthur Arent, from the 1947 novel "Thomas Forty" by Edward Stanley.
Produced by Roger Pryor and directed by Jack Zoller.
Bill Hamilton was the commercial spokesman and Ted Pearson was the announcer.
Music composed by Ardon Cornwell and conducted by Donald Voorhees.
Story: The "hour of decision" came for young Thomas Forty in 1778. A printer's helper on a New York Tory newspaper, Tom found it more and more difficult to conceal his sympathy with the Continentals. Then one day, after he had spoken out against the British, Tom was taken to Sugar House - the notorious Tory prison. Here he was shown the treatment given prisoners, and forced to choose - betray Washington, or be thrown into Sugar House, probably to die as a traitor to the crown. Tom chose prison, resolute in his belief that it is better to die for a cause than to live in hypocrisy. On the day he was to be executed, Tom escaped, and later reached the American lines to fight for freedom.

EPISODE #629 **"SIGNAL TO THE WORLD"** Broadcast on November 8, 1949
    Starring: Cary Grant as Robert Townsend   Joan Lorring as Susan
    Horace Braham as Clinton   Bertram Tanswell as Lieutenant
    Alan Manson as the courier   Berry Kroeger as Roe
    Malcolm Keen as Woodhull   Wilda Hinkle as the woman
Based on a feature entitled "The Quaker and the General" by George Scullin from the August 1949 issue of *True* magazine, and adapted for *Cavalcade* by Russell Hughes. Produced by Roger Pryor and directed by Jack Zoller.
Bill Hamilton was the commercial spokesman and Ted Pearson was the announcer. Music composed by Ardon Cornwell and conducted by Donald Voorhees.
Story: Robert Townsend was a Quaker whose religious principles forbade him carrying weapons. But his courage and ingenuity were weapons that won battles for American liberty in another way. He was the key man in one of the most effective spy rings ever known. During the American War for Independence, Townsend operated in the New York area. Posing as a prosperous merchant with Tory leanings, he made many friend among the British officers. Among these was the commander-in-chief, Sir Henry Clinton, who often confided military matters of extreme secrecy to Townsend, who promptly relayed the information to General Washington. It was soon evident to the British that the spy tapping military secrets was someone they knew and trusted. They seized Townsend's wife, Susan, on suspicion. A man torn between religious convictions and patriotism.

    Trivia: The original title of this script was "White Cockade."

EPISODE #630 **"THE GREATEST RISK"** Broadcast on November 15, 1949
    Starring: Ray Milland as McDaniel   Charlotte Manson as Dorothy
    Barry Thompson as Proctor   John Stanley as Warrell
    Eda Heinemann as Sophia   Reginald Mason as Lathrop
    Dan Ocko as the landlord   John Griggs as the judge
    George Petrie as the coachman   Brad Barker as the voice of the dog
    George Petrie as the jailer
Written for *Cavalcade* by Robert Tallmann and Halsted Welles.
Produced by Roger Pryor and directed by Jack Zoller.
Bill Hamilton was the commercial spokesman and Ted Pearson was the announcer. Music composed by Ardon Cornwell and conducted by Donald Voorhees.
Story: In 1744, the supporters of Bonnie Prince Charlie sent agents to America to promote an uprising against King George II. The leader of the group was an Irishman named James McDaniel, who was sent to Salem, New Jersey. His mission was to organize an overthrow of the local government. This would discredit the rule of King George and win favor for the Stuart preacher. In Salem, McDaniel fell in love with Dorothy Lecroy, who was engaged to the King's attorney. As the months went by, McDaniel's loyalty to the Stuart case wavered. He became convinced that Americans did not need nor want any king. McDaniel finally tried to prevent the rebellion, but was arrested and brought to trial.

EPISODE #631 **"US PILGRIMS"** Broadcast on November 22, 1949
    Starring: George Tobias as Baaraczek   Peter Donald as Joe
    George Petrie as Benny   Dan Ocko as Indian Chief
    Peter Capell as the officer   Peter Donald as Mr. Bauer
    George Tobias as the boss Pilgrim   Mercedes McCambridge as Miss Haskell
    Mildred Clinton Mrs. Hanson, Joe's wife   Rolly Bester as Mrs. Benny
    Written for *Cavalcade* by Frank Gabrielson, who also introduces the drama.
    Produced by Roger Pryor and directed by Jack Zoller.
    Bill Hamilton was the commercial spokesman and Ted Pearson was the announcer.
    Music composed by Ardon Cornwell and conducted by Donald Voorhees.
    Story: same as episode #543, broadcast on November 24, 1947

EPISODE #632 **"SPINDLETOP"** Broadcast on November 29, 1949
    Starring: Henry Fonda as Lucas   Malcolm Keen as Jefferson
    Jack Albertson as Patsy   Gertrude Warner as Caroline
    Butch Cavell as Tony   Roy Fant as Higgins
    Eric Dressler as Hayes   Joe Boland as Galey
    Larry Haines as Hamill   George Petrie as Curt
    Jack Albertson as Campbell
    Written for *Cavalcade* by Irve Tunick.
    Produced by Roger Pryor and directed by Jack Zoller.
    Bill Hamilton was the commercial spokesman and Ted Pearson was the announcer.
    Music composed by Ardon Cornwell and conducted by Donald Voorhees.
    Story: The year 1949 marked the ninetieth anniversary of America's oil industry. From a tiny beginning, it has become one of our country's most powerful assets. This growth has come from men of oil - the drillers in the field, the investors, the engineers. It offered futures for men of vision - like Anthony Lucas. An ex-Captain of the Imperial Austrian Navy, Lucas came to America late in the nineteenth century. Here, he felt, was escape from the tyranny and petty restrictions of the Old World. By 1896, Lucas was a citizen, and a successful mining and mechanical engineer. While drilling for salt in Louisiana, Lucas noticed a peculiar geological formation - an underground range of salt that pointed to Texas. To prove his theory that under one of the domes in this range was oil, he followed the range of salt, drilling as he went. Finally he tackled a dome called "Spindletop" near Beaumont. Succeeding where others had failed, Lucas pioneered one of the country's most fabulous oil wells.

EPISODE #633 **"THE WALL OF SILENCE"** Broadcast on December 6, 1949
    Starring: Gene Tierney as Marie H. Heiner   George Petrie as the undergrad
    Ginger Jones as Flo   Maurice Franklin as the doctor
    Vera Allen as the mother   Joseph Bell as the second doctor
    Charles Seel as the elevator operator   George Petrie as the third doctor
    Cecil Roy as Miss Roy   Charles Seel as the fourth doctor
    Chester Stratton as Henry   Grayce Albert as Mrs. Lewis
    Joseph Bell as Mr. Bell   Grayce Albert as the woman
    Cecil Roy as Betsy
    Adapted from the book "Hearing is Believing" by Marie Hays Heiner, originally published by the World Publishing Company in 1949. Adapted for *Cavalcade* by Morton Wishengrad.
    Produced by Roger Pryor and directed by Jack Zoller.
    Bill Hamilton was the commercial spokesman and Ted Pearson was the announcer.
    Music composed by Ardon Cornwell and conducted by Donald Voorhees.
    Story: One winter night in 1926, Marie Hays went to sleep with the sounds of music and laughter in her ears. When she awoke, the sounds were gone. That morning Marie could not hear. She went from doctor to doctor during the next few years, but the wall of

silence closed in on her steadily. And Marie grew afraid: afraid of not hearing and afraid of others knowing it, afraid of seeming stupid because she could not understand. Then one day a doctor convinced Marie that she must learn to live with her handicap. From that moment began her personal victory over deafness. With this victory came a desire to help others. For the past thirteen years she had devoted her efforts to helping the handicapped. Her program to bring sound into the lives of all deafened persons brought her the 1948 Distinguished Service Award of the Cleveland Community Fund.

EPISODE #634 **"SOUTH OF CAPE HORN"** Broadcast on December 13, 1949
Starring: Mickey Rooney as Nat Palmer   Ian Martin as O'Toole
Rod Hendrickson as Mr. Palmer   Cameron Andrews as the seaman
Arnold Moss as Von Ballingshausen   Parker Fennelly as Phineas
Jimmy Stevens as the Russian Lieutenant   Jack Hartley as Capt. Pendleton
Dorothy Sands as Mrs. Palmer

Based on a portion of the book "Clipper Ship Men" by Alexander Laing, originally published by Duell, Sloane and Pierce in 1944. Adapted for *Cavalcade* by George H. Faulkner.
Produced by Roger Pryor and directed by Jack Zoller.
Bill Hamilton was the commercial spokesman and Ted Pearson was the announcer.
Music composed by Ardon Cornwell and conducted by Donald Voorhees.
Story: Under the command of young Nathaniel Palmer, "The Hero," a tiny sailing ship, set out on a sealing expedition to the South Shetlands. The success of the trip would mean that Nat and his sweetheart, Liza, could afford to be married. After logging nine thousand miles, bad luck overtook "The Hero." The seal fields had been cleared. So Nat sailed on, further south, to look for new hunting grounds. At latitude 68 degrees south, further than man had ever gone, they were finally forced to turn back. They still had found no seals. But they had penetrated the ghostly fog to find and chart a great land mass, whose existence geographers had only guessed at for 200 years - the continent of Antarctica.

EPISODE #635 **"THE DU PONT CHORUS"** Broadcast on December 20, 1949
Under the direction of Frank J. Clark, Jr.
Mr. Crawford H. Greenewalt, President of the Du Pont Company spoke during intermission.
Broadcast from "The Playhouse" in Wilmington, Delaware.
Bill Hamilton is the announcer and master of ceremonies.
Songs performed and sung in consecutive order were: "Silent Night," "Fanfare for Christmas Day," the 1894 song "Lo How a Rose 'er Blooming," "Clear and Calm was that Holy Night," "Behold That Star," "Mary Had a Baby," "Go Tell it on the Mountain," "The First Christmas Candle," "The Sleigh," "Yule Tide Carol," "Hallelujah Chorus," Handel's "The Messiah," and finally a reprise of "Silent Night."

These are just a handful of members of the Du Pont chorus: Arthur J. Hill, Robert K. Weaver, George Tabet, William S. Groundland, Ruth Phelps, S. Elizabeth Long, Eugene Evers, John Mitchell, Jr., Richard V. Lindsey, Edith E. Churchman, Eugenia Hitt, G. Kathryn King, Celeste Martin, Fred L. Johnston, Roger A. Hines, William F. Brondyke, Elva Wells, Kathryn Kane, Katherine Clements, Jessica Reed, Lois Weber, Irma Hushbeck, Thomas Legg, John L. Ludlow, Carl E. Schweitzer, Lucille Williams, Janice Sutter, Doris Huck, Marion Perse, Elizabeth McDonough, A. Frances Edards, Ruth Breslin, Howard F. Berg, John Henderson, Harold W. Arnold, Dorothy Hanway, Elizabeth Klimuc, Margaret Geesey, Sara Freedman, Raymond Fisher, Norman Griffith, E.P.H. Meibohm, William Ulmer, Harry Eatough, Paul S. Pinkney, Thomas A. Ford, Robert N. MacDonald, Suzanne Myers, George L. Smith, Conrad L. Hoover, John C. Coates, Carolyn Swetland, A. Wallace Copeland, and Herman J. Sampson.

EPISODE #636 "A CUP OF COFFEE WITH LEW" Broadcast on December 27, 1949
Starring: Gene Lockhart as Reese
Rolly Bester as the woman
Ginger Jones as the housewife
Julian Noa as Wagner
Alan Hewitt as the salesman
Irving Mitchell as Ed
John McGovern as Harry
Ginger Jones as Lena
Irving Mitchell as Werton
James Goss as the voice
Irving Mitchell as the man
James Goss as Gene
Lon Clark as Don
Joseph Bell as the buyer
Alan Hewitt as Spiker
Dan Ocko as the doctor
Joseph Bell as Miller
John McGovern as Wheeling
Lowell Thomas is the guest narrator.
Written for *Cavalcade* by Morton Wishengrad.
Produced by Roger Pryor and directed by Jack Zoller.
Bill Hamilton was the commercial spokesman and Ted Pearson was the announcer.
Music composed by Ardon Cornwell and conducted by Donald Voorhees.
Story: During the year 1931, an abandoned pottery factory near Scio, Ohio gave Lew Reese an idea . . . to rebuild the factory and provide jobs and money for the people of Scio. Lew's enthusiasm was contagious. The townspeople offered their help, and factory was put back into operation. When the business prospered the owners, the workers, and the town prospered as well. Then disaster struck. A fire reduced the factory to ashes. But once again the men and women of Scio backed Lew with their faith, energy and money. And companies and individuals outside Scio helped Lew Reese make a new start. Today the successful Scio-Ohio pottery Company is a good example of American enterprise at work.

EPISODE #637 "THE INCOMPARABLE DOCTOR" Broadcast on January 3, 1950
Starring: Charles Laughton as Benjamin Franklin
Cathleen Cordell as Sarah
Tommy Rettig as Willie
Scott Tennyson as Adams
Kathryn Grill as the woman
Ivan Cury as Benjamin
Melville Ruick as Goodhew
Elliott Reid as Rutledge
Guy Spaul as Howe
Written for *Cavalcade* by George Faulkner.
Produced by Roger Pryor and directed by Jack Zoller.
Bill Hamilton was the commercial spokesman and Ted Pearson was the announcer.
Music composed by Ardon Cornwell and conducted by Donald Voorhees.
Story: Few men have been more famous or better liked than Benjamin Franklin. His good natured sense of humor, his fondness for all people, and his warm charm won him the affection of everyone he met. Qualities such as these were more than a little responsible for his success as a statesman and diplomat. During the time Franklin followed his hobby of scientific experimentation, he played a major role in a little known episode of American history. As leader of a group of American delegates, Franklin met with Lord Howe in a final, desperate effort to negotiate an honorable peace during the Revolutionary War.

EPISODE #638 "HONOR BOUND" Broadcast on January 10, 1950
Starring: Joan Caulfield as Connie Hardison
Vinton Hayworth as Armstrong
Richard Gordon as Dr. Shaw
Gavin Gordon as the voice
Scott Tennyson as the jailor
Scott Tennyson as the Corporal
James Monks as Zack
John Lund as Sam Davis
Ed Jerome as the Mayor
James Monks as the Chaplain
Ed Jerome as General Dodge
Gavin Gordon as Gray
Kathleen Comegys as Mrs. Davis
Dan Ocko as Wilson
Adapted for *Cavalcade* by George Faulkner, from the novel "On Jordan's Stormy Banks" by Adelaide Rowell, published by Bobbs-Merrill in 1948, and "Sam David,

Confederate Hero" by Edythe Johns Rucker Whitley," published by the Sam Davis
Memorial Association in 1947.
Produced by Roger Pryor and directed by Jack Zoller.
Bill Hamilton was the commercial spokesman and Ted Pearson was the announcer.
Music composed by Ardon Cornwell and conducted by Donald Voorhees.
Story: The story of Sam Davis, one of the Confederacy's great heroes.

Trivia: This broadcast originated from the Ryman Auditorium in Nashville, Tennessee.

EPISODE #639 **"THE GOLDEN NEEDLE"** Broadcast on January 17, 1950
    Starring: Dorothy McGuire as Nell Donnelly   Inge Adams as Katie
    Kathleen Comegys as Mother   Pat Hosley as Martha
    Bess McCammon as Mrs. Herbert   Alan Hewitt as Charlie
    Staats Cotsworth as James A. Reed   Ginger Jones as Elizabeth
    Cameron Prud'Homme as Ballenger
Written for *Cavalcade* by Virginia Radcliffe.
Produced by Roger Pryor and directed by Jack Zoller.
Bill Hamilton was the commercial spokesman and Ted Pearson was the announcer.
Music composed by Ardon Cornwell and conducted by Donald Voorhees.
Story: The story of Nell Donnelly's career, who started and achieved great success as head of a Kansas City factory employing hundreds to make dresses.

EPISODE #640 **"THE INTERCHANGEABLE MR. WHITNEY"** Broadcast January 24, 1950
    Starring: Robert Taylor as Eli Whitney   Bob Dryden as Rowley
    Parker Fennelly as Joel   Robin Morgan as Henrietta
    Raymond Edward Johnson as Edwards   Joseph Bell as North
    Cameron Prud'Homme as Wolcott   Scott Tennyson as Phelps
    Elliott Reid as Rush   Parker Fennelly as Grandpa
    Malcolm Keen as Jefferson
Based on the book "Whittling Boy" by Roger Burlingame, originally published by Harcourt, Brace and Company in 1941. Adapted for *Cavalcade* by Morton Wishengrad.
Produced by Roger Pryor and directed by Jack Zoller.
Bill Hamilton was the commercial spokesman and Ted Pearson was the announcer.
Music composed by Ardon Cornwell and conducted by Donald Voorhees.
Story: In the spring of 1799, Eli Whitney turned from cotton gins to muskets. The young American Republic was in urgent need of arms to protect itself from threatened foreign aggression. Whitney, master mechanic and brilliant inventor, had been commissioned by Congress to turn out 10,000 muskets within two years. He soon found he could never complete the job within the time limits by following customary production methods. For each musket, the gunsmith had to forge the barrel, then make the lock, and then, in turn, all the other parts. It took weeks to complete a single gun. Whitney had only two years to make 10,000! But Whitney solved the problem. And his solution of interchangeable parts helped to change the industrial patterns of the civilized world.

Trivia: Listeners' interests and hobbies were varied, and marked them as experts in specialized fields. A gentleman from Connecticut noted that a script dealing with Eli Whitney used the term "firing pin." "Those were flint lock muskets Mr. Whitney was making," the listener said. "And no flint lock gun ever had a firing pin. Firing pins were never heard of until breach-loading guns were invented . . . twenty six years after Whitney's death." The letter was referred to *Cavalcade*'s historian. "He's right," Dr. Ronalds admitted, checking back on the script. "It should have been 'firing *pans*'."

More trivia: Robert Taylor autographed a copy of this script for Miss "Skippy" Rathburn, while her mother and step-father looked on. Mr. and Mrs. Rathburn were employed by Du Pont Waynesboro Acetate Plant.

EPISODE #641   **"ORDEAL BY FIRE"**   Broadcast on January 31, 1950

Starring: Edward Arnold as Terry   Susan Douglas as Sarah
Jack Manning as Edward   Frank Behrens as Bradley
John Griggs as Nathaniel   Frank Behrens as Ellsworth
Malcolm Keen as Trumbull   Alan Bunce as Bolles
Parker Fennelly as Perkins   John Griggs as the soldier
Dan Ocko as Morrison   Malcolm Ken as Collins

Written for *Cavalcade* by Michael Sklar and Irve Tunick.
Produced by Roger Pryor and directed by Jack Zoller.
Bill Hamilton was the commercial spokesman and Ted Pearson was the announcer.
Music composed by Ardon Cornwell and conducted by Donald Voorhees.
Story: Most insurance companies in the early 1800's were weak compared to present-day standards. One exception was the Hartford Insurance Company, headed by Eliphalet Terry whose guiding principle was "Good faith is good business." Then the great fire of 1835 nearly razed New York City's business district. While other companies went broke and stopped payment on insurance policies, Eliphalet Terry set up offices on the edge of the burned area; every policyholder who had a claim was paid on the spot. Terry's actions gave new hope to the despairing city, helped avert nation-wide panic. And the devastating fire taught the insurance industry another significant lesson: - the need for diversification. By spreading the risks, underwriters established a sound new business that gives added protection not only to policy holders, but also to the companies.

EPISODE #642   **"THE THINKING HEART"**   Broadcast on February 7, 1950

Starring: Raymond Massey as Lincoln   Beatrice Pearson as Ann Rutledge
Griff Barnett as Mentor Graham   Cameron Prud'Homme as the doctor
Ed Max as voice one   Cameron Prud'Homme as voice two
John Griggs as voice three   Gladys Thornton as Mrs. M.
Doris Parker as Augusta   John Griggs as Asa
Ed Max as John W. Booth   Doris Parker as Mary

Written for *Cavalcade* by George H. Faulkner, based on selections from the following:
Carl Sandburg's "The Prairie Years" and "The War Years"
Robert E. Sherwood's stage play "Abe Lincoln in Illinois"
John Drinkwater's stage play "Abraham Lincoln"
E.P. Conkle's stage play "Prologue to Glory"
Edwin Mark-Conkle's poem "Lincoln, Man of the People"
Edgar Lee Masters' poem "Ann Rutledge"
Walt Whitman's poem "O Captain, My Captain"
and Stephen Vincent Benet's "John Brown's Body"
Produced by Roger Pryor and directed by Jack Zoller.
Bill Hamilton was the commercial spokesman and Ted Pearson was the announcer.
Music composed by Ardon Cornwell and conducted by Donald Voorhees.
Story: In honor of Abraham Lincoln's birthday, *Cavalcade* presented a dramatic portrait of Lincoln painted by many skillful hands. Inspired by eight gifted writers, this is the story of a man who loved, and lost the girl he loved; of a man who believed, and fought for his beliefs against many; and of the man who died for those beliefs.

EPISODE #643 **"ENTERPRISE USA"** Broadcast on February 14, 1950
    Starring: Lee Bowman as Eaves   James Monks as Hardy
    Scott Tennyson as Josh   Roy Fant as the barber
    Charles Egleston as Waters   Bill Adams as Newton
    Joe Latham as the banker   Gavin Gordon as Bell
    Roy Fant as Emerson   Butch Cavell as the kid
    Gavin Gordon as Billy   Butch Cavell as Tommy
    Gladys Thornton and Linda Ried as the women.
Written for *Cavalcade* by Doris Frankel. (Arthur Arent contributed only a few lines.)
Produced by Roger Pryor and directed by Jack Zoller.
Bill Hamilton was the commercial spokesman and Ted Pearson was the announcer.
Music composed by Ardon Cornwell and conducted by Donald Voorhees.
Story: In 1945, little Buchanan, Georgia, wasn't even a bus stop. Returning veterans were forced to go to Atlanta and Birmingham to find jobs. But Buchanan was home to Dave Eaves. He had dreamed of returning there all during the long years he'd been in the Pacific; and he was determined to stay and work there. With the help of his best friend, Dave talked the townspeople into building a new, modern factory and then found a business to bring it to life. Attracted by the employment opportunities, people returned to Buchanan. Other new enterprises sprang up. Two young men had proved again that initiative and resourcefulness can make any town in America "Enterprise USA."

EPISODE #644 **"REVEILLE"** Broadcast on February 21, 1950
    Starring: Walter Hampden as Washington   Edgar Stehli as Ben Franklin
    Edwin Max as the first soldier   Larry Blyden as Lafayette
    Staats Cotsworth as the second soldier   Richard Janaver as Hamilton
    Arnold Moss as Von Steuben   Staats Cotsworth as Conway
    Alice Reinheart as Mistress Greene   Ed Max as Wilkinson
    Pat Hosley as Mistress Meade   John Griggs as the Sergeant
    Larry Blyden as Captain Walker   Joseph Bell as Laurens
    John Griggs as Congressman one   Joseph Bell as Congressman two
    William Burbridge and John Harper as the men.
    Anna Maude Morath and Doris Parker as the women.
Written for *Cavalcade* by George H. Faulkner.
Produced by Roger Pryor and directed by Jack Zoller.
Bill Hamilton was the commercial spokesman and Ted Pearson was the announcer.
Music composed by Ardon Cornwell and conducted by Donald Voorhees.
Story: In the winter of 1777, the American Continental Army was in wretched condition. The battles of Brandywine and German town had been lost, and the enemy now occupied Philadelphia. Lack of food, clothing and suitable arms created a critically low morale among the troops. Desertions were an everyday occurrence. In addition to these problems, General Washington realized that his army was not properly trained to meet the British in large scale fighting. Determined to correct this defect before the opening of the spring campaign, he secured the services of Baron Von Steuben - a brilliant Prussian officer and a friend of the Colonial cause. It was the turning point of the war. Under the guidance of the colorful Von Steuben and with the inspiration of General Washington, the American Army at Valley Forge became a strong, confident fighting force that later went forth to win battle after battle until the final victory at Yorktown.

    Trivia: The original title of this script was "Valley Forge Story."

EPISODE #645 **"YOUNG MAN IN A HURRY"** Broadcast on February 28, 1950
    Starring: Virginia Payne as Mrs. Gerber   Cornel Wilde as Joe Gerber
    Mildred Clinton as the clerk   Earl George as the Professor
    Arnold Robertson as Koppleman   Alan Hewitt as the engineer

Richard Gordon as the principal   George Petrie as Norm
Written for *Cavalcade* by Morton Wishengrad.
Produced by Roger Pryor and directed by Jack Zoller.
Bill Hamilton was the commercial spokesman and Ted Pearson was the announcer.
Music composed by Ardon Cornwell and conducted by Donald Voorhees.
Story: In April 1940, Joe Gerber, sixteen-year-old Austrian D.P., arrived in America. Joe's father had disappeared in a concentration camp, and Joe and his mother had managed to flee Germany on one of the last escape boats. From the day he arrived, Joe was determined to waste no time. He wanted to become a useful American, and work hard and to continue his education. Joe's eagerness and ability took him through high school in two years and won him scholarships for advance study. But in his haste to become an engineer as well as an American, Joe hated to spend the long, precious hours that college engineering problems required. His solution has provided a tool which engineers predict will aid production by saving time - in short, will be another lever to help lift still higher the standard of living for Joe's fellow-Americans.

Trivia: The real Joe Gerber made an on-air appearance after the story and was interviewed.

EPISODE #646   "MR. PEALE AND THE DINOSAUR"   Broadcast on March 7, 1950
Starring: Claude Rains as Mr. Peale   Agnes Moorehead as Elizabeth
Alan Hewitt as Dr. Morgan   Parker Fennelly as Masten
Edgar Stehli as Bain   Lyle Sudrow as Peter
Written for *Cavalcade* by Arthur Arent, based on "The Ingenious Mr. Peale" from the 1939 book "America's Old Masters" by James Thomas Flexner.
Produced by Roger Pryor and directed by Jack Zoller.
Bill Hamilton was the commercial spokesman and Ted Pearson was the announcer.
Music composed by Ardon Cornwell and conducted by Donald Voorhees.
Story: Charles Willson Peale of Philadelphia was a man of many interests. His versatility and enormous energy led him into such diversified fields as watchmaking, dentistry, portrait painting and scientific experimentation. But somehow he never managed to accomplish anything of real significance until he acted on the advice of his friend, Ben Franklin. Franklin's suggestion was that Peale start a museum of natural history. "Such a museum," Franklin said, "could help the American people to realize and appreciate the great wonders of the new world." Peale tackled the project with enthusiasm, but had to dig for his star attraction.

EPISODE #647   "CRAZY JUDAH"   Broadcast on March 14, 1950
Starring: Douglas Fairbanks, Jr. as Theodore Judah   Humphrey Davis as the doctor
Gertrude Warner as Anna Judah   Judy Lockser as Elizabeth
George Petrie as the steward   Joseph W. Lewis as the Captain
Arnold Robertson as Gorham   Joseph Bell as Huntington
Humphrey Davis as Hopkins   Arnold Robertson as Crocker
George Petrie as Charley   Joseph W. Lewis as the voice
Written for *Cavalcade* by Arthur Arent.
Produced by Roger Pryor and directed by Jack Zoller.
Bill Hamilton was the commercial spokesman and Ted Pearson was the announcer.
Music composed by Ardon Cornwell and conducted by Donald Voorhees.
Story: For most of his life, Theodore D. Judah dreamed of a railroad that would span the nation. It was 1850 then, and the shortest routes to the West were through the malaria-ridden Panama swamps, of the long, dangerous overland trail. America needed fast, efficient transportation to bind together the interests of the East and West. Judah had pleaded in vain to Congress for funds. Then, with Civil War imminent, fast continental

communication became vital. Congress agreed to help back the railroad, but first Judah had to find a suitable railroad pass over the Sierra mountains.

Trivia: Douglas Fairbanks, Jr. had recently returned from Europe where he had been working with the United Nations Education, Scientific and Cultural Organization.

EPISODE #648   "I, MARY PEABODY"   Broadcast on March 21, 1950
Starring: Elizabeth Taylor as Mary Peabody   Richard Waring as Horace Mann
Susan Douglas as Sophia Peabody   Irene Hubbard as Mrs. Clarke
Anne Seymour as Elizabeth Peabody
Written for *Cavalcade* by Arthur Arent, adapted from "The Peabody Sisters of Salem" by Louise Hall Tharp, originally published by Little, Brown and Company in 1950.
Produced by Roger Pryor and directed by Jack Zoller.
Bill Hamilton was the commercial spokesman and Ted Pearson was the announcer.
Music composed by Ardon Cornwell and conducted by Donald Voorhees.
Story: Of Salem's three famous Peabody sisters, Mary was the shyest and most retiring. She unconsciously let her older sister, Elizabeth, dominate her life - that is, until something of real importance happened. And that "something" was Horace Mann - famous American educator and founder of our modern school system. When the Peabody girls first met him, Elizabeth, in her usual assertive manner, kept Mann's attention diverted to herself. Mary was attracted to Mann, but remained in the background until her younger sister, Sophia, told her: "Decide what you want in this world, and go after it."

EPISODE #649   "GENERAL FORREST RIDES AGAIN"   Broadcast on March 28, 1950
Starring: Richard Widmark as Maury Reynolds
John Gibson as Joker Farrell   John Griggs as Mr. Jorgensen
Joseph Lewis as Captain McIvor   Geoffrey Bryant as Sparks
Roy Fant as Grandpa Reynolds   Ivan Cury as Maury (age 9)
Lester Carr as Dave (age 11)   Geoffrey Bryant as the voice
Written for *Cavalcade* by George Faulkner, adapted from a short story of the same title by Walter Havighurst.
Produced by Roger Pryor and directed by Jack Zoller.
Bill Hamilton was the commercial spokesman and Ted Pearson was the announcer.
Music composed by Ardon Cornwell and conducted by Donald Voorhees.
Story: When Maury Reynolds was a youngster in Nashville, Tennessee, his grandfather told him many an exciting story of the heroic exploits of the great Confederate soldier, General Bedford Forrest. Some years later during World War II, young Maury was signed on as third mate of a Liberty Ship which, by a strange coincidence, was named "Bedford Forrest." Although his ship wasn't a combat vessel, Maury couldn't help remembering the fighting traditions of her famous name. The "Bedford Forrest" was carrying a cargo of drums of vitally needed aviation gasoline when she got behind her South Pacific convoy. This episode tells how Maury used the General's tactics to get his ship through to an air base "first with the most" just in the nick of time to help avert destruction of the base by Japanese aircraft.

EPISODE #650   "DECISION IN THE VALLEY"   Broadcast on April 4, 1950
Starring: Robert Cummings as Surgeon Hunter McGuire
Les Damon as the Yankee   Humphrey Davis as George
Ed Jerome as Gen. Stonewall Jackson   Bob Dryden as Sly
Leora Thatcher as Mrs. Johnson   Les Damon as the Sentry
Grayce Albert as Mrs. Willis   Ginger Jones as Gert
Ginger Jones as Margaret   Roy Fant as the dealer
Anne Seymour as the woman

Based on a sketch written by Arthur Gordon, and adapted for *Cavalcade* by Morton Wishengrad.
Produced by Roger Pryor and directed by Jack Zoller.
Bill Hamilton was the commercial spokesman and Ted Pearson was the announcer.
Music composed by Ardon Cornwell and conducted by Donald Voorhees.
Story: In 1862, when he was a surgeon in the Confederate Army of Stonewall Jackson, young Dr. Hunter McGuire dodged his way through the Union lines to Winchester, Virginia, to reach his sister who was seriously ill. Just as he started to go back to his regiment, he was begged by an unknown woman to visit her seriously wounded son. The young surgeon knew that he risked capture, even death, if he did not return immediately. But the boy would surely die without a doctor's help. Many years later, the outcome of this doctor's heroic decision became introduced to the American people as Dr. Hunter McGuire, President of the American Medical Association. Few knew of this warmly human decision which he had made many years before in an hour of great personal danger.

EPISODE #651   "CITIZEN STRAUS"   Broadcast on April 11, 1950
    Starring: Melvyn Douglas as Nathan Straus   Bobby Nick as the boy
    Parker Fennelly as the vet   Peter Capell as Jacobi
    Bill Zuckert as Simpson   Frank Readick as McClaren
    Bob Dryden as the dairyman   Arnold Robertson as a dairyman
    Alice Reinheart as Margaret   Dean Harens as Green
    Chuck Webster as a third dairyman   Dan Ocko as the man
    Parker Fennelly as the servant   Dean Harens as the clerk
    Arnold Robertson as the Magistrate   Chuck Webster as Smith
    Written for *Cavalcade* by Morton Wishengrad.
Produced by Roger Pryor and directed by Jack Zoller.
Bill Hamilton was the commercial spokesman and Ted Pearson was the announcer.
Music composed by Ardon Cornwell and conducted by Donald Voorhees.
Story: In 1892, on the farm of department store owner Nathan Straus, a pedigreed cow coughed, and then, a few days later, died. Straus, curious, ordered an autopsy, and found the cause to be tuberculosis. Further investigation convinced Straus that milk from a tubercular cow could transmit the disease to humans. Even more important, it was the diseased milk that was responsible for the death of a shockingly high number of infants. Spurred on by his convictions, Straus set out to improve public health conditions. . . a crusade which was met in the beginning with opposition and ignorance.

EPISODE #652   "LADY OF JOHNSTOWN"   Broadcast on April 18, 1950
    Starring: Virginia Bruce as Rose Markward Knox
    Scott Tennyson as the chairman   John Larkin as Charles Knox
    Alan Hewitt as Jimmy   Doro Merande as Sarah
    Joseph Bell as the Lawyer   Scott Tennyson as Simmons
    Rolly Bester as Alice   Bill Lipton as the architect
    Jimmy Sommer as Jimmy (age 13)   Bill Lipton as the man
    Joseph Bell as the member   John Larkin as the second member
    Written for *Cavalcade* by Virginia Radcliffe and Ruth Woodman.
Produced by Roger Pryor and directed by Jack Zoller.
Bill Hamilton was the commercial spokesman and Ted Pearson was the announcer.
Music composed by Ardon Cornwell and conducted by Donald Voorhees.
Story: At the age of fifty, when most women are looking forward to increasing leisure, Rose Knox found herself a widow with two young sons. The boys were not old enough to take over the Knox Gelatine Company of Johnstown, New York, which she and her husband had built. So she decided to take the presidency herself. Rose faced many problems. It was 1908 and a "woman's place was in the home." Mrs. Knox had to prove

she could run a large business efficiently and fairly. But she faced her new responsibilities in her own way - in a woman's way. Under her guidance, the business continued to grow and prosper. Gelatine is now a familiar item on the kitchen shelf. In addition, important new industrial and medical uses for Gelatine have been developed through research sponsored by the "Lady of Johnstown."

EPISODE #653   **"THE FIREFLY LAMP"**   Broadcast on April 25, 1950
Starring: William Holden as William Mahone   Brenda Marshall as Otelia
Cameron Prud'Homme as Dr. Butler   Arnold Moss as Dr. Mallory
Gavin Gordon as Mr. Camp   Scott Tennyson as Sutley
Chuck Webster as Thomas   Gavin Gordon as the voice
Chuck Webster as Jim
Written for *Cavalcade* by Irve Tunick.
Produced by Roger Pryor and directed by Jack Zoller.
Bill Hamilton was the commercial spokesman and Ted Pearson was the announcer.
Music composed by Ardon Cornwell and conducted by Donald Voorhees.
Story: To save costly miles, William Mahone, a young Virginia engineer, proposed building a railroad through the heart of the "Great Dismal Swamp" from Petersburg to Norfolk. His self-assurance and initiative landed him the contract. From the outset, Mahone had trouble. The summer of 1855 brought an epidemic of Yellow Fever to Norfolk and construction came to a standstill. When work was finally resumed, the swamp presented another serious obstacle. Fill for the railroad bed disappeared overnight in the deep mud. Today, the main line of the railroad still cuts through the swamp over the road-bed put down over a hundred years ago. And at the end of the line is a thriving city - Norfolk, Virginia - brought back to life by the enterprise and ingenuity of William Mahone.

Trivia: The title of this script was originally "The Great Dismal Swamp," but changed sometime during the week before broadcast. Brenda Marshall - by the way - is the real life Mrs. Holden.

EPISODE #654   **"I CAN -- AND I WILL"**   Broadcast on May 2, 1950
Starring: Lee Bowman as William Underwood   Eric Dressler as voice one
Marilyn Erskine as Betsy Hale   Jack Kruschen as Meadowcroft
Guy Spaul as Charles Mitchell   William Padmore as voice two
Frank Behrens as Asa Higgins   Ed Latimer as Captain Hale
Written for *Cavalcade* by Doris Frankel.
Produced by Roger Pryor and directed by Jack Zoller.
Bill Hamilton was the commercial spokesman and Ted Pearson was the announcer.
Music composed by Ardon Cornwell and conducted by Donald Voorhees.
Story: Nowadays, American housewives seldom neglect to include an assortment of canned goods in their grocery shopping. But back in the early 1800's, people ridiculed William Underwood for suggesting the preservation of food in jars. "Americans," they said, "will never eat their dinner out of a bottle." Underwood went ahead with his idea. He was convinced that America offered the greatest opportunity for him to prove its soundness. When an old friend - a tinker - suggested packaging food in tin canisters, Underwood gave it a try. However, people were wary of packaged food and it took the Gold Rush of 1849 and a desperate need for food to start Underwood's business toward success.

EPISODE #655   **"NEVER MARRY A RANGER"**   Broadcast on May 9, 1950
Starring: Martha Scott as Roberta McConnell   Nelson Case as McConnell
Donnie Harris as Scott (age 11)   Robin Morgan as Cissie (age 7)
George Petrie as the volunteer   Joseph Bell as the boss

Cameron Andrews as Old Pete   Joe Latham as Oley
Carl Eastman as the radio voice   George Petrie as man one
Joseph Bell as man two   Rica Martens as the woman
Clifford Tatum, Jr. as the kid   Clifford Tatum, Jr. as the baby cry
Written for *Cavalcade* by Virginia Radcliffe, adapted from the book of the same title by Roberta McConnell, as originally published by Prentice-Hall in 1950.
Produced by Roger Pryor and directed by Jack Zoller.
Bill Hamilton was the commercial spokesman and Ted Pearson was the announcer.
Music composed by Ardon Cornwell and conducted by Donald Voorhees.
Story: The Forest Ranger Station on Callina Crib in the Utah mountains is deep in a box-like canyon, at the head of which old Mount Baldy lifts his gleaming crest eleven thousand feet into the air. Fir trees line the creek bed. Under a May sun, it looks beautiful and serene. Such was the sight that met Mac and Roberta McConnell when they arrived to take over the Ranger Station. But the snakes, porcupines, packrats and ticks were another story. So was the icebox that hit 85 degrees in the afternoon sun, and Jughead, the wayward horse. Roberta was about to give up the fight against inconvenience and loneliness. Then a near-disaster helped her realize the importance of a Ranger's job and her part in helping to protect the land and its people.

EPISODE #656 "THE SWORD OF KENTUCKY"   Broadcast on May 16, 1950
   Starring: Wanda Hendrix as Polly Ann McChesney   George Petrie as Major Hay
   Robert Young as George Rogers Clark   Dan Ocko as Vigo
   Lon McAllister as Tom McChesney   Clifford Tatum, Jr. as Davy
   Horace Braham as General Hamilton   Dan Ocko as Simon Kenton
Extras in the cast were Burt Backwell, Herbert Bott, Benjamin Ewing, Marvin Goldman, Jack Nord, Douglas Ramey, and Robert Thompson.
Based on the 1903 story "The Crossing" by Winston Chrucmill and adapted for *Cavalcade* by George H. Faulkner.
Produced by Roger Pryor and directed by Jack Zoller.
William Hamilton and Ryan Halloran were the announcers.
Music composed by Ardon Cornwell and conducted by Donald Voorhees.
Story: As an American frontiersman and soldier, George Rogers Clark won important victories in the Northwest Territory during the Revolutionary War. The Northwest Territory was a vast tract of land dying north of the Ohio River, south of Canada, west of Pennsylvania, and east of the Mississippi River. Clark's victories helped the American negotiators claim the area during peace talks with Britain, ending the Revolutionary War.

Trivia: This broadcast originated from the Memorial Auditorium in Louisville, Kentucky.

More trivia: Danny Ocko has played many varied roles on "Cavalcade" in the past and many varied roles in his stage, screen, radio and television career. He was appeared in such Broadway plays as "Having a Wonderful Time," and "What a Life!" Movie-goers will remember him in *Mission to Moscow* (He was head of the Russian Secret Service, 1943), *Background to Danger* (1943), and *Young Ideas* (1943). His television credits are *Philo Theatre*, *Lights Out!*, *The Eddie Cantor Show*, *The Fred Allen Show*, and *The Jack Carson Show*.

EPISODE #657 "A PORTRAIT OF THE AUTHOR"   Broadcast on May 23, 1950
   Starring: Basil Rathbone as Mr. Burgess   Henry Scott as the garage man
   Ginger Jones as Mrs. Jones   Les Damon as Mr. Jones
   Basil Rathbone as Thomas Jefferson   Denise Alexander as Patsy
   Ronald Long as Benjamin Franklin   Henry Scott as Bob
   Virginia Dwyer as Martha

Written for *Cavalcade* by George H. Faulkner.
Produced by Roger Pryor and directed by Jack Zoller.
William Hamilton and Ryan Halloran were the announcers.
Music composed by Ardon Cornwell and conducted by Donald Voorhees.
Story: It was after hours when two visitors, the Joneses, reached Monticello. They were both surprised and pleased when a Mr. Burgess offered to show them through the home of Mr. Jefferson. In strange detail, old Mr. Burgess painted a word picture for the Joneses - a portrait of Thomas Jefferson in relation to the three great loves of his life: his home, his family and his country. At times the Joneses felt as though they were listening to a man who knew Jefferson very well indeed.

More Trivia: In commemoration of the 174th anniversary of the signing of the Declaration of Independence, *Cavalcade* presented this unusual, dramatic portrait of the author. Also note Basil Rathbone playing two roles.

EPISODE #658   **"MISS VINNIE AND MR. LINCOLN"**   Broadcast on May 30, 1950
Starring: Barbara Bel Geddes as Vinnie Ream   Lyle Sudrow as Lt. Hoxie
Bill Adams as Abraham Lincoln   Ethel Owen as Aunt Samantha
Cameron Prud'Homme as the aide   Bill Smith as the Senator
Leora Thatcher as Mrs. Ream   Sarah Fussell as Tad
Bill Smith as Mr. Ream   Berry Kroeger as Clark Mills
Cameron Prud'Homme as General Grant
Based on the book "Vinnie Ream and Mr. Lincoln" by Freeman H. Hubbard, published by Whittlesey House in 1950. Adapted for *Cavalcade* by Robert Tallman.
Produced by Roger Pryor and directed by Jack Zoller.
William Hamilton and Ryan Halloran were the announcers.
Music composed by Ardon Cornwell and conducted by Donald Voorhees.
Story: Vinnie Ream had two ambitions - one was to be a famous sculptress, the other to marry a General. There seemed to be little progress in either direction until Vinnie tried to free her brother from a Union prison. Her efforts led her to the President's office where she met Abraham Lincoln and a young Army officer. Vinnie went on to become famous for her statue of Abraham Lincoln, and did become the wife of a General.

EPISODE #659   **"THE CONQUEROR"**   Broadcast on June 6, 1950
Starring: William Eythe as Henry Rose Carter   Les Tremayne as Charles Vest
Parker Fennelly as Mr. Whittaker   Dan Ocko as the colonel
Carl Eastman as the sergeant   William Post, Jr. as the Captain
Denise Alexander as Susan   George Petrie as Johnson
Carl Eastman as Spelvin   Ann Tobin as the woman
Ann Tobin as the girl   George Petrie as the man
Dan Ocko as Reed
Based on the book "One-Half the People" by Charles Morrow Wilson, published by William Sloan Associates in 1949. Adapted for *Cavalcade* by David Shaw.
Produced by Roger Pryor and directed by Jack Zoller.
William Hamilton and Ryan Halloran were the announcers.
Music composed by Ardon Cornwell and conducted by Donald Voorhees.
Story: If the sick won't come to the doctor, the doctor must go to the sick. That was the way Henry Rose Carter, young Baltimore physician, felt in 1893. Carter's convictions led him to apply for the post of Assistant Surgeon in the U.S. Marine Hospital Service. He passed his examinations with honors and was immediately assigned to Memphis, where a Yellow Fever epidemic was raging. Medical science, he discovered, was powerless to help the many victims of the epidemic. Hundreds were dying every day while doctors, ignorant of the cause of the dread disease, could do little more than try to ease the suffering. Carter was determined to do something about it.

EPISODE #660 **"THE REDEMPTION OF LOTTIE MOON"** Broadcast on June 13, 1950

    Starring: Lucille Ball as Lottie Moon   Berry Kroeger as General Burnside
    George Petrie as Kemper   Chester Stratton as the second man
    Cameron Andrews as Follansbee   Les Damon as Hanson
    Ian Martin as Stanton   Ann Tobin as the first woman
    Doris Parker as the second woman   Ian Martin as the first man
    Rod Hendrickson as Mr. Moon   Staats Cotsworth as Clark
    Chester Stratton as Myron   Rod Hendrickson as the Minsiter
    Cameron Andrews as Walter

Based on the story "General Burnside's Prisoner" by Walter Havighurst and "Arrest Lottie Moon" by Frank Siedel, both from the book entitled "The Ohio Story," published by World Publishing Company in 1950. Adapted for *Cavalcade* by George H. Faulkner. Produced by Roger Pryor and directed by Jack Zoller.
William Hamilton and Ryan Halloran were the announcers.
Music composed by Ardon Cornwell and conducted by Donald Voorhees.
Story: Lottie Moon was a pretty girl, but she was also temperamental and completely self-centered. One of her suitors - a young West Point Cadet named Ambrose Burnside - made that discovery when Lottie jilted him at the alter. Eighteen years later, in 1863, Burnside, by then a General, was ordered to track down a notorious Confederate spy - a daring woman who had outsmarted the highest Government officials for over two years. The spy turned out to be none other than Lottie Moon. The dramatic story of the second meeting between the General and Lottie, and how she finally learned the real meaning of strength and courage.

EPISODE #661 **"EXPERIMENT IN HUMANITY"** Broadcast on June 20, 1950

    Starring: Edward Arnold as A.R. Glancy   Scott Tennyson as Henry
    Marilyn Erskine as Nora   Joan Shea as Kate
    James Monks as Hull   Gavin Gordon as man one
    Scott Tennyson as man two   Katherine Hart as the wife
    Joan Shea as the nurse   Marilyn Erskine as the woman
    Joseph Bell as the doctor   Joseph Bell as the manufacturer
    Carl Eastman as Mack   Venzuela Jones as Mamie
    Carl Eastman as man three

Based on the magazine article "Miracle Making in the Backwoods" by Harold H. Martin, as originally published in the April 1, 1950 issue of *The Saturday Evening Post*. Adapted for *Cavalcade* by Morton Wishengrad.
Produced by Roger Pryor and directed by Jack Zoller.
William Hamilton and Ryan Halloran were the announcers.
Music composed by Ardon Cornwell and conducted by Donald Voorhees.
Story: "Nobody in his right mind ever claimed A.R. Glancy was a soft touch." So said A.R. Glancy. But he was touched when he heard about the people of Duluth, Georgia. Duluth was in a county of 30,000 people, without a single hospital, and Duluth was trying to do something about it. Glancy sent a little money to help. The result was a dispensary, short on beds, but great in heart. But it was not enough for their needs, and it was not enough for A.R. Glancy. "Buy a tract of land," he said, "and improve it. Then I'll build the finest small-town hospital in the county." When maintenance of the hospital became a costly burden, Glancy suggested starting a business to support it. The whole undertaking was an experiment in humanity that made Glancy feel he could "go on living a hundred years" and brought a new, high standard of living for Duluth.

EPISODE #662 "I SPEAK FOR DEMOCRACY" Broadcast on June 27, 1950
    Starring: Susan Douglas as Gloria Scott Tennyson as General Marshall
    Gertrude Warner as Miss Wright Theo Goetz as Petro
    Virginia Payne as Anastasia Arnold Robertson as George
    Bartlett Robinson as Fulmer Patty Pope as Marian
    Jack Grimes as Wilbur June Allyson as Mary Elizabeth Power
    Scott Tennyson as Smith Bartlett Robinson as the voice
    Jack Grimes as the cab driver Evelyn Juster as Winnie
    Pat Hosley as the girl's voice
    Written for *Cavalcade* by Virginia Radcliffe.
    Produced by Roger Pryor and directed by Jack Zoller.
    William Hamilton and Ryan Halloran were the announcers.
    Music composed by Ardon Cornwell and conducted by Donald Voorhees.
    Story: All over the nation, high school students were competing for top honors in the "I Speak for Democracy" contest. At Wilmington High School, in Delaware, one of the students was seventeen-year-old Gloria Chomiak, a senior of Ukrainian descent. In trying to express herself, Gloria recalled the things America had meant to her - her arrival in New York two short years before from her home in the tiny Canadian outpost of Fort Vermillion . . . the terrifying unfamiliarity of telephones . . . the rush and gaiety of the crowds. But most of all, the freedom and strength of the American people. "I Speak for Democracy," Gloria wrote, "because two generations back my ancestors could not speak of it, there may come a time when we, too, will not have the right to do so . . ." Gloria's essay was one of four national winners. Here is the story behind the essay, the story of Gloria and her fresh and appealing approach to America.

    Jack Zoller: *"The Cavalcade of America* not only dramatizes the stories of the great and the famous but it also tells the stories of those little-known persons who have contributed to our American way of life. Last year, for example, we dramatized the story of Gloria Chomiak, a seventeen-year-old Wilmington, Delaware school girl, who was one of four winners in the national Voice of America contest. The drama, 'I Speak for Democracy,' was highly praised."

    Trivia: As the last program of the season, *Cavalcade* originally intended to present the story of Gloria Chomiak, a Wilmington, Delaware, high school student who came from a remote Canadian outpost. The drama was presented with one change. Peggy Ann Garner was supposed to star as Gloria. The day before, Garner became ill and so radio actress Susan Douglas took over Garner's role as substitute.

EPISODE #663 "JOHN YANKEE" Broadcast on August 29, 1950
    Starring: Basil Rathbone as John Adams Ronald Long as Sewall
    John Griggs as the Clerk * Cathleen Cordell as Abby
    Peter Capell as Sam Horace Braham as citizen two *
    Cameron Prud'Homme as Edes John McGovern as Forester
    Carl Eastman as Quincy Scott Tennyson as Dr. Jeffreys
    Milton Herman as witness three * James O'Neill as the judge
    John Griggs as the watchman * Cameron Prud'Homme as citizen one *
    John McGovern as Crown Prosecutor Carl Eastman as the Bostonian *
    Milton Herman as the foreman James O'Neill as witness one *
    Based on the best-seller "John Adams and the American Revolution" by Catherine Drinker Bowen, originally published by Little Brown, and Company in 1950. Adapted for *Cavalcade* by George H. Faulkner.
    Produced by H.L. Blackburn and directed by John Zoller.
    Bill Hamilton was the announcer.
    Music composed by Ardon Cornwell and conducted by Donald Voorhees.

Story: In Boston of 1770, a historic trial took place. Eight British soldiers were charged with murder. Their offense was firing into an angry, incited Colonial mob. Because mob rule threatened, and feeling against the Crown and its protectors was at a fever pitch, all the great Tory lawyers refused the case. Then John Adams accepted the challenge of protecting the lives and rights of the British soldiers. By this action, he stood to lose the confidence and respect of his fellow-Colonists. Instead, his successful fight for justice gained him a new following and, for the new country, a great leader in her fight for independence.

Trivia: Alice Crocker, secretary of the Du Pont Company, along with Basil Rathbone, cut the program's sixteenth birthday cake. Miss Crocker was a visitor at the opening of "John Yankee," which starred Rathbone in the lead.

More trivia : Those overlooking all of the scripts for historical accuracy were very detailed. Beginning with this episode, the typists and researchers began placing an asterisk beside all of the fictional characters in the script.

EPISODE #664   "THE IRON MOUNTAIN"   Broadcast on September 5, 1950
  Starring: Dane Clark as Latham *   Staats Cotsworth as Lake
  Les Damon as Burrell   Joseph Lewis as Munson
  Peter Capell as Kihlstredt   Luis Van Rooten as Nieto
  Dan Ocko as Sandoval *   Louis Sorin as Grillet
  Joseph Bell as Hollensteiner   Luis Van Rooten as voice one *
  Louis Sorin as voice two *   Dan Ocko as voice three *
  Joseph Lewis as voice four *
  Written for *Cavalcade* by Irve Tunick.
  Produced by H.L. Blackburn and directed by John Zoller.
  Bill Hamilton was the announcer.
  Music composed by Ardon Cornwell and conducted by Donald Voorhees.
Story: In 1945, steam shovels biting deep into Lake Superior's iron-ore deposits pointed up a frightening fact: America's supply of the vital ore would be exhausted within twenty years. A new source must be found to feed industry. So U.S. Steel began one of the most thorough hunts in history for a natural resource. Hundreds of men scoured the world from Quebec to Tunisia, from Sweden to Newfoundland. Ninety-nine per cent of the reports were negative. Then one day in 1947, one of the reports showed special promise. It covered an area in the heart of deep jungle in Venezuela. When the field force double checked, they found "Cerro Bolivar" - a veritable mountain of iron . . . and then they almost lost it. This is the dramatic story of a company's efforts toward supplying America with another source of this vital raw material.

EPISODE #665   "THE MAN WITH THE CARGO OF WATER"   Broadcast Sept. 12, 1950
  Starring: Richard Widmark as Frederic Tudor   Guy Sorel as Toastmaster *
  Arthur Maitland as Reverend Newbury *   Lyle Sudrow as Will Tudor
  Jean Gillespie as Elizabeth Sullivan *   Ronald Long as owner two
  Parker Fennelly as Nat Wyeth   Scott Tennyson as owner three
  Arnold Robertson as owner one   Ronald Long as Mr. Bradford *
  Arnold Robertson as the Captain *   George Petrie as the clerk *
  Scott Tennyson as the ship's mate *   Guy Sorel as Achille Le Blanc *
  George Petrie as Mr. Jones *
  Based on material in "Lost Men of American History" by Stuart H. Holbrook, and adapted for *Cavalcade* by George H. Faulkner.
  Produced by H.L. Blackburn and directed by John Zoller.
  Bill Hamilton was the commercial spokesman and Stuart Metz was the announcer.
  Music composed by Ardon Cornwell and conducted by Donald Voorhees.

Story: One hot August day in 1804, the sound of cool, tinkling ice in a glass gave Frederic Tudor an idea. Why, he thought, couldn't ice be packed and taken to people in tropical countries? His New England neighbors mocked him. "The ice will melt," they said, "and all you'll have left to sell is a cargo is water." Even his fiancee refused to stand by him when he continued with his idea. But Frederic talked his brother and a cousin into helping him. Together they experimented with ways of packing ice, of protecting it for equatorial climates. Finally, with a cargo of 130 tons of ice, they sailed for Martinique. They were then confronted with a completely new problem: the island people, most of whom had never ever seen ice, had to be educated to its use.

EPISODE #666   "GOLDEN HARVEST"   Broadcast on September 19, 1950

Starring: Ed Begley as Father
Irene Hubbard as Mother
Cameron Prud'Homme as McChesney *
Scott Tennyson as the Southern Crator *
Lon McCallister as Cyrus McCormick
Maurice Ellis as Jo *
Klock Ryder as the farmer *
Gavin Gordon as Reverend Greene *

Others in the cast: Doris Parker, Bill Burbridge, John Harper, Douglas Taylor, and Delmar Neutzman.
Written for *Cavalcade* by Halstead Welles.
Produced by H.L. Blackburn and directed by Jack Zoller.
Bill Hamilton was the commercial spokesman and Cy Harrice was the announcer.
Music composed by Ardon Cornwell and conducted by Donald Voorhees.
Story: In the 1820's, and as far back as man could remember, harvest was a time of long days in the field, of tired, aching backs. So it was when young Cyrus McCormick cut and gleaned in his father's fields, year after year, until he was in his early twenties. Then came the first sign of a change. Neighbors began hearing a clickety-click sound of wheels at the McCormick farm; young Cyrus was spending every free moment building a strange contraption. Finally Cyrus thought his reaper was ready for a test. Skeptical neighbors came to watch, and stayed to mock when the machine laid to waste a beautiful golden field of grain. Humiliated by the failure, young McCormick turned from his reaper, and from farming, for many years. But his active mind kept returning to the problem, and he decided to try again. This young man was able to work a modern miracle that made harvest a happier time throughout the world.

EPISODE #667   "YANKEE DOODLE DEBBY"   Broadcast on September 26, 1950

Starring: Joan Caulfield as Deborah Sampson
Bartlett Robinson as Doctor Binney
Staats Cotsworth as Colonel Shepard
Arnold Robertson as McGregor *
Winfield Honey as the landlord *
Parker Fennelly as Williams *
Winfield Honey as Corp. Bean *
George Petrie as Captain Webb
Chester Stratton as Hutton *
Scott Tennyson as Brodie *

Others in the cast include: Rica Martens, Ann Pitoniak, and Palmer Ward
Written for *Cavalcade* by Robert Tallman and Robert Anderson.
Produced by H.L. Blackburn and directed by Jack Zoller.
Bill Hamilton was the commercial spokesman and Cy Harrice was the announcer.
Music composed by Ardon Cornwell and conducted by Donald Voorhees.
Story: In 1781, the American colonies echoed with the din of cannon and musket fire. Independence was at stake as Washington's ragged, out-numbered units fought the well-equipped soldiers of George III. Rallying to her country's need, young Deborah Sampson disguised herself as a man to enlist in the Continental Army. Not only did she distinguish herself in battle, but she also tended her comrades' wounds and cooked their food. Her selfless devotion to duty inspired her entire regiment. Finally, after three years' service, Debby was wounded, and her masquerade discovered.

EPISODE #668 **"SIX MEN OF WOOD"** Broadcast on October 3, 1950
Starring: Robert Young as Albert Wood   Gertrude Warner as Louise
Jimmy Sommer as Moyer (age 14)   Jackie Diamond as Gardner (age 12)
Donny Harris as Bertram (age 11)   David Anderson as Francis (age 9)
Robin Morgan as Margaret (age 7)   Roger Sullivan as Moyer (age 20)
Bob Hastings as Gardner (age 18)   Jackie Diamond as Bertram (age 17)
Donny Harris as Francis (age 15)   Leora Thatcher as Mrs. Scott *

Based on the article "Where Work Is a Pleasure" by Oscar Schisgall, originally published in a 1950 issue of *Nation's Business*. Adapted for *Cavalcade* by Irve Tunick.
Produced by H.L. Blackburn and directed by Jack Zoller.
Bill Hamilton was the commercial spokesman and Cy Harrice was the announcer.
Music composed by Ardon Cornwell and conducted by Donald Voorhees.
Story: Depression year 1930. Albert Wood, successful American architect, suddenly found himself faced with economic disaster. But the Woods were undaunted. Believers in the old American maxim that one's children should understand the value of money and be able to earn their own way, he and his wife, Louise, had trained their five boys as furniture craftsmen. So when disaster hit, they decided to invest their total available funds - $95 - in a business devoted to designing and making new furniture. To begin their new enterprise, they "pioneered" from Michigan to Port Washington, Long Island. There for the first few years it was nip and tuck for the young firm of "Albert Wood and Five Sons." Work came in slowly until, finally, an ad resulted in an order for a whole room of Wood-designed furniture. The new designs gained acceptance and orders pyramided until twenty years later, this flourishing family concern stands as a tribute to one couple's faith on their country's future.

Trivia: The original title of this script was "A Slight Case of Wealth."

More trivia: Albert Wood was a local resident of Port Washington, and since he was within driving distance, Wood paid a visit to the rehearsals, as this episode was about him.

EPISODE #669 **"EMMA"** Broadcast on October 10, 1950
Starring: Ginger Rogers as Emma Edmonds   Larry Blyden as James
James Van Dyck as Dr. Edwards   Staats Cotsworth as the General
Bob Dryden as the rebel *   James Monks as the Captain *
Ozzie Davis as Wilbur   Scott Tennyson as the Sergeant *
Larry Blyden as voice one *   James Van Dyck as voice two *
Maurice Ellis as the negro singer *

Written for *Cavalcade* by Morton Wishengrad.
Produced by H.L. Blackburn and directed by Jack Zoller.
Bill Hamilton was the commercial spokesman and Cy Harrice was the announcer.
Music composed by Ardon Cornwell and conducted by Donald Voorhees.
Story: In 1861, the men in blue and gray were locked in fierce battle near Yorktown, Virginia. At a nearby field hospital, Canadian-born Emma Edmonds served the Union Army as a nurse. Then one day Emma's sweetheart, Lt. James Vernon of the Army of the Potomac, was among those killed. Emma could not bury her grief in caring for the wounded. Instead, she asked for the most hazardous assignment possible - as a spy for the Union Army. To carry out her mission, Emma disguised herself as a plantation worker and crossed through the rebel lines. Though constantly in danger of being captured, Emma carefully memorized gun positions and troop placements. The information she gained helped bring about a Northern victory at Yorktown.

EPISODE #670 **"WIZARDS OF WHITING"** Broadcast on October 17, 1950
    Starring: Ralph Bellamy as Dr. William Burton   Lee Bowman as Dr. Humphreys
    Cameron Prud'Homme as the doctor *   Donny Harris as Claude
    Frances Robinson as Adelaide   Dan Ocko as Schultze *
    Chuck Webster as Rogers   Larry Haines as Ross *
    Alan Hewitt as Kentland *   Chuck Webster as the voice *
    Alan Hewitt as Attison *   Peter Cappell as Kwalicki *
    Written for *Cavalcade* by Irve Tunick.
    Produced by H.L. Blackburn and directed by Jack Zoller.
    Bill Hamilton was the commercial spokesman and Cy Harrice was the announcer.
    Music composed by Ardon Cornwell and conducted by Donald Voorhees.
    Story: In 1909, the specter of a gasoline famine cast a shadow over the future of America's growing automobile industry. A way had to be found to increase the yield of gasoline from petroleum - or the mounting stream of automobiles would eventually stall from lack of fuel. To meet their grave challenge, the Standard Oil Company assigned to its Whiting Plant two top research men - Dr. William Burton and Dr. Robert E. Humphreys - to work on the problem. Burton and Humphreys believed the solution lay in "cracking" petroleum through heat and pressure to increase the yield of gasoline. Working against time - with smoking-hot boilers of oil that often threatened to blow them to bits - they finally succeeded in perfecting the process.

EPISODE #671 **"JULIET IN PIGTAILS"** Broadcast on October 24, 1950
    Starring: Margaret O'Brien as Mary Anderson   John Griggs as MaCauley
    Cameron Prud'Homme as Dr. Griffin   Alan Hewitt as Romeo *
    Bartlett Robinson as Watterson   Alan Hewitt as the Friar *
    Arline Blackburn as Juliet *   Arline Blackburn as the woman *
    Cameron Prud'Homme as the voice *
    Bartlett Robinson and John Griggs played other minor one-line roles throughout the broadcast.
    Written for *Cavalcade* by Morton Wishengrad.
    Produced by H.L. Blackburn and directed by Jack Zoller.
    Bill Hamilton was the commercial spokesman and Cy Harrice was the announcer.
    Music composed by Ardon Cornwell and conducted by Donald Voorhees.
    Story: From the time in 1873, when fourteen-year-old Mary Anderson persuaded her stepfather to take her to see the immortal Edwin Booth in Richard III, Mary wanted to become an actress. Theaters and actors were considered wicked by many at that time. But Mary was so entranced with the performance that she begged for, and finally won, an introduction to Louisville's, great theatrical manager, Barney McCauley. Impressed with the girl's ability, McCauley put her in the part of Juliet when his star became temperamental. With only two days to prepare, Mary was faced with a skeptical Romeo and a hostile cast. On opening night, important stage props mysteriously disappeared. But Mary went through the ordeal like a professional.

    Trivia: This program was presented with the American Legion Auxillary Award.

EPISODE #672 **"WHITHER THOU GOEST"** Broadcast on October 31, 1950
    Starring: Loretta Young as Eliza McCardle   Betty Caine as Ma
    Wesley Addy as Andrew Jackson   Tony Randall as the voice *
    Bob Dryden as Mr. Armitage *   Betty Caine as Mrs. McCardle
    Tony Randall as John Pringle *   Bob Dryden as Chase
    Written for *Cavalcade* by Morton Wishengrad.
    Produced by H.L. Blackburn and directed by Jack Zoller.
    Bill Hamilton was the commercial spokesman and Cy Harrice was the announcer.
    Music composed by Ardon Cornwell and conducted by Donald Voorhees.

Harrison as Thomas Jefferson in "Experiment at Monticello."

Charles Boyer as Albert Gallatin in "Letter from Europe."

Story: In 1826, when Eliza McCardle first saw Andrew Johnson with her mother and stepfather, they were the poorest-looking people she had ever seen. But from the first, Andrew's spunk and eagerness to learn had impressed her. As he sat cross-legged, his deft fingers moving swiftly with needle and thread, Eliza read aloud to him from the Bible, the Declaration of Independence, speeches by Jefferson and Madison, and other classics. Whatever she read, he remembered. Eliza believed in this awkward young man who was so eager to learn. After their marriage, she continued to help him as he first became a lawyer, and then in turn a county judge, Governor of Tennessee, and Vice President under Abraham Lincoln. And then, as America mourned the passing of Lincoln, Eliza saw her beloved Andy, the humble tailor from Tennessee, succeed as President of the U.S., giving new meaning to the words "all men are created equal."

EPISODE #673   **"IMPROVEMENT NOTED"**   Broadcast on November 7, 1950
    Starring: Cornel Wilde as Eliphalet Dennison   Virginia Dwyer as Lydia
    Ian MacAllister as Father   Margaret Burlen as Mother
    Alan Hewitt as Aaron   George Petrie as the customer *
    Ossie Davis as Porter   George Petrie as Metcalf
    Bob Dryden as Stratton *
    Written for *Cavalcade* by Irve Tunick and Philip Lewis
    Produced by H.L. Blackburn and directed by Jack Zoller.
    Bill Hamilton was the commercial spokesman and Cy Harrice was the announcer.
    Music composed by Ardon Cornwell and conducted by Donald Voorhees.
Story: In great-grandfather's day, everyone shopped out of the open cracker barrel, so to speak. Today, however, most everything from soup mixes to father's shirts comes in neat, attractive packages. Behind this revolution lies a story. One day in the late 1800's, after Eliphalet Dennison had lost a sale, he happened to put an unwanted watch in a clean, study box. The customer returned, bought the same watch he had discarded before, and went away beaming with pleasure at his purchase. The only change was the box, and it had been hand-made by Eliphalet's father. Now, at that time, most boxes were imported at a great expense from Europe. Practically all were flimsily constructed. Why not make paper boxes in America, thought young Dennison. So the Dennisons, father and son, started a new business. Supply tags, labels, and even ribbons.

EPISODE #674   **"SIR GALAHAD IN MANHATTAN"**   Broadcast on November 14, 1950
    Starring: Ray Milland as Dr. J. Marion Sims   Helen Claire as Theresa
    Ernest Chappell as Henri L. Stuart   Joan Shea as Tilly *
    Gladys Thornton as Dr. Blackwell   Arnold Moss as Dr. Stevens
    Elizabeth Watts as Mrs. Doremus   Palmer Ward as Dr. Griscom
    Peter Capell as Dr. Buck   Rolly Bester as Mrs. Lezinsky
    Adapted for *Cavalcade* by Virginia Radcliffe, based on the book "Women's Surgeon: The Life Story of J. Marion Sims" by Dr. Seale Harris, published in 1950 by MacMillan.
    Produced by H.L. Blackburn and directed by Jack Zoller.
    Bill Hamilton was the commercial spokesman and Cy Harrice was the announcer.
    Music composed by Ardon Cornwell and conducted by Donald Voorhees.
Story: In the 1850's, Dr. J. Marion Sims was famous in the South as a woman's physician. But few were aware of his reputation when he first set up practice in New York City. And soon, lack of patients forced him to turn his home into a boarding house. It was through his first patient that Dr. Sims learned of the tragic need for local medical facilities to treat women. He decided that a hospital devoted exclusively to the study and treatment of women's diseases would be the best approach to the problem. Dr. Sims' first attempts to get backing for his humanitarian project failed. Then a crusading New York newspaperman mobilized public opinion behind him, and the first woman's hospital in the United States, "The Woman's Hospital of the State of New York," opened its doors in 1855.

Trivia: Ernest Chappell, who plays the role of Henri L. Stuart in this episode, was a radio actor and announcer for many years. One of his early announcing duties was for *The Campbell Playhouse*, a dramatic anthology series starring Orson Welles. A couple of months later, in January, Ernest Chappell would later get the honors of announcing for *Cavalcade* - but for only one broadcast.

EPISODE #675 **"THE STEPPING STONES"** Broadcast on November 21, 1950
Starring: Douglas Fairbanks, Jr. as John Alden

Walter Hampden as William Brewster	Richard Purdy as Capt. Miles Standish
Richard Purdy as James the First	Martin Rudy as Christopher Martin
Barry Thompson as Lord Robert Cecil	William Podmore as Richard Clyfton
Jack Manning as William Bradford	Martin Rudy as John Robinson
Horace Braham as the officer *	Susan Douglas as Priscilla Mullins
Barry Thompson as Captain Jones	William Podmore as Leister
Dennis Hoey as Billington	Horace Braham as Carver

Others in the cast: William Carnell, John Harper, John Lotas, Alvin Sullum, and Francis Saunders.
Written for *Cavalcade* by George H. Faulkner.
Produced by H.L. Blackburn and directed by Jack Zoller.
Bill Hamilton was the commercial spokesman and Cy Harrice was the announcer.
Music composed by Ardon Cornwell and conducted by Donald Voorhees.
Story: It was a tired, curious mixed company that gathered on the deck of the Mayflower, 330 years ago this month, to sign the Mayflower Compact - the first American charter of civil rights. The voyage from England had been a troubled one. William Brewster's congregation numbered but forty-one. Sixty-three others - the "outsiders" - rebelled at being governed by Brewster and his group. Mutiny and disaster were averted when Brewster proposed a compact pledging themselves to "enact, constitute and frame such just and equal laws as it be thought most convenient for the general good." Because of this document, which for the first time proclaimed the equality of man, Americans again, as they do every year, can give thanks for this matchless heritage of freedom, later incorporated into the Declaration of Independence and the Constitution of the United States.

EPISODE #676 **"THE ROSE AND THE THORNS"** Broadcast on November 28, 1950

Starring: Dorothy McGuire as Winnie Davis	Ossie Davis as James *
John Raby as Alfred Wilkinson	Leora Thatcher as Varina Davis
Bill Smith as Jefferson Davis	Joan Shea as Mrs. Peavy *
Ossie Davis as Luther *	

Extras in the cast included Doris Parker and Carl Eastman.
Written for *Cavalcade* by Robert Tallman.
Produced by H.L. Blackburn and directed by Jack Zoller.
Bill Hamilton was the commercial spokesman and Cy Harrice was the announcer.
Music composed by Ardon Cornwell and conducted by Donald Voorhees.
The Melodaires supplied the music and chorus.
Story: In 1885, Jefferson Davis was writing his memoirs - putting down for posterity the dreams and ideals of a defeated cause. But to Alfred Wilkinson, a New York reporter, Davis was an old man trying to resurrect the glories of a vanished past. And Winnie Davis, helping her father in his work, seemed to Wilkinson a young girl wasting her youth, sitting "among archives and documents like a rose among thorns." When Wilkinson wrote these things for publication, Winnie was deeply hurt. But in spite of herself, she fell in love with the young reporter and followed him to New York where they planned to be married. Then love of home, of family, of the South was too strong. At the last moment, she returned home, divided in her affections.

Trivia: Next week's *Cavalcade* was scheduled to be "Mistress of the Congaree," the story of Rebecca Motte who proved her love for freedom with unusual courage during the fight for Independence. It wasn't broadcast. More trivia about this non-broadcast is listed in the next.

More trivia: Dorothy McGuire chatted with Miss Alice McGren of the Sales Division of the Du Pont Plant in Niagara Falls, between the East Coast and West Coast performances of this episode.

EPISODE #677 **"THE GRAND DESIGN"** Broadcast on December 5, 1950
Starring: Charles Boyer as Pierre Charles L'Enfant
Staats Cotsworth as George Washington
Cameron Prud'Homme as the chairman *
Cameron Prud'Homme as Mr. Digges
Richard Gordon as the doctor *
Chuck Webster as Daniel Carroll
Bob Dryden as Burnham
George Petrie as citizen one *
Maurice Franklin as Elihu Root
Maurice Franklin as citizen 2 *
Guy Repp as Isaac Roberdeau
Written for *Cavalcade* by George H. Faulkner.
Produced by H.L. Blackburn and directed by Jack Zoller.
Bill Hamilton was the commercial spokesman and Cy Harrice was the announcer.
Music composed by Adorn Cornwell and conducted by Donald Voorhees.
Story: In 1790 when President George Washington commissioned Major Pierre Charles L'Enfant to design a Capitol city of the United States, L'Enfant submitted plans breathtaking in beauty and magnificent in concept. To finance the building of this city, the Treasury decided to auction off lots adjacent to the proposed Capitol site. One small group of speculators saw a way to turn the project to their own advantage. They tried to obtain from L'Enfant the city design so that they could buy up the best properties. When L'Enfant refused, the group threatened to boycott the sale of land and the project seemed doomed. Reluctantly, President Washington requested L'Enfant's resignation and made the plans public. Despite all obstacles, the original design was adhered to, and in time L'Enfant's vision became a reality - now Washington D.C. Today Americans can justly be proud of this great city which its creator predicted would "stand as an example to the world as a home of liberty under order."

Trivia: The drama "Mistress of the Congaree" was rescheduled for next week, with Ida Lupino in the lead, an exciting story of the Revolutionary War. It was never broadcast.

EPISODE #678 **"ULYSSES IN LOVE"** Broadcast on December 12, 1950
Starring: Ronald Reagan as Ulysses S. Grant
Denise Alexander as Emmy Dent
Kathleen Camegys as Mrs. Dent
Cameron Prud'Homme as Colonel Dent
Dan Ocko as General one *
Martin Rudy as General two *
Lyle Sudrow as Fred Dent
Patsy Campbell as Julia Dent
Adapted from the book "Captain Sam Grant" by Lloyd Lewis, as published by Little, Brown & Company in 1950. Adapted for *Cavalcade* by Arthur Arent.
Produced by H.L. Blackburn and directed by Jack Zoller.
Bill Hamilton was the commercial spokesman and Cy Harrice was the announcer.
Music composed by Adorn Cornwell and conducted by Donald Voorhees.
Story: A few months before the outbreak of the Mexican War, Sam Grant - more formally known as Ulysses S. Grant - met and fell in love with beautiful Julia Dent. But Julia's father, a wealthy planter, opposed the marriage, partly because Grant was an Army man, but mostly because he considered Sam a fortune hunter. After pressure from Julia, however, he reluctantly agreed to the young couple's engagement. Grant was called to duty in the Mexican War, where he served with great distinction and earned the rank of Captain. On his return, he learned that Julia's father has lost his fortune, and Sam was able to convince him that he loved Julia for herself alone.

Trivia: This incident from the life of U.S. Grant is an interesting but little known sidelight on one of our presidents. There's something to be said about actor Ronald Reagan playing the role of a future president . . .

EPISODE #679 "THE DU PONT CHORUS" Broadcast on December 19, 1950

Bill Hamilton is the announcer.
Frank J. Clark is the choral director.
Mr. Crawford H. Greenewalt, President of the Du Pont Company spoke during intermission.
Broadcast from "The Playhouse" in Wilmington, Delaware.
Ardon and Helen Cornwell composed an original Christmas tune for this broadcast, entitled "Christmas, Oh Christmas."
Carols sung by the 116 voices of the Du Pont Chorus.
Songs sung and performed in consecutive order: "It's Christmas!," "Adeste Fidelis," "Joseph Came Seeking a Resting Place," "Carol of the Hills," "Christmas, Oh Christmas," the English carol "Coventry Carol," "Jingle Bells,"Pietro Yon's "Gesu Bambino," and closing with the lyric "Merry Christmas and a Happy New Year."

The Du Pont chorus included: Carolyn Swetland, A. Wallace Copeland, Herman J. Sampson, John C. Coates, Conrad L. Hoover, George L. Smith, Suzanne Myers, Robert A. MacDonald, Thomas A. Ford, Paul P. Pinkney, Harry Eatough, Raymond Fisher, Norman Griffith, E.P.H. Meibohm, William Ulmer, Arthur J. Hill, Robert K. Weaver, George Tabet, William S. Groundland, Ruth Phelps, S. Elizabeth Long, Eugene Evers, John Mitchell, Jr., Richard V. Lindsey, Edith E. Churchman, Eugenia Hitt, G. Kathryn King, Celeste Martin, Fred L. Johnston, Roger A. Hines, William F. Brondyke, Elva Wells, Kathryn Kane, Katherine Clements, Jessica Reed, lois Weber, Irma Hushebeck, Thomas Legg, John L. Ludlow, Carl E. Schweitzer, Lucille Williams, Janice Sutter, Doris Huck, Marion Perse, Elizabeth McDonough, A. Frances Edwards, Ruth Breslin, Howard F. Berg, John Henderson, Harold W. Arnold, Dorothy Hanway, Elizabeth Klimuc, Margaret Geesey, and Sara Freedman.

EPISODE #680 "A MOCKINGBIRD SANG AT CHICKAMAUGA" December 26, 1950

Starring: Lee Bowman as Beasley Nichol
Staats Cotsworth as General Forrest
Claudia Morgan as Hunter Cragwell
Melville Ruick as General Rosecranz
Larry Blyden as Lt. Crockett
Les Damon as M.P.
Bob Dryden as the orderly
Les Damon as Col. Wilder
Tess Sheehan as Mrs. Whitesides
Bob Dryden as Sgt. Goforth

Based on the book "A Mockingbird Sang at Chickamauga" by Alfred Leland Crabbe, as originally published by The Bobbs-Merrill Publishing Company in 1949. Adapted for *Cavalcade* by Robert Tallman.
Produced by H.L. Blackburn and directed by Jack Zoller.
Bill Hamilton was the commercial spokesman and Frank Gallop was the announcer.
Music composed by Adorn Cornwell and conducted by Donald Voorhees.
Story: In 1863, Lt. Beasley Nichol of the Confederate Army was sent to spy out the plans of the Union Commander at Chattanooga, Tennessee. His mission almost ended in disaster when a Northern soldier recognized him as a former Princeton classmate. But Nichol managed to overpower him. Then he learned that the Union Officer was a dispatch bearer from General Grant to General Rosencrans at Chattanooga. Nichol decided to impersonate the Yankee and deliver the dispatch himself. With the help of two accomplices, Lt. Nichol entered Chattanooga and presented himself to General Rosencrans. Only then did he learn that the General expected two identical messages - to prevent just such a ruse. But the Lieutenant found an unexpected ally who helped him escape. And he returned to his own lines with military information which led to an important victory.

Trivia: The announcer for this broadcast, Frank Gallop, was well-recognized not for his voice, but as a floating head, as he was currently the host of television's *Lights Out!*, a horror anthology.

EPISODE #681   "AN AMERICAN FROM FRANCE"   Broadcast on January 2, 1951
    Starring: Joseph Cotten as Irenee   Walter Hampden as Du Pont
    Jack Manning as young Irenee   George Petrie as Victor
    Raymond Edward Johnson as Jefferson   Edgar Stehli as Lavoisier
    George Petrie as the voice *   Guy Sorel as the soldier *
    Joan Alexander as Sophie   Luis Van Rooten as voice two *
    Jack Manning as voice three *   Luis Van Rooten as Etienne
    Santos Ortega as Toussard   Jimmy Sommer as Henry
    Jimmy Summer as Alexis   Raymond Edward Johnson as the man *
    Written for *Cavalcade* by Irve Tunick.
Produced by H.L. Blackburn and directed by Jack Zoller.
Bill Hamilton was the commercial spokesman and Ernest Chappell was the announcer.
Music composed by Adorn Cornwell and conducted by Donald Voorhees.
Story: In the early days of our nation, many men came from other lands, attracted by freedom and the promise of opportunity in America. Among those who came was a young Frenchman named Eleuthere Irenee du Pont. Young du Pont found a nation in urgent need of a domestic supply of quality gunpowder . . . powder to open the wilderness, to protect the pioneers, to put food on the table. And du Pont, a protégé of the great French scientist, Lavoisier, had the technical knowledge to answer the need. In 1802, he built his powder factory on the banks of the historic Brandywine River in Delaware. The first years were hard ones, but the quality of the du Pont powder brought in new orders. The mill was expanded, again and again. At present, the industry employed 85,000 men and women contributing a wide variety of products to the nation's standard of living.

EPISODE #682   "SPINDLETOP"   Broadcast on January 9, 1951
    Starring: Robert Cummings as Lucas   Teresa Wright as Caroline
    Chester Stratton as Patsy   Judy Parrish as Louise
    Chester Stratton as Hayes   Roy Fant as Frazier *
    Eddie Astrich as Tony   Dan Ocko as the minister *
    Dan Ocko as Galey   Les Damon as Hamill
    Written for *Cavalcade* by Irve Tunick.
Produced by H.L. Blackburn and directed by Jack Zoller.
Bill Hamilton was the commercial spokesman and Fred Le Mieux was the announcer.
Music composed by Ardon Cornwell and conducted by Donald Voorhees.
Story; same as episode #632, broadcast on November 29, 1949

Trivia: To participate in the fiftieth anniversary celebration of the opening of the Spindletop Oil Field, this episode originated from the City Hall Auditorium in Beaumont, Texas. Host to the *Cavalcade* company - stars, actors, directors, technicians and announcers - was the employees of the Du Pont Company's Sabine River Works at nearby Orange Texas. The "Spindletop" cast remained in the Beaumont-Orange-Port Arthur area, compliments of Du Pont, for three days of festivities (January 7 - 9).

This Beaumont broadcast marked the first time *Cavalcade* had originated from the Southwest and the eleventh time it had originated from communities outside New York and Hollywood. Four performances of "Spindletop," including the broadcast, were scheduled in the auditorium. They were witnessed by audiences of plant employees, their families and friends, and as many others from the Orange-Beaumont-Port Arthur area as could be seated in the auditorium. This *Cavalcade* script was broadcast over a year ago on this same program, with two changes. The lead roles were played by a different cast and script writer Irve Tunick had completely rewritten the story for the Texas origination.

EPISODE #683 "THERE STANDS JACKSON!" Broadcast on January 16, 1951
Starring: John Hodiak as Thomas "Stonewall" Jackson
Butch Cavell as the boy *   Charles Dingle as the man *
Lawson Zerbe as General Bee   Chester Stratton as the Lieutenant
Maurice Ellis as Jim   Chester Stratton as Captain Douglas
Scott Tennyson as Major Dabney   Lawson Zerbe as Captain Pendleton
Les Damon as Dr. McGuire   Scott Tennyson as General Stuart
Cynthia Stone as Mrs. Jackson   Betty Caine as the woman *
Bill Adams as General Lee   Les Damon as General Rodes
Written for *Cavalcade* by George H. Faulkner.
Produced by H.L. Blackburn and directed by Jack Zoller.
Bill Hamilton was the commercial spokesman and Tom Shirley was the announcer.
Music composed by Ardon Cornwell and conducted by Donald Voorhees.
Story: On the shaded banks of a Virginia stream, some thirty years ago, an old man and a boy rested from their fishing. As they rested, they talked. And the talk was of a great general, of a warrior with whom the old man had proudly served. As the grandsire reminisced over days of past victories and defeats, a portrait emerged of the general - the man they called Stonewall Jackson. "Old Blue Light," the men sometimes called Jackson for the flashing fire in his blue eyes. Stern, he was, and secretive, and the men loved him for his kindness and his courage. History has granted him a place among the great military strategists. In a period of thirty days he marched his intrepid "foot cavalry" five hundred miles, fought five battles and beat four Union armies.

EPISODE #684 "THE METAL OF THE MOON" Broadcast on January 23, 1951
Starring: Montgomery Clift as Charles Hall   Roy Fant as the Chief
Amzie Strickland as Julia   Bill Adams as Jewett
Dan Ocko as Slocum *   Pat Hosley as Lou
Jean Gillespie as Sylvia *   Irene Hubbard as Mother
Dan Ocko as Father   Charlotte Denny as the extra
Written for *Cavalcade* by Irve Tunick.
Produced by H.L. Blackburn and directed by Jack Zoller.
Bill Hamilton was the commercial spokesman and Tom Shirley was the announcer.
Music composed by Ardon Cornwell and conducted by Donald Voorhees.
Story: The parents of Charles Martin Hall showed great patience and tolerance toward their son's chemical experiments. But the last straw was the experiment that nearly burned down their home. Charles took his equipment and his ideas to Oberlin College and worked on them there until his graduation in 1885. Then he set up his laboratory in a woodshed, continued to work at a problem that baffled men of science for centuries: the extraction of aluminum from its compounds. Previous methods had been too expensive for commercial use. Charles sought a cheaper method. For more young men of 22, a moonlight hayride is an occasion for romance. But, according to the story, such a ride gave Charles Hall the answer to his chemical problems. It was something a girl said: "The moon looks like a big, round rock of ice." He rushed back to his laboratory and began using rock ice to dissolve aluminum oxide and produce pure metallic aluminum.

EPISODE #685 **"KEEPSAKES"** Broadcast on January 30, 1951
    Starring: Raymond Massey as Lincoln   Jeanne Elkins as Mary Delahay
    Margaret Draper as Ann Rutledge   Bob Dryden as Marsh
    Scott Tennyson as voice three *   John Griggs as voice two *
    Bob Dryden as voice four *   Les Sterling as voice one *
    Len Sterling as Lemon *   Wesley Addy as the narrator *
Written for *Cavalcade* by George H. Faulkner, based on the following books written by Carl Sandburg and published through Harcourt, Brace and Company: "The Lincoln Collector" (1950), "Abraham Lincoln: The War Years" (1939) and "Abraham Lincoln: The Prairie Years" (1926).
Produced by H.L. Blackburn and directed by Jack Zoller.
Bill Hamilton was the commercial spokesman and Ted Campbell was the announcer.
Music composed by Ardon Cornwell and conducted by Donald Voorhees.
Story: Another stirring story of Abraham Lincoln. A well done story about the lesser known facts about Abe Lincoln, as told through the memorabilia of his life.

Trivia: Two days after this broadcast, Dr. Ray Kellogg of Spokane, Washington, received a check for $1,000 for his prize-winning letter naming *Cavalcade* as his favorite radio program. Radio station's KHQ's president, R.O. Dunning, was the originator of the contest. The program popularity contest, sponsored by station KHQ ran for two months during which 5,000 entries were received. *Cavalcade* tied with *Fibber McGee and Molly*.

EPISODE #686 **"GREELEY OF THE TRIBUNE"** Broadcast on February 6, 1951
    Starring: Brian Donlevy as Horace Greeley   Bob Dryden as Jenkins
    Chester Stratton as Henry Raymond   Ethel Owen as Harriet *
    John Gibson as Thomas Richards *   W. Honey as Webster
    Chuck Webster as reporter two *   Sydney Smith as George Snow
    Chas. Webster as the voice *   Ross Martin as reporter one *
    Lon Clark as Clark *   Ross Martin as the driver *
    Chas. Webster as Davis *   David Anderson as newsboy *
Based on an incident from the book "Horace Greeley, Voice of the People" by William H. Hale, originally published in 1950 by Harper and Bros. Adapted for *Cavalcade* by Morton Wishengrad.
Produced by H.L. Blackburn and directed by Jack Zoller.
Bill Hamilton was the commercial spokesman and Paul Luther was the announcer.
Music composed by Ardon Cornwell and conducted by Donald Voorhees.
Story: Horace Greeley, a prominent American newspaper publisher, founded and edited the *New York Tribune*. He was a leader in the antislavery movement, and his editorials played an important part in molding public opinion, especially during the twenty years before the American Civil War. In this dramatization, we witness a temperance-minded aunt who helped the New York newspaper editor scoop a story about Daniel Webster, which in turn strengthened the free press in America.

Trivia: The original title of this script was "A Gentleman of the Press" when first written. After the second draft and first revision, the script was retitled to "Mr. Greeley's Tribune," and scheduled for a January 30, 1951 broadcast. It was, however, pre-empted for an extra week and the title - once again - was changed to "Greeley of the Tribune."

EPISODE #687   **"FIBER 66"**   Broadcast on February 13, 1951
    Starring: Lee Bowman as Steve Balfour *   Les Damon as Jim Chalmers *
    Wesley Addy as Dr. Carothers   Richard Gordon as Dr. Stine
    Richard Gordon as the manager *   Judy Parrish as Mary Balfour *
    Grayce Albert as woman one *   Ann Tobin as woman three *
    Wilda Hinkle as woman two *
    Written for *Cavalcade* by Irve Tunick.
    Produced by H.L. Blackburn and directed by Jack Zoller.
    Bill Hamilton was the commercial spokesman and Len Sterling was the announcer.
    Music composed by Ardon Cornwell and conducted by Donald Voorhees.
    Story: Wallace H. Carothers, a chemist of the Du Pont Company, was a leader in the development of nylon. In the late twenties, he began to experiment with polymerization. Carothers found that many of the fibers made from compounds that he polymerized could be pulled out to several times their original length after they were cooled. This pulling process made the fibers much stronger and more elastic. Later, chemists referred to this original kind of nylon was "fiber 66" because both chemicals used in making it had six carbon atoms. This broadcast documents the fascinating discovery of the magic yarn.

EPISODE #688   **"MARY OF MURRAY HILL"**   Broadcast on February 20, 1951
    Starring: Joan Fontaine as Mary Murray   Alan Hewitt as Robert
    Ginger Jones as Prudence *   Maurice Ellis as Luther *
    William Post, Jr. as Jonathan *   Bart Robinson as General Washington
    Horace Braham as Sir William Howe   Guy Spaul as Lord Governor Tryon
    Extras in the cast include Carol Pietel, Barbara Murphy, and Grayce Albut.
    Based on material from the book "Women in American History" by Grace Humphrey, originally published in 1919 by The Bobbs-Merrill Company. Adapted for *Cavalcade* by Robert Tallman.
    Produced by H.L. Blackburn and directed by Jack Zoller.
    Bill Hamilton was the commercial spokesman and Cy Harrice was the announcer.
    Music composed by Ardon Cornwell and conducted by Donald Voorhees.
    Story: Mary Murray was a courageous Quaker who helped General George Washington's troops escape from British forces under Cornwallis, by burning the boots of General Cornwallis!

EPISODE #689   **"THE CASE OF HAROLD THOMAS"**   Broadcast on February 27, 1951
    Starring: Dane Clark as John Harvey *   Ann Tobin as Betty Harvey *
    Scott Tennyson as Court Attendant *   Wendell Holmes as Robert Holmes *
    George Petrie as Harold Thomas *   Ed Jerome as the Judge *
    Florence Robinson as Mrs. Thomas *   Dan Ocko as the detective *
    Joseph Kallini as Mr. Fortuno *   Ann Thomas as Janie *
    Scott Tennyson as the district attorney *   Dan Ocko as the banker *
    Written for *Cavalcade* by Robert Anderson.
    Produced by H.L. Blackburn and directed by Jack Zoller.
    Bill Hamilton was the commercial spokesman and Cy Harrice was the announcer.
    Music composed by Ardon Cornwell and conducted by Donald Voorhees.
    Story: The first legal aid agency in the United States was established in 1876 by the German Society, an organization in New York City. The society set up the agency to help German immigrants with legal problems. In 1911, an organization was founded to furnish legal aid to the needy. This group is now called the National Legal Aid and Defender Association. It publishes information and holds conferences for workers in the legal aid field. In this dramatization, a lawyer defends a poor man framed for robbery through the Legal Aid Society.

EPISODE #690 **"WHALE OFF"** Broadcast on March 6, 1951

Starring: Louis Calhern as Samuel Mulford
Torin Thatcher as Sir Robert Walpole
Muriel Kirkland as Martha *
Staats Cotsworth as the hunter
Kathleen Cordell as the Lady of Fashion *
James McCallion as Timothy
Sarah Burton as Lady Mary Montagu
Dick Newton as underling one *
Guy Repp as the pickpocket *
Elliott Reid as Weldon *
Guy Spaul as Blake *
Guy Repp as underling three *
Jack Edwards as underling two *
Humphrey Davis as Miller
John Griggs as the watcher *
John Griggs as the crier *

Based on material from the 1932 book of the same name by Everett Joshua Edwards and Jeannette Edwards Rattray, and from material in the 1908 book "New England Whalers" by J.R. Spears. Adapted for *Cavalcade* by George H. Faulkner.

Produced by H.L. Blackburn and directed by Jack Zoller.

Bill Hamilton was the commercial spokesman and Cy Harrice was the announcer.

Music composed by Ardon Cornwell and conducted by Donald Voorhees.

Story: Thomas Mulford was an early Long Island colonist who fought unfair taxation by taking his complaint case to King George in England. This cantankerous old man who objected so strenuously to the tax on whales, was probably the first man in America to show concern for the preservation of whales and the unfair laws abiding those decisions.

EPISODE #691 **"UNCLE EURY'S DOLLAR"** Broadcast on March 13, 1951

Starring: Juano Hernandez as Uncle Eury
Clifford Smith as Frank *
Cameron Prud'Homme as Pa
Scott Tennyson as Tom *
Robert Santon as the boy *
Roy Fant as the letter carrier *
Venzuela Jones as Emma
Robert Cummings as William Buffington
Dick Wigginton as Willie one
Robert Santon as Willie two
Arnold Robertson as Scott *
Cynthia Stone as Clara
Maurice Ellis as Logan
Emory Richardson as Graham

Written for *Cavalcade* by Morton Wishengrad.

Produced by H.L. Blackburn and directed by Jack Zoller.

Bill Hamilton was the commercial spokesman and Cy Harrice was the announcer.

Music composed by Ardon Cornwell and conducted by Donald Voorhees.

Story: The is the heartwarming story behind the founding of South Carolina and Georgia's "Faith Cabin Libraries."

Trivia: Mr. and Mrs. Joseph Haley of Wilmington received honors to visit Robert Cummings and Juano Hernandez after this *Cavalcade* broadcast. Mr. Haley was in the Polychemical Sales Department, and employee of Du Pont.

EPISODE #692 **"MR. STATLER'S STORY"** Broadcast on March 20, 1951

Starring: John Lund as Statler
Staats Cotsworth as the drummer *
Ethel Owen as the woman *
Cameron Prud'Homme as the driver *
Judy Parrish as Mary
Court Benson as Scratcherd
Richard Gordon as President McKinley
George Petrie as the assassin *
Charles Dingle as Harrison
George Petrie as the reporter *
Jean Ellyn as the nurse *
Bob Hastings as Oscie
Ann Ives as Mamma
Alan Hewitt as the voice *
Scott Tennyson as the man *
Jean Ellyn as woman two *

Written for *Cavalcade* by Robert Tallman.

Produced by H.L. Blackburn and directed by Jack Zoller.

Bill Hamilton was the commercial spokesman and Cy Harrice was the announcer.

Music composed by Ardon Cornwell and conducted by Donald Voorhees.

(cont'd)

Story: Ellsworth Statler was a bellhop with a vision. He dreamed of one day owning a chain of hotels of his own, and wanted to build the biggest hotel in the world. And not just big, but luxurious. From plush red carpets to fanciful wallpaper, Statler's dream came true. This is how he did it.

EPISODE #693   **"THE KING OF NANTUCKET"**   Broadcast on March 27, 1951
   Starring: Robert Preston as Peter Folger   Donald Crisp as Tristram Coffin
   Les Damon as Mr. Jones *   Rolly Bester as Mrs. Jones *
   Parker Fennelly as General Coffin   Court Benson as the voice *
   Staats Cotsworth as Capt. Gardner   Les Damon as Peter Coffin
   Court Benson as Mayhew
   Written for *Cavalcade* by George H. Faulkner.
   Produced by H.L. Blackburn and directed by Jack Zoller.
   Bill Hamilton was the commercial spokesman and Cy Harrice was the announcer.
   Music composed by Ardon Cornwell and conducted by Donald Voorhees.
   Story: Robert Peter Tristram Coffin was an American author best known for his poems about Maine, his native state. Born in Brunswick, many of his writings described the world of his childhood and youth in Maine. The central elements of his poetry were the sights and sounds of the Maine coast. Using his writings, Coffin attempted the overthrow of America's first dictatorship. This is the true story of Tristram Coffin, the would-be King of Nantucket Island.

EPISODE #694   **"THE RELUCTANT PIONEER"**   Broadcast on April 3, 1951
   Starring: June Havoc as Lillian Sholes   Jeffrey Lynn as James Densmore
   Maurice Franklin as the Judge   Bill Adams as Sholes
   Ted Jewett as Glidden   Klock Ryder as Soule
   Roland Winters as Remington   Chester Stratton as Parsons
   Guy Repp as Clough   Guy Repp as the voice *
   Pat Terry as Jenne
   Written for *Cavalcade* by Irve Tunick.
   Produced by H.L. Blackburn and directed by Jack Zoller.
   Bill Hamilton was the commercial spokesman and Cy Harrice was the announcer.
   Music composed by Ardon Cornwell and conducted by Donald Voorhees.
   Story: The story of the first typewriter in America. The story of the invention of the typewriter, and the development of the famous Remington Model #1.

   Trivia: In order to simulate the reality of a Remington Model #1, NBC's sound man Jerry McGee arranged with Remington to bring in a real Remington model, just like the one described in the broadcast. After testing various sound effects, McGee agreed that the sound produced when pushing the typewriter's keys were ideal for broadcast. June Havoc was surprised to learn, when examining the machine, that not only did the typewriter type only capitols, but that it was the very same typewriter Betty Grable used in the 1947 film, *The Shocking Miss Pilgrim*.

EPISODE #695   **"ONCE MORE THE THUNDERER"**   Broadcast on April 10, 1951
   Starring: Laraine Day as Betty Hough   Franchot Tone as Henry Hough
   John Griggs as Professor Marcu Jernegan   Ted Jewett as Ted *
   Scott Tennyson as Steve Scott *   Ann Seymour as Mrs. Mason *
   Wendell Holmes as Captain Bill *   Mary Bennett as the woman *
   Parker Fennelly as George Pope *   Bob Hastings as Jack, Cub Reporter *
   Patty Pope as operator one *   Mary Bennett as operator two *
   Scott Tennyson as Joe *
   Based on the book of the same name by Henry Beetle Hough, originally published by Ives-Washburn in 1950. Adapted for *Cavalcade* by Gerald Holland.

Produced by H.L. Blackburn and directed by Jack Zoller.
Bill Hamilton was the commercial spokesman and Cy Harrice was the announcer.
Music composed by Ardon Cornwell and conducted by Donald Voorhees.
Story: This is the true story of how Betty and Henry Hough, editors of the famous Vineyard Gazzette, a weekly newspaper of Martha's Vineyard Island, went through great lengths to publish and distribute their latest issue on time . . . during a hurricane!

EPISODE #696   "MAN OF ACTION"   Broadcast on April 17, 1951
    Starring: Dane Clark as David Porter   Gene Leonard as Abdul *
    Peter Capell as the Captain *   Joan Copeland as Evelina
    Arnold Moss as Pashaw *   Peter Capell as Mohammed *
    Mercer McCleod as Bainbridge   Dan Ocko as Maley
    Jack Manning as Blake *   Mercer McLeod as the British Sailor *
    Dan Ocko as Mr. Anderson   Robert Santon as David
    Martin Rudy as Downes *   Guy Spaul as Hillyar
    Jack Manning as Knight *
Adapted for *Cavalcade* by George H. Faulkner, from the 1950 book "Preble's Boys" by Fletcher Pratt, originally published by William Sloane Associates.
Produced by H.L. Blackburn and directed by Jack Zoller.
Bill Hamilton was the commercial spokesman and Cy Harris was the announcer.
Music composed by Ardon Cornwell and conducted by Donald Voorhees.
Story: Commodore David Porter was a United States naval officer who fought in the War of 1812. He was captain of the "Essex," which operated in the Pacific Ocean and was the first warship to fly the U.S. flag in those waters. In the war, Porter almost entirely destroyed the British whaling industry in the Pacific. Later, however, porter surrendered to the British ships "Cherub" and "Phoebe." He returned home as a hero and in 1815 became a Navy commissioner, regardless of his valiant but losing battle against the British.

EPISODE #697   "NO DOLL WAS ABIGAIL"   Broadcast on April 24, 1951
    Starring: Joan Bennett as Abigail Dunniway   Les Damon as Joseph Engle
    Elizabeth Watts as Dolly *   Judy Parrish as Dorothy Engle *
    Richard Taber as Rev. Huckins *   Dan Ocko as Mac *
    Charles Dingle as Pomeroy *   Guy Repp as voice two *
    Anne Seymour as Susan B. Anthony   Harry Jackson as voice one *
    Les Damon as the conductor *   Ossie Davis as the porter *
    Dan Ocko as the sheriff *   Guy Repp as editor two *
    Elizabeth Watts as Mrs. Pomeroy *   Harry Jackson as editor one *
Written for *Cavalcade* by Robert Tallman.
Produced by H.L. Blackburn and directed by Jack Zoller.
Bill Hamilton was the commercial spokesman and Cy Harrice was the announcer.
Music composed by Ardon Cornwell and conducted by Donald Voorhees.
Story: The biography of Abigail Scott Dunniway, who fought for the advancement of women's suffrage in the Pacific Northwest by staring a newspaper. Her cause and determination won women of the future, the freedom she requested for all her life.

EPISODE #698   "THE RAFT"   Broadcast on May 1, 1951
    Starring: Robert Montgomery as Rickenbacker   William Post, Jr. as Adamson
    Bob Santon as Eddie Rickenbacker (age 11)   Hazel Logan as Mother
    Larry Robinson as Rickenbacker (age 18)   Melville Ruick as the man *
    James McCallion as Alex   Donald Buka as the pilot *
    James Van Dyke as Lee Frayer   George Petrie as Kraft *
    Melville Ruick as Eastern *   Gene Leonard as the doctor *
    George Petrie as the announcer *   Gene Leonard as the voice *

Based on the books "Eddie Rickenbacker" by Col. Hans Christian Adamson, originally published by MacMillan Company in 1946 and "Seven Came Through" by Eddie Rickenbacker, originally published in 1943 by Doubleday Doran, Inc. Adapted for *Cavalcade* by Irve Tunick and George Fraser.
Produced by H.L. Blackburn and directed by Jack Zoller.
Bill Hamilton was the commercial spokesman and Cy Harrice was the announcer.
Music composed by Ardon Cornwell and conducted by Donald Voorhees.
Story: This is the documentary of an episode in the life of Eddie Rickenbacker, and his ordeal with seven others on a life raft, adrift for twenty-three days in the South Pacific.

Trivia: Several years ago when Bill Hamilton, *Cavalcade*'s announcer was working at a Dayton, Ohio radio station, he saved a girl's life - in the middle of a news program! Bill, who possessed a rare blood type and is a registered donor, had just begun his newscast when he received a frantic call from the hospital. A young girl who was badly injured was bleeding to death - only Bill's rare blood type could save her. Bill, apologizing to his listeners over the air, immediately dashed off to the hospital. During the East Coast performance of this broadcast, the grateful girl recently paid a surprise visit to the *Cavalcade* broadcast to thank him personally.

More trivia: In order to simulate the personality of Eddie Rickenbacker, Robert Montgomery paid a personal visit to Rickenbacker's office, where the two men chatted for hours, and Montgomery admired Eddie's office memorabilia.

EPISODE #699   "A DUEL WITH AUNT REBECCA"   Broadcast on May 8, 1951
Starring: Richard Carlson as James Shields
Charles Dingle as Whiteside   Scott Tennyson as Doctor Merryman
Raymond Massey as Abe Lincoln   Ray Bramley as Simeon Francis
Written for *Cavalcade* by Warner Law.
Produced by H.L. Blackburn and directed by Jack Zoller.
Bill Hamilton was the commercial spokesman and Cy Harrice was the announcer.
Music composed by Ardon Cornwell and conducted by Donald Voorhees.
Story: James Shields served as governor of the Oregon Territory and as a brigadier general of volunteers in the Mexican and Civil Wars. As a Democrat, he also served as a U.S. senator from Illinois, Minnesota, and Missouri. These are the true events of two young political aspirants, Abe Lincoln and James Shields, who found an unusual way to settle their feud. . . and the time Abe Lincoln almost fought a duel.

EPISODE #700   "MILITANT ANGEL"   Broadcast on May 15, 1951
Starring: Margaret Sullivan as Annie Goodrich   Betty Garde as the woman *
Barbara Weeks as Sarah Jennings *   Ann Tobin as Carrie *
Kermit Murdock as the superintendent *   Pat Hosley as Robin Morris *
Scott Tennyson as Gorgas (Surgeon General)   Court Benson as voice three *
Court Benson as Baker (Secretary of War)   George Petrie as voice two *
Arnold Moss as General Noble   Guy Repp as voice one *
Adapted for *Cavalcade* by Morton Wishengrad, from the 1951 book of the same name, written by Harriet Berger Koch, and published by The MacMillan Company.
Produced by H.L. Blackburn and directed by Jack Zoller.
Bill Hamilton was the commercial spokesman and Cy Harrice was the announcer.
Music composed by Ardon Cornwell and conducted by Donald Voorhees.
Story: Annie Warburton Goodrich's life was long and hard. Her long crusade to raise nursing standards in America was fought with verbal and physical aspects. Her beliefs and cause helped create standards for the profession of nursing, during the early years of the century.

EPISODE #701 **"TOP SECRET"** Broadcast on May 22, 1951

Starring: Robert Young as General Clark
Les Damon as General Lemnitzer
Mercer McLeod as the British Colonel *
Ronald Long as General Mason-McFarlane
Ross Martin as Courbet
Berry Kroeger as Murphy
Luis Van Rooten as Mast
Ross Martin as Captain Wright
Glen Langan as Major Thomas
Roderick Walker as Lt. Jewell
Richard Purdy as Campbell *
Berry Kroeger as the lookout
Ed Jerome as the Police Sgt. *

Adapted from an episode in the book "Calculated Risk" by General Mark W. Clark, as originally published by Harper Bros. in 1950. Adapted for *Cavalcade* by Arthur Arent.
Produced by H.L. Blackburn and directed by Jack Zoller.
Bill Hamilton was the commercial announcer and Cy Harrice was the announcer.
Music composed by Ardon Cornwell and conducted by Donald Voorhees.
Story: In 1942, during World War II, Mark W. Clark became a lieutenant general after leading a secret submarine mission to North Africa. He acquired information that was vital to the success of the 1942 Allied invasion of North Africa. Clark commanded the U.S. Fifth Army in its invasion of Italy at Salerno in 1943, during the hard-fought battles at Cassino and Anzio, and during its entrance into Rome in 1944. In 1945, Clark was promoted to a General. In May 1945, in northern Italy, he accepted the first major German surrender.

EPISODE #702 **"THE TORCHBEARER"** Broadcast on May 29, 1951

Starring: Richard Greene as Nathaniel Bacon
Basil Rathbone as Richard Lawrence *
Cynthia Stone as Elizabeth Bacon
Fred Warlock as Peter Henry *
Mercer McLeod as Drummond
Gilbert Mack as the servant
Ronald Long as Colonel Bacon
Richard Purdy as Berkeley

Based on the 1940 story "Tourchbearer of the Revolution" by Thomas Wertenbaker, and adapted for *Cavalcade* by George H. Faulkner.
Produced by H.L. Blackburn and directed by Jack Zoller.
Bill Hamilton was the commercial announcer and Cy Harrice was the announcer.
Music composed by Ardon Cornwell and conducted by Donald Voorhees.
Story: Nataniel Bacon was a leader of Bacon's Rebellion in Virginia. When Governor William Berkeley failed to take quick action in 1676 to repel an Indian invasion, some Virginia planters chose Bacon to lead a force against the Indians. After Bacon's force defeated the Indians, he attempted to make the governor reform colonial policies. Bacon led an army that captured and burned Jamestown. he controlled the colony briefly in 1676. His death ended the rebellion. Bacon was an American Revolutionary born one hundred years too soon.

EPISODE #703 **"PATH TO THE STARS"** Broadcast on June 5, 1951

Starring: Claire Niessen as Phoebe
Sidney Smith as Shaw *
Denise Alexander as Chickie (age ten) *
Guy Repp as Langley
Phyllis Creore as Chickie (age twenty-one) *
Barry Sullivan as Brashear
Roy Fant as Wilkins *
Dan Ocko as Schutze *
Dan Ocko as William Thaw

Written for *Cavalcade* by Irve Tunick.
Produced by H.L. Blackburn and directed by Jack Zoller.
Bill Hamilton was the commercial announcer and Cy Harrice was the announcer.
Music composed by Ardon Cornwell and conducted by Donald Voorhees.
Story: The story of John Alfred Brashear who became famous as a master maker of fine scientific instruments. He became famous as a lens grinder and maker of telescopes, allowing us not only a view, but a path to the stars.

EPISODE #704   "THE SILENT SERVICE"   Broadcast on June 12, 1951
    Starring: Dick Powell as Benson   Larry Haines as Skuyler *
    James McCallion as Gallagher *   Larry Haines as the crewman *
    Staats Cotsworth as Peatross *   George Petrie as File *
    Jack Grimes as Binelli *   Glen Langan as the cook *
    Glenn Langan as the engineering officer *   Cliff Smith as the voice *
    Cliff Smith as the helmsman *

Written for *Cavalcade* by Gil Doud from the book "Battle Submerged" by Rear Admiral Harley Copy, USN and Captain Walter Karig, USNR., published by W.W. Norton.
Produced by H.L. Blackburn and directed by Jack Zoller.
Bill Hamilton was the commercial announcer and Cy Harrice was the announcer.
Music composed by Ardon Cornwell and conducted by Donald Voorhees.
Story: An exciting World War II submarine story dealing with the U.S.S. Trigger and her captain, Lt. Commander Roy Benson. The U.S.S. Trigger was a submarine forced into duty laying mines, due to a shortage of torpedoes. Nevertheless, the Trigger and her crew managed to cause grief for the Japanese.

EPISODE #705   "CHINESE DAUGHTER"   Broadcast on June 19, 1951
    Starring: Diana Lynn as Jade Snow Wong   James Monks as Father
    Rolly Bester as Mother   Anne Seymour as grandmother
    Ann Tobin as the older sister   Kermit Murdock as Mr. Dong *
    Anne Seymour as Dr. Reinhardt   Kermit Murdock as Instructor *
    Berry Kroeger as Mr. Harris   Berry Kroeger as the Comm. *
    Mimi Strongin as Jade Snow Wong (child)

Adapted for *Cavalcade* by Robert W. Soderberg, from the book "Fifth Chinese Daughter" by Jade Snow Wong, originally published by Harper and Bros. in 1945.
Produced by H.L. Blackburn and directed by Jack Zoller.
Bill Hamilton was the commercial announcer and Cy Harrice was the announcer.
Music composed by Ardon Cornwell and conducted by Donald Voorhees.
Story: The heart-warming autobiography of Jade Snow Wong, the fifth daughter of a San Francisco Chinese-American family, and the hardest honor she was able to achieve - the approval of her "daddy."

Trivia: After tonight's broadcast, Ann Tobin (who played the role of the older sister), left for Mexico City for Spanish-speaking Radio and Television appearances. She was the guest of the Lic Rich Co. during the introduction of their American products to Mexico. Since Ann spoke Spanish frequently, she was drafted in wartime to make a series of transcriptions for the Office of Inter-American Affairs. Her understanding of the language and its accents helped here create the role of Maria Chavez "The Cisco Kid," a part she played for over two years.

EPISODE #706   "THEY SHALL HAVE MUSIC"   Broadcast on June 26, 1951
    Starring: Paul Lukas as Theodore Thomas   Dan Ocko as Fay
    Jan Minor as Minna Thomas   Vinton Hayworth as Wilton
    George Petrie as Woodford *   Stefan Schnabel as Carl Eckert
    Chester Stratton as Harper *

Based on a story by Rose Fay Thomas, and adapted for *Cavalcade* by Warner Law.
Produced by H.L. Blackburn and directed by Jack Zoller.
Bill Hamilton was the commercial announcer and Cy Harrice was the announcer.
Music composed by Ardon Cornwell and conducted by Donald Voorhees.
Story: This is the story of America's beloved orchestra conductor, Theodore Thomas, the German conductor who helped to introduce the good music of the Masters to American audiences. Thomas was also the founder of the Chicago Symphony.

EPISODE #707 **"SOUND THE GREAT BELL"** Broadcast on July 3, 1951
    Starring: Lee Bowman as Thomas Jefferson   Susan Douglas as Mistress Graff
    Alan Hewitt as Dickinson   Ronald Long as the Chairman *
    Mercer McLeod as John Adams   John Stanley as Livingston
    Ronald Long as Benjamin Franklin
    Written for *Cavalcade* by Morton Wishengrad.
    Produced by H.L. Blackburn and directed by Jack Zoller.
    Bill Hamilton was the commercial announcer and Cy Harrice was the announcer.
    Music composed by Ardon Cornwell and conducted by Donald Voorhees.
    Story: In recognition of the 175th anniversary of the signing of the Declaration of Independence, *Cavalcade* reprises the ever-old story of Thomas Jefferson, and his struggles to write the Declaration. It was one pact he was most proud of, and he been best remembered for, all the years past, and all the years to come.

EPISODE #708 **"TOWARDS A NEW WORLD"** Broadcast on September 4, 1951
    Starring: Basil Rathbone as Joseph Priestley   Alice Frost as Mary Priestley
    Eda Heinemann as Lady Shelburne   Mercer McLeod as Lord Shelburne
    Malcolm Keen as Brewer *   Malcolm Keen as Winston *
    Ronald Long as Benjamin Franklin   Pat O'Malley as Cartwright
    Ross Martin as Lavoisier   Pat O'Malley as the voice *
    Based on a chapter from the 1930 Simon and Schuster publication "Crucibles" by Bornard Jaffe, and adapted for *Cavalcade* by Irve Tunick.
    Produced by H.L. Blackburn and directed by Jack Zoller.
    Bill Hamilton was the commercial announcer and Cy Harrice was the announcer.
    Music composed by Ardon Cornwell and conducted by Donald Voorhees.
    Story: Your introduction to Dr. Joseph Priestley, an English clergyman and chemist, who shared the credit for the discovery of oxygen with Carl Wilhelm Scheele of Sweden. Priestley called the gas "dephlogisticated air." French chemist Antoine Lavoisier named it "oxygen."

EPISODE #709 **"NO ONE IS ALONE"** Broadcast on September 11, 1951
    Starring: Laraine Day as Laura Wiley *   Thomas Mitchell as Fred Maxwell *
    Les Damon as Rogers *   Dan Ocko as the conductor *
    Grayce Albert as the woman *   Dan Ocko as the man *
    Written for *Cavalcade* by Morton Wishengrad.
    Produced by H.L. Blackburn and directed by Jack Zoller.
    Bill Hamilton was the commercial announcer and Cy Harrice was the announcer.
    Music composed by Ardon Cornwell and conducted by Donald Voorhees.
    Story: The travelers Aid Society is a nationwide network of agencies that provides service to individuals and families who have experienced difficulties related to homelessness, traveling, or moving their place of residence. This a true story from one of the files of the Travelers Aid Society, one of Laura Wiley, who dealt with a "stranger" who came to her town.

EPISODE #710 **"GIRL ON A MISSION"** Broadcast on September 18, 1951
    Starring: Joan Caulfield as Emily   Dick Janaver as Lee
    Henry Norell as Greene   Grant Richards as the scout *
    Dick Janaver as Reade *   Court Benson as General Sumter
    Betty Garde as Mrs. Jenkins *   John Stanley as Captain Gresham *
    Michael McAlloney as the Sergeant *   Richard Newton as Corporal *
    Court Benson as Mr. Phillips *   Irene Hubbard as Mrs. Phillips *
    Written for *Cavalcade* by Robert Tallman.
    Produced by H.L. Blackburn and directed by Jack Zoller.
    Bill Hamilton was the commercial announcer and Cy Harrice was the announcer.

Music composed by Ardon Cornwell and conducted by Donald Voorhees.
Story: A young girl who cannot tell lies well, by the name of Emily Geiger, was used to help the Revolutionary cause with a musical cipher. A woman who risked her life for a great cause.

EPISODE #711 **"LISTEN MY CHILDREN"** Broadcast on September 25, 1951
    Starring: Robert Ryan as Paul Revere   Joseph Bell as Joseph Warren
    Nancy Marchand as Rachel   Rosemary Rice as Deborah
    Jacques Aubuchon as Colonel Ansart   Jim Stephens as Joseph Warren Revere
    Mercer McLeod as Colonel Conant   Brad Barker as the voice of the dog
    Kenny Delmar is the narrator.
Written for *Cavalcade* by George H. Faulkner.
Produced by H.L. Blackburn and directed by Jack Zoller.
Bill Hamilton was the commercial announcer and Cy Harrice was the announcer.
Music composed by Ardon Cornwell and conducted by Donald Voorhees.
Story: Everyone knows about Paul Revere and his famous midnight ride. But that historic night was not the only contribution Paul Revere did for his country. These are a few of his other accomplishments.

EPISODE #712 **"SEQUEL AT SEVENTY"** Broadcast on October 2, 1951
    Starring: Walter Hampden as Dr. Benjamin M. Duggar
    George Petrie as Dr. Ed Ball   Parker Fennelly as Roy Smathers *
    Guy Repp as Dr. Subbarow   Bob Hastings as Pete *
    Sydney Smith as Dr. Lefkowitz   Dan Ocko as Dr. Fischbein
    David Anderson as Albert
Written for *Cavalcade* by Irve Tunick.
Produced by H.L. Blackburn and directed by Jack Zoller.
Bill Hamilton was the commercial announcer and Cy Harrice was the announcer.
Music composed by Ardon Cornwell and conducted by Donald Voorhees.
Story: A story about Dr. Benjamin M. Duggar, discoverer of the new wonder-drug, aureomycin.

EPISODE #713 **"THE FIELDS ARE GREEN"** Broadcast on October 9, 1951
    Starring: Audie Murphy as Walt Carlin   Bob Hastings as Bill Carlin
    Bill Adams as Johnson   Virginia Payne as the mother
    Cameron Prud'Homme as the father   Rosemary Rice as Dorie
    Bill Adams as the driver   Gene Leonard as Arnold
Adapted for *Cavalcade* by Irve Tunick, from the article entitled "Pay-Dirt from Worn-Out Acres" by J.T. Bingham, as originally published in a 1947 issue of *Country Gentleman Magazine*.
Produced by H.L. Blackburn and directed by Jack Zoller.
Bill Hamilton was the commercial announcer and Cy Harrice was the announcer.
Music composed by Ardon Cornwell and conducted by Donald Voorhees.
Story: Formerly known as the Future Farmers of America, the FFA is an organization mainly for students in grades seven through twelve, who study agriculture. This program has helped thousands of youth men and women prepare for careers in agriculture and agribusiness. It has also trained them to become responsible citizens and leaders. Two members of the FFA, Walt and Bill Carlin, use modern methods to successfully run a farm.

EPISODE #714   "THE SHIP THE NAZIS HAD TO GET"   Broadcast on October 16, 1951
    Starring: Ray Milland as Captain Kenneth C. Towne
    Arnold Moss as the German radio announcer *
    Alan Hewitt as the Convoy and Routing officer
    Peter Clure as the radio operator on the ship
    Malcolm Keen as the British Commander at Aden
    Alan Hewitt as the British Lieutenant at Aden
    Santos Ortega as the Italian radio operator
    Victor Chapin as the helmsman
    Guy Repp as Mr. Hoyt *
    Bill Zuckert as Harry *
    Santos Ortega as James Murphy
    James McCallion as Bill Maguire
    Arnold Moss as the Italian Capt.
    Victor Chapin as the Italian

Written for *Cavalcade* by Robert Anderson, adapted from an article of the same title by James H. Winchester, as originally published in a 1951 issue of *The American Legion Magazine*.
Produced by H.L. Blackburn and directed by Jack Zoller.
Bill Hamilton was the commercial announcer and Cy Harrice was the announcer.
Music composed by Ardon Cornwell and conducted by Donald Voorhees.
Story: The British Commander at Aden, in the Red Sea, had received a report that an Italian submarine lay directly in a channel through which the "Seatrain Texas" had to pass. He sent a message to the ship to change course and go around the outside of Socotra Island into the harbor at Aden. This exciting, but true, story of World War II presents a sea-going story about a freighter with a vital shipment of tanks bound for Egypt, and of a journey that had to be made - the hard way.

EPISODE #715   "LOYAL LADY"   Broadcast on October 23, 1951
    Starring: Diana Lynn as Rebecca
    Kathleen Comegys as Mother
    Scott Tennyson as Junius *
    Chester Stratton as Sergeant *
    Kermit Murdock as Sleeth *
    Chester Stratton as Will *
    Bernard Lenrow as Sheridan

Written for *Cavalcade* by Morton Wishengrad.
Produced by H.L. Blackburn and directed by Jack Zoller.
Bill Hamilton was the commercial announcer and Cy Harrice was the announcer.
Music composed by Ardon Cornwell and conducted by Donald Voorhees.
Story: Rebecca Wright, of Winchester Virginia, sympathized with the North and worked for a Union victory during the Civil War. She risked her own life and jeopardized that of the men she loved to serve the cause of the Union during the War between the States.

EPISODE #716   "NAVY BLUE"   Broadcast on October 30, 1951
    Starring: Robert Cummings as Lt. Victor Blue
    Arnold Robertson as Delenhanty
    Carlos Montalban as Pedro *
    Carlos Montalban as the Commandante *
    Arnold Robertson as Captain two *
    Dan Ocko as the Captain one *
    Santos Ortega as Ramirez *
    George Petrie as Reilley *
    Kenny Delmar as Gomez

Based on the 1943 book "The Spy in America" by George S. Bryan, published by J. B. Lippincott and Company, and adapted for *Cavalcade* by Robert Tallman.
Produced by H.L. Blackburn and directed by Jack Zoller.
Bill Hamilton was the commercial announcer and Cy Harrice was the announcer.
Music composed by Ardon Cornwell and conducted by Donald Voorhees.
Story: On the small boat of Lt. Blue, with his crew of twelve men returned to their ship from a mission ashore in Cuba. They were sighted by an enemy gunboat that was bearing down on it. So Lt. Victor Blue, knowing the circumstance of his position, performed an exploit of extraordinary heroism. And this exciting tale of the Spanish-American War ends with Lt. Blue being reprimanded for his heroic actions!

EPISODE #717 "SEVEN HUNDRED BOILED SHIRTS" Broadcast on November 6, 1951
    Starring: Ginger Rogers as India Locke *   Ann Seymour as Maggie *
    Gladys Thornton as the woman *   Dan Ocko as Jeb *
    George Petrie as Baxter *   Ed Jerome as Orr *
    Santos Ortega as the cook *   Dan Ocko as the native *
    Santos Ortega as the first sailor *   Court Benson as Mitchell *

Based on a chapter from "Women Who Went to Sea" by Ora Hinckley, from the book "Barnstable: Three Centuries of a Cape Cod Town" by Donald Trayser, originally published by F.B. & F.P. Goss, Hyannis, Mass. in 1939. Adapted for *Cavalcade* by Virginia Radcliffe.
Produced by H.L. Blackburn and directed by Jack Zoller.
Bill Hamilton was the commercial announcer and Cy Harrice was the announcer.
Music composed by Ardon Cornwell and conducted by Donald Voorhees.
Story: Do you know what it's like to be in love with a seafaring man? Well, if you happen to be a Cape Cod woman, you gather up your skirts, and you climb up through a trap door to the roof - the little fenced-in flat space atop so many Cape houses, called a 'Widows' Walk. You stand up there, gazing out over the dunes until your eyes burned. This is a fictional story of a young New England bride, India Locke, who followed her husband, the Captain of a Schooner, out to sea, because she did not want to do what other women left stranded did, to wait on the Widows Walk.

Trivia: Ginger Rogers makes several mistakes in the first few minutes of the program. Announcer Cy Harrice also played the male lead of Zachary Locke in this broadcast.

EPISODE #718 "A NEW COMMANDMENT" Broadcast on November 13, 1951
    Starring: Douglas Fairbanks, Jr. as Captain Thomas Sullivan
    Gertrude Warner as Margaret   Arnold Robertson as Frank McGinnis *
    Larry Robinson as Sam Martin *   Dan Ocko as Don Juan *
    Alan Hewitt as Watts   Malcolm Keen as the Judge *
    Scott Tennyson as Benson   Malcom Keen as the voice of the pirate
    John Harper as the voice of the jury   Scott Tennyson as the voice of the sailor

Written for *Cavalcade* by Irve Tunick.
Produced by H.L. Blackburn and directed by Jack Zoller.
Bill Hamilton was the commercial announcer and Cy Harrice was the announcer.
Music composed by Ardon Cornwell and conducted by Donald Voorhees.
Story: The YMCA was founded in London in 1844 by a young British clerk named George Williams. Williams wanted to provide clothing store clerks from the countryside with a place in London where they could read the Bible, relax, and find out about decent lodging. The YMCA movement traveled overseas to the United States and Canada in 1851. In that year, Captain Thomas V. Sullivan, a missionary and retired sea captain, founded a YMCA in Boston. The meeting of Captain Thomas Sullivan with a pirate ship and how it led to the founding of the YMCA in America is the incredible but true story documented in this broadcast.

EPISODE #719 "THE PATH OF PRAISE" Broadcast on November 20, 1951
    Starring: Walter Hampden as the voice *   Bobby Santon as Giles
    Bramwell Fletcher as Washington   Frank Readick as Bradford
    Joseph Bell as Reed   Evelyn Varden as Sarah Hale
    Bill Adams as Abraham Lincoln

Written for *Cavalcade* by George H. Faulkner.
Includes a quote by the late Dr. Wilbur L. Cross, governor of Connecticut.
Produced by H.L. Blackburn and directed by Jack Zoller.
Bill Hamilton was the commercial announcer and Cy Harrice was the announcer.
Music composed by Ardon Cornwell and conducted by Donald Voorhees.

Story: As the colors of autumn stream down the wind, scarlet in sumach and maple, spun gold in the birches, a splendor of smoldering fire in the oaks along the hill, and the last leaves flutter away, and the dusk falls briefly, we are stirred and made to ponder the Infinite Goodness that has set apart for us, in all the moving mystery of creation, a time of living and a home. This is the history of Thanksgiving, from George Washington to Abraham Lincoln.

EPISODE #720   "INCIDENT AT LANCASTER"   Broadcast on November 27, 1951
    Starring: MacDonald Carey as Captain Lee   Frank Readick as General Hazen
    Scott Tennyson as Will *   Eugene Francis as a Lieutenant *
    Bob Dryden as the Jailor *   Carl Harbord as Young *
    Betty Garde as the Applewoman *
    Written for *Cavalcade* by Rosemary Foster.
    Produced by H.L. Blackburn and directed by Jack Zoller.
    Bill Hamilton was the commercial announcer and Cy Harrice was the announcer.
    Music composed by Ardon Cornwell and conducted by Donald Voorhees.
    Story: An exciting Revolutionary War tale of how an American soldier, Captain James Lee, went behind the prison walls, pretending to be a Tory P.O.W. to discover the method British prisoners-of-war used to escape.

EPISODE #721   "THE SITTING DUCK"   Broadcast on December 4, 1951
    Starring: William Holden as Lt. (J.G.) Frank Connell *
    Bob Dryden as Jim *   Carl Emory as Chuck *
    Maurice Tarplin as Kim Jong *   Guy Spaul as Lt. Partridge *
    Bram Nossen as Captain Fuller *   Bill Zuckert as Pappadeaux *
    George Petrie as Jackson *
    Written for *Cavalcade* by Robert Mason Pollock and Robert Tallman.
    Produced by H.L. Blackburn and directed by Jack Zoller.
    Bill Hamilton was the commercial announcer and Cy Harrice was the announcer.
    Music composed by Ardon Cornwell and conducted by Donald Voorhees.
    Story: Dramatic story of how an American salvage ship with a U.N. crew, found and salvaged Russia's best jet plane, the MIG-15. Apparently the MIG-15 was brought down by enemy fire during the Korean War.

    Trivia: The role of Kim Jong, a South Korean, was played by Maurice Tarplin. Tarplin was currently heard over Mutual as the host of a creepy radio horror program entitled *The Mysterious Traveler.*

IRENE DUNNE
in
DOCTORA IN MEXICO
MONDAY EVENING   **APRIL 16, 1945**

EPISODE #722 "THE GIANT WHO STEPPED OVER THE MOUNTAIN"   Dec. 11, 1951
    Starring: Tyrone Power as Sevier   Court Benson as Standish *
    Santos Ortega as Baring *   Charles Dingle as Tipton
    Bill Zuckert as Trent *   Chuck Webster as Settler *
    Ted Jewett as the agent *   Floyd Buckley as man one *
    Chuck Webster as man two *   Santos Ortega as the visitor *
    Malcom Keen as the judge *   Ted Jewett as the bailiff *
    Written for *Cavalcade* by Russell Hughes, based on a chapter from "General Washington's Son of Israel and Other Forgotten Heroes of History," by Charles Spencer Hart, as originally published by Lippincott in 1936 and 1937.
    Produced by H.L. Blackburn and directed by Jack Zoller.
    Bill Hamilton was the commercial announcer and Cy Harrice was the announcer.
    Music composed by Ardon Cornwell and conducted by Donald Voorhees.
    Story: An American soldier, frontiersman, and politician, John Sevier served as governor of "The lost state of Franklin" and later became the first governor of Tennessee. In 1796, "The lost state of Franklin" became part of Tennessee. Sevier was elected as it's first governor and served six terms. After the end of his sixth term, Sevier was elected to the state senate for one term and then served again in Congress until his death.

EPISODE #723 "THE DU PONT CHORUS"   Broadcast on December 18, 1951
    Under the direction of Frank J. Clark, Jr.
    Mr. Crawford H. Greenewalt, President of the Du Pont Company spoke during intermission.
    Broadcast from "The Playhouse" in Wilmington, Delaware.
    Bill Hamilton is the announcer and master of ceremonies.
    Cy Harrice is narrator during the musical presentation of "The First Christmas Candle." Songs sung in the following order: "It's Christmas!", "Deck the Halls," "Glory to God in the Highest," "Hark Now O Shepherds," "The First Christmas Candle," "Joyous Christmas Song," the Austrian lullaby "The Shepherds Christmas Song," "The Sleigh," "Christmas is Coming," Adolphe Adam's French classic "O Holy Night," and for the close, the lyric "Merry Christmas and a Happy New Year."

EPISODE #724 "THE DAY THEY GAVE BABIES AWAY"   Broadcast December 25, 1951
    Starring: Bobby Driscoll as Robbie   Natalie Core as Mrs. Eunson
    Sarah Fussell as Jimmie   David Anderson as Kirk
    Lois Volkman as Annabelle   Madeleine Pierce as Jane
    Judy Lockser as Elizabeth   Cameron Prud'Homme as Dr. Delbert
    Eda Heineman as Mrs. Runyon   Sydney Smith as Mr. Tyler
    Robert Santon as Howard, Jr.   Ginger Jones as Mrs. Tyler
    Scott Tennyson as Mr. Stevens   Irene Hubbard as Mrs. Stevens
    Scott Tennyson as the fisherman *   Eda Heineman as Mrs. Clarey
    Based on the 1947 book of the same name by Dale Eunson, and adapted for *Cavalcade* by Frank Gabrielson.
    Produced by H.L. Blackburn and directed by Jack Zoller.
    Bill Hamilton was the commercial announcer and Cy Harrice was the announcer.
    Music composed by Ardon Cornwell and conducted by Donald Voorhees.
    Story: The story of Bobby Eunson's great love for his family. At the age of twelve, Bobby was the man of the house, helping raise five brothers and sisters and working part-time in a logging camp. This touching Christmas story about a twelve year old boy forced to find homes for his brothers and sisters when their mother dies remains a classic.

EPISODE #725 "SIXTEEN STICKS IN A BUNDLE" Broadcast on January 1, 1952
    Starring: Ethel Waters as Mrs. Young   Jester Hairston as Mr. Young
    Norma Jean Nilsson as Josie   H.B. Barnum as Otis
    Kenny Delmar as Collins   Carmen Davis as Flossie
    William Johnstone as the Superintendent   Marie Stansall as Maizy
    Cecil Thompson as the voice of the boy   Shelby Bacon as Hezekiah
    Pat Washington as the voice of the girl   Norma Nilsson as the baby cry
Margaret Hairston, Chester Jones and Florence Cadrez played the rest of the family of fourteen children in the spiritual and ad lib dialogue.
Written for *Cavalcade* by Edith Somner and Robert Soderberg, based on the article of the same name by Richard C. Davids, originally published in the May 1951 issue of *The Farm Journal*.
Produced by H.L. Blackburn and directed by Jack Zoller.
Bill Hamilton was the commercial announcer and Cy Harrice was the announcer.
Music composed by Ardon Cornwell and conducted by Donald Voorhees.
Story: A tribute to the faith of an American woman - Leah Young - and her family. Leah and John Young's fourteen children were all sent through high school and most of them found a way to continue on through college. A poor colored family, only one generation from slavery, put fourteen children through high school, and most of them through college.

EPISODE #726 "A PRISONER NAMED BROWN" Broadcast on January 8, 1952
    Starring: Gregory Peck as Tom Osborne   Staats Cotsworth as the governor
    Scott Tennyson as the keeper   Santos Ortega as Lamb *
    John Griggs as Forrester   Dick York as Jones *
    Maurice Ellis as Two *   Santos Ortega as the guard *
Based on the 1914 book "Within Prison Walls" and "Society and Prisons," both written by Thomas Mott Osborne, and adapted for *Cavalcade* by Warner Law.
Produced by H.L. Blackburn and directed by Jack Zoller.
Bill Hamilton was the commercial announcer and Cy Harrice was the announcer.
Music composed by Ardon Cornwell and conducted by Donald Voorhees.
Story: Thomas Mott Osborne was an American prison reformer. In 1913, as chairman of the New York State Commission for Prison Reform, he spent a week in prison, secretly, so he could understand and help prisoners. He served as warden of Sing Sing Prison from 1914 to 1916 and of Portsmouth Naval Prison from 1917 to 1920. Osborne organized the Mutual Welfare League to help prisoners rebuild their lives.

    Trivia: This was not the only *Cavalcade* presentation to feature an all-male cast.

EPISODE #727 "THE PORT OF MISSING MEN" Broadcast on January 15, 1952
    Starring: Loretta Young as Janet Lord Roper   Harold Huber as Mate *
    Vinton Hayworth as Higgins *   Dan Ocko as Landowski *
    Eda Heineman as Mrs. Lord   Vinton Hayworth as Ed Roper
    Bill Zuckert as Ben *   Harold Huber as the doctor *
    Ruth Yorke as Mrs. Johnson *   Homer Smith as sailor one *
    Maurice Ellis as sailor two *   Grace Albert as the voice *
Scripted for *Cavalcade* by Arnold Schulman, based on the article "Mother of Missing Men" by the late Frank Laskier, as originally published in a 1951 issue of *Lookout Magazine*.
Produced by H.L. Blackburn and directed by Jack Zoller.
Bill Hamilton was the commercial announcer and Cy Harrice was the announcer.
Music composed by Ardon Cornwell and conducted by Donald Voorhees.
Story: Janet Lord (affectionately called, "Mother Roper" by seamen everywhere) and her volunteer work at Seaman's Friend Society and later at the Seaman's Church Institute.

EPISODE #728 **"AS IF A DOOR WERE OPENING"** Broadcast on January 22, 1952
    Starring: John Hodiak as Lafayette   Kermit Murdock as Duke D'Ayen
    Susan Miller as Adrienne   Ross Martin as D'Arcy
    Robert Dryden as Deane   Robert Dryden as the corporal *
    Arnold Moss as Washington   Kermit Murdock as the driver *
Based on the 1951 C. Scribner and Sons publication, "The People's General: The Personal Story of Lafayette" by David Loth, adapted for *Cavalcade* by George H. Faulkner.
Produced by H.L. Blackburn and directed by Jack Zoller.
Bill Hamilton was the commercial announcer and Cy Harrice was the announcer.
Music composed by Ardon Cornwell and conducted by Donald Voorhees.
Story: A tribute to the Marquis de Lafayette, his arrival in the New World, his commission as a major general in the Continental Army and finally his appointment as a member of Washington's staff, his first meeting with George Washington.

    Trivia: This episode was originally entitled "The Lafayette Story."

EPISODE #729 **"THE NIGHT THERE WAS NO PRESIDENT"** Broadcast January 29, 1952
    Starring: Dean Stockwell as Theodore Roosevelt, Jr.   Guy Repp as Elihu Root
    Ian Martin as Theodore Roosevelt   Ed Jerome as Cleveland
    Gertrude Warner as Mrs. Edith Roosevelt   Philip Rodd as Archie
    Parker Fennelly as David Hunter   Sarah Fussell as Quentin
    Robert Dryden as Harrison Hall   Butch Cavell as Kermit
    Jack Edwards as Beverly Robinson
Based on a series of articles by Herman Hagedorn as published in *North American Newspaper Alliance* in 1951, and adapted for *Cavalcade* by Evelyn Nolt.
Produced by H.L. Blackburn and directed by Jack Zoller.
Bill Hamilton was the commercial announcer and Cy Harrice was the announcer.
Music composed by Ardon Cornwell and conducted by Donald Voorhees.
Story: A story portrait of Theodore Roosevelt and his family. When President McKinley's condition grew worse after being critically wounded by an assassin, Roosevelt traveled 440 miles through a blinding rain storm and arrived at Buffalo the next morning. He then learned of McKinley's death and that he was now that 26th President of the United States. The strange conditions under which Theodore Roosevelt became President, as told from the viewpoint of his family.

EPISODE #730 **"THUNDER OF JUSTICE"** Broadcast on February 5, 1952
    Starring: Dorothy McGuire as Beulah Lyon   Grace Keddy as Hattie *
    Cameron Prud'Homme as Senator Mason   Ian Martin as Matthew Lyon
    Wesley Addy as Thomas Jefferson   Bob Dryden as voice one *
    Parker Fennelly as Benjamin Marshall   Sydney Smith as voice two *
    Charles Egelston as Nathaniel Chipman   Bob Dryden as constable *
    Sydney Smith as the driver *   Richard Gordon as the judge *
    Fred Worlock as Governor Chittenden
Based on the book "Crisis in Freedom: The Alien and Sedition Acts" by John C. Miller, published in 1951 by Little Brown and Company. Adapted for *Cavalcade* by William Kendall Clarke.
Produced by H.L. Blackburn and directed by Jack Zoller.
Bill Hamilton was the commercial announcer and Cy Harrice was the announcer.
Music composed by Ardon Cornwell and conducted by Donald Voorhees.
Story: The story of one of the leading opponents of the Alien and Sedition Acts - Representative Matthew Lyon of Vermont, who fought the Allen and Sedition Acts, from behind prison walls.

EPISODE #731 **"WITH MALICE TOWARDS NONE"** Broadcast on February 12, 1952
    Starring: Raymond Massey as Abraham Lincoln   Scott Tennyson as citizen one *
    Charles Egleston as Stanton   Ted Jewett as citizen two *
    Scott Tennyson as Stephens   Ted Jewett as Tinker
    George Petrie as Nicolay   John Griggs as Thatcher
    Based on material from the book "Abraham Lincoln: The War Years" by Carl Sandburg, published in 1939 by Harcourt, Brace and Company, Inc. and adapted for *Cavalcade* by George H. Faulkner.
    Produced by H.L. Blackburn and directed by Jack Zoller.
    Bill Hamilton was the commercial announcer and Cy Harrice was the announcer.
    Music composed by Ardon Cornwell and conducted by Donald Voorhees.
    Story: The true story of President Abe Lincoln and Alexander Stephens, Vice-President of the Confederacy and how they tried desperately to find a common ground of agreement to end the Civil War. . . but the conference failed.

EPISODE #732 **"THREE WORDS"** Broadcast on February 19, 1952
    Starring: Claude Rains as Washington   Bill Lipton as Hamilton
    Richard Purdy as the visitor *   Kermit Murdock as Col. Reed
    Court Benson as General Greene   Jack Hartley as Col. Knox
    Mercer McLeod as Jefferson   Mercer McCloud as Forrest
    Dan Ocko as General Sullivan   Dan Ocko as the hand
    Written for *Cavalcade* by George H. Faulkner.
    Produced by H.L. Blackburn and directed by Jack Zoller.
    Bill Hamilton was the commercial announcer and Cy Harrice was the announcer.
    Music composed by Ardon Cornwell and conducted by Donald Voorhees.
    Story: "Victory or Death" - the three words, the keynote for the most daring strategy of Washington's military career. The origin of those three words, and how Washington used those three words as a password before the Battle of Trenton was told.

EPISODE #733 **"DOCTOR COMMANDO"** Broadcast on February 26, 1952
    Starring: Wendell Corey as General Sams   Les Damon as Lieutenant Drake
    Howard Smith as Chief of Staff *   Chung Yun as Han *
    Dan Lee as Chung *   Dan Lee as the stretcher bearer *
    Jun-Gyu Park as the Korean Marine Captain *   George Petrie as the colonel *
    Jun-Gyu Park as the Korean Guerilla Leader *   Mason Adams as the Major *
    Kisun Yun as the sentry *
    Adapted in part from an article by Peter Kalischer as published in *Colliers* in 1951.
    Written for *Cavalcade* by Robert Anderson.
    Produced by H.L. Blackburn and directed by Jack Zoller.
    Bill Hamilton was the commercial announcer and Cy Harrice was the announcer.
    Music composed by Ardon Cornwell and conducted by Donald Voorhees.
    Story: An exciting story of the U.N. investigation of reports of plague behind enemy Korean lines. Brigadier General Crawford F. Sams, Chief of Public Health for the U.N. forces led the investigation. He landed behind enemy lines in Communist Korea, to investigate those reports of an epidemic of Plague.

EPISODE #734 **"ROMANCE AT FORT CRAWFORD"** Broadcast on March 4, 1952
    Starring: Arlene Dahl as Sarah Knox Taylor   Lex Barker as Jefferson Davis
    Bill Adams as Zachary Taylor   Vera Allen as Mrs. Taylor
    Ginger Jones as Anna   Henry Calvin as Dr. Harper *
    Bill Adams as Johnson *
    Written for *Cavalcade* by Warner Law.
    Produced by H.L. Blackburn and directed by Jack Zoller.

                                                              (cont'd)

Bill Hamilton was the commercial announcer and Cy Harrice was the announcer.
Music composed by Ardon Cornwell and conducted by Donald Voorhees.
Story: These are the true events that led to the courtship of Jefferson Davis and Sarah Knox Taylor. Sarah was one of President Zachary Taylor's five daughters. Their romance ended in tragedy as Jefferson Davis was destined to become the President of the Confederacy. Sarah died three months after their wedding.

EPISODE #735 "ADVENTURE ON THE KENTUCKY" Broadcast on March 11, 1952
    Starring: Richard Widmark as Shryock   Bill Post as Morgan
    Roy Fant as Billy*   Dick York as John *
    Sarah Fussell as Drew *   Les Damon as Watson *
    Neva Patterson as Olive   Don Briggs as Cobbs *
    George Petrie as the voice *   George Petrie as the sergeant *
Based on the story "The Kentucky" by Thomas D. Clark, published in 1942 by Rinehart and Company. Adapted for *Cavalcade* by Irve Tunick and Robert Tallman.
Produced by H.L. Blackburn and directed by Jack Zoller.
Bill Hamilton was the commercial announcer and Cy Harrice was the announcer.
Music composed by Ardon Cornwell and conducted by Donald Voorhees.
Story: Cincinnatus Shryock, an architect and school teacher turned ferryman in order aid the Confederacy by helping to stall a Union pursuit of Confederate soldiers across the Kentucky river.

EPISODE #736 "THE MARINE WHO WAS 200 YEARS OLD" Broadcast March 18, 1952
    Starring: William Bendix as Sergeant Lou Diamond
    Staats Cotsworth as Major Oliver *   Don Briggs as voice two *
    Chester Stratton as the Army Corporal *   Dan Ocko as voice one *
    Chester Stratton as the Aussie *   Ann Tobin as the Nurse *
    Jeff Bryant as Savitt *   Dan Ocko as the army sergeant *
    Bill Quinn as Sgt. Pete Chambers *   Bill Quinn as voice three *
    Don Briggs as Lieutenant Powell *   Bob Hastings as Anderson *
Written for *Cavalcade* by Robert Mason Pollock.
Produced by H.L. Blackburn and directed by Jack Zoller.
Bill Hamilton was the commercial announcer and Cy Harrice was the announcer.
Music composed by Ardon Cornwell and conducted by Donald Voorhees.
Story: The true dramatization of Loud Diamond, a sixty-year old combat Marine, and an indestructible leatherneck. The events in the life of this M/Sgt. proved that age did not matter, when he couldn't be stopped.

EPISODE #737 "BREAKFAST AT NANCY'S" Broadcast on March 25, 1952
    Starring: Susan Hayward as Nancy Hart   Dan Ocko as Sam *
    Gordon Dilworth as the folk singer *   Ivor Francis as Ben *
    Staats Cotsworth as Wilkie Bowman *   Joseph Boland as Benton *
    Cameron Andrews as Tolliver *   James Boles as Elbers *
    Denise Alexander as Sukey *   Jackie Diamond as Morgan *
Based on material from "The Savannah" by Thomas L. Stokes, published in 1951 by Rinehart and Company. Adapted for *Cavalcade* by George H. Faulkner.
Produced by H.L. Blackburn and directed by Jack Zoller.
Bill Hamilton was the commercial announcer and Cy Harrice was the announcer.
Music composed by Ardon Cornwell and conducted by Donald Voorhees.
Story: During the American Revolution, Nancy Hart used her woodland cabin as a station for scouts carrying messages for General Clark of the Continental Army. On one particular day, Nancy hides one of her soldier-husband's comrades from aroused Tories, one of whom she once loved, and her patriotism turned personal. She then had to defend her home and children with a loaded musket.

Trivia: "Breakfast At Nancy's" was originally entitled "The Legend of Nancy Hart."

EPISODE #738 **"THE DEVIL'S STAIRCASE"** Broadcast on April 1, 1952
    Starring: Ray Milland as Frasch   Grace Matthews as Elizabeth
    Luis Van Rooten as Bientout *   Guy Sorel as Morceau *
    Dan Ocko as Toniette *   Joseph Bell as Hewitt
    Maurice Ellis as Henri *   Maurice Ellis as the voice *
    George Petrie as Hoffman   Guy Sorel as Le Clerc *
    Written for *Cavalcade* by Irve Tunick.
    Produced by H.L. Blackburn and directed by Jack Zoller.
    Bill Hamilton was the commercial announcer and Cy Harrice was the announcer.
    Music composed by Ardon Cornwell and conducted by Donald Voorhees.
    Story: Herman Frasch, overcame fear and prejudice in the Louisiana Bayous, when his process of drilling became the laugh of the year. His skill and determination made it possible for America's chemical industry to harness its great sulfur deposits.

EPISODE #739 **"THE NURSE WHO FORGOT FEAR"** Broadcast on April 8, 1952
    Starring: Nina Foch as Bonnie (Jonita R. Bonham)
    John Newland as Tom *   Scott Tennyson as the marine *
    Judy Parish as Vera   Lon Clark as the patient
    Scott Tennyson as Bradley *   John Newland as Bill
    Dick York as Ted *   Bill Zuckert as Al *
    Peter Rankin as Ike *   Lon Clark as Rogers *
    Jack Manning as Tumulty *   Yuki Shimoda as the fisherman
    Sidney Smith as the doctor *
    Based on an article by Karl Detzer in *Everywoman's Magazine* and condensed in *Reader's Digest*, both published February 1952. Adapted for *Cavalcade* by Irving Elman and Arnold Schulman.
    Produced by H.L. Blackburn and directed by Jack Zoller.
    Bill Hamilton was the commercial announcer and Cy Harrice was the announcer.
    Music composed by Ardon Cornwell and and conducted by Donald Voorhees.
    Story: These are the facts of Lt. Jonita Ruth Bonham of the U.S. Air Force Nurse Corps, who shuttled daily between the Japanese Island of Ashiya and the Korean battlefields, nursing evacuated wounded troops across the Korean lines.

EPISODE #740 **"FLY HIGH, FLY LOW"** Broadcast on April 15, 1952
    Starring: Lee Bowman as Thaddeus Lowe   Klock Ryder as the farmer *
    William Podmore as Prof. Joseph Henry   Jimmie Lipton as Jim *
    Parker Fennelly as Fogarty *   Bill Adams as Abraham Lincoln
    Melville Ruick as McClellan   Jimmie Lipton as the soldier *
    John Harper as the telegraph operator *
    Adapted for *Cavalcade* by Warner Law, from material in the 1946 MacMillan publication "Lost Men of American History" by Stewart H. Holbrook.
    Produced by H.L. Blackburn and directed by Jack Zoller.
    Bill Hamilton was the commercial announcer and Cy Harrice was the announcer.
    Music composed by Ardon Cornwell and conducted by Donald Voorhees.
    Story: The story of the ingenuity and heroism of America's earliest pioneer in military air operations - Thaddeus Lowe. Lowe was the first "Aeronaut," who's first balloon ascension for military reconnaissance, in effect, launched the start of the Air Force.

EPISODE #741 "YANKEE AND THE SCALES"   Broadcast on April 22, 1952
    Starring: Mark Stevens as Thaddeus   Alan Hewitt as Erastus
    Robert Dryden as the lawyer *   Eda Heinemann as Mother
    Cynthia Stone as Lucy   Fred Rains as Thompson *
    Cameron Prud'Homme as Billings *   Harold McGee as the Major
    Robert Dryden as Trimble *   Sandra Speiser as the girl *
    Bill Darrid as the boy *
Written for *Cavalcade* by Elwood Hoffman and Irve Tunick.
Produced by H.L. Blackburn and directed by Jack Zoller.
Bill Hamilton was the commercial announcer and Cy Harrice was the announcer.
Music composed by Ardon Cornwell and conducted by Donald Voorhees.
Story: Thaddeus Fairbanks, famed for his invention of the Fairbanks scales, also known as platform scales, became the first improvement on weighing since the Romans!

EPISODE #742 "GOING UP"   Broadcast on April 29, 1952
    Starring: Robert Cummings as Elisha Otis   Judy Parish as Betsy Otis
    Dick Wiggington as Norton   Ivan Curry as Charles
    Fred Irving Lewis as Mr. Maise   Henry Calvin as Mr. Newhouse
    Cameron Prud'Homme as Cavanaugh   Joseph Bell as voice *
    Francine Owen as voice one *   Clifford Owen as voice two *
    Vera Johnson as voice three *   Fred Irving Lewis as the Barker *
Written for *Cavalcade* by David Harmon.
Produced by H.L. Blackburn and directed by Jack Zoller.
Bill Hamilton was the commercial announcer and Cy Harrice was the announcer.
Music composed by Ardon Cornwell and conducted by Donald Voorhees.
Story: Elisha Graves Otis was an American inventor who built the first elevator with an automatic safety device. The device prevented the elevator from falling if the rope that held the elevator broke. Otis demonstrated his elevator in 1854 in New York City by having the rope cut after he had ascended in the elevator. But his invention did not come into wide use until the rise of the skyscraper in the 1870's.

EPISODE #743 "AN AMERICAN FROM FRANCE"   Broadcast on May 6, 1952
    Starring: Walter Hampden as Du Pont   John Lund as Irenee
    Richard Vanaver as Victor   Dick York as Young Irenee
    Haskell Coffin as Jefferson   Edgar Stehli as Lavoisier
    Dan Ocko as Robespierre   Rudolph Justice as the soldier *
    Scott McGregor as Sophie   Haskell Coffin as Etienne
    George Petrie as Toussard   Bobby Santon as Henry
    Dan Ocko as the man *   Leo Cleary as Bauduy
Eleuthere Irenee du Pont also appears (pronounced a-lew-thair ear-ren-ay)
Written for *Cavalcade* by Irve Tunick.
Produced by H.L. Blackburn and directed by Jack Zoller.
Bill Hamilton was the commercial announcer and Cy Harrice was the announcer.
Music composed by Ardon Cornwell and conducted by Donald Voorhees.
Story: It was bound to happen. After more than a decade of dramas sponsored by the Du Pont industry, Eleuthere Irenee du Pont, founder of the Du Pont Company, had to be dramatized. And this was the perfect time to tell the story, as this was the 150th anniversary of the company.

EPISODE #744   "THE PRISONER OF CASTLE THUNDER"   Broadcast on May 13, 1952
    Starring: Robert Taylor as Brown   Gene Leonard as Rev. Carpenter *
    Dick Wigginton as Freddy Brown   Kermit Murdock as Jim Peters
    Sandra Speiser as Molly   Sydney Smith as Captain Porter
    Bill Zuckert as Jake Trussel   Kermit Murdock as the sergeant *
    Scott Tennyson as Sgt. Shank *   Gavin Gordon as Col. Brant *
    Staats Cotsworth as the captain *
    Written for Cavalcade by George H. Faulkner.
    Produced by H.L. Blackburn and directed by Jack Zoller.
    Bill Hamilton was the commercial announcer and Cy Harrice was the announcer.
    Music composed by Ardon Cornwell and conducted by Donald Voorhees.
    Story: A Civil War sailor, Spencer Kellogg Brown who turned a charge of cowardice into a hero's acclaim, the unsung hero for the Union forces during the Civil War.

EPISODE #745   "THE GREEN WALL"   Broadcast on May 20, 1952
    Starring: John Hodiak as Sgt. Curtis Culin   Les Damon as Major Olds *
    Geoffrey Bryant as Gus Aberhauly *   Bill Zuckert as Parodi *
    Chuck Webster as Captain Hanson *   Bernard Lenron as the General *
    George Petrie as Joe Dobson *
    Adapted for Cavalcade by Robert Mason Pollock, from an article by W.L. White published by The Reader's Digest in 1950.
    Produced by H.L. Blackburn and directed by Jack Zoller.
    Bill Hamilton was the commercial announcer and Cy Harrice was the announcer.
    Music composed by Ardon Cornwell and conducted by Donald Voorhees.
    Story: An American soldier, Sergeant Curtis Culin, whose resourcefulness helped make possible the a great breakthrough. This imaginative tank commander came up with the idea that enabled "The Great St. Louis Breakthrough," and eliminated the Normandy Hedgegrows as a tank obstacle.

EPISODE #746   "THE VALLEY OF THE SWANS"   Broadcast on May 27, 1952
    Starring: Dana Andrews as Plockhoy   Louise Allbritton as Katherine
    Luis Van Rooten as Kiphaven *   Charles Dingle as Van Der Goes *
    Gavin Gordon as Carr *   Dan Ocko as Chief Horn *
    Dan Ocko as the voice *   Charles Dingle as the other voice *
    Written for Cavalcade by Irve Tunick.
    Produced by H.L. Blackburn and directed by Jack Zoller.
    Bill Hamilton was the commercial announcer and John Rahe was the announcer.
    Music composed by Ardon Cornwell and conducted by Donald Voorhees.
    Story: Pieter Plockhoy and his wife, Katherine, led a tiny group of Dutch families into the "Valley of the Swans" in 1662 in search of freedom. Early settlers in Delaware were led into the wilderness by Pieter Plockhoy, who gave him the their trust, and Pieter never let them down.

    Trivia: This broadcast originated from Seaford, Delaware.

EPISODE #747   "THE LONG GRAY LINE"   Broadcast on June 3, 1952
    Starring: Cornel Wilde as the narrator *   Staats Cotsworth as Sylvanus Thayer
    Scott Tennyson as Alden Partridge   George Petrie as Adjutant *
    Richard Purdy as Dennis Hart Mahan   Lee Salisbury as the instructor *
    Lon Clark as U. S. Grant   Mercer McLeod as Peter S. Michie
    James McCallion as Dennis M. Michie   Bernard Lenrow as the voice on echo *
    Haskell Coffin as Col. Mills   Lee Salisbury as the sergeant
    Based on material from the 1940 publication "Where They Have Trod" by the F.A. Stokes Company, and "Men of West Point," published in 1952 by Wm. Sloane

Associates, Inc. - both written by Col. R. Ernest Dupay, U.S.A. Ret. Adapted for *Cavalcade* by George H. Faulkner.
Produced by H.L. Blackburn and directed by Jack Zoller.
Bill Hamilton was the commercial announcer and Cy Harrice was the announcer.
Music composed by Ardon Cornwell and conducted by Donald Voorhees.
Story: The story of Sylvanus Thayer, Dennis Mahan, and Peter Smith Michie - the three men who set many of the principles of the United States Military Academy at West Point. Duty, honor and country and the three greatest leaders of West Point.

EPISODE #748 "DAUGHTER WITH WINGS" Broadcast on June 10, 1952
  Starring: Joan Caulfield as Harriet Quimby   Katherine Raht as Mrs. Quimby
  Arline Blackburn as Miss Lynn *   Ethel Owen as Miss Martha *
  Arnold Moss as John Moisant   Dan Ocko as Bill *
  Chester Stratton as Hamel
Written for *Cavalcade* by Robert Soderberg and Edith Somner.
Produced by H.L. Blackburn and directed by Jack Zoller.
Bill Hamilton was the commercial announcer and Cy Harrice was the announcer.
Music composed by Ardon Cornwell and conducted by Donald Voorhees.
Story: "They said it was because I was a woman. Nature did not intend women to fly aeroplanes. The very thought is ridiculous, they said. Laughable. I had only one answer. Rubbish." So wrote Harriet Quimby in 1912. The author was the pioneer aviatrix of America, a girl whose courage, stubborn determination and far-sighted vision opened up the entire field of aviation for women. And Harriet Quimby became the first woman to earn an aviator's license.

EPISODE #749 "THE QUALITY OF COURAGE" Broadcast on June 17, 1952
  Starring: MacDonald Carey as Sergeant Ezra Lee   Dick York as David Bushnell
  Bernard Lenrow as the officer   Alan Hewitt as Jonas *
  William Podmore as Dr. Gale   Ted Osborn as Cyrenus
Based on material from the 1947 publication "Lost Men of American History" by Stewart H. Holbrook, published by MacMillan, and adapted for *Cavalcade* by George H. Faulkner.
Produced by H.L. Blackburn and directed by Jack Zoller.
Bill Hamilton was the commercial announcer and Cy Harrice was the announcer.
Music composed by Ardon Cornwell and conducted by Donald Voorhees.
Story: This is the story of a brilliant inventor and a brave sailor - David Bushnell, who invented the submarine. His failures and successes in accomplishing this feat changed naval warfare for years to come. The first such "underwater vessel" was practiced during the Revolutionary War.

EPISODE #750 "THE DARK HEART" Broadcast on June 24, 1952
  Starring: Jane Wyman as Mary Lincoln   Vinie Burrows as Elizabeth
  Ann Tobin as Lavinia *   Karl Weber as Lincoln
  Dick Wigginton as Willie   Ginger Jones as Mrs. Evans *
  Joseph Bell as Dr. Stone   Dan Ocko as the voice
  George Petrie as Wikoff   Dan Ocko as Major-Domo *
  Haskell Coffin as man one *   Joseph Bell as man two *
Based on material from "Reveille in Washington" by Margaret Leech, originally published by Harper and Brothers in 1941. Adapted for *Cavalcade* by Robert Soderberg and Edith Somner.
Produced by H.L. Blackburn and directed by Jack Zoller.
Bill Hamilton was the commercial announcer and Cy Harrice was the announcer.
Music composed by Ardon Cornwell and conducted by Donald Voorhees.
Story: same as episode #333, broadcast on May 31, 1943

EPISODE #751 **"PATRIOT WITH THE CHESTNUT CURLS"** Broadcast August 26, 1952
    Starring: Joan Caulfield as Sally   Karl Webber as the man's voice
    Cameron Prud'Homme as Mr. Townsend   Vera Allen as Mrs. Townsend
    George Petrie as Robert   Tom Collins as Col. Simcoe
    Richard Newton as Major Andre   Neva Patterson as Audrey
    Sandra Speiser as Phoebe   Karl Weber as Daniel Youngs
    Mercer McLeod as Major Green   Lester Fletcher as the soldier
    Mercer McLeod as the officer
Based on a material from "Sally Townsend, Patriot" by Dorothy H. McGee, published by Dodd, Mead and Company, Inc. in 1952. Adapted for *Cavalcade* by Edith Somner and Robert W. Soderberg.
Produced by H.L. Blackburn and directed by Jack Zoller.
Bill Hamilton was the commercial announcer and Cy Harrice was the announcer.
Music composed by Ardon Cornwell and conducted by Donald Voorhees.
Story: Sally Townsend, helped defeat Benedict Arnold's plan to turn West point over to the British during the Revolutionary War. Battling her own convictions, her courageous act during the Revolutionary War was a tough one. You see, she was in love with the enemy.

Trivia: The American Legion Auxiliary gives the program an award (for the third consecutive year in a row).

EPISODE #752 **"THE MELODY MAN"** Broadcast on September 2, 1952
    Starring: Robert Cummings as Finn   Judy Parrish as Elsie
    Ed Begley as Jamison   Ted Osborn as Salesman
    Dan Ocko as Hans   Ted Osborn as the Professor
    Joseph Bell as the doctor   Cameron Prud'Homme as the cop
    Cameron Prud'Homme as Houstan   Richard Wigginton as Kit
Written for *Cavalcade* by David P. Harmon.
Produced by H.L. Blackburn and directed by Jack Zoller.
Bill Hamilton was the commercial announcer and Cy Harrice was the announcer.
Music composed by Ardon Cornwell and conducted by Donald Voorhees.
Story: This is how a persistent Dane named Finn Magnus, developed the first plastic harmonica. Such noise was not considered a musical instrument, but his invention of an inexpensive, mass-produced harmonica brought joy to thousands of people.

EPISODE #753 **"HOW HIGH THE FLAME"** Broadcast on September 9, 1952
    Story: MacDonald Carey as Squibb   Ginger Jones as Caroline
    Charles Dingle as Bache   Alan Hewitt as Connors
    George Petrie as Yeoman   Court Benson as Tully
    Vera Johnson as Mrs. Simpson   Allan Hewitt as Milton
    Joseph Bell as Remington   Ed Begley as the general
Based on a 1951 manuscript by Harry S. Hammon, Jr., and adapted for *Cavalcade* by Irve Tunick.
Produced by H.L. Blackburn and directed by Jack Zoller.
Bill Hamilton was the commercial announcer and Cy Harrice was the announcer.
Music composed by Ardon Cornwell and conducted by Donald Voorhees.
Story: The founding of the Squibb Pharmaceutical Company began when its founder, Edward Squibb, fought to establish a source of reliable, high-quality drugs.

EPISODE #754 **"MAN OF GREAT IMPORTANCE"** Broadcast on September 16, 1952
    Starring: Lee Bowman as Asa Jennings   Gilbert Mack as Dino
    Ed Begley as Powell   Arnold Moss as Mustafa Kemal
    Dan Ocko as the Greek General   Kenny Delmar as the captain
There were also extras for background voices, the actors for those are not known.
Written for *Cavalcade* by Warner Law.
Produced by H.L. Blackburn and directed by Jack Zoller.
Bill Hamilton was the commercial announcer and Cy Harrice was the announcer.
Music composed by Ardon Cornwell and conducted by Donald Voorhees.
Story: Asa Jennings - who during the Greco-Turkish War saved hundreds of thousands of Greek Nationals from starvation in a Turkish-held port.

EPISODE #755 **"A WOMAN'S WAY"** Broadcast on September 23, 1952
    Starring: Patricia Neal as Catherine Fay Ewing   Howard Reig as the young soldier
    Tom Collins as Archibald Ewing   George Petrie as the soldier
    Cameron Prud'Homme as Dr. William   Roy Fant as the man's voice
    Cameron Prud'Homme as the Chair   Charles Dingle as Knowles
    Scott Tennyson as the old man   Vera Johnson as woman's voice
    Denise Alexander as Nancy   Sarah Fussell as David
    Michael Mann as Tommy   Charles Dingle as Grimes
Based on material from a thesis by Nina E. Rowland, registered 1943 at the Ohio University Library in Athens, Ohio, and adapted for *Cavalcade* by Robert S. Greene.
Produced by H.L. Blackburn and directed by Jack Zoller.
Bill Hamilton was the commercial announcer and Cy Harrice was the announcer.
Music composed by Ardon Cornwell and conducted by Donald Voorhees.
Story: The story of Catherine Fay who founded the first Children's Home in Marietta, Ohio, the first orphanage in the state, taking the little children out of the poorhouse.

EPISODE #756 **"THE GIG OF THE SAGINAW"** Broadcast on September 30, 1952
    Starring: Gary Merrill as Coxswain Halford   Ed Begley as Sicard
    Pat O'Malley as Francis   Elliott Reid as Talbot
Based on material from a then-unpublished manuscript "The Gig of the Saginaw" by Lt. Donald Morris, and adapted for *Cavalcade* by Irve Tunick.
Produced by H.L. Blackburn and directed by Jack Zoller.
Bill Hamilton was the commercial announcer and Cy Harrice was the announcer.
Music composed by Ardon Cornwell and conducted by Donald Voorhees.
Story: The story of five sailors, led by Coxswain Halford (Peter) who sailed a gig from a desolate Ocean Island in the Pacific, to Honolulu, in an effort to get help for their eighty-six shipwrecked comrades. A well done story of survival on the open sea in a small boat.

EPISODE #757 **"ONE WAY OUT"** Broadcast on October 7, 1952
    Starring: John Lund as Danny   Staats Cotsworth as Jersey
    Dick York as Phil   Dan Ocko as Sarge
    Ed Begley as the general   Larry Blyden as Tex
    Ross Martin as the major   Sidney Smith as the corporal
    Sidney Smith as voice three   George Petrie as the lieutenant
    George Petrie as voice four   Maurice Ellis as voice one and five
Based on the article of the same name by Benjamin Blackman, as originally published by *Air Force Magazine* in 1951. Adapted for *Cavalcade* by David P. Harmon.
Produced by H.L. Blackburn and directed by Jack Zoller.
Bill Hamilton was the commercial announcer and Cy Harrice was the announcer.
Music composed by Ardon Cornwell and conducted by Donald Voorhees.
Story: A story of heroism and achievement during the Korean War in November 1950, as told by Marine Danny Parker.

EPISODE #758 **"THE SAGA OF JERRY O'BRIEN"** Broadcast on October 14, 1952
    Starring: Dennis O'Keefe as Jerry O'Brien   Una O'Connor as Mrs. O'Brien
    James O'Neill as Morris O'Brien   Jean Gillespie as Peggy
    Staats Cotsworth as Gideon   Horace Braham as Lt. Moore
    Parker Fennelly as Captain Jones   Guy Repp as voice one
    George Petrie as voice two   James McCallion as voice three
    Based on an unpublished article "The O'Briens Go to Sea" by Colonel R. Ernest Dupay, and adapted for *Cavalcade* by George H. Faulkner.
    Produced by H.L. Blackburn and directed by Jack Zoller.
    Bill Hamilton was the commercial announcer and Cy Harrice was the announcer.
    Music composed by Ardon Cornwell and conducted by Donald Voorhees.
    Story: The story of how the O'Briens and their friends defeated the British in the early days of the Revolution in Maine. The first off-shore skirmish of the Revolutionary War, in Machais, Maine.

EPISODE #759 **"READY ON THE RIGHT"** Broadcast on October 21, 1952
    Starring: Jackie Cooper as Alexander Hamilton   Lyle Sudrow as Troup
    Arnold Moss as Schuyler   Lon Clark as Baggett *
    Rosemary Rice as Betsy   Guy Repp as the doctor *
    Scott Tennyson as Calkins *   Ed Jerome as Washington
    Ross Martin as Lafayette   Staats Cotsworth as Morris
    Written for *Cavalcade* by Robert Mason Pollock and Irve Tunick.
    Produced by H.L. Blackburn and directed by Jack Zoller.
    Bill Hamilton was the commercial announcer and Cy Harrice was the announcer.
    Music composed by Ardon Cornwell and conducted by Donald Voorhees.
    Story: Alexander Hamilton's efforts to obtain a field command and fight the British, rather than remain an aide to General Washington is documented. This is the story of the formation of "The Alexander Hamilton Battery" the oldest unit in the American Army.

EPISODE #760 **"THAT MOORE GIRL"** Broadcast on October 28, 1952
    Starring: Ann Blyth as Bess Moore   Alan MacAteer as man one *
    Roy Fant as man two *   Barbara Townsend as woman one *
    Eda Heinemann as woman two *   George Petrie as Lt. Butler
    Staats Cotsworth as Rhett Nickson *   Bobby Santon as Robbie
    Scott Tennyson as Sam Savage   Alan MacAteer as Treat *
    Dan Ocko as Powers *   Dan Ocko as Sentinel *
    Written for *Cavalcade* by George H. Faulkner.
    Produced by H.L. Blackburn and directed by Jack Zoller.
    Bill Hamilton was the commercial announcer and Cy Harrice was the announcer.
    Music composed by Ardon Cornwell and conducted by Donald Voorhees.
    Story: Bess Moore, whose exploits during the Revolutionary War were the talk of the South. As a young girl, Bess became a Revolutionary War hero when the rebels' plans were overheard, but no one except she would warn the militia.

EPISODE #761 **"ONE NATION INDIVISIBLE"** Broadcast on November 11, 1952
    Starring: Thomas Mitchell as Horace Greeley   Alan Hewitt as Sinclair
    John Barclay as Lincoln   John Seymour as Harrison
    Arnold Moss as Jefferson Davis   Anne Seymour as Mrs. Davis
    Bill Adams as Thaddeus Brown *   Dan Ocko as the judge
    John Harper as John *
    Written for *Cavalcade* by Warner Law.
    Produced by H.L. Blackburn and directed by Jack Zoller.
    Bill Hamilton was the commercial announcer and Cy Harrice was the announcer.
    Music composed by Ardon Cornwell and conducted by Donald Voorhees.

Story: Horace Greeley was one of the first editors to join the Republican Party. He was a delegate to its second national convention, and helped Abraham Lincoln obtain nomination for President. Although he supported Lincoln throughout the Civil War, he urged settling the conflict by compromise. In 1864, he met with several agents of the Confederacy in Canada to discuss peace terms, but the conference failed. In addition, Greeley also urged giving pardons to all members of the Confederacy after the war. This was Greeley's part in getting Jefferson Davis released from prison after the Civil War.

EPISODE #762 "AWAY ALL BOARDING PARTIES" Broadcast on November 18, 1952
    Starring: Wendell Corey as Gallery   Geoffrey Bryant as Jonesy *
    Lon Clark as Johnson   Bob Hastings as Martin *
    Dan Ocko as Henke   Bill Zuckert as the chief *
    Geoffrey Bryant as voice one *   George Petrie as Trosino
    Dan Ocko as voice two *   Les Damon as David
    George Petrie as voice three *   Scott Tennyson as voice four *
    Scott Tennyson as Captain of DD *   Bert Cowlan as Widowiak
    Mason Adams as Knispel
Based on material from the 1951 book "Clear the Decks" by Daniel V. Gallery, published by William Morrow and Company. Adapted for *Cavalcade* by Robert Tallman.
Produced by H.L. Blackburn and directed by Jack Zoller.
Bill Hamilton was the commercial announcer and Cy Harrice was the announcer.
Music composed by Ardon Cornwell and conducted by Donald Voorhees.
Story: "Away all boarding parties" was an age old Naval battle cry, heard only once in the twentieth century, during WWII. As skipper of the aircraft carrier Guadalcanal leading a task group against Nazi submarines in the Atlantic, Captain Daniel Gallery had conceived a daring plan to gain possession of the code books by means of which the movements of all Nazi U-boats were controlled.

EPISODE #763 "THE PATH OF PRAISE" Broadcast on November 25, 1952
    Starring: Walter Hampden as the voice *   Fred Worlock as Bradford
    Vinton Hayworth, Sr. as Reed   Katherine Raht as Sarah Hale
    John Barclay as Lincoln   Mandel Kramer as Washington
    Bobbie Nick as Giles
Written for *Cavalcade* by George H. Faulkner.
Produced by H.L. Blackburn and directed by Jack Zoller.
Bill Hamilton was the commercial announcer and Cy Harrice was the announcer.
Music composed by Ardon Cornwell and conducted by Donald Voorhees.
Story: same as episode #719, broadcast on November 20, 1951

EPISODE #764 "A THOUSAND TO ONE" Broadcast on December 2, 1952
    Starring: Lee Bowman as Steve Balfour *   Les Damon as Jim Chalmers *
    Wesley Addy as Dr. Carothers   Joseph Bell as the manager *
    Joseph Bell as Dr. Stine   Ann Tobin as woman one *
    Judy Parrish as Mary Balfour *   Grayce Albert as woman two*
    Vera Salisbury as woman three *   Francine Owen as woman four *
Written for *Cavalcade* by Irve Tunick.
Produced by H.L. Blackburn and directed by Jack Zoller.
Bill Hamilton was the commercial announcer and Cy Harrice was the announcer.
Music composed by Ardon Cornwell and conducted by Donald Voorhees.
Story: same as episode #687, broadcast on February 13, 1951

Trivia: This same script was performed earlier under the title "Fiber 66."

EPISODE #765 **"LISTEN MY CHILDREN"** Broadcast on December 9, 1952
    Starring: Richard Widmark as Paul Revere   Rolly Bester as Rachel
    Mandel Kramer as Joseph Warren   Dan Ocko as Toby
    George Petrie as Colonel Conant   Dan Ocko as Colonel Ansart
    Jim Stephens as Joseph Warren Revere   Rosemary Rice as Deborah
    Cy Harrice was the narrator during this broadcast.
    Written for *Cavalcade* by George H. Faulkner.
    Produced by H.L. Blackburn and directed by Jack Zoller.
    Bill Hamilton was the commercial announcer and Cy Harrice was the announcer.
    Music composed by Ardon Cornwell and conducted by Donald Voorhees.
    Story: same as episode #711, broadcast on September 25, 1951

EPISODE #766 **"BARBED-WIRE CHRISTMAS"** Broadcast on December 16, 1952
    Starring: Edmond O'Brien as Pete   Garry Walberg as Sid
    George Petrie as Hud   Bill Luckert as Miller
    Ross Martin as Blackie   Harry Jackson as Nick
    Ed Jerome as Captain Moran   Tonio Selwart as the German Underofficer
    Kermit Murdock as the voice on the BBC   Don Craig as the German soldier
    Dan Ocko as the German Hauptmann   Nelson Olmsted as the server
    Kermit Murdock as the German Commandant
    Written for *Cavalcade* by Warner Law.
    Produced by H.L. Blackburn and directed by Jack Zoller.
    Bill Hamilton was the commercial announcer and Cy Harrice was the announcer.
    Music composed by Ardon Cornwell and conducted by Donald Voorhees.
    Story: The story of 4,000 American soldiers, all prisoners of war, who spent Christmas in a German prison camp, destined to attend a midnight mass, even though the Gestapo has forbidden it.

EPISODE #767 **"CHRISTMAS IN AMERICA"** Broadcast on December 23, 1952
    Starring: Walter Hampden as the guest narrator.
    Soloists were Margaret Donnham and Carl Schweitzer.
    Mr. Crawford H. Greenewalt, President of the Du Pont Company spoke in this program.
    The narrative was written for *Cavalcade* by George H. Faulkner.
    William Hamilton is the commercial spokesman and announcer.
    The Du Pont chorus was under the direction of Frank J. Clark.
    Music sung and performed were "Adeste Fidelis," "Deck the Halls," "Away in the Manger," "O Little Town of Bethlehem," "Glory to God in the Highest," "Lo, How A Rose 'Ere Blooming," "White Christmas," and "The Hallelujah Chorus."

EPISODE #768 **"BILLY THE KID"** Broadcast on December 30, 1952
    Starring: Van Johnson as Billy   Michael O'Day as Frisco *
    George Petrie as Harry *   Staats Cotsworth as the skipper *
    Dan Ocko as Canarsie *   Ed Begley as the Colonel *
    Garry Walberg as the Colonel *   Garry Walberg as the soldier *
    Based on material from the article "Korean Sharpshooter" by B.G. Beach, as published in *Air Force Magazine*. Adapted for *Cavalcade* by David P. Harmon.
    Produced by H.L. Blackburn and directed by Jack Zoller.
    Bill Hamilton was the commercial announcer and Cy Harrice was the announcer.
    Music composed by Ardon Cornwell and conducted by Donald Voorhees.
    Story: This is the true story of Sergeant Billie Beach, U.S. Air Force. Along that infamous strip known as Mig Alley, Sgt. Beach in 1950 was high over Korea when he won the nickname "Billy the Kid." Billy was one of a bomber crew of a B-29, during the Korean War, who was attacked by a MIG. It was young Billy, as an aerial gunner, who knocked them out of the sky, and won his respect with the crew.

EPISODE #769 "**A MEDAL FOR MISS WALKER**" Broadcast on January 6, 1953
    Starring: Dorothy McGuire as Dr. Mary Walker   Ed Begley as Bragg *
    Cameron Prud'Homme as Dr. Green *   Alan Hewitt as Finley *
    George Petrie as soldier one *   George Petrie as the guard *
    Larry Robinson as Billy *   Bob Hastings as Phillips *
    Arnold Moss as McCook *   Charles Dingle as Waltham *
    Arnold Moss as Priestley *   Staats Cotsworth as Marsh *
    Written for *Cavalcade* by Irve Tunick.
    Produced by H.L. Blackburn and directed by Jack Zoller.
    Bill Hamilton was the commercial announcer and Cy Harrice was the announcer.
    Music composed by Ardon Cornwell and conducted by Donald Voorhees.
    Story: Mary Edwards Walker was the only woman to receive the Medal of Honor, the highest military award given by the United States government. While serving as a surgeon with the Union Army during the Civil War, she was captured and held for four months in a Confederate prison. She was later exchanged for a Confederate officer. It was because of this she was awarded the Medal of Honor. Why? Because when the Confederates arrived, she refused to leave her patients and insisted on being taken captive with them.

EPISODE #770   "**DOWN BRAKE**"   Broadcast on January 13, 1953
    Starring: Cornel Wilde as Westinghouse   Ed Begley as Father
    Ted Osborn as Leferts *   Malcolm Keen as Mulcahy *
    Dan Ocko as Oscar *   Elaine Rost as Margerite
    Bill Zuckert as brakeman one *   George Petrie as brakeman two *
    Ted Osborn as voice two *   George Petrie as voice one *
    Patti Pope as the girl *   Charles Dingle as Card
    Parker Fennelly as Tate
    Written for *Cavalcade* by Irve Tunick.
    Produced by H.L. Blackburn and directed by Jack Zoller.
    Bill Hamilton was the commercial announcer and Cy Harrice was the announcer.
    Music composed by Ardon Cornwell and conducted by Donald Voorhees.
    Story: George Westinghouse was an American inventor and manufacturer. He produced air brakes for railroad cars. His major inventions include a pipeline system that safely conducted natural gas into homes, and a type of gas meter. Westinghouse also introduced the use of alternating current for the transmission of electric power. By 1886, Westinghouse had already perfected two inventions, a device for replacing derailed railroad cars and a railroad frog, which made it possible for a train to pass from one track to another. This episode dramatizes yet another invention, his perfection of an air brake that led to the formation of his first company, the Westinghouse Air Brake Company.

WASHINGTON AND THE TRAITOR

Starring

HERBERT MARSHALL

MONDAY EVENING   FEBRUARY 19, 1945

EPISODE #771 "**BLESS THIS HOUSE**" Broadcast on January 20, 1953
    Starring: MacDonald Carey as the principal voice *
    William Podmore as John Adams   Irene Hubbard as Abigail Adams
    Jock MacGregor as the watchman   Kathleen Cordell as Dolley Madison
    Richard Purdy as voice one *   Gavin Gordon as voice two *
    Jock MacGregor as Andrew Jackson   Royal Dano as Lincoln
    Anne Tobin as Mrs. Eckley   Joseph Bell as Nicolay
    Kathleen Cordell as woman's voice   Charles Webster as Wilson
    Ed Jerome as Colonel House   Cy Harrice as voice three *
    Written for *Cavalcade* by George H. Faulkner.
    Produced by H.L. Blackburn and directed by Jack Zoller.
    Bill Hamilton was the commercial announcer and Cy Harrice was the announcer.
    Music composed by Ardon Cornwell and conducted by Donald Voorhees.
    Story: These are the stories of the U.S. Presidents and their families, and how they lived in the White House. From the exotic pets, to the wild children, the famed foods, family recipes, and even seasonal traditions.

EPISODE #772 "**THE NUGGET AND THE LAW**" Broadcast on January 27, 1953
    Starring: Glenn Ford as William Coleman   Roy Fant as Scott
    Cameron Prud'Homme as Marshall   Doro Merande as Mrs. Wiemer
    William Zuckert as the loiterer   Ed Begley as James King
    George Petrie as the waiter   Scott Tennyson as Bluxome
    Arnold Moss as Charlie Cora   Arthur Maitland as Judge Palmer
    Bill Zuckert as Casey   Grayce Albert as Mrs. King
    Grayce Albert as the night club singer   George Petrie as the voice
    Written for *Cavalcade* by George H. Faulkner.
    Produced by H.L. Blackburn and directed by Jack Zoller.
    Bill Hamilton was the commercial announcer and Cy Harrice was the announcer.
    Music composed by Ardon Cornwell and conducted by Donald Voorhees.
    Story: California set the pattern for other gold rushes throughout the West. The Pikes Peak gold rush in 1859 opened Colorado, launched the city of Denver, and started a great mining industry. Gold rushes brought people to Alaska, Arizona, Idaho, Montana, Nevada, New Mexico, South Dakota, Utah, and Wyoming. Some mining districts and camps died within a year, but others lasted more than a hundred years. Although people fought like cats and dogs, murdered and stole, gold rushes were important to the development of the West. This is the story of the winter of 1848, at a place called "Sutter's Fort."

EPISODE #773 "**THE SHORT STRAW**" Broadcast on February 3, 1953
    Starring: Irene Dunne as Ann Bernatitus   Les Damon as Moore *
    Robert Hastings as Jones *   Dan Ocko as the corpsman *
    Michael O'Day as Felipe *   George Petrie as the soldier *
    Ethel Everett as nurse one *   Louise Larabee as nurse two *
    Edwin Jerome as the officer *   George Petrie as the sailor *
    Chester Stratton as the orderly *   Dan Ocko as Bosn *
    Chester Stratton as the officer *
    Written for *Cavalcade* by Irve Tunick.
    Produced by H.L. Blackburn and directed by Jack Zoller.
    Bill Hamilton was the commercial announcer and Cy Harrice was the announcer.
    Music composed by Ardon Cornwell and conducted by Donald Voorhees.
    Story: The story of Ann Bernatitus, a Navy nurse on Corregidor during the attack by the Japanese during WWII.

EPISODE #774 "OPERATION MIRACLE" Broadcast on February 10, 1953
Starring: Robert Preston as Captain Edward Elsberg
Charles S. Webster as Joe Hurley *   Craig McDonnell as Admiral Collins *
Donald Buka as Ralph Jarnek *   Guy Spaul as Lt. Thornton *
Sydney G. Smith as the aide *   Allen Desmond supplied all ad lib voices
The British jeep driver was played by an unknown, probably Allen Desmond.
Based on material from "Under the Red Sea Sun" by Rear Admiral Edward Ellsberg, published in 1946 by Dodd, Mead and Company. Adapted for *Cavalcade* by Robert Mason Pollock.
Produced by H.L. Blackburn and directed by Jack Zoller.
Bill Hamilton was the commercial announcer and Cy Harrice was the announcer.
Music composed by Ardon Cornwell and conducted by Donald Voorhees.
Story: This is a story of what happened to a man named Edward Ellsberg, Captain in the U.S. Navy. His assignment was to perform a miracle. It was early 1942, four months after Pearl Harbor. American Flying Fortresses were roaring off the runaways of England. In the Pacific, GI's were hacking a perilous path through the jungles of New Guinea. Ellsberg's job was to salvage a drunken dry-dock, under the worst possible circumstances.

EPISODE #775 "DANGEROUS MISSION" Broadcast on February 17, 1953
Starring: MacDonald Carey as Captain Allen McLane
Jack Manning as Michael *   Felix Deebank as Corporal *
Staats Cotsworth as Wayne *   Elizabeth Watts as Mrs. Smith *
Barbara Joyce as Innay *   Rikel Kent as the man *
Roland Long as the guard *   Roland Long as the double driver *
Edwin Jerome as Washington   Berry Kroeger as Picket
Based on material from "The War of the Revolution: Volume Two" by Christopher Ward, published in 1952 by MacMillian. Adapted for *Cavalcade* by William Kendall Clarke.
Produced by H.L. Blackburn and directed by Jack Zoller.
Bill Hamilton was the commercial announcer and Cy Harrice was the announcer.
Music composed by Ardon Cornwell and conducted by Donald Voorhees.
Story: The story of Captain Allan McLane of Delaware, a daring raider and spy during the Revolutionary War, and how he was responsible for our victory at Stony Point.

EPISODE #776 "LIFE ON THE MISSISSIPPI" Broadcast on February 24, 1953
Starring: Raymond Massey as Mark Twain   Don Curtis as the captain *
Scott Tennyson as the voice *   Klock Ryder as Brown
Scott Tennyson as the leadsman *   Charles Dingle as Bixby
Geoffrey Bryant as Sam   Don Knotts as Henry
Based on the 1923 Harper and Brothers publication of "Life on the Mississippi" by Mark Twain, and adapted for *Cavalcade* by Warner Law.
Produced by H.L. Blackburn and directed by Jack Zoller.
Bill Hamilton was the commercial announcer and Cy Harrice was the announcer.
Music composed by Ardon Cornwell and conducted by Donald Voorhees.
Story: In 1839, Mark Twain's family moved to Hannibal, Mo., a village on the Mississippi River. here the young Twain experienced the excitement of the colorful steamboats that docked at the town wharf, bringing comedians, singers, gamblers, swindlers, slave dealers, and assorted other river travelers. His later profession of riverboat piloting paid well and brought Twain much attention, which he enjoyed. The Mississippi River also rooted much of Twain's writings, such as "Life on the Mississippi" and "The Adventures of Huckleberry Finn."

Trivia: Playing the supporting role of Henry was Don Knotts.

EPISODE #777 **"STAR AND THE SHIELD"** Broadcast on March 3, 1953
    Starring: Broderick Crawford as Campbell   Eileen Merry as Margaret
    Ethel Browning as Grandma   Sandra Speiser as Valerie
    Mary Fickett as Dorothy   Rikel Kent as Whybrant
    Alan Hewitt as Carroll   Les Damon as Kropke
    Staats Cotsworth as Lynch   Staats Cotsworth as Treusch
    Alan Hewitt as Thourot   Rikel Kent as Tobler
    Sarah Fussell as the voice *
    Written for *Cavalcade* by Irve Tunick.
    Produced by H.L. Blackburn and directed by Jack Zoller.
    Bill Hamilton was the commercial announcer and Cy Harrice was the announcer.
    Music composed by Ardon Cornwell and conducted by Donald Voorhees.
    Story: It might happen anywhere, in your town or mine. It actually happened in Union City in the fall of 1952. The New Jersey police force in Union City, under odd circumstances, adopted a little girl named Margaret Leone. During the months that followed, little Margaret Leone literally became a member of the Hudson County Motorcycle Police Corps. And the whole community took Margaret to its heart. Merchants dressed her like a princess. The Holy Family School enrolled her into kindergarten. And everybody repeated her bright little sayings.

    Trivia: *Cavalcade* wished to express their gratitude and admiration to the Hudson County Motorcycle Police Corps for its cooperation in the preparation of this story.

EPISODE #778 **"THE SECRET ROAD"** Broadcast on March 10, 1953
    Starring: Lee Bowman as Captain Grant Ledyard *   Tom Collins as Townsend
    Tom Collins as the voice *   Bob Dryden as the sergeant *
    John Griggs as Austin Roe   Arnold Moss as Washington
    Karl Weber as Major Talmadge   Lily Lodge as Sarah Townsend
    Scott Tennyson as Abraham Woodhull   Bob Dryden as Brewster
    Based on material from "The Secret Road" by Bruce Lancaster, published in 1952 by Atlantic Little Brown Company. Adapted for *Cavalcade* by George H. Faulkner.
    Produced by H.L. Blackburn and directed by Jack Zoller.
    Bill Hamilton was the commercial announcer and Cy Harrice was the announcer.
    Music composed by Ardon Cornwell and conducted by Donald Voorhees.
    Story: This is how two famous spies for General George Washington during the Revolutionary War, saved the French fleet through their daring secret messages.

EPISODE #779 **"THE RIVER FINDS A MASTER"** Broadcast on March 17, 1953
    Starring: Robert Young as Shreve   Jan Minor as Mary
    Cameron Prud'Homme as Ellis   Ed Begley as Long
    George Petrie as Burt   Edwin Jerome as Porter
    Scott Tennyson as Dudley
    Adapted for *Cavalcade* by Warner Law, from "Lost Men of American History," by Stewart Holbrook, originally published in 1946 by Stewart Holbrook.
    Produced by H.L. Blackburn and directed by Jack Zoller.
    Bill Hamilton was the commercial announcer and Cy Harrice was the announcer.
    Music composed by Ardon Cornwell and conducted by Donald Voorhees.
    Story: Henry M. Shreve, a trader and steamboat builder, opened the Red River navigation in the 1830's by clearing it of a logjam that was more than 160 miles long. He contributed greatly to the safe navigation for steamboats. Down in Louisiana is a town named "Shreveport," one of the largest cities in the state, and a major center of industry and trade. It was named after Henry Shreve.

EPISODE #780 **"ONE CAME THROUGH"** Broadcast on March 24, 1953
    Starring: Wendell Corey as William Dawes   Bob Dryden as Peter
    Ed Begley as John Hancock   Ginger Jones as Hetty Dawes
    Staats Cotsworth as John Adams   Chuck Webster as Warren
    Arnold Moss as Paul Revere   Pat O'Malley as the sentry
    Sydney Smith as Phelps   Ronald Long as Smith
    George Petrie as Prescott   Gavin Gordon as MacReady
    Joseph Bell as the voice *
    Written for *Cavalcade* by George H. Faulkner.
    Produced by H.L. Blackburn and directed by Jack Zoller.
    Bill Hamilton was the commercial announcer and Cy Harrice was the announcer.
    Music composed by Ardon Cornwell and conducted by Donald Voorhees.
    Story: "Hardly a man is now alive," recites the famed poem. Hardly a man does not know about Paul Revere's famous midnight ride to Lexington to warn the people that the British were coming. But hardly a man knows about William Dawes, the other man whose midnight ride that same evening, to warn of the Redcoat's approach. This is William's story.

EPISODE #781 **"A TIME TO GROW"** Broadcast on March 31, 1953
    Starring: Thomas Mitchell as Robert Livingston   Ian Martin as Joseph Bonaparte
    Luis Van Rooten as Napoleon   Dan Ocko as Talleyrand
    Guy Sorel as Du Pont   Joseph Bell as Thomas Jefferson
    Scott Tennyson as McKay   Bob Dryden as the clerk
    George Petrie as Victor   Ed Jerome as James Monroe
    Chester Stratton as Lucien Bonaparte   Gene Leonard as Marbois
    Written for *Cavalcade* by Irve Tunick.
    Produced by H.L. Blackburn and directed by Jack Zoller.
    Bill Hamilton was the commercial announcer and Cy Harrice was the announcer.
    Music composed by Ardon Cornwell and conducted by Donald Voorhees.
    Story: The Louisiana Purchase was the most important event of President Thomas Jefferson's first administration. In this transaction, the United States purchased the land from France for about $15 million. But before Jefferson could purchase the land, he had to convince France the necessity of such a need of land - expansion. Jefferson arranged for his friend, Pierre du Pont de Nemours, to carry dispatches to Livingston and to help him influence the French government against acquiring the American colonies.

PARTY LINE

Starring

AGNES MOOREHEAD

MONDAY EVENING   **JUNE 18, 1945**

NOTES ABOUT THE TELEVISION SERIES

The following *Cavalcade of America* log documents all 197 episodes broadcast on television. The dates listed below may vary from town to town, as the program was recorded and broadcast over different local stations at different days and times. The dates listed below are the "official" broadcast dates, when the series was seen over the major national broadcasting stations such as NBC and ABC. Because many of these television episodes remain "lost," it was extremely difficult to find information regarding complete casts and plot descriptions. All of the known information acquired has been compiled below. Please keep in mind that there will always be those inevitable blanks here and there. The following cohere to the broadcast dates below.

       From October 1, 1952 to September 2, 1953, NBC, Wed. evening from 8:30 to 9 p.m.
       From September 29, 1953 to June 21, 1955, ABC, Tuesday evening from 7:30 to 8 p.m.
       From September 6, 1955 to June 4, 1957, ABC, Tuesday evening from 9:30 to 10 p.m.

EPISODE #1   **"POOR RICHARD"**   Broadcast on October 1, 1952
       Starring: Cecil Kellaway as Benjamin Franklin   Dabbs Greer as Lathrop
       Evelyn Ankers as Mrs. Liveright
       Based on the *Cavalcade* radio script "Dr. Franklin Takes it Easy" by Erik Barnouw.
       Directed by Peter Godfrey.
       Filmed at Screen Televideo Productions, studio contract dated April 16, 1952.
       Story: Ben Franklin was one of those rare people who are jacks of all trades and masters of all. His versatility ranged from "Poor Richard's Almanac" to some of the wittiest satire in American letters; from influencing an era in American statesmanship to inventing the long pole with flexible "hands" at the end which storekeepers and librarians use to reach objects on a high shelf. His brilliant mind immeasurably enriched American life. The engaging side of Ben Franklin and his amazing inventive genius was coupled with a new concept of the freedom to be won for the human spirit.

EPISODE #2   **"ALL'S WELL WITH LYDIA"**   Broadcast on October 15, 1952
       Starring: Ruth Warrick as Lydia Darrah   Reginald Denny as Col. Patterson
       John Dodsworth as Lt. Allen   Esther Dale as Aunt Tabatha
       Based on the *Cavalcade* radio script "The House Near Little Dock Street" by Margaret Lewerth.
       Filmed at Screen Televideo Productions, studio contract dated April 16, 1952.
       Story: During the winter of 1777, a small group of Washington's men were camped near Philadelphia at Whitemarsh. In British-occupied Philadelphia, troops were comfortably billeted in citizen's homes. Mrs. Lydia Darrah was the unwilling hostess to colonel Robert Patterson, Adjutant to General Howe. One night Col. Patterson called a meeting of his staff. He ordered the Darrah household to their rooms. Lydia, listened in on the discussion. When she learned that the British planned a surprise attack on the troops at Whitemarsh, she knew she must move quickly to warn the Continentals.

EPISODE #3   **"THE MAN WHO TOOK A CHANCE"**   Broadcast on October 29, 1952
       Starring: Richard Denning as Eli Whitney   Also stars: Rhys Williams
       Based on the *Cavalcade* radio play "The Interchangeable Mr. Whitney" by Morton Wishengrad.
       Commercial entitled "A Home-Made Dress"
       Story: In the spring of 1799, Eli Whitney turned from cotton gins to muskets. Whitney, master mechanic and brilliant inventor, had been commissioned by Congress to turn out 10,000 muskets within two years. Although it took weeks to complete a single gun, Whitney solved the problem of making 10,000 in two years. By taking a risky chance to conform all present-day methods, his solution of interchangeable parts helped to change the industrial patterns of the civilized world.

EPISODE #4 "A ROMANCE TO REMEMBER" Broadcast on November 12, 1952
Starring: Dan O'Herlihy as Nathaniel Hawthorne   Fay Baker as Sophia Peabody
Mary Alan Hokanson as Hawthorne's sister   Dayton Lummis as Ralph Waldo Emerson
Based on the *Cavalcade* radio script "A Valentine for Sophia" by Virginia Radcliffe.
Filmed at Screen Gems Productions, studio contract dated January 29, 1951
Story: After ten years of discouragement, Nathaniel Hawthorne was angrily feeding his "Twice Told Tales" to the fireplace when he learned that a publisher was interested. The book, which he quickly rewrote, gained for Hawthorne recognition as an author, but little financial return. Among the admires of the book was Hawthorne's lovely neighbor, Sophia Peabody, with whom the author fell deeply in love. But with the little money from his writing, the two could not marry. Hard at work, Nathaniel had little time for his writing. But his work brought him, for the first time, into contact with a new kind of America - the men of the docks and ships. From them, he gained a background for his later writing.

EPISODE #5 "WHAT HATH GOD WROUGHT" Broadcast on November 26, 1952
Starring: Edward Franz and Tom Browne Henry
Based on the *Cavalcade* radio script "The Man Who Had Two Careers" by F. Downey and John T.W. Martin.
Commercial entitled "Teflon (Livingston)"
Story: A biography of the famous American inventor and painter. He received the patent for the first successful electric telegraph in the United States. He also invented the Morse code, used for many years to send telegraphic messages. In addition, Morse helped found the National Academy of Design and served as its first president.

EPISODE #6 "NO GREATER LOVE" Broadcast on December 10, 1952
Starring: Mary Anderson as Clara Maass   Arthur Franz as Steve
Based on the *Cavalcade* radio script of the same name by Virginia Radcliffe.
Directed by William J. Thiele.
Filmed at Chertok Productions, studio contract dated January 30, 1951.
Story: Clara Maass, an American Army nurse in Cuba in 1900, was one of many men and women who were trying to stop the mounting toll of death caused by yellow fever. One celebrated Cuban doctor championed the theory that the fever was spread by a mosquito. Clara Maass was among the few people who listened to him, for she believed passionately that without a proven theory or a cure she could do little for the patients who lay dying in her wards. One patient in particular - a Steve Dolan of the Sanitation Commission - she would gladly have given her life to save. Then something happened to make Clara volunteer to take the bite of an infected mosquito . . .

EPISODE #7 "IN THIS CRISIS" Broadcast on December 24, 1952
Starring: Tom Tully as John Honeyman   Richard Gaines as George Washington
Ann Doran as Martha Honeyman   John Hoyt as Colonel Reed
Based on the *Cavalcade* radio script "John Honeyman" by Henry Fisk Carlton.
Story: The story of a plain and simple New Jersey tradesman, John Honeyman, who made it possible for George Washington to plan and carry out successfully the famous Christmas night surprise attack on the British forces at Trenton. In posing as a Tory butcher supplying food for the British forces, this unsung hero won the confidence of the enemy and obtained information which was vital to the success of the American cause. Honeyman started a chain of events that led to a decisive turning point in the struggle for American Independence.

EPISODE #8   "THE ARROW AND THE BOW"   Broadcast on January 7, 1953
    Starring: Sean McClory as Andrew Jackson
    Eleana Verdugo as Mary McDonough
    Others in the cast: Booth Coleman and O..Z. Whitehead
    Based on the *Cavalcade* radio script "Whither Thou Goest" by Morton Wishengrad.
    Filmed at Screen Televideo Productions, studio contract dated April 16, 1952.
    Story: In 1826, when Eliza McCardle first saw Andrew Johnson with her mother and stepfather, they were the poorest-looking people she had ever seen. But from the first, Andrew's spunk and eagerness to learn had impressed her. As he sat cross-legged, his deft fingers moving swiftly with needle and thread, Eliza read aloud to him from the Bible, the Declaration of Independence, speeches by Jefferson and Madison, and other classics. Whatever she read, he remembered. Eliza believed in this awkward young man who was so eager to learn. After their marriage, she continued to help him as he first became a lawyer, and then in turn a county judge, Governor of Tennessee, and Vice President under Abraham Lincoln. And then, as America mourned the passing of Lincoln, Eliza saw her beloved Andy, the humble tailor from Tennessee, succeed as President of the United States, giving new meaning to the words "all men are created equal."

EPISODE #9   "WHAT MIGHT HAVE BEEN"   Broadcast on January 21, 1953
    Starring: Dayton Lummis as Joseph Davis   Ross Ford as Jefferson Davis
    Nancy Hale as Sarah Knox Taylor
    Adapted for *Cavalcade* television by Warner Law, from his *Cavalcade* radio script "Romance at Fort Crawford."
    Commercial entitled "Freon Demonstration"
    Filmed at Screen Gems Productions, studio contract dated January 29, 1951.
    Story: These are the true events that led to the courtship of Jefferson Davis and Sarah Knox Taylor. Sarah was one of President Zachary Taylor's five daughters. Their romance ended in tragedy as Jefferson Davis was destined to become the President of the Confederacy. Sarah died three months after their wedding.

    Trivia: Although this was the ninth episode broadcast in the television series, this was the first episode to be filmed. Contracts were drawn since January of 1951, and filming was completed many months in advance of the actual broadcast date.

EPISODE #10   "NEW SALEM STORY"   Broadcast on February 4, 1953
    Starring: James Griffith as Abraham Lincoln   Jeff Donnell as Ann Rutledge
    Based on the *Cavalcade* radio script entitled "Prologue to Glory" by Arthur Arent and Robert Tallman.
    Story: Here is the Lincoln that few men know - the lank, rugged young man whose giant frame reminded one citizen of New Salem of "the ground plan for a long horse." And here is the picture of Abe Lincoln against the homespun background of a frontier town - the story, full of rich and unexpected humor, of a young man trying to find out where he fitted into the scheme of things. Here we meet his father, Tom Lincoln, a freedom loving American and strong individualist who felt it was time to be moving on to new fields when the day came he could hear the sound of his nearest neighbor's shotgun. Some of Lincoln's most enduring characteristics take on new significance when seen against the background of his early life. We also meet Ann Rutledge and understand perhaps for the first time her tremendous influence upon his life and entire career.

    Trivia: In homage to Lincoln's birthday, *Cavalcade* presented "New Salem Story," based on the *Cavalcade* radio play entitled "Prologue to Glory," originally broadcast on February 7, 1944. Two years after this television episode was broadcast, in February of 1955, this film would be rebroadcast again in homage to Lincoln's birthday.

EPISODE #11   "A MATTER OF HONOR"   Broadcast on February 18, 1953
Starring: Onslow Stevens as Sam Houston   Randy Stuart as Andrew Jackson
Based on two *Cavalcade* radio scripts, "Sam Houston, the Raven" by John Driscoll and
_?_ Milward, and "The Raven Wins Texas" by Driscoll, Milward, and Garrett Porter.
Filmed at Screen Televideo Productions, studio contract dated April 16, 1952.
Story: The somber, dramatic figure of Sam Houston - named "The Raven" by his adopted Cherokee Nation - stalks across the plains and fields of America. As Governor of Tennessee, intimate of President Andrew Jackson, Houston's tragic destiny led him first to renounce his citizenship in the United States and join the Cherokee Indians, then to political ruin in the nation's capitol at the hands of his enemies, and finally to the brink of his greatest adventure - the welding of the United States with the great empire of Texas.

EPISODE #12   "EXPERIMENT AT MONTICELLO"   Broadcast on March 4, 1953
Stars: Brandon Rhodes as Thomas Jefferson   Morgan Farley as James Madison
Barbara Woodell as Martha Randolph   Raymond Greenleaf as Dr. Waterhouse
Based on the *Cavalcade* radio script of the same name by Arthur Arent.
Filmed at Screen Gems Productions, studio contract dated January 29, 1951.
Story: Smallpox was becoming epidemic in 1801, and there seemed to be little that could stop it. In Boston, Dr. Benjamin Waterhouse advanced his theory of vaccination to control the disease, but only a few people, among them Thomas Jefferson, sided with him. When Sally Corcoran, pretty young daughter of Monticello's overseer, arranged a meeting between Jefferson and her friend, John Druce, Jefferson asked the young medical student his opinion of vaccination. John, whose experience was limited to the teaching of his professors, termed Waterhouse a fraud. But smallpox had reached Monticello. Jefferson offered himself not only to be vaccinated, but to inoculate any person on his plantation, including his slaves and servants, with Dr. Waterhouse's serum.

EPISODE #13   "MIGHTIER THAN THE SWORD"   Broadcast on March 18, 1953
Starring: Douglas Kennedy as Peter Zenger   Adele Longmire as Anna Zenger
Based on the *Cavalcade* radio play "Remember Anna Zenger" by Morton Wishengrad.
Commercial entitled "The Science of Seed Treatment"
Story: In America of 1720, certain men from the Old World saw themselves as rulers of the New. They stopped at nothing to build and safeguard their power. Newspapers were powerless. If they spoke in protest the presses were destroyed or the editors jailed. But an unschooled printer named Peter Zenger, and his wife Anna, dared to oppose the corrupt practices in the New York Colony. A trial resulted which established American freedom of the press.

EPISODE #14   "THE INDOMITABLE BLACKSMITH"   Broadcast on April 1, 1953
Stars: Whitfield Connor as Thomas Davenport   Peggy Webber as Emily Davenport
Katherine Warren as Hepzibah Davenport   Frank Ferguson as Barzallai Davenport
Also in the cast: Harris Brown, John Dehner, Robert Fouek, Kathleen Freeman, Paul Keast, Kenneth MacDonald, and Geraldine Wall.
Teleplay by Warner Law, from the *Cavalcade* radio script of same name by John Nesbitt.
Directed by William J. Thiele.
Filmed at Chertok Productions, studio contract dated October 21, 1952.
Story: In the little town of Brandon, Vermont, over a hundred years ago, there lived a blacksmith named Tom Davenport. One day Tom came home with an apparatus for which he had traded much of his worldly goods - a magnetic contrivance of wires and jumping sparks and jars of acid. Tom became absorbed with the contraption. He neglected blacksmithing. Through weeks and months and years of toil, he groped his way toward the incredible marvel of the electric motor. Tom's discovery attracted great attention, but American industry was not yet ready to use it.

EPISODE #15 "THE GINGERBREAD MAN" Broadcast on April 15, 1953
    Starring: Otto Waldis as Christopher Ludwick   William Yetter as Schultz
    Richard Gaines as George Washington   Edith Angold as Katie
John Hamilton as Colonel Norton
Also in the cast: John Wengraf, Tony Christian, Shelton Knaggs, and Myron Healy.
Based on the *Cavalcade* radio script entitled "Lay That Musket Down" by Russell Hughes, and adapted for *Cavalcade* television by Robert Stevenson.
Directed by Robert Stevenson.
Filmed by Screen Televideo Productions, studio contract dated April 16, 1952
Story: Christopher Ludwick, a Philadelphia baker, wanted to serve his country. He had come to America from the Herman state of Hesse-Darmstadt some twenty years before, and he and his family had prospered. Now, during the Revolutionary War, he had a plan through which he might show his gratitude to his adopted land. Ludwick got Washington's approval of his plan. Posing as a deserter from the Continental Army, he slipped through the British lines to the Hessian camp on Staten Island. There he hoped to promote desertion among his former countrymen who were mercenaries serving the British. He was, however, spotted by British officers and forced to disclose of Washington's troops. Without powder the British could not attack Washington. So, as Ludwick made his own escape, he blew up the enemy's arsenal.

EPISODE #16 "NIGHT STRIKE" Broadcast on April 29, 1953
    Starring: Glenn Langan as Captain John Paul Jones
    Richard Garrick as Benjamin Franklin   Russell Simpson as Quartermaster
Also in the cast: Dayton Lummis, John Fraser, Normand Dupont, Maurice Marsac, Robert Osterloch, Ken Murray, James Best, and Dorothea Wolbert.
Written and directed for *Cavalcade* television by Robert Stevenson.
Based on the *Cavalcade* radio script "Captain Paul" by John Driscoll and Arthur Miller.
Filmed by Screen Televideo Productions, studio contract dated April 16, 1952
Story: Like unnumbered thousands who have contributed mightily to the building of the nation, John Paul Jones was not a native-born American. He adopted a nation which, after many years and many trials, formally claimed him as her own. Like millions of other Americans, native and adopted, he was of humble birth. When he was twelve years old, he was apprenticed to a ship's captain who took him on a journey to Virginia. He served as a mate on several slave ships - until finally he became disgusted with the traffic and resigned. Soon we find him in Philadelphia assisting in the earliest efforts of the struggling Continental Congress. The new United States had virtually no Navy, not a single ship worthy of a place in a battle fleet, and certainly no funds or credit with which to purchase any. So John found a ship, acquired a crew, and created a tradition.

EPISODE #17 "SLATER'S DREAM" Broadcast on May 13, 1953
    Starring: Mary Ellen Kay as Hannah Wilkinson
    Terrence Kilburn as Samuel Slater   Howard Wendell as Moses Brown
Howard Wendell as Moses Brown
Based on the *Cavalcade* radio script "Samuel Slater" by _?_ Southworth.
Story: Samuel Slater worked for six years as an apprentice and manager in an English textile mill. At the mill, he learned the workings of the spinning machine developed by the British inventor Richard Arkwright. Slater left England in disguise because the British government prohibited any person who had knowledge of the design and operation of spinning machines from leaving the country. In 1790, Slater agreed to build the Arkwright machine from memory for Almy & Brown, a Rhode Island textile firm that wanted to use the mechanical cotton spinning techniques. Now remembered as the founder of the textile industry in the United States, Slater performed what is probably one of the greatest feats of memory.

EPISODE #18 **"THE PIRATE'S CHOICE"**   Broadcast on May 27, 1953
  Starring: William Bishop as Lafitte   Morris Ankrum as General Jackson
  Also in the cast: John Alvin, Sig Arno, Jan Arvan, Ben Astar, Fred Essler, Douglas Evans, Jim Hayward, Gladys Hurlbut, Peter Mamakos, Donna Martell, Mario Siletti, Philip Tonge, Patrick Whyte, and James Seay
  Based on the *Cavalcade* radio script "Jean Laffite" by John Driscoll, Garrett Porter, _?_ Jackson, and Kenneth Webb.
  Adapted for *Cavalcade* television by Curtis Kenyon and David P. Sheppard.
  Directed by William J. Thiele.
  Filmed at Chertok Productions, studio contract dated October 21, 1952.
  Story: Jean Laffite was the last of the great American freebooters and pirates, a group traditionally present in all frontier society and one which disappeared in American history only with the vanishing of the frontier. Laffite's decisive part in the War of 1812 at a time when the nation was in sore straits. It is a romantic story, dealing with the greatest British force ever sent by the mother country against her errant colonies; a ragged army of frontiersmen led by an Indian fighter named Andrew Jackson, and - the fateful weight that turned the balance in America's favor - Jean Laffite's picturesque band of faithful followers from the Louisiana swamps, an army of smugglers and jailbirds that successfully defended the entrance to the Mississippi Valley. Through the drama swaggers the arrogant figure of Laffite, a daring, suave pirate with a price on his head, whose patriotism led him to the defense of his country on the side of law and order.

EPISODE #19 **"JOHN YANKEE"**   Broadcast on June 10, 1953
  Starring: Whitfield Connor as John Adams   Helen Parrish as Abigail Adams
  Raymond Greenleaf as Dr. Jeffries
  Based on the *Cavalcade* radio play of the same name by George H. Faulkner.
  Story: Lawyer John Adams rejoiced at every expression of popular opposition to the British. But when the treatment of British soldiers who had taken part in the Boston Massacre distressed him, his sense of justice led him to defend Captain Thomas Preston and the British soldiers charged with manslaughter. He felt that the soldiers should be freed, because they had only obeyed orders. Adams feared that his viewpoint would cost him popularity. Instead, his prestige rose. . . and in 1770, the people of Boston chose him as one of their representatives in the colonial legislature.

EPISODE #20 **"THE TENDERFOOT"**   Broadcast on June 24, 1953
  Starring: Edgar Buchanan as Theodore Roosevelt
  Also in the cast: Tom Brown, Robert Courtwaite, John Kellogg, Nolan Leavy, Ludwig Stossel, Lee Van Cleef, and James Young.
  Based on the *Cavalcade* radio script "Sheriff Teddy," by Halsted Welles, and adapted for *Cavalcade* television by Thomas Seller.
  Directed by William J. Thiele.
  Commercial entitled "Safety in Industry"
  Filmed at Chertok Productions, studio contract dated October 21, 1952.
  Story: When Teddy Roosevelt was twenty-five, his doctor ordered him to quit his political life and go out West for a complete rest. The party bosses in Albany agreed with the doctor, for secretly they had felt that the young reformer had been "washed up" for quite some time as far as politics were concerned. Teddy went West, but he found little rest. He soon realized that the Badlands were owned by outlaws and rustlers. There were few laws, and no one to enforce them. Eventually, the young tenderfoot found himself faced with the alternative of playing a crooked game and getting along as best he could or leaving town before he was invited to a "necktie party." Roosevelt risked his life in making a decision and mapping out a plan of action.

EPISODE #21 **"ONE NATION INDIVISIBLE"** Broadcast on July 8, 1953
Starring: Edgar Buchanan as Horace Greeley   Frank Ferguson as Jefferson Davis
Fay Wray as Mrs. Davis
Adapted for television by Warner Law, based on his own *Cavalcade* radio script.
Directed by William. J. Thiele.
Commercial entitled "Du Pont and the Dye Industry"
Filmed at Chertok Productions.
Story: Horace Greeley was one of the first editors to join the Republican Party. He was a delegate to its second national convention, and helped Abraham Lincoln obtain nomination for President. Although he supported Lincoln throughout the Civil War, he urged settling the conflict by compromise. In 1864, he met with several agents of the Confederacy in Canada to discuss peace terms, but the conference failed. In addition, Greeley also urged giving pardons to all members of the Confederacy after the war. This was Greeley's part in getting Jefferson Davis released from prison after the Civil War.

EPISODE #22 **"THE BETRAYAL"** Broadcast on July 22, 1953
Starring: Dan O'Herlihy as Benedict Arnold   Betty Lynn as Peggy Shippen
Also in the cast: Patrick Allen, Lane Bradford, David Cavendish, Bob Clarke, Herbert Deans, Charles Gibb, Kirby Grant, Michael Grant, Robin Hughes, Anthony Jochim, DeForest Kelley, Marshall Reed, Brendon Rhodes, Pierre Watkin, Frank Wilcox.
Based on the *Cavalcade* radio script of the same name by Halsted Welles, and adapted for *Cavalcade* by Curtis Kenyon.
Directed by William J. Thiele.
Filmed by Chertok Productions, studio contract dated October 21, 1952.
Story: The youngest and most beautiful of the four Shippen daughters Peggy dreamed great dreams. In the handsome and arrogant General Benedict Arnold, hero of Saratoga and Military Governor of Philadelphia, she found not only love, but the opportunity to fulfill her hopes. Despite her family's objections, Peggy married Arnold. And, knowing that fame and wealth could come to them if they would hand over to the British the plans for West Point, Peggy was a willing tool for her husband in this - one of the most dangerous intrigues in American history.

EPISODE #23 **"A TIME TO GROW"** Broadcast on August 5, 1953
Starring: Booth Coleman as Robert Livingston
Also in the cast: William Bishop, Raymond Greenleaf, Douglas Marsac, Stacey Kench Toben Meyer, Roy Regnier, and John Wengraf.
Based on the *Cavalcade* radio script of the same name by Irve Tunick, and adapted for *Cavalcade* by William Bruckner.
Directed by William J. Thiele.
Filmed at Chertok Productions, studio contract dated October 21, 1952.
Story: Robert R. Livingston, an American Statesman, helped write the Declaration of Independence in 1776. In 1789, Livingston administered the oath of office to the first President of the United States, George Washington. Even through all this, Livingston was involved in a little-known incident that shaped the history of America forever. As minister to France from 1801 to 1804, Livingston negotiated the Louisiana Purchase, which added a vast new territory to the United States. Livingston's dear friend DuPont de Nemour lends invaluable assistance.

EPISODE #24 **"THE LAST WILL OF DANIEL WEBSTER"** Broadcast on August 19, 1953
Starring: Ray Collins as Daniel Webster   Richard Gaines as George Washington
Ann Doran as Caroline
Also stars: Carl Benton Reid, Roy Harvey, John Hamilton, Kenny Delmar, Everett Glass.
Based on the *Cavalcade* radio script "The Conscience of Black Dan'l" by Russell S. Hughes, and adapted for *Cavalcade* television by N. Richard Nash.

Directed by Robert Stevenson.
Commercial entitled "Fiber E"
Filmed by Screen Televideo Productions, studio contract dated April 16, 1952
Story: Daniel Webster was a loyal and prominent member of the Whig party and he held high hopes of being their nominee for the office of President in 1840. The Whigs, however, chose a more conservative and less controversial candidate, General Harrison. "Black Dan'l" was highly disappointed, but in the interest of his party and his country he accepted the position of Secretary of State that Harrison offered him. When Harrison died in office, and Tyler became President, an important decision Webster made all but ruined his political career. Then eight years later, he was asked to serve in the Senate to help make the Whigs defeat the Clay Compromise. He entered the Senate chamber prepared to do the bidding of the party that could yet make him President.

EPISODE #25 **"THE STOLEN GENERAL"**   Broadcast on September 2, 1953
Starring: Reginald Denny as Lt. William Barton   John Abbott as General Prescott
Barbara Billingsley as Dorothea Meadows
Also in the cast: James Fairfax, William Fawcett, Hank Patterson, Douglas Kennedy, Anna Dewey, Phil Tead, Harlan Warde, Walter Kingsford, Kenny Delmar, Ben Wright, Rex Evans, and John Dodsworth.
Based on the *Cavalcade* radio script of the same name by John Driscoll, Philo Higley and Garrett Porter. Adapted for *Cavalcade* television by Arthur Ripley.
Directed by Robert Stevenson.
Filmed by Screen Televideo Productions, studio contract dated April 16, 1952
Story: In 1777, the new United States of America, on its first birthday hadn't established a routine of celebrations. Perhaps because things looked very dark for the colonies. The British fleet lay at anchor off Newport Island - Newport itself was held by the British Brigadier General Prescott. The capricious Colonel William Barton and a band of Rhode Island patriots decided to make a celebration that would long be remembered. With five whaleboats and a crew of seamen patriots, Barton kidnapped the British general from under the very guns of the British men-o'-war. The daring exploit brought renewed courage to all of New England, and in the words of General George Washington, "at an evil hour, a black cloud was lifted."

EPISODE #26 **"SAM AND THE WHALE"**   Broadcast on September 29, 1953
Starring: Cecil Kellaway as Samuel Mulford   Evelyn Ankers as Lady Mary Montagu
Based on the *Cavalcade* radio script entitled "Whale Off" by George H. Faulkner.
Commercial entitled "How Big Business Helps Little Business"
Story: Thomas Mulford was an early Long Island colonist who fought unfair taxation by taking his complaint case to King George in England. This cantankerous old man who objected so strenuously to the tax on whales, was probably the first man in America to show concern for the preservation of whales and the unfair laws abiding those decisions.

EPISODE #27 **"THE STOLEN GENERAL"**   Broadcast on October 6, 1953 (Repeat as above)

EPISODE #28 **"BREAKFAST AT NANCY'S"**   Broadcast on October 13, 1953
Starring: Amanda Blake as Nancy Hart   Charles McGraw as Wilkie Bowman
Jack Kirkwood as Royston Tolliver   Ronny Hyatt as Morgan
Based on the *Cavalcade* radio play of the same name by George H. Faulkner.
Commercial entitled "Du Pont and the Petroleum Industry"
Story: During the American Revolution, Nancy Hart used her woodland cabin as a station for scouts carrying messages for General Clark of the Continental Army. On one particular day, Nancy hides one of her soldier-husband's comrades from aroused Tories, one of whom she once loved, and her patriotism turned personal. She then had to defend her home and children with a loaded musket.

EPISODE #29 **"SUNSET AT APPOMATOX"** Broadcast on October 20, 1953
    Starring: William Johnstone as General Lee   Henry Morgan as General Grant
    Based on *Cavalcade* radio script "Robert E. Lee" by John Driscoll and Robert Tallman.
    Commercial entitled "Chemistry in Agriculture"
    Story: Honoring the Confederacy's greatest general, and finest citizen, this drama stressed the personal nobility and moral courage rather than the military genius of the Southern hero. Robert E. Lee symbolized all that was noblest a struggle that was more than a war between States and more than a crusade for national union; rather a proud last stand of a great culture and a vanishing way of life.

EPISODE #30 **"AND TO FAME UNKNOWN"** Broadcast on October 27, 1953
    Starring: Rolland Gladieux
    The biography of a high school science professor.

EPISODE #31 **"A TIME TO GROW"** Broadcast on November 3, 1953
    Rebroadcast of episode #23, broadcast on August 5, 1953

EPISODE #32 **"THE MAN WHO TOOK A CHANCE"** Broadcast on November 10, 1953
    Rebroadcast of episode #3, broadcast on October 29, 1952

EPISODE #33 **"THE TIGER'S TAIL"** Broadcast on November 17, 1953
    Starring: Robert Cornthwaite
    Also in the cast: Howard Freeman, William Haade, Paul Harvey, Judy Osborne, Ray Teal, and Robert Warwick.
    Based on the January 8, 1941 *Cavalcade* radio script entitled "Mightier Than the Sword" by Frank Monaghan. Adapted for *Cavalcade* television by N. Richard Nash.
    Directed by Robert Stevenson.
    Filmed by Screen Televideo Productions, studio contract dated April 16, 1952
    Story: When Thomas Nast took to political satire in his cartoons, his influence was powerful. In the interests of civic honor he fashioned a series of cartoons which exposed the ill-famed "Boss" Tweed ring of political corruption in New York, clapped Tweed behind the bars and pointed the way for similar exposures, wherever needed, throughout the country. This work was regarded as the climax of Thomas Nast's career and his great contribution in behalf of decent government to the America of his times.

EPISODE #34 **"THE LAST WILL OF DANIEL WEBSTER"** Broadcast November 24, 1953
    Rebroadcast of episode #24, broadcast on August 19, 1953

EPISODE #35 **"MAJOR PAULINE"** Broadcast on December 1, 1953
    Starring: Gertrude Michael as Major Pauline   Robert Page as General Braxton Bragg
    Also in the cast: Michael Hall, Hank Mann, Harry Cheshire, John Holland, Robert Foulk, Richard Bauman, Fred Beir, William Grueneberg, and Dayton Lummis.
    Based on the original *Cavalcade* radio play "Pink Lace" by Virginia Radcliffe, and adapted for *Cavalcade* television by Robert Stevenson.
    Directed by Robert Stevenson.
    Filmed at Screen Televideo Productions, studio contract dated April 16, 1952.
    Story: During the War between the States, actress Pauline Cushman interrupted her career to do special espionage work which she believed might help save the Union. By openly declaring herself for the South, she was free to move around gathering information. She was eventually caught, however, and arrested as a spy by the South. Can she use her charms to escape across the Union lines?

EPISODE #36 **"THE BETRAYAL"** Broadcast on December 8, 1953
    Rebroadcast of episode #22, broadcast on July 22, 1953

EPISODE #37 **"RIDERS OF THE PONY EXPRESS"** Broadcast on December 15, 1953
Starring: Robert Warrick, Lewis Martin and Ralph Reed
Loosely based on the *Cavalcade* radio script "Speed of Words" by _?_ Longstreth.
Story: The Pony Express was a mail delivery service that operated between St.Joseph, Mo., and Sacramento, California, in 1860 and 1861. These riders could deliver mail to California in ten days of less, faster than any other mail service of that time.

Trivia: The original title of this drama was "Overland Trail," but changed minutes before the opening titles were designed.

EPISODE #38 **"ONE NATION INDIVISIBLE"** Broadcast on December 22, 1953
Rebroadcast of episode #21, broadcast on July 8, 1953

EPISODE #39 **"MR. PEALE'S DINOSAUR"** Broadcast on December 29, 1953
Starring: Lowell Gilmore as Mr. Charles Wilson Peale
Lurene Tuttle as Elizabeth
Also in the cast: Louis Jean Heydt, John Lupton, Anne O'Neal, Hayden Rorke, and Daniel M. White.
Based on the *Cavalcade* radio play "Mr. Peale and the Dinosaur" by Arthur Arent, and adapted for *Cavalcade* television by William Bruckner and Charles Larson.
Directed by William J. Thiele.
Commercial entitled "Titanium (Livingston)"
Filmed at Chertok Productions, studio contract dated October 21, 1952.
Story: Charles Wilson Peale of Philadelphia was a man of many interests. His versatility and enormous energy led him into such diversified fields as watch making, dentistry, portrait painting and scientific experimentation. On one particular afternoon, Benjamin Franklin suggested that Peale start a museum of natural history. Such a museum, Franklin said, could help the American people to realize and appreciate the great wonders of the new world. Peale tackled the project with enthusiasm, but had to dig for his star attraction.

EPISODE #40 **"POOR RICHARD"** Broadcast on January 5, 1954
Rebroadcast of the premiere episode, broadcast on October 1, 1952

EPISODE #41 **"G FOR GOLDBERGER"** Broadcast on January 12, 1954
Starring: Walter Coy as Dr. Goldberger   William Forrest as Dr. Sam Halleck
Emlen Davies as Mary Goldberger   Susan Seaforth as Sarah
Based on the *Cavalcade* radio script "The Red Death" by Ruth Barth.
Story: This is the story of an immigrant boy, raised on New York's east side, who was sent by the United States Public Health Service to investigate the "red death," the mysterious pellagra which had baffled science for two centuries. By unorthodox methods, this American scientist, Dr. Joseph Goldberger, found the cure, then the cause, for the disease. Pellagra, which was a familiar disease in other parts of the world for centuries began to appear in the United States about 1907. It reached alarming proportions, and Dr. Goldberger took charge of the investigation and eventually worked his way through to a brilliant victory over the "red death."

EPISODE #42 **"SMYRNA INCIDENT"** Broadcast on January 19, 1954
Starring: Donald Murphy as Lt. Butler   Carl Benton Reid as Commander Ingraham
Robert Cornthwaite as Koszta   John Wengraf as Captain Von Schwarz
Konstantin Shayne as Koszta's servant   Everett Glass as the American consul
Also in the cast: Albert Szabo, Ted Stanhope, Charles LaTorre, and Otto Waldis.
Written for *Cavalcade* by Robert Stevenson.
Produced by Jack Denove and directed by Robert Stevenson.   **(cont'd)**

Commercial entitled "Neoprene (Livingston)"
Filmed at Jack Denove Studios, studio contract dated October 7, 1953.
Story: U.S. Navy Commander Ingraham, who defies the armed might of the Austrian Empire. By threatening to open fire on units of that nation's fleet, he single-handedly protested Austria's refusal to release an American held prisoner on one of their ships.

EPISODE #43 **"MAN OF GLASS"** Broadcast on January 26, 1954
Starring: Robert Straus as William Stiegel   Carl Benton Reid as Fred Bauer
Jane Whitley as (Stiegel's love interest)   John Eldridge as Jack Huber
Also in the cast: John Alderson, Harris Brown, Phil Chambers, John Eldridge, Charles Evans, Tiger Fafara, and Charles Meredith.
Based on the *Cavalcade* radio script "The House of Glass" by __?__ Longstreth, and adapted for *Cavalcade* by Thomas Seller.
Directed by William J. Thiele.
Filmed at Chertok Productions, studio contract dated October 9, 1953.
Story: People who live in glass houses should not throw rocks. Unless your name is Henry William Stiegel. Stiegel was an important early American manufacturer of fine glass. His factories were the first in the American Colonies to make glassware as good as that being imported from Europe. At the height of his success, Stiegel lived in a large house, wore elaborate clothes, and was called a baron. But his extravagant living and his risky investment in new factories brought financial ruin.

Trivia: The working script title was originally "The Baron and the Rose."

EPISODE #44 **"WHAT HATH GOD WROUGHT"** Broadcast on February 2, 1954
Rebroadcast of episode #5, broadcast on November 26, 1952

EPISODE #45 **"PLUME OF HONOR"** Broadcast on February 9, 1954
Starring: Maurice Marsac as Marquis de Lafayette
Also in the cast: Vincent Pelletier, Otto Reichow, Gabor Curtiz, Albert Szabo, John Banner, Henry Rowland, Larry Winter, and Richard Bauman.
Based on the *Cavalcade* radio script "Lady on a Mission" by Margaret Lewerth, and adapted for *Cavalcade* television by Paul Gangelin.
Directed by George Archainbaud.
Commercial entitled "Du Pont Research Protects the Public"
Filmed at SHA Productions, studio contract dated October 7, 1953.
Story: Paris, 1794: hatred and terror followed in the wake of the Revolution. The prisons were filled. One of those accused of being a traitor was Madame Lafayette, wife of America's great friend, the Marquis de Lafayette. America was shocked, but our Ambassador to France, James Monroe, was helpless. To plead to the Committee of Public Safety for release would mean the loss of prestige for America, and might further harm Madame Lafayette's position. Then the Ambassador's lovely wife, Elizabeth Monroe, suggested a daring scheme. If the people of France became aware of America's concern for Madame Lafayette, the Committee might hesitate to carry out plans for her execution. To make her country's position clear, Elizabeth Monroe, in the face of grave personal danger, called upon Madame Lafayette at the prison. The scheme worked. Madame Lafayette was released, and American diplomacy gained new stature.

EPISODE #46 **"MARGIN FOR VICTORY"** Broadcast on February 16, 1954
Starring: Richard Gaines as George Washington   John Hoyt as William Barton
Also in the cast: Edward Ashley, Richard Avonde, and Francis L. Sullivan

(cont'd)

Also in the cast: Patrick J. McGeehan, Clive Morgan, Guy Bellis, Ronald Bennett, Richard Peel, John M. Kennedy, Scott Lee, Richard Deane, John Patrick, Myrna Fahey.
Based on the *Cavalcade* radio script "The Stolen General" by John Driscoll, Philo Higley, and Garrett Porter, and adapted for *Cavalcade* by Arthur Ripley.
Produced by Jack Denove and directed by Arthur Ripley.
Commercial entitled "Mylar"
Filmed at Jack Denove Studios, studio contract dated October 7, 1953.
Story: In 1777, the new United States of America, on its first birthday hadn't established a routine of celebrations. Perhaps because things looked very dark for the colonies. The British fleet lay at anchor off Newport Island - Newport itself was held by the British Brigadier General Prescott. The capricious Colonel William Barton and a band of Rhode Island patriots decided to make a celebration that would long be remembered. With five whaleboats and a crew of seamen patriots, Barton kidnapped the British general from under the very guns of the British men-o'-war. The daring exploit brought renewed courage to all of New England, and in the words of General George Washington, "at an evil hour, a black cloud was lifted."

EPISODE #47   **"IN THIS CRISIS"**   Broadcast on February 23, 1954
Rebroadcast of episode #7, broadcast on December 24, 1952

EPISODE #48   **"THE ABSENT HOST"**   Broadcast on March 2, 1954
Starring: Don Kennedy as Jack Jouett
Also in the cast: William Adamson, James Horan, Leo Britt, John Patrick, Gil Herman, Nestor Paiva, James Scay, Charles Bastios, Robin Hughes, William Tannen, John Alderson, and John Doncette.
Written for *Cavalcade* t.v. by Russell Hughes, from his radio play "The Darkest Hour."
Directed by Sidney Salkow.
Commercial entitled "Preventive Medicine"
Filmed at SHA Productions, studio contract dated October 7, 1954.
Story: In the dark days of the Revolutionary War, following the invasion of Virginia, the colonies were so disheartened that one more blow would have convinced many that they were fighting against insurmountable odds. Realizing this, the British conceived a bold and daring scheme that might have ended the war in a single stroke. They planned to take prisoner the man who was the heart of the Revolution - the man who wrote the American Declaration of Independence - Thomas Jefferson. If it had not been for the quick thinking of Jack Jouett, a captain in the American forces, all the years of struggle might have been for naught.

EPISODE #49   **"DUEL AT THE O.K. CORRAL"**   Broadcast on March 9, 1954
Starring: Kenneth Tobey as Wyatt Earp   Lee Van Cleef as Ike Clanton
Henry Morgan as Frank McLowry   Morgan Jones as Morgan Earp
Keith Richards as Doc Holiday   Fred Libby as Bill Clanton
Alan Wells as Billy Claiborne   Jim Bannon as Virgil Earp
Based on the *Cavalcade* radio script entitled "Kansas Marshall" by Maurey Robinson and Russell S. Hughes.
Story: When men asked Wyatt Earp what his name was, they often laughed at his answer. They would remark, "What's the matter, Mister? Got the hiccups?" But when this quiet, cool-eyed man with the odd name drew out his six-shooter, they stopped laughing. Even the most hard-bitten criminal of the lawless western frontier respected Wyatt. Marksmanship alone did not qualify a man for the perilous job of town Marshall back in the 1870's. It took courage and continuous devotion to an unpleasant duty. In Tombstone, Arizona, Wyatt met a problem that called for more than courage, more than skill, and more than his fanatic devotion to duty. He discovered that truly civilized community conditions can not be maintained by a single man and his guns.

EPISODE #50 **"THE SPLENDID DREAM"** Broadcast on March 16, 1954
    Starring: Leo G. Carroll as William Penn   Richard Stapley as Lord Mayor
    Based on the *Cavalcade* radio script "Voice in the Wilderness" by Garrett Porter.
    Commercial entitled "Ludox"
    Story: William Penn's "Holy Experiment" was a determined effort on the part of a group of people, calling themselves "Friends," to establish a colony of brotherly love in the New World. Under his gentle guidance and with his charitable appreciation of the problems of settlement in a virgin wilderness in whose silent, strange forests lurked Indian savages who might well have become hostile had not sympathy and understanding won them over to the colonists' side, the colonization of Pennsylvania was sensibly and prosperously achieved. William Penn's signing of the Constitution of 1701 was to become the frame of the Constitution of the United States.

EPISODE #51 **"YOUNG ANDY JACKSON"** Broadcast on March 23, 1954
    Starring: Billy Gray as Andrew Jackson   Lisa Lindgren as Rachel
    Based on the *Cavalcade* radio script "Young Andrew Jackson" by Erik Barnouw and Robert Tallman.
    Story: One of the early rumblings of Secession in the United States was heard in South Carolina during the administration of Andrew Jackson. But the powerful voice of "Old Hickory" stilled the incipient tumult with the words, "The Union; it must and shall be preserved." Forthright, fiery, vigorous in mind and body was this dynamic President. Hero of Indian wars, the Battle of New Orleans and a waxing hot political career, Andrew Jackson was a mighty force in shaping the destiny of our Republic.

    Trivia: A few months after this broadcast, Billy Gray, who starred as Andrew Jackson in this broadcast, would later star as James Anderson, Jr., referred to as "Bud," on television's *Father Knows Best*, which premiered on CBS television in October of 1954.

EPISODE #52 **"ESCAPE"** Broadcast on March 30, 1954
    Starring: David Alpert as Carl Schurz
    Also in the cast: Robert A. Paguin, Frances Morris, Kenneth Alton, Virginia Lee, Lawrence Ryle, Ashley Cowan, Dabbs Greer, and Vincent Pelletier.
    Written for *Cavalcade* by Paul Gangelin.
    Directed by George Archainbaud.
    Filmed at SHA Productions, studio contract dated by October 7, 1953.
    Story: Carl Schurz, a Prussian student comes to America in 1852 to become advisor to presidents from Abraham Lincoln to Theodore Roosevelt.

EPISODE #53 **"RIDDLE OF THE SEAS"** Broadcast on April 6, 1954
    Starring: John Hoyt as Matthew Fontaine Maury   Ruth Robinson as Ann
    Also in the cast: Shiela Clark, Laura Elliott, Len Hendry, Lamont Johnson, Vincent J. Pelletier, Roy Roberts, John Stephenson, and Alan Wells.
    Based on the *Cavalcade* radio script "The Pathfinder of the Seas," and adapted for *Cavalcade* television by William Bruckner.
    Directed by William J. Thiele.
    Filmed at Chertok Productions, studio contract dated October 9, 1953.
    Story: In the pilothouse of every ship that sails the seven seas the master mariner has a collection of charts, charts which hold for him priceless information; charts which tell him what he needs to know about the winds and the waves, the ocean currents, the pathways of the sea. And down in a corner of most of these charts, in very small type, is a legend which reads: "Founded upon the researches made in the early part of the 19th Century by Matthew Fontaine Maury, while serving as a lieutenant in the United States Navy." That legend today is printed on every pilot chart issued by the United States Hydrographic Office.

EPISODE #54 "CRAZY JUDAH"   Broadcast on April 13, 1954
    Starring: Ross Elliott as Theodore Judah   Frances Rafferty as Anna Judah
    Also in the cast: Snub Pallord, Salvador Boguez, Lou Nova, Leo Curley, Roy Bennett, Robert Carson, Gabor Curtis, William O'Neal, Ted Von Eltz, Hugh Sanders, Forrest Taylor, Frank Wilcox, Beverly Washburn, and Patrick McGeehan.
    Teleplay by Louis R. Foster, from the *Cavalcade* radio script by Arthur Arent.
    Produced by Jack Denove, and directed by Louis R. Foster.
    Filmed at Jack Denove Studios, studio contract dated October 7, 1953.
    Story: For most of his life, Theodore D. Judah dreamed of a railroad that would span the nation. It was 1850 then, and the shortest routes to the West were through the malaria-ridden Panama swamps, of the long, dangerous overland trail. American needed fast, efficient transportation to bind together the interests of the East and West. Judah had pleaded in vain to Congress for funds, but first Judah had to find a suitable railroad pass over the Sierra mountains.

EPISODE #55 "THE ARROW AND THE BOW"   Broadcast on April 20, 1954
    Rebroadcast of episode #8, broadcast on January 7, 1953

EPISODE #56 "THE PAPER SWORD"   Broadcast on April 27, 1954
    Starring: Patrick O'Neal as James King   Also starring: Margaret Field
    Story: Newspaper editor James King crusades for a clean government during brawling San Francisco's lawless days.

EPISODE #57 "THE GENTLE CONQUEROR"   Broadcast on May 4, 1954
    Starring: Wilton Graff as Father Serra
    Also in the cast: Rico Alaniz, Richard Beymer, David Bond, Russ Conklin, Ted de Corsia, Pitt Herbert, Lamont Johnson, Vincent J. Pelletier, Donald Randolph, Gil Warren, Alan Wells, Chief Yowlachie, and Dorothy Sky Eagle.
    Based on the *Cavalcade* radio script "The Colonization of California" by John Driscoll, and adapted for *Cavalcade* television by Thomas Seller and William Sackheim.
    Directed by William J. Thiele.
    Filmed at Chertok Productions, studio contract dated October 9, 1953.
    Story: Father Junipero Serra was a Franciscan missionary who in 1769 founded the first mission in present-day California. He founded the California Missions and laid the foundation for the colonization of the state of California.

EPISODE #58 "SPINDLETOP"   Broadcast on May 11, 1954
    Starring: William Bishop as Captain Lucas   Nancy Hale as Mrs. Lucas
    Richard Eyer as Tony Lucas   Burt Mustin as Galey
    Richard Gaines as Dr. Hayes   Stanley Andrews as Guffey
    Russell Gaige as the bank president   Renny McEvoy as the clerk
    Based on the original *Cavalcade* radio play of the same name by Irve Tunick.
    Story: The year 1949 marked the ninetieth anniversary of America's oil industry. From a tiny beginning, it has become one of our country's most powerful assets. This growth has come from men of oil - the drillers in the field, the investors, the engineers. It offered futures for men of vision - like Anthony Lucas. An ex-Captain of the Imperial Austrian Navy, Lucas came to America late in the nineteenth century. Here, he felt, was escape from the tyranny and petty restrictions of the Old World. By 1896, Lucas was a citizen, and a successful mining and mechanical engineer. While drilling for salt in Louisiana, Lucas noticed a peculiar geological formation - an underground range of salt that pointed to Texas. To prove his theory that under one of the domes in this range was oil, he followed the range of salt, drilling as he went. Finally he tackled a dome called "Spindletop" near Beaumont. Succeeding where others had failed, Lucas pioneered one of the country's most fabulous oil wells.

EPISODE #59 **"MOONLIGHT SCHOOL"** Broadcast on May 18, 1954
Starring: Emlen Davies as Miss Prescott   George Nader as Royce Emery
Also starring: Lon Chaney, Jr.
Based on the *Cavalcade* radio script "The Petticoat Jury" by Joseph Cochran.
Story: When Miss Euphemia Prescott left Boston to teach school in the wide open spaces of the West, she was prepared for a different sort of life. She had heard much of the great new land of opportunity and she was prepared to live there and like it. But when she arrived at her new home, she was rudely shocked for it was a lawless community, when a man's rightness and worth were judged by his speed and accuracy with a six-shooter. Euphemia had lived all her life in staid and civilized nineteenth century Boston, and this new land confused and disgusted her. She decided to go back immediately, but something happened . . . and Miss Euphemia Prescott decided to stay on and bring law and order to the town, no matter how she had to do it.

EPISODE #60 **"MIGHTIER THAN THE SWORD"** Broadcast on May 25, 1954
Rebroadcast of episode #13, broadcast on March 18, 1953

EPISODE #61 **"A STRANGE JOURNEY"** Broadcast on June 1, 1954
Rebroadcast of episode #48, broadcast on March 2, 1954

EPISODE #62 **"THE SKIPPER'S LADY"** Broadcast on June 8, 1954
Starring: Paul Langton, Sally Brophy, Harvey Stephens, Harry Bartell, Richard Crockett, Paul Keast, Vincent J. Pelletier, John Pickard, Paul Stader, Harvey Stephens, Houseley Stevens, and Lee Van Cleef.
Written for *Cavalcade* television by William Sackheim.
Directed by William J. Thiele.
Commercial entitled "Du Pont is a Good Neighbor"
Filmed at Chertok Productions, studio contract dated October 9, 1953.
Story: With a woman in command, the clipper Neptune's Car races to reach California to prevent an uprising.

EPISODE #63 **"A MATTER OF HONOR"** Broadcast on June 15, 1954
Commercial entitled "Du Pont and the People of a Good Cummunity."
Rebroadcast of episode #11, broadcast on February 18, 1953

Trivia: A memo from R.M. De Graff dated June 16, 1954 reads: "You heard me speak about the blooper on the network last night. We ran an old repeat film which closed with 'and we'll be back two weeks from tonight, etc.' I have asked the agency to wire all delayed stations to cut off the sound at the end of the picture and George Neilson is taking care of WDEL-TV. The main point, I believe, is this - let's try and make sure this does not happen again."

EPISODE #64 **"COURAGE IN CONNECTICUT"** Broadcast on June 22, 1954
Starring: Booth Colman, Anne Kimbell, and Sean McClory
Based on the *Cavalcade* radio script "Yankee Independence" by Henry Fisk Carlton, based on his 1932 story "The Charter Oak."
Story: The story of Connecticut's determined effort to keep its identity and protect its charter was one that has become a New England tradition. The facts of the story of the Charter Oak are clouded in legend but many believe that the main events were substantial. New England was colonized by people who put self-government above all ideals. though officially under the rule of the British crown, extensive rights and privileges were given to the colonists by their charters.

Trivia: The Freedoms Foundation recognized Du Pont's contributions in "bringing about a better understanding of the American way of life." "Courage in Connecticut" was the *Cavalcade* program that won the award. *Cavalcade* had been given seven Freedoms Foundation awards in six years . . . under the Foundation's rules, no one may be awarded top honors more than five times!

EPISODE #65   **"MOUNTAIN MAN"**   Broadcast on September 28, 1954
   Starring: Gregory Wolcott as James Ohio Pattie
   Also in the cast: Vincent Pelletier, Charles Stevens, Henry Escalante, Paul Picerni, Edward Colmans, Larry Johns, Eugenia Paul, Guy Prescott, and Keith Richards.
   Written for *Cavalcade* by Paul Franklin.
   Directed by Robert Walker.
   Commercial entitled "Our Improved Standards of Living."
   Filmed at SHA Productions, studio contract dated October 7, 1953.
   Story: Story of James Ohio Pattie, a Kentuckian who crossed the rocky mountains into California, in 1828, and was imprisoned there.

   Trivia: First episode of the new season.

EPISODE #66   **"THE GREAT GAMBLE"**   Broadcast on October 5, 1954
   Starring: Whitfield Connor as Cyrus Field   Marjorie Lord as Mrs. Field
   Susan Oden as Mary Field
   Also in the cast: Florenz Ames, Logan Field, Robert Middleton, Vincent J. Pelletier, Herbert Rudley, and Harry Shannon.
   Written for *Cavalcade* by Warner Law.
   Directed by William J. Thiele.
   Filmed at Chertok Productions, studio contract dated October 9, 1953.
   Story: The story of the great faith and fortitude of Cyrus Field in his attempt to lay the first telegraph cable beneath the Atlantic Ocean. Field was labeled a swindler when his first play failed, but he continued his work, and succeeded.

EPISODE #67   **"SPINDLETOP"**   Broadcast on October 12, 1954
   Rebroadcast of episode #58, broadcast on May 11, 1954

EPISODE #68   **"NIGHT STRIKE"**   Broadcast on October 19, 1954
   Rebroadcast of episode #16, broadcast on April 29, 1953

EPISODE #69   **"THE FORGE"**   Broadcast on October 26, 1954
   Starring: George Nader as Eliphalet Remington, II   James Seay as William Paddock
   Walter Sanda as Eliphalet Remington   Madge Meredith as Lavinia Paddock
   Kathleen Crowley as Abigail Paddock   Vernon Rich as Morgan Jones
   Roland Varna as Capt. Von Holst   Russell Simpson as Eleazer Grant
   Based on the *Cavalcade* radio script of the same name by Joseph Cochran.
   Commercial entitled "The Benefits of Competition."
   Story: Eliphalet Remington didn't have enough money to buy a new rifle, but he did have his father's forge, and his own high standards of workmanship. So he spent weeks carefully machining the parts of a gun (as carefully as though he were sharpening fine silver pieces for his mother). His gun completed, Remington entered a nearby target-shooting contest and found himself scheduled to shoot against the state champion, who owned one of the most expensive rifles made. Eliphalet Remington didn't win the match but he did win something that soon proved far more important.

Fact... and Fiction, Too

NEW APPROACH FOR 'CAVALCADE' AS IT RIDES INTO THE PRESENT

Cavalcade of America, a show from which dignity and prestige drip in kingsize drops, is on the verge of a change of pace. While no one connected with the operation would say the show is switching from the historical to the hysterical, that is about what it amounts to. Cavalcade of America, in short, is about to depart the wonderful sanctity of circa 1776 and move boldly into 1954. In these times, this could be suicidal.

Sponsored for 17 years on radio by

Out of the past: Cecil Kellaway and Evelyn Ankers in a Cavalcade historical play.

the Du Pont people, Cavalcade came to TV in 1952. It has been devoted, of course, to depicting events of American history, with a warmth and understanding so often lacking in the cold print of textbooks. It has dedicated itself to Americana, dealing in both fact and semifiction, and has finally reached the point where it seems wise to move on, at least occasionally, and lock horns with the immediate present.

"This, of course," says Jack DeNove, who is currently producing the bulk of the Cavalcade films, "means we must deal more in fiction than in fact. There is nothing tougher than trying to depict a person who is still alive—or even a person whose heirs are still alive. They can be worse, in fact."

For the first "modern" film, Cavalcade has chosen to memorialize the American doctor, genial practitioner variety. Titled, sensibly enough, "The Doctor," it is scheduled to be telecast on ABC Dec. 7. Dean Jagger, an Academy Award winner (for his adjutant's role in "Twelve O'Clock High"), makes his TV film bow in the episode.

Du Pont, with characteristic caution and a magnificent eye for detail, commandeered no less a personage than Dr. Dwight Murray, chairman of the board of trustees of the American Medical Association, to examine set and script for complete authenticity. The only thing the good doctor missed was the prop diploma on the office wall—a veterinarian's.

DeNove, despite the built-in headaches of any costume picture, would still rather do them dead than alive. "In this doctor film, for instance," he sighs, "we had a real simple little bit where the wife hums a snatch of melody from 'Oklahoma!' which reminds her husband that he's forgotten to go out and buy tickets to the show. We had so much trouble trying to get clearance on that one bit of music that we had to scrap the whole

Cavalcade in stride: an episode from days when British Redcoats battled the Yankees.

thing and change it to 'Carmen.' More cultural, anyway. Also in the public domain."

Future *Cavalcades*, to be dealt with strictly as fiction, will include a salute to the American newspaperman, the policeman, the football coach, the farmer, the public servant, the aviator (possibly based on Charles Lindbergh) and other subjects designed to tell the story of present-day America.

Most affected by the shift is one Richard Gaines, an actor. His specialty is playing George Washington, whom he resembles in face if not in fortune, and whom he has depicted in no less than six *Cavalcades* to date.

"When *Cavalcade* decides again that this country has a history," he says, a little forlornly, "I will be available."

The year is 1954: Dean Jagger as 'The Doctor' advises patient Nancy Hale in Cavalcade's first portrait of the present.

EPISODE #70 **"MOONLIGHT WITNESS"** Broadcast on November 2, 1954
  Starring: Bruce Bennett as Abraham Lincoln   Walter Reed as William Herndon
  Clair Du Brey as Hannah Armstrong   Rhys Williams as Hugh Fullerton
  Also in the cast: Jimmy Mesley Dodd, Sam Flint, John Force, Melbourne Ford, Byron K. Foulger, Jonathan Hale, Maurice Everett Hall, Jr., Frank Joquet, Robert Walter Quarry.
  Based on the May 19, 1947 *Cavalcade* radio broadcast "Witness by Moonlight," by Henry W. Denker. Adapted for *Cavalcade* television by Maurice Geraghty.
  Directed by Maurice Geraghty.
  Filmed at SHA Productions, studio contract dated October 7, 1953.
  Story: Lincoln and Herndon, attorneys-at-law, in closing their ledgers, were puzzled by an item, "one book - fifty cents." Then the lawyer who was about to become president recalled the expenditure. It had, indeed, been a small price to pay for a life . . . In defending young Duff Armstrong against a framed murder charge, Lincoln learned that the prosecution was hinging everything upon the testimony of one witness who claimed he had seen the victim murdered and that he possessed the weapon Armstrong had used. Shrewdly, Lincoln proceeded to attack the witness's story, producing finally his "trump card" - the fifty-cent book.

EPISODE #71 **"SATURDAY STORY"** Broadcast on November 9, 1954
  Starring: Otto Graham as himself   Dabbs Greer as Mark Wilson
  Joyce MacKenzie as Idele Wilson   Ralph Moody as the high school principal
  Charles Meredith as the high school superintendent
  Also in the cast: Mark Wilson, Idele Wilson, George Wallace, Morgan Jones, Dick Schackelton, Frank Leahy, and Franklin Bingman.
  Written for *Cavalcade* television by Mervin Gerard and Joel Murcott.
  Produced by Warren Lewis and directed by Francis D. Lyon.
  Commercial entitled "Job Continuity at Du Pont."
  Filmed at Four Star Productions, studio contract dated October 7, 1953.
  Story: Cleveland Browns football player Otto Graham, former All-American known as "Mr. Quarterback," plays himself in this drama. This is a tribute to high school coach Mark Wilson, who taught Graham the values of manhood as well as the skills of football. Frank Leahy, former of Coach of Notre Dame, will introduce the show.

  Trivia: Critics branded this episode "more or less a television version of a slick magazine type of sentimental yarn that did not come off as well as it should have." Mark Wilson was apparently a Mr. Chips of Midwestern high school football. The coach, played by Dabbs Greer, taught the fundamentals of the game to Otto Graham, played by himself, who was currently the quarterback of the professional Cleveland Browns. Critics also said that "the weakness of the show lay in the fact that the coach was not portrayed as an individual, but rather as a saintly type, spouting undeniably good advice on all occasions."

EPISODE #72 **"JOHN YANKEE"** Broadcast on November 16, 1954
  Commercial entitled "The Important of the Plant Manager."
  Rebroadcast of episode #19, broadcast on June 10, 1953

EPISODE #73 "AMERICAN THANKSGIVING" Broadcast on November 23, 1954
    Starring: Ann Doran as Mother   Regis Toomey as Father
    Walter Coy as Abe Lincoln   Richard Gaines as George Washington
    Also in the cast: Larry Johns, Dick Rich, and Helen Van Tuyle.
    Based on the *Cavalcade* radio script "The Path of Praise" by George H. Faulkner.
    Story: As the colors of autumn stream down the wind, scarlet in sumac and maple, spun gold in the birches, a splendor of smoldering fire in the oaks along the hill, and the last leaves flutter away, and the dusk falls briefly, we are stirred and made to ponder the Infinite Goodness that has set apart for us, in all the moving mystery of creation, a time of living and a home. This is the history of Thanksgiving, from George Washington to Abraham Lincoln.

    Trivia: The original script title for this teleplay was "The American Thanksgiving - It's History and Meaning."

EPISODE #74 "ORDEAL IN BURMA" Broadcast on November 30, 1954
    Starring: Toni Gerry as Ann Judson   Donald Murphy as Adoniram Judison
    Richard Lee as the Governor   Noel Drayton as Gouger
    Story: The scene is Burma and the date is 1824, during the British-Burmese War. Medical missionary Adoniram Judison is caught between the two opposing armies, and finally is imprisoned by the Burmese forces.

EPISODE #75 "NIGHT CALL" Broadcast on December 7, 1954
    Starring: Dean Jagger as the doctor   Sheila Bromley as the doctor's wife
    Donald Murphy as the intern   Alyn Lockwood as the ex-GI
    Rita Walsh as the nurse   Nancy Hale as the female patient
    Also appearing in the cast was Paul E. Burns.
    Story: The camera follows a small-town doctor through the day and reveals the excitement and drama of the daily life of a general practitioner. A contemporary drama of a doctor's fight to save an ex-GI from dying of an unknown disease.

    Trivia: Leaving the area of historical dramas at this point, *Cavalcade*'s first "modern" film chose to memorialize the American doctor, genial practitioner variety. Originally, this drama was entitled "The Doctor," but changed to "Night Call" before broadcast. Dean Jagger, an Academy Award winner for his adjutant role in *Twelve O'clock High*, made his first filmed television appearance on this *Cavalcade* broadcast.

EPISODE #76 "A MEDAL FOR MISS WALKER" Broadcast on December 14, 1954
    Starring: Maura Murphy as Mary Walker   Frank Ferguson as Dr. Green
    Roy Rogers as Col. Carson   Hugh Sanders as Gen. Bragg
    Walter Reed as Captain Marsh
    Based on the *Cavalcade* radio play of the same name by Irve Tunick.
    Commercial entitled "Unfinished Business in Scientific Research."
    Story: Mary Edwards Walker was the only woman to receive the Medal of Honor, the highest military award given by the United States government. While serving as a surgeon with the Union Army during the Civil War, she was captured and held for four months in a Confederate prison. She was later exchanged for a Confederate officer. It was because of this she was awarded the Medal of Honor. Why? Because when the Confederates arrived, she refused to leave her patients and insisted on being taken captive with them.

EPISODE #77 "THE GINGERBREAD MAN" Broadcast on December 21, 1954
    Rebroadcast of episode #15, broadcast on April 15, 1953

EPISODE #78 **"A MAN'S HOME"** Broadcast on December 28, 1954
    Starring: Ross Elliott as James Otis   Hillary Brooke as Mrs. Otis
    Dorothy Green as Mercy Warren
    Commercial entitled "Dragon Fur"
    Story: James Otis, a Boston lawyer serving as advocate-general to the British crown just prior to the Revolution, resigned just prior in protest against the illegal invasion of American homes.

EPISODE #79 **"THE MARINE WHO WAS 200 YEARS OLD"** Broadcast January 4, 1955
    Starring: Ward Bond as Sgt. Lou Diamond   John Cuff as the medical officer
    Larry Winter as M.P.   John McGovern as Pfc. Bob Wardelle
    Gregg Palmer as Captain Collins   Mary Alan Hokanson as the Nurse
    Based on the *Cavalcade* radio script of the title by Robert Mason Pollock.
    Story: The true dramatization of Loud Diamond, a sixty-year old combat Marine, and an indestructible leatherneck. The events in the life of this M/Sgt. proved that age did not matter, when he couldn't be stopped.

EPISODE #80 **"A ROMANCE TO REMEMBER"** Broadcast on January 11, 1955
    Rebroadcast of episode #4, broadcast on November 12, 1952

EPISODE #81 **"A MESSAGE FROM GARCIA"** Broadcast on January 18, 1955
    Starring: Donald Murphy as Lt. Andrew Rowan
    Peter Mamakos as Major Wagner   Salvador Baguez as General Garcia
    Also in the cast: Cheryl Callaway, Alberto Mariscal, Alex P. Montoya, George Navarro, Vincent J. Pelletier, James Seay, Jonathan Seymour, Randy Stuart, Phil Tend, James Todd, and Murvyn Vye.
    Based on the *Cavalcade* radio script "Mission to Cuba" by Halsted Welles, and adapted for *Cavalcade* television by Charles Larson.
    Directed by William J. Thiele.
    Filmed at Chertok Productions, studio contract dated October 9, 1953.
    Story: Lt. Andrew Rowan accepted one of the toughest assignments ever handed out by our Military Intelligence. His was the task of bringing a message from the United States Government to General Garcia, leader of the Cuban rebels, just before the then imminent Spanish-American War. Rowan had never been to Cuba; he did not speak the language of the country and he was to proceed without any idea as to the whereabouts of the rebels, and without identifying credentials in case of arrest.

EPISODE #82 **"PETTICOAT DOCTOR"** Broadcast on January 25, 1955
    Starring: Willis Bouchey as Dr. Evan Morgan   Minerva Urecal as Mrs. Creel
    Betty Caulfield as Dr. Emily Blackwell   Edgar Buchanan as Horace Greeley
    Paula Raymond as Dr. Elizabeth Blackwell
    Commercial entitled "Du Pont Quality Control"
    Story: Dr. Elizabeth Blackwell is befriended by New York newspaperman Horace Greeley in her struggle to obtain recognition and respect for professional women. Dr. Blackwell was the nation's first woman doctor.

EPISODE #83 **"TAKE OFF ZERO"** Broadcast on February 1, 1955
    Starring: Lamont Johnson as Marine Corps Col. Joseph Coleman
    Marjorie Lord as Lee Powell Coleman   Edgar Dearing as Fitz
    Steve Pendleton as Beecher   James Seay as Lt. Wells
    Also in the cast: James Flavin, John Holbrook, Nelson Leigt, Fred Libbey, Alyn Lockwood, and Rory Mallinson.
    Written for *Cavalcade* television by Harold Shumate.
    Produced by Jack Denove and directed by Charles Bennett.   **(cont'd)**

Filmed at Jack Denove Studios, studio contract dated August 20, 1954.
Story: These are the true events of Marine Corps Lt. Col. "Skeets" Coleman, who was assigned to the then top-secret "flying pogo" plane, an experimental model. Coleman made the first test run in the Navy's specially designed plane that took off horizontally instead of vertically.

EPISODE #84 "NEW SALEM STORY"   Broadcast on February 8, 1955
Rebroadcast of episode #10, broadcast on February 4, 1953

EPISODE #85 "DECISION FOR JUSTICE"   Broadcast on February 15, 1955
Starring: Jeff Morrow as John Marshall
Commercial entitled "Film: Today's Explorer"
Also in the cast: Marilyn Erskine, Marjorie Lord, and Dayton Lummis
Story: In honor of the 200th anniversary of Chief Justice John Marshall's birth, the story of his part in the establishment of the American judicial system is told.

EPISODE #86 "THE HOSTAGE"   Broadcast on February 22, 1955
Starring: Glenn Langan as Captain Richard Stobo
Also in the cast: Peter Adams, Paul Bryar, Peter Cainlio, Iron Eyes Cody, Suzanne Dalhart, Claudia Drake, Abel Fernandez, Laurette Luez, Maurice Marsac, Eugene O. Roth, Paul Sorensen, George Spaulding, Leoin Sullivan, and Phil Tread.
Written for *Cavalcade* by Harold Shumate.
Produced by Jack Denove and directed by Charles Bennett.
Commercial entitled "Miracle of the 20th Century."
Filmed at Jack Denove Studios, studio contract dated October 7, 1953.
Story: Captain Richard Stobo, of the Virginia Militia, is given as a hostage in the surrender of Fort Necessity. This is the story of his daring action during the French-Indian attacks, prior to the Revolutionary War.

EPISODE #87 "WHAT MIGHT HAVE BEEN"   Broadcast on March 1, 1955
Commercial entitled "Petroleum Research Helps Bring You Better Fuels."
Rebroadcast of episode #9, broadcast on January 21, 1953

EPISODE #88 "THAT THEY MAY LIVE"   Broadcast on March 8, 1955
Starring: Booth Coleman as Dr. Abraham Jacobi
Emilyn Davies as Dr. Mary Putnam Jacobi
Also in the cast: Peter Adams, Louise Arthur, Claire Du Brey, Paul Harvey, Louis Jean Heydt, John F. Holbrook, Natalie Norwick, William Pullen, Norbert Schieles, Fred E. Sherman, and Stephen Wootten.
Written for *Cavalcade* television by Gwen Bagni.
Produced by Jack Denove and directed by Robert Stevenson.
Commercial entitled "Your Test of a Trademark."
Filmed at Jack Denove Studios, studio contract dated August 20, 1954.
Story: Dr. Abraham Jacobi and his doctor-wife wage a battle against prejudice in an attempt to gain special treatment for sick children. Dr. Jacobi believed the treatment of children's diseases should be a separate branch of medicine. His wife, Mary, worked with him to lay the groundwork for the modern science of pediatrics.

Trivia: This episode was broadcast on the ABC Network only, March 8, and not on spot channels from March 9 to 14, like the other broadcasts.

EPISODE #89 **"MAN ON THE BEAT"** Broadcast on March 15, 1955
    Starring: William Campbell as Off. Clyde Bannon   Constance Ford as Mrs. Bannon
    Harry Lauter as Ray Marshall   Vincent Padula as counterman
    Len Lesser as the prisoner   Richard Crane as Fred Gage
    Sara Harte as Joyce Leonard   Stacy Keach as the sergeant
    Hal Baylor as the lumberjack   Joe McTurk as newsstand operator
    Commercial entitled "The Deep Freeze Suit"
    Story: A typical day in the life of a big-city policeman. We follow a big-city policeman through a normal day and see the various duties he must perform. A day of danger in which a killer is hunted and a day of service in which he does his assigned job.

    Trivia: This film was produced with the aid of the Los Angeles Police Department.

EPISODE #90 **"ALL'S WELL WITH LYDIA"** Broadcast on March 22, 1955
    Commercial entitled "Our Improved Standards of Living"
    Rebroadcast of episode #2, broadcast on October 15, 1952

    Trivia: This episode was broadcast on the ABC Network only, March 22, and not on spot channels from March 23 to 28.

EPISODE #91 **"THE SHIP THAT SHOOK THE WORLD"** Broadcast on March 29, 1955
    Starring: Alex Gerry as John Ericsson   Carl Benton Reid as C.H. Bushnell
    Robert Warwick as Gideon Welles   Lumsden Hare as Commodore Smith
    Carleton Young as Commodore Davis   Richard Hale as President Lincoln
    Based on the *Cavalcade* radio script entitled "Man of Iron" by Robert L. Richards and Robert Tallman, originally broadcast on July 13, 1942.
    Commercial tells how chemical science combined sand and imagination, and came up with an important new product, "Ludox" colloidal silica.
    Story: When the Civil War broke out the Federal Government learned, to its great dismay, that the Confederates were building an iron-clad ship, the Merrimac, which promised to sweep the Union Navy from the seas. John Ericsson, one of the greatest inventors of the nineteenth century, came forward and offered to build, in the incredibly short period of one hundred days, a vessel that would destroy the Merrimac. Ericsson's "Cheesebox on a Raft" appeared and engaged the new menace in successful battle. Ericsson had introduced a basic new principle of naval warfare to the world.

    Trivia: In Connecticut, "The Ship That Shook the World" was originally scheduled for WNHC-TV in New Haven on March 31. It was not presented. In its place, WNHC-TV carried "A Man's Home" as a special preview for one of the commercials. A commercial entitled "Letter to a Child" was broadcast on this station with "A Man's Home" to test out the viewers' response. Other television stations in the New Haven area showed "The Ship That Shook the World" as scheduled.

    The commercial "Letter to a Child" introduced what might be called a primer of Du Pont's man-made fibers. Bill Radebaugh of the Public Relations Department created it especially for a girl whose third grade class was studying clothing. It was a simplified description of how our new textile fibers contribute to today's better living.

EPISODE #92 **"NO GREATER LOVE"** Broadcast on April 5, 1955
    Commercial entitled "How Are We Doing?"
    Rebroadcast of episode #6, broadcast on December 10, 1952

Pictured above is an artist's perception of the *Cavalcade of America* television series. Sketched in 1957, the picture features: (listed clock-wise) Rev. Bob Richards as himself from "Leap to Heaven," Michael Landon and Harry Townes from "The Man From St. Paul," Peter Reynolds as Nicolo from "The Two Worlds of Nicolos," Caroline Craig as Billie Davis from "The Hobo Kid," Skip Homeier as Jacob Shazier from "The Return of the Bombardier," John McIntire as Johnny Appleseed from "Wild April," and Susan Kohner from "Bed of Roses."

EPISODE #93 **"THE GIFT OF DR. MINOT"** Broadcast on April 12, 1955
    Starring: Walter Coy as Dr. George Minot   Aline Towne as Marion Minot
    Phyllis Coates as Barbara Leland   Richard Erdman as Harry Jordan
    Noel Toy as Mrs. Nomura
    Story: Dr. George Minot is a diabotic who won the 1934 Nobel Prize for his contribution to the development of a cure for pernicious anemia. Neglecting his own health in an effort to find a cure for pernicious anemia. Life of Dr. George R. Minot, 1934 Nobel Laureate in Medicine for his liver treatment of anemia.

    Trivia: For the year 1954, Du Pont had again won the National Safety Council Award. This was the eleventh time that the Company had been so honored. Presentation of the award to Mr. C.H. Greenewalt was shown on the network telecast of this broadcast.

EPISODE #94 **"THE INDOMITABLE BLACKSMITH"** Broadcast on April 19, 1955
    Rebroadcast of episode #14, broadcast on April 1, 1953

EPISODE #95 **"HOW TO RAISE A BOY"** Broadcast on April 26, 1955
    Starring: Paul Kelly, Erin O'Brien-Moore, Gordon Gilbert, and Tommy Ivo.
    Written for *Cavalcade* by Edith Somner and Robert Soderberg.
    Story: A childless farm couple takes a city orphan under its wing.

EPISODE #96 **"STAY ON, STRANGER"** Broadcast on May 3, 1955
    Starring: Peggy Converse as Ann Robertson   Lon Chaney, Jr. as John Cockrill
    Edgar Buchanan as Lem
    Based on the *Cavalcade* radio script "Frontier Widow" by Agnes Eckhardt and Priscilla Kent.
    Story: When Ann Robertson's husband was killed by the Indians, she and her three young daughters joined a small pioneer band that was preparing to leave Fort Caswell for the Cumberland Bluffs in the Territory of Tennessee. She felt certain she could earn her place with the settlers by teaching their children and helping the other women, but she had to reckon with John Cockrill. As one of the leaders of the expedition, he did not believe that pioneer settlements needed education or that a widow with children should undertake such a dangerous journey. A surprise Indian attack gave Ann a chance to prove she was more of a help than a hindrance to the colony.

EPISODE #97 **"SUNRISE ON A DIRTY FACE"** Broadcast on May 10, 1955
    Starring: Jack Kelly as James E. West
    Also in the cast: Lois Collier and Peter Reynolds
    Story: Half a century ago a young attorney named James E. West became interested in juvenile delinquents. and his efforts to help them.

    Trivia: Another repeat test in New Haven was conducted this week (see episode 91). This time, a repeat of "The Marine Who Was 200 Years Old" was broadcast with a commercial entitled "Your Test of a Trademark." That commercial won favorable reviews from viewers and was later added to a different broadcast later in the series.

EPISODE #98 **"EXPERIMENT AT MONTICELLO"** Broadcast on May 17, 1955
    Rebroadcast of episode #12, broadcast on March 4, 1953

EPISODE #99 **"SIX HOURS TO DEADLINE"** Broadcast on May 24, 1955
    Starring: John McIntire as Tom Geary   King Donovan as Paul Jordan
    Will Wright as Will Barton   Sara Haden as Jenny Smith
    Forrest Taylor as Mr. Forrest   **(cont'd)**

Story: The managing editor of a small-town newspaper, is faced with a difficult problem. From behind the iron curtain comes the news that the daughter of a respected college professor has made unflattering remarks about her former home town. She has chosen the life of Communism and the hard choice of reporting falls on his shoulder as he doesn't want to hurt his friend - but he'll be choosing the other side if he doesn't.

EPISODE #100 **"SLATER'S DREAM"** Broadcast on May 31, 1955
Rebroadcast of episode #17, broadcast on May 13, 1953

EPISODE #101 **"THE PALMETTO CONSPIRACY"** Broadcast on June 7, 1955
Starring: Richard Hale as Abe Lincoln   Rhys William as Pinkerton
Also in the cast: Dorothy Bruce, Joseph Greene, Howard Neyley, Byron Palmer, John Pickard, Lonie Pierce, Vic Rodman, Piene Watkin, and Rush Williams.
Based on the *Cavalcade* radio script "The Pinkerton Man" by Russell S. Hughes, and adapted for *Cavalcade* television by Charles Bennett.
Produced by Jack Denove and directed by Charles Bennett.
Filmed at Jack Denove Studios, studio contract dated August 20, 1954.
Story: In 1850, Allan Pinkerton, an American detective, established one of the first detective agencies in the United States. He first won fame for exposing the activities of a band of counterfeiters. In 1861, Pinkerton guarded Abraham Lincoln as he journeyed from Springfield, Ill., to Washington D.C., to be inaugurated as President. His accomplishments also include smashing several Western gangs. His earliest "Wild West" case ended with the capture of the Reno brothers, a gang of train robbers.

EPISODE #102 **"THE PIRATE'S CHOICE"** Broadcast on June 14, 1955
Rebroadcast of episode #18, broadcast on May 27, 1953

EPISODE #103 **"THE RESCUE OF DR. BEANES"** Broadcast on June 21, 1955
Starring: Donald Murphy, Paula Raymond, Christopher Dark, and Griff Barnett
Based on *Cavalcade* radio script "Stephen Foster" by John Driscoll and Robert Tallman.
Commercial entitled "The Private File of a Salesman"
Story: Although Stephen Collins Foster began his career as a bookkeeper, he was soon spending all his time and energy at song writing. While in the midst of a rescue attempt, Stephen Foster was captured and imprisoned. These are the events leading up to his composition of the "Star Spangled Banner."

Trivia: This was final episode of the season. *Cavalcade* would return officially in September to begin its newest season. Some stations across the country decided to present rebroadcasts of previous episodes to fill the time slot, until new episodes were made available in the fall. Other stations decided to broadcast a different television program until the fall. In Baltimore, Maryland, for example, the ZIV Productions *Science Fiction Theatre* took *Cavalcade*'s time slot.

EPISODE #104 **"A MAN'S HOME"** Broadcast on July 6, 1955
Commercial entitled "Shopping Made Easier."
Rebroadcast of episode #78, with a different commercial, broadcast December 28, 1954

Trivia: For the summer of 1955, no new episodes were featured. Instead, reruns of previous broadcasts were shown every other week until the new season would pick up in the fall. This was the first of the summer season.

EPISODE #105 **"PETTICOAT DOCTOR"** Broadcast on July 20, 1955
Commercial entitled "New Adventures in Film."
Rebroadcast of episode # 82, with a different commercial, broadcast January 25, 1955

EPISODE #106 **"THE GREAT GAMBLE"** Broadcast on August 3, 1955
Rebroadcast of episode #66, broadcast on October 5, 1954

EPISODE #107 **"MOONLIGHT WITNESS"** Broadcast on August 17, 1955
Rebroadcast of episode #70, broadcast on November 2, 1954

EPISODE #108 **"THAT THEY MAY LIVE"** Broadcast on August 31, 1955
Rebroadcast of episode #88, broadcast on March 8, 1955

EPISODE #109 **"THE HOSTAGE"** Broadcast on September 6, 1955
Rebroadcast of episode #86, broadcast on February 22, 1955

EPISODE #110 **"A TIME FOR COURAGE"** Broadcast on September 13, 1955
Starring: Hugh Beaumont as Jack Cody   Gloria Talbot as Nancy Merki
Noreen Corcran as Nancy
Story: Nancy Merki was a gallant little girl crippled by polio and Jack Cody the coach of the famous Multnomah, Oregon girls' swimming team. Cody taught the little girl to swim and helped her overcome her disability and, eventually, to represent the United States in the 1952 Olympic games. He felt keenly the disappointment of not being picked as coach of that team, but four years later Jack Cody was called out of retirement to fulfill his lifelong ambition, and named coach of the Olympic women's swimming team for 1956. She was the 1948 Olympic swimming star, and her battle against polio.

Trivia: Although "A Time for Courage" was the original title presented during the opening credits and listings, the script lists "The Nancy Merki-Jack Cody Story" as the alternative title.

More Trivia: This was the first show in a new series succeeding *Cavalcade of America*. Now as *DuPont Presents the Cavalcade Theatre*, and as before, it still concentrated on dramatizing events from American history. But unlike the older show, it would concentrate on fairly recent events.

EPISODE #111 **"DECISION FOR JUSTICE"** Broadcast on September 20, 1955
Rebroadcast of episode #85, broadcast on February 15, 1955

EPISODE #112 **"THE TEXAS RANGER"** Broadcast on September 27, 1955
Starring: Jim Davis as Jim Armstrong   William Talman as Wesley Hardin
Produced by Jack Denove.
Commercial entitled "Fundamental Research."
Filmed by Jack Denove Productions.
Story: Texas Ranger Jim Armstrong is faced with the task of escorting Wes Hardin, a known killer, across four states to stand trial for murder. Hardin boasts that friends of his are waiting to rescue him, and Jim finds that no one will accompany him on the dangerous task.

EPISODE #113 **"TOWARD TOMORROW"** Broadcast on October 4, 1955
Starring: James Edwards as Bunche (as a man)   Ruby Goodwin as grandmother
McHenry Norman as Bunche (as a boy)   Also in the cast: Maidie Norman
Written for *Cavalcade* television by Joel Murcott.
Produced by Warren Lewis.
Filmed at Four Star Productions.

(cont'd)

EPISODE #106 **"THE GREAT GAMBLE"** Broadcast on August 3, 1955
Rebroadcast of episode #66, broadcast on October 5, 1954

EPISODE #107 **"MOONLIGHT WITNESS"** Broadcast on August 17, 1955
Rebroadcast of episode #70, broadcast on November 2, 1954

EPISODE #108 **"THAT THEY MAY LIVE"** Broadcast on August 31, 1955
Rebroadcast of episode #88, broadcast on March 8, 1955

EPISODE #109 **"THE HOSTAGE"** Broadcast on September 6, 1955
Rebroadcast of episode #86, broadcast on February 22, 1955

EPISODE #110 **"A TIME FOR COURAGE"** Broadcast on September 13, 1955
Starring: Hugh Beaumont as Jack Cody   Gloria Talbot as Nancy Merki
Noreen Corcran as Nancy
Story: Nancy Merki was a gallant little girl crippled by polio and Jack Cody the coach of the famous Multnomah, Oregon girls' swimming team. Cody taught the little girl to swim and helped her overcome her disability and, eventually, to represent the United States in the 1952 Olympic games. He felt keenly the disappointment of not being picked as coach of that team, but four years later Jack Cody was called out of retirement to fulfill his lifelong ambition, and named coach of the Olympic women's swimming team for 1956. She was the 1948 Olympic swimming star, and her battle against polio.

Trivia: Although "A Time for Courage" was the original title presented during the opening credits and listings, the script lists "The Nancy Merki-Jack Cody Story" as the alternative title.

More Trivia: This was the first show in a new series succeeding *Cavalcade of America*. Now as *DuPont Presents the Cavalcade Theatre*, and as before, it still concentrated on dramatizing events from American history. But unlike the older show, it would concentrate on fairly recent events.

EPISODE #111 **"DECISION FOR JUSTICE"** Broadcast on September 20, 1955
Rebroadcast of episode #85, broadcast on February 15, 1955

EPISODE #112 **"THE TEXAS RANGER"** Broadcast on September 27, 1955
Starring: Jim Davis as Jim Armstrong   William Talman as Wesley Hardin
Produced by Jack Denove.
Commercial entitled "Fundamental Research."
Filmed by Jack Denove Productions.
Story: Texas Ranger Jim Armstrong is faced with the task of escorting Wes Hardin, a known killer, across four states to stand trial for murder. Hardin boasts that friends of his are waiting to rescue him, and Jim finds that no one will accompany him on the dangerous task.

EPISODE #113 **"TOWARD TOMORROW"** Broadcast on October 4, 1955
Starring: James Edwards as Bunche (as a man)   Ruby Goodwin as grandmother
McHenry Norman as Bunche (as a boy)   Also in the cast: Maidie Norman
Written for *Cavalcade* television by Joel Murcott.
Produced by Warren Lewis.
Filmed at Four Star Productions.

(cont'd)

Story: The true, heart-warming story of the highest ranking American in the United Nations - Dr. Ralph Bunche. This tells of the relationship between Ralph Bunche and his grandmother, whose love, sacrifice and personal example provided the training that led him to high honors.

Trivia: Dr. Bunche himself cooperated in the planning and production of episode #113.

EPISODE #114 **"SIX HOURS TO DEADLINE"** Broadcast on October 11, 1955
Rebroadcast of episode #99, broadcast on May 24, 1955

EPISODE #115 **"DISASTER PATROL"** Broadcast on October 18, 1955
Starring: Steve Brodie, Robert Anderson, and Jean Ruth
Story: Steve Brodie stars in a tale of the Civil Air Patrol. A wartime flier has promised his wife he'd never fly again. But he is needed for a mercy mission.

EPISODE #116 **"SWAMP MUTINY"** Broadcast on October 25, 1955
Starring: Hans Conried as General Francis Marion   Paul Brinegar as Flint
Nancy Hadley as Nancy Croft   Ron Randall as Captain Stewart
Based on the *Cavalcade* radio script "The First Commando" by Alan Lomax and Peter Lyon.
Story: In the early days of the war, the world began to hear of brilliantly executed punitive raids against the enemy in occupied territories. From England came stories of the deeds of the Commandos. From Russia - stories of the Guerrillas. From the U.S., stories of the Marine Raiders, of the Army Rangers. But such bands of fighting men, and their methods of fighting, are not new in the history of the war. They are the latest of a long tradition . . . a tradition that began in America, with American soldiers, more than 170 years ago. These are the events of these first Commandos, of their General, Francis Marion, and of the courage of this band as it fought in the swamps of South Carolina.

EPISODE #117 **"CHAIN OF HEARTS"** Broadcast on November 1, 1955
Starring: Charles Bronson as John Staniszewski
Joyce McClusky as Dolly Staniszewski
Written for *Cavalcade* television by Frederic Brady.
Story: True story of merchant seaman John Staniszewski and his wife Dolly, and their efforts to gain citizenship here in the United States - experiences which rival anything fiction has to offer. It took them eight years and the aid of a "chain of hearts": many wonderful people, before they obtained the evidence which enabled John to become a citizen in 1954.

EPISODE #118 **"SATURDAY STORY"** Broadcast on November 8, 1955
Rebroadcast of episode #71, broadcast on November 9, 1954

EPISODE #119 **"ONE DAY AT A TIME"** Broadcast on November 15, 1955
Starring: James Daly as Bill   James Bell as Dr. Bob
John Litel as Dr. Silkworth   Eve March as Ann
Barbara Eiler as Lois   James Best as Harry
Hugh Sanders as Burton   Herbert Lytton as Jack
Jack Reitzen as the bartender   Nolan Leary as the minister
Sam Gilman as Charlie   Tyler McVey as man one
Robert Bice as man two   Edward Earle as man three
Napoleon Whiting as the colored man   Virginia Christine as the housewife
Charlotte Lawrence as the laughing girl
Teleplay by Larry Marcus, from the *Cavalcade* radio script "Thirst Without End."
Produced by Warren Lewis and directed by Laszlo Benedek.   **(cont'd)**

Filmed at Four Star Productions.
Story: The true story begins in 1934 when doctors tell a man named Bill that he'll die in six months unless he stopped drinking. Bill's home-life had become a nightmare and his promising career in the financial world halted by his illness. He had to stop drinking or die. And Bill found a way from his association with "Doctor Bob" and the organization that has helped many thousands - Alcoholics Anonymous.

EPISODE #120 **"AMERICAN THANKSGIVING"** Broadcast on November 22, 1955
Rebroadcast of episode #73, broadcast on November 23, 1954

EPISODE #121 **"CRISIS IN PARIS"** Broadcast on November 29, 1955
Starring: Howard St. John as Benjamin Franklin   Leslie Gray as Madeleine
Noel Drayton as Wentworth   Liam Sullivan as Andre Leray
Based on Dr. Morgan's *Cavalcade* radio script "Dr. Franklin Goes to Court."
Story: Dr. Franklin was the first American to achieve a world-wide reputation. When asked if he would serve as envoy to France he replied that his services could be worth but little - that he was like the end of a bolt of cloth on a merchant's shelf - "You may have me for what you will." But as America's Emissary in Paris, Ben Franklin managed to go to court and walk away with the treaties that ultimately resulted in the independence of the United States, and brought two young lovers together at the same time.

EPISODE #122 **"TAKE OFF ZERO"** Broadcast on December 6, 1955
Rebroadcast of episode #83, broadcast on February 1, 1955

EPISODE #123 **"DOCTOR ON WHEELS"** Broadcast on December 13, 1955
Starring: Lamont Johnson as Paul Shearer   Betty Lynn as Beth Shearer
John Deere as Bobbie Jeffers, Harry Wilcox as Dr. Banner, and Ike Jones as Charles
Story: Paul has dreamed of becoming a doctor since childhood. He and his young wife overcame family difficulties to enable him to finally enter medical school - and then polio robbed him of the use of his legs. It seemed as if his career was over. Then he devised a power-driven wheel chair which helped him get around freely by himself.

EPISODE #124 **"BARBED-WIRE CHRISTMAS"** Broadcast on December 20, 1955
Starring: Chuck Connors as Harry   Strother Martin as Wilkins
John Bryant as Fred
Adapted for *Cavalcade* television by Warner Law, from his *Cavalcade* radio script.
Story: The story of 4,000 American soldiers, all prisoners of war, who spent Christmas in a German prison camp, destined to attend a midnight mass, even though the Gestapo has forbidden it.

EPISODE #125 **"POSTMARK: DANGER"** Broadcast on December 27, 1955
Starring: Barry Atwater, Scott Forbes and Stacy Keach
Story: Swindlers have been approaching the parents of boys missing in Korea. They claim to be able to return the boys to their homes in exchange for a fee. A postal agent gets on the racketeers' trail, and helps smash their profitable business.

EPISODE #126 **"THE BOY WHO WALKED TO AMERICA"** Broadcast on January 3, 1956
Starring: Danny Chang as Little Joe   John Dennis as Sgt. Sam
John Stephenson as the Colonel   Hugh Beaumont as Father Werr
Tyler McVey as the Captain
Story: A Korean war orphan who learned of America's wealth from magazines around the Korean Army bases, was determined to share in it, even if it meant walking all the way to America. He did reach this country in time, but from Sergeant Sam, Chaplain Werr and the others who helped him on his way.

EPISODE #127   "NIGHT CALL"   Broadcast on January 10, 1956
Rebroadcast of episode #75, broadcast on December 7, 1954

EPISODE #128   "THE PRISON WITHIN"   Broadcast on January 17, 1956
Starring: Gloria Talbott as Mary   Claire Carleton as Mrs. Carlson
Joi Lansing as Florence   Mark Damon as Bill
Ed Platt as Dr. Banner
Based on a story by David Dresser, and adapted for *Cavalcade* by John Meredyth Lucas.
Story: In the strange case of Mary Fletcher, a convicted forger, parole officer Edith Carlson gave sympathetic help to free the girl not only from the physical prison but from the mental turmoil that caused her to break her parole. The girl is overcome with remorse when the soldier she refused to marry is killed in Korea. Her unusual guilt complex leads her to commit a series of crimes, the cause of her imprisonment.

EPISODE #129   "STAR AND THE SHIELD"   Broadcast on January 24, 1956
Starring: Walter Sande as William Campbell   Cheryl Calloway as Margaret
Elizabeth Patterson as Mrs. Couche   Gordon Jones as Lt. Treusch
Also in the cast: Joi Lansing and Mark Damon
Based on the *Cavalcade* radio script of the same title by Irve Tunick.
Story: It might happen anywhere, in your town or mine. It actually happened in Union City in the fall of 1952. The New Jersey police force in Union City, under odd circumstances, adopted a little girl named Margaret Leone. During the months that followed, little Margaret Leone literally became a member of the Hudson County Motorcycle Police Corps. And the whole community took Margaret to its heart. Merchants dressed her like a princess. The Holy Family School enrolled her into kindergarten. And everybody repeated her bright little sayings.

EPISODE #130   "THE MARINE WHO WAS 200 YEARS OLD"   Broadcast January 31, 1956
Rebroadcast of episode #79, broadcast on January 4, 1955

EPISODE #131   "THE SECRET LIFE OF JOE SWEDIE"   Broadcast on February 7, 1956
Starring: Chick Chandler as Joe Swedie   Ed Platt as Terry
Linda Sterling as Ella   John Hensley as Andy
Story: Chicago-based Joe Swedie never forgot the yearning and need for love and attention of orphans and lonely little sick kids. Having been an orphan himself, Joe became a child-therapist who helped bed-ridden children in hospitals to retain an interest in life. Sometimes parents, not as perceptive as their children, questioned his motives. In this episode, one such parent began an investigation and learned an unusual, true story of unselfishness.

Trivia: In 1955, the Variety Club of Chicago voted Joe Swedie its "Man of the Year." This television story shows why.

EPISODE #132   "MAJOR PAULINE"   Broadcast on February 14, 1956
Rebroadcast of episode #35, broadcast on December 1, 1953

EPISODE #133   "CALL HOME THE HEART"   Broadcast on February 21, 1956
Starring: Teru Shimado as Koturo Sulo   Chiyoko Baker as Masa Sulo
Richard James as the newsboy   Donald Curtis as Pete
James Seay as Frank Catzentine   Kristine Miller as Jane Fisher
Roy Roberts as Carl Fisher
Story: The tale of a Japanese gardener, who, under the sponsorship of a pioneer civic leader, beautified the Miami Beach area with his imaginative planting of lush greenery. He eventually became one of the city's honored citizens.   **(cont'd)**

Trivia: "Call Home the Heart" entailed the use of a special production crew in Miami Beach. Filmed with the cooperation of the Miami Beach Chamber of Commerce and prominent members of the community, this broadcast featured the true story of how a Japanese-American repaid his country for the opportunities it gave him.

EPISODE #134 **"SMYRNA INCIDENT"** Broadcast on February 28, 1956
Rebroadcast of episode #42, broadcast on January 19, 1954

EPISODE #135 **"THE LISTENING HAND"** Broadcast on March 6, 1956
    Starring: Barbara Eiler as Mrs. Hathaway   John Craven as Mr. Harold Hathaway
    Edith Evanston as Mrs. Pipes   Ruth Lee as Nurse Edwards
    Nan Boardman as Mrs. Van   Morris Ankrum as Judge
    Arthur Space as Dr. Ellis   Tom Brown Henry as the editor (Mr. Lane)
    William Leicester as Collins   Aline Towne as the nurse
    Jack Daly as the man   Jack Carol as Lucas
    Eddie Ryder as Johnson   John Alvin as Mr. Brown
    Written for *Cavalcade* by Dick Carr.
    Story: This is the true story of the Hathaways, a young couple of parents who had serious physical handicaps. They were blind, deaf-mute parents and there was a great deal of doubt on the part of the public welfare agency that they could provide proper care for their newborn baby. The parents fought for the right to keep their own child, by proving their competence to a compassionate neighbor, a capable nurse, a spirited reporter and finally an understanding judge who was willing to consider things as they are, not as they might be.

EPISODE #136 **"BREAKFAST AT NANCY'S"** Broadcast on March 13, 1956
Rebroadcast of episode #28, broadcast on October 13, 1953

EPISODE #137 **"A LIFE TO LIVE BY"** Broadcast on March 20, 1956
    Starring: John Ericson as Leon Patterson   Sally Fraser as Dixie Patterson
    Russ Conway as Coach O'Brien   Chris Warfield as Joe Wilson
    Shirley Bernard as Betty Wilson   Alec Campbell as the doctor
    Written for *Cavalcade* by Laszlo Gorog.
    Story: A California schoolboy who, in spite of the knowledge that he has an incurable and fatal kidney disease, married and lived a happy, fruitful life together before death overtook him. Before he passed away, Leon somehow managed to set a new world's record for the high school shot-put.

    Trivia: Filmed on location at the University of Southern California campus where Leon Patterson lived with his pretty wife, Dixie.

EPISODE #138 **"MAN ON THE BEAT"** Broadcast on March 27, 1956
Rebroadcast of episode #89, broadcast on March 15, 1955

EPISODE #139 **"THE DOLL WHO FOUND A MOTHER"** Broadcast on April 3, 1956
    Starring: Cheryl Callaway as Kathy   Peggy Webber as Stella
    Mort Mills as Frank   Ross Bouchey as the Judge
    Scotty Morrow as John   Jeanette Nolan as Mrs. Corbitt
    Story: There is a unique public service agency which was founded in Los Angeles, California and has since become widespread. It is the Toy Loan Library where instead of books, children can borrow toys and learn to care for them properly. From one of these private libraries comes a true story of a lesson taught in love to a little girl and her family. It is the story of how a marriage was saved; and how the little girl learned that her step-mother really did love her.

EPISODE #140   "YOUNG ANDY JACKSON"   Broadcast on April 10, 1956
   Rebroadcast of episode #51, broadcast on March 23, 1954

EPISODE #141   "THE JACKIE JENSEN STORY"   Broadcast on April 17, 1956
   Starring: Jackie Jensen as himself   B.G. Norman as Jackie (age 13)
   Gary Gray as Jackie (age 17)   Ross Elliott as Coach Kerchum
   Vivi Janiss as Mrs. Jensen   Lorna Thayer as Miss Holmes
   Filmed by Four Star Productions.
   Commercial entitled "Competition."
   Story: Boston Red Sox outfielder and former football All-American Jackie Jensen stars in his biography. As a small boy in Oakland, although a natural athlete, Jackie was well on his way toward being a misfit until a school athlete instructor, Ralph Kerchum, took an interest in him. Ralph helped Jackie grow up, how to govern his temper, give him companionship that the fatherless boy learned for - and forced him to remember his goals in life.

EPISODE #142   "THE STOLEN GENERAL"   Broadcast on April 24, 1956
   Rebroadcast of episode #25, broadcast on September 2, 1953

EPISODE #143   "DIPLOMATIC OUTPOST"   Broadcast on May 1, 1956
   Starring: John Hudson as Ed Connors   Richard Loo as Ho Chung
   Cynthia Stone as Pat Connors   Willis Bouchey as Carver
   Bob Karnes as Saunders
   Story: A young Vice-Consul on his first foreign assignment finds himself put to the test. Ed Connors is Vice-Consul in Byaka where, on election eve, tension grips the city as a local strong-arm man makes a bid for power. Riots threaten American life and property. But when an epidemic breaks out among the native children, Connors' instinctive and quick action helped provide a dramatic climax and did the Consular Service proud. This is the story of the Far East, and how this young American diplomat and his wife coped with a polio epidemic and the threat of Civil War.

EPISODE #144   "DANGER ON CLOVER RIDGE"   Broadcast on May 8, 1956
   Starring: Robert Horton as Ranger Norm Keller   Ray Howell as Sheriff
   Howard Negley as Fred Lewis   Jean Howell as Mary Keller
   Harry Shannon as Pop Smith   Gordon Mills as Ben Johnson
   Story: The rangers who are in charge of this country's vast public forests do an important multi-faceted job. Guardians of the great areas of virgin country, they lead a life of responsibility and yet freedom such as is reminiscent of the early American West. Your introduction to one ranger and his activities during a forty-eight hour period during which we not only see the beauty of his domain, but also some of the scope of his work. Interwoven is a highly personal tale of a hunter who unwittingly starts a forest fire. A forest ranger works to clear the name of an eccentric guide who is suspected of robbery, attempted murder and arson.

EPISODE #145   "THE GIFT OF DR. MINOT"   Broadcast on May 15, 1956
   Rebroadcast of episode #93, broadcast on April 12, 1955

EPISODE #146   "WHO IS BYINGTON?"   Broadcast on May 22, 1956
   Starring: Henry Morgan as Byington   Dan Tobin as Graffon
   Tom Powers as Wilkeson   George Chandler as the proprietor
   Anthony Jochim as Trone
   Story: A quick-thinking reporter becomes an important factor in the rescue of hundreds of Union troops during the Civil War.

Trivia: Henry Morgan, who plays Byington, works with another Byington (Spring, that is) each week on television's *December Bride*.

EPISODE #147   **"SUNRISE ON A DIRTY FACE"**   Broadcast on May 29, 1956
Rebroadcast of episode #97, broadcast on May 10, 1955

EPISODE #148   **"THE MAJOR OF ST. LO"**   Broadcast on June 5, 1956
Starring: Peter Graves as Major Tom Howie   Nick Dennis as Sgt. Chiaco
Robert Cossen as Lt. Morgan   Ed Kemmer as Major Bingham
Morris Ankrum as General Gerhardt   Frank Gerstle as General Cota
Written for *Cavalcade* television by Al C. Ward.
Produced by Warren Lewis.
Commercial entitled "Fundamental Research."
Filmed by Four Star Productions.
Story: The Normandy invasion's greatest battle, the key victory in the Allied offensive. On the eve of the American attack on the German-held bastion, Major Tom Howie who had led his men through forty-one days of fierce fighting in the hedgerows of Normandy, was killed just before the assault on St. Lo. Howie had promised his men he would lead them into the city. And so loved was the Major that, even though dead, he did lead them in the dramatic, crushing attack.

EPISODE #149   **"STAY ON, STRANGER"**   Broadcast on June 12, 1956
Rebroadcast of episode #96, broadcast on May 3, 1955

EPISODE #150   **"DUEL AT THE O.K. CORRAL"**   Broadcast on June 19, 1956
Rebroadcast of episode #49, broadcast on March 9, 1954

EPISODE #151   **"HOW TO RAISE A BOY"**   Broadcast on June 26, 1956
Starring: Paul Kelly, Erin O'Brien-Moore, Gordon Gabert, and Tommy Ivo.
Written for *Cavalcade* by Edith Somner and Robert Soderberg.
Story: A childless farm couple takes a city orphan under its wing.

EPISODE #152   **"THE RESCUE OF DR. BEANES"**   Broadcast on July 3, 1956
Rebroadcast of episode #103, broadcast on June 21, 1955

EPISODE #153   **"SUNSET AT APPOMATTOX"**   Broadcast on July 10, 1956
Rebroadcast of episode #29, broadcast on October 20, 1953

EPISODE #154   **"MAN OF GLASS"**   Broadcast on July 17, 1956
Rebroadcast of episode #43, broadcast on January 26, 1954

EPISODE #155   **"G FOR GOLDBERGER"**   Broadcast on July 24, 1956
Rebroadcast of episode #41, broadcast on January 12, 1954

EPISODE #156   **"THE SHIP THAT SHOOK THE WORLD"**   Broadcast on July 31, 1956
Rebroadcast of episode #91, broadcast on March 29, 1956

EPISODE #157   **"THE FORGE"**   Broadcast on August 7, 1956
Rebroadcast of episode #69, broadcast on October 26, 1954

Trivia: *Cavalcade* was pre-empted, along with numerous other television programs, on August 14 and 21, due to Democratic and Republican Conventions.

EPISODE #158 **"DOCTOR ON WHEELS"** Broadcast on August 28, 1956
Rebroadcast of episode #123, broadcast on December 13, 1955

EPISODE #159 **"THE BOY WHO WALKED TO AMERICA"** Broadcast September 4, 1956
Rebroadcast of episode #126, broadcast on January 3, 1956

Trivia: This television film won a special award from the Freedoms Foundation "for outstanding service in bringing about a better understanding of the American way of life."

EPISODE #160 **"THE PRISON WITHIN"** Broadcast on September 11, 1956

EPISODE #161 **"MONUMENT TO A YOUNG MAN"** Broadcast on September 18, 1956
Starring: Perry Lopez as Pete Salavedo   Michael Fox as George Wooley
Miguel Landa as Armando Castro   John Beradino as Julio Gonzales
Written for *Cavalcade* by A.I. Bezzerides.
Story: Armando Castro was a youth from the east side of Los Angeles, a tempestuous teaming area of many racial groups. As a superior athlete and high school hero, his ambition to work among and help the people of the area commanded respect. He was killed in a needless tragedy when trying to help the youth of this area. From this sprung an organization dedicated to his memory and to the work he wanted to do: The Armando Castro Memorial Scholarship Fund.

Trivia: This was the first episode of the new season (and what was to become the final season of the series). The title of the program changed once again, to *The DuPont Theatre*.

EPISODE #162 **"BED OF ROSES"** Broadcast on September 25, 1956
Starring: Susan Kohner as Lorrie
Also in the cast: Kathryn Card, Dick Foran, and Greta Granstedt
Commercial was entitled "Stretch Yarns."
Story: A charming and romantic story of a young girl on the verge of marriage. Lorrie wanted her approaching marriage to be something better than the dull and colorless life she thought her parents had. Surely, she believed, there must be romance and beauty for a marriage to endure. In the days before the wedding she began to learn what actually grows in the garden of love. An engaged girl disagrees with her parents about the kind of wedding ceremony she should have. She wants an elaborate church wedding; her parents insist on a simple home ceremony.

EPISODE #163 **"STAR AND THE SHIELD"** Broadcast on October 2, 1956
Rebroadcast of episode #129, broadcast on January 24, 1956

EPISODE #164 **"THE PEOPLE AND GENERAL GLANCY"** Broadcast on October 9, 1956
Starring: Minor Watson as General Glancy
Based on the *Cavalcade* radio script "Experiment in Humanity" by Morton Wishengrad.
Story: In the little town of Duluth, Georgia, a retired industrialist, A.R. Glancy, was persuaded by his daughter to build an urgently needed hospital in Duluth. Unfortunately, General Glancy was used to big city ways and he and the other people of Duluth had to learn to adjust to each other before the hospital became a reality. Then General Glancy discovered that it cost so much to maintain that he was forced to build a factory whose profits would support the hospital. All of this meant a lot to Duluth and its general pros and over five thousand babies that have been born in the hospital.

EPISODE #165   **"WILD APRIL"**   Broadcast on October 16, 1956
    Starring: John McIntire as Johnny Appleseed   Jessie White as Link Barren
    Based on the *Cavalcade* radio script "The Gift of Johnny Appleseed."
    Story: Dreaming of a place of his own, Link Barren turned West to wild, unsettled Illinois - with its vast stretches of unbelievably rich black soil. Passing through Ohio he paused at the farm of Fleming Greenup, and there fell in love with honey-haired Sally Greenup. But Sally, while deeply attracted to Link, had often heard of heartaches and toil which pioneer women endured. Her parents reminded her of the easy life offered by Ike Hyar, owner of the richest farm in the district. Knowing he had only his love and ambition to offer Sally, Link decided to leave. Enter Jonathan Chapman, the gentle, kindly man known as Johnny Appleseed. Through his sympathy and understanding, Johnny Appleseed offered Sally and Link the precious gifts of courage and truth, and faith in the future.

EPISODE #166   **"THE HOBO KID"**   Broadcast on October 23, 1956
    Starring: Caroline Craig as Billie Davis (child)   Penny Carpenter as Vi (child)
    Caroline Craig as Billie Davis (teen-ager)   Robert Foulk as Dad Roberts
    Melinda Plowman as Vi (teen-ager)   Adrienne Marden as Ma Roberts
    Story: Billie Davis was dissatisfied with her way of life. As daughter of an itinerant peddler, in town after town, Billie saw children on their way to school and longed to join them. But her parents didn't believe in school and never stayed in one place long enough. When they did settle done for a longer-than-usual period, Billie managed to attend her first school. After that, whenever they moved, Billie always managed to go to school. The story is a tribute to America's school teachers. The story of the daughter of migratory farm workers, and her stubborn fight to get her education.

EPISODE #167   **"DATE WITH A STRANGER"**   Broadcast on October 30, 1956
    Starring: Arthur Franz as Casimir Pulaski   Judith Braun as Julie
    Madge Blake as Mrs. Morrissey
    Filmed by Hawthorne Productions.
    Story: A young immigrant girl and a young lawyer meet in Philadelphia's Independence Hall. From then on it seems as if the spirits of George Washington and General Casimir Pulaski take a hand in the love affair as it progresses among the wonderful old historic spots in Philadelphia. The Australian girl is desperate because she is about to be deported from the U.S. She prays to George Washington for help and this results in a mysterious encounter with a man named Casimir.

    Trivia: A delightful romance, this film required the use of a special camera crew to photograph our national shrines in Philadelphia, Pennsylvania.

    More trivia: *Cavalcade* was pre-empted on the week of November 6, due to election results.

EPISODE #168   **"THE INNOCENT BYSTANDER"**   Broadcast on November 13, 1956
    Starring: Don Taylor as the reporter   Reba Tassell as Joan
    Story: A chain-of-events story about a newspaper reporter who is injured while investigating a neighborhood fight. Angered and upset because the injury could have been fatal and because the circumstances surrounding his involvement seem to refute his personal philosophy, he begins probing into the cause of the fracas to determine who was responsible. As clue succeeds clue the reporter learns many things about his neighbors and, more important, about himself - all leading to a surprising and yet charming denouement. You see, this newspaper reporter has lived his whole life believing in the biblical maxim of "As Ye Sow, so Shall Ye Reap." But he is seriously injured while investigating a juvenile gang fight, and he begins to lose his faith.

EPISODE #169 "WOMAN'S WORK" Broadcast on November 20, 1956
    Walter Brennan as Link Morley   Mary Murphy as Rowena Morley
    James Best as Slate Morley   Jane Darwell as Minna
    Written for *Cavalcade* by John Weaver.
    Filmed by Hawthorne Productions.
    Story: A comedy about a terrible-tempered old man and the slip of a girl who cuts him down to size and makes him like it. Link Morley has a habit of throwing anything he can put his hands on when he gets his ire up. When his son, Slade, married lovely Rowena Thornton, the town sees Link throw a giant-sized tantrum. One thing Link can't stand is a woman who thinks she had some rights, especially if she is a Thornton. But Rowena thinks just that, although she has to butter a battle of wits for supremacy in the household.

EPISODE #170 "THE RETURN OF THE BOMBARDIER" Broadcast November 27, 1956
    Starring: Skip Homeier as Jacob Shazier   Bob Kino as Captain Kuto
    James Dobson as Sgt. Spatz   Don Kennedy as Lt. Farrow
    Jon Shepodd as Lt. Hays   Sue Carlton as Florence
    Story: Based on the true story of Jacob De Shazer, a young gunner on one of the courageous crews that flew with General Doolittle on his historic Tokyo raid in 1943. Forced to bail out, De Shazer and other crew members were captured. During his imprisonment in a Japanese P.O.W. camp, De Shazer was given a Bible. Never religious, he read and reread it for there was nothing else to do, and it was the words that enabled him to survive, and to vow, upon his release at the end of the war, to return to Japan as a missionary. And he did just that.

EPISODE #171 "IN PURSUIT OF A PRINCESS" Broadcast on December 4, 1956
    Starring: Brian Aherne as John Kirk   Fred Clark as Ollendorf
    Ida Moore as Miss Liz   Dick Elliott as Williams
    Paul Burns as Joseph   Percy Helton as Stevens
    Mary Lawrence as Ann   Oliver Blake as Detwiler
    Commercial entitled "The Voice of America."
    Filmed by Hawthorne Productions.
    Story: A whimsical comedy of two middle-aged antique collectors and their rivalry over an Indian princess. The princess is a wooden Indian of the cigar store variety, for these men collect wooden Indians. The wooden Indian princess they both want is owned by a destitute little old lady who likes both men but dislikes what their foolish rivalry is doing to them. She douses them with cold water and refuses to sell either of them her beloved Indian princess, even though she needs the money - and she plans to make them friends again.

EPISODE #172 "ONCE A HERO" Broadcast on December 11, 1956
    Starring: Ward Bond as Harvey Kendall
    Also in the cast: Richard Eyre and Ben Johnson
    Written for *Cavalcade* television by Jack Schaefer.
    Commercial entitled "Porcelain Enamel."
    Filmed by Hawthorne Productions.
    Story: A modern western about one Harvey Kendall, a man who in his youth had been the world's champion cowboy. The story is told against the background of a small western town rodeo in terms of a father, Harvey Kendall, and his small son. Egged on by circumstances, Harvey attempts to use the rodeo to prove his son that he is as good as ever at the game. He fails miserably, but out of this failure, the little boy learns a lesson and gains new respect for his father that is based on solid values.

EPISODE #173 "THE BLESSED MIDNIGHT"   Broadcast on December 18, 1956
    Starring: Maureen O'Sullivan as the aunt   Danny Richards, Jr. as Teddy
    David Saber as Billy   Carole Wells as Marilyn Hayes
    Frances Bavier as Mrs. Hayes
    Filmed by Hawthorne Productions.
    Story: Two little Irish-American boys, steadfast companions despite the fact that Billy enjoys a well-to-do, happy family life and Teddy is poor and miserable with a ruffian for a father. On Christmas Eve, Billy discovers unhappily, that he is to be featured in the procession at Midnight Mass. Teddy, desperately anxious to find a gift for an aunt, the one person whom he wants to love him, steals a bar mitzvah cake - because it is beautiful and he wants to give his aunt a beautiful gift. Billy speaks up for his friend and finds allies in a Rabbi and a Monsignor.

EPISODE #174 "THREE YOUNG KINGS"   Broadcast on December 25, 1956
    Starring: Nestor Paiva as Senor Alverez   Alma Beltram as Mrs. Diaz
    Edward Colmans as Senor Montoro
    Also in the cast: Tony Terry, Robert Hernandes, and Carlos Vera
    Story: A touching Christmas story based upon the Christmas custom in Latin American countries of distributing gifts twelve days after Christmas Day by men representing the Three Kings of biblical lore. Three young boys ride through the towns distributing gifts purchased by well-to-do families for their own children. But instead, the boys give the presents to the poor children. . . which causes a stir among the public.

EPISODE #175 "THE TWO WORLDS OF NICOLOS"   Broadcast on January 1, 1957
    Starring: Peter Reynolds as Nicolo   James Seay as Mr. Watson
    Sheila Bromley as Mrs. Watson   Gary Gray as John Sargent
    Susan Odin as Martha Watson   Joe Perry as William Dircks
    Inspired by the American Field Service Exchange Student program.
    Produced by Warren Lewis.
    Commercial entitled "Business Ownership."
    Filmed by Four Star Productions.
    Story: A sensitive Italian boy, Nicolo, selected by competitive examinations to visit the United States, lives with a typical American family. He spends a year as a senior student in an American High School. But Nicolo has personal problems which make it seem imperative that he return to Italy in the middle of the year. Torn between the fulfillment of his ambition and his family's need for him, Nicolo finds a solution that teaches him things about America - including the fact that this country has a big heart.

EPISODE #176 "THE HOUSE OF EMPTY ROOMS"   Broadcast on January 8, 1957
    Starring: Ann Harding as Margaret Milgrim   Ross Ford as Bill
    Helen Westcott as Christine   Carol Veazle as Hattie
    Robert Crosson as Ron   Beverly Long as Dilly
    Judith Ames as Carol
    Commercial entitled "Going Into Business."
    Filmed by Hawthorne Productions.
    Story: Margaret discovers that a large house that was once a happy home, is an empty shell when the husband is gone and the children have married and moved into homes of their own. Because she has the courage and ingenuity and wants to keep her life full, she opens her heart and home to a young musician and a teen-age girl. Before long, things are humming for Margaret and her house once more becomes a happy place in which to live.

EPISODE #177 "LEAP TO HEAVEN" Broadcast on January 15, 1957
    Starring: Rev. Bob Richards as himself (Adult)   Louise Arthur as the mother
    Hal Stalmaster as Bob Richards (as a child)   Gloria Castillo as Mrs. Richards
    Richard Tyler as Bob Richards (as a youth)
    James McCallion as Rev. Merlin Garber
    Produced by Warren Lewis.
    Commercial entitled "Porcelain Enamel."
    Filmed by Four Star Productions.
    Story: Bob Richards, the famed "pole-vaulting person," a young man who has represented the United States in three Olympiads, won the vaulting championship twice and holds the Olympic record for the event. This is the story of how this vital young man and of the Reverend Merlin Garber, the man who took an interest in Bob Richards the boy, who took him into his home, who inspired him and molded him into a man of great accomplishments.

EPISODE #178 "DOWRY FOR ILONA" Broadcast on January 22, 1957
    Starring: Oscar Homolka as Jeno Reinitz   Caroline Craig as Ilona Reinitz
    Based on the story of the same name by Al Martin, and adapted for *Cavalcade* by Laszlo Gorog.
    Commercial entitled "All Size is Relative."
    Filmed by Hawthorne Productions.
    Story: A cheap violin, the bombastic head of a Hungarian-American household, and a love affair combine to make this a delightful, amusing story. Jeno Reinitz rashly promised his daughter, Ilona, a dowry of fifteen hundred dollars. The solution to this problem revolved around the cheap violin and a prospective son-in-law who didn't intend to let old world ideas about dowries affect his marriage plans. At the same time the son-in-law was fully aware that the pride of Jeno had to be considered.

EPISODE #179 "THE MAN FROM ST. PAUL" Broadcast on January 29, 1957
    Starring: Harry Townes as John Norton   Michael Landon as Frank "Tex" Benson
    Bonnie Franklin as Alice Benson   Aline Towne as Katherine Fink
    Commercial entitled "Junior Achievement."
    Filmed by Chertok Productions.
    Story: Principal John Norton befriends a youngster who is accused of robbery, and obtains a parole for the boy. He even gets him a job as cashier in the school lunchroom. When money is stolen from the lunchroom, the boy becomes the number-one suspect, and Norton again comes to his assistance.

EPISODE #180 "ARE TREES PEOPLE?" Broadcast on February 5, 1957
    Starring: Ruth Donnelly as Mary Dolan
    The three children were played by Jean Howell, Ed Brophy, and Marjorie Bennett.
    Commercial entitled "Growth of a Nation."
    Filmed by Hawthorne Productions.
    Story: Soon after Mary Dolan went to live on the country with her married daughter she realized how much she missed the noisy friendliness of the city and it caused her to raise the question, "Are trees people?" Mary needed people around her, people to talk to. When on one of many secret excursions to her beloved Bronx, she met three frightened orphans and took them back to the country with her. She found the excitement, laughter and sense of being needed that she lacked. But she had no knowledge about the adoption laws, and took the children to her home without notifying the proper authorities.

EPISODE #181 "**DECISION FOR A HERO**" Broadcast on February 12, 1957
    Starring: John Ericson as Joe Loring   Joan Evans as Dianne Elton
    Lurene Tuttle as Mrs. Elton   Donald Freed as Lew Bradley
    Commercial entitled "National Electric Week."
    Filmed by Hawthorne Productions.
    Story: To most people, Joe Loring is just a typical big time athlete, but Joe has a private life which he successfully concealed for a long time. Joe Loring, a college football player, doesn't know it, but Dewey Elton, a fellow student, has been writing letters home saying that they are "best friends." When Dewey during his sophomore year, dies in the college hospital unexpectantly, his parents arrive on campus and want to talk about him with Joe. Joe decides to carry on with the deception for the sake of Dewey . . .

    Trivia: The working script title for this episode was "The All American."

EPISODE #182 "**THE FRIGHTENED WITNESS**" Broadcast on February 19, 1957
    Starring: Dan Duryea as Joe Kohler   Harold J. Stone as Craig
    Barbara Billingsley as Harriet Kohler   Ed Jerome as Doc Staples
    Christian Pasques as Jimmy   Wendy Winkleman as Betty
    Also in the cast: Herbert Rudley
    Commercial entitled "Lucite."
    Filmed by Hawthorne Productions.
    Story: The chairman of the Citizens Committee Against Crime is murdered by a gangster. Joe Kohler, the only witness to the hit-and-run murder, has to describe whether to remain silent and accept a payoff or identify the killer and risk the lives of himself and his family. His sense of personal freedom compels him to overcome the fear which force and threats have created, and to defy the racketeers.

EPISODE #183 "**THE BOY NOBODY WANTED**" Broadcast on February 26, 1957
    Starring: Johnny Crawford as Billy (as a boy)   Ron Hagerthy as Billy (as a man)
    Jean Inness as Martha Wheelock   Virginia Gregg as Mrs. Sherman
    Roy Barcroft as Mr. Wheelock   James Nolan as Nick Brandon
    Produced by Warren Lewis.
    Commercial entitled "Business is Creative."
    Filmed by Four Star Productions.
    Story: This true story began when a playful tussle between two small boys ended in a tragedy that left one dead and the other alone in an unfriendly world. Nine-year-old Billy Brandon had already been involved in another accidental death of a playmate. His father was in prison. No one wanted to take a chance on him until a childless farm couple opened their home and their hearts to him. Through their love Billy found a new life and in later years fully justified that love.

EPISODE #184 "**THE MAN WHO ASKED NO FAVORS**" Broadcast on March 5, 1957
    Starring: Lew Ayres as Matt Benham   Sandy Descher as Joanie Slade
    Rhodes Reason as Jacob Mott   Morris Ankrum as Peter Slade
    Whitney Blake as Sabina   Howard Wright as Orcutt
    Commercial entitled "Big League-Little League."
    Filmed by Hawthorne Productions.
    Story: Matt Benham, a newly arrived preacher, refuses to pray for rain even though the people of this backwoods community are suffering because of a prolonged drought. It is not drought, but the truth about themselves that the townspeople must face, and when Matt succeeds in leading the town to face the truth, he loses the one person who understands him.

Trivia: The original script for this drama was entitled "The Preacher Rebelled," but for reasons unknown, it was rejected and retitled "The Man Who Asked No Favors."

EPISODE #185 **"ONE DAY AT A TIME"** Broadcast on March 12, 1957
Commercial entitled "Voice of America."
Rebroadcast of episode #119, with a different commercial, broadcast on Nov. 15, 1955

EPISODE #186 **"DAN MARSHALL'S BRAT"** Broadcast on March 19, 1957
Starring: Patty McCormack as Trudy Marshall   Russ Johnson as Dan Marshall
Barbara Eiler as June Marshall   Paul Fix as Grandfather Barton
Written for *Cavalcade* by Warner Law.
Commercial entitled "All Size is Relative."
Filmed by Hawthorne Productions.
Story: A little girl from the East, Trudy Marshall, is enchanted with her new home in the West. Trudy saves the life of an old man who claims to be the Calaveras Kid, one of the old West's most infamous badmen. Then she finds out that the kid is pledged to kill her grandfather, Old Man Barton, who had disowned her parents. When Barton takes the water supply away from Trudy's father, the little girl finds a way to mend the rift between her father and Barton - and to stop the Calaveras Kid from carrying out his pledge.

EPISODE #187 **"THE WIDOW WAS WILLING"** Broadcast on March 26, 1957
Starring: Anne Jeffreys as Lucinda Teffy   Robert Sterling as Charles Jerrold
Jean Inness as Mrs. Spooner   Dee Carroll as Myrtle Jones
Commercial entitled "The Benefits of Productivity."
Filmed by Hawthorne Productions.
Story: An enjoyable comedy of manners played against the background of Cincinnati, 1868. Charles Jerrold, a nineteenth century writer who is always hungry, ill-clothed and out of paper, exists by writing letters for the residents of the squalid Strawberry Walk in sweeping Spencerian penmanship at four cents a piece. One of his steady - and most beautiful - customers is the prim young widow Teffy. The fun begins when the Widow Teffy decides that Charles is too shy to ask her to marry him and plans her moves accordingly.

EPISODE #188 **"THE LAST SINGER"** Broadcast on April 2, 1957
Starring: Kevin McCarthy as Frank O'Keefe   Vladimir Sokoloff as Jake Bartosh
Barbara Woodell as Miss Bronson   Brad Morrow as Jerry
Also in the cast: Lisa Montell
Written for *Cavalcade* television by Warner Law.
Commercial entitled "Pursuit of Air Safety."
Filmed by Hawthorne Productions.
Story: The whole town is outraged when a strange, new name is found signed to the City Hall's copy of the Declaration of Independence. A reporter, trying to get to the bottom of the story, finds not a jokester, but a serious old man and his beautiful daughter. The old man won't talk and the daughter doesn't trust the reporter, but in a dramatic courtroom scene the reporter arranged for everything to come out all right.

Trivia: This episode was originally scheduled for broadcast on March 12, but was pre-pre-empted for April 2 instead. A rebroadcast of a previous episode was aired in the March 12 time slot.

EPISODE #189 **"THE TEXAS RANGER"** Broadcast on April 9, 1957
Rebroadcast of episode #112, broadcast on September 27, 1955

EPISODE #190 "THE JACKIE JENSEN STORY" Broadcast on April 16, 1957
Rebroadcast of episode #141, broadcast on April 17, 1956

EPISODE #191 "THE SHARK ON THE MOUNTAIN" Broadcast on April 23, 1957
Starring: James Gleason as Noah   Richard Eyer as Brian Beck
Produced by Warren Lewis.
Commercial entitled "Business Gears."
Filmed by Four Star Productions.
Story: No one believed ten year old Brian when he said he overheard a man admit to murder. Even his best friend, old Noah, who was given to telling tall tales of his own, turned a deaf ear - but the killer knew, and thereby hangs a tale.

EPISODE #192 "CHICAGO 2-1-2" Broadcast on April 30, 1957
Starring: Frank Lovejoy as Ed McCook   Roy Thinnes as the boy
Tomi Thurston as Mickey   Franklyn MacCormack as Keno
Commercial entitled "Going Into Business."
Filmed by Hawthorne Productions.
Story: A firebug is loose in downtown Chicago and it is up to the Fire Inspector to track him down. Millions of dollars in property and many lives are in peril unless the arsonist is trapped quickly. The files of the Chicago Fire Department provided the story of the Inspector who thought of studying newsreel pictures of spectators at the fires until he thought he had the man spotted. Then his job really began - to track down the man and place him under arrest.

EPISODE #193 "DOWRY FOR ILONA" Broadcast on May 7, 1957
Commercial entitled "The Teacher Goes to School."
Rebroadcast of episode #178, with a different commercial, broadcast January 22, 1957

EPISODE #194 "ONCE A HERO" Broadcast on May 14, 1957
Rebroadcast of episode #172, broadcast on December 11, 1956

EPISODE #195 "IN PURSUIT OF A PRINCESS" Broadcast on May 21, 1957
Rebroadcast of episode #171, broadcast on December 4, 1956

EPISODE #196 "THE FRIGHTENED WITNESS" Broadcast on May 28, 1957
Commercial entitled "National Electric Week."
Rebroadcast of episode #182, with a different commercial, broadcast February 19, 1957

EPISODE #197 "THE MAJOR OF ST. LO" Broadcast on June 4, 1957
Rebroadcast of episode #148, broadcast on June 5, 1956

TELEVISION LISTING (ALPHABETICAL ORDER)

"The Absent Host" 3/2/54
"All's Well With Lydia" 10/15/52, 3/22/55
"American Thanksgiving" 11/23/54, 11/22/55
"And to Fame Unknown" 10/27/53
"Are Trees People?" 2/5/57
"The Arrow and the Bow" 1/7/53, 4/20/54
"Barbed Wire Christmas" 12/20/55
"Bed of Roses" 9/25/56
"The Betrayal" 7/22/53, 12/8/53
"The Blessed Midnight" 12/18/56
"The Boy Nobody Wanted" 2/26/57
"Boy Who Walked to America" 1/3/56, 9/4/56
"Breakfast at Nancy's" 10/13/53, 3/13/56
"Call Home the Heart" 2/21/56
"Chain of Hearts" 11/1/55
"Chicago 2-1-2" 4/30/57
"Courage in Connecticut" 6/22/54
"Crazy Judah" 4/13/54
"Crisis in Paris" 11/29/55
"Danger on Clover Ridge" 5/8/56
"Dan Marshall's Brat" 3/19/57
"Date With a Stranger" 10/30/56
"Decision for a Hero" 2/12/57
"Decision for Justice" 2/15/55, 9/20/55
"Diplomatic Outpost" 5/1/56
"Disaster Patrol" 10/18/55
"Doctor on Wheels" 12/13/55, 8/28/56
"The Doll Who Found a Mother" 4/3/56
"Dowry for Ilona" 1/22/57, 5/7/57
"Duel at the O.K. Corral" 3/9/54, 6/19/56
"Escape" 3/30/54
"Experiment at Monticello" 3/4/53, 5/17/55
"The Forge" 10/26/54, 8/7/56
"The Frightened Witness" 2/19/57, 5/28/57
"The Gentle Conqueror" 5/4/54
"G for Goldberger" 1/12/54, 7/24/56
"The Gift of Dr. Minot" 4/12/55, 5/15/56
"The Gingerbread Man" 4/15/53, 12/21/54
"The Great Gamble" 10/5/54, 8/3/55
"The Hobo Kid" 10/23/56
"The Hostage" 2/22/55
"The House of Empty Rooms" 1/8/57
"How to Raise a Boy" 4/26/55, 6/26/56
"The Indomitable Blacksmith" 4/1/53, 4/19/55
"The Innocent Bystander" 11/13/56
"In Pursuit of a Princess" 12/4/56, 5/21/57
"In This Crisis" 12/24/52, 2/23/54

"The Jackie Jensen Story" 4/17/56, 4/16/57
"John Yankee" 6/10/53, 11/16/54
"The Last Singer" 4/2/57
"Last Will of Daniel Webster" 8/19/53, 11/24/53
"Leap to Heaven" 1/15/57
"A Life to Live By" 3/20/56
"The Listening Hand" 3/6/56
"The Major of St. Lo" 6/5/56, 6/4/57
"Major Pauline" 12/1/53, 2/14/56
"The Man From St. Paul" 1/29/57
"Man of Glass" 1/26/54, 7/17/56
"Man on the Beat" 3/15/55, 3/27/56
"A Man's Home" 12/28/54, 7/6/55
"The Man Who Asked No Favors" 3/5/57
"Man Who Took a Chance" 10/29/52, 11/10/53
"Margin for Victory" 2/16/54
"Marine Who Was 200 Yrs. Old" 1/4/55, 1/31/56
"A Matter of Honor" 2/18/53, 6/15/54
"A Medal for Miss Walker" 12/14/54
"A Message from Garcia" 1/18/55
"Mightier Than the Sword" 3/18/53, 5/25/54
"Monument to a Young Man" 9/18/56
"Moonlight School" 5/18/54
"Moonlight Witness" 11/2/54, 8/17/55
"Mountain Man" 9/28/54
"Mr. Peale's Dinosaur" 12/29/53
"New Salem Story" 2/4/53, 2/8/55
"Night Call" 12/7/54, 1/10/56
"Night Strike" 4/29/53, 10/19/54
"No Greater Love" 12/10/52, 4/5/55
"Once a Hero" 12/11/56, 5/14/57
"One Day at a Time" 11/15/55, 3/12/57
"One Nation Indivisible" 7/8/53, 12/22/53
"Ordeal in Burma" 11/30/54
"The Palmetto Conspiracy" 6/7/55
"The Paper Sword" 4/27/54
"The People and General Glancy" 10/9/56
"Petticoat Doctor" 1/25/55, 7/20/55
"The Pirate's Choice" 5/27/53, 6/14/55
"Plume of Honor" 2/9/54
"Poor Richard" 10/1/52, 1/5/54
"Postmark: Danger" 12/27/55
"The Prison Within" 1/17/56, 9/11/56
"The Rescue of Dr. Beanes" 6/21/55, 7/3/56
"The Return of the Bombardier" 11/27/56
"Riddle of the Seas" 4/6/54
"Riders of the Pony Express" 12/15/53
"A Romance to Remember" 11/12/52, 1/11/55
"Sam and the Whale" 9/29/53

"Saturday Story" 11/9/54, 11/8/55
"The Secret Life of Joe Swedie" 2/7/56
"The Shark on the Mountain" 4/23/57
"Ship That Shook the World" 3/29/55, 7/31/56
"Six Hours to Deadline" 5/24/55, 10/11/55
"The Skipper's Lady" 6/8/54
"Slater's Dream" 5/13/53, 5/31/55
"Smyrna Incident" 1/19/54, 2/28/56
"Spindletop" 5/11/54, 10/12/54
"The Splended Dream" 3/16/54
"Star and the Shield" 1/24/56, 10/2/56
"Stay On, Stranger" 5/3/55, 6/12/56
"The Stolen General" 9/2/53, 10/6/53, 4/24/56
"A Strange Journey" 6/1/54
"Sunrise on a Dirty Face" 5/10/55, 5/29/56
"Sunset at Appomatox" 10/20/53, 7/10/56
"Swamp Mutiny" 10/25/55
"Take Off Zero" 2/1/55, 12/6/55
"The Texas Ranger" 9/27/55, 4/9/57
"The Tenderfoot" 6/24/53
"That They May Live" 3/8/55, 8/31/55
"Three Young Kings" 12/25/56
"The Tiger's Tail" 11/17/53
"A Time for Courage" 9/13/55
"A Time to Grow" 8/5/53, 11/3/53
"Toward Tomorrow" 10/4/55
"The Two Worlds of Nicols" 1/1/57
"What Hath God Wrought" 11/26/52, 2/2/54
"What Might Have Been" 1/21/53, 3/1/55
"Who is Byington?" 5/22/56
"The Widow Was Willing" 3/26/57
"Wild April" 10/16/56
"Woman's Work" 11/20/56
"Young Andy Jackson" 3/23/54, 4/10/56

BOOKS

In November of 1937, two years after *Cavalcade* premiered on radio, the Milton Bradley Company (then also a publishing company located in Springfield, Mass.), published a small 5 by 8 hard cover book entitled The Cavalcade of America. The dark blue cover pictured an imprint of a covered wagon pulled by oxen. The book featured three hundred pages of short stories, in text format, adapted from actual *Cavalcade* scripts. Edited by Dixon Ryan Fox (then President of Union College and President of The New York Historical Society) and Arthur M. Schlesinger (then President of History at Harvard University). The short stories were penned by numerous writers, many who wrote for *Cavalcade*. William Sanderson illustrated.

In September of 1938, Milton Bradley published another anthology, The Cavalcade of America, Series 2. This volume was almost a twin to its predecessor, only with a dark red cover instead of dark blue, and thicker - about three hundred and fifty-eight pages. Again, same editors, same illustrator. Both books featured a full-color book jacket, with pictures of Buffalo Bill, Benjamin Franklin, Nathaniel Bowditch, and Sarah Hale.

Although few radio scripts had been published in book form during the late thirties, Cavalcade was the first program to supply subject matter for two full volumes. Milton Bradley Company brought out the first volume in 1937, the second in 1938. Cavalcade was thus the first radio program to be used as a fully accredited text in American history. The Texas State Board of Education in 1940 purchased 40,000 copies of the first volume!

"We were indebted to the Du Pont Company for the generous co-operation we had received in publishing the collection of stories on dramatic sketches, presented over the radio as *The Cavalcade of America*," one figure from Milton Bradley wrote, "to the authors of the original stories, and to the historians who had collaborated to make this volume outstanding in its field for historical accuracy and interest."

Table of Contents:

The Cavalcade of America, published in November 1937, 300 pages.
Chapters:
1. "The Pine Tree Shilling" by Osmond Molarsky (previously broadcast on June 23, 1937) - page 3
2. "Benjamin Franklin" by Ann Barley (April 8, 1936) - page 23
3. "The Declaration of Independence" by Kenneth Webb (January 1, 1936) - page 34
4. "George Washington, The Farmer" by Katherine Seymour (April 28, 1937) - page 55
5. "Stars of Destiny" by Edward Longstreth (June 16, 1937) - page 76
6. "Steamboat Builders" by Edward Longstreth (June 24, 1936) - page 98
7. "The Golden Touch" by Edward Longstreth (April 21, 1937) - page 119
8. "Abraham Lincoln" by E.R. McGill, Dixon Ryan Fox and Kenneth Webb (Feb. 12, 1936) - page 138
9. "Samuel F.B. Morse" by Fairfax Downey and John T. W. Martin (December 16, 1936) - page 154
10. "Tillers of the Soil" by Edward Longstreth (May 13, 1936) - page 171

11. "The Story of Rubber" by Laurence Hammond (November 18, 1936) - page 195
12. "The Story of Dynamite" by Innis Osborn and John T.W. Martin (May 12, 1937) - page 215
13. "Luther Burbank" by Osmond Molarsky (June 30, 1937) - page 229
14. "P.T. Barnum" by Laurence Hammond (September 30, 1936) - page 246
15. "The Speed of Words" by Edward Longstreth (January 22, 1936) - page 266
16. "Transcontinental Journeys" by E.R. McGill (November 11, 1936) - page 283

The Cavalcade of America, published in September 1938, 353 pages.
Chapters:
1. "The Charter Oak" by Henry Fisk Carlton (previously broadcast on December 30, 1936) - page 3
2. "William Penn, and the Holy Experiment" by Edward Longstreth (October 13, 1937) - page 23
3. "The Story of the Constitution" by Kenneth Webb (December 8, 1937) - page 40
4. "Benjamin Franklin, the First American Citizen" by Mann Page (May 18, 1938) - page 63
5. "Junipero Serra - The Colonization of California" by Winifred Willis and John Driscoll (May 11, 1938) - page 85
6. "Thomas Jefferson, Pioneer in Education" by Edward Longstreth and Kenneth Webb (April 13, 1938) - page 102
7. "The Louisiana Purchase" by Edward Longstreth and Kenneth Webb (February 16, 1938) - page 120
8. "Nathaniel Bowditch, the Master Navigator" by Katherine Seymour (December 22, 1937) - page 136
9. "Francis Scott Key, the Story of the Star Spangled Banner" by John Driscoll (February 2, 1938) - page 154
10. "Heroes of Texas" by Edmund Robert McGill (June 17, 1936) - page 174
11. "Mary Lyon, Pioneer Woman Educator" by Katherine Seymour (October 6, 1937) - page 193
12. "Noah Webster, the Nation's Schoolmaster" by Ruth Adams Knight (February 23, 1938) - page 211
13. "Sarah Josepha Hale" by Ruth Adams Knight (November 24, 1937) - page 228
14. "Elizabeth Blackwell, Pioneer Woman Physician" by Ann Barley (January 27, 1937) - page 244
15. "Edwin Booth" by John Driscoll (September 29, 1937) - page 262
16. "John C. Fremont, the Pathfinder" by John Driscoll (January 26, 1938) - page 275
17. "Buffalo Bill" by Ruth Adams Knight (March 9, 1938) - page 291
18. "Edward Livingston Trudeau, the Beloved Physician" (December 15, 1937) - page 308
19. "Oliver Wendell Holmes" by John Driscoll (February 9, 1938) - page 324
20. "The Seeing Eye" by Ruth Adams Knight (November 17, 1937) - page 340

(More books on the next page)

In 1956, Crown Publishers, Inc. *and* the Lothrop, Lee and Shepard Publishing Com., Inc. released an 8 by 11 hardback entitled Cavalcade of America: The Deeds and Achievements of the Men and Women who Made our Country Great, edited by Carl Carmer, based on the broadcasts of *The Cavalcade of America* program. Prepared under the editorial supervision of Carl Carmer, all of the stories in the book were written especially for the publication, but were based on the original radio plays produced for and broadcast on the *Cavalcade* radio program, sponsored by E.I. du Pont de Nemours Co., Inc.

Many of the illustrations were full-color reproductions of portraits, and paintings of dramatic scenes by famous American artists - Gilbert Stuart, Benjamin West, Peale, Copley, Audubon, Whistler, Remington and many others. There were also engravings, etchings and drawings in wash and line. Two hundred illustrations in all, of which fifty were in full color. The book was 382 pages thick, with a United States flag imprinted on the front cover. A color book jacket was included. This book sold for $4.95 in the book stores.

Table of contents:
CREATORS OF THE NEW WORLD
THE SEEKERS
"The Discoverer" *Christopher Columbus* - page 13
"They Planted the Seed" *The Mayflower Compact* - page 18
"The Holy Experiment" *William Penn* - page 22
"Old Pegleg" *Peter Stuyvesant* - page 26
"A Passage to Georgia" *James Edward Oglethorpe* - page 29
"Colonizer of California" *Junipero Serra* - page 32

MAKERS OF THE REPUBLIC
"The Father of His Country" *George Washington* - page 34
"Farmer from Virginia and First President" *George Washington* - page 38
"Apostle of Freedom" *Thomas Jefferson* - page 42
"Scientist, Writer, Inventor" *Thomas Jefferson* - page 46
"The First American" *Benjamin Franklin* - page 50
"The Laziest Man in the World" *Benjamin Franklin* - page 54
"The Clarion Caller" *Patrick Henry* - page 58
"America's Most Famous Duel" *Alexander Hamilton* - page 61

PATHFINDERS FOR A NATION
"The Right to Petition" *John Quincy Adams* - page 66
"Old Hickory" *Andrew Jackson* - page 69
"Daniel Webster, Statesman" *Daniel Webster* - page 73
"The Great Compromiser" *Henry Clay* - page 77
"Honest Abe" *Abraham Lincoln* - page 81
"With Malice Toward None" *Abraham Lincoln* - page 86
"The President and the Calculated Risk" *Grover Cleveland* - page 92
"The Man Who Carried a Big Stick" *Theodore Roosevelt* - page 95

FREEDOM'S WARRIORS

THE FIGHTING MEN
"The Known Soldier" *Sergeant Curtis Culin* - page 101
"From Failure to Success in Three Sad Years" *U.S. Grant* - page 105
"Retreat to Victory" *Sam Houston* - page 109
"Water Girl" *Molly Pitcher* - page 113
"Our Country, Right or Wrong" *Stephen Decatur* - page 116
"The Victories at Manila Bay" *George Dewey* - page 121
"Father of the American Navy" *John Paul Jones* - page 126
"President Robert E. Lee" *Robert E. Lee* - page 130

THE PATRIOTS
"The Midnight Rider" *Paul Revere* - page 133
"The Battle Hymn of the Republic" *Julia Ward Howe* - page 138
"The National Anthem" *Francis Scott Key* - page 142

THE CHAMPIONS OF HUMAN RIGHTS
"Freedom of Worship" *Roger Williams* - page 145
"The Champion of Common Sense" *Tom Paine* - page 149
"He Led the Way to Reunion" *Horace Greeley* - page 153
"The Great Feminist" *Susan B. Anthony* - page 157

THE MEN OF VISION

THE EXPLORERS
"He Won the Pacific Northwest for the U.S." *Robert Gray* - page 163
"The Way West" *Lewis and Clark* - page 167
"The Pathfinder" *John C. Fremont* - page 171
"The Top of the World" *Robert E. Peary* - page 175

BREAKERS OF THE WESTWARD TRAIL
"The First Frontier" *Daniel Boone* - page 179
"Founding Father of Texas" *Stephen Austin* - page 183
"How to Find Gold" *John A. Sutter* - page 186
"He Led the Way" *Kit Carson* - page 189

PIONEERS IN SCIENCE
"The Man Who Understood Madness" *Benjamin Rush* - page 191
"The Epidemic Fighter" *Benjamin Waterhouse* - page 195
"The Master Navigator" *Nathaniel Bowditch* - page 198
"The Conquest of Pain" *William Morton* - page 201
"Doctor in Crinoline" *Elizabeth Blackwell* - page 205
"First American Woman Scientist" *Maria Mitchell* - page 207
"The Plant Wizard" *Luther Burbank* - page 211
"The Fight Against Yellow Fever" *Walter Reed* - page 214
"He Mapped the Mind of Man" *Harvey Cushing* - page 217

THE BUILDERS

THE INVENTORS
"The Inventor of Interchangeable Parts" *Eli Whitney* - page 223
"The Farmer Who Hated Harvest Time" *Cyrus McCormick* - page 228
"Inventor of the Telegraph" *Samuel F.B. Morse* - page 23
"From Flying Kites to Flying Machines" *Wilbur and Orville Wright* - page 236
"The First Flight" *Jean Pierre Blanchard* - page 241
"First Airman of the Army" *Thaddeus Lowe* - page 244
"Inventor of the Telephone" *Alexander Graham Bell* - page 248
"The Great Inventor" *Thomas A. Edison* - page 251

THE MEN OF ENTERPRISE
"First American World Trader" *Stephen Girard* - page 256
"The Tremendous Triffle" *Edwin Drake* - page 259
"The Greatest Show on Earth" *Phineas T. Barnum* - page 262
"The India-Rubber Man" *Charles Goodyear* - page 265
"He Drew the Nation Together" *Hiram Sibley* - page 268
"Powder for Progress" *Eleuthere Irenee du Pont* - page 272
"Pure and Sure" *Edward Robinson Squibb* - page 277
"Pioneer American Engineer" *James B. Eads* - page 280
"His Monument Is Under Water" *Clifford Holland* - page 284

PURSUERS OF THE AMERICAN DREAM

THE EDUCATORS
"The Nation's Schoolmaster" *Noah Webster* - page 291
"The Great Educator" *Horace Mann* - page 294
"Pioneer Woman Educator" *Mary Lyon* - page 297
"New Times, New Training" *Peter Cooper* - page 300
"Up from Slavery" *Booker T. Washington* - page 304

THE HUMANITARIANS
"Medicine's Great Friend" *Johns Hopkins* - page 308
"Angel of Mercy" *Clara Barton* - page 311
"Social Servant" *Jane Addams* - page 314

THE ARTISTS
"Novelist of Our American Scene" *James Fenimore Cooper* - page 317
"The Good Gray Poet" *Walt Whitman* - page 320
"The Birds of America" *John James Audubon* - page 324
"Museum Piece" *Charles Willson Peale* - page 330
"Pioneer in Painting" *James A. McN. Whistler* - page 333
"Recorder of the Last Frontier" *Frederic Remington* - page 337
"We'll Always Sing His Songs" *Stephen Collins Foster* - page 342
"The Tradition of Great Acting" *Edwin Booth* - page 345
"Champion of Humor" *Mark Twain* - page 349

APPENDIX

The Declaration of Independence is reprinted beginning on page 355.
The Constitution is reprinted beginning on page 359.
The Bill of Rights is reprinted beginning on page 365.
The Seals of the original thirteen colonies were reprinted on pages 369 and 370.

In 1958, Crown Publishers, Inc. and Lothrop, Lee and Shepard Company, Inc. published a second book based on the popular radio / television series. Again edited by Carl Carmer, this book was entitled A Cavalcade of Young Americans, subtitled "The Deeds and Achievements of Boys and Girls who Won a Place in Our Country's History." Howard Simon drew the color illustrations. This 8 by 11 hard cover edition was 260 pages thick with a dark blue spine, and dark red cover. 200 illustrations of which 50 were in full color.

Again, this book featured text adaptations of previous scripts, but this publication was aimed towards younger readers.

Contents:

1. "Pocohontas: First American Princess" by Mildred Smith Koskinen - page 11
2. "The Two Boys of Haverhill: Escape from the Indians" by Margaret Rockwell Finch - page 19
3. "Benjamin West: America's First Painter" by Anita Resko - page 28
4. "Nathan Beman: The Boy Guide at Fort Ticonderoga" - page 35
5. "Peter Francisco: The Virginia Giant" by Anne Gibson Sands - page 42
6. "Jemima Boone: She Outwitted the Shawness" by Jane Parker - page 48
7. "Mary Redmond: She Carried a Message" by Winifred Nies Northcott - page 55
8. "Three Patriots on Martha's Vineyard: They Saved the Liberty Pole" by Mildred Smith Koskinen - page 62
9. "Sybil Ludington: Her All-Night Ride to Rouse a Regiment" by Adele Smith - page 68
10. "The Drummer Boy: He Helped General Clark to Victory at Vincennes" by Anita Resko - page 75
11. "Betty Zane: Heroine of Fort Henry" by Hilda L. Barnum - page 82
12. "The Experiment: a Pioneer Voyage to China" by Frances Westgate Butterfield - page 89
13. "Sarah Barker's Voyage: The Youngest Passenger on the First Steamboat" by Frances Westgate Butterfield - page 99
14. "A Boy, A Girl, and a Star-Spangled Banner: The Story of the Flag that Inspired the Song" by Hope Lacy - page 106
15. "Two Indian Boys and the Seneca Chief: The First Trip Down the Erie Canal" by Virginia Stephenson - page 116
16. "Kit Carson: The Boyhood Days of the Famous Scout" by Mildred Smith Koskinen - page 124
17. "Maria Mitchell: The Girl Astronomer" by Virginia Stephenson - page 133

18. "Yankee in Russia: How an American Boy Won the Friendship of the Czar" by Anita Resko - page 140
19. "Jimmy Cotter: The Stowaway from Ireland" by Anne Colver - page 145
20. "Midshipman John Maffitt: The Sailor Who Danced with the Queen" by Marguerite Uman - page 153
21. "Allen Jay: The Quaker Boy and the Runaway Slave" by Margaret Rockwell Finch - page 160
22. "Abby Hutchinson: The Girl Singer who Became World Famous" by Mary Hutchinson Westland - page 169
23. "Joseph Jefferson: The Great Rip Van Winkle" by Elaine Davies Bylund - page 177
24. "Cordelia Howard: The First Little Eva" by Elaine Davies Bylund - page 187
25. "Ida Lewis: Heroine of Lime Rock Lighthouse" by Mary Hutchinson Westland - page 195
26. "Grace Bedell and Lincoln's Beard: Why the President Wore Whiskers" by Margaret Rockwell Finch - page 202
27. "Little Giffen: The Tennessee Hero of Eighteen Battles" by Anita Resko - page 210
28. "John Philip Sousa: The Pied Piper of Patriotism" by Mitchell Vincent - page 216
29. "Henry Devereux: The Spirit of '76" by Willard Connolly - page 223
30. "Thomas Alva Edison: The Boy Wizard" by Jeremy M. Harris - page 232
31. "An Educated Heart: The Story of Helen Keller" by Winifred Nies Butterfield - page 239
32. "Byron Unteidt: School Bus Hero" by Frances Westgate Butterfield - page 247
33. "Stephen Temby: The Radio Ham Who Saved a Town" by Hervey Berman - page 253

Of the authors who wrote the short stories: Mary Hutchinson Westland was the great-niece of Abby Hutchinson, and herself a singer and an actress of wide experience. She was persuaded to write the story of her famous aunt. A substantial part of her material was based on family records and papers belonging to the family. Hervey Berman, author of the story on Stephen Temby, ham radio operator, was himself a well-known member of the Ham Radio Operators Association, which included such famous hams as ex-President Herbert Hoover, and Amos and Andy of radio and television renown. Hilda Barnum, author of the story about Betty Zane, was a direct descendant of Elder William Brewster, religious leader of the Mayflower Pilgrims. Margaret Finch, herself a Quaker and a student of Quaker history, wrote a story about Allen Jay, whose courage and ingenuity enabled him to send a runaway slave to safety, without violating his Quaker principals, against telling a falsehood. Anne Colver, author of the story of Jim Cotter, was a professional author. Her adult biography, entitled *Mr. Lincoln's Wife*, was a choice of the Literary Guild and a best seller.

BROADCAST TIMES

October 9, 1935 to June 29, 1938
  East Coast: Wednesday on CBS from 8 to 8:30 p.m. (EST)
  West Coast: Wednesday on CBS from 8:30 to 9 p.m. (PST)
December 5, 1938 to May 29, 1939
  Monday on CBS
  8 to 8:30 p.m. (EST), 7 to 7:30 p.m. (CST)
  10 to 10:30 p.m. (MST), 9 to 9:30 p.m. (PST)
January 2, 1940 to April 23, 1940
  Tuesday on NBC
  9 to 9:30 p.m. (EST), 8 to 8:30 p.m. (CST)
  7 to 7:30 p.m. (MST), 6 to 6:30 p.m. (PST)
  with the following exceptions during these months . . .
  WOW in Omaha, 9:30 to 10 p.m., CST on Friday starting January 5
  WAVE in Louisville, 6:30 to 7 p.m., CST on Tuesdays starting Jan. 9
  WLW in Cincinnati, 3 to 3:30 p.m., EST on Sunday, Jan. 7 and 14 only
  WSM in Nashville, 6:30 to 7 p.m., CST on Fridays starting January 5
    Beginning Jan. 21, WLW broadcast *Cavalcade* Sun. 5:30 to 6 p.m., EST.
April 30, 1940 to June 25, 1940
  Tuesday on NBC
  9 to 9:30 p.m. (EST), 8 to 8:30 p.m. (CST)
  6 to 6:30 p.m. (MST), 5 to 5:30 p.m. (PST)
  with the following exceptions during these months . . .
  WOW in Omaha, 9:30 to 10 p.m., CST on Friday
  WAVE in Louisville, 9 to 9:30 p.m., CST on Sunday
  WSM in Nashville, 9:30 to 10 p.m., CST on Fridays (Thursday in May)
  WLW in Cincinnati, 7 to 7:30 p.m., EST on Friday
October 2, 1940 to March 26, 1941
  Wednesday on the Red Network
  7:30 to 8 p.m. (EST), 6:30 to 7 p.m. (CST)
  7:30 to 8 p.m. (MST), 6:30 to 7 p.m. (PST)
  with the following exceptions . . .
  WHAM in Rochester, 8 to 8:30 p.m., Friday (EST)
  WHO in Des Moines, 3 to 3:30 p.m., Sunday (CST)
March 31, 1941 to June 16, 1941
  Monday on the Red Network
  7:30 to 8 p.m. (EST), 6:30 to 9 p.m. (CST)
  8:30 to 9 p.m. (MST), 7:30 to 8 p.m. (PST)
June 23, 1941 to August 30, 1943
  Monday on the Red Network
  8 to 8:30 p.m. (EST), 7 to 7:30 p.m. (CST)
  8:30 to 9 p.m. (MST), 7:30 to 8 p.m. (PST)
September 6, 1943 to June 27, 1949
  Monday on NBC
  8 to 8:30 p.m. (EST), 7 to 7:30 p.m. (CST)
  10 to 10:30 p.m. (MST), 9 to 9:30 p.m. (PST)
August 30, 1949 to March 31, 1953
  Tuesday on NBC
  8 to 8:30 p.m. (EST), 7 to 7:30 p.m. (CST)
  10 to 10:30 p.m. (MST), 9 to 9:30 p.m. (PST)

AWARDS

These are just a few of the awards *Cavalcade* won during it's early years.

1935 - 1938
Following a nation-wide poll among women's clubs and parent-teacher associations, *Cavalcade* was selected by the American Legion Auxiliary as "the radio program most acceptable and worthwhile to the general family audience."

Radio Guide, a leading fan magazine, awarded the program its Medal of Merit as "one of the truly distinguished radio programs of all times, which combines the warmth and vitality of living drama with the dignity and integrity of scholarship. It is good entertainment and good history."

The Women's National Radio Committee mentioned *Cavalcade* as one of the programs outstanding for "good taste in advertising" and selected it as the only sponsored program on the networks "having particular value to children."

In September of 1937, *Cavalcade* was designated "the radio program most acceptable and worthwhile to the general family audience" by the Radio Committee of the American Legion Women's Auxiliary.

1938
The Women's Press Club voted *Cavalcade* to be "the best program for older children."

In 1938, the Women's National Radio Committee rated *Cavalcade* an award for being one of five air shows having educational value for young people, and commended the DuPont Company for its good taste in advertising.

1939
The Women's National Radio Committee cited *Cavalcade* as the "outstanding radio offering of the year." It was the only commercially sponsored program to be cited in the adult education group. This was the third consecutive award.

1940
For the first time in the eleven-year history of the Institute for Education by Radio, a commercial program - *The Cavalcade of America* - won a first award. On April 30, 1940, at the eleventh annual meeting of the Institute, held at Ohio State University, *Cavalcade*'s broadcast of February 13, "Abraham Lincoln: The War Years" presentation, was pronounced "the best dramatic program designed for general use by adults."

In interesting contrast to this citation by a group of experts, was the award received by *Cavalcade* on May 8, 1940. The *Cavalcade* series was the only radio program chosen for an award by Youth-builders, Inc., a New York City children's organization, in a poll which covered the radio, book, motion picture, and periodical field. The selections were announced after open balloting among more than one thousand school children who were members of Youth-builders, Inc. The actual award was presented by a fourteen-year-old Youth-builder who said: "We have chosen this program because it shows how American democracy grew up by telling us true stories about real Americans."

INDEX

"Abigail Open the White House" 512
"Abraham Lincoln" 19
"Abraham Lincoln: The War Years" 174, 213, 265
"Accent on Youth" 268
"Action at Santiago" 580
"The Admiral" 410
"Admiral Perry Discovers the Pole" 77
"The Admiral who had No Name" 539
"Adventure on the Kentucky" 735
"The Adventures of Mark Twain" 381
"Alaskan Bush Pilot" 471
"Alaska Under Arms" 305
Albert, Eddie 563
Albritton, Louise 506, 746
"The Alerting of Mr. Pomerantz" 555
"Alexander Graham Bell" 149
"Algerian Adevnture" 484
"Allan Pinkerton" 152
"All That Money Can Buy" 249
"Ambulance Driver, Middle East" 377
Ameche, Dana 519
"American for Christmas" 415
"An American From France" 681, 743
"An American is Born" 262
"American Journalism" 38
"Amerigo Vespucci" 168
Anderson, Judith 246
Andrews, Dana 435, 464, 518, 746
"Angels on Horseback" 271
"Anna Ella Carroll: The Woman in Lincoln's Cabinet" 229
"Anne Hutchinson" 235
"Anne Royall" 175
"Anne Rutledge and Abraham Lincoln" 197
"Anne Sullivan Macy" 124
"Annie Oakley" 231
Arlen, Richard 363
Arnold, Edward 249, 292, 309, 357, 497, 641, 661
"Arrowsmith" 267
Arthur, Jean 480, 602
"Artistic Impulse" 20
"Artist to the Wounded" 434
"As a Man Thinketh" 209
"As If a Door Were Opening" 728
"Assignment for the Professor" 442
"Autobiography of an Angel" 382
"Away All Boarding Parties" 762
Bainter, Fay 6, 411, 489, 581
Ball, Lucille 573, 660

"Barbed-Wire Christmas" 766
Barker, Lex 734
Barrie, Wendy 346
Barrymore, Ethel 175, 338
Barrymore, Lionel 260, 515, 533
"Baseball Centenary" 162
"Battle Hymn of the Republic" 203
"Battle of the Ovens" 284
"Battle to Stay Alive" 446
Baxter, Anne 429, 521
Baxter, Warner 359
Beal, John 479
Bel Geddes, Barbara 658
Bellamy, Ralph 293, 315, 321, 339, 343, 506, 561, 617, 670
Bendix, William 324, 425, 476, 736
"Benedict Arnold" 181
"Benjamin Franklin" 135
Bennett, Joan 254, 697
Bergman, Ingrid 272
"Bernadine, I Love You" 425
"The Betrayal" 588
"Between Them Both" 312
"Big Boy" 535
"Big Boy Blue" 457
"Big Brothers" 118
"Billy the Kid" 768
"Black Duster" 557
"Black Rust" 217
Blair, Janet 465, 601, 607
"Blazing Trails for Science" 117
"Bless This House" 771
"Blessings of Liberty" 383
"Bluecockade" 584
Blyth, Ann 760
"Bob Hope Reports" 352
Bogart, Humphrey 451
"Bolivar, the Liberator" 247
Bondi, Beulah 356
"Boomerang" 392
Booth, Shirley 361, 396, 505, 563
Bowman, Lee 498, 514, 526, 531, 541, 643, 654, 670, 680, 687, 707, 740, 754, 764, 778
Boyer, Charles 261, 604, 677
"Boy Wanted" 605
"Breakfast at Nancy's" 737
"Break the News" 576
Brennan, Walter 426, 439, 460
Brent, George 355
"Bridge Builders" 20

Brown, Joe E. 375
Bruce, Virginia 528, 534, 605, 652
"Bryant's Station" 583
"Builders of the Bridge" 452
"Builders of the Soo" 507
"Building and Architecture" 15
"Build Me Straight" 461
"Bullseye for Sammy" 364
"Burma Surgeon" 355
"Burning Bush" 586
Cagney, James 254, 477
Calhern, Louis 570, 690
"The Camels are Coming" 463
"Captain Paul" 250
"Captain Robert Gray" 126
"Captains of the Clouds" 264
Carey, MacDonald 570, 720, 733, 749, 753, 771, 775
"Cargo Over Burma" 443
Carlson, Richard 699
Carroll, Madeline 224, 263, 281, 290, 291, 299, 301, 303, 307, 596, 613
"Case for the F.B.I." 322
"Case of Harold Thomas" 689
"Case of the Tremendous Trifle" 469
Caufield, Joan 561, 638, 667, 710, 748, 751
"The Cavalcade of Music" (series) 90 through 101
"Change for Jimmy" 508
"Charlotte Cushman" 128
"Chautauqua Fable" 572
"Check Your Heart at Home" 361
"A Child is Born" 310, 362
"Children of Ol' Man River" 465
"Children, This is Your Father" 449
"Child Welfare of the U.S." 136
"Chinese Daughter" 705
"Christmas in America" 767
"Cimarron" 255
"Circus Day" 474
"Citizen Mama" 606
"Citizen Strauss" 651
"City of Illusion" 244
"Clara Barton" 281
"Clara Louise Kellogg" 106
Clark, Dane 479, 510, 627, 664, 689, 696
"Clifford Holland" 237
Clift, Montgomery 684
"Clipper Ships" 157
Coburn, Charles 341
Colbert, Claudette 279
Collins, Ray 187, 212
"Collossus of Panama" 282

"Commencement in Khaki" 464
"Common Glory" 574
"Community Self Reliance" 8
"Conquerer" 659
"Conquest of Pain" 413
"Conquest of Quinine" 394
"Conscience of Black Dan'l" 550
"The Constitution of the United States" 112
Conte, Richard 388, 443
"Continental Uniform" 274
"Continue Unloading" 351
"Cook of the P-T Boat Writes Home" 324
Cooper, Jackie 564, 759
Corey, Wendell 762, 780
Cotten, Joseph 316, 386, 461, 524, 681
Coulouris, George 380
"Country Lawyer" 497
Craig, James 356
Crawford, Broderick 777
Craven, Frank 4
"Crazy Judah" 647
Crisp, Donald 611, 693
Crosby, Bing 421
"Cruise on the Cashalot" 485
Cummings, Robert 614, 650, 691, 682, 716
"A Cup of Coffee with Lew" 636
Dahl, Arlene 734
"Daniel Boone" 183
"Dangerous Mission" 775
"Danger: Women at Work" 488
"Dark Angel" 266
"Darkest Hour" 582
"Dark Heart" 750
Darnell, Linda 584
Darwell, Jane 353, 372, 610
"Daughter with Wings" 748
"David Crockett" 227
Davis, Bette 262
Day, Laraine 463, 578, 695, 709
"The Day They Gave Babies Away" 546, 724
"D.D.T." 441
"Dear Brutus" 270
"Dear Funnyface" 346
De Camp, Rosemary 575
"Decision in the Valley" 650
"The Declaration of Independence" 13
De Corsia, Ted 393
"The Defiance of Nature" 11
Delmar, Kenny 199, 225, 240, 243, 296, 618, 622
"The Devil's Staricase" 738
"Diamond in the Sky" 545
"Diamonds in the War" 341

"Diary of a Saboteur" 320
"Diary of a Pig Boat" 313
"Dinner at Belmont" 607
"Direction Home" 456
"Doctora in Mexico" 431
"The Doctor and the President" 520
"The Doctor Gets the Answer" 400
"Doctor in Crinoline" 414
"Doctor John Gorrie" 139
"The Doctor Shoots A Cannon" 367
"The Doctor With Hope in his Hands" 470
"Dolly Madison" 166
Donlevy, Brian 347, 360, 373, 387, 413, 429, 469, 490, 535, 621, 686
"Double Play" 347
"Doughnut Girl" 412
Douglas, Melvyn 567, 651
"Down Brake" 770
"Down to the Sea" 219
Drake, Alfred 332, 346, 364, 378
"Dr. Commando" 733
"Dr. Franklin Goes to Court" 200
"Dr. Franklin Takes it Easy" 211
Driscoll, Bobby 724
"Drums Along the Mohawk" 252
"Duel with Aunt Rebecca" 699
Dunne, Irene 255, 431, 568, 583, 606, 773
"The Eagle's Nest" 311
"Eagle to Britain" 297
"Edgar Allan poe" 215
"Edward Bok" 147
"Edward MacDowell, Pioneer in American Musical Training" 55
"Edwin Booth" 102, 220
"The Eighteenth Captain" 321
"The Eighth Wonder of the World" 86
Eldridge, Florence 251
"Elizabeth Brooks" 159
"Elmer Ambroise Sperry" 107
"Eluthere Irenee Du Pont" 141, 167
"Emma" 669
"The Enemy is Listening" 334
"Enlightened Professor" 569
"Enoch Crosby" 176
"Enterprise" 17
"Enterprise USA" 643
Erwin, Stu 388
"The Evolution of Dance Music in America" 46
"The Exiled Heart" 575
"Experiment at Monticello" 594
"Experiment in Humanity" 661
Eythe, William 603, 659

Fairbanks, Jr., Douglas 494, 520, 590, 600, 647, 675, 718
"Faith in Education" 5
"Fame in Literature" 26
"Family Circle" 590
"The Farmer Takes a Wife" 201
"Fat Girl" 330
"Father of Plastics" 65
"Feast from the Harvest" 306
Fennelly, Parker 391
Ferrer, Jose 390
"Fiber 66" 687
"The Fields Are Green" 713
"First Commando" 378
"Firefly Lamp" 653
Fitzgerald, Geraldine 331, 434, 483, 559
"Flame" 540
"Flight Nurse" 424
"Fly High, Fly Low" 740
"Flying Tigers" 315
"Flying Tigers Fly Again" 495
Flynn, Errol 253
Foch, Nina 739
Fonda, Henry 252, 448, 456, 517, 536, 632
Fontaine, Joan 406, 688
Fontaine, Lynn 277, 310
Foran, Dick 471
Ford, Glenn 599, 772
"Footlights on the Frontier" 616
"The Forge" 537
"The 4-H Club Movement" 131
Foster, Preston 367, 384
"FRA Junipero Serra" 134
Francis, Arlene 305
Francis, Kay 248, 329
"Francis Scott Key" 120
"From Emporia, Kansas" 391
"Frontier Widow" 521
Gable, Clark 407
"The Gals they Left Behind" 396
"Garden Key" 585
Garfield, John 177, 351, 383
Garner, Peggy Ann 502
"General Benjamin Franklin" 489
"General Forrest Rides Again" 649
"The General's Wife" 472
"The General Wore Calico" 353
"The Gentleman From Paris" 261
"Geronimo" 243
"George Gershwin" 91, 154
"George Washington, Farmer" 80
"George Washington Rides Again" 649
"George Washington Refuses a Crown"

163

"Gettysburg" 577
"G.I. Circuit" 375
"G.I. Valentine" 370
"The Giant of the Meadow" 293
"The Giant who Stepped Over the Mountain" 722
"The Gift of Johnny Appleseed" 593
"The Gig of the Saginaw" 756
"The Girl Who Ran for President" 534
"The Girl Lincoln Loved" 406
"The Girl on a Mission" 710
Gish, Dorothy 549
Gleason, James 365
"Glory of the Vanquished" 113
Goddard, Paulette 259, 283
"Going Up" 742
"Golden Harvest" 666
"Golden Needle" 639
"The Golden Touch" 79
"Good Morning, Miss Tychman" 553
"Gorgeous Hussy" 259
"The Great Man Votes" 257
"The Greatest Risk" 630
"Green Pastures" 206, 258
"Grand Design" 277
"Grandpa and the Statue" 428
Grant, Cary 629
"Great Mcgraw" 475
"Greeley of the Tribune" 686
"Green Wall" 745
Gwenn, Edmund 319
Hall, John 328
Hampden, Walter 1, 597, 616, 644, 675, 681, 712, 719, 743, 763
"Hardiness" 33
Harding, Ann 416, 500
Harrison, Rex 594
Hasso, Signe 454
"Hated Hero of 1776" 350
Havoc, June 694
Hayes, Helen 188, 285, 333, 362, 382, 478, 481, 540, 553, 562
Hayward, Susan 737
"Heard 'Round the World" 611
"The Heart and the Fountain" 224
Heflin, Van 544
"Helping Hand" 52
Hendrix, Wanda 656
Henreid, Paul 620
"Henry Bergh, Founder of the ASPCA" 223
"Henry Clay of Kentucky" 212
"Here is Your War" 365
Hernandez, Juano 206, 258, 586, 691
"Heroes of Texas" 36

"Heroes of the Sea" 21
"Heroism in Medical Science" 9
Hersholt, Jean 284, 499
"The Hickory Tree" 493
Hodiak, John 384, 444, 465, 501, 523, 530, 584, 683, 728, 745
Holden, William 437, 507, 653, 721
"The Homecoming of Sou Chan" 618
"Home to the Heritage" 581
Homolka, Oscar 608
"Honest John Gaminsky and the Thriteen Uncle Sams" 608
"Honorable Titan" 496
"Honor Bound" 638
Hope, Bob 405
"The House Near Little Dock Street" 612
"The House of Glass" 75
"How High the Flame" 753
"How to Build Paradise" 436
Hull, Henry 176, 216
"The Humanitarian Urge" 12
Hunt, Marsha 424, 450, 507
"Hurry Up Yost" 542
Hussey, Ruth 622
Huston, Walter 169, 178, 249, 282, 379, 401 - 420, 422
"Hymn From the Night" 285, 401
"I Can and I Will" 654
"I Count the Days" 454
"I Guess It's Here to Stay" 482
"I, Mary Peabody" 648
"I, Mary Washington" 291
"The Immortal Blacksmith" 623
"Immortal Wife" 418
"Improvement Noted" 673
"Incident at Lancaster" 720
"Incident at Niagara" 579
"The Incomparable Doctor" 637
"Indigo Girl" 592
"The Interchangeable Mr. Whitney" 640
"In the Best Tradition" 302
"In This Crisis" 275
"I Remember Mama" 606
"Iron Camels" 348
"Iron Horse" 529
"Iron Mountain" 664
"I Sing a New World" 218
"I Speak for Democracy" 662
"I Was Married on Bataan" 299
Jaffe, Sam 171
Jagger, Dean 287, 288, 304, 336, 342
"James Fenimore Cooper" 74
Jameson, House 394, 578
"Jane Adams of Hull House" 188, 408

"Jean Laffite" 173
"Jean Pierre Blanchard" 233
"Joe Dyer Ends a War" 356
"Joel Chandler Harris" 232
"Joe Palmer's Beard" 621
"John Bartram's Garden" 108
"John Brown" 204
"John Fitch" 180
"John Honeyman" 146
"John Howard Payne" 160
"John Jacob Astor" 105
"John James Audubon" 127
"Johns Hopkins" 228
Johnson, Van 768
"John Sutter" 190
"John Winthrop, Pioneer in Chemical Science" 54
"John Yankee" 663
"Johnny Comes Home" 450
"Josephine Baker" 238
"Journey Among the Lost" 602
"Juarez" 298
"Juliet in Pigtails" 671
"Juliette Low" 164
"Junior Angel" 372
"The Justice and the Lady" 549
"Justice Oliver Wendell Holmes" 165
"Kansas Marshall" 517
"Keepsakes" 685
Kelly, Nancy 201, 312, 464
Kibbee, Guy 371
"King Coal" 138
"The King of nantucket" 693
"Kit Carson" 153
"Kitchen Scientist" 532
"Knute Rockne" 142
Kruger, Otto 367
Ladd, Alan 377
"The Lady and the Flag" 283
"The Lady Becomes a Governor" 624
"The Lady of Distinction" 527
"The Lady of Johnstown" 652
"Lady on a Mission" 609
Lancaster, Burt 582
"Landing of the Swedes in Delaware" 140
Langford, Frances 370, 405
"Last Frontier" 571
Laughton, Charles 294, 409, 428, 489, 637
"Law of the Scouts" 125
"The Law West of the Pecos" 439
"Lay That Mucket Down" 620
"The Laziest Man in the World" 409
"League of the Long House" 158
"Lee of Virginia" 565

"Leif Ericsson" 242
"The Lengthening Shadow" 326
"Letter From Europe" 604
"Lifeline" 627
"Life on the Mississippi" 776
"Lifetide" 323, 402
"A Light in the Hills" 202
"Listen, My Children" 711, 765
"Listen to the People" 338
"Listen to the Sound of Wings" 327
Lockhart, Gene 636, 545
Lockhart, June 545
Lockhart, Kathleen 545
"The Long Gray Line" 747
"Lost Colony" 194
Louise, Anita 518, 579
"The Louisiana Purchase" 122
Lovejoy, Frank 392, 395
"Lovely Lady" 393
Lowe, Edmund 345
Loy, Myrna 271
"Loyalty to the Family" 18
"The Lieutenants Come Home" 348
Lukas, Paul 327, 486, 556, 564, 706
Lund, John 576, 593, 638, 692, 743, 758
Lupino, Ida 418, 445, 468, 512, 527, 532
"Luther Burbank" 89
Lynn, Diana 705, 715
Lynn, Jeffrey 694
"The Magnificent Failure" 509
"The Magnificent Meddler" 458
"The Major and the Mules" 344
"Make Way for the Lady" 335
"Man Against the Mountain" 511
"Man of Action" 696
"Man of Design" 289
"Man of Great Importance" 754
"Man of Iron" 287
"The Man Who Had Two Careers" 61
"The Man Who Stepped Aside" 516
"The Man Who Taught Lincoln" 412
"Man Who Took the Freedom Train" 563
"Man Who Wouldn't Be President" 309
"The Man Who Wouldn't Grow Old" 69
"The Man With the Cargo of Water" 665
"The Man With the Green Fingers" 515
March, Frederic 251, 270, 326, 381
"Marie Dressler" 156
"The Marine Who Was 200 Years Old" 736
"Mark Twain" 150
Marshall, Brenda 653
Marshall, Herbert 389, 423, 487
"Mary Lyon, Pioneer Woman Educator"

103

"Mary of Murray Hill" 688
"The Mask for Jefferson" 379
Massey, Raymond 174, 205, 213, 265, 278, 369, 619, 642, 685, 699, 731, 776
McAllister, Lon 656, 666
McCrea, Joel 463, 551
"The McGuffey Readers" 76
McGuire, Dorothy 558, 588, 609, 624, 639, 676, 730, 769
"A Medal for Miss Walker" 769
"Meet Artie Greengroin" 476
"Mehitable Wing" 170
"Melodies of Stephen Foster" 182
"Melody Man" 752
"Men in White" 256
Meredith, Burgess 168, 245, 246, 427, 442, 504, 509
Merkel, Una 514, 526
Merrill, Gary 756
"Metal of the Moon" 684
"Mightier Than the Sword" 208
"Militant Angel" 700
Milland, Ray 218, 227, 230, 571, 630, 674, 714, 738
"Minute Men of the Air" 68
"Mission to Cuba" 531
"Mister Navigator" 114
Mitchell, Thomas 180, 380, 456, 516, 542, 550, 560, 565, 709, 761, 781
Mitchum, Robert 410, 539, 579, 698
"Mockingbird Sang at Chickamauga" 680
"Modern Orchestral Music" 48
Montgomery, Robert 410, 539, 579, 698
Moorehead, Agnes (starring roles) 186, 202, 229, 231, 235, 238, 244, 440, 472, 493, 646
Morgan, Dennis 314
Morgan, Frank 459
Morris, Chester 430, 511
"Mother of Freedom" 500
"Mr. Conyngham Sweeps the Sea" 494
"Mr. Lincoln Goes to the Play" 554
"Mr. Lincoln's Wife" 333
"Mr. Peale and the Dinosaur" 646
"Mr. Pullman's Palace Car" 513
"Mr. Statler's Story" 692
Muni, Paul 220, 247, 311, 555, 585
Munsel, Patrice 374
Munson, Ona 368
Murphy, Audie 713
Murphy, George 366, 484, 495
"My Fighting Congregation" 387
"My Friend Monair" 390

"My Freshman Husband" 483
"My Hunt After the Captain" 603
"My Son John" 451
"The Mystery of the Spotted Death" 234
"My Wayward Parent" 429
Nagel, Conrad 603
"Name, Rank, and Serial Number" 417
"Names on the Land" 459
"Nancy Hanks" 186
"Nathan Hale" 151
"National Parks Pioneers" 72
"Native Land" (Parts I and II) 245, 246
"Navy Blue" 716
"Navy Doctor" 360
Neal, Patricia 755
"Nellie Was a Lady" 445
Nesbitt, John 623
"Never Marry a Ranger" 655
"New Commandment" 718
"The Night There was No President" 729
"Nine Men Against the Arctic" 342
"Noah Webster" 123
"No Doll was Abigail" 697
"No Greater Love" 558
Nolan, Lloyd 359, 455
"No One is Alone" 709
"The Nugget and the Law" 772
"The Nurse Who Forgot Fear" 739
"Nurses Under Sealed Orders" 331
"Oath" 538
Oberon, Merle 266
O'Brien, Edmund 766
O'Brien, Margaret 671
O'Brien, Pat 376, 447, 475, 589
"Ode to a Nightingale" 221
"Odyssey to Freedom" 373
"Of Such is the Freedom" 536
"The Old Fall River Line" 490
"O. Henry" 236
O'Keefe, Dennis 758
"Oliver Wendell Holmes" 121
"Oliver Wendell Holmes MacLanahan" 589
"Once More the Thunderer" 695
"One Came Through" 780
"One Foot in Heaven" 251
"One Last Romance" 597
"One Nation Indivisible" 761
"One Wagon Westward" 491
"One Way Out" 757
"Operation Miracle" 774
"Opportunity" 27
"Orchestra of Today and How it Grew" 49
"Ordeal by Fire" 641
O'Shea, Michael 332, 443

O'Sullivan, Maureen 337, 520
"Ottmar Mergenthaler" 111
"An Ounce of Prevention" 70
"Page One" 523
"Paging Miss Ellen" 559
Paige, Gail 471
"Parade" 499
"Party Line" 440
"A Passage to Georgia" 222
"Passport to Freedom" 486
"The Path of Praise" 719, 763
"Path to the Stars" 703
"Pathfinder" 119
"Pathfinder of the Seas" 196
"Patrick Henry" 161
"The Patriot With the Chestnut Curls" 751
"Paul Bunyon" 145
Payne, John 595
"Peanut Vendor" 519
Peck, Gregory 467, 522, 726
"Penny Fancy" 419
"The Perfect Tribute" 317
"Perfect union" 552
"Perserverance" 23
"Peter Stuyvesant" 143
"The Petticoat Jury" 480
"Pharmacist's Mate" 332
"The Philippines Have Never Surrendered" 433
Pidgeon, Walter 268, 402, 466, 581
"The Pine Tree Shilling" 88
"The Pinkerton Man" 498
"Pink Lace" 601
"Pioneer American Engineer" 116
"Pioneer Woman-Physician" 214
"Plain Mr. President" 214
"The Plot to Kidnap Washington" 319
"Port of Missing Men" 727
"The Portrait of the Author" 657
Powell, Dick 368, 577, 704
Powell, William 538, 572
Power, Tyrone 267, 273, 280, 628, 722
"Powhatan's Daughter" 548
"Prairie Burner" 506
"The President and the Doctor" 560
Preston, Robert 693, 774
Price, Vincent 420
"The Printer was a Lady" 277
"The Prisoner at Castle Thunder" 744
"The Prisoner Named Brown" 726
"Prologue to Glory" 369
"Prophet Without Honor" 294
"Proud Way" 578

"The Purple Heart Comes to Free Meadows" 371
"Quality of Courage" 749
"Queen of Courage" 749
"The Queen of Heartbreak Trail" 568
"The Queen's Handmaid" 596
"A Race for Lennie" 410
"The Raft" 698
"Railroad Builders" 28
"Rain Fakers" 504
Rains, Claude 181, 209, 250, 275, 295, 646, 732
Rathbone, Basil 274, 350, 508, 549, 560, 574, 657, 663, 708
"The Raven" 169
"The Raven Wins Texas" 178
Raye, Martha 329
Readick, Frank 185, 391
"Ready on the Right" 759
Reagan, Ronald 537, 678
"Recon Pilot" 437
"Red Death" 198
"The Redemption of Lottie Moon" 660
"Red Lanterns on St. Michaels" 239
"Red Stockings" 530
Reed, Donna 510
"The Reluctant Pioneer" 694
"The Reluctant Rebel" 614
"Remember Anna Zenger" 626
"Remembered Day" 279
"Report from the Pacific" 405
"Resourcefulness" 34
"Return to Glory" 533
"Reveille" 644
Revere, Anne 472
Reynolds, Marjorie 424, 438
"Ridin' Shotgun" 617
"The River Finds a Master" 779
"Road to Berlin" 411
"Road to Victory" 308
"Robert E. Lee" 184
"Robinson Crusoe, U.S.N." 430
Robinson, Edward G. 322, 403, 433, 470
Rogers, Ginger 612, 669, 717
"Roger Williams" 187
"Romance at Fort Cramford" 734
Rooney, Mickey 634
"The Rose and the Thorns" 676
"Roses in the Sun" 561
Russell, Rosalind 401, 625
Rutherford, Anne 564
Ryan, Robert 711
"Sacajawea" 241
"Safety First" 29

"The Saga of Jerry O'Brien" 758
"The Sailor Takes a Wife" 368
"The Sailor who had to Have a Horse" 453
"Sam Davis" 179
"Sam Houston" 169
"Samuel Slater" 137
Sanders, George 458
"Sara Josepha Hale" 110
"Sawdust Underground" 444
Schildkraut, Joseph 320
"School for Men" 522
"Schoolhouse at the Front" 340
Scott, Martha 655
Scott, Zachary 598
"Search for Iron" 129
"Secret Operation" 595
"Secret Road" 778
"The Seeing Eye" 59, 108
"Self-Reliance" 30
"The Sentinels of the Deep" 53
"Sequal at Seventy" 712
"Seven Hundred Boiled Shirts" 717
"Seven Iron Men" 426
"Sheriff Teddy" 551
"The Ship the Nazis Had to Get" 714
"A Ship to Remember" 384
Shirley, Anne 222
"Short Straw" 773
"Shortcut to Tokyo" 343
"Showboat" 189
"Showmanship" 51
"Signal to the World" 629
"Sign Here, Please" 427
"The Silent Heart" 272
"Silent Service" 704
"Sing a War Song" 385
"Sir Galahad in Manhattan" 674
"Sister Kenny" 307
"Sitting Duck" 721
"Six Men of Wood" 668
"Sixteen Sticks in a Bundle" 725
Skinner, Cornelius Otis 192, 590
"Skylark Song" 573
"Sky Nursemaid" 337
Sloane, Everett 334, 378, 390, 392, 395,
         397, 482, 485
Smith, Kent 347
"Soldier of a Free press" 295
"Soldiers in the Greasepoint" 329
"Soldiers in High Boots" 328
"Soldiers of the Cloth" 339
"Soldiers of the Soil" 358
"Soldiers of the Tide" 314
"Song for Spokane" 374

"Songs of Home" 35
"Songs of Sentiment" 58
"Songs of the American Indian" 84
"Songs of the Sea" 66
"Songs of the South" 81
"Songs that Inspire the Nation" 22
"So Red the Rose" 254
"So Sorry - No Mercy" 376
Sothern, Ann 375
"Sound the Great Bell" 707
"South of Cape Horn" 634
"Speed of Words" 16
"Spindletop" 632, 682
"Spin a Silver Dollar" 481
"The Spirit of Competition" 3
"The Spy on Kilocycles" 448
"The Star and the Shield" 777
"Star in the West" 468
"Stars of Destiny" 87
"Steamboat Builders" 37
"Stephen Arnold Douglas" 240
"Stephen Foster" 148
"Stephen Girard" 73
"Stepping Stones" 675
Stern, Bill 542
Stevens, Mark 741
Stewart, James 453
"The Stirring Blood" 514
"The Stirring Blood" 526
Stockwell, Dean 729
"The Stolen General" 177
"The Store That Winked Out" 598
"Storm" 479
"The Story of American Dyes" 85
"The Story of Canine Joe" 397
"The Story of Christmas Songs" 60
"The Story of Dynamite" 82
"The Story of Penicillin" 380
"The Story of Rubber" 57
"Strike a Blow for Liberty" 628
"Submarine Astern" 325
Sullivan, Barry 702, 703
Sullivan, Margaret 700
"Susan B. Anthony" 192
"The Sword of Kentucky" 656
"Take Her Down" 354, 407
Taylor, Deems 385
Taylor, Elizabeth 648
Taylor, Robert 552, 640, 744
"Ten in Texas" 460
"Terrence O'Toole, MP" 366
"The Texas Rangers" 155
"That Moore Girl" 502
"That Skipper From Stonington" 518

"That They Might Live" 301, 492
"Theodore Roosevelt, Man of Action" 292
"Theodosia Burr" 226
"There Stands Jackson" 683
"They Also Serve" 24
"They Died with their Boots On" 253
"They Shall Have Music" 706
"The Thinking Heart" 642
"Thirst Without End" 477
"This Little Plot of Ground" 625
"This Our Exile" 290
"This Side of Hades" 276
"This Way to Tomorrow" 556
"Thomas A. Edison, the Man" 83
"Thomas Jefferson" 172
"Thomas Jefferson and American Education" 130
Thomas, Lowell 636
"Thomas Paine" 185
"A Thousand to One" 764
"Three Words" 732
"Thunder of Justice" 730
"Thunder on the Hudson" 566
Tierney, Gene 572, 633
"Tillers of the Soil" 32
"A Time to Grow" 781
"Tisquantum, Strange Friend of the Pilgrims" 171
Tobias, George 340, 543, 587, 631
"Tokyo Spearhead" 388
"Tomorrow and Tomorrow" 263
Tone, Franchot 3, 256, 462, 569, 695
"A Tooth for Paul Revere" 278
"Top Secret" 701
"Torch Bearer" 702
"Torpedo Lane" 304
"To the Shores of Tripoli" 316
"Toward a Farther Star" 303
"Towards a New World" 708
"Towards the Horizon" 544
"Transcontinental Journeys" 56
"Traveller to Arkansas" 455
"Treason" 386
Trevor, Claire 419, 452, 461
"The Trials and Triumphs of Horatio Alger" 225
"A Tribute to Ernestine Shumann-Heink" 62, 115
"Troublesome Jane" 622
Trout, Robert 580
"Twelve Desperate Miles" 357
"200,000 Flyers" 447
Turner, Lana 412
"U-Boat Prisoner" 363

"Ulysses in Love" 678
"Uncle Eury's Dollar" 691
"The Undefended Border" 205
"Under the Big Top" 525
"The Unheroic Hero" 600
"The Unnatural Death" 541
"Unsinkable Marblehead" 336
"The Unsinkable Mrs. Brown" 473
"U.S. Pilgrims" 543, 587, 631
"A Valentine for Sophia" 599
"Valley Forge" 195, 260, 404
"Valley of the Swans" 746
"Vengeance of Torpedo Eight" 349
"Venture in Silk Hat" 462
"Victor Herbert" 39, 191
"Village Doctor" 567
"Vinnie and Mr. Lincoln" 658
"Voice in the Wilderness" 216
"Voice of the Wizard" 510
"Voice on the Stairs" 403
"Wait for the Morning" 210, 269
Walker, Robert 450
"Walk in the Sun" 395
"Wall of Silence" 633
"Walter Reed" 193
"War Comes to Dr. Morgan" 318
"Washington and the Traitor" 423
Waters, Ethel 725
"Waters of the Wilderness" 248
"Weapon 4-H" 432
"The Weapon That Saves Lives" 345
"Weather is a Weapon" 435
Welles, Orson 257, 298, 300, 302
"Westward the Women" 416
"Whale Off" 690
"What Makes a Hero?" 399
"What Price Freedom?" 389
"When Cupid Was a Pup" 473
"When We're Green We Grow" 610
"Whither Thou Goest" 672
"Who Walk Alone" 570
Widmark, Richard 399, 615, 649, 665, 735, 765
"Wild Bill Hickcock" 199
Wilde, Cornel 473, 557, 625, 645, 673, 747, 770
"The Wild Young Man" 288
William, Warren 344
"The Willingness to Share" 7
"Will Rogers" 144, 207
"The Will to Conquer Distance" 2
"The Will to Explore" 10
"The Will to Rebuild" 4

"William Penn and the Holy Experiment" 104
"Wings to Glory" 501
"Winner Takes Life" 564
"Winning Prestige for the American Stage" 64
"Winning Recognition for American Singers" 71
"Wire to the West" 619
"The Wise Mad General" 359
"With Cradle and Clock" 487
"With Malice Toward None" 731
"Witness by Moonlight" 524
"Witness for the People" 411
"Wizards of Whiting" 670
Woollcott, Alexander 203
"Woman Alone" 528
"Woman of Steel" 562
"The Woman of Lime Rock" 505
"The Woman with a Sword" 613
"Woman's Emancipation" 6
"A Woman's Way" 755
"Women in Public Service" 14
Wright, Teresa 682
Wyman, Jane 750
"The Yankee and the Scales" 741
"Yankee Doodle Debby" 667
"Yankee from Olympus" 398
"Yankee Independence" 63
"Yellow Jack" 273
"Young Andrew Jackson" 230
Young, Loretta 194, 276, 408, 414, 449, 672, 727
"Young Major Washington" 467
"Young Man in a Hurry" 645
Young, Robert 354, 436, 446, 492, 496, 513, 525, 554, 656, 668, 701, 779
"Young Tom Jefferson" 280

ABOUT THE AUTHOR

Martin Grams, Jr. is the author of the highly-acclaimed publication *Suspense: Twenty Years of Thrills and Chills*, and co-author of *The CBS Radio Mystery Theater: An Episode Guide and Handbook to Nine Years of Broadcasting, 1974-82*. Having written a few books on horror and mystery programs, Martin has decided to venture into American history with this publication. He has also written articles for a handful of film, television and radio related magazines such as *The MacGuffin* and *OTR Digest*.

His love for Hollywood, television and radio is beyond comprehension. He is currently at work on other publications, one of them documenting the history of the radio and television series *Have Gun, Will Travel*. He is also currently hard at work on another television program, which will bring him back to his love of mystery and horror, *The Alfred Hitchcock Presents Companion*, both of these books are due for an early 2000 release.

* For information regarding any of these books, including the books he is currently working on, check out the next page.

THE HISTORY OF THE CAVALADE OF AMERICA

Written by Martin Grams, Jr.

* Did you borrow this book from your local library?

* Has your friend been looking for a copy of this book?

* Looking for that perfect gift or want a copy of your own?

ORDER INFORMATION

Please provide the following information:

1. Name, address, city, state, zip, and a phone number in case we have any questions about your order.

2. Check or money order for $24.95 for each copy. (wholesale orders are available for dealers and bookstores, write and ask.)

3. Add $3.00 to cover postage and handling, and $1.00 for each additional book.

4. Visa and Mastercard orders are accepted. Call (717) 456 - 6208

Mail all orders to CAVALCADE OF AMERICA, PO BOX 189, DELTA, PA 17314

Other books written by Martin Grams, Jr. are also available through this address and phone number. Just write or call!

Suspense: Twenty Years of Thrills and Chills $29.95   460 pages

The CBS Radio Mystery Theater: An Episode Guide and Handbook to Nine Years of Broadcasting, 1974 - 82
$50.00   320 pages

ANN HARDING
in
WESTWARD THE WOMEN
MONDAY EVENING   JANUARY 1, 1945

"Great Stars . . . . Great Radio Plays"

LORETTA YOUNG
in
Jane Addams, Woman of Courage
MONDAY EVENING   NOVEMBER 6, 1944

"Great Stars . . . . Great Radio Plays"
IN CAVALCADE'S 1944 FALL SERIES